DISPARITY:

An Autobiography of a Man with a Hungry Heart

Enjoy an inside look at my crazy life.

Peter M. Talty

ptalty@keuka.edu

Peter M. Talty

Copyright © 2016 by Peter M. Talty.

Library of Congress Number		2016903751
ISBN:	Hardcover	978-1-5144-7237-8
	Softcover	978-1-5144-7236-1
	eBook	978-1-5144-7235-4

All rights reserved. No part of this book may be reproduced or transmitted in any form or by any means, electronic or mechanical, including photocopying, recording, or by any information storage and retrieval system, without permission in writing from the copyright owner.

Any people depicted in stock imagery provided by Thinkstock are models, and such images are being used for illustrative purposes only. Certain stock imagery © Thinkstock.

Print information available on the last page.

Rev. date: 04/19/2016

To order additional copies of this book, contact:
Xlibris
1-888-795-4274
www.Xlibris.com
Orders@Xlibris.com
725893

Contents

Author's Note vii
Introduction ix

Disparity Is a Very Compelling Force 1
We Were Rich Once! We Were? 5
Rich No More 8
The Sad and Insane Confluence of Two Families 11
The Talty Flu 20
Why Didn't Ma Contract the Talty Flu? 28
Our First Flat: Knotty and Nutty Times 30
The Travails of the Flat 37
That Awful Night! Our Titanic! 42
Life with Sue and Jim 46
A New Dad Emerges 51
Behavioral and Emotional Land Mines Explode 55
We Become Home Owners! Us? Really? 58
Our Move Back to a Flat and Other Tragedies 75
The Beginning of Pat's Lifelong Affliction 91
Back with Sue and Jim 95
Tough Guy Pete Emerges 100
A New Ma Emerges 117
Crazy Pete Emerges 121
Polishtown 124
The Demise of Tough Guy Pete 128
A Better Pete Emerges 137
The Trial 141
Life on Probation 147
Life after Probation 156
Back to Our Old Neighborhood! 159
Pat's Sad Life Goes from Travesty to Tragedy 168
We Become Suburbanites! 179

College? Me? Really?	186
Marriage: What a Concept!	195
Our First Apartment	199
Janitor No More! I Become a Steelworker, Sort of!	202
Janice and I Move to the Old Neighborhood!	209
The West Side	211
Now Back to the University and Some Big Changes	219
Another New "Job" for Me in the Steel Plant	227
OT School	238
Hardships and Fun in the Family	241
My Junior Year of College	245
Our Pleasant Way of Life Deteriorates Fast	249
A Crisis for Me at the University	257
11:00 p.m.	262
Ma Moves On	264
My First OT Internship	266
Sadness and Joy in My Senior Year!	269
My Last Two Internships	279
A Big Change for Ma: Back to the Old Neighborhood!	284
Pandora's Pizzeria	287
My First OT Job	290
The Ramifications of My Unbridled Disparity	301
And Suddenly, Ma Was Gone	306
"The Eve of Destruction"	310
Egregiously, I Now Wreck Many Lives	318
From Disparity to Annihilation	328
Was I Now a Bachelor or a Bastard? I Was Both!	331
From Disparity to Devastation to Discovery	336
Rebuilding a Life	345
Challenges and Successes in the Boondocks Home	348
A Scary Time for Our Baby	374
The Grand Geriatric Facility	376
A Sad Distraction	395
The Grand Ain't So Grand!	398
Moving On	404

Moving On! Really? Really!	411
We Become Bernie and Annie's Neighbors	413
The Medical Center and the University	422
ARMI	429
The University	432
Oh No, They're Moving Again!	437
Wellington Woods	446
Bedlam Hospitals*	452
Unique Relationships and Special Times	459
More success at Bedlam Hospitals	461
The Parlay!	467
Up, Up, and Away: Part 1	470
Two Possible "Lifesavers"	478
Up, Up, and Away: Part 2	480
The Process of My Rehabilitation	485
I Become an Entrepreneur and Live the Life	491
The Talty Family's Interest in the Macabre	498
Merging Entrepreneurism with Academia	500
Ah, Wilderness!	511
Down But Not Out	516
Chair of Occupational Therapy	522
Riding a Bike from Niagara Falls to Lake Placid, New York	525
Let the Juggling Begin!	536
Marco Island and MFR	542
Crises in the Wilderness	549
Big Surprises for Janice	567
Peter Jr. Comes Home!	571
Janice's Mom	576
Changes to My OT Private Practice	582
Pat Becomes a Trailer Owner	588
Out of Town Again	593
A Simpler Life That Was a Godsend	598
"Morning Has Broken"	606
A Tribute to Anne Marie	610
Grandparents? Us?	616

My Sabbatical	619
Pat's Mercurial Life as an Adult	625
Sleazy's Final Blow	641
More Grandkids?	646
The Sale and the Search	648
"Peter, I Think I Found Our House"	651
Walton Woods and Audubon	655
Hey, Papa?	657
A New Home for Beth and Dan	660
A New Home for Peter and Kathy	662
A Grandkid We Didn't Know We Had	666
The Unexpected and Abundant Joys of Grandkids	668
A New OT Job!	672
Ah, Wilderness! No More	676
Alaska: First-Class Style!	680
The Great Opportunity I Didn't Get to Seize	685
Retirement!	691
Florida!	697
My Dreadful Past Roars Again!	703
Immersions into the Idyllic Lakes Community	706
Going Forth on Faith	708
Life in Shangri-La II	715
A Real Sod (Not Sob) Story	719
Teaching Again!	722
Sadness amid the Joy	725
The Craziest of Days for Janice and Me!	728
New Frontiers	733
Move Number 20	737
Surprises!	739
Oh, Danny Boy	743
St. Therese of Lisieux to the Rescue Again	752
What If . . . ?	754
Conclusion, Maybe	756

Author's Note

My life has been more like a chase than a journey. My chase has taken me and my family to highs and lows that will surprise some, disappoint others, and perhaps bring forth a bit of rage in a few. Many people accompanied me on my chase, and because of the role they played, they may wish to remain anonymous. Out of respect for their privacy, I have chosen to use pseudonyms to protect their identity. I have done the same with organizations where I worked and the cities where various episodes took place.

INTRODUCTION

Peter Talty and I met a few years ago in a retirement community along the gulf coast of Florida. We quickly became friends, partially because of our common background: we both were born and raised in the northeast, and we both had long careers as college professors. Nonetheless, I was surprised when, several months ago, he asked me to read his life story. I had no idea that writing this had become a major retirement project for him. I did not even know that he was interested in being a writer, which I now consider him to be.

I found Peter's long and detailed life story to be interesting and engaging in so many ways. His approach is akin to the "Dear Reader" author/reader relationship in which he consistently guides his reader. He invites the reader on a long journey, one that has not yet ended. There are many very effectively developed episodes or stories along the way.

As is common with many autobiographies, except for those written by noted personages or witnesses of significant historical events, the primary readers of Peter's autobiography are intended to be members of his family. There is a strong sense of family throughout his entire life story—in a family that many may consider dysfunctional. (Alcoholism and mental illness are family afflictions.) Peter remains the "man in the middle" in any family feuds that develop throughout the narrative.

He often initiates actions that cause tension in the family but then ironically works effectively to resolve the tension. A particular type of cynical humor, known as the Talty humor, prevails as a bonding agent whenever family members get together. Peter's family (and true friends) always remains dear to him. Nor does he ever take them, particularly his wife, Janice, for granted.

Throughout the autobiography, Peter demonstrates his ability to analyze and verbalize what motivates him. *Disparity* is the ever-present theme, and the majority of the action is initiated by him because, from his own unique viewpoint, he has a driving need to improve his situation and that of those he cares about. He is forever striving to reduce or eliminate his acute sense of disparity. He doesn't simply report what is happening. In most cases, he causes it to happen.

Others in his life (e.g., his sister Sue, his brother Bernie, or his wife Janice) play major supporting roles, but Peter always remains the protagonist. This is mainly because of how his mind operates. He gets an idea for a change, identifies potential obstacles, develops a plan to overcome those obstacles, and immediately begins to put that plan into action. (Action is always better than inaction.) Only at this point does he inform others of the change he is unilaterally attempting to bring about—no matter how close to him they are or no matter how much the change may affect them.

A corollary to the "disparity" theme is that of "risk-taking." If one is driven to act—and act quickly—one must be prepared for, or even seek, high risks. As a teenager and young adult, this meant adopting the role of Tough Guy Pete and engaging in highly questionable, even illegal, behaviors. But while he provides his rationale at the time for these behaviors, he never attempts to justify them to the reader and often reflects upon the lack of wisdom and common sense behind them. He often expresses regret for hurting those who love him and whom he loves. Particularly in his later years, the possible negative consequences of his risk-taking seem to have resulted in a strengthening of his faith.

All autobiographies are written accounts of their authors' memories of their personal experiences. A major feature of Peter's autobiography is the very impressive memory for the detail it displays. Names of numerous people and places fill its pages. Pseudonyms are provided for those who most likely would prefer anonymity. (In such cases, the pseudonyms are not always complimentary.) Most noticeable is the exactitude with which he presents details of the many places he has lived, mostly in the northeast, and the many places he has worked.

The flow of life is filled with joys, challenges, sorrows, and regrets. I know that much of what Peter has written in his autobiography was difficult for him to write. But it takes courage to remember and then to present those memories fully and honestly. This autobiography reveals that courage.

It is obvious that this autobiography is written by an experienced health-care professional, not only because the narrator recalls his studies, his employment, his self-employment, and his teaching in the field of occupational therapy but also because he consistently views his life as a professional through the eyes of an occupational therapist, and he provides appropriate explanations for the reader. As Peter teaches his students, he teaches his readers.

During most of his adult life, Peter's recreational passion has been hiking and canoeing, most often in his beloved Adirondack Mountains, and he entertains us with memorable stories of wilderness adventures. In recent years, he has begun a foray into acting, and just as he has sought to improve himself in all his life's endeavors by reading and studying, so it has been with acting. Although his actual stage experience in this relatively recent activity is still rather minimal, all acting is not done on stage. His autobiography reveals that he has been playing various roles throughout his life and that he has much experience cultivating his vivid sense of the theatrical.

Although Peter's focus is upon himself and upon those with whom he has come into contact throughout his life, I believe his autobiography will appeal to a wider audience than those included in his story. He not only remembers but he also reflects deeply upon those memories, and in so doing he invites the reader to make personal applications. Having read Peter's life story and despite now knowing more of what we do not have in common, I have been enriched by my friend's life.

Robert J. Margrett
Professor Emeritus
University of Wisconsin Colleges

Disparity Is a Very Compelling Force

According to Dictionary.com, disparity is *"The lack of similarity or equality; inequality; difference."*

Being acutely aware of what others have and what I don't have in terms of possessions and abilities has been like a surging engine within that has goaded and propelled me ever since childhood. For example, growing up, I hated the fact that the Conger[*] and the Kramer[**] kids in my neighborhood had orange juice every morning. Hated? Seems strange, doesn't it? Milk and cereal, or in my case six slices of buttered toast (with crusts secreted on a shelf under our table), was our breakfast. Why should it matter what other kids had for breakfast? Because of that damned disparity thing, that's why. It has generated strong emotions in me that has served me well and not so well throughout my life, and still does today. Crazy? Yes!

I love Dictionary.com's definition of disparity because it cuts right to the gut of it all. Disparity: *the lack of similarity or equality; inequality; difference.* The word "disparity" itself sounds a bit like dissatisfied, desperate, disparate, disparage, disconcerting, dispassionate, and my old friend dispirited. They all have that "dis" sound. I was acutely aware of differences early on in my life that others in my family were

---

[*] To protect the people who would prefer not to be associated with my experiences, I have chosen to use pseudonyms to safeguard their identity.

[**] Ibid.

1

unaware of or unaffected by. Not me. Ours was a different life from that of the other kids in our neighborhood, and early on, I saw and felt the differences fiercely. I guess I knew it couldn't be any different. No sense in pointing out these disparities to anyone. Who could change them? But still, why were these other kids' Dads washing and waxing their cars when we didn't even own one? Why did these Dads come right home after work? That was a puzzle for me and also generated more of that disparity stuff that came cascading down all around me from about eight years of age onward.

Was I never happy or satisfied? Of course, but I was the happiest when I could bring about a change in my circumstances. Living with disparity was never my way. It still isn't, but the paths I took to dispel disparity were at times bizarre and often not the most productive. However, it makes for a rich reservoir of experiences to ruminate about and share (I think).

Now, looking back, I don't think I was overly concerned about the myriad inequities I was constantly observing or perceiving around me (people with OCD [Obsessive Compulsive Disorder] never do). Do you? Also, I don't think I was psychotic while making these perpetual comparisons. Do you think? But then again, do people with paranoid schizophrenia know that their thoughts are disordered and out of sync with the rest of the world? Don't worry. I have not, so far, been diagnosed with either of these conditions and therefore believe that my view of disparity wholly deserves my reverence. The worst and the best of my life's decisions and actions can be attributed to my discerning (another "dis" word!) disparities between what I had or could do in comparison to the possessions and abilities of others. And get this. I think this disparity stuff can drive people to achieve great and dumb things. I have ample proof of both.

How did and how does disparity ignite and motivate me? Conversely, how could trivial differences between me and others cause me to be depressed? I'm looking crazier and crazier, aren't I? Where did this orientation to life come from, and where did it lead? These are questions that I can now answer after a massive dose of introspection. I now know it wasn't from my mother. Disparity was just not a factor for her. She either ignored what others had or possessed or, when she did notice them, was sincerely happy for them. Not me and not my Dad. Differences gnawed at us like an abscessed tooth. It was actually at times kind of annoying to me to see how Ma was genuinely thrilled with what her friends and their family members had acquired or accomplished. If they bought a new car, she didn't despair (there's another of those words like disparity), she rejoiced and relished telling others about it. And get this, she did this when we did not even own a car and the possibilities of us ever being able to own one was beyond bleak. So you see, the "disparity gene" did not come from Ma. What about my Dad's genes? Possibly. He often hated and openly disparaged the successes and acquisitions of others in the most acerbic of terms. A typical conversation between Ma and Dad when he was not drunk and was not giving us all "the silent treatment" would go something like this:

Ma: "I talked with Mrs. Steadfast* the other day and she said her son Goody* took college courses and got a big promotion in the army."

Dad: "Who gives a shit about that suck-hole? He always was a brownnoser and a spoiled brat. You know why he always gets ahead? Because he looks like a Jew, that's why."

Ma: "Oh, Tom, don't say that. I think it's wonderful that he is doing so well and serving our country."

Dad: "Bullshit!"

Talk about a difference in worldviews. Even today, after seventy-three-plus years, whenever I gravitate toward a narrow and negative view of a situation or person, I can feel my Dad cheering me on from his grave. Thankfully, I get counter-messages from Ma and others like my wife, Janice, but I at times also value the cynicism I got from Dad. He had been right not to trust everyone and not to believe all the stuff that people spiel. However, he was so wrong about so many things that his has become an almost inaudible voice in my life. This may have been due to the happenstances of my Dad's short life and my slow and often regressive path to adulthood. By the time I became a saner version of myself, my Dad had become quite debilitated, and then he died without us having had the chance to fully appreciate each other and our different perspectives on life. Several years after Dad died, I had to absorb Ma's more positive view but with some serious adjustments to accommodate for the realities she usually ignored.

So how much alike were my Dad and I when it came to disparity? Similar, but it was our responses to disparity that were so vastly different. We both noticed who had what, but what we did in response to these perceived differences and inequities were where we diverged. He became disgusted, envious, resentful, and then went out and got drunk. He also did not work in a disciplined and focused way to change the situation or himself.

As an adult, I too drank when disappointed or frustrated, but just briefly, and then it was on to changing the situation, me, or both. The successes and failures that came from my efforts to decrease disparity has been the driving force throughout my life.

WE WERE RICH ONCE! WE WERE?

I had always heard that we were once a fairly wealthy family, but recalling the surroundings of our bleak flat growing up, I really found that hard to believe. The actual evidence that we were once rich was totally lacking. The fact was we were poor. Also, if we were once rich, then where did all the money go? Why didn't we own our house like my friends' parents did in this Irish neighborhood in this northeast industrialized city? Or why didn't we have a car? Why were we living so close to, and often actually in, poverty?

In doing the research for this book, I did find some recorded evidence to support the idea that my mother's side was once a wealthy family. We were always told that her family was a beneficiary of the Plant's largesse. The Plant, which was the vernacular for the large steel corporation in an adjoining state, had planned to build a massive steel-production enterprise in the early 1920s. They sought a location on the shores of one of the Great Lakes in order to take advantage of the lakes for the shipping of raw materials and the finished steel products.

Ma's family's fortune came about when the mega out-of-state steel enterprise decided to expand and acquired a local steel company in 1922 for $60 million. No, we did not have a piece of that transaction. However, my great-grandfather, Samuel Wasson, owned 117 acres of farmland that was in immediate proximity to the shores of their chosen Great Lake. So, the company that was to become known as The Plant purchased this land from him for $170,000 in 1899.*

This would amount to about $4 million in 2011 and, of course, even more when you factor in the absence of income tax back then. In addition to this money, he apparently also invested in various companies, including coal mines that further enhanced the family's financial position. Ma always told us that her father was a civil engineer, and I remember as a kid playing with a bunch of his instruments kept in a wooden case that was lined with felt or maybe even velvet. Perhaps his civil engineering work enabled him to ferret out some other lucrative deals.

As I grew up and heard stories from Ma about "sleeping on bags of gold," I was puzzled and enchanted by this image even though it didn't sound too comfortable or very practical. Why were they sleeping on bags of gold? Were they afraid of the banks failing? It's possible. Whatever it was, I don't remember her ever explaining it, but the image sure stuck with me, and so I repeatedly checked the three mattresses in our destitute home just to be sure no bags of gold were left behind. There weren't.

Another compelling memory was that of the Big House. My mother grew up in what she always called the Big House, which really was the largest and most prestigious house in their village at that time and where Ma, as a young lady, "entertained with two sets of china, one in blue and one in yellow." I don't know, but the image of this life as she described it was quite vivid in my young mind and in great contrast to the life we lived as kids. I also remember seeing that very impressive Victorian home built on the main street coursing through the village, which had become a city by the time we came around. It was also one of the first houses to be outfitted with electricity. So impressive was this home that it was even on a postcard with the phrase "The Wasson Family Home the Showplace of Lackawanna."

---

* The History of Lackawanna, Lackawanna Bicentennial Commission, December 10, 1976, p 55.

I remember seeing both the postcard and the house itself when we lived for a time in a trailer on the outskirts of the city. My seventh-grade teacher taught us the history of our state, and when the topic moved to our city, my social standing in the class went up a few notches. "Peter Talty's great-grandfather was an important person in our city, and the mansion that he built is now the clubhouse for the Knights of Columbus on the corner of Ridge Road and Rosary Avenue." She then passed around the postcard. The Big House was an impressive house, and we would always watch for it as we rode by on the bus (remember, we didn't have a car). My oldest brother Tommy and my sister Sue got to live in the Big House during the early years of my parents' marriage, and they always told us younger guys what it was like. Of course, when they lived there, most of the wealth was gone, and the Big House was all that was left from the previous years of my family's prosperity.

Unfortunately, the taxes and expenses of maintaining such a large home became more than my aunt Dory could handle. My great-grandfather and grandfather had died, and my aunt Dory had inherited the house, but out of necessity, she was forced to sell it and most of its contents to a local organization in the 1950s. I know it must have greatly saddened my mother to see her family's mansion in the hands of an organization and us living in a trailer, but she never belabored this. She always had a positive outlook and focused more on the future and the present, choosing to only recall the positive aspects of the past. I do, however, remember her expressing great sadness when her former home was accidentally destroyed by fire on December 21, 1954. I remember her crying quietly as she read about the fire and looked at the photographs of her former grand home in the newspaper. As a kid, I remember us having a few cut-glass bowls in our china cabinet and a wicker furniture set on our porch that was the few remnants of Ma's other life in the Big House. Otherwise, that was it. Even the postcard has since been lost.

Rich No More

So how did our family go from "sleeping on bags of gold" to struggling to remain in a flat in a house in the 1950s that my father's brother (Uncle Bern) owned? And with a rent of just $35 per month that we could seldom pay? There has always been a lot of guessing among my adult siblings and me about where all the money went. We always assumed that the money was not invested successfully and that the family just lived off the gains from the sale of the farmland and stock dividends or sales. The crash of 1929 must have also been devastating. Regardless of where and why the money went, it was clear that by the time my mother married my father, there was little left. My mother received a trust fund when she became twenty-one, but it was only a few thousand dollars a year and was quickly consumed by my father's impulsive buying and increasing alcoholism. This assumption was based on the fact that when I was a kid, there were certainly no funds to purchase a car or a house or, in many instances, even pay the expenses of nominal family living.

So was my father going to be the one to rebuild the family's wealth? No, but perhaps he could have. He was intelligent enough, but he was distracted by other forces. For example, he seemed unaffected by the culture surrounding him where most husbands and fathers worked hard in the steel plant, took advantage of overtime opportunities, and built solid financial bases and home lives for their families. Not our Dad. He was unmoved by the thriving industrial economy following the depression that surrounded him. Add to this time of emerging prosperity was the war effort with the advent of World War II. Burgeoning affluence was everywhere. In my college days, I worked in the Plant with men that were contemporaries of my Dad's who had seized those opportunities and bought homes and cars, went on vacations, and sent their kids to college. Again, this was not our Dad. Ma cogently captures in a joking way where Dad's time, energy, and money went when she often said, "He was always too busy drinking and carousing."

~~~~

My Dad, Tom or Thomas Edward Talty, worked as an engineer on a small railroad that operated mainly within the Plant, and provided all the movement of steel, its waste products such as slag, and also the raw materials like iron ore required to make steel, as well as the steel end products throughout the Plant. This was an extremely well-paid position, and Dad worked his way up through the positions of office clerk, fireman, and eventually engineer. Besides the money, he had prestige far above the laborer and hooker roles that I occupied for eighteen months during my college days. Of course, when I worked there, this steel behemoth was beginning its decline, leading to its inevitable subsequent death.

In my Dad's day, he was part of a thriving production giant with twenty-three thousand steelworkers employed at the Plant's local operation alone that generated prosperity for all those working there. Driving past it today and seeing the vacant buildings and desolate landscape, it is hard to imagine what it once was. At one time, the Plant and its other operations were producing almost all the steel for the nation's emerging skyscrapers, bridges, and, subsequently, for cars and steel plates for ships and tanks as World War II unfolded. It was a great time to be a steelworker and an even better time to be a railway engineer.

But unfortunately, we did not enjoy the standard of living and quality of life that Dad's paychecks could have commanded and that his contemporaries enjoyed. No, Dad's mind, interests, and energies were deployed elsewhere. Alcohol and other distractions held far more power than a loving wife and six kids. As a result, our young lives were frequently ones of want and near poverty because he seldom brought home his handsome pay. Instead, he bought alcohol and immersed himself in a somewhat nefarious lifestyle. Who dealt us this mess of cards? I don't know, but I was always acutely aware of the disparity between what my peers' families and homes were like and the impoverished life we were living.

I have often thought what could have been if my great-grandfather's money had been invested differently or if my father's obsession with alcohol was instead directed toward forging a solid work history and the foundations of family stability. How different our lives might have been? Or would they? We can never know. Perhaps the more intriguing question is, would we have been different as kids and then as adults? These are all questions we ask that have no answers. However, an even far more compelling question to me is, how did my mother cope with all the disappointments that she had to experience as she witnessed the decline of her family's wealth and then see her own family being immersed in a life of poverty? This was, of course, all facilitated by her marrying a man who was unable to take hold of life and provide for his family as most of his contemporaries did. And I have to ask, how did Ma deal with a lifetime of such adversity and still keep a positive outlook? In spite of all her losses and a life of despair, she somehow maintained a sense of optimism and dignity. How did she do this? My brothers and I still marvel at this even today.

The Sad and Insane Confluence of Two Families

Ma and Dad had six kids, but our ages resulted in there sort of being two distinct family configurations. Ma and Dad married young in 1927; he was eighteen, and she was seventeen. They quickly had two kids, Tommy in 1928 and Sue in 1929. Between 1929 and 1939, Ma had three miscarriages. The end result was that Ma, Dad, Tommy, and Sue lived life as a family of four for ten years until 1939 when Bernie was born. I followed in 1942, Danny in 1945, and then Pat in 1946. Also, in 1946, Tommy joined the air force, and in 1948, Sue married Jim Riley. So with Tommy and Sue out of the house, this gave Ma and Dad a sort of second family ("the four boys") to raise and be responsible for. Because of the age difference between Tommy and Sue and the four of us, they were propelled into the role of surrogate parents to us at far too early of an age. This was especially true of Sue because Tommy was usually living abroad during his military service days.

Ma was always the one to pick up the yoke of these two struggling families with Sue as her ally and confidant. Dad was disengaged from both families as he wandered through a life of alcoholism, mental illness, gambling, physical deterioration, and then an early tortured death at age fifty-four. As Ma's second family struggled and almost perished a number of times, it was Sue and Jim who were the "first responders" [*a person (as a police officer or an EMT) who is among those responsible for going immediately to the scene of an accident or emergency to provide assistance]*. Of course, they were not really police officers or EMTs, but they certainly were pulled into the morass of Ma's second family's chaos throughout Sue's life that ended at age fifty-nine. It was Sue and Jim who ended up being the ones *"going immediately to the scene of an accident or emergency to provide assistance."* Tommy helped from afar with financial assistance and support through his plenteous letters and phone calls. He also provided a respite for all of us at various times when we went to visit or stayed with him and his wife Karoline. Trying to help Ma deal with the ongoing convulsions of this second family was unfair to Sue and Jim. It cheated them out of having a stable, peaceful, and happy life of their own. They were true heroes.

~~~~

Ma wrote a letter to Sue when I was born that really shows Ma's perspective on her family in 1942 as well as the beginnings of her second family. It is a significant letter that survived and stands by itself in terms of content and time. It begins my life story and gives us Ma's perspective on our family at that time. This particular letter was written while she was in the hospital recuperating from delivering me on April 16, 1942. She wrote this letter to my sister Sue, who was thirteen years old at the time. Over the years, Sue became Ma's best friend, confidant, co-conspirator, advocate, and rescuer. In troubled times, it was Sue who was summoned to the scene and whose counsel Ma sought. I view this particular letter as a sort of transition letter as Ma began the laborious effort to establish and maintain a stable family against all the destructive forces surrounding her. I don't know how this letter survived because so much of our family photos, letters, and other personal treasures have been lost as a result of our frequent moves and turbulent lives.

April 19th, 1942
Dear Sue,

Daddy has been telling me what a good girl you've been. I know it is bad enough to have to take care of

The Sad and Insane Confluence of Two Families

Bernard without Dory picking on you, but you know how she is when she is tired so try to take it until I come home. I'll make it up to you some way. We know Dory doesn't feel well and is so darn good to us, but I wish she wouldn't work so hard. It makes me nervous just laying here worrying about it.

I hope you don't feel bad about the baby, but after I get home he'll have to be handled as little as possible. I'll let you hold him once in a while but it will have to be gentle. I miss Bernie so; I can hardly wait till I get home to show him the baby. I named him today, Peter Michael. I hope you didn't tell Mrs. Caldwell or Harriet about Peter's foot. Because I don't want anybody to know until the Doctor operates on it. He will have to wear a cast for a while, but I don't care because it will help him a lot in his walking.

We are going to get Castor oil this morning, and it is getting pretty near time for it, so I guess I'll close. Will write more next time, and tell you who came to see me. So far just Daddy and Tommy. I haven't had anybody in the afternoon, so I sleep as much as I can. Well goodbye until the next letter.

Mother and Peter

Tell Dory I said not to work so hard, and tell me if Daddy went out at all since I've been here. He won't say so for fear I'll worry. If he spends the money I can't help it now.

M & P

Our family: Thomas Stephan, Susan Ann, Bernard Francis, and Peter Michael Talty

~~~~

Oh yeah, that stuff about my foot. Yes, I was born with a clubfoot. I have no idea why I thought you would know this but thought it would be a good way to lead into talking about my foot and subsequent "foot adventures." For example, years later when I was in college taking a freshman literature course, I found a hero of sorts in W. Somerset Maugham's Philip Carey. Philip, like me, was born with a clubfoot, and he was also the protagonist in Maugham's masterpiece novel *Of Human Bondage*. How do you like that? Actually, our clubfeet were the only thing we actually had in common. However, I was so impressed with our clubfoot connections that I made it the focus of the writing assignment we were given. My professor wrote "irrelevant" in heavy red pencil right next to this disclosure about my clubfoot on my analytical essay about the book. Screw him!

Anyway, they did some cutting-edge surgery (get it?) back in 1942 that gave me a solid ankle that enabled me to walk, run, jump, and slide into the bases on the playgrounds that actually had bases. I loved to slide. In fact, I was better at sliding than I was at anything else in baseball. Philip Carey didn't have surgery and had to wear a big shoe and limp around. No baseball and sliding for him. I bet that was what my Ma was thinking would be my life if this new surgery wasn't successful. However, that vanguard surgery wasn't perfect. I ended up with two different size feet. As an adult, shopping for shoes to fit a size 13 on the left and a size 9 on the right was a test of patience and economics, but it led to me getting my picture and my shoe story in the *National Enquirer*. Really! I know Philip Carey can't say that.

Ma's concerns in her letter about our aunt Dory were very appropriate because she did do a lot to offset my Dad's refusal to bring his hefty wages home, and she also helped Ma with the ponderous work involved in trying to feed and clothe an unstable, unruly, unappreciative, and poorly funded family living in a low-life kind of flat. It wasn't low-life when we moved in, but it certainly evolved in that direction in a short time due to a combination of neglect and abuse, especially by me and my brothers. In reality, I hardly remember Dory at all, but I must have been extraordinarily moved at her funeral to the extent that I screamed out "Dory!" and tried to jump into the grave when they were lowering her coffin. My elder brother Bernie saved me from further embarrassment by pulling me back just in time, coupled with a harsh message to "Shut up!" I must have seen this grave-jumping business happen on some TV show or in a movie and impulsively decided to replicate a bit of it myself. Bizarre, I know.

Doesn't Ma's letter sound like the beginnings of a nice family with perhaps just a few minor inklings about my Dad's drinking and a couple of nagging financial concerns? She almost makes us look like the emerging Waltons or the Huxtables. From my view today, I think Ma was either dreaming or maybe even a bit delusional. Sorry, Ma. Maybe it was the impending dreaded castor oil.

If Ma knew the kind of family strife that was going to unfold over the subsequent years, she may have opted to run away with a hospital orderly or someone else. We would have understood (not that we were real understanding kids; it's just that it would make sense to flee from the crazies we were going to become). No, we were not like those cute Cleaver kids or Fred MacMurray's mischievous little guys on *My Three Sons*. We were more like the three sons of bitches (I exclude Bernie because he was always a good boy). Dad often described Danny, Pat, and me as such.

Remember those other nice families on TV like the one on *Lassie* with the loving and sexy mom, or that fine, stable, and hardworking Scandinavian Hansen family on *I Remember Mama*? Well, they sure as hell weren't us. Actually, we were the total opposite of those TV fantasy families that we watched on our twelve-inch Philco TV that we had no business owning.

It really was ludicrous for us to be the only family on our street to have a TV when Ma did not even have money for food or clothes for us. Now what I would really love to do is wrest those perfect people right out of their wonderful family tableaus and thrust them right into the midst of our chaotic lives of that time. That would be so delicious. Oh yeah, and make a show about some force ripping those perfect bastards out of their wonderful lives and then thrusting them into my life at that time. I would really like to watch a show like that.

~~~~

Now it may seem incongruous that we would have a TV when we couldn't even pay our rent or buy food. Well, we had the first TV on the block because Dad was both impulsive and persuasive. Regardless of other family needs, in 1949, he (they?) decided to buy a twelve-inch Philco TV that was delivered one evening when Dad was home and not drunk. I remember it arrived with the four of us yelling questions and trying to see what this thing was. Dad responded by yelling, "Get back, you bastards. You'll wreck it" and then shifting to a voice of obsequiousness when thanking the guys who delivered this marvelous box. This was when TV was so new that there was only one channel, and the broadcasts didn't come on until 5:00 p.m. and then went off at 10:00 p.m. For the first and only time, we were the envy of our peers (reverse disparity?), but we were quite magnanimous in that we welcomed the entire neighborhood of kids into our debacle of a home every afternoon to watch *Howdy Doody* and *Cactus Jim* for an hour from five o'clock to six o'clock, Monday through Friday.

These shows so captivated us kids that my best friend Georgie left me in a field with a broken wrist when I was seven or eight years old and rushed home to my house to catch the latest episode of *Howdy Doody*. He had been watching me jump out of a second-story window of a house under construction into a pile of dirt. I had done it a couple of times successfully but mistimed my jump and landed on my hand fracturing my wrist. In response to Ma's question of "Where is Peter?" my friend said, "Oh, he's down in the field. He hurt his arm." Before any more information could be elicited, I arrived in a kind neighbor's car who took Ma and me to Mercy Hospital to have my arm put in a cast. Oh, the mesmerizing power of *Howdy Doody*!

~~~~

The broken wrist was just one of several injuries I sustained as a kid because I was impulsive and liked taking chances. For example, one day, while playing in a field with my brother Bernie and my cousin Tyke*, I showed these characteristics from high up in a tree.

Tyke and I had each climbed parallel trees while Bernie watched from below. We climbed as high as we could and then crawled out on big limbs that were about ten feet from one another. Without thinking or any hesitation, I yelled to Tyke that I would swing over to his tree using a branch hanging below my limb. Unbeknownst to me, the branch was quite dead, and so was I, almost. Holding firmly on to the branch that I envisioned would be my "Tarzan swing," I instead plummeted the twenty feet to the ground, striking my head on a rock. Bernie and Tyke, having witnessed this terrible fall, were just glad I wasn't dead. I just had a bad scalp wound with a lot of blood. They probably would diagnose it as a concussion if this happened to a kid today, but I just went home, and Ma washed it off, and off I went to play.

I have a whole list of injuries like this, including running into the side of a moving car when Bernie was chasing me, tearing my armpit on a broken tree limb during another fall that required five stitches, getting a fishhook in my eyelid from a deviant cast by my cousin Tyke, getting a cut across my upper lip from a ragged tuna fish can top wielded by a kid I was fighting with, and on and on.

People often said that I was accident-prone as a kid. I disagree. Actually, it was more that I was reckless and crazy, doing things saner kids would shun. Perhaps these were the foundations of my need to engage in risky behavior that became my hallmark throughout my life and manifested itself in a myriad of ways.

~~~~

As one of my first efforts at decreasing my feelings of disparity, I tried to get a paper route. However, you had to be at least twelve years old to get one, and I was only seven or eight at the time. So I volunteered to help an older kid who delivered the local newspaper to our house, the houses on my street, and some other nearby streets in the neighborhood.

Initially, I didn't get paid, but I gained prestige because my "supervisor" gave me a newspaper bag, and I felt pretty important bringing the newspaper to my own house plus twenty-eight friends' houses each afternoon. I was puny as a kid, and my newspaper bag often dragged on the ground when it had all the papers I had to deliver neatly stacked in it, but I didn't care. To me, I was now a paperboy! (Sort of.)

Because I was always trying to lessen the disparity between what I had and the possessions of others, I became an opportunist early on. This was apparent at a baseball game I was watching in the park being played by older kids like my "supervisor." Anyway, my "supervisor" who I'll call Max* was involved in a close game, and Max's team had a chance to win it, but it was time for him to leave to pick up his newspapers and deliver them. Since Max was one of the best players, his teammates were begging him not to leave. Max was conflicted because he was also a responsible kid. As they were all pleading with him, I ran up and said, "Hey, Max, I'll go to your house and get your wagon, go out to the paper house and get your papers, and start delivering them. You can stay here and finish the game and catch up with me." Max was at first hesitant, but everyone else convinced him to let me do it. I did such a good job that Max "hired" me for 50¢ a week to deliver my twenty-eight newspapers six days a week. I did this for a while until Max gave up the route, and the new kid said he didn't need me.

My next venture into working revealed a regression of sorts in my burgeoning work ethic. My brother Bernie had a paper route of a different kind. Each week on Mondays, about one hundred shopping slingers were delivered to our house. Bernie had to roll each one, put a rubber band around them, place them vertically in a newspaper bag, and then deliver them to the houses designated on his route. He was paid $2 for this. We would all help with the rolling, except Pat because he just never liked to help and Dad because he wasn't home.

After a few weeks, Bernie decided to give up the slinger, and I saw an opportunity for me. I suggested that he keep the slinger in his name—you had to be twelve for this too—and I would take care of delivering it, and then I would get the $2 per week. He was fine with it, and so was Ma, so I was in business. The first three weeks did not go so well. In fact, if it hadn't been for Ma diligently rolling and banding all the slingers while she watched TV, it would have gone much worse much sooner.

I found that many people didn't want the slinger; some even threw them back at me when I threw them on their porch. I also realized that the "customers" would not know or even care if I delivered their slingers or not. So I took the next logical step and dumped them all off the Cazenovia Street Bridge into the shallow creek below. I did this for a few weeks, but I noticed how they were bunching up in the shallow water. So I changed my dumping spot to an empty field. This worked for a few more weeks, but then my observant sister Sue, while coming home from shopping, spotted the pile of slingers in the creek and another pile at the edge of the field. I was too lazy to take them further on in so they would be less visible. So that ended that business venture, and it was all due to my laziness and deceitfulness. I still feel bad that Ma rolled and banded all those slingers while watching *Lights Out* and *Martin Kane*, and I just callously dumped them all. In those beginning days of my trying to decrease my economic disparity, I was driven to earn money but lacked the discipline, fortitude, and energy to achieve it in an honest way.

The Talty Flu

Being a member of this non compos mentis household had the potential of infecting all the inhabitants with what I now refer to as the Talty flu. This really wasn't the flu in a medical sense, but more of a constellation of attitudes and behaviors that we Taltys seemed to possess. It was my experience and observations that this strange malady usually went undiagnosed and thus untreated (continuing the medical analogy). Now if you view life's problems as hopeless and unsolvable and the work of fate and if you find yourself overreacting to stress (and "blowing your stack"), you may have also contracted this malady. You have my sincerest of condolences because life's journey is made so much more arduous when you have a bad case of the Talty flu.

Oddly, Hallmark has not come up with an appropriate card to comfort those with this affliction, but they should. On the cover, I'm picturing an image of a downward spiral with a sad and angry face depicted struggling through the stages of life. I must give credit to my Uncle Bern who was our landlord and then my employer for almost ten years (seven full time and three years part time) who first sort of identified this condition in his terse and gruff way. He didn't call it the Talty flu, but he was certainly describing a sort of disease. I heard it described numerous times during the several years I worked for him as a janitor in the school where he was the stationary engineer. Whenever I would screw up, he would say disgustedly, "Pete, you're getting just like the Taltys. They are the stupidest creatures ever put on this earth. They can't learn from experience, and they keep making the same mistakes over and over." I was hurt by his characterization of me and my family this way, so I came up with what I thought was a brilliant comeback: "But you're a Talty too!" It seemed brilliant back then, at least to me. He was not impressed; he would just let out a low-level growl and mutter something unintelligible as he walked away. His kids, Tyke and Bood*, told me that he often said the same thing to them whenever they erred. The point is that there seemed to be a sort of disease, or constellation of attitudes and behaviors, that "infected" us Taltys that needs to be delineated because we are all fighting it to varying degrees throughout our lives.

Some of the compounding signs of the Talty flu that I have identified by observing many of my family members, including myself, are procrastination, the avoidance of active problem solving through data gathering in favor of bitching, avoidance of facts in favor of assumptions, and yes, that's right, blowing one's stack. A more subtle sign is the inability to learn from other people's mistakes, scientific facts, and thus recklessly hastening ahead down the highway to "the city of disappointments, errors and failures" by refusing expert advice because objective fact-finding was just not the Talty way.

This maladaptive way of attacking problems was not due to a lack of intelligence. We Taltys are a fairly bright people; it's just that our brains are encumbered by history and too much exposure to too many poor navigators and pilots of the sinking ships of life in our family and not enough of those who have it really figured out. In fact, when any of these latter kinds of these potentially good role models came into our fields of awareness, we usually ignored, ridiculed, and laughed at them amongst ourselves while consuming lots of alcohol. Do you think this dumb and childish? Yes, of course, but that's the Talty way, and thus the Talty flu. I know you are wondering if there is a prophylaxis to prevent one from getting the Talty flu, and if one does become infected, is there an antidote? Yes! Definitely! Ma's spirit and positive outlook was one form of defense.

~~~~

The Talty Flu

I have a great example of the Talty flu. This crazy thing happened around 1960 and, for once, did not involve me directly. It happened during one of our many moves where a few Taltys and a friend were all helping move our stuff from one flat to another. For this move, there were just two family members and a friend involved. I had to work that day; otherwise, I would be immersed in another Talty fiasco.

One of the benefits of this move was that our family would no longer have to see or have any further dealings with their next-door neighbor, Apollo Creed (a fake name that fits this story, but protects his identity). They had a lot of stuff to move, requiring two truckloads. Throughout the whole day, Apollo kept snapping pictures of them and also filming them with a movie camera without saying a word. These were taken from his front porch and backyard, so he was always on his own property. This was bizarre, but throughout his time next door, an extensive list could have been made of his bizarre behaviors.

Our family's relationship with Apollo and Mrs. Creed had not always been adversarial. In fact, the two couples had once been good friends, visiting back and forth at each other's homes and going out drinking together. The relationship became strained and then eroded after Apollo tore the phone off the wall and beat his wife too many times. When this occurred, Mrs. Creed would run next door to our family member's flat to use their phone to call the police on Apollo and actively seek the support and counsel of whoever was available. After too much of this drama, we, in our usual direct and no-nonsense way, told her not to come back. From that time on, there was coldness and outright arguments over many things too many times. And now, on the last day, Apollo had to continue harassing us.

Some of us in the family had the proverbial hot Irish tempers in those days and a history of physically fighting with little provocation. However, some showed great restraint throughout this emotional day. But once they closed the doors on the last load and were driving away, they suddenly stopped the truck and said, "Let's go back to ask Apollo what he was doing taking pictures of us." Some cooler heads in the truck tried to dissuade the hotheads, but to no avail. The driver turned the truck around and drove back into what was their own driveway. Apollo was still standing on his porch.

Besides going back, the trio made a second mistake that day by walking onto Apollo's property in order to confront him from the sidewalk as Apollo remained on his porch. The conversation was brief. When asked, "Why were you taking pictures of us?" Apollo, who was a heavyset, large man, simply said "I'll show you." With that he reached inside his front door and quickly came off his porch swinging two baseball bats held together in his two thick hands. Apollo struck one guy two or three times before the other two jumped in and grabbed him in a vain effort to restrain him. According to another family member, who had also returned when she saw the truck turn around, a "battle royal" had ensued with the four men rolling on the ground. Efforts to restrain Apollo were fruitless as he lashed out with his bats. This convulsing turmoil of bodies and bats commenced across Apollo's front yard and onto the side of his house. There must have been much yelling because an older woman who lived on the other side of Apollo and had been recovering from a heart attack looked out her bedroom window. When she saw three men attacking her friend Apollo Creed, she called the police.

In the midst of trying to wrest the bats away from Apollo, he bit one of the family members on the forearm as well as struck him with the bats. The main protagonist in this drama absorbed most of the hits from the bats. Finally, they got the bats away from Apollo and had wrestled him to the ground just as a police car pulled up. With the police present, everyone stopped fighting. When they were told what had just taken place, the police confiscated the bats, put them in the police car, and ordered all parties to stop fighting or arrests would be made. They also said that if any of them wanted to bring charges against the other parties, they needed to go to the local police precinct to file a complaint.

The late-arriving family member who was not involved in the fracas but witnessed most of this bizarre event called Atticus Finch,[*] who was actually their friend besides being their lawyer. He advised them to file a complaint specifying that Apollo had attacked them first with a deadly weapon (the baseball bats). He also directed them to go to the hospital or a doctor to have their injuries treated and recorded. So off they went to the hospital and then to the police precinct to file the complaint.

I did not personally witness any of this "main event" but did get the play-by-play from the "Talty Battlers" when I came from work. They were all there in our living room flat describing the foray in detail for Ma and Dad, who seemed aghast at it all. As directed by their lawyer, the complaint had been filed at the police station and injuries recorded at the hospital. According to their lawyer, they had an excellent case and were therefore going to sue Apollo for their injuries plus "pain and suffering". There was much glee on everyone's part except for Ma and Dad. They seemed more subdued about the pending lawsuit. Revenge and satisfaction was not on their mind that day; it was simply relief that the fight was over.

~~~~

I was curious and also wanted to show support for the injured victims, so I went to two of the preliminary hearings. My boss (Uncle Bern) was not happy to hear why I wanted a few hours off to attend the hearings. He asked his usual rhetorical question after I gave him a synopsis of the Apollo Creed incident: "What the hell's the matter with you people? Don't you have enough problems?" Also, as usual, I viewed his questions as rhetorical, and therefore didn't answer them. I just explained how my work would get done and left for a few hours.

The hearings did not have the outcome we had all anticipated. We all believed the lawyer when he said that my family members, the injured parties, had clearly been injured by Apollo Creed and that he was going to be made to pay for all damages. However, there was a sad surprise awaiting us. When our main protagonist was on the stand and being questioned by Apollo's lawyer, he gave a detailed history of the years of harassment by Apollo culminating in the attack on that fateful moving day. Two key pieces of the case were Apollo's use of the baseball bats with the intent to cause bodily harm, and that Apollo had initiated the attack. This was looking good. The only questions in my mind were would Apollo go to jail, and how big was the cash settlement for damages going to be? I was the one now feeling gleeful, but it was premature.

"Where are these supposed baseball bats now?" Apollo's lawyer asked in a sarcastic tone as our protagonist sat defiantly in the witness chair. When he explained that "Officers Sneak and Snake" (these pseudonyms are just me inserting some ireful humor into this humorless situation) put them in their car and took them as evidence." I thought this was it! Wow, was I wrong!

The rest of the testimony was painful to watch. Skewered, I think, is the term for it. Apollo's lawyer must have known about our sometimes explosive personalities and his skilled questioning elicited it. Although he didn't leave his chair and attack the lawyer, I thought he might do so at any moment. Our lawyer remained quiet as the skewering went on and on. "*Object!*" That's what my mind was yelling even though I had no idea what our lawyer should object to. Atticus tried on redirect to bring out our protagonist's patient and kind side and all the times he had helped Apollo and his wife when they were fighting and tearing phones off walls, but I think the judge already saw the potentially-pouncing-angry posture threatening to erupt.

After our last family member and friend left the stand Apollo's lawyer called the senior police officer Sneak who first arrived at the "fight arena." He brought his written report and was asked to read it into the record. When he finished, Apollo's lawyer said, "Your report makes no mention of two baseball bats. Did you take two baseball bats from the scene and put them in your car as evidence?" The officer should try out for Broadway. He looked very perplexed and said incredulously, "Baseball bats? Neither I nor my partner, Officer Snake, put any baseball bats in our car. We didn't see any bats." Thus began the painful and rapid slide toward dismissal, but the nail in the coffin was yet to be seen or heard. It was to be presented in a most dramatic fashion.

The Talty Flu

After all the witnesses had been heard; the Court adjourned until the following week. However, Apollo's lawyer had a request that was outside of the norm for court procedure, which is what got this case in the local newspapers and on TV. It seems that what was in dispute was who had actually initiated the attack? The only person who could determine this was an objective eye witness, and Apollo's lawyer announced that they had found such a person. It was the woman who called the police and saw the scuffle outside of her bedroom window who had this key information, or so Apollo's lawyer said. However, he went on to say that "she was too ill to come to court, but she wants to tell the court what she saw. If she could not come to court, could the court go to her?" The judge agreed to directly hear from this witness the following week when the case would be continued in her bedroom!

Lying in her bed, she told the judge, lawyers for both sides, and the court recorder what she had witnessed. She didn't see the whole fight, only the portion that took place on the side of the house outside her bedroom window. She saw three men (the Talty gang) "all attacking poor Apollo Creed." That was it. The case was dead, but the actual pronouncement of death would not occur for a few months. It was, of course, dismissed! We waited anxiously to see if Apollo would sue the Taltys for false arrest, but thankfully, he did not. The sympathy aroused and attention garnered from the "bedroom testimony," coupled with the missing baseball bats, killed what seemed to be an open-and-shut case. It was, but just not in our favor. Thus, another chapter in the annals of the history of the crazy Taltys with doses of the Talty flu in ample supply.

Today, when I think back on this bizarre incident, of course, questions abound in my mind. The key question is what made them go back? They could have been all done with the annoying Apollo Creed and moved on with their lives. What really became of the baseball bats? They were not something that our group just imagined. Did Officer Snake and Sneak get paid off to "lose" the bats, or did they just honestly misplace them? Was it intentional for some reason? Why was the lady in the bedroom's testimony given such incredible credence? If Apollo was as an innocent victim as he claimed, why didn't he sue us for false arrest, slander, or something else after the court ruled in his favor? All questions for which we have no answers.

This whole crazy and sad tale has all the elements (or signs and symptoms) of the Talty flu. It is replete with things like making a bad situation worse, overreacting to stress, ignoring the prudent thing to do and just walking away, blowing one's stack and engaging the perceived enemy, and not seeking counsel from experts earlier on when Apollo first began harassing them with his bizarre cinematography.

One last note on the Talty flu: I kind of think it's contagious. My evidence is admittedly weak because it is nothing more than a hypothesis. However, I observed how previously sensible, rational, and calm people married into our family were changed forever the more they were exposed to our ways. They were calm and logical problem solvers no more. Over the years, they worked tirelessly trying to help us all using a voice of reason whenever problems arose. No more. It was like those who helped treat lepers (people afflicted with Hansen's disease) and supposedly contracted the dreaded disease themselves.

Why Didn't Ma Contract the Talty Flu?

You would think that Ma, having spent all that time with Dad, would have contracted a severe strain of the Talty flu. Miraculously, she did not. My mother tried her best to approach problems differently and to give us a more optimistic perspective on life. However, the Talty flu was far too virulent a disease for one person to eradicate. But like an unfortunate early settler or Native American Indian wrapped in a smallpox-infested blanket, avoidance of the Talty flu would seem impossible, but remarkably, Ma did it. How do I know all this? It is by living in the midst of our family's chaos and through reading Ma's letters that I discovered Ma's antidote or prophylaxis of sorts.

We have clear evidence of Ma's great optimism and resiliency in the abundant letters that she wrote to my brother Tommy over a twenty-year period. Tommy was a supportive mainstay of the family from afar, and perhaps living overseas for much of his adult life enabled him to also avoid contracting our strange affliction. It was always a cause of great anticipation and celebration whenever Tommy returned home. Ma would talk about his pending return for days, working us all into a frenzy of anticipation. My first recollection of Tommy's return home was when I was very young—young enough to be riding tricycles with my cousin Tyke. We had ridden the half block to the corner of our street watching for Tommy when I saw a yellow Van Dyke taxicab go by with the back window rolled down and a soldier in uniform yelling out my name. I exclaimed to Tyke, "That's Tommy!" With that, we pedaled down the street as fast as we could. By the time we got to our house, he was assembling his luggage including a big duffel bag and paying his fare. I still remember the excitement I felt in seeing him in his air force uniform; even Tyke got caught up in it too.

I think Tommy avoided contracting the Talty flu because he was exposed to different role models who approached problem solving in a whole different way. Living overseas, he was removed from the chaos of our early lives and interacted on a daily basis with more rational and mature people whom he liked and respected.

Ma's letters serve as the historical backdrop for our lives as Taltys, and coupled with my own observations, depict a convoluted trail of entanglements that still surprise and depress me and my brothers even today.

~~~~

Yes, our early lives were lacking in both stability and normalcy. However, Dad was not drunk all the time, and he did come home a lot of nights. It seemed that paydays were his and our worst times. When he was home and sober, he would make feeble forays into the roles of husband and father but with little persistence or success. Of course, we kids sure didn't help. I know he was surely disappointed in our poor performance as students and our lack of concern about it further enraged him. We also were not very responsible or dependable regarding any home chores. In fact, our unruly behavior may have even helped propel him out the door (if he was even home) and into the taverns.

My life story is organized around the numerous places where I lived and, later on, where I worked. Interspersed are what to me are very significant experiences and events that coincided where I lived or worked. My response to the disparity I encountered in each of these venues and the results of my efforts to dispel it are my story as I lived it. I tried to adopt more of Ma's ways, but I was seriously encumbered by the proclivities inherent in having been stricken with a severe dose of the Talty flu.

Our First Flat: Knotty and Nutty Times

Although we do not have Ma's letters from this era, we do have our collective memories of life as kids in our dysfunctional family. Poverty, uncertainty, anxiety, sadness, and strife had become a way of life for Ma and us kids because of my Dad's unwillingness to bring home a steady pay or, on some nights, to even come home at all. He also became more threatening and verbally abusive to the extent that life was hell whether he was home or on one of his alcoholic binges. Thankfully, I don't ever remember him being physically abusive. His way was to punish Ma and the rest of us with what my sister Sue astutely labeled "the silent treatment". He would not speak to any of us, no matter how much Ma tried to please and cajole him. We all wanted so badly for him to talk, to laugh, or to just be good because that's what Ma wanted.

Dinnertime with Dad was, in some ways, like having dinner with a silent ominous presence at the head of the table. He could not be pleased and was easily further angered. Sometimes it would take much cajoling from Ma to just even get him to come to the table from their bedroom. He would come silently (what else?) to the dinner table while we kids remained scared and quiet. These were anxious moments for us all.

Ma was a good cook, but without grocery money, she often had to improvise. Dad would scrutinize with scorn whatever Ma had concocted and then, with a growl of disgust, take his plate and angrily scrape his food into the kitchen garbage can. I personally thought he was crazy because it tasted fine to me. However, Ma would cry quietly, and we kids would sometimes giggle for some crazy reason.

He then would go abruptly into their bedroom and slam the door. We kids would eat, but I felt so bad for Ma and somewhat ambivalent about Dad; I often felt a bit sorry for him not having anything to eat. After a few minutes, he would open the bedroom door and have his coat and hat on. It was clear he was going out, and then he would walk right past us all without speaking. His going out did mean a far less stressful night, but I was always anxious about what it would be like whenever he did come back. Even though he was exiting quickly on these nights, Ma would plead with him not to go out, and she would pitifully promise to make him something else to eat, but to no avail. Out he went. We figured out later on in life that he was intending on going out even before he sat down to eat and intentionally used the food that didn't meet his standards as his reason to depart. That's our Dad!

Having been in other kids' houses at suppertime I, of course, saw a vivid contrast in terms of food as well as family dynamics. The covert anger that resided within Dad and permeated the whole kitchen was not what I saw in my friends' homes. Lots of vivid instances of disparity remain in my memory bank! The peace and cordiality that I witnessed in their homes was a lot like those Ozzie and Harriet–type families I saw on TV. So there really were families like that? Their fathers were home at night, worked hard, owned cars, bought homes, did home repairs, talked, and went on family vacations. These kids did not have to be ashamed of themselves, their homes, or their parents. These parents and kids actually talked and listened to each other. Do you hear it? Do you hear my dear old friend disparity emerging? Emerging? Hell, it was raging!

~~~~

As a way of dealing with these disparities I often outright lied about my family life. I remember returning to class in the fall of fifth grade where each kid had to stand up and tell what they had done on their summer vacation. There were stories of family trips, summer camps, visiting Washington DC, and so forth. It was about to be my turn. I had to come up with something, and so I did. My story sounded good, almost normal. "My Dad drove us all up into the Adirondack mountains in our 'Woody' station wagon. I saw three meadowlarks and seven Baltimore orioles." We had been studying ornithology in the previous year, and I wanted to impress the class with my bird-watching prowess. However, Georgie Kelly,* my neighbor and closest friend, put up his hand and, in an instant, destroyed my nice story while practicing his burgeoning language skills of the lawyer he was to become as an adult.

"Peter Talty is a liar," Georgie said with disdain. "His Dad doesn't even have a car, and he comes home drunk all the time, and one time he even crawled down the street on his hands and knees when we were playing baseball." That son of a bitch with the perfect family life and his mom, the president of the PTA, needed a beating that I could not administer because he was bigger and stronger than me. So I vehemently stood up and, in a tearful voice, said, "Georgie is the liar." My teacher chose to ignore me and just moved on to the next kid. I don't remember anyone ever asking me again about my family vacations. I wonder why.

~~~~

Early on I discovered that I had a silent ally in combating this ubiquitous force of disparity. My mom inadvertently gave me information and perspectives that strengthened my efforts to lessen disparity. Differences in housing have always been a fertile place for my disparity to thrive. Renting our flat from my Dad's brother (Uncle Bern) gave us some security because no matter how poorly we acted as kids or how much we damaged his property, and despite the fact that we seldom paid our $35 a month rent, he didn't evict us. Add to this the drunken ranting of my Dad when he made his middle-of-the-night appearances followed by some loud pounding and kicking on the back door, it is a wonder he didn't throw us out.

In my nine-year-old mind, although we were lousy tenants, it still did not give my cousin Tyke the authority to prevent us from playing in the backyard. His authority may have come from his ability to beat me up, and so wisely, rather than fight him for yard privileges, I chose to go crying to Ma when he stood guard at the big gate and would not let us go into the yard. She was appalled at this violation of our tenant's rights and sent me back out to give Tyke one hell of a message. "My Dad has a better job than your father ever thought of having." Oh, that was good! As a nine-year-old I felt intrepid power in saying what I thought was a very demoralizing statement of fact. In fact, at the time, I think this may have been even better than if I had kicked his ass. However, his retort was the knife in my gut. "Oh yeah, then how come you don't have any shoes?" I responded with some more crying and ran down the street so I wouldn't have to tell Ma the hurtful (but accurate) thing Tyke had said.

Of course, he was right. I didn't have shoes, which was not good from a medical perspective because my clubfoot required support from custom orthopedic shoes. Instead, I wore sneakers because the orthopedic shoes cost $35 a pair (one month's rent), and it was an all-day excursion to the store by bus and a streetcar to a northern suburb just to get fitted. There was no money for this kind of extravagance or a car to take us. Ma knew I needed the shoes, but trying to put food on the table and cover the myriad other expenses of the family took precedence. So sneakers it was for me in spite of my discomfort, and Tyke knew this well from all the times we played together. The problem with my sneakers is that we could only buy one pair that fit my big foot, which was three sizes bigger than my small foot. Thus, I had a big sneaker and a sneaker stuffed with tissues, flopping around on my small foot. This did not support my weak ankle structure, caused pain, and made running slow and cumbersome. Tyke knew all this and delivered that terrible verbal salvo at the gate. It is interesting that he remembers none of this today, but conversely, it's embedded in that part of my brain where I store all instances of disparity.

Long before the gate-guarding incident, Tyke and I were good friends. We played together as did my brother Danny with Tyke's younger brother Bood, who was just five days older than him. Living right upstairs from us made it very convenient. Bood and Tyke also joined the throng of other neighborhood kids who flocked into our living room each weeknight from five o'clock to six o'clock to watch our favorite shows on the first TV on the block. I had often wondered what some of these kids thought when they looked around at our worn-out couch and chairs with springs and stuffing protruding, unpainted walls (we removed the wallpaper but had no money for paint), and barren floors (Ma preferred linoleum in those days, but it was pretty beat with lots of holes and little color).

Picture eight or so kids trying to find a seat on furniture where springs did not protrude or lying on a hard floor with eyes transfixed as the nightly *Howdy Doody* and *Cactus Jim* stories unfolded. Then add my Dad. He would sometimes come home at suppertime, be quite drunk, and fall down among us kids on the living room floor. He would sleep right there where he fell. At Ma's request, we would go through his pockets in hopes of finding some money, but I remember only finding cigarette butts and pieces of pretzels. This didn't happen a lot where he joined us for afternoon TV in this state, but it happened enough to be forged in my brain as a sad tableau.

~~~~

Was Dad ever not drunk? Yes, of course. He would sometimes go for weeks at a time without drinking, and we would approach normalcy. Approach but never really arrive. A few weeks with him home and a couple of paychecks cashed but not spent in a bar gave us the feeling that we were thriving. There would be hard rolls and ham, chocolate milk, Clark candy bars, a roast, apples, but for some reason never orange juice. It was during such hiatuses from drinking that Dad would do some painting or fix our bikes. I wanted to shout

out to the other kids, "Hey, look at what we have over here at our house! Here's a real Dad doing real Dad things!"

~~~~

It was during these times of Dad's abstinence that we slept through the night, went to school, played with our friends, and ate dinner as a family with just the usual disruptions that we kids generated. What also seemed to occur during these good days was the purchase of some unexpected things. Without regard for our immediate needs like clothes, shoes for me, dental care, paying off the corner store charge accounts, rent, and so forth, Ma and Dad would surprise us with some amazing things. The TV that we revered like it was the Pieta was at the top of these unexpected and thrilling purchases.

On another night Ma and Dad had us stay out of the kitchen just before supper, and it remains a wonderful memory. We watched TV sporadically as we anxiously awaited and wondered what was going on behind the closed kitchen door. Pat was being his usual demanding and uncooperative self, trying to open the door to see what the surprise was. Dad finally opened the door, and in we went to receive another spectacular gift. My brothers and I each received a set of Hopalong Cassidy dishes complete with mug, cereal bowl, and plate with pictures of our hero Hoppy beautifully emblazoned. There was no explanation given as to why we were granted these spectacular gifts, but I could see that Ma and even Dad were very proud to be able to bestow them upon this unworthy lot. We loved those sets. Just like the TV, no other neighborhood kids had such treasures.

The same night that the Hoppy sets appeared, Ma announced a new program in behavior management (my words, not hers). "From now on, Dad and I will decide which one of the four of you behaved the best during the week, and whoever is the best boy of the week will get a special gift. We decided that this week the best boy was Bernie!" What the hell was this! Bernie was always well-behaved, and he would win this phony "Best Boy" award every week. This was no competition. Then, to make this new program even more bizarre, Ma gave Bernie an imitation leather portfolio as his prize. For what? He wasn't a lawyer or a businessman; he was a thirteen-year-old kid!

Where had this whole concept come from? Had they heard about B. F. Skinner's research on learning using rats in laboratory experiments, and how well the rats responded to positive reinforcement? If so, did they then see some application to us? Were the unexpected gifts and "Best Boy" awards their venture into behaviorism? No, no, and no. I believe these were just some other examples of their impulsive, immediate gratification, non-thinking buying, usually driven by Dad. Whatever the motivation, we sure liked those days (except for that crock about the "Best Boy" award). Regardless, the "Best Boy" program only lasted that one week for some reason, which actually surprised me at the time.

~~~~

This impulsive buying was a constant of Ma and Dad's way of life. It seemed Dad was the one that needed to buy these things like a little kid who wants something and doesn't care about the consequences. One of the ways they facilitated their impulsive buying was the reliance on two loan companies where they could repeatedly refinance their loans, albeit with exorbitant interest rates. Dad's impulsive buying usually resulted in poor decisions, and he often paid the full amount or higher for inferior merchandise.

Ma probably tried to dissuade him, but he was so persuasive in those days that he would get his way. When the poor quality of the purchase became apparent, he would become enraged and depressed, which usually led to his going out and getting drunk. Of course, these purchases, coupled with his drinking, pushed them further into debt, generated even more angst for Ma, and surely must have infuriated our creditors including his brother and landlord, Uncle Bern, who still received no rent.

The Travails of the Flat

Until 1953, life in our flat had a predictable albeit sad rhythm to it. Dad seldom came home after work on paydays. Sometimes he would be gone for two or three or four days. Where did he go? Why did he go? Ma had no money and was trying to feed us and do what she could to pay the bills without much success. We had charge accounts at the two small neighborhood grocery stores, but that stopped because we seldom paid anything on what we owed. My brother Bernie remembers the shame he felt for Ma when the owner told Ma that she could no longer charge food at his delicatessen, and then he made Ma put all the things she had placed on the counter back on the shelves.

Now my experience with this charge account system was a bit different from Ma's and Bernie's because of my despicable ways. Here's how I used the charge system (when it was still available to us) to lessen another form of my sense of disparity. I envied the boys who could buy a Coke or RC (Royal Crown) and a bag of Wise potato chips (the best) after a hot game of baseball. I would beg them for a "swig" and some chips, but then I got the idea to get my own and just "put them on Ma's charge." What a great concept!

In the beginning of Ma and Dad's charge account era, we kids would go to the store for Ma, select the food items on the list she gave us, and just say, "Put it on the charge, Dick*" (I boldly called the owner by his first name just like Ma did). I learned early on that I could also get candy or a Coke and just add it on to the food charge.

Ma never asked for receipts, and so I saw an opportunity to satisfy my sweet tooth and lessen some disparity. To make my sneaky purchases appear more legitimate, I would never just get the contraband stuff by itself. No, I would always add something like a package of Kraft's Swiss cheese to make it look more legitimate. Then to make this dastardly deed even worse, I would throw the non-treat items over the fence into the alley next to the store.

Yes, I was a sneaky, selfish, and brazen bastard. I not only added to my parents' financial woes by inflating their debt but I also deprived my family of food items they needed and would have loved. This definitely falls into the category of making a bad situation worse, which was one of the signs of the Talty flu. I am still very sorry for this and for the even worse troubles I will cause as I somersault through my troubled adolescence.

~~~~

Throughout my family's mercurial life, we were fortunate to have a benevolent individual who was really unappreciated and was at times even resented by us. The resentment was caused by his possessing things that our family did not. Dad's brother and our landlord, Uncle Bern, owned the house and lived in the flat upstairs from us. Over the years, he stepped forth on a number of occasions with jobs, a few dollars, a ride, hand-me-down bikes, and other stuff for many members of our family. He must have viewed Dad with consternation, which morphed into disgust mixed with some pity as he witnessed Dad's decline into alcoholism. The cumulative result was that we would never win the tenant of the year award. In spite of not receiving our $35 a month rent, Uncle Bern still tried over the years to help Ma and Dad out by giving Dad jobs and money when he wasn't working. Alas, he was unsuccessful. So during these days, we hoped that Dad would come home, not be drunk, have his full pay with him (fat chance), and then we would all live happily ever after (even fatter chance). This unrealistic thinking on my part was proof that I was adopting some of Ma's "la-la land thinking" in that maybe this time he would come home, and it would be different. He didn't, and it wasn't.

Actually, Dad often came home in the early morning hours with everyone asleep except Ma. If he was too drunk to work the key in the lock, he would yell and pound on the door, waking Uncle Bern, who would yell back from his upstairs doorway. To prevent this level of uproar, Ma would stay up waiting to let Dad in. Then the peace of our night would soon explode with him yelling and things falling. They would argue, and Ma would plead with him to go to bed. It was a good night when he would collapse into bed and sleep it off. Other nights the arguing and yelling seemed to go on throughout the night. We four boys were too young, too small, and too scared to alter these fights that my mom called "set-tos" (*a usually brief and vigorous fight or debate*). Have you ever tried listening to a "debate" at three o'clock in the morning when one of the parties is very drunk and belligerent? Not good.

Whenever Tommy would return home on leave from the air force, he would valiantly try to ameliorate our family's life by dealing with Dad. He would take charge and provide a more proactive approach by calling the police when Dad arrived home in a drunk and belligerent state. Having Dad arrested gave us a peaceful night's sleep but did not resolve the long-term problems we were living with on a daily basis.

Was Ma really trying to communicate with Dad, trying to get him to be introspective and insightful, and then change his ways when he was so drunk? Yes, of course! Ma would dauntlessly try to reason with and even confront Dad in his drunken and volatile state because she still loved him and believed in him. More fantasy thinking? Yes, I think so.

~~~~

Our poverty, coupled with Dad's drinking, made for a challenging childhood for us all, but in spite of this, I still recall a lot of kid-generated fun and adventure. I had my brother and buddy Danny to play with on rainy and snowy days, and we were both creative with building expansive "towns" out of plastic bricks and Lincoln Logs. Ma respected our good work and would let us keep our elaborate array of constructed buildings and roads in place, occupying large chunks of our living room while inconveniencing other members of the family. Pat would always want to build with us, but would not listen to our directives as we constructed our magnificent edifices. Thus, we were vigorous and hostile in our quick dispatch of Pat, which saddens me today.

Our neighborhood was great for peer companionship but typically short on diversity. In the 1940s and 1950s, our city's neighborhoods, like many other cities, tended to form around ethnic and racial lines. Our neighborhood could have easily been designated "WASP City" because of the paucity of diversity within it. We were almost all White, Catholic, and Irish (not protestant and Anglo-Saxon) and only played with kids of the same ilk. The only diversity we encountered were some Protestants, Germans, and some kids of English heritages. I never knew any black people until I went to high school, no Jewish people until college, and no Hispanic people until I began practicing occupational therapy as an intern at the county hospital in 1969. So while I think this sense of neighborhood sameness engendered harmony for baseball games, hide-and-seek, red rover, and other kids' games, it unfortunately gave us a too strong sense of egocentrism. Conversely, it did provide a level of comfort and familiarity in just talking and hanging out with a lot of kids just like us. We seldom had fights or even arguments because we liked one another a lot and saw the world through the same lenses, as narrow as they were.

~~~~

But thanks to Frederick Law Olmsted we had a treasured paradise almost in our backyard. In 1887, Olmsted, the famous landscape architect who designed Central Park in New York City, also designed our local city park that was one block from where we lived. This was a wonderful playground for kids and adults nestled in a pastoral expanse of woods and ponds with a pretty creek meandering through the center. This park was the center of our activities once we left our street. Swimming in the expansive pools, walking and exploring along the creek, fishing, ice skating, tree climbing (my favorite), playing games and sports with my brothers, cousins, and friends was the principal source of joy in my life. I think it certainly helped me lessen the sequelae of Dad's drinking. I said, I think.

This cycle of drinking and poverty continued for several years. Ma was certainly immersed in a quagmire as well as a major quandary that must have overwhelmed her for many reasons. She faced an economic dilemma and that, of course, was the underlying obstacle to normalcy. The quandary was that because my Dad was employed in a high-paying position as a railroad engineer, we could not qualify for public assistance ("Welfare") or assistance from other organizations like Catholic charities. The court system perhaps could have helped, but in this, my mom was the major obstacle that intensified the quagmire. If someone in the family like one of Dad's brothers or my brother Tommy got inspired to try and fix our mess, and thus had Dad arrested for drunkenness, assault, abuse, or neglect, Ma would cave the next day. She would appear in court with him and never press charges. As a result, they would then release him, and things would be good for a few weeks. Then Dad would resume his drinking-carousing-abusing lifestyle all over again. That is until "that night."

That Awful Night! Our Titanic!

"Hey, kids! What time is it? It's Howdy Doody time!" The hell it was! It was the time of our family's implosion and fragmentation. It was a few days before Christmas in 1953, and Ma's mind was probably on how she could possibly give us kids a nice Christmas when she had no money. She and a quite drunk and belligerent Dad were in the kitchen arguing. He was sitting at the table with his winter coat and hat on, and Ma was standing at the stove stirring tomato soup. Dad would sporadically yell out, "You son of a bitch" and "You bastards" and other mean things, a lot of which we couldn't really understand because of his drunken speech. His mutterings were interspersed with low-volume growling.

He had come home late in the afternoon that day (surprise!) and was quite drunk (no surprise!). He was arguing with Ma while she was making tomato soup for supper to go with our grilled cheese sandwiches. Because his yelling was not that unusual, we just turned up the TV sound as we usually did so we could hear all about Howdy's latest dilemma. But then we heard something above the arguing and howling, and even above Howdy Doody and Mr. Bluster. It both confused and terrified us all. It was a loud crash and then lots of dishes breaking that brought us all running to the kitchen door.

In the kitchen, we saw something that none of us will ever forget: Ma crying softly but still stirring the tomato soup, and my Dad teetering drunkenly over an upside down kitchen table. Where were our grilled cheese sandwiches? They were all over the floor mixed in with the shattered images of our beloved Hoppy mugs, bowls, and platters that were bought at another time when our Mom and Dad felt differently about themselves, us, and their lives.

Now the room was filled with a mixture of silence, fear, and sadness. What would he do next? Who would protect us from this crazy man? I was the one who panicked first. I ran to the phone in the dining room and called my sister Sue who always knew what to do whenever things got crazy. I doubt that my voice was firm or clear for an eleven-year-old as I exclaimed, "Dad is real drunk, and he flipped the kitchen table over. He broke all our Hoppy bowls. Can you come over?" I didn't hear her full response, just "That bastard!" as she hung up. I too hung up and merged my fear with that of my brothers viewing the mess from the kitchen doorway. We were also ready to run out if Dad came at us. He was trying to talk, but I couldn't hear or really understand his muttered ramblings. I knew if he went after my mom that I would run outside. I was too small to stop my Dad and too afraid to oppose him. So I was going to save myself. What a brave son I was!

Dad's voice was different that night. It was a pitiful mixture of unintelligible sadness and rage. One I never heard from him. Just weaving and stumbling about the kitchen, but not moving toward my mom who continued to just stir the soup and cry. What about our grilled cheese? He stepped on them and unintentionally destroyed more of our prized Hoppy stuff. He almost fell a few times until he navigated out of the Hoppy-grilled cheese morass, inching toward the bathroom. And still she stirred and cried. I cried too, but I guess my brothers were stronger.

Then things changed, as did all of us. Our heroes, Sue and Jim, arrived and quickly resolved the crisis Dad had created. I can still see him sitting on the bed and staring but not really seeing. I was now crying for my Dad because he looked so small, pitiful, and, I think, ashamed. I felt so bad for him and still do today. Jimmy continued to berate Dad from the kitchen doorway telling him he was "chicken and weak." In the midst of this hiatus of sorts, Ma brought out the new pair of corduroy pants she managed to buy Bernie for Christmas to show Jimmy. Regardless of Ma's strange timing, Jimmy agreed that they were nice, and as the conversation in the dining room continued on beyond corduroy pants we heard a loud slam of the kitchen door as Dad left without even wishing us a merry Christmas. I bet you wouldn't see a scene like this on *Father Knows Best* or *The Waltons*.

~~~~

The pathos of that night still reverberates with me every Christmas, especially when those ubiquitous carols first come forth on the radio. Added to this residual emotional trauma was the realization on Ma's part that she was helpless and our family situation had really become hopeless. We all lived in great fear each of the days after that Christmas because Dad never came back after Jimmy stripped him of his pride in front of his family. I don't know where he went, but we had developed a great sense of dread about his return. We knew that the more days he was gone, the worse it was going to be when he finally did come home. If he came back in the middle of the night, which was his wont, we wouldn't have Jimmy there to protect us.

We were terrified of going to bed on those nights after Christmas. So when Ma and Sue told us of the plan they had concocted, we were all scared and confused. It had been decided that Ma would take Danny and Pat, the youngest boys, and go to San Antonio, Texas, to live on the air force base with my brother Tommy and his wife, Karoline. Ma would finance this New Year's Eve getaway partly through my Dad's railroad pass and whatever money Sue and Jimmy could quickly put together. The pass would only get them to St. Louis, and then Tommy would have to somehow find the money to get them the rest of the way. Bernie and I would go to live with Sue and Jim.

Ma and I cried while she packed, and then it was time to go to the train station. Then more and more tears. At the time, everybody viewed this as a permanent solution to our family's ongoing crises, and the thoughts of not ever seeing Ma, Danny, and Pat again, coupled with the anxiety over Dad and his whereabouts, just overwhelmed

Ma and me. Ma and I have always been the biggest crybabies in the family, and I still am.

Getting Ma, Danny, and Pat to San Antonio from St. Louis presented Tommy with a prodigious challenge because he did not have any extra money. This was pre–credit card access and his fellow air force pals were as broke as he was. So off he went to the nearby grocery store, where he hardly knew the owner, to ask for a loan. After hearing Tommy's plight, he lent Tommy $100, which was a substantial loan in 1953, to enable them all to get to San Antonio after he wired Ma the money in St. Louis. Tommy paid the grocer back and still marvels today at the grocer's trust in someone he hardly knew.

Life with Sue and Jim

While Ma, Danny, and Pat settled in with Tommy and Karoline in the great state of Texas, Bernie and I were trying to adjust to life without Ma. We, at first, lived with Sue and Jim in their nice rented flat, and then in a few weeks, we all moved into their new home that they bought. It was a little over a mile away from our old flat, but it put Bernie and me outside of our familiar neighborhood and the geographic boundaries of our public school. This was disconcerting for me because they could transfer me to another school where black kids were enrolled. My Dad had instilled feelings of superiority in me as well as a strong fear of black people (he preferred to refer to them as niggers, shines, darkies, coons, jigaboos, and so forth). Of course, both the feelings of superiority and the associated fear were without justification. Regardless, the idea of going to a new school where black kids were prevalent still scared the hell out of me.

Sue and Jim's purchase of a new home was quite a remarkable accomplishment for twenty-four-year-olds, and they were deservedly proud. It was a small Cape Cod–style house, and with everything all brand new, we were quite amazed. I had never been in a house so grand. I also had never lived in a house with a shower and knew nobody that did. The kitchen sink had a sprayer and that, along with hardwood floors and new storm windows and doors, felt like we were living in a little mansion.

Although we were only a little over a mile from our old flat and neighborhood, it proved to be more like an enormous chasm for me.

Life with Sue and Jim

My friends were no longer immediately available, and I missed them a lot. In addition, we had to completely clean out our flat so my Uncle Bern could move into the more desirable downstairs flat. This would enable him to rent his upper flat to an actual paying tenant. That would be a new experience for him.

The saddest of days occurred when Sue, Jimmy, Bernie, and I returned to our former flat to clean it out. I didn't know it at the time, but it was the same feeling I got later on in life when I had to clean out my Uncle Wasson's room and also Ma's flat after they died. I felt like an intruder in my own home, and it looked even sadder without Ma, my brothers, and even my Dad there. It was so quiet in our old flat. So many memories. The feeling of sadness was so heavy that we were at first unable to do anything. I went from room to room seeing remnants of our sad lives, crying (of course), and missing everyone so bad.

Then Jimmy took charge. "Lay these army blankets out on the dining room floor." Bernie and I did as he directed, and he brought drawer after drawer of our ragged clothes that Ma couldn't take with her to Texas and dumped them in the center of the blankets. He was fast and ruthless as he filled blanket after blanket and then fiercely tied the four corners into large bundles for donations to Goodwill. When I asked why he was giving Bernie's and my clothes away, he said grandiosely, "I will buy you all new clothes." I'm still waiting.

It was so pitiful to see how few possessions of value we actually owned. I bet even Goodwill wouldn't keep the ratty underwear, shirts, towels, sheets, pillowcases, etc. that Jimmy was throwing into his contrived blanket bundles. The same thing happened as we moved from room to room. Apparently, according to Jimmy, there were few sacrosanct items in our home. We did wrap Ma's dishes and kitchenware in newspapers and packed them in bushel baskets. I was hoping this meant that someday Ma was going to come back from Texas and make a new home for us. I was always a dreamer as well as a schemer. Hey, that rhymes!

To me, the cleaning out of our sad flat in this way was as if our place, our home, and our stuff had no value at all. Jimmy told Bernie and me to only take a few of our toys and things. Everything else was going to Goodwill because I think they were less selective than the St. Vincent de Paul Society, and also because Sue was mad at Catholic charities because they wouldn't help us in the days when we didn't have food. I wanted to take some of Danny's and Pat's toys too, but Jimmy said, "No. A lot of that's junk. It will fall apart in a week. If they ever do come back, they won't miss them." I loved and revered Jimmy, but at that time, I really resented him being so disrespectful about our stuff. However, he was right about it being junk. Ma had little money to work with in those days, so she tried to get us what we wanted for Christmas, but she had to buy really cheap things. Danny and my new and cheaply made hockey sticks were broken beyond repair one Christmas Day in just one game of street hockey. Danny's wooden fort of balsa wood was broken in several places from Dad stepping on it when drunk. My new basketball was more like a beach ball, and it abruptly collapsed in a pitiful heap when one of Danny's new darts accidentally punctured it. What was still intact I put in a box and took it to the car, and was my wont, crying all the way. I thought I was going to suffocate from the great lump stuck in my throat.

After a few more tearful days of packing and sorting, the Goodwill truck arrived, and most of our household goods were loaded on board except for our living room set, mattresses, and box springs. These were in such poor shape that they wouldn't take them. Then with cruel finality, Ma's beloved wicker set, a remnant from the veranda of the Big House and her days of wealth, was tied onto the back of the truck and down the street went our family's glorious and not-so-glorious past.

~~~~

Living with Sue and Jim had many elements of those TV families I envied and sometimes hated. Many times the despair that accompanied my sense of disparity was so great that it short-circuited the potential for joy in my new life. This, unfortunately, became the framework for my life. I couldn't really enjoy the peace and stability of Sue and Jim's nice home because I missed the rest of my family so much. However, it was fun playing with Kathleen, Sue and Jim's three-year-old daughter, and joining in the excitement of moving into their newly purchased home. It almost made me feel at times like I was "that irrepressible Ricky Nelson". Was this the sense of normalcy I so craved? Yes, I think it was.

~~~~

Unfortunately, Bernie and I now had to walk a little over a mile to school because of the location of Sue and Jim's new house. The direction we took also precluded our walking with our friends who went back to our old neighborhood. I was further stressed by the fact that our school did not have cafeteria privileges for students in the fifth grade. This necessitated my carrying a lunch bag, but even with this, I was not allowed to remain in school to eat it.

My sister Sue tried to mitigate my lunch dilemma by giving me money to buy a soft drink at a local restaurant and eat my lunch right there. I got to walk with my friends who were going home for lunch while I earnestly entered a small diner-like restaurant. Sitting at the counter, I ordered a Coke and opened up my lunch but was then shocked and grief-stricken when the man behind the counter brought my Coke and then, in one action, scooped up my sandwich and the rest of my lunch and handed it to me saying, "Get out. You can't eat a bag lunch in here." I sat on the curb on the busy street outside the restaurant, cried (what else?), and ate my lunch.

That night, when I told Sue what had happened, she rescued me as always. The next day she went to my school and convinced my fifth-grade teacher to let me eat my lunch in her classroom. My teacher didn't like it because she had to spend her lunch break supervising me. I don't know if it was the fear of her bridled rage or my sandwich's dryness, but chewing and swallowing were not easy. We were both very happy once my lunch was eaten and I could head to the playground and she to the faculty lounge.

Tommy and Karoline kindly provided a home for Ma, Danny, and Pat as their contribution to helping us out of our desperate living situation. If the responsible adults in our family could not get Dad to change, then Karoline and Tommy provided a stable home instead, as did Sue and Jim for Bernie and me. What heroes these young people were to make rooms in their homes for all of us. It was also not viewed as temporary; apparently, adoptions for each of us were part of the discussions.

A New Dad Emerges

When school was out each day, I often opted to take a route to my new home that took me painfully past my old home. I don't know why. It made me very sad to go past the house where once sadness and turbulence prevailed. I missed everyone, but strangely, I was also worried about my Dad. We learned later on that Dad eventually tried to come home a few days after everyone had gone, but he didn't quite make it. In his drunken state, he mistakenly tried to enter the house next door instead. He apparently figured out that he was at the wrong house and tried to leave but lost his balance and fell down the stairs. The fall itself was not the problem, but the broken bottles of beer that he was carrying when he fell cut him up a bit. He was bleeding from several cuts and bruises to the extent that someone called an ambulance. It was determined that he should go to the hospital where he was subsequently admitted. We didn't know about any of this until Dad called Sue the next day from the hospital looking for Ma. He was devastated when she told him the sequence of events that had transpired. Hearing that Ma, Danny, and Pat were in Texas; Bernie and I were living with Sue and Jim; and that Ma and Dad's flat was no more must have been quite a shock.

The present-day hospital and health insurance regulations that determine who can be admitted to a hospital and how long they can stay were nonexistent in 1953. Thus, Dad spent at least six weeks in the hospital for conditions that would most likely not even qualify him for admission today.

A New Dad Emerges

I don't know how it happened, but Bernie and I, along with Sue and Jim, began visiting Dad at the hospital as he "dried out" and his wounds healed. He was also quite debilitated and required rest as well as proper nutrition to regain his health. The hospital was right next to the school we attended, so stopping by every day became routine for me. When sober, my Dad could be funny, kind, clever, and caring—traits usually hidden from us under all the booze.

Coincidentally and conveniently, our school had an ongoing service project for the hospital where cupcakes were baked in our cafeteria, and then students would frost and decorate them for different holidays. The cupcakes then went to the patients at the hospital where Dad was one of those patients. In a deeply appreciated gesture, he would save his cupcake plus any extras he could scrounge for me and Bernie when we stopped by for a visit on our way home after school. I was very pleased that he would think to do this little thing for us.

~~~~

With Ma, Dan, and Pat having left on New Year's Eve and this now being late February, Dad was ready to be discharged from the hospital. The problem was that his flat was no more and his family broken in ways none of us could have ever imagined. Dad still had his great job as a railroad engineer and was ready to return to it. However, even though he was sober, Dad had no options in terms of a place to live. His brother Bern, who owned the house, moved his family into our flat and rented out his upstairs flat, so there was no going back there. With nowhere else to go, he asked Jimmy if he could live with them until he "got straightened around." The magnanimousness of Jimmy showed itself once again, as he agreed to let Dad move in with the rest of us, but he stipulated that Dad could not drink. Dad agreed, but because of his history of generating chaos, we were all still anxious about his moving in with us.

~~~~

Thankfully, there was no need for us to be concerned. Dad really was a changed man and showed far more tolerance for adversity than I had ever seen in him. He had to sleep in a single bed in Sue and Jim's unfinished and unheated attic. There were only enough boards in place to accommodate the width of a single bed, which made his getting in and out of bed somewhat precarious. He jokingly, but accurately, referred to it as his garret [*generally synonymous in modern usage with a habitable attic or small (and possibly dismal or cramped) living space at the top of a house*]. We didn't know the word garret at the time, but I know now that Dad sure did aptly name it. However, he was so happy to have a place to live and his own space, as adverse as it was, that he never complained, which was a face of Dad that we had not seen before.

It seemed that he was only home a few days when he returned to work. Seeing him either going or coming from work made me so happy. He was happy too. There was also a pride in his bearing that I also never saw before.

After he had been working a few weeks, he showed me his paycheck. He not only was working his scheduled hours but was also working overtime at a significantly higher hourly rate. I don't remember the amount, but I do remember being quite amazed. The amount must have been something way beyond what I thought possible. Dad paid Sue and Jim something each week for his room and board, but he also would go shopping for food and pay for it all. He also began writing to Ma and sending her money.

This new Dad also shocked me in other ways. I was struggling with multiplication and long division in math, and he helped me comprehend what my teacher could not. He was always patient and supportive while helping me with my homework (who was this guy?).

I think the initial reason he never drank in those days, let alone got drunk, was because he knew that Jimmy's no-drinking rule would result in eviction from his garret. However, I think he was also enjoying life without the booze and what it brought. He was enjoying his new sense of self and the new way of life that he was forging. With his high wages, he was able to pay off many of the bills, but he was especially beaming the day he showed me the "paid in full" receipts from the two corner grocery store charge accounts that had grown precipitously. I thought this was the pinnacle of his many accomplishments in this era of sobriety, but he proved me wrong.

One of the things Dad did was to write to Ma reporting all his accomplishments along with what I assume were large doses of remorse and pleading. He missed Ma far more than I (and probably he) thought possible. His pleading worked, and Ma agreed to return home. However, our flat no longer existed. So once again, our guardian angels Sue and Jim invited Ma, Danny, and Pat to join the rest of us in their small Cape Cod–style house. So a house with one bathroom and built to comfortably house a family of four was about to be burdened with four adults, five kids, a dog, and a parakeet.

Behavioral and Emotional Land Mines Explode

There were a number of unforeseen land mines waiting to explode at the Riley residence that severely worked against us all living happily ever after. Besides the sheer number of people living in a small house with just one bathroom, we had dysfunctional relationships that were already present and were then greatly exacerbated in the few months we all lived together.

There was the predictable strife when two families move in together, but our situation was even more fractious. One of the biggest problems was that Ma reverted to coddling Dad, and this irritated Sue to no end. Sue, being outspoken, would say to Ma with Dad sitting right there, "He can fix his own goddamn soft-boiled eggs. His arms aren't broken. He did it himself while you were in Texas." Ma would just respond in an ingratiating way, "I know, but he doesn't feel too good today." Dad had also returned to his sulking ways, which, of course, triggered Ma's ever-constant pleasing efforts, which further enraged Sue. Tick, tick, tick.

Another land mine was my brother Pat's complicated behavior emanating from his "sick spells," which apparently was due to his yet undiagnosed epilepsy. Ma overprotected and defended Pat because of feeling sad and guilty over his daily struggles and rejection by us all.

Pat was spoiled, but his difficult behavior was often also driven by loneliness and rejection. He was always a great and easy target for ridicule, and there was a pile-on mentality operating among us when it came to Pat. He said and did crazy things, so we always had ample fuel for making Pat look even more foolish. He was also very temperamental and easy to enrage. It's like we would set him up, and he would react in very predictable, intense, and bizarre ways, and then we would sit back and enjoy the show. This was more of that old saw of us Taltys making a bad situation worse. There were numerous other land mines just waiting to explode, not least of which had to do with space and possessions.

My feelings about our whole living situation certainly did change. Initially, it was fun and, to me, very comforting to have most of the people I loved all living together under one roof. It did take some organizing to get everyone in and out of showers, planning meals for all these hungry mouths, and trying to respect Sue and Jim's nice furnishings when we were more accustomed to far more forlorn stuff. We kids now had to live with more structure and rules than ever before. Bernie was older and was never as problematic as Danny, Pat, and I were. "Rambunctious" was Ma's euphemistic word to describe us. We missed our beloved park and had to make the most of a lesser city park that lacked a swimming pool and all the amenities we were so used to having at our old park. Our new park served us well enough for baseball and basketball but little else. To supplement our sports activities, my brother Danny and I would hone our pitching skills by playing catch every day for hours in front of the house.

Initially, there was a lot of laughter and kidding at the Riley residence as we good-naturedly struggled to accommodate the complexities of two different families trying to adjust to each other's habits and idiosyncrasies. However, before long, the land mines began to explode.

With Ma and Dad occupying the second bedroom that should have been Kathleen's, it was now necessary for her to sleep with Sue and Jim. This was not good for their relationship, and Sue saw this as so unfair to Kathleen. We also did not really respect Sue and Jim's furniture and were constantly told to stop jumping on it or putting our sneakered feet on their new sectional sofa. We were bad.

So in just a few short months, Sue, in her usual direct way, told Ma that we had to go. Besides, with Dad sober and working steady, it was time for us to venture out and do what Ma referred to as "going housekeeping" again. Sue and Jim needed to have their own space, as did we. Ma cried when she told us what Sue had said, and of course, I cried too. I didn't cry a lot at first because I think I knew on some level that this present living situation was never going to work.

We Become Home Owners! Us? Really?

The Trailer Park

As Ma and Dad began to search for a new place to live, they started contemplating buying a house rather than renting a flat, which was all they had ever done. However, they had little in the way of a down payment, and their credit rating must have been dismal in spite of Dad's recent payoffs of some of their creditors. These realities must have impacted their search. Certainly providing impetus to the search was the covert and, at times, overt pressure for us to get out of Sue and Jim's house and fast.

The pressure probably came from Sue as she desperately tried to manage her own anxieties while trying to preserve her own family. She was emotionally exhausted from all that we had put her through. Realizing all these dynamics, Ma and Dad were doing their best to find a place that we could afford and also accommodate the five of us as fast as possible. I say five because Bernie had decided to stay with Sue and Jim so that he could finish high school without transferring. He did eventually transfer from a vocational school where he was learning auto mechanics to a regular high school, but he still continued to live with Sue and Jim.

Finally, Ma and Dad found a trailer that they could actually own. It was an Ironwood, used, and nine feet wide and thirty-five feet long.

We Become Home Owners! Us? Really?

It was compact, cozy, and mostly furnished with built-in beds and dressers. All they needed to buy was a sleeper sofa for Ma and Dad to sleep on in the living room and a TV. We would be living in another city that Ma and Dad knew well. It was over three miles from our familiar surroundings, and I was fearful of such a big change. We would have to change schools, churches, neighborhoods, and friends. These changes, plus leaving Sue and Jim, made me very sad to the extent that I couldn't stay in a room without crying if anyone talked about us moving. Regardless of my reticence and unstable emotional state, we moved. I, of course, cried all the way to our trailer in a modest trailer park. What an adjustment we all had to make, and how unexpectedly wonderful did my life become for the next three years. I was surprised every day with the rewards of this new habitat and the exciting but somewhat dangerous lifestyle that ensued.

~~~~

Surprisingly, the whole trailer park experience gave me a different form of disparity. Surprise! We were on top! Or at least near the top! We were not "trailer trash" like some of the people that occupied some of the trailers in the park. We were actually one of the most stable families in the whole trailer park. Although the majority of the families were permanent residents, there were several transient families that came and went, often following the local farm harvests or the carnivals. Of the approximately sixty trailer lots, about fifteen or so were occupied by trailers that appeared some time during the night and just as mysteriously were gone in a few months, again in the night. The kids from these families gave us a bit of diversity, but more importantly to my brothers and me, these kids brought adventure in many forms, and we loved it all.

With Dad working steady and taking good care of us, he was looking pretty good in contrast to the transient families. In fact, he became a respected member of the trailer park community. Can you believe it? He bought things to improve the trailer, puttered around,

We Become Home Owners! Us? Really?

fixed things, kept the trailer clean and neat, and interacted with other Dads in the park. He was now a real Dad and not a drunk!

We also went up a social notch in school. Ma enrolled Danny, Pat, and me in a Catholic school that was about a mile from our trailer in the adjacent village. We were the only kids from the trailer park that didn't go to the public school. We were almost getting "uppity." We had to wear blue shirts and ties that Ma purchased from the school with dark pants as our uniforms. Since we were the only kids from the trailer park who went to this school and wore uniforms, I felt for a while like we had become one of those nice families like on TV. Disparity was arrested for a bit.

~~~~

I can never think of or drive by that church and school without thinking of Terrance (not Terry) O'Connor.* He was the nicest boy in the sixth grade, maybe in the whole Catholic school. He was never late or absent, did his work, always said "Yes, Sister" when answering the teacher's questions, got good grades, and was probably the best example of what students at this school were supposed to become. He sat across from me and was always friendly in his quiet way. Then one afternoon Terrance shocked us all.

It began at lunchtime when we were allowed outside to play after eating our lunch. Richard Brownout,* one of the rowdier kids in the eighth grade, brought a hunting knife to school. This was not allowed, but we all were quite taken with this magnificent knife, including Terrance. Richard let some of us hold the knife, which was quite thrilling. When the bell rang signaling us to return to class, Richard quickly hid the knife under his coat, and in we went.

Our classroom shared a common wall of sliding doors with the eighth-grade classroom taught by a tyrannical and feared nun who was also the school principal. Whenever the sliding doors opened and she strode menacingly down the aisle to the front of our class, it was usually bad news for somebody. On this day, she seemed especially irate as she turned and, in a loud voice, commanded that

I and six other boys she named, including Terrance O'Connor, come to the front of the room. She roughly pushed and arranged us in a semicircle facing the class with herself in the center.

We were all wondering what we had done wrong, and then she explained that she had seen each of us holding Richard's hunting knife out on the playground. Her window was right above where we "did the deed," so of course, she saw us. We were dumb, knife-struck kids. Then she announced our punishment. We were ordered to each put out our hands, palm up, and receive four whacks to each hand with Sister's infamous yardstick.

Really? For just touching a knife? This seemed like a cruel and unusual punishment to me, but I did not raise the issue. We knew Sister never held back when using her yardstick, and we were all terrified of the pain that was about to be inflicted upon us.

She was moving efficiently around our semicircle administering her whacks, leaving crying boys, including me, in her wake. When she got to Terrance and he was ordered to put out his hand, he shocked us all by refusing. Instead, he said in a straightforward, confident, but still respectful way, "I didn't touch the knife, Sister. I just looked at it, so you shouldn't hit me." This was indeed amazing. Sister's face was beet red as she bellowed, "Put out your hand." Terrance didn't and, in the same confident voice, said without one shred of defiance, "No, Sister, I won't." With that, Sister reached behind Terrance and forcibly pulled his hand out in front of him and brought her yardstick down with all the cumulative rage she was feeling. Oh, but Terrance, quick as a cobra, grabbed Sister's yardstick, broke it in half over his knee, and dropped it at her feet. There was no one breathing at this point, let alone speaking. To say Sister was shocked would be a great understatement. She lost both this public battle and her poise. With tears in her eyes and unable to speak, she walked to the sliding doors, exited, and slid the doors closed behind her. It was over. Our teacher told us to return to our seats, and she resumed whatever lesson she was teaching.

We all sat in awestruck admiration of Terrance. He was our hero. However, this incident did not change him. He was still the best behaved boy and a very good student. To do something so brave like Terrance did is something we all aspired to do. I wonder how many of us did something to equal Terrance's courageous stance against someone as formidable as our principal on that day long ago. I know I never did.

~~~~

It was a new life for us in the trailer park. Dad stayed sober, went to work, came home (with his pay!), and worked at being a conscientious home owner, good neighbor, husband, and father. He and Ma enjoyed being home owners, and he did his best to upgrade our trailer. He was handier than I ever knew. He erected a little fence around our side yard, bought and assembled a canvas and metal rod wading pool for Pat, and tried to grow grass. He also consulted with some other men in the park and arranged to have a shed built on the side of our trailer and a gravity-fed kerosene fuel system installed that made our furnace safer and easier to maintain. Dad was really settling into family living, not drinking, being home every night, and interacting with us all in a pretty normal way. Everything was going well, and he was handling the stress of being a responsible adult quite well, but it wouldn't last. My brothers and I would see to that.

~~~~

Ma worked full-time days in the central supply department in a local hospital, which she enjoyed very much. She formed strong relationships with "the girls" in her department, learned and told dirty jokes (I overheard her telling Dad some of them), acquired a quasi-level of medical knowledge that made her the medical go-to person for all things medical in the family, and earned money that helped the family with our increasing expenses. The worst thing about Ma working is that she worked from seven o'clock to three o'clock, and Dad worked from three o'clock to eleven o'clock. This meant that a lot of the housework fell to Dad to which he vacillated between pride in his work and disgust with how we so casually messed up his neat trailer each day. It wasn't intentional; we were just "rambunctious".

Overall, it was us three kids who gave Dad "a mountain this time." The "mountain" was our unruly behavior. The three of us—Pat, Danny, and me—all did poorly in school and were always getting caught doing things that were against our parents' rules, the regulations of the trailer park, the law, and what was considered just normal respectful behavior. We were bastards, and I was the worst of the three of us. Something happened to us kids in the trailer park in that we quickly followed any kid who had an exciting new thing to try. We were curious and had a lot of free time to explore even if it meant stepping outside of the rules. It also didn't help that we played with some kids who routinely did dangerous things for fun. I was especially eager to participate in these nefarious activities.

Perhaps as a carryover from what we witnessed in our old neighborhood, and unbeknownst to Ma and Dad, we even had charge accounts at the local delicatessen. How could this be that kids were allowed to have charge accounts? A store that we frequented on the way to school allowed kids to charge their candy and other snacks. Pat, Danny, and I started accounts as soon as we heard about this unusual credit program. Danny and I would pay off our accounts whenever we got close to or just over a dollar using whatever money we could find. Pat, on the other hand, didn't grasp this aspect of the credit system. His charge account was approaching $5 when Pat panicked and told Dad about the economic mess he had generated.

Like always, the first thing Dad did, like all crazy Taltys, was to "blow his stack", and then bizarrely, he went down to the store and paid off all our debts. Why? I don't know, but thanks, Dad. Unfortunately, Dad also demanded that the store owner never grant us credit again. Dad also called Ma at the hospital and told her about our charge accounts and how he had handled it. Ma gave us hell when she got home, but I don't remember any real punishment. Years later Pat jocularly often asked in wonderment, "What was that guy in the store thinking?"

~~~~

We Become Home Owners! Us? Really?

You would think that if we were enjoying some elevated social status in our new surroundings that I would not feel that old disparity thing gnawing at me. Wrong! What drove me to become an incorrigible kid were my newly discovered outlets for adventures, thrills, and risk-taking. I wanted to catch up with my new friends who had been doing risky things for a while. It did help my burgeoning wild streak that our trailer park was positioned between two sets of railroad tracks, very convenient for hopping freights. There also was a small creek running directly behind our trailer for rafting and wading in the springtime, and two big farmer's fields nearby with plenty of fresh vegetables available for our illegal procurement. Besides the kids in the trailer park being far more adventurous than those in our old neighborhood, there was the absence of baseball diamonds, basketball courts, and swimming pools. This all commingled and caused us to explore other pursuits.

These new kids were not fearful of many things, and I became best friends with Ray Cordowski* who proved to be the most fearless and resourceful of them all. He taught me how to smoke cigarettes, how to run along the side of a moving freight train, grab the ladder attached to the side of a selected freight car, and swing myself aboard. It was both terrifying and exhilarating to be hanging on to the freight car's ladder as the train gained speed and then to time jumping off before the speed became too great to safely let go. This ladder-freight hopping maneuver was mainly for short rides; for longer all-day excursions, we would select an empty boxcar or gondola car while the train was stopped. Once on board, we could relax and watch the scenery. These were usually fast-moving trains where we had to wait a few miles for the train to slow down in order to safely disembark.

For these all-day journeys, sometimes into an adjoining state, we would stock up on fresh carrots and beets from the adjacent farmer's field. I was doing all these perilous things when I was only ten or eleven years old. I fantasized that we were Spin and Marty from the Mickey Mouse Club TV show, but they didn't really engage in the high risk and illegal activities that we did.

The elevated railroad tracks also provided us with thrills in the winter as we engaged in a different kind of sledding. I don't know who or how, but someone took the hood from an abandoned 1940s car, turned it upside down, and attached a twenty-foot long, thick rope to the front of this V-shaped "sled." It took three or four of us to pull and push this monster up to the top of the railroad embankment where three of us would climb in (one in front and two behind). With a speed I can still feel, we flew down that steep embankment and across the icy field. That ride was worth the hard work of getting our car hood-sled back up for the next breathtaking descent.

There were also less dangerous things that engaged us, and one of my favorite things to do was to sit high in a tree fort or on top of a huge pile of hay in a farmer's field talking with my superhero Ray. Some of my best memories were listening to Ray. He was very smart about many things of which I was pretty ignorant. It was great to sit or lie in these special places and tell dirty jokes, plan our next venture, or relive our past acts of recklessness. We could make each other laugh outrageously while engaging in the simplest of activities like peeing down on my unsuspecting brother Pat from high up in our difficult-to-access tree house.

I also loved the tamer things we did like building all kinds of forts above and below ground, high in trees, and even a small shack. The dangerous part came when we swiped things like kerosene lanterns and other useful items from underneath people's trailers or from construction sites. Once we multiplied the level of danger by trying to heat our shack by lighting a bucket of kerosene that was in the bottom of a homemade (not by us) stove that we found in the dump. Thank God we couldn't light it or there would have been an inferno in our small shack killing four little boys, two of which were in the same family (Danny and I).

A day that still makes me nauseous when I think of it today is the time I tried to teach Danny the art and science of hopping a moving freight train. I almost got him killed or severely injured. After demonstrating the proper way to grab the ladder on a boxcar while running alongside a moving train, he tried to imitate me. However,

We Become Home Owners! Us? Really?

instead of trying to grab the ladder of a boxcar, he foolishly selected a flatcar that only had a two-rung ladder that made boarding much more difficult. Only a seasoned freight-hopper would try this. Also, he did not see the elevated track switch looming ahead that he hit while running alongside the train. The force of his running right into the switch threw him under the moving wheels of the train. Luckily, he held onto the ladder and was able to pull himself up onto the flatcar. It terrified him so much that he did not ask to go freight-hopping again, and that was fine with me.

Because the roads in the trailer park were not paved and the sharp gravel ruined our tires, we no longer rode our bikes. We walked every place (actually ran). We were now living in a more rural area where the potential for outdoor thrills and adventure were so plentiful that bike riding was actually too tame for us.

In winter, we could walk a mile or so to a fairly busy road where we could spend a pleasant afternoon hitching on the backs of cars and trucks for a fun ride sliding along the icy streets in a crouched position. One of my fun winter Saturdays was ruined by a policeman who grabbed me off the back of a truck, put me in the back of his police car, and drove me home to also ruin Dad's Saturday. However, I did get a lucky and astonishing break as a result of being captured.

~~~~

I do need to explain how another of Ray's and my activities miraculously played a part in saving me from my getting punished for more than car hitching. We had discovered that we could pry the coin machines open with our pocket knives (we all carried them) at the trailer park's washhouse. Everyone in the park had to rely on the washers and dryers in the washhouse because no one had them in their trailers. It became routine for Ray and me to stop by late in the day to "collect the day's receipts." It was so easy. Then one evening Stan,* the owner of the trailer park, a mean and explosive man, unexpectedly pulled up in front of the washhouse. He got out quickly and was moving toward the door when one of the tenants thankfully intercepted him. I heard him ask in his strong Polish accent, "Are those kids in there?" The tenant talked lower, so I couldn't hear what he said, but I could hear Stan, and he was really agitated about something.

We knew that if he caught us in there and with his coin boxes empty once again, we would be his prime suspects. There was only one door that opened into this small room containing the washers and dryers, a sink, and a table for folding clothes. It seemed there was no escape or place to hide, and so I told Ray, "Get inside that dryer, and I'll get in this one." He said, "You're crazy. What if they turn it on?" I wasn't worried about that, but I was worried about getting caught by Stan. He always scared me.

These were large front-load dryers, and they could save us. I pushed him toward one, and I got in the other one just before Stan walked in. Ray and I were both small enough to fit in these big dryers, but I still tried to get as far back as I could. I could see Stan the whole time through the dryer window as he went around in escalating rage to each coin box and discovered them all empty. He repeatedly yelled, "Sons of bitches!" after he slammed each coin box closed. He then stormed off, probably to the local office of the FBI. Ray and I waited about two minutes, and then out we ran with our pockets full of quarters and dimes jingling away. Oh yes, we laughed our asses off on the way to the store to buy some candy such as green leaves, potato chips, and "pop."

~~~~

Now here is how my winter car hitching capture and the washhouse caper resulted in my lucky break. Ma and Dad's work schedules put a lot more homemaking and parenting responsibilities on Dad during the day than he would have liked. Actually, I think it was a lot more than he was capable of handling mainly because of the unruly behavior of Danny, Pat, and me, and his poor preparation for this demanding role. However, it was on the day that the police brought me home that Dad became the most distraught. The policeman was pretty nice about it, but it didn't placate Dad.

He yelled in anguish and rage, "You bastards! I'm calling your mother at work. I don't give a goddamn anymore. Get the hell to bed." So I started to head to Danny's and my bedroom in the back of the trailer. The police had just left when there came a loud pounding on the trailer door. I recognized Stan's angry voice as he was yelling, "Talty, Talty, Talty! Is that boy in there? I want that Peter boy!" Dad was shaking as he opened the door, and Stan caught Dad's full blast of his anxiety-filled voice as he blurted out, "Stan, don't bother us now, please. The police just brought Peter home, and we have so much trouble. I don't know what we are going to do." I heard Stan's response and could not believe it! He said quietly in his broken-English, "I'm sorry, Talty. I not bother you. I go. I go." He just left, and I never heard another thing about the coin boxes. I was given some hell from Ma the next day for car hitching and couldn't go out and play for a week. It was a light penalty compared to what could have been if Stan had gotten his way. However, right after that, Stan had heavy duty locks installed on each of the machines, and our washhouse source of revenue was terminated.

~~~~

While living in the trailer park, I fell in love with the outdoors and the whole idea of being in the wilderness and could not wait to go on long all-day hikes into what we called "Old May Woods" or sometimes to "Charlie's Woods" where a real hermit—whose name, I guess, was Charlie?—lived in a shack. I have no idea where the name Old May Woods came from, but this was an enchanting and somewhat vast area with ravines, a raging creek in the spring that coursed through a big tunnel, large trees to climb, and without marked trails—a fun place to get lost. I took Danny and Pat there a few times, and they also loved it. Because it took us an hour and a half to walk there and there was so much we wanted to do once there, these trips became all-day escapades. These types of hiking and exploring days established a pattern for our Saturdays when Danny and I or Ray and I would be gone from eight o'clock in the morning until sometimes eight o'clock at night.

Remember, Ray and I were only ten years old and Danny eight. Ma trusted us, and she really shouldn't have. We were always doing reckless things until my adventurous and joy-filled lifestyle ended, spurred on by what, for me, were three cataclysmic events. These events were unrelated except for their impact on me. They did not happen all at once. Their impact on me was insidious, and their relationship to one another was obscure except in my mind.

~~~~

The first cataclysmic event happened while Ma, Danny, Pat, and I were spending part of our summer vacation visiting my brother Tommy and his wife Karoline in Texas. Dad stayed home to take care of our trailer and go to work on the railroad. This was our second summer in the trailer park, and going to Texas was another kind of adventure for us. Although I missed the trailer park and my friends, we had fun in Texas living on an air force base outside San Antonio.

Dad wrote to Ma quite often and kept us informed about life in our much-loved trailer park. However, one letter that summer brought terrible news. Enclosed was a newspaper clipping that shocked and devastated me. Ray, my best friend and mentor was dead at eleven years of age. He died tragically doing something he and I did on a regular basis as part of our crazy daredevil repertoire. We routinely climbed high-tension wire towers and challenged each other to touch the large insulated coils anchored on an elevated platform more than eighty feet in the air. We stood close to the powerful wires themselves but had an unspoken rule to not touch them. You could hear the deep hum of the high-voltage electricity being transmitted and just knew they were too dangerous to touch. That awful day Ray must have forgotten our rule and touched the wires. Sixty-nine thousand volts went through his body and hurled him into the air. The fall of eighty or more feet broke his neck. He was pronounced dead at the bottom of the tower. I read all this in the newspaper article that was on the front page, along with his picture. This can't be true. I knew that tower so well and could imagine my friend falling.

Out of some weird sense of curiosity, one of the first things I did when I got back to the trailer park at the end of summer was to go the tower, but I couldn't climb it ever again. I went back several times to stare up and envision the path his body took to the ground. One time I got Ray's sister to come with me so she could show me where he had hit the ground. She said his arm and hand were all black. Rest well, my friend.

~~~~

The second cataclysmic event was a convoluted set of interactions that exposed my deceitful and reckless ways of behaving. I had a sense of bravado after Ray was killed that resulted from fighting bigger kids and usually winning. I was puny but fast. When bigger kids tried to bully me or my brothers, I took them on. The last three fights I had were significant because I was victorious in two where I was absolutely the underdog and one where I was publicly humiliated in front of my friends and family.

This last fight was with a sixteen-year-old athletic kid was over quickly as Carl Boyer* flipped me over his shoulder (I said I was puny) three times. I pretended I was dead or at least knocked out (I wasn't) after his last flip until my Dad came rushing out to rescue me. Ma and Dad saw the whole thing from the trailer's back window. I really think they knew that I was faking and went along with my heroic acting. No, this was not the second cataclysmic event, but it was the thing that took away my public persona of bravado and led to the next related big event.

~~~~

Periodically, when Tommy was being transferred by the air force, Karoline would come and stay with us in the trailer for a few weeks during the transition. Well, she was a physically and mentally strong woman who absolutely believed that children must respect and obey their parents. She was also very astute. She was wary of me and my brothers and would not tolerate any of our usual shenanigans.

On a cold late winter day, almost spring, when there were still some sporadic patches of snow on the ground, I was trying to get my status back as a fearless, tough kid. The Carl Boyer whipping aroused my old friend disparity from that compartment in my brain where it had lain dormant. We had transferred to the local public school after just one year at the Catholic school after Dad had a big argument with a nun. I don't remember what the issue was, but I remember him yelling at her as he left the room. "You should be ashamed to wear the habit!"

Whatever transpired led Danny, Pat, and me to being transferred to the public school, and I was now among bigger and tougher kids. No room for a wannabe tough guy here.

So I took to the railroad tracks one Saturday afternoon in an effort to recapture my other self. I had with me a younger kid who thought very highly of me and wanted to learn how to hop freights. I felt like I was wearing the mantle of Ray as I took this novice through the proper freight-hopping procedures including how to spot railroad police or what we called "Dicks".

As I imparted my vast knowledge of train yards and their workings, we met two kids I didn't know but who had watched me demonstrate freight hopping and were very impressed. When they asked, "Where are you two going?" I responded, "We're running away from home," and with that, I hopped into an open boxcar on a slow-moving freight train heading south and pulled my protégé up with me. How's that for driving my friend disparity back into the closet while resurrecting my old bravado? Unfortunately, it wouldn't last because of some unanticipated results from that last conversation.

Unbeknownst to me, my Dad usually walked these same tracks where we were freight-hopping on his way into the steel plant for his 3:00 p.m. to 11:00 p.m. shift. Furthermore, it was fortuitous and not-so fortuitous that when I got dressed that morning, I elected to wear a black-and-white Holstein cowlike pattern winter coat that

Karoline gave me when it no longer fit her. Wearing this coat made me stand out, and that's how Dad spotted me showing off in the moving boxcar.

When I saw Dad, I whispered, "It's a Dick" and told my protégé to jump out of the boxcar on the opposite side of Dad and to just run. I knew it wasn't a Dick and that it was my Dad. I just wanted to get this kid to move and fast. We did, but once on the ground, I looked under the passing freight cars and saw Dad's legs as he hurried toward the end of the train to come around and catch me. Pushing my protégé in the opposite direction, I ran, tumbled down the embankment, and landed sprawled in the mixture of snow and dirt below. My Holstein coat served as the perfect camouflage as Dad scoured the ground of sporadic snow patches from the tracks above looking for me. We were only twenty or so feet away from each other, but he couldn't see me! Thank you, cow coat! That's the fortuitous part; the not-so fortuitous part is that the coat also made it easy for Dad to spot me riding on the train in the first place. Now we are getting to the cataclysmic part of this event.

Dad couldn't find me, but he did catch my "trainee" who had turned around and came face-to-face with Dad. Of course, my "trainee" believed that Dad was one of those railroad Dicks I had scared him about. He panicked when Dad asked him where I was, and he repeated my message, "He's running away from home." This frightened Dad terribly, and he hastened to the plant and the nearest phone and called Ma to tell her of my intended departure. Karoline was with Ma when Dad called, and she took off looking for me.

I had no idea that this conversation had taken place and was feeling pretty good about avoiding Dad's search. Happily, I came bouncing down off the railroad trestle only to encounter an infuriated Karoline. It became immediately clear how very strong she was for a small woman. Grabbing my Holstein coat (formerly hers) with one hand, she double slapped me across the face saying, "This is for going on the railroad tracks, and this is for running away from home." They were stinging slaps that made me cry, and she ordered me to get home. I got slapped again by Ma when I got home and ordered to bed with the warning "Wait until your father gets home." This whole thing was cataclysmic as is. I didn't need a beating from Dad too. I was scared when he came home at eleven thirty that night, and so I resurrected my coma act that I used at the end of the Carl Boyer whipping. He tried in vain to wake me with some vigorous shaking and shouting. "So you don't like it here? You want to run away from home?" In spite of lots of shaking and yelling, I pretended that I could not be woken. I think I could have gotten a job acting like a corpse! He finally gave up and let me really sleep.

Although I was relieved that I had bested Dad twice in one day, I approached morning fearfully. Thankfully, it all worked out because I felt great shame and remorse (really) over everything and sincerely apologized to them all. They forgave me. Ma said I was grounded for a month, and I accepted it. I also learned that Ma, Dad, and Karoline really loved me. They were more worried than mad about my freight train fiasco and declaration about leaving home. This I will never forget.

~~~~

The etiology of my third cataclysmic event was the work of Ma and Dad. They, unlike me, did not view the trailer park as an exciting playground with the neatest playmates a kid like me could ever have. Likewise, our trailer that they once viewed as cozy and quaint was now cramped and old. Also, the rural setting was now viewed as too far away from Sue and Jim and our roots. Apparently, these insights were discussed between them when I was out of earshot because I felt like I had been punched hard in the stomach when they announced their plan to sell the trailer and move us back into our old neighborhood.

Oh my god! Moving from this great place? How could they do this to me? I had never been so happy and had the least pangs of disparity while we lived in our little trailer. I loved it especially on cold wintry nights when we were all home and safe. The wind coming across the open fields behind us would rock the trailer while we were warm and so snug inside. Also, things were good with Dad working and staying sober. Why when we were more normal than we ever were, do we now have to move? None of my questions or misgivings about moving did any good. We were going to move back into our old neighborhood and return to our previous grammar school. This intended move devastated and enraged me, and I handled it poorly. I stayed mad and sad for over a year while disparity raged within me.

These three unrelated cataclysmic events were compounded for me because I was on the brink of adolescence. Change was my enemy, and it made a great partner with my usual disparity. What a formidable partnership they made; I was no match for them. I found out later on that this move was partially initiated when a co-worker of Ma's told her that her son had a flat for rent in our old neighborhood. When Ma shared this information with Sue, they both became enthused about the possibility of living closer to each other once again. It surprised me that Ma and Dad, having enjoyed the freedom and independence of home ownership for three years, were now considering renting and once again experiencing the capriciousness of landlords and landladies.

Regardless of this and the long list of objections I had of why they should not sell the trailer, they put a deposit on the flat and put the trailer up for sale. They wanted out of the trailer park badly and quickly and thus took the first firm and reasonable offer they received. It must have been a cash deal because Dad showed me a bunch of money that he and Ma had hidden in a RyKrisp box and secreted away in the back of a kitchen cupboard. Regardless, in what seemed like a few short weeks, we were out of the trailer and into a flat much closer to Sue and Jim.

Our Move Back to a Flat and Other Tragedies

This next flat was where many sad things occurred beyond my silent rage against the whole move itself. The flat Ma found was nice and right around the corner from where I spent the first eight years of my life. It was on a very busy street with a bus stop right across the street. We were coming back to our old neighborhood. We were not transferring to a new school; we were returning to our familiar grammar school. Once told of our imminent transfer, the teachers and principal at our present school were concerned that we would not show up at our new (actually old) school. They kept telling me, "Peter Talty (why the first and last name?) they are expecting you at that school, so you make sure you and your brothers go there." I guess if you lived in the trailer park, the teachers assumed that education was not a high priority. According to this perspective, they thought we would all just abandon school once we left that school. They were actually right about the three of us abandoning school, but not for a few years yet.

Another puzzling thing about this move was that Ma put me, a thirteen-year-old, in charge of getting Danny, Pat, and me transferred. So I asked each of our teachers for our records to take with us, but they said they would send them. So we left there on a Friday and arrived on the following Monday at our old-new school. So there! We did show up!

However, they were not expecting us. Not only were they not expecting us, but our records had not been sent. I made this situation worse by becoming anxious and mixing up the words "expecting" with "waiting." I confused the hell out of the office staff when I said, "We are Peter, Daniel, and Patrick Talty, and I know you are waiting for us." Stupid! I tried to assure the principal that our records were being sent, and that we were in the grades I specified. So after a phone call to our old school, she assigned us to our classrooms pending receipt of our records. I was in eighth, Danny in sixth, and Pat in fourth grade.

~~~~

Oh, how things had changed in our old school and my old friends in the three years since we had moved away. I knew most of the kids in my room from having gone through the first through fifth grades with them, but their growth academically and level of maturity was in dramatic contrast to my own stagnation. Their language skills and seriousness about education were extraordinary and strange to me. I was never a good student, and this was going to be embarrassingly revealed over the remaining weeks of the semester of eighth grade. This school had each class as a group change classes each period. Our first class was science, and one of the students, Mary Densmore,* explained the circulation of the heart using a big plastic model. It was quite dramatic, and I was even more shocked when the teacher handed Mary her pointer so she could point to the long and strangely named vessels and chambers for complete edification of the class or some such bullshit. I knew nothing of which she spoke and had never seen a peer conduct a lecture as if she were the teacher. Where was I? Who were these kids?

With feelings of nausea, anxiety, alienation, and, of course, full-blown disparity, we next went to English. This teacher actually looked and acted like an English teacher. He was friendly and explained to me specifically (why me?) that the class had been engaged in contrasting two different books they had read this past year. I stared blankly when he asked the class, "What factors do you feel should we use in our contrasting work?" I shifted my gaze to my old best friend Georgie Kelly[*] when I recognized his voice. He looked so grown up in his sport coat and tie (I owned neither). He said something eloquent, the specifics of which I don't remember, but at the end he used a word I had never heard before: "locale."

What the hell was locale? But the teacher loudly clapped his hands together and exclaimed, "Excellent, George!" That class and the rest of the day were agony for me. How did my old friends get so smart and sophisticated? Regardless, I thought my old friends would be glad to see me (they weren't) and would welcome me back (they did not). They were really into their studies. Imagine!

I then thought of a way to impress and reconnect with my old pals. It was drawing on my prior success at my old school as the class clown. Back there I said and did silly things on purpose that made everyone laugh, even the teachers. I was also used to being a leader of sorts in which I led my peers and brothers on perilous adventures like hopping freight trains, climbing high on trees and high-tension wire towers, and hitching on the bumpers of cars in the winter. Telling them in between classes and at lunch about my trailer park experiences did not have the impact I anticipated no matter how funny I tried to make it sound.

I then had an epiphany of sorts when I realized that although my old friends had grown intellectually, they had no idea how I had grown in terms of recklessness and gross motor skills. So instead of paying attention in social studies class, I planned out how I would reveal my prowess to them at the end of the first day in a spectacular way while walking home.

As soon as the bell rang signaling the end of classes, I bolted ahead of my classmates out onto the adjacent street. Knowing that this was the way my old friends would be walking, I ran ahead and selected a tall tree with limbs that did not start for at least twenty-five feet up. This made climbing it really difficult and impossible for most, but not me. I shinnied up that tree like an orangutan and awaited my friends. This was going to be good! As they came by below, I began calling loudly to each by name: "Georgie! Georgie Kelly! Sharon! Sharon! Sharon Butler*!, Ernie Wells*!" and so on.

Each looked up briefly as I called their name, but no one stopped or called anything up to me. I was confused more than disappointed and slid on down after they had all gone by. What a disastrous first day! It was replete with rampant disparity. The great differences between me and my old friends were now painfully apparent.

I didn't ask Pat or Danny how their first day went. I didn't care about theirs, and I sure as hell didn't want to talk about mine. We all did get a break in that the instruction we got in math at the old school put us ahead of the new-school kids. Everything else we were behind on and the teachers were not real motivated to catch us up coming in so late in the year. So all three of the Talty boys commenced to struggle in the rest of our classes, and in addition, I was also foundering socially.

~~~~

The contrasting cultures between the trailer park I had left and the school and friends I now experienced were far greater than I could have ever imagined. These kids had changed a lot. They were far more mature than I was, and they valued education way beyond my interests. I was really just interested in having fun, showing off, taking risks, hopping freights, playing in the woods, and enjoying other things that didn't fit in with my old friends. So what did I do when confronted with these multiple disconnects? I tried to fit in as best I could but lacked the social skills and confidence to even talk to these kids. I felt that they viewed me as a jerk, and that is why my feeble attempts to join in were rebuffed. So I gave up and moved myself socially and psychologically to the periphery of the class.

It was necessary at this time to choose a high school. The smart kids like Georgie Kelly* and Mary Densmore* were going to attend a nearby high school to prepare themselves for college. Neither I nor my teachers viewed me as college material, so a vocational school seemed to be my destiny. I looked over all the possible trades and settled on baking. My brother Bernie had been befriended by a baker, whom I'll call Mr. Donut,* and I think, subconsciously, this played a part in my decision. However, the manner in which Mr. Donut and Bernie became great friends screams for a digression back to our days in our first flat. At least I think it does.

~~~~

When we were living our life of poverty due to Dad's drinking, I did something that is still shameful to me today. The Donuts were a new family to our neighborhood who bought a home behind us and worked very hard in fixing it up. They had put in a lot of plants and flowers, creating a picturesque garden in their backyard. For some reason, inspired by Satan, I guess, my brother Danny and I, when we were about eight and ten years old, respectively, went over to the Donuts' and tore out every plant and flower in their beautiful yard. I can still see a stunned Mrs. Donut watching out her bedroom window as we rampaged about. What bastards we were! And stupid too! I can't blame this diabolical act on disparity.

We were not home long before Mrs. Donut called Ma and told her the whole story about us kids having gone mad in her once lovely yard. Ma took me and Danny back over there and had us apologize to Mrs. Donut. Bernie went too because he was older and always a good boy, plus I think he was kind of nosy about our latest escapade. Mrs. Donut was far more understanding than she should have been toward Danny and me and about this whole horrible incident. It is still a mystery to me how she could be so nice about it all.

After some discussion with Ma, it was decreed that Danny and I would clean up the yard and salvage whatever flowers that could be replanted. Now comes the part that led to the Bernie and Mr. Donut compact: it was further decreed that Bernie would be the overseer as Danny and I restored the yard as best we could. So we spent a couple of days that summer working in their yard and drinking lemonade and eating homemade cookies that Mrs. Donut served us. Was this the way to treat garden-wreckers? Crazy! Meanwhile, the

Donuts embraced Bernie, especially Mr. Donut, and they forged a strong relationship that lasted until Mr. Donut's death many years later. When we finished our work, the yard was neat and clean, but the garden itself would take a few years to recover. However, Bernie would be the beneficiary of Mr. Donut's largesse for many years. I forgot to mention that Mr. Donut was a baker and owned three successful bakeries. Bernie worked for Mr. Donut periodically and often brought home lots of day-old baked goods that we devoured like locusts. I don't think Bernie ever properly thanked Danny and me for initiating this beneficial relationship with Mr. Donut.

~~~~

So, anyway, back to my education and choice of career. I decided to go to a vocational high school to become a baker. Now do you see the Mr. Donut connection? It's not that we ever really had a conversation about my becoming a baker, I just didn't know of any other trades. My peers that were college-bound elected to attend a non-vocational high school because there they could follow a college preparatory track. I thought they were dumb because that path seemed vague, whereas mine had a clear direction leading to a specific trade and a job: a baker!

I attended my grammar school graduation ceremony, and Ma organized a small (very small) family celebration party at our house. A few of Bernie's friends came too. Now in those days, it was sort of customary for the graduates to seek out their friends to celebrate with and to eschew their family party as soon as possible. However, since I had no friends to seek out, I stayed at my little family party until the end.

~~~~

The next day began my summer vacation that I'm sure I spent in a way far different from my peers. I mostly stayed in the house for the summer because I was still pissed off about the move out of the trailer park and depressed about my low social standing amongst my peers. That was a strange summer for a thirteen-year-old boy. I went to Sue and Jim's for almost all the weekends and helped with housework, did yard work for Jim, babysat Kathleen, and then went with them to drive-ins, miniature golf, amusement parks, the beach, and so forth. So my schedule was one where I pretty much stayed in my room from Sunday night until Thursday afternoon and then went to Sue and Jim's from Thursday to Sunday. I had no friends. I failed at connecting with my old ones even when employing my prowess in tree climbing. I was also too shy and inept to make any new ones. That summer established my dysfunctional early life pattern, whereby, when my sense of disparity was enormous, and my perceived chances of my being able to decrease the differences between myself and what others could do or things they possessed, I would just withdraw and shut down. I was ashamed of not having any friends. I was also embarrassed to be completely dependent on Sue and Jim for any kind of social life that summer. However, I felt that by being helpful to them, I would not be a burden. I also loved and admired Sue and Jim very much and just enjoyed hanging out with them. The anger that I irrationally felt toward Ma and Dad for uprooting us from the trailer park was at the center of my summer withdrawal from life. Bemoan, bemoan, bemoan.

~~~~

One of my efforts to help Jimmy with yard work was disastrous. Jimmy had bought a new gas-powered lawn mower from a local hardware store. It was a beauty! Jimmy loved it, but he did not particularly love grass cutting itself. So in an effort to help Jimmy and elevate myself to being a man, I offered to cut the grass the next day while he was at work. I had watched him cut the grass several times and assured him that I could do this. He went over the procedure of filling the mower with gasoline, making sure the spark plug was connected, adjusting the choke, and giving it a few strong pulls on the starting rope. This was all reviewed in Jimmy's living room without us going into the basement where he kept the mower and gasoline. Apparently, neither he nor I felt the need to go over these simple procedures with the mower present—a big mistake. I couldn't wait for the next day to get mowing and moving forward on my path to manhood.

Confidently, I went into the basement the next morning and hauled the lawn mower upstairs, through the kitchen, and outside. They didn't have a garage, and so to keep his mower safe, Jimmy kept it in his basement. I went back downstairs and picked up what I thought was the gasoline can. Following Jimmy's precise directions, I opened the gas cap, filled it to the brim, put the cap back on snug, attached the spark plug wire, and gave the starting cord a pull, adjusted the choke, pulled the cord a couple more times, and it started right up. Off I went, but it stalled after only a few minutes. No matter how many times I tried, it would not start. Frustrated and saddened, I came back in and told Sue what happened. She didn't know what to suggest, so she called Jimmy at work. He took the time to patiently walk me back through all the steps but nothing worked. Jimmy said to leave the mower outside, and he would look at it when he got home.

At this time Jimmy had not contracted the Talty Flu, and thus he was still a good problem solver. With calmness and deliberateness, he went about figuring out why his beloved mower would not start. As part of the process, he opened up the gas cap on the mower to be sure there was plenty of gas in the tank. He was shocked to see not gas in the tank; I had filled it with oil instead—a bigger mistake. Oil? In the gas tank? Yes, I know. I was an idiot! I didn't even know the difference between oil and gasoline.

Typical of Jimmy, he did not blow his stack, scream at me, swear, kick the mower, or go get drunk in a true Talty Flu fashion. No. Instead, he proceeded in a deliberate way and just calmly set about trying to get the oil out of the gas tank. I helped him turn it upside down in an effort to drain out the oil. He left the mower outside overnight and tried to start it several times the next day but with the same dismal results. After a few days, I helped him move the mower back into the basement to wait. Wait for what? A miracle? That's sure what we needed.

After several days of Jimmy repeatedly trying to start his mower with real gasoline and a new spark plug, it started! The problem now was that the mower was billowing black smoke in his basement, and he was afraid to shut it off. He let it run for about five minutes, shut it off, took it outside, started it again (on the first pull!), and this time let it run for a half hour. It ran fine that day and every day after that when I cut the grass. Yes, he let me use his mower and never once yelled at me about my dumb mistake.

~~~~

Going back to my bleak social life, you would think I would have followed Bernie's excellent example and overcome my loneliness and frustration by getting involved. He really was a model of social success. He was socially competent and confident, resulting in a large circle of friends, girlfriends, as well as adult friends like Mr. Donut and Uncle Bern. He also went to dances, had dates, and became involved in social organizations that were directed toward teens. I had the false belief that his social success, especially with girls, was because of his attending a co-ed high school, whereas my intended high school was an all-boys school. That's some of that old Talty Flu thinking at work: blaming the problem on the wrong thing.

~~~~

Attending the vocational school that fall did prove to be disturbing for a number of reasons. First, it was an all-boys school located in the inner city and about 50 percent of the students were black. Interacting with black kids was new to me coming from that lily-white neighborhood where we were so biased that we would quickly climb out of the public swimming pool if some rare black kids happened to jump in. This seldom happened because they had their own pool in another section of the city. What were we afraid of? Whatever it was, I carried that fear along with a distrust of Polish people who also abounded at the vocational school but not in our neighborhood into my high school experience.

Race and ethnicity were important factors but only to the extent of keeping a distance geographically, physically, and mentally. We just didn't think about it until someone different came into our field of awareness. I had a hierarchy firmly embedded in my mind about who to like and respect. White Irish Catholic people were at the top. Under them came English, German, and Scandinavian people in a cluster. Next were the Polish. Under them were the Italians, Jews, and Greeks. As color came into my perception, I saw a sub-hierarchy of Hispanics and then blacks. All the pejorative and stereotypical terms of Nigger, Polack, Dago, Wop, Spic, and so forth were how we referred to people different from ourselves. We were at the top looking down with scorn on just about everyone else. Bizarre thinking considering the impoverished way my family lived growing up.

Another difficulty I had entering the vocational school, besides this bundle of biases, is that only one other student from my grammar school was attending that school. He too was intending to become a baker. He lived in another neighborhood and thus took a different set of buses, so I really didn't get to interact with him except at school. He was also Italian, so he would not have been a person I would normally seek out to become my friend. Coincidentally, his last name was Pepe, and this name would become an amazing and unanticipated part of my life as well as Bernie's. Just wait!

~~~~

I think I decided to adopt a new persona at the vocational school because no one knew me. I had always been enchanted with the tough guy persona of James Dean in *Rebel Without a Cause*, Marlon Brando in *The Wild Ones*, and anyone who was tough and really good-looking. I had also read a book titled *Knock on Any Door* by Willard Motley where the tough guy died in the electric chair after having committed murder. So I had adopted a sort of silent hero worship of tough guys and was ready for the new me as Tough Guy Pete.

However, in reality, I lacked several essential traits for the role of a tough guy: I was neither tough nor good-looking, and I was also a wimp in every respect. Talk about rampant disparity!

The other thing that worked against my tough-guy aspirations was that I initially liked school and was having success in my freshmen year. I liked the baking program, and the other courses I had to take were not very hard. There was also no homework. This is where disparity was operating in my favor. There were a lot of poorly motivated students at the vocational school, so anyone who made a moderate effort went to the top of the class. The tough guys I wanted to emulate were anti-education, so this gave me another significant obstacle to overcome. I was a good student in my freshmen year, not a tough guy. Unfortunately, this would cease before my sophomore year.

~~~~

Besides my depressing summer prior to entering high school, I and the rest of the family were staggered by the portentous medical crises that hit Dad, Ma, and Pat all in a short period of time. Our new flat in our previously beloved neighborhood became the site of much grief for us all.

It started with Dad's psychological collapse that was preceded by radical lung surgery. Back in 1954, Dad had become increasingly ill with emphysema and underwent major chest surgery to remove much of his emphysema-diseased lung tissue in an effort to alleviate his symptoms.

Unfortunately, his chronic shortness of breath, fatigue, irritability, chest pain, and great anxiety when he could not get his breath were not improved by the surgery. He tried to resume working on the railroad, but the winter cold was his enemy. Because he still did not have a car or a driver's license, it was necessary for him to stand outside in the bitter cold waiting for buses. He had been a two- to three-pack-a-day cigarette smoker throughout his adult life, and as crazy as it sounds today, he continued to smoke even with his debilitating emphysema. It gets even crazier when I recall that even Dad's doctor was a smoker. His lame advice to Dad to "just cut back" seems insane in light of today's knowledge about smoking.

~~~~

He did recover physically from the surgery, but then an alien condition struck Dad and presented me with a real-life mystery. Dad had been readmitted to the hospital, but not to our usual hospital right across the street from our flat. For some unknown reason, he was now a patient at an uptown hospital that required two buses to reach. The other part of this mysterious hospitalization was, why was Ma crying all the time, and why were Ma and Sue the only ones allowed to visit Dad?

I hate mysteries. I repeatedly pressed Ma to tell me what was wrong, but she was so emotional that she couldn't tell me and just waved me away with a handkerchief to her face. Finally, one day after coming back from visiting Dad, she blurted out in response to my persistent questioning, "Your father's lost his mind!" What the hell did that mean? Apparently, Dad had become very depressed around the same time his longtime girlfriend committed suicide. He was admitted to the psychiatric unit of the uptown hospital because Ma, Sue, and Dad's doctor were afraid Dad might do the same. His elder sister had killed herself when she became pregnant as an unwed teenager, and this might give Dad the same idea. I was eventually allowed to visit him, and he seemed fine. He was "going to OT" and made me a pair of moccasins. He must have forgotten about my anomalous feet because the moccasins were both the same size.

After about two weeks, Dad was transferred to a private psychiatric hospital in order to receive shock therapy. I also visited him there, and he seemed just the same. We thought he was improving, but we were apparently wrong. His psychiatrist told Ma that Dad needed long-term institutional treatment in a state hospital. Of course, Ma felt terrible about this but believed she had no choice but to sign the papers for his admission. There were two large state hospitals in our area, and admission was determined by the patient's residence in relation to a river that divided the region. Since we lived south of this river, Dad was assigned to go to the state hospital that was about forty miles from where we lived. So off he went. It was a sad and pitiful thing for Dad as well as us. People admitted to a state hospital in those days seldom ever came home again.

~~~~

Another sad event for me was Bernie joining the army. He had graduated from high school but was frustrated with his job situation, finding it hard to get hired and then soon after being laid off. It seemed the army was the best option for him. I was very sad. I always found good-byes difficult, and the idea of Bernie going off to who knows where was very difficult for me. We were very close, having always been together whenever our family broke up, and we were also usually room and bedmates. The morning he left for the army, I wouldn't get out of bed to say good-bye. I was crying (like usual) when he came in and forced me to shake his hand. Bernie's leaving for the army was one of the personal tragedies I associate with that flat, not least of which was Dad being admitted to the state hospital so far from home.

~~~~

There was, however, some fun and joy for me while living in that flat, thanks to my cousin Tyke. He only lived two blocks from us in our old flat, and he and his brother Bood attended the local Catholic high school also right near our flat. Tyke often took the time to stop by to see me, and he and I engaged in some mildly reckless behavior by going to the local burlesque theater. This was pretty exciting stuff to see women provocatively removing their clothes and to watch the performance of outrageous comedians replete with sexual innuendos. It was great fun!

Tyke also was instrumental in initiating my lifelong love of college basketball. This was back in the late 1950s and early 1960s before the NCAA organized colleges and universities into conferences. In those days, there was a great rivalry between the local colleges. Every Saturday night one or more of these teams would play in the downtown auditorium ("the Aud"). Sometimes they played each other, which were always a sellout, and on other nights the opponents were teams from distant universities like Arizona State, Duquesne, St. John's, Temple, and so forth. I found it really exciting to watch these highly competitive games featuring great athletes. Tyke was often able to get free general admission tickets, and he and I would take the bus downtown to the Aud. An unanticipated corollary to the game was my becoming enamored with college itself. I never considered that I would ever go to college, and I viewed the athletes, the cheerleaders, and the students with wonder and envy. Predictably, this caused another grim arousal of disparity as I envied the life these young people were enjoying in contrast to the small, boring life I was experiencing.

However, my intense interest in college basketball was still pleasurable to watch and read about in the newspaper. Not only was the 1960–61 season memorable in that one of our local colleges rose to the rank of second in the nation but they also achieved this with the help of a kid from our neighborhood. He would sometimes play basketball at the YMCA or on the local playgrounds. I even played against him once, but of course, he killed me. To go from watching him in the gyms and playgrounds to seeing him play at the Aud and then on national TV was quite a thrill for me.

So my long and boring summer preceded the basketball season where the excitement of great games was often overshadowed by that comparing thing I constantly do. Of course, depression naturally followed.

~~~~

I was able to get two part-time jobs that gave me some spending money, but neither job was anything I enjoyed. The first came once again through our family's benefactor, Uncle Bern. He needed someone to clean several of the classrooms in the school where he was the stationary engineer. So when his wife called and asked me to come to their house because Uncle Bern wanted to talk with me, I was hoping it was about a job. He wanted me to come to his school each day after I finished my high school classes. After I finished cleaning the classrooms, I could ride home with Uncle Bern. He didn't pay me a lot of money, but it was a convenient way to earn some money. He said I would get more hours during the Christmas, Easter, and summer vacations. I started the following Monday, and then I seized another opportunity that doesn't even exist today.

I became what was known as a "pin-sticker". By 1956, almost all the bowling alleys in our area had converted to electronic pin setters and ball returns and thus had eliminated the need for someone to manually place the pins in the rack and return the bowling ball. However, there remained one small bowling alley a few blocks from where we lived that still used the old system. I saw an ad in the newspaper and applied in person the same day I saw the ad, but I was not alone. There were about five or six of us that wrote our name and phone number on the sheet of paper that the owner passed around.

With only sixteen alleys and one guy could take care of two alleys, there was really only the need for eight pin-stickers. Also, he already had a cadre of eight homeless men whose drinking problems prevented them from getting a regular job. The only way I would ever get a chance to work was if one of the regular men were too drunk to work or failed to show up.

So rather than sit home and wait for the call that may never come, I decided to go to the bowling alley every night after school and wait to see if he needed me. Unfortunately, all the other boys decided to do the same thing. Sitting around the bar area waiting and hoping that one of the regulars wouldn't make it was what we did. Then I noticed that the number of replacements was dwindling, and by the end of the second week, I was the only one. It worked out that I became the number one sub and got to work three or four nights a week and often on Saturdays.

Once engaged in the work itself, I saw how grueling it actually was. I had to quickly move continuously back and forth between my two assigned alleys in order for the bowlers to bowl their games in a timely manner. It also proved quite dangerous. One night, while I jumped into the pit and began picking up the pins, a guy threw the ball down with a great deal of force and hit me in the face. It knocked me out for a few minutes, but I went right back to work. There was no way I was giving up my alleys. On another night the sixteen-pound bowling ball caromed off the rack above me and struck me on the back of the head. I was unconscious longer this time, and they wouldn't let me continue working that night.

Except for these two mishaps, I became a steady pin-setter for about six months. The work was hot, hard, dirty, loud, and did not pay very well. For four or five hours of setting pins, I would earn $7 or $8. Occasionally, the bowlers would throw coins down the alleys for a tip but not enough to make it all worthwhile. The hours were another factor. I often didn't get home until after midnight and had to get up for school at six thirty each morning.

As crappy as this job was, I did take pride in outlasting the other replacements and impressed the owner with my consistency. I also became fairly skilled and could handle two alleys with no problem. It was also interesting talking with the homeless men before the bowling started. It gave me a glimpse into a sad lifestyle. In comparison, I did not feel any disparity during these conversations. In fact, I felt that my sad life away from my cherished trailer park was now looking a lot better. I did eventually quit being a pin-setter in favor of juvenile delinquency.

The Beginning of Pat's Lifelong Affliction

Danny and I did not know what awaited us when we turned the corner onto our street that summer day and saw the flashing lights from the ambulance, rescue squad (paramedics hadn't come into being yet and interns rode in the ambulances), and two police cars all parked in front of our house. We had just walked home from the park after a day of swimming. Our front door was propped open. Why? What was going on? We rushed upstairs.

Many people we didn't know were gathered around the doorway of Pat and Danny's bedroom, but we rushed on by them and were shocked to see Pat in the throes of his first of what we learned later was a grand mal epileptic seizure. We had never witnessed such an event. He was on his bed, shaking all over, tongue out, drooling, and his eyes rolled back in his head. Ma stood at the bottom of his bed as they tried to put an oxygen mask over his big head. "He's dying, help him," Ma said over and over to anyone and everyone in the room. Danny and I just stared and cried. Then the crowded room got more crowded as two Franciscan brothers from the local Catholic high school appeared. They began to pray over Pat, which I just assumed was giving Pat his last rights to go along with Ma's declaration of his dying.

In a few minutes, Pat stopped shaking and began to come out of the seizure. He was scared and confused when he saw all the people

The Beginning of Pat's Lifelong Affliction

in his room. He had also wet himself and was now crying. With that, they put him on a stretcher and took him off to the hospital. None of us knew how this day would change us all forever, especially Pat, as he embarked on a life of unpredictable and uncontrollable seizures and all their sequelae. He was admitted to the hospital right across the street from our flat, which was very convenient. We all frequently went to see him while he underwent a number of tests over a two-week period to find out what caused his seizure.

We were so glad when Pat was able to come home and especially thankful that he had not died. Ours, and especially Pat's, lives were certainly going to be changed once again because Pat's seizures occurred without warning throughout his life and were terrible to witness. They also robbed him of a normal and happy life.

Ma continued to work in central supply at the hospital where she picked up some information about various medical conditions and their treatment. This, plus the experience of raising six kids, gave her the confidence to dispense medical advice without even being asked. This was evident as she readily interpreted the information provided by Pat's neurosurgeon, Dad's psychiatrists, and her own doctor. She asked the nurses at work, and they freely shared what they knew of the various afflictions that befell our family, which Ma then brought back to us. Then came the dangerous part. Sometimes the information Ma brought home wasn't completely accurate. Panic and despair would ensue in typical Talty fashion whenever Ma presented us with the grimmest and often most graphic description of one of our loved ones' conditions. She loved phrases like "He'll be a vegetable the rest of his life" or "She was filled with cancer," and so on.

~~~~

Sadly, I did not lessen Ma's burdens during these troublesome times. I was bored and frustrated with my dismal social life. The highlight of my day was watching *American Bandstand*. After that, the only interesting thing for me to do was to harass Pat. I would

The Beginning of Pat's Lifelong Affliction

make him crazy with all kinds of schemes and antics. He would become so distraught that he would call Ma at work to report my latest efforts to antagonize him. We would also sometimes wrestle without concern for the owners of the house who lived downstairs. So here Ma was so worried about Pat and Dad's health, her precarious financial situation, and I compounded it all because I was bored and frustrated. Not good, I know, but I will do much worse things.

These stressful times must have certainly contributed to Ma having her worst heart attack to date that necessitated an extended hospitalization of almost six weeks. With Dad in the state hospital, Bernie in the army, Pat staying at Sue's because of his seizures, and Ma now in the hospital, there was just Danny and me left in our new flat. We would go to Sue's after school for supper and then walk home to our dark, quiet, and lonely flat.

I would take the mail up to Ma at the hospital along with the checkbook so she could pay the bills. In those days, doctors strongly believed that the best treatment after a heart attack was complete bed rest, and so that's what Ma got. Apparently, in those days, Ma's physicians feared that any strenuous activity could bring on an even more severe heart attack resulting in her death. Even sitting up in bed to write checks and letters was not permitted, but she did it anyway. I was trying to be a better person and helping out where I could and not generating any more angst for Ma and Sue.

~~~~

During her hospitalization, Ma then got some devastating news from her doctor. He decreed that Ma could never return to work nor could she ever take care of a home by herself. Knowing what I know today about heart attacks (myocardial infarctions) and how lifestyle is such a large contributing factor, I marvel at the medical thinking of those days. Not once did the doctor emphasize that Ma should lose weight, stop smoking, adhere to a low-fat diet, and engage in mild exercise to prevent future attacks. No! It was stop working and caring for a home. Rest was king in those days to the detriment of many patients. She did not have a bad doctor; they just lacked the scientific knowledge of today.

So, unfortunately, this "complete rest" perspective was the way Ma's health was going to be managed. She was scared and was now going to strictly follow her doctor's orders. With great sadness, Ma resigned from the only full-time job she ever had. She always referred to it as "my little job," but she loved it and took great pride in it. As far as a living situation, Sue and Jim once again saved us by inviting Ma, Danny, Pat, and me to move in with them. How much more could they take? To be sure, besides just all these bodies invading their cute little home once again, we brought tons of emotional baggage and generated even more once we got settled in.

We had lived in the new flat for less than two years, but what great sadness I associate with that place. Besides my poor adjustment to the move, Ma had two very severe heart attacks that hospitalized her for a total of three months; Dad had a mental collapse, was no longer able to work, and was admitted to a state hospital; Bernie left for the army; and Pat began his lifelong struggle with uncontrollable seizures.

Back with Sue and Jim

Before we moved back in with Sue and Jim, Tommy and Karoline had come home to help sort out the present state of the family and especially our finances. With Dad and Ma both hospitalized and Pat in and out of the hospital because of his uncontrollable seizures, Tommy asked to have a family meeting in order to figure out what could be done. I had seen business meetings on TV and in movies, and so I naturally assumed that it was this kind of meeting that we were going to have. I cleaned off the dining room table, put glasses of water at each person's place, along with a piece of paper and a pencil. It must have looked a bit strange to Bernie, Sue, Jim, Tommy, and Karoline when they walked in and saw my preparations for the meeting.

 Even though no one drank their water or took any notes, the meeting was successful. It was confirmed that we would give up our flat and once again move in with Sue and Jim. I do not know what would have happened to us if Sue and Jim didn't welcome us into their home once again. We kids may have had to go into a foster care home, but what would have become of Ma? She was too young and nowhere near debilitated to the point where nursing home placement would have been an option. Thank you, Sue and Jim, once again!

 Both Ma and Sue knew from their prior experience that combining two families under one roof has the potential for extreme stress, strain, and upheaval for everyone culminating in damaged relationships. So in anticipation of these pending problems, Sue and Ma tried to plan out how we could do it differently this time.

Besides the anticipated strife, add to it the incendiary mixture of Jimmy's venture into business and Sue becoming pregnant. He tried to operate a gas station with two partners while they all worked full-time jobs on one of the local railroads. The gas station was fairly successful mainly due to Jimmy's commitment and work ethic, which significantly overshadowed that of his partners. I helped him on weekends and during the week in the summer trying to increase his chances for success by working for free. It truly was remarkable the way Jimmy and his partners were able to take a gas station that had been closed up for years and essentially abandoned and turn it into a thriving business.

One example of Jimmy's industriousness was his digging of a pit in the once-abandoned gas station. He had learned from a man that used to have work done at the gas station by one of the long-ago owners that they at one time had a pit where they could do mechanical work on the undersides of cars. Before there were the hydraulic lifts of today, service stations had pits that cars drove over and thus gave mechanics access to the undersides of their cars. For some unknown reason, one of the previous owners filled the pit in and sealed it over with cement. Undeterred, Jim used a pickax to break through the cement, and then he dug and shoveled all the stone and dirt out of the pit. This was a sizable amount of dirt and stone to remove because when finished, the pit measured three feet wide, six feet long, and five and a half feet deep. The pit enabled them to expand their services beyond just selling gasoline. Now we could provide the more profitable services like grease jobs, oil changes, exhaust system replacements, and so forth. That pit really did enhance their business, but not enough to support three guys on a full-time basis, which was their dream.

~~~~

Back with Sue and Jim

Jimmy was working all the time between the gas station and the railroad, which left little time for anything else. His partners were not as heavily invested in making the gas station a success as Jimmy was, and this became more evident with each passing day. Working there, I saw how much longer and harder Jimmy worked than his other two partners, but I never heard him complain or be critical of them.

In spite of the success of the pit, Jimmy subsequently left the partnership. He also quit his job on the railroad and assumed independent ownership of a large Esso (now known as Exxon) gas station. It was an even further distance from his house, but he believed that he could be successful on his own. It was also about this time that Sue had a new baby (Shawn Patrick Riley) to care for in their increasingly stressful and crowded home. The driving distance to the Esso station caused him to be gone every day for fifteen and sometimes eighteen hours. Sue and Jim's relationship progressively eroded, and with the economic strife of not having the consistent pay from Jimmy's railroad job, coupled with all of us around, it was a terrible time for Sue.

~~~~

Prior to us moving in, Jimmy had put a wooden floor down in the attic with the intent of creating two large bedrooms with Danny and Pat on one side and Bernie (when he was home on weekends from the army) and me on the other. The walls were never constructed as Jimmy got consumed by his gas station ventures, but we didn't mind. It was nice having our own space, and we could do what we wanted with it. I decorated my side with posters and pennants to give it some color and help cover some of the tin foil insulation. Downstairs, things were not so harmonious because Kathleen lost her private bedroom again, as she and Ma shared a bed. Sue was always sad and resentful about this.

In those days, I was still somewhat committed to being a good student. I completed my freshman year with perfect attendance and got good grades. However, I had to miss my first day in the spring of my sophomore year when I had to help Jimmy and his friend and partner from the gas station move Ma's furniture into Sue and Jim's basement. I was rapidly losing interest in school at this point anyway, and I do not believe missing out on my perfect attendance record was the cause of my subsequent academic decline.

Ma and Sue had formed a plan whereby we would move Ma's refrigerator, stove, kitchen set, and living room furniture into Sue's basement. This would give us our own apartment of sorts so that we wouldn't wreck Sue's nice furniture, and they would have separate areas in case Ma and Sue "got on each other's nerves". Jimmy was going to finish off the basement with drywall, but this idea was sacrificed when all Jimmy's spare time and money went into the gas stations, especially the new one.

After supper each night, Sue and I would go down to Ma's flat to pack it all up. This dismantling of our home wasn't as emotional for me as when we did it before because we were not going to split the family up this time. With Sue pregnant and having a lot of nausea coupled with Jimmy being gone so much, she became very depressed. We were not of much help to her, and in fact, I know at times we made it worse, especially me.

~~~~

Every Sunday Sue drove Ma out to the state hospital to visit Dad. Sometimes some of us kids would go with them, but it was usually just the two of them that made the eighty-mile round trip without the aid of expressways. They often made the drive in treacherous weather on isolated roads through the center of what became known as "the snow belt" and, worst of all, in a poorly running car. Numerous times they had to turn back because of the weather and, on other occasions, they had to deal with flat tires without a spare.

When they did make it to the state hospital, Dad would constantly complain about his having to live there, his being unable to leave, and Ma not giving him enough spending money for cigarettes—yes, he still smoked—and candy. He was also very critical of Ma and wanted to know what she was doing with all the money that she was getting from his disability pension. Ma and Sue would try to explain everything to him about their financial struggles and what a terrible time they had getting out there, but he was only concerned about himself. Because he was this way and the trip itself so unpleasant, my brothers and I never wanted to go with Ma and Sue. Since Ma didn't have a driver's license, Sue had to do all the driving all the while going through a very difficult pregnancy.

Something else that made the trips to the state hospital so unappealing was that sometimes Dad didn't know us. This happened after he had received several shock treatments (ECT: electroconvulsive therapy), which I think were administered in a series of twenty over a few weeks. I remember being so upset seeing Dad with a vacant look and responding to Ma and the rest of us like we were strangers. No one told us that this was a frequent and temporary result of shock therapy. We just assumed that his brain had deteriorated or some other dramatic explanation that we probably got from Ma. It was very upsetting to see Dad like this, especially with the limited information we had about what his confused state really meant.

There were times when Dad's physical condition took precedence over his mental state. His emphysema, which they thought at the time was asthma, put a great strain on his heart, and he went into cardiac arrest. When this happened, they discontinued shock therapy. His psychiatrists told Ma that Dad would be a patient out there for a very long time because he still had suicidal and homicidal thoughts. I suppose they had him on some medication to help him now that shock therapy was no longer an option.

Tough Guy Pete Emerges

One day, soon after we moved in with Sue and Jim, Sue suggested that I join "the Y" (the Young Men's Christian Association) in order to meet new friends. I know Bernie enjoyed swimming at the Y and going to the dances that they held under the auspices of a youth group known as the "Hi-Y". I was desperate to decrease my social disparity, so I said, "Sure, I'll try it." Sue paid for the membership, but if she could have foreseen what was to follow, she surely would have quickly withdrawn her offer.

Most guys join the Y to take advantage of their athletic facilities, like Bernie did with the swimming pool and others the basketball court. None of these for me! I just liked the idea of playing pool (pocket billiards) partly because that's what Nick Romano, one of my heroes from a book I loved (*Knock on Any Door*), did, and my other real-life hero Jimmy also was a pool player. I wasn't very good at pool, but I did become good friends with Freddie Crane* and Marty O'Brien.* They weren't tough guys, but they were risk-takers. Freddie was very good-looking and always had girlfriends, and they, in turn, had girlfriends, so through them I began to have dates. Marty was very funny and clever.

Something the three of us had in common was the lack of money to do the things we would like to do. None of us had a car, not even driver's licenses. We were only fifteen years old. The disparity I felt when I would see guys my age or a little older driving their own cars and spending money in the local pizzeria made me crazy. It did the same to Freddie and Marty, but not to the same extent.

To me, the most direct way to lessen this new brand of disparity was through stealing. Freddie and Marty felt the same way. It started in the locker room, where we noted that many of the basketball players left their wallets in their pants with their lockers unlocked and sometimes wide open. Because this was an older adult group that played here, these guys had jobs and money.

Our "MO" (modus operandi) was for Freddie and me to go swimming and then to change clothes in the locker room while a pickup basketball game was going on in the gym. Marty would be our lookout. Since he was a basketball player and often stood around the edge of the court to watch the games when he wasn't playing, there was nothing suspicious about him. He positioned himself near the locker room door and would walk in before anyone else, thus alerting Freddie and me who were rifling pockets of the players who left their lockers unlocked. We never took all of anyone's money, not because we felt guilty; we didn't. It just made sense to take "a little from a lot" and thus not be readily discovered.

We did our stealing two nights a week, but we were at the Y every night playing pool. To throw suspicion off us, we would go swimming on the off nights and not take any money. On one of our off nights, I did deviate from our "program," and I took the car keys from a guy's coat pocket while he was playing basketball. I knew which car was his, so on a snowy and slippery evening, Marty and I went for a ride. I drove, but I had very little experience except for driving cars in and out of the bay at the gas station for service. Of course, driving on icy streets was a complete mystery to me. I drove too fast, skidded on the ice, and ended up off the road just missing a tree. We stalled and were stuck in deep snow. Not knowing what else to do, we ran. I still remember that the song we had blasting on the radio as we ran down the street, "Mr. Blue" by the Fleetwoods. Weird things I remember!

Around this same time, we were able to get served beer in a local tavern. The legal age for drinking in 1959 was eighteen, and we were three years from it. No matter. We had phony draft cards that we got from someone that showed our age as eighteen. The names on the cards were not our own, but no bartender in those days ever went that far as to match some other form of identity with someone's proof of age.

So there we would sit drinking beer and sometimes observe some of our victims discovering their loss. "Son of a bitch! I know I had a twenty! Where the hell did it go?" We would try not to laugh, but we were feeling pretty invincible and clever beyond our years.

Another source of revenue was the cash drawer at the Y. They had a drawer under the counter where they kept money from the sale of candy, potato chips, etc. There was never a lot in it, but we could usually reach over and take out a dollar or two when the clerk was occupied in the back.

~~~~

Was I a tough guy yet? No, but I was on my way. I carried my thieving ways over to my vocational high school where I was becoming more and more of an unmotivated student. My school day was divided up by working in the bakeshop all morning, and then I went to academic classes like English, science, history, and so forth in the afternoon. We "bakers" made all the baked goods for the cafeteria and sold the extra stuff at a little store where we took orders each day from teachers, staff, and students.

We had bench partners that we worked with every day, baking the items directed by our teacher Mr. Dough.* My partner, Dick Pratt,* was a good kid who would not have done anything wrong if not enticed by me. Since we rotated through all jobs in the bakeshop on a weekly basis, we had to take orders and sell the baked goods in the store when it was our turn. I saw quickly that Mr. Dough kept the money from the store in an unlocked metal cashbox in his desk (also unlocked). At the end of the week, he would turn the money into the office.

On a daily basis it was often necessary for us to go into Mr. Dough's desk to get cake decorating utensils or some of the knives he kept in there. Dick and I had to use some special knives one day, and so I told Dick to watch the office when I went in there and to come in front of anyone who attempted to walk in on me. I told him I would split the money with him, and he thought it was a great plan. So now I had another source of revenue. I was also becoming more of a tough guy, at least in my mind.

Dick and I ran our little scheme for several weeks until one day the sky fell in on us. It happened on a day when I did something all tough guys do—I skipped school. When I got to school the next day and was in the shower room changing into the white shirt and pants that we wore while working in the bakeshop, Dick came rushing up to me, almost in tears. He was talking so fast in a whisper that it took me a bit to figure out just what was going on.

According to Dick, yesterday, Mr. Dough lined up all the guys in the bakeshop. He said, "There are crooks in this class, and we are going to find out who they are. Some of you have been taking the store money out of my desk. I sprayed the money with an invisible powder that can't be washed off no matter how hard you try. This powder can only be seen with an infrared light that the police have. If you admit it right now, we will go easy on you. If not, I will have the police come in with their special light, and we will find out who the crooks are, and they will be sorry." Wow! Dick said Mr. Dough had each guy put out his hands as he went from one to another, examining each closely.

I told Dick to calm down. I reasoned that Mr. Dough must have been bluffing. He knew he lost money and was desperate to get it back in any way he could, and so he came up with the infrared light bullshit. It seemed to me that if he really had such evidence, they would be having this conversation with a police officer and not Mr. Dough. So I decided that if Mr. Dough confronted me, I would bluff him right back.

We were just setting up to make doughnuts that day when Mr. Dough told me to come into his office. He ran the whole thing down for me just like he did with the class, and I responded not like a tough guy but like an innocent guy. "I did not take the money. Bring the police in with their camera, and you will see that I didn't do it." He looked at me for a bit, and I looked right back at him. I must have been convincing because he told me to go back to work. I wasn't 100 percent certain that we were okay, but I told Dick to keep denying it no matter what. We never heard any more about it. Regardless, it was enough of a scare for Dick to go straight, but not me. I was continuing on with my life goal of becoming a tough guy. I just wasn't going to take any more money from Mr. Dough's desk. He also began locking the cashbox.

~~~~

Besides stealing, tough guys fight a lot. At least that was my perception based on the movies I watched and books I read. However, the obstacle I faced when I tried to fight is that I was not very good at it. I would fight just about anyone and without much provocation. There were a lot of real tough guys at my vocational high school, so finding a fight was no problem. The problem was the beating I would take in every one of them. I was smart in only one respect. I would always fight in a public place, like the cafeteria or bakeshop, where teachers would quickly separate us before I was beaten too badly. Of course, I didn't get the reputation that I wanted of being known as a tough guy; I think I was just viewed as a crazy guy.

I was intrigued and attracted to another negative role model that I read about in the newspaper: "the Capeman". His real name was Salvatore Agron, and when he was sixteen years old, he stabbed to death two innocent teenage boys who he mistook for rival gang members in New York City. He received the death penalty, so in my assessment, he qualified as an authentic tough guy and someone I wanted to emulate. However, I was not attracted to the stabbing, killing, and death penalty aspects, but I did like his persona. I didn't own a cape yet, but I did have a porkpie hat, and my own personal pool cue and case. The idea of wearing a cape was the only piece of my crafted tough guy ensemble that was missing. In my delusional thinking, I really thought I was achieving the tough guy image I desired, but I was not. I was just getting crazier and crazier.

~~~~

I was able to keep my tough guy persona a secret from Ma, Sue, and the rest of the family until the day I attacked one of my teachers, Mr. Tyson.* He also happened to be a neighbor of ours, which made the whole incident even more distasteful. He taught us bakers a course on the science of baking. It was boring, and some guys slept throughout his class. Although he was a short man, he was very tough and thus the pseudonym of "Tyson" that I chose.

I saw him get the best of many students who were much bigger than he. He was wiry, fast, and strong. In contrast, I was thin, weak, and slow.

One day, because I was tired from all my "nighttime activities" that I will detail later on, I folded my arms on my desk and went to sleep. Nodding off in his class was one thing, but blatantly sleeping like I did angered Mr. Tyson, and he lost it. Before I realized what was going on he had pulled me from my seat and my peaceful slumber and just about threw me into the hall. I was stunned. Then he reopened the door and dropped my notebook and textbook noisily onto the floor. Everyone in the room was laughing loudly and applauding for Mr. Tyson. I debated whether to just walk out of school and never go back or stand there in the hall humiliated. So of course, I chose another even more stupid way to respond.

When I pulled the door open, I immediately saw that Mr. Tyson was seated at his desk, arm on the chair, and his chin resting on his hand. He was staring straight ahead and ignoring me. I went right for him and tipped over his chair and all into a shelf of science equipment next to his desk. As I tried to get at him I was struck from behind by an enraged Ima Badger,* and I was fortunate it was a glancing blow or I would have been unconscious, I'm sure. Ima was a lineman on the football team and usually a quite easygoing guy. Apparently, he liked Mr. Tyson and was out to avenge my attack on him. I knew I had no chance against Ima. My only weapon was speed. Ima was lumbering but persistent in his objective of pummeling me.

In the chaos, I was able to get past Ima and out the door. I was down the hall before the monitors (these are seniors whose job was to make sure that only guys with passes were allowed in the halls when classes were in session) could react, but they did. They were yelling at me to stop, and I was yelling back that Ima Badger was after me. I was no match for the speed of these guys, and they caught me. They took me to Mr. Enforcer's* office, who was the assistant principal in charge of discipline.

Ima Badger, relentless in his pursuit of me, followed us all the way and kept saying, "Poor Mr. Tyson. Talty hit him. I'm going to beat up Talty bad." Mr. Enforcer told me to sit in his office (safe from Ima!) while he took Ima back to class and to check on Mr. Tyson. We still had two hours of school left, and then I had to survive a trip to my locker to get my coat and try to elude Ima.

When Mr. Enforcer got back, he asked me what happened. I don't remember what I said, but I know it was neither coherent nor persuasive. He told me to go on to my next class, and he was going to call my parents and tell them what I did. He also said I could not come back to school unless a parent came with me. I explained to Mr. Enforcer that my mother had a heart condition, but he said he would take that into consideration when he called her.

I went to my last two classes, but as soon as the last class was over, I was out the door. I flew to my locker, but too late. Ima was waiting. Luckily for me he had calmed down some. He grabbed me by the neck and pushed me up against the lockers and then up right off the floor. I don't know what he thought I could possibly do in terms of fighting this powerful guy. Then a miracle! He let me down, shook his big head in disgust, and just walked away to catch his bus.

~~~~

Because this happened on a Friday, I had the whole weekend to think about what Monday would bring. Ma and Sue were very sad over what I did. They said I had to stay in except for helping Jimmy at the gas station and doing my after-school cleaning job. I was dreading seeing him, not knowing what he might say or do. One thing I did do that showed some level of humanity is to walk the mile to Mr. Tyson's house and apologize. I did this on my own without being ordered by Ma or Sue to do it. It was a mistake on my part to think that Mr. Tyson would be moved by my appearing at his house early Friday evening. He was not welcoming or warmhearted at all. He just said in a cold voice, "Okay, you apologized. Now let me get back to my family." I think he was still pissed!

I rode with Jimmy out to the gas station, and he didn't say anything about the incident. He also treated me fine just like he always did. I wonder if he understood because he did a similar thing when he was a junior at a different vocational high school. He punched his English teacher, and it led to his being suspended. He never returned to school except for a week or so of wandering the halls at a nearby high school, at least that's how my sister Sue described his lackluster effort to finish high school.

Finally, Monday morning arrived. Sue drove Ma and me up to school to meet with Mr. Enforcer. It was a cool and quiet ride. No radio and minimal talking. Once in Mr. Enforcer's office, he described in painful detail what I did to Mr. Tyson. He said I should start by apologizing to Mr. Tyson. Then he was shocked and quite pleased to hear that I had already gone to his house the night of the incident and tried to apologize. Mr. Enforcer was shocked again when Ma started saying that "we have had a lot of problems at our house". Out poured the whole story! "Peter's father has a lot of mental problems, and they had to put him in the state hospital. I can't work because of my heart condition, and we had to move in with my daughter who has her own problems. Peter's brother has bad seizures, and we are afraid one of the bad ones will kill him. I think all these troubles caused Peter to do that awful thing to Mr. Tyson, and Peter doesn't say much, but I know he's very sorry. Please don't throw him out of school."

Wow! Where the hell did that come from? Thanks, Ma. You saved my ass! Mr. Enforcer was very moved by our family's plight. He said, "Don't worry. I'm not going to suspend Peter. I think he's learned his lesson. Go to class, Peter, and stay out of trouble."

Off I went to the bakeshop. Everyone wanted to know what happened, but I just said, "Nothing" and went to work helping my partner Dick make puff pastry. Even Ima Badger came up to me to see if I was okay. What a strange day! Certainly not what I expected!

~~~~

I resumed my "night activities" of stealing money from wallets at the Y and engaging in more underage drinking. We had found a few other taverns, some downtown in bad but exciting areas that would serve us without any proof of age. These latter places were the kind that I envisioned a tough guy would be hanging out in. So, these were my kind of places.

~~~~

As I write all this, fifty-seven years after these events occurred, a number of words come to mind to describe my attitude and behavior at that time: despicable, reprehensible, disgraceful, shameful, dishonorable, unforgiveable, criminal, sinful, vitriolic, repugnant, and so forth. I didn't feel these attributes at the time because I was so self-centered and consumed with my distorted need to decrease disparity in my life by becoming a supposed tough guy.

Yes, I was still trying to become a tough guy in a futile effort to lessen my disparity even though I was not being very successful at it or even happy trying. The next thing I did was more brazen and even dumber. One night, when Freddie, Marty, and I were in a seedy part of downtown playing pool, we decided to hot-wire a car to get us back home. A few months ago, an older guy had showed me how to do it using three wires with an alligator clip soldered on each end, which he made for me, and that I always carried with me. When no one was around at the gas station, I practiced starting different cars without their keys. Some cars were easy to jump and others impossible.

I spotted an "easy car" parked on the street about two blocks from the pool hall. It was not locked, and so I hopped in and attached the alligator clips under the dash, pressed the starter, and we had a car! I drove carefully back to our neighborhood while Marty rummaged through the glove compartment and Freddie worked the radio. Then the shock of all shocks! The car owner left his wallet in the glove compartment. It only had about $10 in it, but there were some credit cards that could be useful. So I dropped Marty and Freddie off and drove to a closed restaurant near Sue's house. I left the car in the parking lot and walked home. This was during Easter vacation, and it was good to know I could sleep in the next morning. But this was not to be.

Around ten o'clock the next morning Danny woke me up to say that a bunch of my friends were here. I said send them up. There was Marty and Freddie, but they added our friend Chuck McMahon[*] with them who had his own car. Chuck was not interested in becoming a tough guy or doing illegal things, but he was easygoing and enjoyed being with the three of us. I got dressed and we headed out for the day.

~~~~

While we had breakfast on the wallet's owner at a cheap diner, we surreptitiously examined the contents of the wallet. The two credit cards that we decided might have potential were the Gulf Oil gasoline credit card and a credit card from what I'll call the Classy Men's Store[*].

The first thing we did when we got back in Chuck's car was to pull into a Gulf gas station and get Chuck's tank filled. This was in the days when attendants pumped your gas for you and took your credit card inside for processing. We were all nervous but not as much as Chuck as he signed the card owner's name. It worked! Off we went with a full tank of gas and the whole day ahead of us. The only thing we didn't have was money because we spent what little was in the "found" wallet on breakfast. So we just went to the Y and shot pool for a few hours, and then Chuck dropped me and Freddie at his house and then took Marty home.

After an hour of boredom at Freddie's house, we decided to catch a bus and go downtown to do some Easter shopping using the Classy's Men's Store credit card. Classy's at that time was a high end men's clothing store situated in the center of downtown. Freddie always had nice clothes, but even he got caught up in selecting shirts, pants, several sweaters, and a really nice spring jacket for each of us.

The saleswoman must have been working on commission because she got very excited with each selection we made as our pile of clothes and total bill mounted. I don't remember the total amount that I signed for, but she quickly processed the stolen credit card, and out the door we went with several shopping bags full of very nice clothes.

We had no place to put all these clothes without arousing suspicion at our homes, so we spread the clothes around at our various friends' houses until we could phase them into our own wardrobes. Oh yes, I forgot to mention that I hot-wired another car to enable us to get around to disperse our new clothes.

Then I really got greedy. Marty was one of the guys' homes where we had dropped off some of our loot, and while we were up in his bedroom with the door closed trying on some of our new clothes, greed did indeed take over. I suggested that we hot-wire another car and go out to a suburban plaza where they had a branch of the Classy store and see if we can get more clothes but with a different salesperson. So off we went, and this trip was even more successful than the first.

We now had way too many new clothes to take home and didn't have any more friends we could trust. So we decided to rent two lockers in the Greyhound bus terminal. This was going to require one of us to load more quarters once a week to maintain the locker, but we didn't know what else to do with the clothes. There was no one else we could think of who would hide clothes for us.

The next day was Holy Saturday, and when Freddie heard what we did last night at the suburban branch of Classy's, he wanted to do it again but back downtown. I don't know why I thought this was a great idea. I was stupid because I agreed to go back there again. This time we took the bus because stealing a car in daylight was even crazier than what we were about to do.

We walked in like we were the rich kids of the card owner and began to make our selections. Unbeknownst to me, the saleslady from the day before recognized me (porkpie hats on fifteen year-olds are memorable) and was curious about our spendthrift ways. When we had our stuff all piled up on the counter Freddie said, "You know, we really should get something for Dad for Easter because he let us use his credit card to buy all these great clothes." I was almost ready to burst out laughing, but I agreed, and we selected a nice sweater-vest for "Dad."

Just before the saleslady started to put "our" credit card through, the saleslady from yesterday came over. This is where this dumb escapade became even dumber. Freddie stepped forth to sign for our purchases, and the saleslady from yesterday picked up on it right away and came right over. She said to me, "You were in here yesterday with another boy, and I waited on you, and I know that you (me) were the one who signed this credit card, and now today this boy (pointing to Freddie) signed as this person. What is going on?"

I nonchalantly turned to Freddie and said under my breath "Tear ass!" We ran out the side door, turned right and ran into bumper-to-bumper Easter holiday traffic blocking the street we needed to cross. Behind us we could hear the saleslady standing in the doorway yelling as loud as she could, "Mr. Wheeler*! Mr. Wheeler! Mr. Wheeler!" We got across the street by running across the hoods of some cars and then as fast as we could down the street on the other side trying to get as far away from Classy's as we could. We turned right at the next intersection and then ran into the first alley we came to. This proved to be a dead end with no way out, and so we returned to the same street. I then tried a door at the back of the big downtown library, and it was unlocked. We realized that we were in the library's storage room containing row upon row of empty bookshelves. There was no place to hide because of the openness of the shelves, but we scrunched down behind them anyway.

We heard men talking outside, and I heard one of them ask, "Did you see two boys running through here?" Someone else said, "Yeah, they ran in there." With that, a large man came in, bent down, immediately saw Freddie and me, and said "All right, you two, come on out of there! Right now!" We came out, and he grabbed each of us by the necks of our coats so tightly that there was no way for us to escape.

As he walked or half dragged us back to the store, he kept asking us to tell him what we stole. He thought we were shoplifters! How dare he! Freddie, with his Harry Potter glasses, had an angelic look and was quite believable when he lied. He looked directly at Mr. Wheeler and, with a voice and face oozing innocence, said, "Sir, I've done nothing wrong. You don't have to hold me." Hell, I would have believed him! But as soon as Mr. Wheeler released his grip Freddie bolted. It was fortunate for Mr. Wheeler that another manager-type man was coming out to help and caught Freddie before he had gotten to the street while Mr. Wheeler held me even more tightly.

We were dragged up to the counter where all our "purchases" were still sitting. The saleslady explained what we had tried to do with the credit card. We found out the other man's name was Mr. Krolas,* and I think he was the store manager. They took us up to one of their offices, but on the way up on the elevator Freddie motioned to me to cry. Freddie was quite the actor, and when he began to cry, I could see by the way the two men looked at each other and by their facial expressions that they were fooled. So I joined in too, but of course, I was not as convincing as Freddie.

These men must not have watched many police stories because they made the tactical error of interviewing us together. They first asked where we got the credit card, and I said (after I had calmed down from my fake crying), "We found it Thursday night on Pearl Street." I went on to explain that we still have the wallet and all the credit cards and papers, but that there was no money in it when we found it.

Freddie caught right on and got specific as to just where on Pearl Street we had found it. He also assured them that he would bring the wallet in so that it can be returned to its rightful owner. Freddie should have been on Broadway!

They asked us to show them some identification. I had the good sense to show them my recently obtained Junior Red Cross membership card, which seemed to impress them. Mr. Krolas asked, "What do you do with the Red Cross?" Lying, I said, "I volunteer two afternoons a week at the Veterans Hospital and help pass out trays and things like that." The truth was that I only joined the Junior Red Cross to get my picture in the yearbook as a joke. I never went to a meeting and wasn't even sure where the Veterans Hospital was.

Freddie brought out his DeMolay membership card for his identification because he told me later that Mr. Wheeler was wearing a Masons ring. I learned later on that the DeMolay was a sort of junior version of the Masons. Freddie was not only a good actor but he was also smart and observant. This prompted Mr. Wheeler to quiz him about which Masonic Lodge was the sponsor and whether or not he knew two men that Mr. Wheeler knew. Freddie didn't know them, but it didn't seem to matter. They were getting to be buddies.

I then made a plea that they not call our parents because my Dad was in the state hospital and my mother had a bad heart. I expressed how sorry we were and how stupid we were to try such a thing. Freddie dramatically said, "This was the worst thing I've ever done, and I am so ashamed and so sorry. This could ruin our lives." His performance was Oscar worthy! In the spirit of full honesty we told them about the purchases we made at the suburban plaza Classy store. They hadn't known about that, and thanked us for our honesty.

Mr. Wheeler and Mr. Krolas left us alone for about five minutes, and we were smart enough to make sure all our verbalizations were about us being stupid and scared and about what was going to happen to us. This was in case they were just outside the door and listening.

Apparently, all our acting and fabricating paid off. When they came back in, Mr. Krolas said, "All right, we think you are both good boys and that you realize your mistake. Now can you locate all the clothes?" We said yes. Then he gave us the bad news! "We want you boys to leave here now, locate all the clothes and the wallet, and be back here by the time the store closes at five o'clock. If you don't come back in time, we will call your parents and the police." Oh hell! It was already 2:30 p.m., but we weren't going to argue.

We quickly took the elevator down and went directly out of the store (no more browsing for us) in search of a taxi. We were desperate to meet Mr. Krolas's demands and deadline. Between the two of us we had enough money for the taxi, but we had to work fast, so the bus was out. When we were riding along in the taxi, Freddie showed his quick wit even under these circumstances. The taxi driver asked conversationally, "You boys got your Easter outfits yet?" In a flash, Freddie responded with "Yes, stripes!" His alluding to prison garb was really pretty funny, and in spite of the strain we were both feeling, we laughed like crazy—maybe because we were both crazy at the time.

With us directing the driver, we made the circuit of our friends' homes hoping they would all be home so we could collect all the clothes. It required five stops including each of our homes where we had stashed stuff. It was tricky walking back out with the clothes under our coats, and of course, everyone was curious about us riding in a cab. With a loud "We'll explain later," we were out the door. We unloaded the lockers at the Greyhound bus terminal last because it was also downtown and not far from the store. At quarter to five, the taxi driver dropped us off at Classy's and even helped us carry in the mountain of clothes we had assembled. He was confused throughout the whole wacky journey and even more confused with the way it ended in that we took clothes into the store and not out like normal people. We offered no explanation; we just thanked him and tipped him well, which he appreciated.

The salesladies did a quick inventory of what we brought in, and then announced that we had brought back every single item. I think Mr. Wheeler and Mr. Krolas were quite impressed.

They thanked us and warned us to stay out of trouble in the future. We thanked them, shook hands, wished them a happy Easter, and left. We caught the bus because we had no extra money for any more taxis. What a day!

~~~~

Although I had just experienced three pieces of good fortune from potentially disastrous situations (the attack on Mr. Tyson, the thefts from Mr. Dough's office, and the now Classy's Men's Store caper), you will see I did not learn what I should have from these close calls. However, Freddie and Marty did learn that the path we were on was not a good one, and they decided not to become tough guys. They were still friendly to me, and we laughed a lot about our misadventures whenever we saw one another, but they were not interested in doing any more "activities" with me.

~~~~

I then met Mike Jeffords* and Joe Russell,* two guys my age who were similar to me in that they were also not interested in school. Something else we had in common was the desire to do things other guys would not. Together we stole cars, skipped school, and drank beer in any tavern that would serve us. We also took money from just about any place we could without getting caught. This included houses when no one was home and some small businesses after they closed like gas stations (never Jimmy's), liquor stores, and so forth. I was the one that mainly did these latter "activities" because I was more desperate for cash than my compatriots.

Things at home were becoming more stressful, and there was a lot of tension from many quarters. Sue and Jim were struggling with their relationship. With all of us there all the time, they had little time for private talks. Also, Jimmy's long hours and unpredictable pay at the gas station caused Sue to feel insecure and anxious about their increasing debts. Home maintenance was no longer something Jimmy had time to do and the same goes for their car. As a result, Sue had to call in repair people that they couldn't afford or simply live with things not working properly (like her car).

The long rides to the state hospital to see Dad put Ma and Sue at serious risk because the car they were driving on those isolated country roads was neither dependable nor safe. I still remember how far it was between the little towns and how few cars traveled that desolate road in those days. Without cell phones, they would have to wait for some Good Samaritan to stop to help them whenever their car quit running or they had a blowout without a spare.

Ma and Sue's relationship became strained as old issues resurfaced (Pat and Dad) and new ones popped up (mostly mine). One thing was different from the first time we moved in with Sue and Jim, and that was Ma. She had become a different woman.

A New Ma Emerges

Because she was not burdened with the Talty Flu, Ma was now ready to take charge of the family. I'm certain her doctor was surprised about how Ma regained her strength on her own. After she could wash and dress herself, albeit slower than she would have liked, she started taking short walks outside. Each day she would walk a little bit further as she measured it by the number of houses she could reach and then return. This progressed to where she could walk the equivalent of a full city block without stopping on a daily basis.

By being patient with herself, she did a little bit more each day until she was also able to handle a full day of housework. She took her time and did little jobs around the house like light cleaning, preparing meals, washing dishes, and doing the laundry. It was interesting to see how she prudently used her limited energy and time. An example of this was while in the basement waiting for each load of wash to get done, she knew she could not take climbing the stairs on a repeated basis. On some days she would iron a few shirts while sitting on a stool, and others she would sort through her housewares that Sue and I had packed when we moved us all from the flat. Then she got the idea of painting her kitchen set. She decided to paint the set black and then buy new pink cushions for the chairs. She thought her choice in colors quite daring. It looked like new when she finished, and she was quite proud of the way it turned out.

After several weeks of a slow but progressive recovery, she felt she could return to work in central supply at the hospital. Her doctor was impressed with her recovery but at the same time was skeptical about her ability to work full time. She convinced him that she was ready, and so he reluctantly signed her papers enabling her to return to full-time work. Her return to work was something neither her doctor nor the rest of us thought we would ever see.

The next thing she did was to take driving lessons. She went to a driving school because she realized that neither Sue nor Jim had the time to teach her. So a few days each week, her driving instructor picked her up, and out she went for her lessons. She got additional practice when she would drive out and back to the state hospital with Sue. Opportunities for additional sessions of driving practice came from a surprising source.

~~~~

This next development was something Ma was quite conflicted over. It started when she began socializing after work with some of her co-workers with whom she had become very close. Once or twice a week "the girls" would take Ma to a tavern where they would have a sandwich (usually beef on wick) and some beer. These were great nights for her even if she was pretty tired the next day. Her socialization also included some company picnics, and get-togethers at one of the girls' houses. Going out socially without the burdens of kids or a moody husband who got drunk was a new experience for Ma. She was like a teenager going out socially for the first time.

Then the socializing got complicated. One of the girls had recently remarried, and her new husband had a friend that he thought Ma might enjoy meeting. Was Ma going to have an affair? With Dad in the state hospital? Could this be? Not really. Ma stipulated that she was not interested in getting involved with a man, and she emphasized that she was still married and was not planning on getting a divorce. So with these stipulations in mind, Ma went out on a date with Bart Niceguy (my pseudonym for him that fits). He was a retired police detective whose wife had died a few years ago, and he was now living with his daughter and her family. He was very nice to Ma, and she had a great time.

Bart and Ma went out a lot after the first date. They loved to go for long rides in the country and stop for dinner. This gave her more time to practice her driving of which she was becoming increasingly competent and proud. Soon after she took her road test for her license and passed. Now she was really proud. Her next idea was to buy a car.

Tommy had organized a budget for Ma, which gave her a structure and something that she never had when it came to money: control. She now had the full responsibility for managing our family's income and expenses. The structure of the budget was comforting for her, and she was always figuring and refiguring her bills in hopes of finding a way to buy a car. She did not have a lot of income to work with, but she was much better at controlling expenses than when she and Dad spent what little he brought home in frivolous ways. No more impulsive spending for her. The budget served as her plan, and she was committed to working her plan.

~~~~

However, before she could seriously consider buying a car she had to find a place for us to live. She felt that if we moved out, then Sue and Jim could work out their problems. For income, she had Dad's disability pension, her pay from her central supply job, and military allotments from both Bernie and Tommy. I had started getting paid (not much) from Jimmy for my weekend work at his first gas station and working a couple of hours each day after school for my Uncle Bern at a grammar school, so I was also paying Ma and Sue a small amount each week. Ma put all this together and decided that maybe we could get our own place. It was going to be a stretch, and so I volunteered to quit school and go to work full time for Jimmy and his partners at the gas station. In reality, my offer was driven more by my intense dislike of school rather than a desire to help Ma out. Regrettably, I was still a self-centered bastard.

~~~~

Looking back, I think Ma was a marvel as she led our family through some terrible times with me as the primary cause of her latest traumas, stress, and strain. I experienced her new assertive persona as we repeatedly warred over my going out, my skipping school, and my other aberrant ways.

Of course, besides me, Ma also had all the worries about my Dad and the demands he continued to put on her, Pat's seizures and infantile tantrums, Danny's poor school performance, Sue and Jim's marital struggles, and the ongoing stress of trying to manage her infamous budget. Her friend Bart and her expanded social life were some of the ways she survived these difficult days. Most people would have withdrawn and succumbed if immersed in such a mess, but not Ma. She soldiered on in spite of it all.

Then things changed. I had become a really difficult person for Ma to deal with, but then I went completely out of control bringing tragedy after tragedy to Ma's door and breaking her heart. It's a wonder it didn't kill her.

Crazy Pete Emerges

I was still doing illegal things for fun and to make extra money, and I was also on the verge of getting kicked out of high school. My grades were poor, my attendance erratic, and my attitude worse. I had stopped getting into fights, but I stayed out all night (some of my "activities" required night work) and skipped school to the point that they had stopped calling Ma. This was nearing the end of my junior year, and no matter what, I knew I wasn't going back to school in the fall. Jimmy talked with his partners, and they decided they could give me a full-time job, but the problem was that even though the gas station was doing well, I knew there was not enough income for three owners and to also pay me. Consequently, their pay offer was pretty low.

So Sue, Jim, Ma, and me had a meeting, which went very bad and was very sad for all of us. I had to tell Jimmy that the money they were offering me was not enough for me to pay Ma to enable us to move out. Talk about dropping a bomb! Jimmy really got pissed. He thought I was being greedy and ungrateful after all he had done for us. Guilty! Confronting Jimmy was very hard for me, and I couldn't do it without crying, and then Sue and Ma cried too. Then Sue defended me, which got Jimmy really pissed, and so he just got up and went out. So Sue said it was up to me, and that I shouldn't do it just because Jimmy was mad. So I went to bed and cried some more.

The three lives I was leading (student, thief, and worker) were now going to change. I announced to everyone the next morning that

I would quit school and go to work for Jimmy. I think everyone knew (especially me) that I was done with school, but they made some lame statements of hope like, "You could always go back later and finish up" (fat chance!) or "You could go to night school and become an automobile mechanic." My nights were already full with my ill deeds, and they were about to get fuller.

~~~~

Through a friend of mine at high school, I met his older brother who was about twenty-five and way ahead of me on the path to becoming a tough guy. Yes, I was still on that path but had been on it alone since my other pals got smart and stayed out of trouble. My friend worked part time in a large neighborhood bakery, and he told us that on Sunday nights, they had a lot of money in the safe. So he, his brother, and I were planning to rob it. His brother had guns that he would let us use. There were five large bakers working there, and we figured we wouldn't be able to control them if we didn't have guns. I had never shot anything, except an air rifle (BB gun), and admitted this to my friend's brother. He solved that, sort of, by taking us into the part of the city that was in ruins where we shot the guns with no one who cared around. They were louder than I thought they would be, but it sure was exciting to shoot those guns.

This planning was still going on just before school ended for the year, but I kept in touch with them, and we got more detailed in planning each time we met. I had identified two cars that I could easily hot-wire so we could have two getaway cars, and we each had gone into the bakery separately to get a handle on the setup. I was feeling like a real big-time criminal. Events transpired that prevented us from engaging in an armed robbery that was most fortunate for me as well as the bakers. Who knew what Crazy Pete would have done with a loaded gun if the bakers had rushed us during the robbery?

So I quit school and started working full time at the gas station. My schedule was to open the gas station each morning at seven o'clock, work until three o'clock in the afternoon, hitchhike to the grammar school to clean for a couple of hours, and then ride home with my Uncle Bern. I paid Ma enough money that she could plan on moving us out. Dad was still in the state hospital, and with Bernie in the army, there would just be Ma, Danny, Pat, and me in the new place.

Polishtown

With Ma's new take-charge attitude and emerging organizational skills, it didn't take long for her to find us a place to live. We had hoped to stay in our beloved old neighborhood, but the best she could do was get us a flat adjacent to it in a section of the city known as "Polishtown". It was, of course, an area highly populated with Polish people who made us a bit uneasy because of the comfort level we had always found in living among Irish people like ourselves. This prompted Danny and me to always go back to the old neighborhood to be with our friends. One thing that was convenient is that the bus stopped right in front of our flat. We could sit inside on our enclosed porch until we saw the bus coming over the hill and then run out and hop on. Very nice! The flat was clean and well-maintained. The landlord's daughter lived upstairs, and she made life difficult for us at times. However, Ma's new assertiveness enabled her to confront this difficult person at every instance. Go, Ma!

Once we were all moved in, Ma began earnestly searching for a used car. She found a 1953 Dodge on a used-car lot owned by a friend of one of her co-workers. It seemed to be in good shape, but to be sure, she had both Jimmy and Bart check it out separately, and they both concluded that it was a good car at a fair price. So Ma bought her car and was she ever pleased. She loved having a car. It gave her a level of independence and stature that she had never experienced in her life. Driving back and forth to work, taking Pat for rides, and when Sue's car wasn't running, she was thrilled to be able to drive her to the doctor's or take her shopping. When she drove out to the state hospital to see Dad for the first time, he was completely enraged, yelling at her and saying, "Yeah, you're a big shot now with your car while I sit out here and rot." This verbal haranguing didn't bother the new Ma. She just said, "Tom, you can make a life for yourself out here or even get yourself better so the doctors will release you. It's all up to you. I'm leaving." He must have been shocked at her response. Regardless, she got in her "little car" and drove home to her new flat that she had fixed up real nice.

~~~~

It was right after Ma got her car that I really went crazy. She sometimes let me take the car to work at the gas station on Saturdays and Sundays provided I got home in time to take her to work. While I had the car at the gas station, I washed and waxed it, decorated the inside with decals and funny signs, painted the wheel rims red, and put artificial white walls on it called "Portawalls". The car looked great, and Ma and I were real pleased with it. Actually, I was more than pleased; I was obsessed. The car instantly decreased my disparity, and I was addicted to the feeling it gave me. I had two girlfriends, but looking back now, I really think I liked them a lot more than they liked me. In fact, in reality, they both liked the car a lot more than me, but I was too self-absorbed to see this.

I relentlessly tormented Ma to have the car. It was her car, and she loved driving it, but in my self-centeredness, I didn't care. To make it worse, I drove in a reckless fashion, and within a few months, I had had three accidents. Each time I had an accident, they would cancel our insurance, and we ended up in a risk pool with higher rates, which I had to pay.

I was also crazy at the gas station. I was bored, and for something to do, I would take a Jeep pickup truck out for rides, but it did not have a registration, plates, or insurance. Jimmy bought the truck so he could provide road service and plow snow, but it needed work before that was possible. I didn't care; I just wanted to drive it because it was a standard shift on the floor and a lot of fun to drive. It was fortunate that I was never stopped by the police nor had an accident while on my little excursions. Oh yeah, I left a ten-year-old kid who hung around the gas station in charge while I was gone. He would pump the gas and collect the money, so it freed me up to go off on my little half-hour jaunts.

Besides driving Ma's car way past posted speed limits, I would show off to my friends by running traffic lights and stop signs, and that was when I was sober. I drove after and while drinking without regard for my passengers or other cars and their passengers, property, or pedestrians. I could have been the cause of numerous fatalities including my own. Thus, I view this as a miraculous time in my life because of the disasters I could have caused but didn't. This is not to minimize or say that the disasters I did cause were of small consequence. They were not.

~~~~

Of course, I continued to steal cars and other things with my usual non-thinking bravado. Once, late at night, my new friend Jack Hill* and I threw a concrete block we took from a nearby construction site through the front window of a liquor store. The sound was so loud we thought for sure it would awaken those nearby. Unwilling to take any more of a chance, we each quickly grabbed only two bottles of whiskey and drove away in a car we had stolen earlier that night. After an hour or so, we decided to drive past the liquor store to see what was going on, and we were quite surprised to see no one there. With that we stopped, opened the trunk, and emptied out the store window. We had over twenty bottles of whiskey and gin, one of which would play a major role in one of the worst nights of my life.

This was in the winter when the worst of my goings-on were happening. Our night "activities" (burglaries) had led to an accumulation of various items that we took from homes and businesses, including the twenty bottles of whiskey. Our plan was to sell the stuff on our own because we had learned through experience that a pawnshop was not giving us anywhere near what our items were worth. They probably knew they were all stolen.

As a temporary storage area, I found a shed in a park that the city used for storing their grass-cutting equipment, but it was not being used during the winter. So we got the lock off the shed and put one that we bought on it instead. We figured if we came back and saw our lock gone, we would assume the authorities had found our stuff, and thus we wouldn't try to enter. It worked well for us at the time.

~~~~

Ma and I were in a constant war over the car, my accidents, my late hours, and my whole attitude. As an example of my combined recklessness with good and bad fortunes, one night I drove Ma's car backwards for four miles in morning traffic. It wasn't done intentionally. When two friends and I were driving around downtown, I could not get the car to go forward. I could only back up. We had been out all night, but I had to get the car home and then go to work at the gas station. So I proceeded to drive backwards through downtown and back to Polishtown and into a transmission shop that was just opening up for the day. This was where my bad luck turned to good. The mechanic knew exactly what the problem was and said he "could fix it for about six bucks using parts from a junkyard." Ma was not happy that she would be without a car until later in the day, but I got it back for her before she had to leave for work at 2:30 p.m.

The words I used earlier to describe myself during this time (despicable, reprehensible, disgraceful, shameful, dishonorable, unforgiveable, criminal, sinful, vitriolic, repugnant, and so forth) still applied, but now to a much greater degree. In those days, I was in denial and therefore had little feelings of disparity as long as I had the car. Then, as can be seen by what I did next, all my previous escapades will all pale in comparison to my subsequent deplorable acts.

The Demise of Tough Guy Pete

I did two even more horrible things to Ma, to the rest of the family, and to myself. The first was getting arrested. I was driving a car I had stolen earlier, and I never should have kept it as long as I did. My usual habit was to ditch a stolen car after three hours max, but I had foolishly driven this one for more than six. I remember the whole thing so well. I was stopped by the police at an intersection right near downtown. I had two friends with me: Jack Hill* who helped me steal the car, but the other guy, Joey Zorn,* didn't even know the car was stolen. Amazingly, I wasn't really scared at all. I think it had to do with how I had gotten away with a number of things in the past like the bakeshop thefts at the vocational school, the Classy Men's Store caper, and so forth. So I was thinking I will get out of this too.

The cops knew the car was stolen because the owner had reported it missing a few hours ago, and they had been watching for it. There were cops on both sides of us with their hands on their guns as they ordered us out of the car. I told my friends to let me do the talking (what was I going to say? I was delusional!). The cop on my side told me to shut the car off. I said, "I don't have a key, sir (this extreme politeness worked in the past), and I have go underneath (the dashboard) to shut it off." He told me to do it, which I did. It was a quiet ride to police headquarters for booking. I found out later that the only reason we were brought to headquarters was because it was close by and they had open holding cells. They didn't ask us any questions on the way, and we didn't volunteer any information.

The Demise of Tough Guy Pete

They interviewed us separately, and we all told the truth. Jack and I both admitted to stealing the car and that Joey was completely innocent. They weren't sure about this and locked us all up, each in separate cells but next to each other. Knowing that they would have to call Ma (I was only sixteen and thus still a minor), I urged them to call Sue (poor Sue) instead because of Ma's heart condition.

It was a long and anxious night, but I did have a visitor in the middle of the night that I thought was going to be my rescuer (silly me). A guy who was a detective whose last name was also Talty came up to my cell and said in a friendly way, "Which Talty are you?" I thought, *This is it. It's going to be okay, and I'm getting out!* I said, "We're from the Irish section of the city. My Dad is Tom Talty." Then the big piece of encouraging news, "Your Dad and me are cousins. I'm Fran Talty." I remember hearing Dad talk about him and heard that he was a big detective or something. I'm thinking, *Hey, I'm getting out. Just give me a minute to get my things together.* Wrong! He just said something like, "Say hello to your Dad for me," and then he was gone.

Jack was in the cell on my right and Joey on the left. We talked for a bit and made some jokes, but none of us were feeling very jovial, and we didn't even have the gumption to fake it. After a couple of hours, just as I started to go to sleep, there was some commotion. They were letting Joey go home. They believed our story that Joey was innocent, and his parents were there to take him home. It was sad, his leaving and us not, but it was only right. I tried to go back to sleep, but I couldn't stop thinking about what it must have been like for Sue when she got that phone call, and then the call she had to make to Ma. I was very sad and ashamed.

We got a bologna sandwich and black coffee for breakfast, and then at nine thirty, they came for us. They told us that we were being arraigned (whatever the hell that meant) at ten o'clock in city court. There were about twelve of us. Then they lined us up and handcuffed us so that each of my wrists was handcuffed to the guy on each side of me. Someone made a joke about us being a "chain gang," and then we were marched outside and put on a dark green bus with no windows. It was only a few blocks, and then we stopped in front of the city court.

The Demise of Tough Guy Pete

One of the saddest and indelible images in all my life was seeing the looks on Sue's and Ma's faces when they saw me in handcuffs as part of the "chain gang." They were both crying, and I was struggling to not cry in front of Jack especially. They uncuffed and de-chained us and sat us on long benches until they called our names for the arraignment process. Sue had called a friend of hers (Atticus Finch), who was the lawyer who represented our family members in the Apollo Creed fiasco. She called Atticus because when the police called her the night of my arrest, they told her that if we had a lawyer, they could get me released in my mother's custody. He was there, and when they called my name, he came up to the judge with me. I didn't know I even had a lawyer and that he was it.

Atticus told me with a reprimanding tone to keep quiet and let him talk for me. The judge said, "Peter Talty, you are charged with second-degree grand larceny. How do you plead?" Atticus answered for me, "Your Honor, this is his first offense, and to which he pleads guilty. I ask that a probation report be prepared and that he be released in the custody of his mother and that sentencing not take place until the court has reviewed the probation report." The judge then said, "Request granted. Hearing to be scheduled pending receipt and review of the probation report." Atticus gave me a stern look and warned me to stay out of trouble, and then we left.

~~~~

Ma drove (in her treasured car), Sue rode in front, and I got in the back (it should have been the trunk). I got more bad news when Sue told me that Jimmy had fired me from the gas station not because I had been arrested but because of what happened at the gas station last night. Apparently, Jimmy let one of his good customers leave his snow-plowing truck in the gas station overnight because there was some problem with the radiator and he didn't want it to freeze up. Jimmy told the guy that I would be there at 7:00 a.m. to open up. He had snow-plowing contracts that necessitated that he be able to get his truck out. Jimmy was still working on the railroad, so he couldn't go and open up, and so he had to pay the guy for the money he lost. Also, Jimmy had found out about me taking the unlicensed truck out and leaving the young kid in charge of the gas station. What a fool I was in so many ways.

All the way home Ma was telling me that I had to stay home, not go out all night anymore, and on and on. Also, that I had to pay for the lawyer. Please let this ride end.

~~~~

As could be expected, the cumulative effect of getting arrested, spending a night in jail, being humiliated as part of the "chain gang," and then being fired from the gas station, along with being alienated from Jimmy changed me. I was smart enough to know that getting arrested while awaiting the outcome of my arrest would be ruinous. So I stopped stealing cars and stealing in general. Of course, now my disparity raged with little way to appease it. I did not have a full-time job and had dismal results when I tried to get one with just three years of high school and no references. I still worked for my uncle, cleaning at the school, but this was only for about ten hours a week at minimal pay.

~~~~

My disparity was now all centered around Ma's car even if it was looking rather ragged, thanks to my three accidents. However, it was the car that still enabled me to feel whole and self-confident. Through begging and manipulating, I got Ma to relent, and I was able to take her car each morning to pick up my sort of girlfriend (in my mind) at the time and drive her to school. She hated walking the mile or so distance to high school and loved it (but not me) when I drove her. Sometimes Ma let me take her to work at three o'clock, then to my janitor job, and then I had the car for the evening as long as I was back at the hospital in time to pick her up at 11:00 p.m. This arrangement enabled me to get some self-respect back and lessen my disparity at least for a few hours. Of course, it also gave me the opportunity to continue driving recklessly in my vain efforts to impress people. One of the crazy things I did was to drive straight through at least four red lights on a busy street with five other teenagers in the car. I was not drunk or even drinking at the time. How disastrous that could have been.

~~~~

One of the rules Ma had set forth was that I was not to hang out with Jack Hill because she erroneously felt that he had led me to steal the car that night. I wanted her to believe that was the only car I ever stole. However, I didn't have a large number of friends, so Jack was it.

So I would still go to the Y some nights, shoot pool, and hang around with Jack. That was until his brother-in-law, Mickey Dorrance,* confronted us. About a week and a half after our arrest, Jack and I walked into the Y and encountered Mickey playing pool. I said, "Hi, Mickey," which caused him to stand up from his pool-shooting position and say to me with all the venom he felt, "Hi, thief." I don't remember what I said in response, but it didn't matter.

Mickey actually was a full-grown man, not a teenager like us. He was about twenty-five years old, had been in the army, was married, and had been working as a crane operator in the steel plant for a couple of years. He was also quite large, sort of fat, but powerful and fast. I had a prior connection with Mickey, which was kind of strange. Strange in that why would a twenty-five-year-old guy want to hang out with sixteen-year-olds? It had to do with sex. He was married but still loved going to downtown taverns where prostitutes hung out and to the houses of ill repute, or whorehouses, but he didn't like to go alone. He also liked to go far more frequently than his peers. Therefore, he dropped down a few notches and often asked Jack and me, or sometimes just me, to go with him. I went because it was fun and because he was well-known in these places, and so none of them ever asked me for proof of age.

As a person, he was bombastic and overbearing. For example, if we were riding in his car and the Marty Robbins song "El Paso" came on the radio, he would blast the radio and sing the whole song loudly and poorly. It was especially weird that at certain points of the song he would lean way over while driving and sing in my face. Oh well, he had a car, and I got to go to some exciting places and interact with some interesting people. This background makes the rest of the present incident even more peculiar.

So here was this raging mass right in front of me and, in a very threatening way, says, "You stay the hell away from Jack (remember, he was married to Jack's sister). If you come near him again, I'll kill you." I tried some bravado that I wasn't really feeling and said something like, "Oh yeah? We'll just see about that" and nonchalantly walked out the door to go into the next room to get a Coke. I didn't quite make it into the next room the way I intended. I was propelled into the room by Mickey's big fist as he punched me in the back so hard that I fell into the room out of breath. I thought, *Hey, weren't we were buddies? Not anymore!*

While lying half in the room and half in the connecting vestibule, Jack attempted to intervene. This delighted Mickey who now put his pool cue against the wall and said, "Come on, punks. I'll beat the hell out of both of you at once." He assumed a crouched boxer's position with his massive fists ready to pummel us. I knew we were done, so I got up and walked out of the Y, leaving Jack alone with his angry brother-in-law. How is that for a tough guy?

I never called Jack again and only saw him at our various court dates. Not surprising, Mickey never called me to go downtown with him anymore either. At least I didn't have to listen to him sing that damn "El Paso" anymore.

~~~~

My life was crap. The lack of money was a big problem for me as well as for Ma. She was dependent on the money I paid her for room and board, which was about half of what Jimmy was paying me at the gas station. My contribution was the difference of staying with Sue and Jim and us getting our own place. So, in addition to Ma's burdens of Dad, Pat, me, Sue and Jim; juggling her relationship with Bart and the related guilt; and her car, she now had a serious financial threat to sustaining our new flat. Because Jimmy paid me under the table, I also could not collect unemployment.

Did I appreciate Ma's load and try to help? Was I consumed with my pending court case and lack of a full-time job? No, I was filled with disparity and related despair. I continued to be a selfish bastard.

~~~~

Sue suggested that I go around to all the big companies in the area and put in job applications. She also said I should go downtown to the civil service commission and see if there were any positions I could qualify for or tests I could take. Ma said I could use her car because I had a legitimate reason. So for the next few days, I filled out applications at the phone, electric, and gas companies; the Chevy and Ford plants; and the steel plants. I heard the same sickening phrase over and over, "We are not hiring at this time, but we will keep your application on file and notify you if something comes up." This response was depressing enough, but then there were worse responses I had to suffer. Some looked at my application, saw that I wasn't a high school graduate, and told me that they only hire high school graduates. I then lowered my sights and went to supermarkets, small companies, and even a few gas stations. Nothing! Without a high school diploma, there were no civil service jobs for me either. Surprisingly, I was more mad than depressed over all this rejection. Mad at myself for screwing up high school and my life in general.

~~~~

I then dealt Ma the worst blow of all. I told Ma that I had a date (a lie), and so she let me take the car on a Saturday night. Then, ignoring Mickey's threat to kill me if I didn't stay away from Jack, I called him up to go out. I also called my cousin Tyke, and he was free too. Not having very much money to go out drinking, I got one of the bottles of whiskey from our illicit storage shed I had left over from the liquor store window-breaking episode. We were riding around and passing the bottle back and forth and getting drunker and drunker. I seldom drank whiskey, but it made me feel better about me and my sad life, and to me, that's all that mattered.

We ended up driving through the inner city with no specific destination, moving in and out of neighborhoods surrounded by demolished houses and rubble that was part of urban renewal. We were all in the front seat—Tyke in the middle and then Jack riding "shotgun". I was driving in my usual reckless, fast, and crazy way. This was especially crazy because the streets were narrow with cars parked all along them. Suddenly, we hit one car with such a force that it drove it into another car. We next careened across the street striking still another car where we came to rest, forever wrecking Ma's beloved car. The horn was blaring and there was steam (I thought it was smoke) all around. I said, "Run!" We were all out in a flash, and as I started running, I told Tyke and Jack that we should split up.

Getting away proved a challenge because of the rubble of the demolished houses. I was trying to get over and around what resembled a war zone. In my drunken state, I was lost once I got off the street where I had hit all those cars. After wandering in an aimless way, I returned to the streets because they were easier to navigate. I then saw Jack coming toward me with blood all over his face. This got me sober for a moment, and I told him that we had to get him to a hospital. We were fortunate that we found a small hospital a few blocks from "the scene." We walked into the emergency room, but this time the whiskey was having its full effect, and I was incoherent and nauseous. I vomited all over me, the nurse, and the stretcher they laid me on, and then I passed out.

They called Ma, and of course, she called Sue. I guess they told Ma that I didn't appear to be injured, but they were keeping me overnight for observation. Jack was stitched up, and he called Mickey (oh no!) to come pick him up. That must have been an interesting ride home. I bet there was no singing about "Out in the west Texas town of El Paso . . ."

When I woke up the next morning, I was nauseous with a bad hangover (are there really any other kind?), but I was anxious to know about my cousin Tyke. I worked for his father (Uncle Bern), and if Tyke was hurt and Uncle Bern found out about it, that would be the end of the only job I had left. So when Ma came in with Sue (of course, poor Sue got pulled in once again) to pick me up, Danny was with them. After some well-deserved condemnation and denouncements from Ma and Sue, they went to talk with the nurse about when I could be discharged. Just before they went out the door, I gestured for Danny to come back and asked him to find out if Tyke was all right. He said he would, but Ma saw Danny and me whispering, and so on the way home, she demanded that he tell them what the whispering was about. He told all. Hearing that Tyke was with me just infuriated Ma and Sue even more. I found out later that Tyke wasn't hurt at all and was able to catch a bus and got home safely. Tyke was a good kid, and I never should have put him in such a dangerous situation.

~~~~

The police interviewed me at the hospital and then Ma at home on the day after the accident. I had always said that I blacked out, and so Ma picked up on this and told her investigating officer the same thing I told the policeman at the hospital. Surprisingly, I did help my situation in an accidental way. When I got out of the wrecked car, I continued to hold on to the bottle of whiskey for some dumb reason, but it actually turned out to be beneficial. Realizing I had the bottle, and not wanting any more of it, I threw it into an abandoned house as I was stumbling on by. Another thing that helped was that because I had walked to the hospital and not been apprehended by the police in the car, a sobriety test was never administered. Without the results of a sobriety test, the only thing police had as evidence that I was drunk was the report from the emergency room. Apparently, this wasn't enough to issue me a citation for a DWI (driving while intoxicated) or whatever was the terminology at the time. God was looking out for me once again.

A Better Pete Emerges

Ma had her car towed to a collision shop right near our Polishtown flat. Sadly, this location was right on the bus route Ma took to work. I can't imagine the rage she must have felt toward me and the great sadness she would have felt every time she passed her beloved car on the bus on her way to and from work and every other time she went to visit Sue. The collision mechanic pronounced that her car was wrecked beyond repair, and he recommended that Ma just junk it. Unable to make this anguishing decision, she did nothing as her car sat there, torturing her each time she went past for at least a month. Eventually, the collision mechanic pressured Ma to junk it, and so she did with more pain than one could imagine.

Now do you think I got it? Did I come to the realization that my life was a disaster and that I needed to make big changes? Was the loss of the respect of my family enough shame to abandon my old ways? No, no, and no. Unbelievable! However, I was scared of the repercussions from the accident combined with the arrest for the stolen car. My lawyer made it clear that I would most likely get probation and not be incarcerated, but this was dependent on my staying out of trouble. The accident could be what puts me in jail, and that's what really kept me from doing anything else of a criminal nature.

These were sad days for me, but why not! For everything I did, I deserved to be sad. I had alienated and lost the trust of everyone. Bernie, home for a weekend from the army, was so disgusted with me that he beat me up. I felt so bad for both of us, but especially me because I caused everyone so much sadness and pain. However, there was a bright spot. I still had my afternoon cleaning job, and that led to the biggest reversal of my crazy life. It so happened that the fireman who took care of the boilers at the school where I worked was retiring and Herman Helpr,* my friend and the full-time janitor (the actual term was "porter"), wanted to move up to the position of fireman.

~~~~

My Uncle Bern promoted Herman and asked me if I wanted the full-time job of porter. Of course, I said yes! It would give me enough money to pay Ma and help us stay in our new flat in Polishtown. It also would look good on the probation report that I was employed full time.

I started immediately and had a great sense of pride in my title (porter or janitor didn't matter) and in my role as a full-time worker. Herman was very organized and a fine trainer who taught me how to systematically handle my different janitorial duties. It felt so good to have a job! I didn't care that I had to clean thirty-two toilets, sweep and mop several rooms including the gym and cafeteria, haul all the garbage downstairs and burn it, rake leaves, shovel snow, and whatever else my uncle or Herman told me to do. It did bother me a bit that I was the guy they called every time a kid threw up ("get Pete the janitor"), but I was now working full time, so the rest didn't matter.

When my uncle noticed that I didn't have a lunch bucket and thermos, he advanced me a few dollars of my first pay so that I could go over to a nearby store and buy one. Never was one as proud of a lunch bucket as I. It was black with a rounded top typical of the ones steelworkers, autoworkers, and other working men carried, and now I was one of them in a way.

~~~~

My revered lunch bucket played another important role in my resurgence of self-esteem and long-overdue maturation process, and it came from an unexpected source. Each morning my uncle picked me up and dropped me off at the end of the day, but on some days I had to take the bus for various reasons. On one of my no-ride days, I boarded the bus and was surprised to hear someone call my name. It was my childhood friend Georgie Kelly, all dressed up and on the way to his classes at the university. As we sat and talked about what we were each doing now, he was able to see my pride in my job and was happy for me. I was also glad that he was going to college. He was always very bright. In spite of our different journeys in life at this time, I was as proud of my lunch bucket sitting on my lap as Georgie was of his thick college textbooks on his.

~~~~

Now all was not "happy, happy, joy, joy" with my life. I still was very worried about what was going to be the result of my two pending legal problems. My sentencing on the second-degree grand larceny charge was postponed twice, which generated much anxiety for me as well as my family. My Dad had improved enough that he was being considered for discharge to home. In preparation for his return home, he was given weekend passes to try out family living once again. I think he must have wanted to return to the safe haven of the state hospital when Bernie told him all the evil I had done and my court cases still pending. This happened before I got my full-time job as a janitor, so his disclosures about my actions and bad decisions had even more of a traumatic impact on Dad. I think he actually did ask to be taken back to the hospital earlier that week because of the stress he was feeling.

The accident investigation progressed to where the department of motor vehicles served Ma and me with subpoenas ordering us to report downtown to the state office building for separate interviews once again. We arrived separately because I came from work and she from home, but we decided the night before to stick with the "blackout story" that I had concocted in the hospital. They pressed me on any prior incidents of blacking out and also inquired as to what subsequent medical evaluations had been done to determine the cause of the blackout on the night of the accident. Of course, there were no subsequent medical evaluations and no actual basis for my claim of a blackout, and they knew it.

A few weeks later I received a letter stating that they were suspending my driver's license for sixty days. Since I no longer had access to a car, I did not see this as a problem. I just had to send my license to the department of motor vehicles. Similarly, when our insurance company cancelled our insurance because of this being my fourth accident, this too was of little consequence. I remember in those days how we hated going to the mailbox because it brought only bad news, mostly because of me.

The Trial

The main determining factor as to whether or not I would go to jail or just get probation was contingent upon my staying out of trouble, and I was. Another good thing that happened at this time was that Jimmy asked me to help him at his new Esso gas station that he had just taken over. I was ecstatic because it gave me the chance to apologize to him for all the trouble I had caused him and Sue and everyone else. He was good about it and said he was glad I learned my lesson. It was a good day, and it felt very good to be of help to him. We set it up that I would work at the gas station every Saturday and Sunday and be paid $5 per day. These were usually twelve- to eighteen-hour days, so he was getting a real bargain, but it was all he could afford at the time. I didn't mind either the long hours or the low pay because in the parlance of AA, "I was making amends." I also saw this as a form of well-deserved penance.

Looking back, it seems there were interminable visits to the city court for different reasons, so it was in this vain that I told my uncle that I had to go downtown for another court appearance. I also said that my lawyer said it wouldn't take long, just be there at 10:00 a.m. He always got angry with me whenever I had to ask off for anything court-related; it seemed to remind him of my stupidity. He never understood why I did the things I did (who did?). I had to tell him about the charge against me, and he asked the gruff questions he usually asked, "Don't you have enough trouble in your family? What

The Trial

the hell is the matter with you?" I always pretended these were rhetorical questions, and so I didn't answer them.

~~~~

If you have ever read *The Trial* by Franz Kafka, you may be able to appreciate what happened to me on that Monday. I went to work with my uncle in the morning, did my usual early duties, and then took a bus downtown arriving at the city court about fifteen minutes early. Jack was already there. We never did see each other anymore except at these appearances, and we didn't have much to talk about in those days. I didn't see my lawyer, and Jack said he didn't see his either. When it got to be ten o'clock, a clerk came out, read our names, and told us to stand along the back wall with a bunch of guys in handcuffs. I explained to the guard that we were supposed to meet our lawyers here for some kind of court appearance. He was not unfriendly but certainly more firm when he said again, "Stand over there and keep quiet."

After about twenty minutes, they told us to line up, and we walked single file out the back door and boarded a bus with no windows (we rode one of these the morning after we were arrested). I asked a different guard, "Please check your list because we were not supposed to be going any place. We were supposed to meet our lawyers, but they weren't there. They won't know what happened to us." This guard really seemed concerned and did check his clipboard. He asked our names, and he said we were where we were supposed to be. What the hell was going on?

After a short distance, the bus stopped. When the doors opened the guard told just Jack and I to go up to the green door of this large building and give the guards our names. Then "The Trial" really began. We knocked, gave our names, and the guard let us in. It was a big room apparently used to process new prisoners (this certainly wasn't us!). With Jack and I both talking at once trying to explain our plight, we were told "Take off your clothes and put these on." Am I losing my mind? We put on the khaki shirts and pants that

The Trial

wouldn't stay up because they were too big, and there were no belts, and then paper slippers instead of our shoes. All our street clothes were checked in at a big wire-caged room along with our wallets, keys, and whatever else we had in our pockets. The little money we had was counted in front of us. We signed that it was accurate, and everything was then put in a basket with our names on the attached tags.

Next, we got our mug shots taken and were fingerprinted. I then began thinking that they must have found out about all the other stuff we had stolen, and we were now being brought up on additional charges. This was very scary. If I had known that this was the situation for sure, I would have really panicked. But if we were being hit with the burglaries and everything else, there would have been a formal arraignment on these additional charges. So that wasn't why we were walking around in jail garb, or so I hoped. For now, I just kept calm and kept asking anyone and everyone if they could please help us. Most of the guards just ignored me. Others listened, nodded, and walked away. I think the worst were the guards who seemed genuinely concerned that there was an error made and that we were, in fact, not supposed to be locked up. They promised to look into it and get right back to us. They never did anything that I could tell, and so when we asked the same guards again later on about our situation, they said something like, "We're looking into it," but I could tell they really weren't.

Then they took us on an elevator up to the sixth floor when it suddenly hit me! I figured out the error! We were in the county jail, and we were supposed to have been in city court not in here at all! I couldn't shut up about this great insight and told every guard we encountered about the mistake that was obviously made, but it was to no avail.

~~~~

Holding blankets and a small pillow they gave us downstairs, Jack and I were told to step up and wait at the doorway of bars that was the entrance into the cell block to which we were assigned. We each had tags that indicated the cell to which we were assigned. Mine was "1A'" and Jack's "1B". They pushed a button, and the gate slid open, and we walked through looking for our assigned cells. We walked all the way down the row of cells numbered 1 through 16, but did not see any with A or B designations. The guys in the cells ignored us, but I asked the guy in cell number 1 who at least smiled at us, "Can you tell me where cells 1A and 1B are?" His smile immediately became a loud belly laugh as he pointed to the areas on the hallway floor in front of his cell and said, "That be 1A and that there be 1B. We is all full up, and so you boys get the floor until one of these cells opens up." Are you kidding me? We don't even get a cell or a cot?

We sat on the floor on our folded-up blankets, but I repeatedly jumped up to explain our plight and this awful error that they had made to every guard who passed by whether they listened to me before or not.

Then we got more bad news. The guy in number 1 who was black explained, "This jail be overcrowded and the whites been fighting with the coloreds, so they don't let us out together anymore. Every three hours they let the coloreds out and keep the whites in, and then after an hour out in the hallway, wees go back in and the whites come out. You boys be careful when the coloreds come out, you being white and all." He sure scared the hell out of us.

It turned out, however, that everyone, black or white, continued to just ignore us. They yelled, joked, and swore at each other, but no one seemed to notice we were even there although they did have to walk around us and our assigned 1A and 1B floor areas. It was the longest, most confusing, and most frustrating day of my life. Later on in college when I read *The Trial*, I could completely identify with the prisoner's situation. Josef K. and I were two very confused and worried guys.

Finally, about two thirty that afternoon, they called our names and told us we were being released! It was like we got a reprieve from the governor just before we were to be strapped into the electric chair. Overly dramatic, I know, but we were very relieved. No one in our cell block wished us well or promised to write.

The Trial

~~~~

So it was back downstairs. We got our own clothes back on, counted our money, and were told to follow two guards who would take us back to city court. This time the guards took us through a tunnel that ran under the streets and up the stairs into a courtroom. The judge was there along with our lawyers and a few clerks. It was not surprising that our families weren't there because we had, of late, been going to these "routine" appearances by ourselves. The judge gave us his ruling, and Jack and I were both given indefinite probation. His next words were to become the most important in my life: "Because of your age at the time of your arrest and your favorable probation reports, I am granting you youthful offender status. This means this will be a sealed record and can never be disclosed unless you commit a second offense. You made a mistake, but you now have a second chance to lead decent lives." With that he whacked his gavel and said, "Case closed." The clerk then gave us a form with the names of our probation officers and instructed us to go there immediately to a building right across the street from the court to meet with our respective probation officers. So off we went. Jack and I had different probation officers, so we split apart once inside the building.

~~~~

The waiting room outside my probation officer's office was another shock on a day full of shocks. There were about fifteen guys of ages sixteen (like me) to forty all lounging about and some sound asleep. Two of them were quite drunk, but even though the others appeared sober, they all seemed far more familiar with the criminal justice system than I ever wanted to be. I didn't try to speak to anyone, and they ignored me.

It was about three o'clock when I sat down in the dank and smelly waiting room, and then finally, just before five o'clock after everyone else was gone, I got called into the office. My probation officer was Mr. Con Troller,[*] and he was not a warm and friendly guy. He did not stand up or offer to shake hands. I don't think he even looked up at me. His cold message started off by saying, "You're lucky you got probation. Don't ruin it. Now (handing me a sheet of paper) here are the rules you must follow or your probation will be revoked and you will be put in jail. Do you understand?" I told him I did, and then he gave me a form that listed all the conditions of my probation. He demanded that I give him my driver's license, which he said I would get back when I was off probation. I explained that the DMV had it, and he said that I had to surrender it to him when I did get it back. I don't remember all the rules (I think there were eighteen of them), but the main ones were that I could not hang around with known criminals, especially the guy I was arrested with, I had to work full time or go to school, I could not drink alcohol or use drugs, I could not go to taverns, I had to be home every night by ten o'clock, and so forth. I also had to report to him every Monday at 6:00 p.m.

I was more than sad walking up that windy street to catch a bus home, but not because of the restrictions of probation. It was because of the way the whole process made me feel. Being on probation was embarrassing and infantilizing. I could tell that Mr. Troller thought I was just like everyone else on his caseload in that waiting room. To him, none of us deserved his trust or his respect. Oh well, it sure beat spending my days and nights like I just spent this day. I suspected this day was all prearranged to catch us off guard and show us what being in jail would be like. I did get it, but I had gotten it before that day in jail. I was already committed to being a decent person and not a tough guy or thief anymore. So the day in jail was not a revelation; it was just a frustrating inconvenience. That's how I looked at it anyway.

When I got home and told Ma what had happened that day, she didn't act too surprised about our being jailed. This made me suspicious that she had been informed by my lawyer about what was going to happen to me and was instructed not to let on to me about it. I often wondered if my boss (Uncle Bern) was in on it too because when I explained to him the next day as to why I didn't come back to work, he just smiled. He was not a smiley person, especially when interacting with me when the topic was me missing work for a court appearance.

Life on Probation

I had actually tired of my other life as a low-life criminal awhile before it actually ended. I was tired of always feeling so desperate and acting so rash and foolhardy. It was quite a mess I had made of my life to this point, and I was definitely done with living it that way. Being committed to earning the trust and respect of my family was what compelled me now, but I had no idea of how I was going to do it except to keep my job and see my probation through to a successful end.

Working at the gas station gave me another place to demonstrate to my family that I had changed. I sought no praise or recognition for my efforts because I was doing the measuring myself and knew when I fell short. Besides the emotional debt I had to work off, I had also incurred some hefty financial debts that I had to resolve. In an effort to ease Ma's stress and be a better son, I took over the payments on her car loan. It seems feeble to say now that it was the right thing to do, but it absolutely was the right thing to do. One of the cars I damaged sued me personally for the loss of their car and the judgment said I had to make restitution through my probation officer. This was established at my next appointment, and from that time forward, I had to bring him a payment, which he forwarded on to the guy who lost his car. My lawyer also gave me a sizable bill but was willing to let me pay it off over a six-month period.

I needed a vision of a better day to get me through probation, and so I crafted my vision around a Corvette. I loved Corvettes ever since an affluent guy I sort of knew took me for a ride in his new Corvette a couple of years ago. It was amazing in every way. The design and power of that car captivated me, and I made it my goal to save enough money so that when I got off probation, I would have enough to buy a new Corvette. I had to pay off my debts first, but then I would open a bank account and start saving.

In the meantime, I occupied myself by painting and building model cars. Surprisingly, I never built a model of my hallowed Corvette, focusing instead on customizing antique cars like a 1932 Ford, 1950 Mercury, and so forth. Those early cars were fun to build and modify using a creativity and skill I didn't know I had.

Because I worked Monday through Friday from 7:30 a.m. to 4:30 p.m. and Saturday mornings as a janitor for my uncle at the school and then worked twelve hours on Saturday and eighteen hours on Sunday at the gas station, the time on probation went by faster than I thought it would. I spent my evenings painting and building model cars and hanging out with my family. My previous friends never called me, and I didn't feel they would like to hear from me, so I never called them.

Dad had been discharged to home and was doing okay mentally, but now his breathing was a major issue for him. Ma had to end her relationship with Bart, as well as the exciting social life she had just gotten to enjoy, but she was happy to have Dad home. Bernie had gotten out of the army on a hardship discharge in order to help the family, and he was working all night at Jimmy's gas station. This was the first time in several years that we had our whole family (except Tommy and Sue, of course) under one roof, and I really enjoyed it.

~~~~

I worked hard cleaning the school and applied all the time-saving ideas Herman taught me to get everything done each day without any real strain. My plan was to just stay employed for a short time at the school and then get a high-paying job in one of the local big factories or with one of the utilities. I tried these before, but now I thought I could do it because I presently had a full-time job. Some friends of Bernie's encouraged me to put in another application at their places of work, but I couldn't leave my present job to do it. My sense of disparity was aroused. My job did not pay very well in comparison to the big companies, and I didn't get any benefits like hospitalization, retirement, or sick leave. The previous pattern of my life was that once my sense of disparity got going, a period of dissatisfaction usually precedes a big change (usually spectacularly disastrous in my previous life). The problem was that the probation rules did not permit changing jobs without my probation officer's approval. Also, having Ma call the various companies requesting applications (I was not allowed to use the phone at work) and then mailing them back completed was not working for me. It may have proved impossible because I only had three years of a less-than-stellar high school education, or maybe they still weren't hiring. So, it thus looked like I was stuck as a janitor for the rest of my life. The pride I had felt in having this job was fast dissipating.

~~~~~

Then one morning, while having coffee with my Uncle Bern and Herman, I saw an article in the morning newspaper that related to an epiphany I had just had: education was the key! I know this was not a spectacular epiphany for most people, but I never really got it until I got all those rejections of my job applications. This article said that a high school, which was about a mile from the school where I worked, offered a high school completion program at night. It was not a GED. It was for students who had some high school, and courses were offered three nights a week.

I knew where this high school was, but I didn't know how to get there from the school where I worked. My uncle Bern told me how to get there, which turned out to be quite simple. When I explained why I wanted to know where it was, Herman said with pride, "Yes, I think that would be good for you." My uncle had a different response: "Yeah, and you're going to shit too!" This was a phrase he often used whenever someone told him they were about to do something that he felt was a mistake or beyond that person's abilities. He was not very supportive, but I didn't really deserve his support. I got a similar response from my Dad (of course, I did; he's my uncle's brother) and Bernie when I told them about my going back to high school. I guess they didn't see my potential. I remember thinking that they might be right. At least Ma and Sue thought it was a good idea.

Before I could enroll, I had to tell my probation officer about what I planned to do because depending on my bus connections, I may not be getting home from night school before my ten o'clock curfew. I also would have to change my reporting night from Monday to either Tuesday or Thursday because the night school courses ran on Mondays, Wednesdays, and Fridays. So on my next appointment, I told Mr. Troller about my intentions and was shocked at his lack of support or encouragement. He said, "You better be going to school and not out running around with your old pals. You know probation is a privilege, and I can withdraw it anytime and have you put right in jail." My old crazy self suddenly appeared as I stood up and just about yelled, "You should be glad I'm not like all the other guys you got coming in here. I have been working full time in the same job, plus a part-time job in a gas station, obeying all the rules of probation, and now I am trying to get my high school diploma. What's the matter with you?" Talk about shock! He was very shocked! But he recovered quickly and said, "You're right, and I'm sorry. What about Tuesday at six o'clock starting next week? Also, don't worry about missing your curfew on school nights." We got along fine after that confrontation, and I actually came to like him.

~~~~

Regardless of these less than encouraging responses, on the following Monday I walked over to my new high school (about twenty minutes away) and registered for world history, general science, and an elective course in bookkeeping. I was always interested in how businesses operated and thought bookkeeping would help me understand this. I still was not certain how this was all going to work out because I had not liked school very much in the past.

Each course met for one hour three nights per week. I figured out that if I took three courses each semester, I would have my high school diploma at the end of two years. It seemed like a long way to the end, but I was getting a second chance to finish high school, and I was determined to complete it and not mess it up again. However, an incident occurred in the second week of the bookkeeping class that almost ended it all.

As I said, the bookkeeping class was interesting to me because I had never understood about how a business ran with balance sheets, ledgers, debits, credits, and so forth. Jimmy's two gas stations were the only personal experiences I had with business, but his was mostly an informal operation with none of these formal business practices operating. To help students understand the whole process, we each had to buy a packet that contained all the bookkeeping materials for a small business. It was my first class each night, and I had little confidence in myself as a student, but the structure of the packet and the course itself was helping me to think that maybe I could do this. I completed the first week and was establishing a routine with school three nights a week after working all day and then taking the bus home.

The bookkeeping course was taught in a large room in what was referred to in those days as a "Study Hall". It had about fifty of the old-type desks with the tops that flip up so you can put your books and stuff inside. Only fifteen students were in the course. Most were about fourteen or sixteen years of age, while I was the old man of eighteen. I kept to myself and just did my work because the other students were too immature for me. Imagine that!

On the Monday night of the second week, I arrived early, as was my wont, and put all my books on my usual desk. Four or five students were gathered near my desk near the front of the room talking and laughing like they typically did. Also, as usual, I ignored them and they me. I took my bookkeeping workbook and went to the bathroom. When I returned, all my other books were gone. I tried asking the group of students, but they were all laughing and would not respond to my questions or even look at me.

I then frantically started to search each of the fifty vacant desks, flipping up the tops to see if the immature students had perhaps hid them from me as a joke. I was methodically checking each desk and was about sixteen desks down the second row when the teacher came in to start the class. He told me to sit down because the class was going to start. I tried to explain that I had to find my books. He then yelled, "*Sit down!*" I just about ran to the front of the room, yelled "*Fuck you!*" at the teacher, threw my bookkeeping workbook in the wastebasket, grabbed my coat, and stormed out the door. I didn't bother going to my other classes that night; I just went out and got on the bus. I was so mad at myself for walking out the way I did and swearing at the teacher. I concluded that my brief return voyage back into academia was sunk. This was the typical Talty catastrophic thinking at work.

When I got home so early, Ma and Dad figured something had gone wrong. So I announced to my family that I had quit school, and they were not surprised. My parents said, "At least you have a job. Don't mess that up." Their response was to be expected because I had such a bad performance record throughout grammar and high school, plus all my behavioral aberrations. I was despondent beyond what I thought I could tolerate.

~~~~

The next day it was back to the mop. It looked like I would be a career janitor. Then later on in the morning, my uncle interrupted my mopping to tell me that I had a phone call. He also bitched at me for getting a call at work, even though it was the first one in my two years there. I was scared that something bad had happened to Ma, or Dad, or maybe it was Pat. They were all pretty vulnerable in one way or another.

So I went down to the office with anxiety about my family being hurt or something else tragic. On the phone was my bookkeeping

Life on Probation

teacher! He called my home and got my work number from Ma. I will always remember his exact words: "Peter, this is Mr. Rescuer* from night school, and I want to apologize for last night. I didn't know what was going on when I yelled at you to sit down. After you left, the girls in front told me that they hid your books as a joke. I have your books and your bookkeeping packet right here, and if you can come to the next class tomorrow night a half hour early, I can catch you up on what you missed." I said, "I'll be there." A second chance! I wasn't done yet.

When I told everyone that I was still going to be attending school, they were happy for me. I came to the next class on Wednesday a half hour early, and my bookkeeping teacher did exactly what he said he would do. He had all my books and went over everything that he covered on Monday. The other students came in, but no one said anything to me. That's okay. I was just glad to be back.

As the semester progressed, I noticed the number of students in each class became less and less. For some reason, their dropping out invigorated me. I now had such resolve that I knew nothing was going to deter me. Also, the mishap with my books taught me to have more faith in people to do the right thing like my bookkeeping teacher did.

I did not find the courses overwhelming. It seemed my level of learning was right in sync with the level of instruction. Remarkably, I was even feeling smart. My days were long, and I often fell asleep on the bus coming home, but never in class. Was I becoming one of those "goody-goodies" that I always despised? Maybe I was in a way, and that was a good thing.

The janitorial work was now very boring and not very satisfying, but the teachers at the school were very encouraging when I told them that I was working at completing high school. As my academic successes increased, my family seemed to look at me differently as did my probation officer. He smiled broadly when I showed him my report card and he saw how well I was doing. I had become a serious student, and my confidence in the classroom soared. Becoming very responsible with my money and paying off my debts and building a bank account also helped build my self-esteem. Each payday when I went into the savings bank, made my deposit, and looked at my new balance, I was so proud because every cent of it was earned honestly.

~~~~

My social life was limited to family gatherings, which almost always included Sue and Jim who were a lot of fun. We all have a similar sense of humor (the Talty humor) that is marked by a lot of sarcasm, finding humor in tragic family events, and lots of reminiscing. Also, out of boredom, I bought a folding pool table that was regulation length and width. Danny, Jimmy, Pat, and I all enjoyed playing pool, which gave us another fun activity to do together.

The pool table was purchased without a lot of forethought in terms of space. It was way too big for our dining room/TV room, which was its intended place. So with Ma's approval, Danny and I moved the TV, easy chair, and couch into the former dining room and set up the pool table in what previously was our living room. It worked out great, and to add to the bizarreness of a pool table in our living room, Bernie set up his drums at the other end of this big room.

~~~~

Finally, after almost sixteen months on probation, Mr. Troller told me that he was going to move ahead to have it end. Hallelujah! In the wonderful words of Dr. Martin Luther King, Jr., I felt "free at last, thank God almighty, free at last." Mr. Troller said that it would take a few days for him to write and submit his report to the judge, but he said for me to come back in two weeks and that should do it. That night I was so elated I flew up that windy street, caught the bus, and brought great joy to our Polishtown flat when I told them what Mr. Troller had said.

~~~~

The first thing I did was start looking for a car. I had abandoned my dream of buying a Corvette and was now looking at more practical cars. Bernie drove me to a few used-car lots, and then I saw the car I had to have. It was a red-and-white 1956 Buick Super hardtop. I think I was subconsciously drawn to this car because it was an almost duplicate of the car my hero Jimmy owned a few years previous. His was also was a 1956 Buick, red and white, and a hardtop. The only difference was that his model had been a Century and mine was a Super.

Because I did not yet have my driver's license back (Mr. Troller had it) I had to register the car and take out the insurance all in Bernie's name. I still can remember the excitement and pride I felt when Sue drove Bernie and me to pick up my first car. Bernie drove, I rolled down all the windows, and I set all the push buttons on the radio to my favorite stations. It was a beautiful car, and I had Bernie drive slowly past any large store windows so I could admire my car and me in it. Ma and Dad were enthralled to see such a fine car parked outside of our flat in Polishtown. I told Ma that she could take it to work, shopping, or just to take Dad out for a ride. She beamed, but not as much as I.

True to his word, when I went for my scheduled appointment with Mr. Troller at the two-week mark, he gave me my driver's license back, told me I was free to go, wished me luck, and shook my hand. Now I really was free! I took the bus home for the last time.

Life after Probation

Having a car, working full-time, being essentially debt-free, and moving forward with my education should have made me a pretty happy guy. Right? I was to some extent, but when I compared myself with other guys my age that were progressing through college or advancing in their chosen careers, disparity reigned. I was behind, and I didn't like it. I also couldn't do much about it except to just bear down and get my high school diploma.

    I did like being in a position to help other people in the family with rides or small loans. Just not being the burden was such a relief, and so anything beyond that was a bonus. Working at the gas station came to an emotional end for Jimmy as well as the rest of us who worked there. Apparently, he was unable to generate the amount of business necessary to meet his lease agreement. As a result, the Esso oil company locked him out of the station and seized all his tools and equipment as assets against his debt. He was devastated, and we all wondered how he and Sue would ever survive this catastrophe, but they did.

    He went out a couple of days later and got a job doing some of the most physically demanding work imaginable. I know because I tried to do it one night and only lasted four hours. The work was moving by hand and back large sides of beef that were hanging in refrigerated boxcars out onto a dock and then into designated trucks for delivery to supermarkets the next day. Each side weighed well over 150 pounds, and so he had to lift and carry these monstrosities all night. Then he would often work additional hours the next day to drive a truck and deliver the meat.

~~~~

Not having to work at the gas station gave me time and energy to expand my social activities. I went out on a few dates and went to college basketball games with my cousin Tyke. It wasn't much because I was now really committed to finishing high school in a strong way.

~~~~

Things had stabilized quite a bit for our family. Dad was fully discharged from the state hospital, and he was able to draw his railroad pension, which, combined with Ma's hospital pay and Bernie's and my board, gave Ma and Dad more financial stability than they ever had. Dad, however, struggled terribly with his emphysema without any relief. In the good news department, Pat's doctor seemed to have found the right combination of medications to control his seizures, and he was functioning better. He was a big help to Ma and Dad by doing their shopping and running local errands.

It was while we were living in our Polishtown flat that Ma got reconnected with her long lost brother Myles. His actual name was Myles Wasson Farnham, but we always called him "Wasson" or "Waddy." What happened was that one day Jimmy and I were driving to the gas station when Jimmy spotted Waddy standing on the corner. We told Ma about seeing him, and she was very pleased to hear that he was still alive. They had not had any contact for at least ten years, but Ma never stopped thinking about her only sibling. We saw him a few more times, but Ma was ambivalent about us stopping to talk with him, and so we never did.

Apparently, our not stopping to talk with Waddy was not a factor in his and Ma's reconciliation. Waddy, independent of any contact with us, wrote to Ma describing how desperate his life had become. He was no longer able to work because of problems with his knees and his heart, and he was renting a room from a woman who had a small boardinghouse. It was a pathetic letter in that he described not having much to eat, getting 50¢ a day from a local barber for sweeping the shop floor, and wanting to find out how he "could get on the Welfare." He closed by asking Ma to send a "few bucks if she could spare it." Ma responded with $5 and asked him to call her. He called and then came to visit us in our Polishtown flat on a regular basis, sometimes every Sunday for a while. He loved playing pinochle, and so did Ma and Dad. It always made me happy when I would see the three of them at the kitchen table playing cards and drinking beer.

Back to Our Old Neighborhood!

Ma had decided to look for a flat for us back in the locale we all loved. The main impetus for this move seemed to come from Ma's and Sue's needs to have more frequent and convenient access to each other. Although the distance between our flat and Sue's house was only two and a half miles, without a car, it was forty-five minutes by bus. Their thinking was that if we were closer, Sue could help Ma out with cleaning and housekeeping. Sue had had her son Shawn Patrick in December, and Ma and Dad loved babysitting him. So the hunt was on for a flat near Sue that would facilitate all this.

The hunt was successful. Ma found a place that she thought was so nice that she feared she wouldn't get it, and she didn't. Initially, the owner who lived upstairs had a verbal agreement with a woman, so he had to tell Ma that the flat was already taken. After a week of disappointing viewing of less desirable flats, he called Ma and said that the woman had decided not to take it, and so if she was still interested, the flat was hers. Ma enthusiastically said she would take it. The next day she gave notice to our present landlord, and then the packing and cleaning out commenced. The new flat was really nice. It was clean and had an updated kitchen and bath. Overall, it was probably the nicest place (besides the Big House and Sue and Jim's) in which Ma and Dad had ever lived. It was also a convenient walk to Sue and Jim's, so everyone was happy.

Using Sue's, Bernie's, and my cars, we were able to move a lot of the small stuff quickly. We then rented a truck and the "moving crew" of Jimmy, Bernie, Danny, Pat and I together made the first of many moves within the family. We quickly got settled into our new flat, and Ma and Dad got to be good friends with our landlord and landlady. They took Ma, Dad, and Pat on a lot of day trips, which they all enjoyed very much.

A real bonus for Ma and Sue was not only the proximity to each other but also the new flat was only a few steps from the shops on their favorite street. At that time, this street not only was a network of diverse shops and stores but also included the convenience of banks and the post office. This was all within four city blocks where safety was not a concern whatsoever. A great day for Ma and Sue was to meet to window-shop, do their various errands, and then go to their favorite drugstore for coffee and visiting. No matter which of them said they had to go run errands, the other jumped right in. It was obvious these were highly valued days for Ma and Sue. Dad hated Ma being gone, but secretly, he really enjoyed Shawn's antics as he babysat him while "the girls" went shopping, visiting friends, paying bills, etc.

~~~~

It was about this time that Sue and Jim went through an awful time. With Jimmy working all the time and me working my two jobs and going to school, there was no one Sue could get to do the routine maintenance work on their home. She liked things neat, orderly, and in good repair, but she now saw the house as too much of a burden. So when Jimmy suggested that they sell the house and that they use some of the money to finance a trip to England for Sue and the kids to visit Tommy and Karoline, she jumped at it.

Unfortunately, the money from the sale of the house had to be sunk into the gas station and used for living expenses when Jimmy lost the gas station. They were renting an upstairs flat not far from their former house. Their debts from the gas station venture were so great that they had to declare bankruptcy. Jimmy was working full time, but his pay was not equal to their creditors' demands. Of course, the trip to England was off.

~~~~

Finally, in 1962 after two years of night school, I received my high school diploma. I was very proud of my academic success. I had hoped to now get a better job, but the job market just then was in a state of decline. Bernie and I were becoming big social drinkers frequenting several of the local taverns. Two in particular played a monumental role in my social life and, also later on, in Bernie's. The first was a pleasant tavern located in one of the suburbs. They had a bowling machine and pool table, plus the typical jukebox—all the amenities we needed for nights of great fun and laughter coupled with lots of beer. It was during this time that I became good friends with Bob Wrestler.* He had gone to high school with Bernie and did not live far from us. It just sort of evolved that he and I would go almost nightly to play pool and drink. One night a guy who I didn't know asked me, "Are you Peter Talty?" When I said yes, he added, "Well, I'm Eric O'Brady.* I lived right near you when we were kids." I remembered him well, and he might even have been one of the many neighborhood kids who frequently joined us to watch *Howdy Doody* and *Cactus Jim*. We had a good time reminiscing about the old neighborhood and catching up on each other's lives.

Through Eric I met four other guys with whom we all connected. We six became drinking buddies and took many vacations together, building memories that I will never forget. This was what I missed out on in my teenage years—having a group of friends to which I really belonged. Even though they were all established on solid career paths while I was in a sort of holding pattern with mine, it didn't matter. I felt no disparity. I saw the first two or so years that we spent together as a hiatus on my career development plan in favor of camaraderie and fun. Because most of this group worked at a large department store that I will refer to as the "Big Store*", we referred to them as

---

* The Big Store is a fictitious name I created to indicate this large department store that played a large role in my family's life.

the "Big Store crowd". After they finished working at nine o'clock each night, we would all gather at our favorite tavern for drinking, pool playing, and lots of joking and laughter. This carried over into weekends when we would venture downtown or any place where we thought we could meet girls. When we eventually found steady girlfriends, they joined in our festivities with the parties shifting to private homes, local parks for picnics, and any other place where we could drink and have fun. I had found a place socially, just as Ma and Dad had found a nice home back in our old neighborhood. Our family was doing well.

Unfortunately, I did return to some of my old risk-taking behaviors and also served as the clown for the group, especially in conjunction with too much alcohol. Besides the alcohol, I was also fueled by the need to "turn it up a notch" so that whatever we were doing became even more fun if I did something reckless. It was a miracle that in spite of our heavy drinking and driving, none of us were ever involved in a serious accident or got a DWI. Today, with the police being so vigilant about drinking and driving, we would have all been paying a lot of money and maybe have lost our driver's licenses or even our freedom or our lives.

I knew I was concerned about drinking and driving somewhat because when a kid from our old neighborhood was killed in an auto accident, I was morbidly intrigued. I went to where his car was towed to a collision shop and saw the engine in the front seat intertwined with the dashboard and unrecognizable twisted parts of the car. The windshield was smashed with blood all over it. He was just eighteen years old. He had hit a tree at such a high rate of speed that the whole front of his car formed a "C" around where the tree and his car came together. The guy at the collision shop said disrespectfully, "he must have been drunk as a skunk." Regardless, he did give me directions as to where the accident happened, and of course, I had to find the tree. It was surprising to me how little the tree was damaged in comparison to the car and, of course, my friend.

Did all this preoccupation serve as my "wake-up call" for me to stop drinking and driving? Of course not. We were all just lucky. I wasn't a regular attendee at church, but God was certainly in charge of my car on a lot of those nights. When it came to church and God, mine was sort of a crisis connection. That is, if I or someone in my family was in crisis, I was in church or on my knees.

Besides the drinking, we played basketball a lot in the local playgrounds, went to football games, and to week-long vacations together in Canada, New York City, and the Adirondack Mountains. The owner of the other tavern where we hung around even sponsored our basketball team so we could play in a league.

Many of our girlfriends at the time were college students like mine, and so some of our social activities had to revolve around events at their respective colleges. I didn't like these latter kinds of activities because my sense of disparity became aroused, as I felt unworthy of being with guys and girls who seemed far smarter than I and were enrolled in college unlike me. My new group of drinking buddies was more in sync with my place in life, and none of them held college in high regard. This was fine with me because I just finished high school, and I didn't see college in my future.

However, as this lifestyle of frivolity continued on, there came a time when my close friend disparity emerged on a far more frequent basis. It would emerge whenever I was unable to participate in all the activities with my friends because I earned less than all of them. On a small scale, they could order whatever they chose when we went out to eat, while I had to always search for the cheapest thing on the menu. Disparity also raged when it came to cars. I had since sold my Buick in favor of cheap cars that were basic transportation at best while they were all driving new or fairly new cars. Some of the lowest points were when I would have to borrow one of their cars when I had a date where I wanted to impress the girl. None of the cars I drove during that time would impress anyone.

~~~~

Here is the good thing about the disparity I felt in those days: not once did I ever consider stealing as a way of augmenting my income in an effort to lessen my disparity. What I did instead was to ask my friends at the Big Store to recommend me for a part-time job there, which they did gladly. Their recommendation was very effective, and soon I began working as a stock boy Monday through Friday from six to nine and then twelve to nine on Saturdays. This was in the midst of the Christmas-shopping chaos, and my first assignment was to the toy department and report to the department head, Frank Pepe. Little did we know how our paths, along with Bernie's, would become inextricably linked in just a short time and then throughout our lives. On that night, Frank was in complete control of the chaos prevailing in the toy department, working the cash register, answering customers' questions, directing his sales staff, and speaking calmly and pleasantly to each person. He directed me to his assistant manager who put me to work organizing the shelves and putting displaced toys back in their proper place. I didn't get to work just in toys again; I was permanently assigned to the job of distributing stock throughout the store.

It was good having the extra money, and the work wasn't very hard. I just had to distribute the various items to the different departments or stock the shelves in the storeroom with the things that were too large for the storeroom areas behind each department. The hardest part was the seventy plus hours in total that I spent working and, of course, the late hours drinking and socializing with my friends. The alcohol consumption did not make me the most productive employee at either job or the most attentive.

~~~~

It was during one of these times of inattentiveness that I sustained one of the most painful injuries of my life, and I had several to which to compare because of my chronic recklessness. One Thursday evening while moving freight off the dock at the Big Store, I was using a manual forklift. I slid the forks under the pallet, jacked up the load, and proceeded to maneuver the load around objects in a lackadaisical manner. Not realizing how close I was to the edge of the dock, I stepped back and fell off. I continued to hold on to the handle of the forklift that was spring-loaded, so as I went down, the handle sprang back up when I let go of them. Thus, there were two moving forces going in opposite directions—me going down and the handles going up. There was an abrupt and painful end to our opposing trajectories as the handles smashed with a nauseating sound into my face.

    I was stunned, but surprisingly, the handles hitting me in the face was not the source of the sickening pain I was feeling or the reason for the blood pouring out of my mouth. My teeth had been driven deep into my tongue, and I was spewing blood and reeling from the most intense pain. There were customers standing about waiting to pick up large items that they had just purchased in the Big Store. They were horrified because of what they witnessed with some only a few feet away when I fell. They saw and heard it all. I still can see the shock, concern, and look of nausea on their faces. My supervisor was called, who was a very intense former naval chief petty officer who was always confusing us by directing us about like we were on a ship. "Take this topside." "Police the deck." "Who's got the watch?" "I'm going to the head." Well, if he uttered a naval idiom when he saw the mess I was, I don't remember what it was. He just said, "Boy, you best get your ass to the hospital." So off I went holding a wad of paper towels someone gave me over my mouth as I drove myself to the hospital.

    By the time I got to the hospital, I must have looked pretty bad because they took me right in ahead of the other six or eight people waiting in the emergency room. They took some X-rays, and everyone was surprised, including me, that nothing was broken, not even any of my teeth. The only injury I had was a lacerated tongue for which sadly they could do nothing. It couldn't be stitched, which was fine with me. The thought of a needle being pushed in and through my tongue was more unsettling than the injury itself. So they gave me some pain pills and sent me home. When I got home, I had a hard time telling Ma and Dad what happened because my tongue was so swollen and painful. I then just went to bed.

However, before retiring, I was cognizant enough to anticipate that Bernie might wake me up when he saw the towel across my face (we shared a bed), so I left him a note: "I got hurt at work. If I'm asleep, don't wake me. I'm in a lot of pain." It was to no avail. He woke me anyway! "What happened? Are you okay?" I explained the best I could, took two more pain pills, and eventually fell back asleep. Surprisingly, the next day I felt a lot better. The copious blood supply to the tongue must serve as a quick fixer because it was amazing how quickly I healed. I went to work the next day to both jobs.

~~~~

Now besides the extra money from my job at the Big Store, there were some surprising other benefits and coincidences that ensued from my working there. Its impact on so many people is just so uncanny it still astounds me today. One of those happenstances was in 1963 when I met and then got to know Corey Matthews.* Corey was black (back then, even he referred to himself as "colored") and one of only two black people (the other was the janitor) employed in the Big Store. This was prior to the Civil Rights Act of 1964 when hiring practices where unregulated. Corey worked with me as another stock boy, but he was far more than that. He was a full-time student at the university studying to become an occupational therapist and a second lieutenant in the U.S. Army Reserve. Corey was not a braggart. It took a while to find out all this stuff about Corey. It was over a period as we worked side by side and took our breaks and dinners together that I learned who Corey Matthews really was. Corey was going to become an occupational therapist, but this was not a spontaneous decision. Corey really believed that people could become anything they chose, and he encouraged me to also think like that. When Corey resigned from the Big Store to concentrate more fully on the demanding curriculum he had chosen, I thought we would not see each other again. I was gratefully mistaken.

Life was good in our new flat for my family and me for the first year, but things there did get very bad very fast. It started with strained relationships with our landlord. He became strange and overbearing. Ma and Dad hated to hear him come home because they were tired of his constant presence and repetitive off-color jokes. They declined invitations for rides using my Dad's poor health as an excuse, which sadly was the case. Dad's progressive decline in health due to his emphysema made life very difficult for us all but especially for him. He was in and out of the hospital without any seeming benefit. He was miserable and demanding. On our part, we were all insensitive to his decline and annoyed with what we referred to as his constant bitching.

He had terrible coughing and choking spells and an awful time getting his breath. If he felt we were ignoring his plight, he would let us know the rage he felt by exclaiming in between painful breaths, "I wish you had it (his lung disease), you bastards!"

It had become quite common for us to have Sue and Jim and the kids at our place for Sunday dinner, or occasionally, we would all go over to Sue's. Tommy and Karoline were back in the States and were also staying with us. We had a house full, which Ma absolutely loved. Even Dad was pleased to have Tommy and Karoline home. He knew that the New York Yankees and Notre Dame were playing on TV the weekend Tommy first came home, and so he and Ma went out and bought a new TV. It was another of their impulsive purchases but one appreciated by us all, especially Tommy.

Pat's Sad Life Goes from Travesty to Tragedy

Thankfully, Sue and Jim were able to resolve their marital problems and stay together. We hated the idea of them separating because to us they were a couple. It was always a good day when we all got together no matter what the reason. There were, however, now some undercurrents of tension unrelated to Sue and Jim's difficulties that were ever present in our lives: Pat and Dad were feuding with increasing frequency and intensity. Pat had gotten quite heavy, and Ma and Dad were fearful of his fits of rage now compounded by his size. Jimmy was always the enforcer, and Pat maintained a calm demeanor whenever he was present. On this particular Sunday, the friction between Dad and Pat escalated beyond anything we had ever seen before. Even Jimmy's presence could not deter Pat's belligerence and outright hostility directed at us all. Also, Pat had a vacant look about him, something we hadn't seen.

As the day progressed, something happened, I don't know what, but it caused Pat to run into the kitchen, pull open the drawer where Ma kept her sharp knives, and before we could respond, he pulled out a large carving fork while screaming, "I'll kill you!" What caught us off guard was that he was not going to attack Dad; he went after Jimmy. I think Bernie and I grabbed him and got the fork out of his hand, and then Tommy and Jimmy joined in the fray as we wrestled Pat to the floor.

Then a progression of events followed that made Pat's attempted attack even more tragic. Ma or Sue called the police because they knew we had to be protected from Pat's uncontrollable rage. He was also no longer a little kid; he was a large and obese man. By the time the police arrived, Pat was calm but scared. It was the policeman's assessment that this was more of a mental health case than a criminal one and recommended that we take Pat to the specialized hospital where people with mental health issues could be assessed and treated if necessary (how well we knew). So Jimmy drove with Tommy in front and Pat in the back between Bernie and me. Typical of the Talty nature, we talked of other things like Tommy's next air force assignment and news about Tommy and Jimmy's contemporaries and changes in the neighborhood. This was a great example of us Taltys verbally meandering through la-la land while embroiled in an evolving tragedy.

Since we had been through this type of assessment in the past with other family members, we knew how the process worked. While Pat sat in a cubicle waiting for a psychiatrist to evaluate him, he gave me a knowing grin and said in a way that we always thought crazy people talked and mouthed "Psych ward!" This got us all laughing, which probably made the staff think we should all be evaluated.

The psychiatrist talked with Pat and then separately talked with us all as a group to find out Pat's history and what precipitated the attack. To our collective but sad relief, they decided to admit Pat to the psychiatric ward for further observation. We were told that we could leave, and the staff would take Pat to his room. They gave us the visiting hours and his doctor's name. Leaving Pat was very sad, as we all wondered to ourselves about what was to become of him. It was a quiet trip back to Ma's.

When we got back home, Ma and Dad were still very upset and even more so when they heard that they had admitted Pat. I think it was so hard for Ma because she was always Pat's main support and advocate, and it was hard for Dad because he knew firsthand what it's like to be admitted to a psychiatric ward. Ma could not stop crying and begged us to take her to the hospital so that she could see for herself that he was okay. So that night Bernie and I drove her to the hospital, where we visited a contrite Pat in very depressing surroundings. We talked with his doctor, but he was not able to tell us anything of substance because the assessment and observation process had just begun. However, Ma did feel better for having seen Pat, and she also was able to make Dad feel better when she explained that Pat was in the best place. She always liked to take a positive view of things no matter how forlorn a situation may look. This definitely was not the Talty wont.

We went back to our regular lives of work and stuff, but I could not get Pat out of my mind. Looking at his messed up bed and his meager possessions scattered about the bedroom he shared with Danny made me cry, and it still does today whenever I think of it. But then I learned there was a far greater reason to cry when we got the results of the psychiatrist's evaluation.

It was the psychiatrist's opinion that Pat had suicidal and homicidal tendencies. Because Pat was dangerous to those around him, he needed long-term treatment in a state hospital. I don't remember what we were told about his diagnosis, but knowing what I know about these things today, I would guess he was diagnosed with adolescent adjustment reaction. Today, people with this diagnosis are rarely hospitalized, but when this happened to Pat in 1962, this sadly was the only treatment option available at that time. So once again, we waited for one of our own to be driven out to the state hospital just as they did with Dad in 1956. It seemed far more tragic this time because Pat was only fourteen years old.

~~~~

Just as she was with Dad, Ma was relentless in getting anyone to drive her out to the state hospital each Sunday to see Pat. If Bernie or I had something we were planning to do, or sometimes just too hungover to drive out there, or Sue's car was not running, Ma would call up friends of Bernie's. I was always impressed that they never said no, which didn't make Bernie or I look too good. So out of shame or love (I hope it was love), we tried to be more responsive to Ma's requests. We both took our girlfriends at the time along for the ride, which was not always a good thing. Sometimes he was so medicated and lethargic that he slept through the whole visit.

The girl I once took out there with me was confident that she "knew from her college psychology courses just what Pat needed." She said in her usual all-knowing and annoying way, "Psychiatric patients like to look through the the Big Store catalog," and in spite of Pat's consternation, she presented him with the large catalog. In later years, we laughed about this bizarre idea, and Pat would remark, "What the hell was I going to do with the Big Store catalog out in the state hospital? I didn't have any money."

This particular girlfriend of mine was very nice and very smart. My whole family loved her and could not understand why I broke up with her. The Big Store catalog incident should have explained it. What actually annoyed me so much about her is that she was always the expert regardless of the situation. Then what made it doubly annoying was that most of the time she was right. The Big Store catalog fiasco was definitely the exception.

~~~~

Another thing we did that disgusts me now to recall was to laugh and ridicule the other patients that resided with Pat in the state hospital. My brothers and I did this among ourselves and, hopefully, not to the extent that the patients were aware of it. If patients talked to themselves or tried to talk with us about their delusions or hallucinations or gestured energetically in bizarre ways, we would get out of their presence and laugh and laugh. On Pat's rational and less stuporous days he would join in the fun. Pat had a keen wit and excellent skill at imitating his fellow patients. If the staff was aware of our antics, they may have determined that more than one Talty brother needed psychiatric care.

We were becoming increasingly concerned that Pat may never be able to return home. The inconsistency of his behavior and lack of progress was what convinced us. The way the hospital helped patients prepare for life outside of the hospital was to permit patients a level of autonomy commensurate with their behavior. The more appropriate and cooperative they were, the more privileges they received. This level of freedom directly corresponded to their level of residence in the high-rise tower where Pat lived.

Some days we would arrive for a visit and Pat would have been given full grounds privileges, and we would have to wait for his arrival as he flitted about the grounds. Strangely, it was on these days that he was in the worst mood, very demanding and argumentative. Then the next week he may get into a fight with some other resident or refuse to do his work, and the staff would put him in seclusion, restricting him to one of the upper floors. When in seclusion, he couldn't wear his own clothes; hospital pajamas and a bathrobe were the usual attire. He was often so sedated during these times that he would sleep throughout the visit and not even be aware that we were there in spite of our best efforts to arouse him.

Never knowing what we were going to find after making the long, non-expressway trek to this gloomy place, none of us were eager to take Ma out there. Pat's inability to follow the rules and his frequent meltdowns caused us all to be pessimistic about his ever being released.

~~~~

Adding to the anguish of those days, Ma had another of her heart attacks and was hospitalized. Her condition seemed to worsen as she worried so much about Pat, especially since she could not get out to visit him. However, she too was coming to the anguishing conclusion that the state hospital would be Pat's home for the rest of his life. She said as much in one of her letters to Tommy that she wrote from her hospital bed: "As I said before I will have to see him myself. I am so glad that it is over. I mean that he is being taken care of. Now he really has to take his pills. Tomorrow he starts school. If he goes only 3 hours a day, he has a job to do. I don't know what it is because Peter couldn't remember. But if he goes all day he won't have that job to do. One day or night last week he was allowed to go to their dance. Another night he was going to Bingo, and then he goes to Occupational Therapy every day I think. I told Peter that Pat is making a whole new life for himself and he told Sue and Jim that he is having more fun out there than he ever had at home." Thankfully, we were all proven wrong about our pessimistic outlook.

~~~~

My blossoming social life was dealt a major blow when Bob Wrestler and I were banned from our favorite tavern. It was due to our drinking (it was a bar!) and refusing to be quiet, some grossly inappropriate practical jokes, or some other such juvenile behavior on our part. I was very saddened by the ban because all my Big Store friends usually gathered at this tavern every night after work, and now I couldn't join them. Here, I finally gain entrée into a great social group, and now I was denied access to them. However, another of my guardian angels stepped forth, and once again I was saved.

When one of my good friends, Mike Savior,* who worked at and had a lot of influence at the Big Store, said he would fix this (my being banished from the tavern), I wondered if he really could. Miraculously (strange word), his way of fixing it was to convince the whole crowd from the Big Store (about eighty people) to eschew our old tavern and to instead gather at a tavern just down the road. So I was still banned, but it didn't matter because Mike was able to move the gathering throng on down the road to a new tavern where I was welcome. My social life was once again back on track. Thanks, Mike.

~~~~

During this time the number of us living in our flat decreased by one. Danny joined the navy. He had been pestering Ma to sign for him, and finally, she did. It was her thinking that since he was not interested in school, he might as well go in the navy. We all missed him terribly when he went, but this was what he wanted. He seemed so young to be going so far away. He spent the majority of his time aboard the USS *Enterprise*, the first nuclear-powered aircraft carrier. There was much about the navy that did not appeal to him, plus he had a girlfriend back home. So, thus began a tumultuous time for Danny, all of us, and the navy itself.

~~~~

While Pat continued to live at the state hospital and I continued to work both at my janitor's job at the school and as a stock boy at the Big Store, Dad worsened significantly and was admitted to the hospital. I wasn't able to get up to see him because of my work schedule, but a fortuitous incident at the Big Store's fence lot changed that. One of my responsibilities when working on the dock at the Big Store was to accompany customers to the fence lot where fencing and all the accessories were kept. One Saturday afternoon I had to cut some fencing and help a customer load the fencing and railings onto his pickup truck. I left a long pipe (called "top rail") leaning against the gate of the fence lot while I was kneeling down cutting the fencing with large wire cutters.

Unbeknownst to me, the customer leaned against the gate causing it to swing away from him and for the top rail to rapidly slide down and then off ending with a resounding blow to the top of my head. It almost knocked me out and gouged my skull a bit, producing some blood. The customer went back to the dock and told my boss what happened. He told me to drive to the hospital, tell them this happened on the job, and then go home for the rest of the day. So, off I went to a very familiar facility.

I was x-rayed at the hospital, got a couple of stitches, and told to go home and rest. Instead, I went upstairs to visit with Dad. He was feeling better and glad to see me. We had a good visit, and as it turned out, it was the last chance I would have to speak with him. I didn't go to see him on Sunday, and then on Monday morning while cleaning the gym, Herman came to tell me that I had to go right to the hospital; "Your Dad is dying." I was in shock. We had had no deaths in our family since Aunt Dory died over fifteen years ago, and the idea of Dad dying was just so hard to comprehend.

~~~~

It was so sad for all of us sitting in the hospital's waiting room waiting for Dad to die. They gave us no hope. His lungs had given out, and the doctors said that in a short time, his heart would too. He was essentially in a coma and unresponsive to our voice and touch. We got confusing information from his doctors, "He's holding his own" and "He's responding to treatment." What did these mean? We didn't have the courage to ask for clarification or elaboration. We saw that his chest was very large giving us a frightening view of his labored breathing. None of this mattered because he died on the morning of April 24, 1963, at the age of fifty-four just five days before his fifty-fifth birthday.

I remember being overwhelmed with grief and guilt when Dad died. Thinking of all the times I found his physical complaints so annoying and his simple requests ("Take out the garbage," "Bring in the newspaper," etc.) so unworthy of my time or attention, I was repulsed with myself. How could I have been so insensitive to his needs?

Carrying a shopping bag home from the hospital with his clothes and slippers along with an almost empty wallet was so depressing. It all seemed so little. Was his life also so little? He spent most of his adult life getting drunk or recovering from being drunk. He then spent three of what should have been his prime years in the state hospital. Not long after he was discharged, he was diagnosed with the emphysema, which eventually killed him.

What may have been the proudest major possession he ever had was when he owned the trailer for three years. He never owned a car that I can remember. The furthest he ever traveled was the thirteen-mile ride on the Canadiana across Lake Erie to the Crystal Beach amusement park in Ontario, Canada. His honeymoon was going to Niagara Falls. That was it.

Recalling him sitting in the front seat of my Buick, I was moved and even depressed at how he looked. He seemed so small and frail, which, of course, he was. Was he aware and pained that his life may also have been so small? I hope not. He got to be a part of the lives of his six kids and three grandkids, but was it enough? He did enjoy our successes like Tommy's service in the air force; my finishing high school; Bernie's multiple achievements in music, athletics, and joining the army; and Danny joining the navy. However, he never came to watch Bernie swim or run cross-country or Danny swim for their high school. He tended to shun social events of all kinds even before he got sick. It was the adversities of life that were the hardest for him. When bad news came to our door, Dad would crumble or get drunk, and Ma would deal with it.

Dad did have a dry sense of humor and was like Sue in terms of being able to astutely (not that they were always accurate) perceive people. His wry nicknames for everyone, including us, were very clever and funny. He called Sue "the lawyer" because she would always argue Ma's case against him. I was the "dizzy bastard" because of my erratic behavior. Bernie was "the wanderer" because of his busy social calendar. Pat was just plain "wacky" because of his demanding and self-centered behavior. Danny was "mud socks" because of the frequent times he came home to the trailer with mud caked all over his shoes and socks. Tommy was "the promiser" because of his pledges to improve our living conditions. Even when Dad was dying and Bernie went up to the hospital to shave him, his dry sense of humor was at work. He told Bernie to "save some for the undertaker." It was Talty humor to the end.

We were all bereft when Dad died, but for me, pity was also a major accompanying emotion. Pity for all that he never got to do with his life and pity for the way he was physically, mentally, and spiritually. He never seemed able to enjoy the life he had. Perhaps the only time he experienced anything approaching joy was when he was high on alcohol. A sad life indeed, and now it was over. I'm sure this awareness compounded the grief we all felt.

Prior to the funeral, we had to notify Danny who was in the navy and bring Pat home from the state hospital. Dad was waked at a local mortuary a few blocks from our flat, and we had his funeral mass at our parish's church where Ma had previously registered them, even though he never went to church. He was buried in Ma's family's cemetery, but in one of two graves for him and, eventually, Ma. Dad's death was very hard for us all, especially for Ma. In spite of the challenges that being married to Dad brought, she loved him and was going to have a hard time finding a place in the world without him. Seeing his vacant chair, lamp, and TV was so sad. His was a small world and even more so in his final days.

~~~~

Then, as if to eradicate my belief that Dad's life was so small, we were awakened at twelve thirty in the morning the day after Dad's funeral with a call that Dad's name had been drawn and that he had won a new car! We had just buried Dad that morning, and so when I answered the phone, I was very disoriented and confused. All I could do was take down the name and number of the guy who called to arrange to pick up the car, which was in his barn in a rural town not far from us.

The next morning Bernie helped us all to understand what took place with the car. Bernie had bought two tickets from a friend of his on the railroad where he was presently working. This was a fundraiser that was being run by the fire department in a small town where this guy was a volunteer fireman. Bernie knew Dad would like to participate but knew he didn't have the money for a ticket. So Bernie bought two tickets and each week for twenty weeks he would check to see if either of them won the cash drawing, but they never did. It was beyond ironic that Dad's ticket was drawn on the last Saturday and he won a new 1963 Dodge 440 worth almost $3,000. The guy who called was at the party but hadn't known that Dad had died, but he knew Bernie had been buying the tickets each week. I guess he wanted to be the one to tell Bernie that Dad had won the car. So Bernie called the guy, and Tommy drove him out to pick it up. I'm sure Dad was smiling down from above uttering one of his sarcastic witticisms about his winning a car from the grave.

~~~~

It was a short time after Dad's death that Tommy proposed the idea of buying a house for Ma so that she would not have to ever deal with landlords again. Ma loved the idea. So, Tommy contacted a real estate agent to begin the search. After looking at some houses in our neighborhood that were not satisfactory, they decided to look at new homes because none of us had the time, skill, or inclination to take on a house that needed fixing up. Because of this, Tommy decided that a new house would be best, and so the search was expanded beyond our neighborhood. They eventually found a new three-bedroom ranch home in a suburban village that Ma loved. So Tommy bought it, and once again, we got ready to move.

We Become Suburbanites!

Great news! After a year in the state hospital, Pat was discharged to home! We were all pleased to be wrong about all our dismal prognostications that he would live there the rest of his life. He was only fifteen years old; spending his life in an institution at that young age, considering his intelligence, would have been such a waste. Pat was bright, but he lacked the discipline and confidence to be successful in school. He was thrilled to be home and to start the hunt for a full-time job, which unfortunately proved very difficult for him.

He was home in time to join Ma in the excitement of moving into a new home in the suburbs. So on October 1, 1963, we moved, and Ma got her dream house. The "Talty-Riley moving crew" that now also included Pat was assembled once again, and we got all our furniture and stuff moved out to the new house in just one day. The house was very nice with everything brand new. Its location in suburbia was a distance from Sue's, but this did not detract from Ma's excitement about having her own home. She enjoyed decorating it and setting it all up just the way she wanted it. Not having to contend with landlords and landladies gave her a freedom she never experienced.

Ma had her own room, Pat had the middle bedroom that he would share with Danny when he was home from the navy, and Bernie and I shared the larger back bedroom. It all worked out quite nicely. I had a bit further to go to work, but there was an expressway near us that made it a pretty easy commute.

We Become Suburbanites!

In spite of the abounding good feelings, the location of Ma's new house was problematic for Sue. She and Jim's relationship had not improved to the extent we had hoped, and she now needed Ma's companionship and support more than ever. The problem was that she did not have a reliable car to make the five-and-a-half-mile trip from our old neighborhood to suburbia. They talked on the phone every day, but they both missed their in-person visiting, or "kibitzing", as Ma referred to their conversations.

Sue and Jim eventually decided to separate. The way they worked it out was that they would vacate their flat, Jimmy would leave Sue and the kids and get a room, and Sue and the kids would move out to suburbia with the rest of us. We had to do some juggling of the rooms and furniture, but we were glad to do it. After all, Sue had done so much for us over the years that being inconvenienced now was the least we could do for and her kids. The bedrooms were reorganized. We put three single beds in the large bedroom for Bernie, Pat, and I. Ma kept her bedroom to herself but took the smallest one. Sue and the kids were set up in the last bedroom using her bedroom set and Shawn's crib. She had sold her dining room and living room sets and kitchen set, and we moved the rest of her stuff into our basement. Kathleen transferred to a Catholic school and rode the school bus for the first time. Shawn had gotten so cute, and we loved playing with him. It was all working out. Ma loved having Sue and the kids there, and Sue was a big help to Ma.

Tommy and Karoline had provided a major resource for the family when they were able to buy the suburban house for Ma. It provided a modern home that the family could move in and out of as needed without having to deal with landlords. What's the problem with landlords? Nothing for most families, but we did not fare well with them for a myriad of reasons. We were a rambunctious lot who needed a home free of landlord scrutiny, and suburbia was the place.

~~~~

My social life had gone through another transition. About the same time that I was tiring of just going to taverns and hanging out, our group began to fragment. Some of the guys entered the military, while most of the others became much more serious about their relationships including getting married. So at the same time when there was no one available to go out with, I really no longer had the desire to go out. I read a lot and took two continuing education courses at the local high school: typing and the stock market. I really enjoyed both courses and found a thirst for learning that was way beyond anything I ever experienced before. So, with motivation and confidence rising, I applied to the university through their night school division. I had no idea about a course of learning or major to pursue. It was just the desire to get a college education that drove me. I knew from reading the information that the university sent me that I could explore a number of fields for quite a while before having to declare a major.

~~~~

My job at the Big Store at that time became a bit diverse when they asked me do some promotional work. It was easier than the stock work I was doing, and it gave me an outlet for my need to perform. The first assignment was for me to dress up in a clown's costume (how appropriate) and lead a parade around the shopping plaza welcoming Santa Claus to town. I did it, had fun, and the people who asked me to do it were very satisfied.

Then my next assignment had unbelievable consequences. The Big Store was having a sale on electric blankets, and my job was to wear green-and-white striped flannel pajamas, walk around the store, and distribute coupons for a drawing to win an electric blanket. I quickly realized that I wasn't being very effective in handing out my coupons by wandering around the store trying to approach individual customers. So instead, I positioned myself just at the bottom of the escalator and kept up a constant banter about the value of electric blankets while handing out lots of coupons. At one point a friend of mine, Annie Pepe, who ran the tobacco and candy department at the Big Store, came up to the escalator with her sister. I made a buzzing sound and gave her sister a coupon proclaiming that she had a winner. Annie introduced me to her sister Janice as they went on up the escalator and out of sight.

A few weeks after this encounter, I was getting ready to go out. Bernie was curious as to where I was going this particular night, and when I told him "to my new favorite nearby tavern," he rolled his eyes. He then asked, "Who's going to be there, that crowd from the Big Store, Annie Pepe, and them?" I said yes and encouraged him to come down and join us, but he was noncommittal. Well, later on that night, he did come in, and I introduced him to the people at our table, and one of them was Annie Pepe. They got along great and talked together the whole night (Pepe was the last name of the kid I went to high school with, but they were not related). Also, Annie's brother, Frank, was my first supervisor when I started at the Big Store in the toy department. So there are a few "Pepe connections."

Bernie and Annie quickly became a couple and spent a lot of time together. With Bernie's birthday coming up on April 2nd, Annie decided to throw a surprise birthday party at her house. She invited Sue and Jim (they had gotten back together by this time), several of Bernie's close friends, and me. However, she asked if I would be willing to come to the party as her sister Janice's date. I said sure.

Bernie thought he and Annie were going out on a date and was, of course, very shocked when we all jumped out yelling *"Surprise!"* Bernie then proceeded to demonstrate what serious drinking was all about. He always drank beer, but for some reason, this night he chose to drink scotch and lots of it. It all culminated in him collapsing on the dining room floor and then curling up asleep under the large dining room table. A bunch of us picked him up in his unconscious state and carried him into a back bedroom. That is where he was sleeping it off when Annie's mom came home. I doubt she had had as much experience with drunks in her house as we did and thus decreed that "He cannot stay here!" Annie convinced her that there was no way we could get him up and out, so her mom uneasily acquiesced. In spite of this now infamous beginning, the Annie and Bernie relationship prospered. It went so well, in fact, that they decided to marry on July 25th of that same year, 1964.

~~~~

My next "special assignment" for the Big Store played another significant part in my life that I never would have expected. They were having a children's clothing sale, and so this time I donned a Magilla Gorilla costume and walked around the store greeting any kids I met. In the midst of my rambling about the store, I was approached by Janice Pepe (Annie's sister), and she asked if she could talk to me. So we went outside, and I took off my big Magilla Gorilla head so I could see and hear her better. She wanted to know if I would be willing to take her to her senior prom. I said yes, and we had a good time at the prom and the picnic the following day.

We had a few other dates after the prom. On one of our first dates, I took Janice for pizza at a fancy pizzeria in my neighborhood. We ordered a medium pizza assuming it would be a good size for the two of us. As we sat and talked, our pizza came, and we commenced to eat. At least I did. I kept urging Janice to take a piece, but she kept refusing. After my prolonged insistence, she told me that she wasn't really very hungry. So as we talked, I ate, and I consumed the whole pizza. This shocked Janice, but I didn't know this until months later. It was also later that I learned the real reason why Janice did not eat any pizza: she had gum in her mouth. We were given cloth napkins, and thus she didn't know how to get rid of her gum. She was also very hungry and shocked that I ate the whole thing. We had other dates where she demonstrated a very good appetite, but I never knew about the gum and pizza incident until much later on in our relationship.

~~~~

It did concern me that there was a five-year difference in age between Janice and myself. Also, in some ways it was greater than five years because of the crazy life that I had already experienced in contrast to her somewhat sheltered life. That summer when I visited her at a cottage she and her sorority sisters rented in Canada, I began to think that maybe she was too young for me. Even so, I continued to call her and take her out. In those days, people gave "couples showers" and Annie asked me to be Janice's escort once again. So as Bernie and Annie moved closer to the altar, Janice and I continued to amplify our relationship.

~~~~

While dating Janice and talking with Bernie, I learned that Janice and Annie came from a very remarkable family. Besides Janice and Annie, there was their elder brother Frank who graduated in accounting from a local Jesuit college and was progressing in upper-level management at the Big Store. Janice's mother was widowed when her husband was killed while riding in a taxi while out of town on business. He was just forty-four years old and left Janice's mother to raise Frank who was sixteen at the time, Annie who was thirteen, and Janice who was only five. Janice remembers she and Annie being taken out of dancing class by an uncle when they received the terrible news. The way the large families on both sides rallied around Janice's devastated mother was emblematic of their concern for one another and of their compassion. The more I got to know Janice's Dad's side of the family (the Pepes) and her mom's side (the Siracuses), the more I admired and respected them.

Coming from an unstable and chaotic family wrought with crises and dissension, I was always surprised at how much these two families respected and supported each other. Things like divorce, abuse, alcoholism, criminal behavior, unwanted pregnancies, neglect, suicide, mental illness, drug abuse, and other aberrant behaviors were negligible among the Pepes and the Siracuses. Unfortunately, we Taltys were way too familiar with people whose lives involved these tragic situations. I suspect that Bernie was the only person who ever got drunk and collapsed under their dining room table and had to be carried off to bed.

In spite of the travesty of Bernie's party, I was always so grateful that the Pepes and the Siracuses welcomed Bernie and me into their respective families without hesitation. We both often remarked about how we never felt disrespected or uncomfortable in any way when we were with them. They were mature and stable, and they were hardworking, family-oriented, law-abiding, and churchgoing people. Education was valued in this large extended family, but at the same time, if a person chose another path such as becoming a salesperson or factory worker, no one thought any less of them. As long as their focus was on being responsible, being a good citizen, being a churchgoer, and taking care of their families, how one chose to do it was up to them.

Although Janice and Annie came from impressive and stable families, my old biases about people different from me came to the fore when Janice invited me for Sunday dinner. Concerned that they might be eating something strange, like squids or leeches or other things bizarre and consistent with their culture as I perceived it, I was worried and conflicted. I really didn't know what to say. I wanted to go, but what if they served something I just couldn't eat? Unlike Bernie, I was never an adventurous eater. He had already eaten at their home several times, and he survived. So when I asked Janice what they were going to have that particular Sunday, her answer terrified me. "I don't know, probably sauce." Sauce? Who the hell ate just sauce? I envisioned lots of old men and women talking Italian and drinking bowls of spaghetti sauce. Not me! I declined more than a few invitations without asking for any clarification about sauce. Later on, I found out that "sauce" was a generic term they used to refer to some type of pasta (spaghetti, rigatoni, lasagna, etc.), and it was delicious. Stupid, bigoted, and provincial me missed out on a lot of fine meals!

College? Me? Really?

1964

I loved everything about going to college. It was only one course, but I felt like this is now where I was supposed to be. There were several colleges and universities within the area, but none of them had such a well-established night school program as did the university I chose. Also, because it was a state university, the tuition was very cheap. I also had a vivid memory of a tour of the campus that my friend Bob Wrestler took me on a couple of years earlier when he was an engineering student there. It was just after they had opened several new buildings, and as Bob took me through them, I was impressed with the campus while at the same time envious of those who could enter there. Never did I think that I would ever be one of them.

It did gnaw at me, however, that I hadn't started going to college sooner than age twenty-two. This was the age when most people were finishing college, not starting. There was old disparity trying to get into my thought process, but I shut it down with counter-thoughts like, *At least I'm doing it, Better late than never, I'll get more out of it because of my other life experiences,* and so forth. It worked! In my mind, I was telling, and sometimes yelling at, my old nemesis disparity to shut up and get the hell out! This worked too. Most of the time.

Putting the university parking sticker on my car, buying a university sweatshirt, and going to the bookstore were thrilling experiences for me. Thrilling? Yes, because these were actions that further convinced me that bit by bit I was, in fact, becoming a college student. Buying a notebook with the university shield on the front with the philosophy encircling it was something else that emboldened me: "Let each become all he is capable of being." This was for me! It was also reminiscent of my friend Corey Matthews' message that "you can be anything you want to be."

So I was back to my old routine where I worked as a janitor all day, fixed and ate dinner there at the school, and drove to the university for my class in English composition. I think I chose this course to start with because in high school I usually didn't struggle as much with English as I did other courses. My friend Herman at the grammar school helped me create a fine study area in the electrical room. This room would serve as my study place for the next few years as I continued on my college journey. It was clean and, best of all, quiet. It also was conveniently located if my uncle or anyone else needed me.

My Uncle Bern was once again saving me. Five years ago, he not only gave me a job when I desperately needed it but he also didn't fire me when I got arrested and was put on probation. He also tolerated my "party days" when I was often late or worked in a lethargic and hungover condition. Now here he was again, letting me study on his time as long as my work was done. Uncle Bern gave me the chance more than once to save my own life and become all that I could be. Thanks, Unc.

Ma and the rest of the family were proud of me going to college, but as is the wont of the Taltys, they were hesitant to get too excited because we often didn't finish things we started. However, Tommy was always encouraging because he too started and completed college later in life. His letters always let me know that he was proud of me, and there was an implied confidence that I could do this. With a common bond around the theme of using education to improve ourselves, we enjoyed a lifetime of many rewarding conversations.

~~~~

Although I was now officially enrolled in a college course, before I could engage in the learning process, I had to stop being so damn nervous. Disparity reigned as I watched and listened with great intimidation to how well other students responded to the professor's questions. Typically of me at the time, I generated my own profound level of anxiety whenever I felt like I didn't belong. My English professor was a nice guy, but he had expectations for us that were especially daunting for me. He expected us to read the books he had us buy. There were seven of them. Besides just reading them, we had to interpret and analyze them. Then we had to discuss them in class and write analytical papers about them. Reading itself was onerous for me because I was never made to read with this level of intensity and discernment. No matter, I just had to bear down and get it done.

My reading was made more laborious because of my weak vocabulary. I spent a lot of time looking up words I should have known. Because reading was not something I had done enough of, there were numerous words I had never seen. There certainly could not be much analysis going on if I didn't even understand the words. It was a slow-going and cumbersome process as I looked up six to ten words on each page in the large dictionary Tommy gave me. Then in the university bookstore, I found a little dictionary that defined thousands of words using just one or two words. This greatly sped up my reading because I could quickly define the word and write the terse definition right in the book. Then, each time I reread the book as part of the analysis, I could use my handwritten little definitions to understand the passage. My vocabulary also grew in this process, so I didn't need to look up as many words as the semester moved on. Hey, I was getting educated!

I now know that I made my college experience more difficult because of always doing it on my own. I read the course catalog carefully and followed the directives put forth. However, I never sought out a tutor or went to an adviser. I was embarrassed that I did not have the academic background that my fellow classmates had. I may have been thinking something crazy, like if they find out how poorly prepared I was, they would throw me out. I also

College? Me? Really?

made it harder by never asking any of my professors for help or ever consulting with the stronger students.

Although I overcame the laborious way I was reading and defining words, I got discouraged with the writing assignments themselves. That is, until I got some wonderful advice from a good friend of Bernie's, Bob Wizard.* Bob really was smart. He also liked to relax in a tavern after working all day as a caseworker. He would sometimes come into my favorite tavern where I only went once in a while now. With his college education and great command of language, he was a good person for me to talk to. He gave me a piece of advice I never forgot and have used repeatedly for over fifty years.

It was back in 1964 on a hot summer night when I was struggling to write an analytical paper about one of the seven books I had to read for my English course that I decided to take a break and go out. I went to my old hangout and was delighted to see Bob Wizard there. He was always very encouraging about me going to college. However, before I could have the life-changing conversation with Bob, I got whacked by a casual comment by a guy I didn't know sitting to my right at the bar. He overheard Bob asking me about college when this guy asked me how far along I was in my studies. Before I could answer, he followed with the fact that he had gone to the university for three years but dropped out. When I told him that I was just taking my first course, he did some quick and depressing math and then sarcastically said, "Let's see, you're taking English 101, worth 3 credit hours, and you need 128 credit hours for a bachelor's degree. So you only have 125 credit hours to go. At this rate of taking 9 credits a year, you will graduate in about 14 years." This depressing description of the long road ahead was not what I needed to hear.

Bob shifted the conversation away from this doom-and-gloom guy by asking specifically what kind of paper I was working on. When I explained what I was trying to write and how frustrating and unproductive my time had been, he gave me a real pearl. He said, "Remember, writing is 80 percent thinking and 20 percent writing. Don't try to write until you have done the thinking. The writing goes much easier after that." He didn't tell me where he got this from or if he made it up. It didn't matter because I found out that he was absolutely right. I never forgot this approach and have used it throughout my career with very rewarding results. Thank you, Bob!

This was all long before computers and word processing, so having to type all my papers was also a problem. I didn't own a typewriter, and even if I did, that typing course I took last year would not have enabled me to meet the deadlines imposed by the professor. Once again, my sister Sue was my savior. I asked her if she would like to type my papers, and I would pay her per page. She said sure. She had a manual typewriter, was an excellent typist, and found typing enjoyable and relaxing. So I would write all my papers in longhand as neatly as I could (cursive writing was also never one of my strengths), take them to Sue's, and then pick them up when she was done. As time-consuming as the whole process was, it was well worth it because I never lost points for typographical errors.

As the course progressed and my confidence grew, I went ahead and registered for three courses for the fall. It was easy to follow the path toward a college degree just by reading the college catalog. I knew what distribution requirements I would need regardless of my major. Because of my perception that I was so far behind other people my age, I decided to take courses year-round in an effort to catch up. It took organization in my scheduling to not take courses during the year that were also offered in the summer, therefore assuring that there would always be the courses offered in the fall and spring that I needed.

I took required courses but often added an elective in fields that I was curious about. The readings were difficult and extensive, but I didn't mind. I loved learning stuff that helped me understand myself as well as the world. Reading the classics and all the great authors like Kesey, Hemingway, Thoreau, Faulkner, Steinbeck, Melville, and so forth as well as the poets like Whitman and Emily Dickinson all made me feel and think differently. Then I really came to comprehend and love their writings when I went to class. The university had wonderful professors, and they all helped me really appreciate the messages in the readings. Talking with Tommy about books we had read in common gave an added benefit to my studies.

I also loved the social sciences like sociology, psychology, and anthropology. These helped me better understand my own human behavior and society as a whole. I learned from these social science courses that I was well on my way to becoming a racist and a bigot before I got to the university. Apparently, I had absorbed or internalized the perspectives of the people that raised me and that I hung around with growing up. My old neighborhood was almost entirely a white community. Dad often used the terms "nigger" or "darkie" to refer to black people. He would scrutinize performers on TV, like Eartha Kitt, to ascertain if they had "nigger blood" in them. If he liked them as performers, he would say something like, "Boy, that nigger girl can sing." Even my kind and accepting mother played a part in communicating how people who were not white were inferior. This got a bit outlandish as she explained in passing about how much worse the smell was of a bowel movement of a "colored baby" as opposed to a white baby in the nursery at the hospital. She was always quick to add in recalling this perspective gained at her hospital job: "That's even what the nurses said." My sister Sue had a whole layering of the races delineated when it came to housing: "Whites that sell their houses to niggers are the lowest, but if they do, then the niggers who buy them will sell to spics (Hispanics), and the spics to dagos. Each one moves in and wrecks the places so bad that the only people that will buy them are people poorer than themselves." Wow! What a culture for me to understand but discard!

I remember when the Big Store decided to be forward thinking in 1965 and hired a black man, but not as a janitor or stock boy but to work on the floor selling shirts and ties. It was a difficult time for many of the white employees who held on to stereotypes, but they modified their thinking when they saw the poise and professionalism in which this young man carried out his responsibilities. He was also a college student, and that further exploded the myths that were operating among them (us). These powerful messages are just some of the perspectives I was carrying when I entered college. Thankfully, this was an added benefit of my education. I learned how ridiculous and unfounded those perspectives were and was able to discard them one by one.

The History of England course where I read all four volumes of Winston Churchill's take on England's fascinating history gave me a whole different view of American history. When I took biology, botany, and other "hard sciences," I found out why they were so termed. They were hard! The preparation for each lecture was hard, and then I had the lab sessions each week that was just as demanding. No matter, I dug in and got through them all.

Along the way I discovered what the word "sophomoric" meant; it sure did fit me regardless of what year I was in. Here is the definition of sophomoric that described me in those days with my newly discovered "wisdom": *"suggestive of or resembling the traditional college sophomore; intellectually pretentious, overconfident, conceited, etc., but immature."* That sure was me. I remember being like that a lot, and I must have been a burden for my family, especially poor Janice. Thankfully, she loves me and has a very forgiving nature. Also, thankfully, the rest of the family tolerated this phase of my education and later on even came to value and draw upon my burgeoning expertise throughout the years.

~~~~

As I was emerging from my sophomoric phase, I happened to read an article in *Reader's Digest* while waiting in the dentist's office that galvanized me and provided a focus and less sophomoric approach to my education. This article talked about a guy about twenty-five years old who was taking college courses without a concentration (sounds like me). He then decided that helping people was his mission in life, and he decided to become a social worker. This article inspired me to do the same. The idea of helping people fit with my early life experience of growing up in a troubled family. I felt these experiences would give me empathy that would then enable me to be highly successful in this role. I never intended to go to college to become rich, and so becoming a social worker would certainly be consistent with this ethos of helping people. Actually, I felt the learning I was acquiring was enough of a reward in itself, but to have it all result in a satisfying career was a bonus.

~~~~

Things were stable at home and enabled me to really focus on my studies. Everyone was in good health for a change. Although Pat was now home, he encountered a tight job market. Jobs were not plentiful for someone in his situation, but he doggedly applied to all kinds of organizations. He found jobs as a dishwasher, shoe salesman, grocery store stock boy, magazine salesman, and so forth, but none of them lasted long. I did his income taxes for him that year, and he had thirteen W-2 forms that illustrated how much he persevered without permanent results.

Danny and his girlfriend, Susie, decided to marry even though he still had a few years of service required in the navy. Subsequently, Susie gave birth to a baby boy (David) and a little girl (Lisa) a couple of years later. They struggled on through some difficult times with Ma and the rest of us often getting pulled into their turbulence.

~~~~

Bernie and Annie married on July 25, 1964, with Janice as the maid of honor and me as the best man. It was a big wedding. Actually, it was a wedding like no one in our family had ever attended or even heard about except with rich society people. In our minds we viewed it like a high society kind of wedding, and we were very proud to be a part of it in some way.

Janice and I continued to "go together" as I progressed along at the university. I found that our age difference was not a factor because Janice was very mature and flexible. She had to be flexible because my schedule did not allow for a lot of social time. With most of my former social group now married, it was a natural transition to now do couples things with house parties where I took Janice as my date.

She got along great with all of them besides being a good fit with my family. Of course, with my brother married to her sister, she had easy entrée.

I had given up my job at the Big Store soon after I had one more interesting assignment diverging from my stock boy and entertainer roles. They asked me to guard the furs in the better dresses department while a big sale was going on. I had to dress up in a suit, which was a problem because I didn't yet know how to tie a tie. A friend at the Big Store would tie it for me each night as I rushed over to where he was selling shoes just before I went on duty.

Another coincidence with this assignment was that Janice had a job in the same department putting the dresses back on the racks after they were left in the dressing room. My job was easy but very boring. I had to keep circling among the few racks of furs and repeatedly count them. When it appeared that no supervisors were in the area, I would put a chair in an area between some coats and take a nap. Janice would remain alert and sometimes awaken me if one of the managers came around. Although Janice witnessed how quickly I could fall asleep, it would not be the last time she would observe this phenomenon. This was just a two-week sale, so when it was done, so was I.

My course load was about to intensify with the addition of biology with a lab to my full-time load at night school. This would mean that I would be in school four nights a week, so I gave my notice at the Big Store. I had a car payment and other expenses, so I took on some freelance gardening and painting jobs. These gave me some additional income, and I could decline them when my courses got too demanding.

Marriage: What a Concept!

With Bernie and Annie and most of my friends all married, Janice and I were also discussing getting married but in vague and general terms, but I never actually proposed to her. Without talking to anyone (especially Janice!), I reasoned out that it would be a good idea for us to get married for a whole lot of reasons and that we should do this soon. Why wait? With my work and school schedule, we didn't get to see each other as much as we would have both liked to and living together would save all that time of me going back and forth from my house to hers.

Another reason I did not want to wait, albeit a selfish one, was because I didn't want Janice to find someone else. I was worried that with her being younger and having friends closer to her own age that she may become wary of this "old guy" who kept coming around and instead look for a young stud.

There was also the compatibility factor. With my tendency to jump into things and then figure it out as I went, I needed someone to ask questions in a way that I could hear them and stop and better assess what I was about to do. One of Janice's many strengths was her logical and practical view of everything, all done with her calm demeanor. However, she was more comfortable staying at the analysis level without taking any action, so she needed someone like me who was unafraid and actually sought risks. Compatibility was the strength of our relationship from the beginning, and I could see us going far with such a strong and consonant base.

So the only part I needed help with was in selecting an engagement ring. I think most guys make this purchase in concert with their intended, but I thought it would be better to surprise her. My sister Sue and Ma were the only ones who knew what I was planning. Sue went with me to a local jewelry store, and together we found an engagement ring that we both felt Janice would like. It did seem pretty strange to Sue that I was getting engaged in the way I planned without an actual proposal and acceptance, but she still helped me select the best ring I could afford.

~~~~

My plan for giving Janice the ring was something else I thought up, and I have not met anyone else who has done it this way. I decided I would do it on a Friday night (August 6, 1964). I was painting apartments as one of my side jobs in a large building that a friend of mine owned. I didn't have classes on Fridays and this house was located very near Janice's home. So we had gotten into the habit of me joining Janice and her mother and Aunt Florence for dinner on Fridays.

To prepare for the presentation of the ring, I bought a box of candy. I then took out two pieces of candy, put the ring box in their place, and wrapped everything back up. When I came in, I gave the candy to Janice, and I said, "Oh, here. The lady who lives in the apartment I'm painting gave me this. You can have it." She said, in her logical way, "You should have said you bought it."

Then my plan went a bit awry. Janice put the candy away! So to get the plan back on track, I said, "Why don't you open the candy? I'd like a piece." Ever practical and ever mature Janice responded in typical fashion and admonished me that I might "spoil my dinner." After one more bit of my whining, she opened the candy and immediately saw the ring box. She asked, "Is it real?" Janice's response may seem odd, but just a few days earlier I had given her a fake ring as a joke. But when she saw this ring, she was pretty sure it wasn't a fake. She then showed the ring to her mother and aunt who witnessed all this while sitting at their kitchen table. It then got real crazy as the three of them started crying and rushed into a back bedroom. I figured I screwed this up, and they were all mad at me for not informing any of them of my intentions. It turned out that they were actually overcome with joy. Whew! Janice then called her sister Annie and surprised her and Bernie also. Since I had to get back to my painting, I could not join them for a celebratory dinner. This happened on the following Friday when Bernie and Annie were able to join us.

It may seem rash and unusual that I would proceed with buying the ring and sort of rushing us into marriage, but this was more thought out than it may appear, at least on my part. I had had some experience with girlfriends and girls in general, but I had not gone out with anyone like Janice. She was so different. Her reasonableness and what a friend of mine described as "a steady and balanced nature" was not something I saw in other girls or in even women with whom I interacted. I knew that a person like me, who was impulsive, a big risk-taker, and so focused on things that I often missed the essence of people could not marry someone just like me. It would have been cataclysmic. Instead, I envisioned a partnership based on compatible strengths, and in Janice I believed I found such a person. And on top of all that, I loved her tremendously.

So now we had to put the plan to work. The next day Janice and I got together and organized a schedule for our getting married. It seemed that the only day where I could be off from work at my janitor's job was in conjunction with Election Day. I had off that Tuesday, and if I stayed late on Friday to do my Saturday work, the only day I would have to ask my uncle to be off was that Monday. It would be a brief honeymoon, but it's all the time I could afford away from my classes.

The time from August 6th when we got engaged until October 30th when we were married went by very fast. To expedite the planning process, I abdicated. I was very busy and confident that they did not need me to make the myriad decisions that had to be made. Janice and her mother handled the wedding, while Janice and I concentrated on finding and furnishing our first apartment.

My already strong relationship with Bernie got even stronger, as the four of us (Bernie, Annie, Janice, and me) became a family within the family. The four of us had so much in common at this stage of our lives that the sister and brother bonds became tighter as we married and remained each other's best friends. It was always a unique and treasured part of my life whenever the four of us got together, regardless of the purpose.

Our First Apartment

In planning where we were going to live after we got married, Janice and I decided that it made sense to find a place near the university and the school where I continued to work as a janitor. Because I spent sixty or more hours per week between these two places, it made sense to live close to them. We just had one car, so we also had to find an apartment close to a bus route for Janice. The place we finally found was just six blocks from my job, so I could walk it, and Janice could take the car to her job in the accounting department of a downtown department store. She would be home in plenty of time for us to have supper together before I headed off to the university for my night classes.

We were not getting married until October 30th, but the apartment was available for us to move our furniture and stuff into beforehand. With some careful shopping and the generosity of friends and relatives at Janice's showers, we were able to get everything we needed and in place before the wedding. In the process, I had confirmation that Janice was a practical and thrifty shopper.

We were married in the same church as Annie and Bernie the previous summer. After a quick drive through the Adirondack Mountains, we ended up in a beautiful resort area. Because it was late in the fall most of the places were closed and the leaves were off the trees, but it was still beautiful, and we had a great time. Too soon we were back home, settled into our little apartment, and engaged in the full craziness of my schedule. One of the things we bought was a small desk that we put in the closet off the living room. It was this place where I spent many hours studying. Janice showed great fortitude and patience in giving me the time to work on my studies. I did not find college easy and was working very hard just to maintain a C+ or B- average.

In spite of my busy schedule, we still found time to attend a lot of family functions, and go out to dinner most Fridays with Annie and Bernie, Janice's mother and Aunt Florence. We also attended most the Talty family gatherings at my mother's house often to watch football games on Sundays. There was a great contrast between our families. Janice's family may have a glass of wine or two at dinner, but no one ever got drunk. The Taltys were very different. When we gathered, we drank, and it was never just a glass or two. Oh, no! We Talty boys got very drunk and had a lot of laughs while doing so. Once again, we were fortunate that our drunken gatherings did not end in any auto accidents or other tragedies.

~~~~

A sequence of events took place that posed somewhat of a financial strain for Ma. When Dad died, the railroad pension Ma received was reduced significantly. Then she lost the money Bernie and I had been paying her for our room and board when we got married and moved out. Add to this Pat's inability to find a steady job. All of it together forced Ma to go out and find a job.

She went to the nearby plaza and put in applications at several stores. She got a call a few days later and ended up working at a department store as a saleslady. It wasn't a well-paying job, and she had to always be on her feet, but it gave her the financial relief she needed. Getting back and forth to work proved to be quite a challenge because she did not have a car and the bus connections were not very compatible with her work schedule. However, she stuck with it until an unexpected opportunity came her way.

Bernie's wife, Annie, after she returned from their honeymoon, had resumed her duties managing the tobacco and candy concession department within the Big Store. On busy days, she would hire Ma for extra assistance, which Ma did in addition to her department store job that she had come to dislike for a number of reasons. Then she got a break. One day, while she was working for Annie, she decided to put in an application at the Big Store, which was a separate entity from Annie's tobacco and candy concession. Ma had become a familiar face to the store personnel, and so they hired her. Quitting her prior department store job was no problem. It was actually a delight.

Ma's job at the Big Store was not full time, but they said they would move her into a full-time position in a few months and thus into their excellent profit-sharing plan. Sadly, this was not the way it went. Ma was assigned to what the Big Store called their "Flying Squad". She was not given forty hours or benefits, and her schedule was as erratic as the departments to which she was assigned. It might be pets one day or sometimes only part of a day and then to dresses or housewares. On other days, she could be selling hardware or sporting goods. She never knew where she would be working. This was all very stressful and chaotic for her. However, she needed the job and had hopes that any day they would move her into the position they originally promised her.

One good thing that happened when she joined the Big Store is that she met people with cars who lived near her and were happy to pick her up and bring her home. After several months of what I called "Flying Squad hell", the Big Store finally relented and gave her the position she so desperately wanted and needed. She was now a forty-hour-per-week employee with benefits, including her coveted profit sharing.

Janitor No More!
I Become a Steelworker, Sort of!

One day, while at work, Ma encountered a man who was married to Ceil, a good friend of hers and also my godmother who had died a few years ago. Ceil was originally married to Ma's brother Wasson, but they had divorced long ago. Theirs was a tumultuous relationship due to his drinking. They also lost a little girl, Alice, to cancer when she was only ten years old. Alice was Sue's best friend, and she often spoke of her and the difficult life and death she had. Ceil subsequently married Steve Steelguy,* and that is who Ma saw at the Big Store that day. They talked a bit, and he asked if she would like to go out sometime, and Ma said sure. This chance encounter would change my life so dramatically that I still marvel about it all today.

Around this same time I began thinking that perhaps I could earn more money if I had a different job. Janitors were not highly regarded or rewarded. I also did not receive benefits like health insurance or retirement (sounds to me like a lot of disparity was operating). It was in this disgruntled state that a social situation turned into a career opportunity. Besides my working and going to school, there were social commitments that I felt compelled to host at times. It was when Janice and I invited Ma and her new "beau" (our term) Steve to spend the evening with us in our little apartment that opportunity knocked. No, it really didn't! I sort of pushed open the door but in a respectful way. This was in the summer of 1966.

Janitor No More! I Become a Steelworker, Sort of!

The evening was pleasant, and Steve was a nice person who seemed to care a lot about Ma. In fact, he cared a lot more about Ma than she did about him. Ma was lonesome since Dad died, and Bernie and I had gotten married, but apparently Steve was not the person to fill the void. At this stage of their relationship, he was unaware of her true feelings toward him, which worked in my favor.

Because Steve had been married to my godmother, Ceil, I knew him a bit growing up, as he and Ceil would come visit us at various times. I guess this prior connection and his attraction to Ma, coupled with a few bottles of "beer-courage" all helping, I asked him if he could get me a job at the steel plant. He had worked at the plant for over thirty years and had a well-paying job as a "roll turner." This, I came to learn, was a skilled craftsman. He said he would see what he could do and that he would call me in a few days. He took my phone number, and I waited. I knew that this was a downward turn for employment at the plant, so I wasn't expecting much to come of my request.

Surprise! Surprise and anxiety! Steve called me and said it was all set. He gave me specific instructions about how I was to go about the application process. When I handed in my application, I was told to say, "Fred Friend* said for me to tell you to call him about this (my application)." I had no idea of who Fred Friend was. The anxiety I felt was also about asking my crabby Uncle Bern for time off without telling him what it was for. In the past, the only time I had to ask for time off was when I had court dates related to my earlier misdeeds. I didn't want to lie to him in case I did get the job and had to have another anxious conversation when I resigned. So after I brought him his lunch that he paid for from the local restaurant (which I did every day, plus getting his morning coffee) I just said with great apprehension and rapidity, "On Monday, I have some stuff I have to take care of, and the office I need to visit isn't open at night." Okay, got that out. "Would it be okay if I left for a few hours after I got the gym and shower rooms all cleaned? I should be back in time to clean the cafeteria." Then came a jolt! He said pleasantly, "Sure, go ahead." This absolutely was not the way he responded to any of my previous requests for anything, but who cares. I was free, without having to lie, to go and apply for the steel plant job.

That Monday I went out to the steel plant's employment office, wondering what the hell I was doing. Will I get the job? If I get the job, could I handle it and go to school full time during the day if necessary?

The employment office had a large open room with about thirty desk chairs set up in rows. Almost all the chairs were filled with guys filling out application forms. I picked up the form from the man at the desk who seemed to be running things and took an open seat in the front row right across from the guy in charge. This was not going well. After completing the application, you had to hand it in to the guy at the desk. He looked over each application as if it were a pizza with the wrong toppings. He then seemed to enjoy saying in the most droning and punctilious way to every applicant, "We are not hiring at the present time. We will keep your application on file and notify you if something opens up." Each application was added to the growing stack as more guys entered the room and filled out their applications.

So now I am figuring that Steve Steelguy is either mistaken about the hiring situation or his ego drove him to get me out here just to impress Ma for some reason. I had myself convinced that this was a waste of time, but I knew I had to see what happens doing it Steve's way. I handed in my application and said my practiced phrase, "Fred Friend said for you to call him about this" as I gestured to my completed application. Surprise! He didn't say his repetitive statement. Instead, he immediately dialed the phone, talked for about a minute to someone, hung up, filled out a card, and said, "Go out this door (not the one I came in), turn right, walk straight back until you see the infirmary on the left. You're hired, but you got to pass our physical. It's not an extensive physical." He was smiling the whole time he said this, which is something I hadn't seen him do prior to his making that phone call.

He was right. The physical was pretty cursory; all done in ten minutes. I was then sent back to the employment office with a card saying I was physically ready to work. I filled out some more forms and was then taken to a supply room where I was given my first pair of "Metatarsals" (heavy work boots with a steel flap covering the top of the foot), a pair of safety glasses, and a brown hard hat that signified that I was a laborer. I didn't dare ask for work boots in two different sizes, I was just happy to have the job. He told me to be there at 7:00 a.m. on Monday, which was not possible. I had the pressure of giving my notice to my gruff uncle of whom I was always intimidated. I told them that I could start in two weeks from Monday. I think if I had not had Fred Friend's blessing, they would not have held the job for me, but I did, so they had to accept my stated start date.

I got back to work in time to talk to my uncle. I explained that I had gotten a new job at the steel plant. He said, not in a kind way, "What the hell did you do that for? They'll lay you off in a few months, and then where will you be?" I started to thank him for the job he gave me seven years ago, but he walked away muttering (growling?) before I could get it out. He turned around after a few feet and asked in a surprising calm voice, "When are you leaving?" I said in two weeks, to which he growled something unintelligible and then really did walk away. His response really didn't matter. I was no longer a janitor and excited to be a steelworker. At least I was until I started working there.

~~~~

I started work at the steel plant as a laborer in the Roll Shop in September of 1966. It was a dirty, hard, noisy, hot, and boring job. The part of steelmaking that I was involved in was not steelmaking at all. It was more of a maintenance or support operation. Once steel was forged into thick blocks, it was then run through a series of rollers to increase its length without increasing its width until it was the proper thickness for a customer's specifications. After several tons of steel had been run through these giant rollers (picture a series of rollers on a giant wringer washing machine), the rolls became worn

Janitor No More! I Become a Steelworker, Sort of!

in an uneven way. The rolls were then removed and transported with a large overhead crane to one of two Roll Shops via railroad cars (coincidently the railway was my Dad's former employer) where they were then placed in giant lathes where roll turners (like Steve Steelguy) would skillfully grind and restore the rolls to their specified working condition.

The grinding process produced shavings of steel scrap that fell into a pit under one of the thirty or so mega lathes that stretched on down the mill. My disgusting job as a laborer was to climb down into these pits and—using a shovel, rake, and pitchfork—get the steel scrap pieces up and out into a large wheelbarrow and then into dumpsters. Being the newest person I didn't expect to be embraced and welcomed into the group, but there was a coldness in the way they that these men interacted with me. I was puzzled by it.

And then I got it! I didn't figure it out on my own. This came about after a few weeks while I was being trained on a new job as a "Hooker". Hookers (not that kind) were the guys that followed the high overhead crane running up and down the shop and hooked objects onto large cables for the crane to lift and move to their intended place and then unhooked. It paid more, and I didn't have go down in those damn pits and "shovel scrap." I could walk around, breathe cleaner air, and even talk to people like the guy training me. This guy was pretty friendly, and as we got to know each other, he asked, "When are you leaving to go back to college?" I was surprised that he thought I was leaving, and so I explained that I went to college at night and worked here during the day. I wasn't leaving. When he heard this, he changed completely and helped me understand why no one talked to me.

It seemed this department hired several college students who were home for the summer. The problem was that many of them were sons or somehow related to the senior guys in the shop. He described these college students as "spoiled brats, lazy, and immature as hell." Because they were "connected" to guys with influence in the shop, no one could tell them what to do, and if they did, they would tell their Dad or whoever who would then berate them and their supervisor. As a result, this group of workers hated summer college students, and they assumed I was one of them who was just leaving a little later than all the others. I told this guy to let them know that my story and status was different, and so was I. He said he would. I didn't know if he did or not because my situation changed due to the timely intervention by another guardian angel that I didn't even know I had.

~~~~

As it turned out, I wouldn't need my fellow hooker's intervention. One day after I punched in and started to head over to one of the pits, a foreman called me over and said, "You're now working out at the Strip Mill at 6 gate. The roll shop is the first building on the left. Go in the office and ask for Mike Shamrock.*" I asked why I was being transferred, but he had no other information. He was just the messenger. I had no idea what was going on, but I had no choice but to head out to 6 gate.

~~~~

Anyway, I found the office. There were actually two offices with a connecting door. The outer office had some guys doing paperwork, and they told me to go through the connecting door to find Mike Shamrock. He was a leprechaun of a man, short in stature, with a red face, a kind smile, and a soft voice. When he asked if I was Catherine Talty's son, it was in a way that I felt he was really hoping and praying that I was. The warmth he exuded when I told him that I was indeed Catherine's son filled the room. He asked, "How is your mom? She is a fine person. I have known her almost all my life. I knew your Dad too." He didn't have anything to say about Dad, but he knew he had been sick and wondered how he was. When I told him Dad had died, he seemed genuinely sad and offered his condolences.

This pleasant conversation moved on to what I was going to be doing at 6 gate. He had heard that a Peter Talty was working at the main Roll Shop and was pretty sure I was Catherine and Tom's son.

So he arranged to have me transferred to his department. He was the general foreman and wielded a lot of power and influence within the plant. He had also heard that I was going to college and wanted to know what I was studying. As I sat there chatting with this kind man with high status, I found it rather funny. It was quite different from shoveling scrap out of a pit. I couldn't wait to get home to tell Janice about this unexpected and miraculous reassignment.

I quickly learned that Mike Shamrock was a lover of education, loyal to his longtime friends, and greatly respected people who were putting themselves through college. He liked me right away, as I did him. His next words are with me still today: "I got you out of that scrap-digging job. That's no place for a man with a good brain. I want you to work here in our office. Sammy will show what to do. It's not hard. A chimpanzee could be trained to do it." He then introduced me to Sammy Corigliano,* the senior clerk who would supervise me and another clerk named Joey.* What a break this was! The job was easy, and the guys I worked with were fun and funny. I was taking my night school courses and now had an easy day job that was paying me much more that I earned as a janitor. Plus, I wasn't a janitor anymore!

Janice and I Move to the Old Neighborhood!

One day, after about a year at the Big Store, Ma got to talking with one of her supervisors, and he asked her if she knew of anyone who might like to rent an apartment in our old neighborhood. She said she would ask me and then get back to him. Her timing was pretty good because Janice had taken a new job as a teacher's assistant in a Catholic grammar school close to this area. Her sister Annie had the same job title in another Catholic school right near Janice's. In the old neighborhood, I would be further from the university, but closer to the steel plant. However, it was all very manageable. As Janice and I talked, the more it made sense for us to also be closer to her job as well as very close to Bernie and Annie, Sue and Jim who lived just a few houses from them, as well as Ma and Pat. Ma's suburban house had become the epicenter for Talty family gatherings, and being closer to this center of family activity was not only practical but also great fun.

So we decided to move. Our landlady did not take it well when we said we were moving at the end of October having only having been there a year. She ranted, "What am I going to do for tenants? Only trash moves in winter!" I'm not sure what this made us because we were doing just that: moving in winter. Regardless, we were moving.

The usual moving gang of Bernie, Pat, Jimmy and me was assembled, and the move went smoothly until we tried to get our queen-size mattress and box springs up the stairs. It just wouldn't fit. We even tried standing on the top of the U-Haul moving truck while trying to put it through an upstairs window that we had disassembled, but this too was unsuccessful. Then Bernie suggested that we temporarily switch our mattress and box springs with theirs that was a standard size. What a great idea! That's exactly what we did. What a brother! What a sister!

~~~~

The mattress trade was just one of thousands of good things that came from these sisters marrying these brothers. It was a most potent alliance that we forged. We supported and helped each other through some very difficult times. This was in addition to a lot of fun and laughter along the way. The four of us got closer with each year of marriage. We built a trove of joint family memories that enriched all our lives. I also loved telling people that my brother and I married sisters. It was something that gave each of us our uniqueness. Annie always loved telling people about it and ending the tale with: "Peter introduced me to Bernie, so I had to pay him back by introducing him to my sister Janice."

Janice and I then established a routine whereby we each went to work—she took the bus and I the car. She got done earlier than me, and so she got home in time to fix supper. I would get home an hour or so after her, shower, have supper together, and then I would head off to the university four nights a week for my classes. This was a little hectic, but we got it down to a system that worked. One of the things I discovered about Janice was that she liked systems and structure just as much as I, so creating systems and avoiding chaos as much as possible became the way we lived. We found we could handle the occasional chaotic situation if we were organized in our daily lives. I got this from my sister Sue and Herman who trained me in my janitor's job, whereas I think Janice was just born with it.

The West Side

Adding to the emotional stress of those days of my working full time and going to school full time, Janice and I decided to move once again. Janice's mother was getting married on May 8, 1967, and then moving to Philadelphia with her new husband, Tom DePaul. She said we could move into the downstairs flat of the house that she owned at a really cheap rent. It was her thinking that this might help us financially while I finished college. It also saved her from having to move all her stuff out, and she would not be abandoning Janice's Aunt Florence who had lived in an apartment upstairs and had done so before Janice was born. So we gave our landlord our notice, called the "Talty-Riley moving crew" and moved into the West Side. This is the house where Janice grew up. Besides Aunt Florence, Janice's brother Frank's mother-in-law, Blanche McCarron, lived in the other apartment upstairs. Everyone was pleased that we were moving in, especially us. The low rent we would be paying was going to help us a lot.

It may seem like I was always and unfairly drawing on the "Talty-Riley moving crew" to move us, but in between my moves, I helped Bernie move a couple of times, Jim and Sue twice, and Danny about five times. So it was a good deal for all of us to help each other move. I also enjoyed working and joking with my brothers and Jimmy as we did each move. My brothers, Jimmy, and I all got along well and really enjoyed one another. These were great days, as we started the day with a box or two of delicious doughnuts, and a beer or two or seven at the end of the move. In between, we caught up on each other's lives as we passed each other carrying boxes or shared each end of a piece of furniture. There was also a lot of teasing and reminiscing throughout the day.

The only move that put us all in a rotten mood was on one of the several times we moved Danny's family. When we were all done with one memorable move, he told us that now we had to go move all of his mother-in-law's stuff. She was moving in with him. The Talty rage was ubiquitous and overt and got much worse when we also found out that his mother-in-law didn't know the move was that day. She asked us to go to the grocery store to get boxes. We had to pack for her! The bitching was loud and frequent as we finished the day with what we always referred to pejoratively as "the double-move day."

~~~~

Around this time Pat landed a steady job at a paint manufacturing plant where he received a fairly good pay and benefits. However, the plant was in the city, which made it challenging to coordinate buses to get him there on time. Luckily, he did make friends with a guy who would often pick him up and bring him home. This job really was a lifesaver for Pat, and he really appreciated it. It enabled him to purchase things like his new color TV, stereo, clothes, and to take two vacations. He went to New York City by himself, and he took our nephew Shawn with him to California to visit Tommy and Karoline and go to Disneyland. This was a happy time for a guy who had little joy before and after these rewarding working years ended for him too prematurely.

With Ma and Pat now both working, they began to buy things for the house like a lawn mower, a snow blower, an outdoor picnic table, a barbecue grill, and so forth that all enhanced their home. Ma loved being able to have her own home and the freedom to do what she wanted to do with it. The responsibility of dripping faucets and furnace issues produced some angst for both Pat and Ma, but these minimally impacted Ma's joy of home ownership. Both Pat and Ma got very adept at becoming friendly with some very helpful neighbors who either taught Pat how to fix different things or they fixed them themselves. Pat was pretty handy, so many times, a little guidance was all he needed.

~~~~

Danny, after getting out of the navy in June of 1967, found himself in a chaotic marriage with two very cute kids (David and Lisa). During his and Susie's frequent separations for a multitude of reasons, he would move back in with Ma and Pat. The moving in and out was unsettling for Ma, and then rather suddenly, Danny decided to move to Maryland outside of the Washington DC area by himself. We all missed him, but not nearly as much as his two kids. This was a crazy time for Danny.

Early on in Danny's marriage, Bernie and I made a feeble and futile attempt to help Danny get on track. Because of my own epiphany about education being the path out of a troubled life, I stupidly assumed this applied to everybody.

So, prior to Danny moving to Maryland, with ignorance and arrogance as my partners, I looked into a GED program that could enable Danny to finish high school. I deduced that because he essentially only had one year of high school, it would take him too long to go to the evening high school as I did. I also didn't think he had the patience and fortitude (at least I was right about this) to sustain three hours of classes for three nights a week for at least three years. So I enlisted Bernie's support to help pay for the six-week GED preparation course plus the cost of a book. It wasn't a lot of money, but at the time, for Bernie and I, it was enough that we expected to see some results. Naiveté was also at work here on both Bernie's and my part.

So with all this great information and enthusiasm for education spilling out of my dumb (sophomoric) mouth, I talked with Danny. He was impressed and appreciative of this opportunity I presented to him. I gave him the money (Bernie's and mine) and the information about the course and drove home with what was I'm sure was a very smug look on my dumb face.

A week or so later, I had to drop off something Janice wanted to give to Danny's wife. I was on my way someplace and decided to stop in even though I remembered it was the night Danny went to his GED review course. Surprise! He was home! They had bought new living room furniture that was delivered that day, and he "was so excited that he wanted to get it all put together." So he decided to skip class that night. I wasn't excited. The furniture was very cheaply made and wouldn't last as long as the payments. This was not me being haughty. It was drawing on what Janice had taught me about quality, and I was sad to think how sad they will be as their furniture deteriorated while they were still paying for it.

I wasn't just sad about him skipping his class; I was quietly enraged. Knowing how important it is to immerse oneself in the educational process, especially when he, just like me, had done it so poorly the first time through, I was enraged because this said to me that my great epiphany had not transferred to him. How could this be? I thought I was so clear and so convincing; how could he flippantly skip a class. I think I also was doing a bit of prognosticating. If he missed a class and then when he returned found himself far behind, he would quit. What a foreseer I was! That is exactly what happened. Bernie was as enraged as I, but I don't think either of us cared about the money. It was self-rage over our own naiveté that put us both in a funk. Little did we know that a greater tragedy would befall Danny that would make his dropping out of the GED course pale in comparison. This upcoming tragedy would greatly challenge and change us all.

~~~~

Another of my ventures into helping people was far more successful. One day, while I was still working as a janitor, I got my second ever on-the-job phone call. This time it was not my high school bookkeeping teacher calling to encourage me to return to class; it was Ma calling about her brother Waddy (Myles Wasson Farnham). His landlady called Ma because Waddy was acting strange, talking to himself, yelling at everyone on the street in a threatening way, and pacing about in an agitated manner scaring the neighborhood kids. We had encountered Waddy's unusual behavior before, but it was always in conjunction with his being drunk. Since it was summertime and my work was finished, my uncle did not mind my leaving early to go see what was going on with Waddy.

As I drove to Waddy's street, I wondered what I would find and how I was going to handle it. I knew I was destined for a career in helping people, but I had had no real training to be jumping into this present situation. Was this my disparity working or just common sense? I would know soon enough.

Waddy was sitting on the front steps of his boarding house when I pulled up and he was really glad to see me, which was a good beginning. I sat next to him on the steps and chatted about I don't know what. He was repeating himself a lot, like he kept saying "Pete, Pete, Pete" and then laughing uproariously. I noticed that the kids who came by looked at him with fear as they rushed on by. When I asked how he was feeling, his response gave me an opportunity to act. He said, "I don't feel so good. I have a little 'sugar,' and I think that's acting up." I knew from experience that he had a high regard for the Veteran's Hospital, so I said, "Let's take a ride up to the Vets and get you checked out." He surprised me by readily agreeing, getting up, and heading to my car.

At the Veterans Hospital, they talked with him briefly, but they told me that his was not a medical condition. They told me to take him to another hospital because they felt he needed psychiatric care. He also liked the hospital they suggested, so again there was no resistance when I said we had to go there. It was just a ten-minute ride. He was still in a pleasant mood, talking in a hard-to-follow way and then laugh, laugh, laugh.

I was very impressed with the kind and respectful way the staff treated my uncle in the emergency room. Having been through this process before with a few family members I knew what the psychiatric assessment would entail and waited patiently with Waddy for the psychiatrist to appear. He was a young resident whose name no longer exists in my memory bank, but I will never forget how he handled himself and respectfully interacted with us. After talking with Waddy for about twenty minutes in a side room, he then talked to me out in the hall.

The psychiatrist told me that he thought the best thing to do was to admit Waddy to the psychiatric unit. It was his thinking that Waddy was very lonely as well as very depressed. This surprised me because I always thought he was a loner and liked being alone. It made me very sad to think of him alone while we were enjoying a rich and fun life with the rest of the family. He would show up at some family gatherings but often in a drunk and annoying state.

Regrettably, we were not warm and welcoming. In fact, I physically threw him out of our Polishtown flat when he was so drunk and belligerent that he had Ma crying. I sure regretted that then and still do now.

When I went in to see Waddy after I left the psychiatrist to see how he was doing, he was pretty upbeat. He liked the doctor and was glad they were going to take care of his "sugar" (diabetes). That was fine with me that he was okay with being admitted, and I didn't explain about the type of hospitalization he was about to experience. In any event, I told him I would come see him tomorrow, and with that, they took him to the psychiatric unit.

I drove home in a pretty depressed state myself. The thoughts of him being unable to work, his trying to subsist on his small Welfare check, and then being alone in his little room, and then finding out that he was sad most of the time was quite distressing. As I called Ma, Bernie, Sue, and Danny and repeated what had transpired with Waddy that day, I was only further entrenched in my saddened state. Poor Janice had to hear me tell Waddy's sad story four times. By the time I finally got off the phone we were both firmly committed to helping Waddy when he went home. We were determined to get him connected to our family and to as many other components of the extended Talty family as we could generate.

It turned out that I did not have to do any generating. Bernie was up to see Waddy the next day and talked to his doctor who reinforced how lonely he had become. Waddy was doing much better because of the antidepressants that were prescribed and the kindness of the staff. He was liked by the staff, and they enjoyed how appreciative he was of any attention shown him. Bernie told Waddy that after he was discharged, he was going to have him out to his house for dinner as much as he could.

Waddy was, in fact, discharged after about two weeks. I picked him up and took him to our house for dinner. Janice, being a naturally warm and effusive person, was just what he needed. I sat and talked with him about anything that he showed energy around. He was an avid reader who walked two miles each way to check out several library books once a week. The details about the books he read seemed to be forgotten soon after he had read them. I had not talked with him much about anything, and now that I was trying to get to know him, I was the one challenged. I had never tried to closely listen and understand someone like Waddy. He was usually content and actually quite happy to float along through life with few concerns in spite of living at or below the poverty level.

~~~~

My obsession with sports carried over to Janice. She never followed sports growing up but was an apt student as I relayed information about the backstories of the athletes, game strategy, and the basics of football and college basketball. There was no such thing as taping games in those days, and if I was taking a night class or had a meeting, my able "sports apprentice" Janice would watch some athletic event I was interested in on TV and then fill me in on what I had missed when I got home. Janice's knowledge of and interest in basketball, hockey, and football surpassed that of her sister Annie and my sister Sue, which I loved.

So I decided to dial down my intensity about basketball, and just enjoy Waddy without putting any pressure on him to be anything but himself. Bernie and I had made a pact to not let Waddy wither away in isolation. We also learned that it was best to pick him up early on Sunday mornings before he could get drunk. This way he was coherent and pleasant to be around for the day even if he did have a few beers.

He loved to play pinochle, and a fun day for him was to spend a Sunday afternoon with Ma or Jim and Sue doing just that. Neither Bernie nor I were card players, so when he came to our houses, the entertainment was watching football or some other sports. Then as our kids grew, it gave him another dimension to his life. However, I always wondered if he was ever saddened to watch our kids play (especially Jill and Beth), if he thought about his deceased little girl, Alice. If he did, he never said. But we also had the warmth and love emanating from our wives that all made his Sundays and holidays to help dispel any sadness he might have felt. Our program of "orchestrated inclusion" of Waddy in the family worked very well for several years. How well this simple idea worked was a surprise. With a small effort on each of our parts, Waddy was a changed man. He wasn't depressed, and there were no more incidents like the one that precipitated his psychiatric admission.

There was however a bit of a gap that happened in our "Waddy care system" when Bernie moved out of town and Danny's family life became so unstable that having Waddy for Sunday dinner was no longer possible. This took two homes out of our planned rotation. Rather than have him just languish alone on Sundays and holidays, Janice and I took him to our house more frequently. He also still had visits to Ma's where he often stayed for a few days. Also, Sue and Jim's was sometimes a viable option for Sunday afternoon pinochle games.

Now Back to the University and Some Big Changes

Going to the university was getting increasingly more difficult as I moved into the upper-level courses, but I was also getting better at reading the voluminous assignments and writing the different papers I was assigned. I kept shifting my major back and forth between psychology and sociology. I had thought either one of these majors would be appropriate for my objective of becoming a social worker. However, this objective was fading fast with each conversation I had with practicing social workers. They bitched a lot about how unfulfilled they were and the frustrations of trying to help people who couldn't or wouldn't be helped. The frustrations also came from clients who were not motivated to help themselves, or from not having access to enough resources to have an impact on people's lives. So I decided to change my major to anthropology because I really liked the courses and I thought the nature of the work would be interesting. I had come to the conclusion that if I had to work all my life, I should find a career where I would enjoy going to work each day. I saw myself as becoming a cultural anthropologist where I could do research out in the places where different people lived in order to better understand them. This lasted for about two semesters, and then one of those things happened that took my life in a whole different direction.

~~~~

While in this state of transition, bordering on disparity, I was at the university in one of the academic buildings, waiting for the students to empty out of the room where my anthropology class was held. I was about twenty minutes early, so I was reading bulletin boards. One was all about occupational therapy (OT) as a major and career. The only thing I knew about OT is that it was something that Dad and Pat went to when they were patients at the state hospital and where they made bird houses and moccasins. This was a career? It required a college education? What the hell was it? Then I remembered that my friend Corey Matthews from the Big Store was studying to become an occupational therapist, and he spoke with great reverence and enthusiasm about it. There were a bunch of brochures, so I took one and began to look at the course requirements. I had already taken a lot of courses as I jumped in and around different majors, but fortuitously, I had taken the entire load of prerequisite courses that the OT program required. With that realization, I decided to skip my anthropology course and go up the hall and visit the OT office.

The OT secretary was very nice and suggested that I talk with one of the faculty members about the program. She then called someone who said they could see me. I don't remember who I met with, but she was also very nice and seemed very excited that I was interested in OT. Apparently, there was a need for more males in OT but few were interested. However, everything she said had a very positive effect on me. I still wanted to help people, and OT looked like an exciting way to do it. I also still had the memory of my friend Corey Matthews from my stockroom days at the Big Store. He was an impressive person in every regard. He also spoke glowingly about how occupational therapists help people overcome disabilities. Between Corey's words and those of that friendly OT professor, I felt I had found the major and career for me. There were, however, some concerns that I needed to talk over with Janice when I got home that night.

One big obstacle facing me if I were to switch from anthropology to OT was the schedule. There were no part-time options, and OT was only offered during the day. I needed to work full time, so this shift to OT as a major may not be feasible. Perhaps I could switch to the night shift at the steel plant. I just didn't know. The other concern was the timeline. I was in a four-year major with only a year and a half to go before I would earn my bachelor's degree in anthropology. OT was a five-year program including two summers, which meant I was looking at an additional hunk of time in college.

Of course, my intimate friend disparity was whispering that I was older than the other students and that I should have been graduating from college long before this. So Janice's pragmatic analysis was the key for me in this decision. She said, "So what if it takes you longer? At least you will be doing what you want to do." Well, that took care of the guilt and sense of disparity I was feeling. Gross anatomy was looming in the upcoming summer, and this was going to be a major course made even more excruciating because of my need to work full time.

Now what about my job? While I was sorting this out, I examined the OT brochure and the other materials I got from the OT department. The courses were daunting as was the nine months of internships in three different facilities. These internships were disconcerting not because of the anticipated rigors, but how would I work to support us for those nine months? I assumed these were unpaid. So how would I do an internship and work a full-time job? Lots of stressful questions that I would need to figure out.

~~~~

My troubles were still unresolved when they instantly became insignificant. Ma's phone call awoke me on a Saturday morning to say that Danny's wife, Susie, had called her to say that he had been in a very bad auto accident about forty miles out of town. She did not know anything except that he was in critical condition and in the hospital there. Susie had two little kids, plus a great deal of anxiety and other problems that precluded her from making the trip with us. So, I told Ma that I would call Bernie and that I would then pick him, her, and Pat up as soon as I could. Bernie was waiting on his porch, and we quickly made the twenty-minute ride to Ma's, and the four of us drove the forty miles to the hospital. We didn't talk much as we all imagined what we were going to find. How bad was he hurt? Would he even be alive when we got there?? What the hell was he doing there? He didn't own a car, so whose car was he driving? Was he driving?

I was driving as fast as I could because we were all so anxious about Danny's condition, but not so fast as to alarm anyone further than they already were. Whenever one of us would engage in the typical Talty catastrophic thinking, Ma would offer one of her calming idioms. "Let's not react until we get the facts" or "We cannot start going crazy until we get all the particulars." These wacky expressions did actually help us to "keep calm and carry on."

I was glad but also afraid when we finally walked into the emergency room. We were not able to see him right away, but after about twenty anxious minutes, the doctor came out to talk with us. He started by saying, "He's a very lucky boy. He is badly injured with a fractured neck, a jaw fractured in four places, and numerous cuts and bruises. He needs a team of specialists, and he needs to be transferred to a hospital with a trauma center where he can get that kind of expert care." The reason we found out later that the doctors repeatedly said "he was a very lucky boy" was because he was driving such a little car when he hit a tree. He could have easily been killed or paralyzed.

~~~~

We were finally able to see Danny but just for a few minutes because they wanted to get him ready to be transported. It was devastating for us all when we went in to see him. He was conscious and in a great deal of pain. With his fractured jaw hanging down almost to his chest, it was impossible for him to talk, and what he said we couldn't understand. With no shirt on for some reason, he looked like such a little kid to me, just like he did when he was a kid. We were all too emotional to speak ourselves, but Bernie saved us by telling Danny that we loved him, that he was getting the best of care, and that we would see him when he got to the medical center.

Bernie and I did not know what was going on when we overheard Ma approach a nurse in the hall and ask, "How is Mrs. Dimwitty*?" Dimwitty? Who the hell was Mrs. Dimwitty? Pat explained that it was a friend of Danny's named Marcy Dimwitty, and she was married to his best friend Hank. Bernie and I had never heard Hank and Marcy's last name, so we had no idea who she was inquiring about. It turned out that she only had a fractured arm and had already been discharged. Pat hung around with this group a lot more than us, so he wasn't as confused as Bernie and I when Ma inquired about Mrs. Dimwitty's condition. Of course, I think we all thought the same thing but didn't ask where were Danny and Marcy going and why?

We were all crying out in the hall as we waited for them to prepare him for the ambulance ride to the medical center. Our plan was to follow the ambulance, but the nurse said it would be better for us to wait until he is there and settled and then go up to see him in the afternoon. None of us liked that idea, so after I called Janice and Susie and Bernie called Annie, we decided something different. We stopped for breakfast on the way, which took some time, and then proceeded to the medical center. It turned out that Danny was already there, and he was sleeping. We decided to go home and come back that night.

~~~~

I often wondered how much Danny's accident brought back for Ma the memory of Tommy's devastating accident. On that awful night many years ago, a car Tommy was riding in with four other young guys struck the caboose on a moving train. Tommy was just sixteen years old, and the driver who was killed had just turned eighteen. Tommy sustained severe facial trauma and other injuries that made his survival questionable. The morbid and captivating details surrounding Tommy's accident came from Ma and Sue, which they told us in detail over the years. Ma told of Dad being taken off his engine and whisked across the vast steel plant while trying to get his work clothes off in an emergency vehicle of some sort. The steel plant officials had gotten word of the accident and of Tommy's precarious condition and were doing everything they could to get Dad to the hospital in time.

Ma also told of being in the waiting room at the hospital when the doctor gave the parents the terrible news that their only child was dead. According to Ma, the boy's father threw his hat on the floor and proceeded to jump all over it in his inconsolable grief. It was Ma's way to add a wry comment at the end of such tragic stories, and for this she pointed out that "he also ruined a perfectly good hat."

Tommy's injuries required several surgeries, extensive hospitalization, and a very long period of convalescence at home. It was a traumatic time for Tommy and the whole family. He has little memory of the accident, which was a good thing. I think Ma must have been able to divorce her feelings from Tommy's accident and thus concentrate on what Danny needed at the time.

After numerous X-rays, the specialists decided to take him to surgery. The first surgery was to drill two holes in his head and attach a clamp to his skull with a cable-and-pulley apparatus attached, which in turn held a fifteen-pound weight off the back of his bed. This grotesque apparatus provided the necessary traction on his cervical spine so it would heal and not cause damage to his spinal cord making him paralyzed. Later on in my training to become an occupational therapist, I learned that this was established treatment for cervical fractures and the apparatus was known as Crutchfield tongs. But in our ignorance at that time, we were traumatized when we saw this bizarre contraption in place. With his head shaved and the tongs so visible, it was hard for us not to be traumatized.

We were all so emotional that it was necessary for us to only be in the room with Danny for fifteen or twenty minutes. Our sister Sue could not go up to see Danny at all because it just reminded her so much of Tommy's accident. Tommy's jaw was also fractured along with a number of facial and eye injuries. We, who were at the hospital with Danny, would have to slip into the hall and cry. It was just so sad to see him in this condition, and it was about to get even worse.

~~~~

The following day Danny underwent a six-hour surgical procedure to set his fractured jaw. This necessitated the wiring of his upper and lower teeth together and the placing of permanent wires to secure the fragments of his jaw in place for healing. They also had to do a tracheotomy and insert a tube for his breathing. His lung had collapsed, and so he had a tube put in his side to get that reinflated. I will never forget the awful way he looked when they brought him down from surgery. We were able to see him just for a few minutes in the ICU, and that was really all any of us could take. I think what made the whole thing so sad for me was that his family life was so tumultuous and his life in general in such disarray that to now have this tragedy befall him seemed to just compound my sadness. It was so hard for me to study or do anything without thinking about Danny.

Before we left the hospital we organized a system of visitations. We didn't want him to be alone if we could help it. So between Bernie, Pat, Ma, and me, we set up a schedule. After a few days, Sue as well as Danny's wife Susie was able to visit Danny, and this gave us more people to join our rotating visitor system.

Miraculously, but slowly, Danny got better each day. He was very anxious about being unable to breathe because his trach tube kept clogging up. This required the nurses to suction him frequently, which was not a pleasant experience for any of us, especially Danny.

He was in the hospital for over six weeks and was discharged with what they call a halo to keep his spinal column secure as it continued to heal. Just like the Crutchfield tongs, the halo took some getting used to. He had a steel ring encircling his skull attached with four screws to his skull. Then, there were four steel rods, two in front, and two in back, each running from the ring (the halo) to his chest and back padded steel plates. This looked bizarre, but it was highly effective. He was able to walk around and do everything for himself without pain or his healing spinal column being at risk. He and Susie and the kids moved in with Ma and Pat until he would be able to return to work.

It was so good to finally see Danny get better and be discharged. It seemed his accident consumed us all, and we sort of put our own lives on hold throughout his hospitalization. For myself, I had to finish up my present courses and get ready for a challenging phase of my own life in the occupational therapy program and day school.

Another New "Job" for Me in the Steel Plant

Knowing that I had to work full time and that in a few weeks I would be starting gross anatomy, I approached Mike Shamrock about transferring to a night job at the steel plant. He was his usual encouraging and curious self. He wanted to know all about OT and was impressed that I wanted to help people with this career. It turned out that there was no night job where I was presently working (6 gate, strip mill), but there may be something back where I started at the main roll shop at 1 gate. I would have to go back to being a laborer, which meant going down in those damn pits again and shoveling scrap all night, but I had no choice. If he could get me transferred to nights doing no matter what, I was going to do it.

It worked out that I was transferred the following week, which was the beginning of my descent into hell. Nothing had changed since I was there before. It was just hotter, dirtier, and noisier than I remembered it, and the guys were not any friendlier. I spent the first night shoveling scrap, but about three o'clock in the morning when I climbed out of the pit, I was surprised that it was so quiet. What was going on? I walked around and saw all the guys sleeping on the benches behind their machines. So off I went to find a bench for me. The benches were so narrow that you had to lie on your side. I didn't care. I fell right to sleep for over an hour. I was rudely awoken when the big overhead crane started up and noisily moved down the mill to make a lift at one of the machines. I tried to go back to sleep, but in another half hour or so, the shop came alive. The big lathes started rolling, guys were yelling, and the crane, moving up and down the shop, prevented anyone from sleeping any longer.

I was exhausted from being up most of the night, but I got to sleep for six hours before I ate supper and headed off to my night classes. I was finishing the spring semester, and then I would have a week off before starting gross anatomy in the first week of June. This gave me the chance to do all the things that I would not have time to do after June like getting a haircut, having the car serviced, and any other time-consuming things. I had to be ready. Janice was also gearing up for what I was about to take on. So we got ourselves ready in any way we could, which included letting the family know that we would probably not see them much over the next six weeks.

I got a break of sorts at the steel plant because I was getting more and more opportunities to do the job as a hooker. It paid more, and I could stay above-ground and take breaks in between the lifts. I had to do it in concert with the crane operator high above. He was too high up to hear anything being said, so he relied on the hand signals that they had previously taught me. Also, he was too far up to see exactly what was going on below, so the hooker and the crane operator had to be alert to remain safe. This was a lesson I sadly forgot one critical night.

~~~~

The luxury of a job without school was over. After working all night as a laborer and sometimes hooker, I left the steel plant at the end of my shift at 7:00 a.m. I got home, showered, drank a breakfast shake and two cups of coffee, and drove to the university. I was very excited. This to me was the big time. Now I really felt like I was in college. It was day school, and I was a full-time student. Gross anatomy was taught in the main building where the medical school was housed. I was going to be in the same lecture hall and lab where medical and dental students learned anatomy.

Another New "Job" for Me in the Steel Plant

My initial excitement quickly morphed into anxiety, confusion, and outright terror. There were about sixty students in the class equally divided between OT and PT. The students seemed to already know one another, and many of them did because they had taken many of the prerequisite courses together and had been at the university since freshman year. I took a stool at one of the tables facing the front and waited for the professor to come in to start the class. As I looked around the room, I saw that many of the students had already purchased their lab coats, books, and dissection kits. Disparity was screaming "What is the matter with you? Don't you see you are not prepared (worthy)? Who do you think you are kidding?" In an effort to catch up with everyone and to shut up my rapidly escalating sense of disparity, I asked the girl next to me, "Where did you get your lab coat and stuff?" It was bad timing because the professor came in, and she angrily shushed me. This was not a good beginning. In spite of this bad beginning, we became friends over the years and ended up working together but in a way she could not tolerate. But none of that was relevant to my panic that morning.

One thing that was good was that any lethargy I was feeling from the night before quickly dissipated as I tried to take everything in. The professor gave instructions about the structure of the course, exams, lab protocol, and so forth. We would have lecture Monday through Friday mornings from eight thirty to ten thirty, have a fifteen-minute break and then the lab part of the course would run until twelve thirty. He said that there was too much material to grasp in the allotted lab time, so the lab remained open into the evening for our use. There were two rules that he stated in a severe way, "No parts of the cadavers could be removed from the lab and taken into the student union, for example." Really? "You also cannot eat your lunch in the lab." What? Who the hell would want to?

He then launched into a lecture about the anatomical position, axes, planes of motion, and numerous anatomical terms. Some of it was stuff I had gotten before, and the anatomy course I took in anthropology helped me to not get too overwhelmed. I felt just a tiny bit better when he gave us time to have lunch and go to the bookstore to buy our books (four of them including *Gray's Anatomy* and all very expensive), a lab coat, and a dissection kit. There were several dissection kits of varying prices available, but I chose a medium-priced kit. Who knew how long I was going to last, and what would I do with it after?

We returned to the lab where the professor told us to wait for him before entering. Precisely at 12:30 p.m. the professor arrived and unlocked the doors to the lab and to our anxiety. The dissection I did in my earlier courses of rats, frogs, a shark, and a pig did not prepare me for what was to come. The smell of formaldehyde hit me as soon as I walked in the room. There were four stools situated around each of forty or so large steel ominous "tanks." These were stainless steel containers about six feet long and three feet wide with a curved top. We were told to arrange ourselves in teams of four around each tank. I knew no one but saw a group of three guys who said yes when I asked if I could join them. They were all PT students consisting of Davis* from Georgia who was about my age (twenty-five), married, and had just gotten out of the air force, and two guys about twenty (Joe* and Bob*) who had been at the university since their freshman year. I would be tied to these guys throughout my next six weeks of hell. Davis and I also became very close and stayed friends throughout our time at the university.

~~~~

The next step was a surprise. The professor told us to open the tanks, which we did with trepidation, thinking that we were about to encounter a dead body. Surprise! The tanks were all empty. Each team had to go into a large refrigerated room where numerous (seventy-five?) dead bodies (cadavers) were hanging upright, held in place by steel tongs in their ears. We had to lift the cadaver up while a lab partner opened the tongs to release it, and then carry it out and place it on the perforated plate extending the length of each tank. It was a macabre and bizarre scene consisting of young people (70 percent girls) lifting and carrying cadavers about the gross lab. I learned on the first day that the term "gross" did not mean the way it is used today to describe something offensive or disgusting (even if that was what this was). No, in this context, "gross" meant the entire body.

Davis and I carried our cadaver to our tank and tried not to be appalled by it. We found out that some of the cadavers had been willed to the medical school or to science, while others were homeless people who had no one to claim their bodies. It was also unsettling to learn that some of them may have been dead for over a year. All had been embalmed with formaldehyde to delay the process of decay. This would prove to be a real issue because this was summer, the temperatures outside were in the eighties but much higher in the lab because we were on the fourth and top floor with a flat roof and there was no air conditioning.

There was a systematic way of learning that we all followed. Since the human body is symmetrical with two identical sides, dissection can occur on each side of the body simultaneously. We worked in teams of two—one guy reading information from the dissection manual and *Gray's Anatomy* and the other guy doing the actual dissection. Bob and I worked on one side of the body, alternating days of reading and dissecting, and Davis and Joe worked on the opposite side in the same way.

Using my scalpel, I made my first incision down the back and began the process of separating and identifying muscles firmly encased in fat and fascia. It was tedious work made more difficult by the heat of the room and the intensity of Bob, my lab partner. He was an intelligent and excellent student who tolerated nothing less than perfection. I was exhausted from everything so far and was very relieved when my group decided at three o'clock that we had done enough for today. Yes, I would say so!

~~~~

Driving home I thought of all the homework I had to do to prepare for lecture and lab the next day. I felt overwhelmed, inundated,

Another New "Job" for Me in the Steel Plant

engulfed, and every other word to describe someone beaten down, and this was only the first day. I was also pretty smelly from the heat and fluids in the lab, so I had to shower. Janice was getting supper ready, and I tried to go into my little office and study. I failed. I was asleep with my head on my books when Janice came to get me for supper. I ate and went back to the books with more success. After a couple of hours, I quit, lay down for a quick nap, got up, and drove to the steel plant to begin work at eleven o'clock.

The foreman said I would be shoveling scrap that night. I tried to pace myself and conserve my depleting stores of energy. I just kept moving and sleeping every few minutes down in the pits I was supposed to be cleaning out. I got yelled at a lot for being slow, but I didn't care. I watched, and as soon as I saw the crane operator climb down the long ladder for his nap and the other guys settle down on their benches for their naps, I went looking for a vacant bench.

I got to sleep for only a half hour when the foreman came and found me. He kicked the bench and told me to get to work. I had no choice. I could not afford to get fired.

This cycle of hell continued of shoveling scrap or hooking all night, going to school from eight thirty in the morning until three o'clock in the afternoon and sometimes later, getting home, showering, eating, and then trying to study in between napping at my desk. During the second week, my nightmarish life became even more so. I was hooking one night but not giving it my full attention. One of the giant rolls that I was readying for the lift shifted and crushed the end of my index finger. The crane operator must have known what happened because without me signaling, he immediately raised the roll, and I pulled my hand free. The pain was intense. I got the big hooking glove off and my finger looked like a hot dog. Crazily, all I could think of is that they are going to send me home with pay, and I will be able to sleep. With those delicious thoughts on my mind, I walked the couple hundred or so feet to the infirmary and woke up the doctor who was sleeping on a gurney. He looked at my finger, took an X-ray, and said I had a "longitudinal fracture of the distal phalanx." Rummaging through some drawers he put a metal splint on my finger and wrapped it with an elastic bandage. Next, he had me put my large hooker's glove back on, and told me to go back to work. This can't be! But it was! I had to choose between going home sick and losing the rest of the night's pay or suck it up and deal with the pain. Back to work I went, but it was a long night between my awkward movements with the splinted finger, the pain, nausea, and exhaustion. I did get through it someway.

They didn't give me anything for pain, so as soon as I got home, I started taking Bufferin, which was supposed to be the strongest over-the-counter pain medication available at that time. I took the splint off to shower, ate, and Janice wrapped my finger back up. I glanced at the reading for the day recalling that it was my turn to dissect. Hopefully, Bob will be okay with us switching off for a few days. I was wrong. He said in response to my request to switch, "Oh no, it's your turn to cut, and you have to cut. I won't do it." I wanted to beat him with my *Gray's Anatomy*, but again, I had no choice but to dissect. Keeping the wrapped finger out of the fluid was not possible, so I ended up going without the splint. The Bufferin did help the pain. I dissected the shoulder musculature and avoided severing the brachial plexus, which was a cluster of nerves that we were instructed to keep intact for future study. I did the day's dissection successfully! Screw you, Bob!

~~~~

After about three of the worst weeks of my life a wonderful thing happened. Janice discovered that she was pregnant. This was probably not the best timing, but we knew we wanted a baby. It was just a bit earlier than optimal, but I knew Janice and I would be fine with having a kid around to accompany us on the difficult path I had chosen.

~~~~

Then after another week of hell, a second wonderful thing happened, but the beginning of this incident was both confusing

Another New "Job" for Me in the Steel Plant

and disconcerting. It began when I went to punch in at the steel plant that night. There was a note paper-clipped to my time card telling me to call Jimmy Boing* in the roll shop office the next day. His phone number was included on the note, but I had no idea who Jimmy Boing was and why he would want me to call him. Anyway, I worked all night, and the next day during the break between lecture and lab, I made the call. He was pleasant and explained that they needed someone to record the tonnage at night and wondered if I was interested. Was I! This was the easy job I had at the strip mill. I said yes, and we worked out for me to meet him in the office the next morning. He would come in early at 6:00 a.m. and show me what to do and still have me out on time at 7:00 a.m.

Jimmy was the nicest guy. He had heard about me from my old friend, protector, and guardian angel Mike Shamrock. Apparently, Mike was still watching over me because he and Jimmy created this job for me! In Jimmy's terms, "this was a job that didn't need to be done, and if anyone did do it, no one would care." It seems there were boxes upon boxes containing years of tonnage reports that had data relevant to the amount of wear and tear in terms of the tons of steel rolled on the thousands of rolls the steel plant owned.

The rolls were very expensive, and thus keeping track of how much steel ran across each roll was a way of monitoring the conditions of each roll, plus a worn roll could damage the new steel being run across it. All this was true when the plant's operations were producing at a high capacity, but now as an organization it was entering its death throes, so now no one seemed to care about the conditions of old rolls from a record-keeping perspective.

My "job" was to take the numbers of tons rolled off the roll turner's production sheets and enter them onto the five-by-eight cards reserved for each roll. I had done this at the strip mill, so I really didn't need to be trained. However, as Jimmy explained, there was a lot of good news about my new job, the first of which was that I would not have a supervisor. I would report to Jimmy who worked only days. We would communicate through notes left on his desk. The office was on the third floor above the roll shop and the shop

234

foremen did not have a key. I was given my own key. The office was heaven, especially when compared to hooking or shoveling scrap out of the pits. It was clean, quiet, and best of all air-conditioned. I now could study and sleep at work without interruption. I was saved! I really believe that I would have failed gross anatomy if Mike Shamrock and Jimmy Boing had not rescued me from those pits. Thank you, Mike, and thank you, Jimmy!

~~~~

Initially, when I punched in I was very anxious about how this whole office thing was going to go over with the foremen. Jimmy had assured me that this had all been worked out and that no one would bother me. Still, I was anxious. I felt I had to resurrect some of my old Tough Guy Pete persona to pull this off. The time clock was right outside the foremen's office, so they could visually keep track of the men and communicate with them as needed as they entered and left the shop. So the routine was to punch in, turn left, and go into the shop, but not me. I went right and headed for the stairs. The sound of a rolling desk chair and the opening of the office door were followed by a loud, "Hey, Talty, where the hell do you think you're going? You're hooking tonight." During my criminal days, I had learned early on that if you're caught doing something wrong, the best response is to first vehemently deny it, and if that doesn't work then become aggressively confrontational. So I just yelled back, "Look, I was transferred upstairs to work on some important reports for Fred Friend (this was a risk because although his name got me hired eight months ago, I doubt he even remembered who I was). I continued in my old Tough Guy Pete persona as I started up the stairs yelling back, "If you have a problem with what I was told to do, you can take it up with Jimmy Boing or Fred Friend. I got work to do." Then it was up the stairs, key out, door unlocked, inside, and door locked!

In spite of my bravado downstairs, I was scared as hell when I opened the office door and turned on the office lights. I double-checked to be sure the door was locked behind me, and then I had the delicious task of turning on the air conditioner! Jimmy left me a note about enjoying my new job and not to "work too hard." I don't think he included a smiley face, but he should have.

To continue the ruse that this was a real job that really needed to be done, I laid a bunch of production sheets out on Jimmy's desk, put two other open boxes of them on the floor, and started entering my little numbers on the five-by-eight cards. I kept waiting for a fierce pounding on the door (he didn't have a key), but it never came. Did my bluff work? Was the foreman going to call Fred Friend in the morning and blow me out of the water? Nothing I could do now but continue on this brazen path.

Although I was anxious throughout the night, I did manage to get three hours of sleep and almost the same amount of studying. I had two of the smaller anatomy texts and my lecture notes in my big "lunch bag" and thus had plenty of material to go over. I arrived home quite refreshed as well as prepared for class. What a job! It truly was a miracle!

When I punched in the next night, I was not confronted. I went right up to "my office" and went right to work. I was not bothered the rest of the week, but I was not yet feeling fully confident. With the foremen on a rotating shift schedule, I was concerned that my bluffing would not work as well with the rest of them (there were four or five of them). As it turned out, no one bothered me either when I punched in or out or throughout the night. The word about my special assignment right from Fred Friend must have gotten to each of them. However, there was one younger foreman who did come knocking and yelling while I was sound asleep with the lights out one night, but I didn't open the door. That was Tough Guy Pete in action once again, or actually nonaction. I was never bothered again.

My routine was now so different. Instead of being consumed with disparity and rage toward my lab partners and fellow students who got to sleep all night, I was more like them. The only difference was that they were sleeping in beds, whereas I was making a mattress of sorts by arranging a pile of new mopheads from the janitor's closet on the top of a desk complete with a nice mop-pillow. This was after an hour's worth of tonnage recording (sometimes less), and three hours of studying. It was a great setup, and to this day, I do not specifically know how it came about or who actually orchestrated it. I do know I will always be grateful.

OT School

I passed gross anatomy, but not with any distinction. It didn't matter. I would continue into my junior year in the fall after six glorious weeks off from classes. We spent the month of August at "the Florence." This was a cottage we rented across the lake in Canada.. There were quite a few of us in this little cottage including Bernie and Annie and their newly adopted baby Jill, Sue and Jim, and then Janice and me. In addition, Danny joined us for a week or so as part of his recuperation, which was going well. He was even throwing and catching a football with us.

Even though I still had to "work" at the steel plant and drive back and forth for my 11:00 p.m. to 7:00 a.m. shift, it was a great vacation. I did not have to study! So now at work I was reading novels for pleasure, not *Gray's Anatomy*. I got to sleep more and arrived back at the cottage fairly refreshed. I would sleep a few hours in the morning and then join everyone for fun-filled and relaxing days. We would go to the big amusement park nearby that was within easy walking distance, walk around the town, and otherwise just hang out as a family. Having Danny healthy again made us all so grateful, and the whole vacation was enhanced by his presence. He brought his young son David up there for a few days, and we even brought Waddy, Pat, and Ma along. We laughed a lot and enjoyed one another very much.

Then, as in most situations like this, the month at "the Florence" became too long. We all tired of the cramped quarters with only one bathroom, and the longer commutes Bernie, Jimmy, and I still had each day to work. Tensions began to build, and we Taltys did what we often did, we got quiet and withdrew. I don't remember who left first, Bernie or I, but whoever, the other followed soon after. There was probably two weeks of good times, a few tense days, and then we left. Sue and Jim loved "the Florence" and were happy to stay for the rest of the month. They must have loved it even more with all of us out of there. Thankfully, the tenseness never led to any arguments, and we all left on good terms and resumed our good relationships once we were all back in our own homes.

~~~~

Previously, while going to night school at the university I become good friends with a guy named Larry Shrewd.* We met initially in a psychology class. He and his wife, Kim,* came up to visit us at "the Florence" and they fit in nicely with my family. Larry and I had discovered that we had a number of parallels in our lives. Although we grew up thirty miles away from each other, once we connected, we followed similar academic paths and enrolled in many of the same courses. For a brief time he was in the OT program, a year behind me, but then he switched to PT. Throughout the years it was always great being in classes with Larry because we both saw things in the same way. It also helped that we had the same sense of humor.

The parallels between Larry and I were numerous and eerie. He grew up in a small town and spent many summer days at a lake where Janice's family had a cottage. He had worked at the steel plant also at the strip mill. We were both planners and opportunists; schemers and dreamers may have better described us. Neither one of us had been married long; both a bit over two years and both of our wives became pregnant within a short time of each other. Another eerie parallel is that we had both taken up pipe smoking before we met, and both independently discovered a wonderful pipe store. We loved buying pipes and showing them to each other. In those days, smoking in class was not an issue (imagine?) and so we both lit up and smoked our way through hundreds of hours of classes.

When we both entered our separate day school curricula, we didn't see each other much, but we both did land jobs in the same medical library of a large hospital, which gave us plenty of time to study. All we had to do was reshelve books and journals, help doctors find stuff, and keep track of how many people used the library. We could work any schedule we liked, and this served us both quite well.

Getting home from "the Florence" was really good. Janice was feeling fine and was not experiencing any morning sickness. We would spend the rest of my vacation which was for me in an atypical relaxed state. Janice and I got to visit Ma and Pat as well as friends and relatives who we had put on hold during my crazy time. I also could play basketball as much I wanted to in our backyard without feeling guilty.

Hardships and Fun in the Family

The year 1967 turned out to be a better time for Sue and Jim. Their goal was to recover from the bankruptcy that the failed gas station had put them in by paying off all their creditors. It was a way of reestablishing their credit record as well as their good name. Jimmy worked a most demanding job unloading large heavy pieces of meat from railroad cars all night long, and then he performed an even more Herculean feat during the day by driving a truck to deliver this meat to grocery stores, which sometimes were over one hundred miles away. However, this horrible job did enable him to obtain the special driver's license required to drive the large semi-trucks. With this license, he was earning significantly higher wages, and he turned his family's life into a far more secure and prosperous one. I was, and still am, so impressed that he was able to accomplish this. Then when a new trucking company opened a branch in the area, he was one of their first hires as a driver. This was a prestigious and well-established company that enabled Jimmy to prosper even more. He took great pride in his new job, and as the operation grew and they added more drivers, he became the number two driver in terms of seniority among fifty or so other drivers. This gave him the right to pick the best runs and an elevated status, which he enjoyed and deserved.

~~~~

Ma was both rejoicing and suffering at the same time. Soon after the Big Store gave Ma her coveted full-time position, she developed severe pain in her legs. It was so severe that when taking the bus to work, she now had to time her arrival at the bus stop to allow enough time for her legs to recover after a three-block walk. If not, she would be unable to get up the bus steps, and thus have to wave the bus on by and wait for the next one. This latter outcome made her late for work besides giving her a large load of stress and aggravation.

Ma's doctor erroneously believed that it was arthritis that was causing her so much pain and weakness. Her condition unfortunately progressed without the correct diagnosis, making for miserable days for her. The only thing that relieved the pain was to sit down and rest after she had exerted herself, but the Big Store would not look kindly on a saleslady sitting down when on duty, so she just soldiered on.

Economically, she was in a desperate situation. Her income from my Dad's pension was greatly reduced when he died, and so a full-time job was what she needed, and now that she had it she was not going to jeopardize it for anything. Of course, her job in sales gave her no opportunity to relieve her pain by sitting down (except for her lunchtime and coffee breaks). It was constant standing and walking. Her financial plight was worsened when Pat lost his job. He had been paying Ma for room and board, but not anymore. Pat's resulting depression gave Ma even more to worry about.

I did not realize how difficult Ma's life had become until many years later. She wrote all her worries in extensive and detailed letters to my brother Tommy that I didn't get to read until a few years after her death. After venting to Tommy about her troubles, she always followed with quick and firm denials that she expected him to do anything. This was Ma's way of dealing with her problems. She would vent to someone, which I knew was therapeutic for her, but then she would reject assistance because she never wanted to "put anyone out." It was Ma's way to just pick up the load and carry it. Each of us "kids" (actually we were all adults at this time) back here in the States were unaware of how much Ma was suffering and the amount of emotional stress she was experiencing. Sue may have known to some extent because they talked on the phone almost every day. However, Ma's quick rejection of any offered help was reluctantly accepted by us without argument even as her condition worsened.

Sadly, I think my brothers and I were at an even lower level of awareness of Ma's health and financial burdens than Sue was. We were each consumed with our own lives and troubles, which Ma was acutely aware of because we often vented to her. I was guilty of this myself and get depressed today when I reread her letters to Tommy delineating her worries, pain, and frustrations.

Of course, we all have our own justifications for not being aware of Ma's plight, with some being more valid than others. Bernie and Annie were given very bad news in late November of 1967 that her facial tumor had returned. She had a history of recurring parotid gland tumors that were always benign, but their surgical removal left her face increasingly more disfigured. They were living about an hour and a half away from where her doctor had his practice. So their time and energies were consumed with fear that this time it may be malignant or that the surgery may be so extensive that she would lose her ability to talk or swallow. On January 25, the tumor was removed, it was not malignant, but the surgery resulted in the removal of nerves that controlled her eyelid, and the whole left side of her face was essentially paralyzed. Jill stayed with us on the West Side while Annie was in the hospital and Bernie worked. When Annie came home, she was greeted with Jill walking.

~~~~

Danny and Susie continued their chaotic lives with Danny moving back and forth between Ma's and being with Susie and the kids. Ma was very sad about all this, but felt powerless to help them because of her own troubles.

Pat's job woes did not improve. He got and lost five jobs in December alone. These were menial jobs as a dishwasher, housekeeping work in a restaurant, and so forth, but to not have a full-time steady job was very hard for him. He was not employed at any one job individually or collectively long enough to qualify for unemployment and thus became even more depressed and disgusted with no income.

My Junior Year of College

I had two very demanding courses in the fall of my junior year: kinesiology and physiology. These were made more difficult because each one had a lab attached to it, which was as much work as two separate courses. Because kinesiology was an extension of anatomy, it enhanced my knowledge of applying anatomy to human motion, but it also challenged me to work extra hard to comprehend it all. Physiology was hard because of the chemistry involved, and these were all new concepts for me. It was apparent that the other students had taken high school or college chemistry and were not struggling as much as me.

The OT courses themselves were manageable, and I enjoyed them. We had about twenty-eight students in the junior year with only four males. One of the males dropped out during the semester, so it was just me and two other guys among all the girls. This was my first experience of being a member of a minority, but far from being my last.

One of the courses I took was Orientation to OT, and it included spending a half day each week in OT clinical settings on a four-week rotation. This gave me the chance to work with kids at a children's hospital, a psychiatric unit where my Dad and other family members spent some time, a rehabilitation center where I got to work with people who had strokes and spinal cord injuries, and the Veteran's Hospital to see how occupational therapists helped people with chronic conditions. These experiences really cemented the idea in my brain that I had found the right profession for me.

A cluster of one-credit courses fell in the realm of medical sciences. These were taught at one of the major teaching hospitals where doctors specializing in neurology, orthopedics, psychiatry, and so forth presented various conditions to us using slides of actual patients. These were interesting classes but a bit overwhelming because of trying to remember all the facts about each condition like etiology, signs, symptoms, epidemiology, prognosis, the kinds of medical and surgical treatment that was appropriate for each diagnosis and what we could expect from an OT perspective.

At the time I went to OT school, occupational therapists used a lot of crafts in their work with patients. As a result we had to learn how to do all kinds of crafts. These were taught in the evening in an obscure university building located off campus. These buildings were isolated and were not easily accessible by phone, which became significant in the subsequent semester. They were older buildings that the university used, but in the past, this complex was used to house and treat kids with polio during the epidemic. Just as I was in the last OT class that was five years in length, ours was one of the last classes required to take these four one-hour lab craft courses. They were one hour of credit but met for three hours each week. We learned weaving, copper tooling, woodworking, ceramics, leather craft, and so forth. They weren't difficult, just time-consuming. Most of the students did not like these courses, but I found them interesting and relaxing. This was in spite of the fact that these classes met from 7:00 to 10:00 p.m., and so when they ended, I had to hustle out to the steel plant to make my 11:00 p.m. punch-in time.

Yes, I still had my wonderful steel plant job where I could sleep and study after doing a minuscule amount of actual work that no one checked on or cared about. An unexpected but appreciative by-product of working at night is that I grew accustomed to getting by on four hours of sleep. The ability to function quite well in spite of having little sleep has been a real asset throughout my life.

~~~~

While working (sort of) at night and going to school during the day was manageable, I began to explore other options. With Janice pregnant and due to deliver in February or March, I wanted to be around as much as I could, especially at night. Her aunt and her brother's mother-in-law lived upstairs, but neither owned a car, and Janice getting herself to the hospital by bus when she went into labor didn't seem like a good idea.

So we looked at our finances and figured out that if we could put together a combination of income sources, I could quit the steel plant. With my mother-in-law letting us pay so little for rent, our expenses were not that great. I searched for scholarships, loans, and part-time jobs that might work for us. At that time, they had what were called National Defense student loans that were interest-free, and I would not have to repay them until after I graduated. Along with this loan application, I also submitted applications for the AMBUCS (American Business Clubs) scholarship, as well as any other scholarship where demonstrated financial need was a big factor. Being married with a baby coming gave me an advantage.

After a month or so, I was notified that I was awarded two scholarships and a National Defense loan. Now I just needed to find a part-time job to implement our new plan. As part of my job search I went to the university's student employment center. In their files I found a gardening/handyman job working for an elderly couple living near the university, and I did this for a few weeks. However, the pay and hours were not going to be sufficient for our needs. Then I did find the job in the files for a medical student to work at the medical library at the hospital near where we lived. In talking with my friend Larry Shrewd, I discovered that he was looking to do the same thing I was trying to do (quit working full time), and he too saw the same job in the files (two more parallels for Larry and I!). However, he took it to the next step and submitted an application, and he got the job. Apparently, they had this position designed for a medical student, but when none came forth, they hired Larry. He encouraged me to apply because the librarian said they needed a second person. I did apply, and I too was hired (and still another parallel!).

Now Janice and I had all the pieces to go forward with our plan. I waited until my semester break was over before I quit the steel plant, but I did it in an unusual way. I say unusual based on the reactions of the guys who witnessed my last day. After working through the night, I left my key and an effusive thank-you note on Jimmy Boing's desk and pulled the locked office door shut for the last time at 7:00 a.m., just as I usually did. Then I went to the shower room and threw my hard hat, safety goggles, and Metatarsal work boots into the garbage can in the center of the room. The guy who I knew from my hooking and scrap-handling days asked, "What the hell are you doing?" My response was not said with arrogance or scorn but more with exhilaration. "I'm done with this stuff." And then I left. No one cared that I left, maybe they were a little bewildered by my manner of departure but not that I left. Why? Because I was doing a job (sort of) that didn't need to be done, and apparently, only one guy (Jimmy Boing) knew I was even doing it.

Our Pleasant Way of Life Deteriorates Fast

How did we go from madness to complacency? I'm not sure. I do remember that in the beginning of 1968, Janice and I had one of our most rational periods of our married life to date. I was home and got to sleep in a bed every night. We resolved our unstable transportation issues by using some of the loan money to buy a new Volkswagen Beetle for $1,620. Remember this was 1968 when I just left my steel plant job paying me $8,400 a year. Initially my courses and work schedule were very manageable. Larry Shrewd and I were both working as "Pages" (that was our job title) at the medical library, and each got about twenty hours a week at minimum wage. The library was open twenty-four hours a day through the use of a card key system so that the doctors and we all had access to it. There were no computers in those days or Google, so all the research was done through the card catalog and thumbing through the hundred or so current and bound journals for which the library had subscriptions. We also participated in the interlibrary loan system to obtain back issues of journals and books not on our shelves. In reality, there wasn't a lot for us to do because the doctors all did their own research. This left us plenty of time to study.

I also had time to engage in other sources of revenue. At various times I drove an ice cream truck, served summonses and subpoenas for an attorney, and delivered pizzas. Each of these provided interesting and humorous experiences that will be shared later on as deemed appropriate.

~~~~

On March 3, 1968, at 2:03 p.m., Janice and my lives were changed forever when she gave birth to our son, Peter Michael Talty Jr. I always liked my name, and so did Janice, so we did not have to go through an extensive search for just the right name. Annie and Bernie came in from out of town, and Annie got a thrill when Janice's doctor invited her to come with me to see Peter for the first time. He was a marvel and a joy right from the beginning. We had a great time watching him grow and develop. Unfortunately, Ma was in the hospital when Peter was born, and so she still hadn't seen him.

I was busy but not really overwhelmed. We got to visit with everyone and usually spent Sundays with Ma and Pat (before she was hospitalized) and anyone else who decided to join us. Ma's leg pain became so severe that she could no longer work as a saleslady on the floor. The Big Store, to their credit, did not fire Ma. Instead, they transferred her into the catalog department where she could sit all day and take orders over the phone. Although still glad to have a job, she missed the interaction she had on the floor and the commission she earned on her sales. I was only vaguely aware of Ma's pain and misery because I was enjoying the normalcy of my own life at that time. The abrupt way that I learned of how bad life had become for Ma has become a searing memory for me.

~~~~

On March 20, 1968, at around nine o'clock in the evening, Janice got a phone call from my sister Sue saying that they had to find me right away. Ma had been in the hospital for a few weeks and had undergone surgery that day to replace the clogged arteries in her upper legs with plastic tubing of some sort. I had classes all day and did not go to the hospital during the procedure, but why I did not go, I do not know. The actual procedure had gone very well, but in the elevator on the way to recovery, she had a massive heart attack and was now in the ICU in very critical condition. Sue said Janice had to find me because they didn't know if Ma would live or not. I had talked with Sue earlier in the day, and she told me that Ma was doing fine, but that was the last I knew.

Janice knew I was in class at one of those obscure off-campus buildings that the university owned, but she did not have the phone number. Also, I had our only car, so she couldn't drive over there and try to find me. Plus, she had just had a baby. Cell phones had not been invented yet, nor had the Internet or e-mail. She was not deterred. Janice has great persistence, and so she just started with the university's operator and persevered until she got campus security to get the message to me.

Firmly entrenched in la-la land, I was blithely weaving on a loom as part of one of those evening craft courses I had to take when an agitated security officer rushed in asking for me. I was shaken and panicking that it was about Janice or the baby. A bunch of horrible things were running through my mind. When I said I was Peter Talty, he said, "There has been a family emergency. You have to call home immediately." I was confused as to where to call from. There was no phone in the lab we were in. He took me upstairs to a pay phone, and I called Janice. She was calm but intense as she said, "Ma had a massive heart attack during her surgery and is in very critical condition. You have to go right to the hospital." She told me to go right to the floor where Sue and Pat were in the waiting room. I ran down to the lab, grabbed my books and coat, and ran out. I didn't stop to explain to the instructor as to why I was leaving so abruptly. I also ignored the questioning and concerned looks from her and the other students. If I had tried to explain, all they would have gotten was a gushing slobbering fool.

I drove the seven and a half miles to the hospital as fast I could, crying uncontrollably. Why didn't I go to the hospital for her surgery? What if she dies before I get there? What if she never gets to see Peter Jr.? What business did I have being content and happy and going to classes when Ma was . . . ? Please, God, don't let her die. There was no disparity operating here. No, this was pure despair at the thoughts of losing Ma.

What a dreadful trip to the hospital. Everything seemed to take so long in spite of the fact that I was speeding and slinking quickly through red lights. Parking and walking into the hospital was a mere few seconds, I'm sure, but it felt like I was moving through mud. Waiting for the elevator took forever. Then suddenly, I was in the waiting room. Pat was crying inconsolably. Danny looked like he had been crying. Bernie was on his way from out of town, and Tommy from overseas. Where was Sue? Pat said through his tears, "Oh, she's down in the emergency room with Jimmy. He might have had a heart attack!" What the hell! How much more can we take?

After fifteen minutes or so, Sue came in. She looked terrible. She said they didn't know if Jimmy had a heart attack or not, but he was on a stretcher down in the emergency room with excruciating back and chest pain. Poor Sue. She was afraid to leave the ICU floor to check on Jimmy because Ma's condition was so precarious. There were no jokes of the Talty humor variety or of any other type. We were all so quietly scared.

Finally, we got some news. The surgeon who did the surgical procedure of replacing Ma's femoral arteries with plastic (Dacron?) tubes talked with us. He was kind but direct. No false hope here. I could see that he was genuinely doubly shocked—first, that she had not had the heart attack during the procedure, and second, that she had survived it. I don't think his intent was to reassure us, and he surely didn't. It seemed he was trying to prepare us for Ma not making it. How could we get prepared for life without Ma? He said we could go in to see her but just for a few minutes because he wanted her to rest as much as possible. Knowing how I usually cannot stop myself from crying in these situations, I didn't object when Sue and Danny asked to go into the ICU first to see Ma.

While we waited our turn to go in, I tried to convince Pat, and probably more so me, that we had to be strong for Ma and not cry. We will have plenty of time to cry after. Now it was our time to go in. The ICU was freezing and very bright. Ma looked so little and so old in the bed, and the machines and multiple tubes going in and out of her looked massive in comparison. She was awake, and her eyes were wide with joy (could it be?) and what looked to me like fear. She had a big tube in her mouth, so she could not speak. I did the talking. What got me through it was focusing on my son. She had not seen him yet, and I knew this was a place for both of us to go and keep control. So after reassuring her that we talked with her doctor and he said she was doing great (a lie!), and that the best thing he said she could do for herself was not to get upset and to just rest (half a lie!). Then it was on to telling Ma about Peter Jr. and how he slept in a fetal position but up on his knees and his arms stretched out over his head. It was evident that this is what she loved hearing about. After about five minutes, we left her to sleep. Pat and I did well; we didn't cry until we got out in the hall. Bernie had just arrived, and so they let him go in for a few minutes.

We then went down to see Jimmy in the emergency room. They were quite full down there; Jimmy couldn't even get a cubicle. He was lying on a gurney in the hall after having gotten the good news from the doctor that he had not had a heart attack. Apparently, it was just a severe back spasm that radiated to his chest, but his heart was fine. They were going to give him a prescription for pain medication and send him home. Sue was conflicted about staying with us or taking Jimmy home, but we convinced her to leave. Bernie, Pat, Danny, and I returned to the waiting room.

We took turns going down to the cafeteria for something to eat. The ICU visiting schedule was very strict, only two family members at a time every hour, and we could only stay for five minutes. Knowing that each time we went in might be our last time to see Ma, none of us wanted to miss a visit. I called Janice and Bernie called Annie. Our message was the same to the Pepe sisters married to the Talty brothers: "Ma's hanging in there."

Sometime after midnight one of the nurses came out and suggested that we go home, get some rest, and come back in the morning. She promised to call one of us if anything changed. It was something we needed to hear. We were exhausted. So two at a time we went in to say good night to Ma, not good-bye. Ma was sleeping peacefully. After making sure the nurse had our phone numbers, we headed for home. Bernie went to Ma's with Pat and slept there rather than driving back home. This was so good because Pat was so upset that to be alone in Ma's house would have been terrible for him.

When I got home, Janice was asleep. I quietly went into Peter's room and sat in the rocker watching him sleep. As I watched him, I couldn't keep the idea out of my mind what someone had once told me. It might have even been Ma. "When someone dies, a new life is born." I had the new life in front of me, but it was unbearable to think that Ma would now die. To dispel this thought, I went back to the hospital about ten the next morning. I had to see her to affirm that she was still alive. I didn't go to school. Before I left, I watched Janice feed Peter and then just watched this incredible little guy do what one-month-old babies do.

Ma was still alive! In fact, she was doing better. No one else was there yet from the family, and the ICU was as busy as usual. I talked to the nurse before I went in to see her. She said Ma's vital signs were becoming more normal and that she was responding well. She was still critical but stable. This was mostly great news to me.

Buoyed by the nurse's good words, I entered the ICU. It was more terrible than last night. Ma looked even worse to me. She was sleeping and looked so old and I hated to think it, but she almost looked dead. A different nurse working with another patient yelled over to me (Yelled? In the ICU? Was she crazy?) "Go on, you can wake her up. We want to keep her awake more." So, I gently shook Ma's thin little shoulder and said tentatively, "Ma?" Nothing. I shook her a little harder. She was so thin. Her eyes opened and she tried to smile around the big tube in her mouth. She was better! I could see and feel it.

I told her what both nurses had said about her getting better and wanting her to stay awake more. She shook her head in response to this last part, but I assured her that she would also be getting plenty of rest as per her doctor's directive. I was probably trying to infuse as much positive energy into her as possible. I told her about Peter and what a great mom Janice was. This made her smile. I kept my talk light. Knowing that she would be thinking about me missing school, I assured her that I was going to go back tomorrow, and that I could catch up on anything I missed from today.

~~~~

I just was so desperate for her to live and to get well. It may have been at this time that I made a silent promise to Ma and to God that I would never abandon her or ignore her needs ever again. This promise drove how I would spent my time both today and in the future. I, of course, was not going to ignore Janice and Peter or my schoolwork, but I was already mentally moving Ma from the periphery into the center of my responsibilities.

When I came out of the ICU, Sue and Danny were in the waiting room. Since no one could go in for about forty-five minutes, we went down to the cafeteria for coffee and doughnuts. I told them what the nurses said, and their spirits were lifted just like mine. Jimmy was doing much better too. The muscle relaxants they put him on were a big help. He was able to get up, shower, and have breakfast. Against what Sue thought was the best idea, he was planning on going to work tomorrow. Jimmy was always a hard worker, and so I was not surprised to hear this. The three of us seldom got to talk together, and so I enjoyed our little coffee klatch.

Bernie and Pat were in the waiting room when we got upstairs. In a few more days, Tommy arrived, and the six of us rotated our visiting times with Ma. Of course, the first time Tommy went in to see Ma we had to prepare both of them. We didn't want Ma to know how close she had come to dying, so we lied and said Tommy was in the States on military business and was able to squeeze in a visit home. Even when Ma was in good health, she would go to pieces every time Tommy came home, departed, or called on the phone. Knowing how bad Ma looked, we shored Tommy up with how good she was actually doing so he could keep it together in Ma's presence.

Tommy now stayed with Pat at Ma's, thus enabling Bernie to return to his home and back to his family and his sales job. With

Ma a bit more stable, we all returned to our lives while keeping a close vigil on her. After about a week with us, Tommy had to leave for Germany where he was stationed at the time to rejoin Karoline and his daughter Thea. As always, it was sad to see him go, but it was great having all six of us together again in spite of the emotional trauma surrounding Ma's current health crisis.

~~~~

Ma got stronger each day, and it seemed like every day whoever was at the hospital visiting Ma would call the rest of us with a positive progress report. After almost three weeks of hospitalization, on April 11, 1968, she was discharged. I brought her to our house to recuperate and also so that she could see her latest grandson, Peter Jr. She progressed slowly at our house and enjoyed Peter. I know it was Janice's loving and calm demeanor that facilitated Ma's recovery. At first Ma was very depressed over how weak she was, but typical of Ma, she rallied and announced after about a week that she wanted to go home. She wanted to be back in her own home and bed, plus she was worried about Pat. That afternoon I drove her back to her beloved home, which seemed to be just what she needed.

On April 23, I took Ma to see her surgeon for a follow-up appointment. He was encouraged about the strong pulse in her legs and her ability to walk pain-free. However, he said she could not return to work for at least three months. This upset Ma, and she started to cry. Her doctor was somewhat brusque when he said she should be glad she was alive. I wanted to punch his face in but restrained my fist and my words. What he didn't know was that Ma not only wanted to get out of the house and back to work, but she had to work to pay her bills. On the way home, I suggested that maybe we (the six of us "kids") could all contribute to her income until she was back to work. She rejected this on the grounds that "you all have your own bills and families to take care of, so don't worry about me." She was the same old Ma, thinking of us before herself.

A Crisis for Me at the University

I was momentarily distracted from Ma's crisis with a crisis of my own. What happened caught me off guard. Maybe I got too complacent again; I don't know. Perhaps it was because I did not find the courses in the spring of my junior year as vexing as in previous semesters. The most demanding course was pathology where I had to learn the details of the disease process that related to all the conditions that an occupational therapist may encounter in practice. Regardless of how much I had to learn, it was interesting and I was doing well in it.

My crisis came in an OT course I was taking involving mental health. It was a four-credit course where we had two lectures per week, and once a week we had what was known as a practicum at a local psychiatric hospital. During the practicum, we were in groups of four or five students, and we got to work alongside the OTs treating patients with different psychiatric diagnoses. The practicum sessions required us to be there for three hours each week.

I suspect I had far more personal experience with this facility than my peers. Having gone through the admissions process here with five of my family members over the past three years gave me an edge, or so I thought. These experiences, plus my twenty-seven credit hours of psychology courses caused me to take the practicum way too casually. When the midterm grades came out, we were given two separate grades—one for the lecture part of the course and the other just for our performance during the practicum. I got an A for the lecture and an F for the practicum. F? The F was certainly a shock, but the narrative evaluation was even more devastating. There was a checklist evaluation about how I performed during the practicum along with a narrative written collectively by the OT staff. They said I did not take the practicum seriously (I didn't), I joked around with the patients (I did) and did not contribute to the clinical reasoning process that followed each patient group experience discussion with the staff (How could I? I had no idea about what I was supposed to be saying or doing). I was very embarrassed but also confused about the write-up.

I was very sad and withdrawn that night but didn't say anything to Janice about it. This has always been one of my shortcomings. When I am worried, angry, depressed and so forth I tend to keep it all in for what I think is a very good reason: Why bother telling somebody about a problem you have if that person does not have the expertise or resources to help you resolve it? It took several years for me to see how faulty my logic was on this. I am better about this now, thanks to Janice. I have never known a better listener than Janice or a person more logical or a better problem solver. These are just a couple of her many strengths.

So burdened with anxiety, I joined my other junior students in our pathology course the next morning. The professor had not arrived yet, which gave time for some expression of emotion. My peers were all enraged. It turned out that the staff of OTs had failed or given Ds to the whole class for the practicum part of the course. This all came out in the fifteen or so minutes we had waiting for the professor to arrive. What was reassuring to me is that I was not the only one that received an F. Some of the brightest and most assertive people in the class were in the same position as me and were inconsolable with rage. I loved it! Yesterday when they got their grades, they had demanded and were granted a meeting with the chair of the OT department (this was the 1960s and students spoke out whenever they felt they were being treated unjustly). It was set for that day at three o'clock. The students wanted everyone there, but I was in a dilemma.

I shared their anger over the arbitrary and capricious way (don't I sound like a lawyer?) the grading was done, but I had a big reason for not wanting to alienate the OT staff at this facility. I was scheduled to be an intern there for three months on a full-time basis for the upcoming summer. There were three of these internships ahead, and each was known as a level II fieldwork experience. This was to be my psychosocial fieldwork experience, and then at the end of my senior year, I would need to complete two more—one in physical dysfunctions and the last in general medicine and surgery. So completing each of these successfully and on time was critical to me and my family's future. However, there was a major reason why this particular facility was the only place for me to go, and I didn't want to blow it.

Through some diligent research I had discovered that you could sometimes be paid for these fieldwork internships. These were only a few in number, but I was able to be paid for each of mine because I was married and had a child. This facility was one of the very few facilities in the local area that paid students in the form of a stipend. I needed to get paid in order to support my growing family. I had successfully lobbied to be assigned there before I got unceremoniously thrashed by the OT staff. Although conflicted, I still went to the meeting.

~~~~

The best thing that happened to me was that I didn't have to say a word. The enraged pack took the lead. They were eloquent and unrelenting in their criticisms and demands for justice. However, the chair sought the opinions of the quieter members of the class and called on me (damn!). I tried to soften the harsh message of my peers. "Yes, everything they said was true, but I think it was a problem in communication (isn't everything?). The OT staff wasn't clear about their expectations, and feedback throughout the practicum was minimal and vague. None of us knew where we stood until the evaluations were distributed." This was the first time I used my "reasonable voice" in a public forum and was surprised with the result. It seemed to provide a path for the chair to take to resolve the problem, and she said she was going to meet with the OT director at the facility to get this cleared up.

So I left feeling pretty good about my situation, first, because I was not alone in failing the practicum and, second, because several students thanked me for saying what I did. They said they felt the same way. I didn't realize how powerful a simple, clear, and unemotional response could be. Since it was only the midterm grade, the chair had the opportunity to work with the person responsible for the course to make the necessary adjustments to result in a more equitable and less subjective grading system. No promises were made except that the chair did say she would look into it and get back to us. Fair enough.

I was scheduled to return to the practicum in two days and was anxious (nervous, not eager) about how the staff was going to react to the angst our meeting with the chair may have generated. I was also concerned about them being vengeful in some way. To their credit, they handled our harsh criticism with professionalism. However, they didn't admit to being neglectful in any way and put it all on us to change our ways or risk failing the course. Failing any OT course means delaying graduation by a whole year because each OT course is only offered once per year. This wasn't going to happen to me. I couldn't afford another year. Plus, my sense of disparity was aroused. I was older than the typical college junior, and I needed to get done and get started on my career.

~~~~

So I stopped joking with the patients, and tried to imitate the therapists as best I could in both the group and the one-on-one treatment sessions. Also, during the discussion following each treatment session, I asked questions that I was genuinely curious about and also would impress the staff. Was I sucking up and playing the game? Damn right! I needed to be successful in this course so that I could continue into the paid internship in the upcoming summer, plus I needed to graduate on time. I wanted to be done with school and begin getting established in my career as an occupational therapist.

My "new behavior" was viewed by the OT staff as meeting their criteria, and I passed. In fact, I earned an A in both the practicum and the course. So the crisis was resolved, and I was able to move on but still nervous about what it was going to be like to spend forty hours a week for three months with these people versus three hours, once a week, for fifteen weeks. Well, whatever. I had to do it, and I did.

11:00 P.M.

As part of keeping better connected to Ma I made a commitment to call her every night at eleven o'clock. This gave us a chance to catch up with each other, but more importantly for me, I was able to go to sleep each night knowing that Ma was okay. If she was troubled about something, I would try to help her problem solve it or just offer assurance that things will get better. I personally never found platitudes like "It will be fine" or "Things always look better in the morning" very beneficial, but she did, so I said them. Sometimes it was something tangible I could do for Ma, like taking her shopping or to one of her many doctor's appointments. I would rearrange my work schedule to take her to the doctor's, or if it was shopping or errands she needed done we would do those on Saturdays.

Regardless of the stress and strain I was experiencing that semester, I did not share it with Ma. As was my wont at the time, the only person who knew what I was going through was Janice, and even she was shielded from many of my fears. So it was with that thinking of protecting Ma that was paramount when I always said to myself, Ma had her own stress; she didn't need any of mine.

Just like in the hospital when I was trying to will Ma back to good health and away from death's door, I was now trying to keep her going with my eleven o'clock phone calls. Was I grandiose? Probably, but I had to be doing something to assuage the guilt of neglecting Ma prior to her almost fatal surgery. I don't think I was cognizant at the time as to why I was trying to do all this; I just did it. Also, Janice

11:00 p.m.

joined me in this commitment. When I had to work or study, she would call Ma at eleven o'clock. She also would take her shopping. Ma much preferred Janice taking her because she had Peter with her, and she was far more patient shopping than I. This was especially true when Ma went shopping without a list or a meal plan for the week. What amazes me now looking back is that Janice filled in the gaps for me with Ma because she knew how worried I was about her. We never discussed my plan for Ma, probably because even I didn't know I had one.

Ma Moves On

For the rest of 1968, Ma got stronger and stronger. She really did regain her health. She even progressed to where she could babysit Sue's son, her first grandson Shawn, during the summer while Sue worked. He had a good time and was company for Ma, as he stayed for several days at a time. After Shawn returned home and to school in the fall, Ma took the train to visit Bernie, Annie, and Jill for a week or so. When Ma went to see her primary physician, he was very impressed with her recovery. He told her that she was being written up in a medical journal, and that she was the topic of grand rounds at the local hospital. Ma was thrilled to be viewed as a "star." At the end of the summer, on September 7, 1968, she returned to work full time at the Big Store in the catalog department. It was necessary for her to return to work full time because of what she called her "money troubles". Regardless of her financial stress, she did enjoy being back to work and was well-received by her many friends. In early October, she got another good report on her medical condition when she went back to her doctor.

    Her social life was altered when she told Steve Steelguy, her "boyfriend," that she didn't want to see him for a while. She loved going out and being with people whereas he preferred to just sit in Ma's living room and fall asleep. They were also arguing a lot over what she referred to as "his getting a little too friendly." She told him, "Let's just take a break. I have had my share of arguing in my life, and now I want some peace and quiet." This is the guy that got me into the steel plant and may have even contributed to me getting those soft jobs, so I'm glad I got to thank him before Ma gave him the boot.

Ma loved a houseful of people, and we provided it. Whenever Bernie was playing drums in a band locally, he would often stay all night at Ma's, or even better, he would bring Annie and Jill in to stay the weekend. Janice, Peter, and I would often join them on Sunday afternoons for dinner and to watch football games on Pat's new color TV. Sometimes we would pick up Waddy on the way and, in the process, give him a fun day also. Sue, Jim, and Shawn would often come out, and Ma had her wish granted of having a houseful. Of course, we consumed plenty of beer to enhance the whole "get-together" (Ma's term).

Some of the gatherings would be a work project like the time that Jimmy, Pat, and I painted Ma's living room, and at another time the outside of the house. We had fun, and Ma loved having us there and getting her painting done. For us, it was a chance to catch up with what was going on with each of us coupled with lots of kidding sprinkled with large doses of Talty humor.

My First OT Internship

I successfully completed my spring semester of my junior year bringing me closer to being a college graduate and a registered occupational therapist (OTR). This success included my passing the infamous psychiatric practicum but under some constrained feelings on the parts of both my classmates and the OT staff at the psychiatric unit. More than one of my peers asked me if I was worried about going back to the place that made life so difficult for us all. I was honest in telling them that I was worried but also committed to doing everything necessary to complete this first level II fieldwork (internship) successfully. I was adamant that I was going to not only get through it but also do it at an excellent level.

This hospital had an interesting history having at one time been a TB (tuberculosis) sanatorium. It was a large, sprawling facility with multiple buildings and was the primary teaching hospital for the university's medical school. There were numerous specialized units for every medical condition, plus a trauma center, burn unit, spinal cord unit, cardiac and pulmonary unit, and far more. The ninety-bed psychiatric center was in one of the more recently built buildings where several of my relatives had been inpatients. It was the hospital where people with the most challenging of conditions were hospitalized, but only for a short time (ten or twelve days). At the end of that time, patients were either discharged to home or transferred for long-term treatment at one of two state hospitals in the area. As a result, students from every profession anticipated having a rewarding but demanding learning experience if assigned here for their clinical experience. These certainly were my expectations.

With all this in mind, plus the emotional baggage surrounding the practicum, I arrived eager to learn and work. I then got another of those breaks in my life that was directed from above. The director of OT, Maria Hamlin,* was also the primary instructor for the infamous practicum.

Regardless, she greeted me warmly and explained the plan for the next three months.

I would spend the first month on the medical-psychiatric unit working with Joyce Schmidt.* She was a fairly new therapist who graduated from a highly regarded OT program one year ago and was the only therapist on this unit. The second month would be working under a former university graduate, Helene McCourt,* on one of the teams on a psychiatric unit, and the last month doing some advanced work on various units depending on how the first two months went. I liked the structure of the experience with some built-in flexibility depending on my ability and interests.

~~~~

Joyce Schmidt had to be one of the most professional, caring, and brightest therapists I ever worked with, and it proved to be my good fortune to be assigned to her unit. Coming off my disastrous performance on the practicum, albeit passing, she was just the kind of clinical supervisor I needed. She was extremely organized and had the respect and friendship of all the doctors and the rest of the staff on the unit. The patients were interesting and challenging because they all had medical as well as psychiatric diagnoses. For example, one young man had a diagnosis of paranoid schizophrenia, plus multiple fractures of his pelvis and both legs due to an auto accident.

I progressed well on this unit and on all the subsequent assignments. It was so rewarding to see that I had the knowledge and skills to be highly effective with this population. The staff, who previously perceived me as a jokester (I was, but no longer), now admired my work and sought my counsel on difficult cases. They also liked my ideas for new treatment programs. One idea in particular on how to use work as the treatment media was so intriguing to the staff, that they asked me to research and write it up for the OT department's future use. The final paper was well received and forwarded on to the university for inclusion in the OT department's files for future students' use.

This was a great experience, culminating with all the OT staff taking me out to dinner on my last day. In the afternoon, Maria, the director of OT, went over my last evaluation with me that was all As, coupled with superlative comments throughout. At the conclusion, she not only offered me a position upon graduation, but she also was close to begging me to take it. She said, "You are just what the department needs to grow to the next level." Considering how this association and fieldwork experience started, my stellar ending was just that much sweeter. Then besides taking me to dinner, they surprised me further by picking up Janice (we only had one car) and brought her to the restaurant. It was a great night and made even better by having Janice there.

Sadness and Joy in My Senior Year!

It was with great pride and confidence that I returned to campus to begin my senior year. I still carried the feeling that I was a high school dropout, so being a real college senior was surreal. My classmates and I were all curious about one another's internships, but mine was even more of a curiosity because of the history and residual feeling everyone had surrounding our disastrous practicum. We had a class session where we exchanged experiences. They were surprised and found it incredulous that my experience went so well. It wasn't that they doubted my ability to be successful; they just didn't think anyone could be successful at that facility. No matter. I was moving on.

My medical library job continued to be great jobs for both my friend Larry Shrewd and me. The hours were flexible and the ample time to study was a bonus. Janice and I were still struggling financially, so on October 10, 1968, I started an additional part-time job delivering pizzas and other food on Friday and Saturday nights for Pandora's[*] Pizzeria. This pizzeria was located in the downtown area, and a lot of their delivery business came from the poorer and more dangerous sections of the city. There were two other pizza drivers when I started, but they were fearful of being robbed and beaten, so they often refused to make deliveries in these high-crime areas.

---

[*] I fabricated this pseudonym for reasons that will become very apparent as the story of the next few months unfold.

Having spent quite a bit of time in these areas for various reasons, I told the owners that if they took the orders, I would deliver them. They, of course, were pleased to hear this, and their delivery business grew quite a bit. I also would do other things like make boxes, put sauce on the pizzas, bring cases of beer up from the basement, and so forth while waiting around to make a delivery just because I was bored. There were three drivers initially, but after they left, they were not replaced. So I was the only driver for both Friday and Saturday nights, which was fine with me because this meant I got all the tips.

~~~~

I got through the fall semester without difficulty. My grades for that semester were four As, three Bs, and two Cs. I continued to make my daily phone call to Ma at 11:00 p.m., and she was always so pleased to hear about my grades and my other accomplishments. These phone calls were not always joyful, as Ma struggled with her finances and getting rides to and from work. We also went out to Ma's for dinner on many Sundays, picking up Waddy on the way. The family was very pleased with my progress in college, and it was apparent that I had reestablished the trust they once had in me. Fortunately for me, Janice and Annie didn't know me during my "bad times" as Tough Guy Pete or Crazy Pete, so they always viewed me as a trustworthy and responsible person. Actually, my past and upcoming disclosures in this book may surprise a lot of people.

~~~~

During the break in between my fall and spring semesters, I had a bit of misfortune while delivering pizzas. Around the middle of January of 1969, I skidded on the ice while approaching a red light and slid into the back of a car stopped at the light. I was driving our fairly new Volkswagen Beetle, which afforded little protection for me or my car. My head hit the windshield after my teeth hit the steering wheel. There was no damage to the other car, and my car was still drivable. It was not an accident that either I or the guy I hit wanted to report to our insurance companies for fear they would raise our rates. So, we just went our separate ways, and I made my delivery. This was my last delivery for the night, but I was in too much pain to continue working. I stopped back at the pizzeria and told them what happened, and that I had to go to the hospital. It was very hard for me to talk; they may have even thought I had been drinking.

While driving, I discovered that my four front lower teeth were still attached to my jaw, but the steering wheel had pushed them into a horizontal position with my tongue lodged underneath them. It was hard for me to talk and be understood, but I was also concerned that I might have a fractured skull or a concussion because of the force with which I hit the windshield. So I drove myself the half a mile or so to the hospital and went into the emergency room. This was about one o'clock in the morning. They weren't very busy and took me right in. There wasn't much blood on my jacket when I took it off and lay down on the examination table. They took a bunch of X-rays after the first doctor looked me over. He then told the nurse to call the oral surgeon that was on duty. So I waited and worried about how bad my car was damaged as well as my head. I also mobilized that old Talty cataclysmic kind of thinking. What about the consequences beyond the car like my head? What if for some reason I couldn't go back to college for my last semester? Then what? Lots of worries besides lots of pain!

The oral surgeon finally arrived, looked the X-rays over, examined my mouth and teeth while I lay on a gurney, and then without any preamble got his fingers under my horizontally displaced front teeth and forced them back into their original vertical place. It hurt somewhat, but not as bad as one might think because my teeth and jaw were already hurting so bad before he did his "adjustment." I was given some pain pills and a card with instructions to call another oral surgeon on Monday morning. Coincidentally, this was the specialist who did the surgery on Danny's jaw after his accident. I was given my X-rays to take with me for the appointment. They wanted to call a family member to come get me, but I refused and walked out.

Regardless, they did call Janice even though I asked them not to; I didn't want to awaken her or the baby, or upset her.

When I got home, Janice was waiting up for me and was very worried. I reassured her as best I could that I was all right, took some of the pain pills they gave me, and went to bed. The next day, Sunday, the pain was bad in between the dosages of pain pills, which made doing anything productive or even socializing impossible. A wasted day!

I didn't go to school on Monday because I was able to get an appointment with the oral surgeon for that afternoon. I used the morning to get an estimate for repairing my car from a local collision shop. The news about the damage to my car was not good. The estimate was $500! This made me sicker than I was if that were possible. From there I went to see the oral surgeon. I didn't ask if he remembered Danny in case he still owed him any money. I then got surprised with more bad news. My jaw was broken. He explained that the oral surgeon at the hospital probably saved my teeth with his draconian "adjustment." He also said that the best way to set the fracture was to wire my lower teeth together, which in turn put the jaw fragments in their proper alignment for healing. So that's what he did. He also told me that when he took the wires off in about six weeks my teeth might come with them in spite of "Dr. Draconian's" best efforts. Great! More potentially bad news! All this from an icy street!

I knew we had no choice. Getting the car repaired was something we just did not have the money to do. I needed the car for school, my two jobs, shopping, taking the baby to the doctor's, and getting out to see Ma and to take her places, and so on. There was no way we could function without a car. So I looked at driving it as it was. Everything still worked. It just looked bad from the front, and the bumper and fender were rubbing against the right front tire. To eliminate the rubbing, I hooked one end of a big chain that was in our garage to a sturdy chestnut tree in front of our house and the other around the bumper. By slowly driving the car backward and Janice supervising from a distance, I was able to free the wheel. That was it. We had our car back! It just didn't look very nice.

~~~~

After six weeks, the oral surgeon took the wires off my teeth. The good news was that my teeth stayed in place and did not come out as he had foreshadowed. However, he did say that the teeth may still die because of the trauma; the teeth had been separated from their blood and nerve supply and therefore may not recover. He praised the oral surgeon at the hospital who pulled my teeth from the horizontal to the vertical position in order to reestablish their blood supply. Apparently, this barbaric procedure may have saved my teeth. Time would tell if it was successful or not. An X-ray confirmed that at least the jaw itself had healed properly.

So I had my teeth, a fixed jaw, and a functioning car. I didn't miss any work at the library or the pizzeria, and so our fragile financial ship was still afloat. My last semester of classes went well, and I earned good grades once again. I just had to go through one more self-induced trauma in between my last class and the beginning of my next level II fieldwork experience (internship).

~~~~

One of our OT professors invited the senior class to her house for dinner on the Friday after our last week of classes. She apologized that her home was not large enough to accommodate more people than the twenty-eight students in our class. So without Janice, I went to the dinner. It was a disaster on many fronts. The professor and her husband had gone to a lot of trouble to prepare a nice meal and provide us with plenty of beer. We were not very appreciative; we were actually quite rude. Whether it was the stress we had all been living with or the freedom from classes, we ran amuck. We ignored our hosts, got sloppily drunk, spilled food and drinks all over their nice home (not intentionally), used profanity freely, and drank far more beer than we ate food. This was the first time the whole class had gotten together socially, and we had a lot of things to laugh and talk about without any concern for anyone but ourselves. It sounds like that son-of-a-bitch Crazy Pete was back, and he found twenty-seven friends of the same ilk.

To the relief, I'm sure, of our hosts, the drunken crowd was leaving because we had drank all the beer. All the mess was made, and we were on our way out the door at just after nine o'clock. I got in my battered VW Beetle, started it up, and, without looking, pulled out onto their busy street and proceeded to make a U-turn. I did not see the large Oldsmobile come around the turn that was just past our host's house. The driver could not stop and hit me broadside on the passenger side resulting in what is known today as a T-bone collision. I wasn't hurt, but I was scared as hell. It also scared the hell out of my classmates and professor who had witnessed my stupid move and heard the resounding crash.

The driver and his passenger weren't hurt, but they were sure enraged. "Didn't you see us? You could have killed us!" Then came their undeserved concern for me. "Are you all right? Ohhh! Look at your poor car!" Recognizing that their car had sustained some minor damage but nothing as bad as mine, the nice man suggested that we exchange information for our insurance companies. I didn't care. I just wanted to get out of there before the police arrived. I would have been arrested for drunk driving for sure. We exchanged the information quickly, and he left. My classmates were in a state of shock, and it was not just from witnessing the accident. Viewing the side of my car with the door crushed in onto the passenger seat and the window broken and glass lying all over the inside was unsettling for us all. They couldn't believe that I was going to drive it, but I did.

Once again I made a disaster out of an evening of fun and celebration. What was I going to tell Janice? What would we do without a car? The Beetle was certainly in no condition for us to drive it. I decided to go with Ma's philosophy: "Things always look better in the morning." I thus said nothing about the accident to Janice, watched TV for a bit, and then went to bed very depressed.

The next morning, while looking at my car in the daylight, I realized things were not better. They were, in fact, much worse. So much for Ma's philosophy! I was hungover, nauseous, and had a bad headache. In spite of my condition, I had to go out and look the car over in the daylight. Maybe it wasn't as bad as my drunken recollection? It was a sad-looking mess. What was remarkable was not the severity of the damage, which was pretty bad, but the containment of the damage. The brunt of the collision was all on the passenger door and window. After looking it over, I came back in and gave Janice the bad news. It is in situations like these that Janice is so unique. She did not go crazy. Her calmness in difficult situations is one of the many things I love about her. She was mainly concerned about me, probably thinking back to my broken jaw accident just five months previous. Once she knew I wasn't hurt and that the people in the other car were okay, she said, "I'll finish getting Peter dressed, and we'll go look at it together. How bad could it be if you're okay?"

I shifted into fix-it mode and went back outside. By the time she came out, I had cleaned the broken glass out of the front seat and determined that the door was crushed in so far that it was impossible to open. All Janice said was "Oh my god! You could have been killed. I'm just glad you weren't hurt. We can always get another car or maybe get this one fixed." She was wrong about these last two statements. There was no money in our tight budget to buy another car, and repair was not an option either. We did not have collision insurance, so our insurance would not cover the repair or replacement of our car. But I did have some good news for her, sort of. I said, "I'm thinking of figuring out some way to get a window in the door, close up the openings all around as best I can, and drive it until it has to be inspected next year." Janice laughed because she knew I do crazy things like this to resolve messes, and this sure was a mess.

~~~~

I had two weeks off before I had to start my six months of internships at the last hospital, and I would need that time to make the car "functional." I knew it was no longer going to be a pretty car and that we would only have one operating door. It was not due to be inspected for another eight months, and it certainly would not pass because of just having one working door. This would give me time to get through the two back-to-back internships at the same hospital, graduate, and get a job as an occupational therapist. I would then be in a better position to get another car. Now how do I make my badly damaged VW bug "functional"?

My first priority was to keep the rain out and the warmth in once the cold weather started. So I bought a piece of Plexiglas that was flexible enough to contour around the irregular shape of the crushed door, and after caulking all around, I screwed it directly to the window frame with about twenty metal screws. I then used some of my knowledge from one of those craft courses I took and fitted copper sheeting all around the rest of the openings around the crushed-in door and attached that with metal screws as well. It looked like hell, but we were dry and warm. Getting in and out for Janice was a challenge as she had to climb over the gear shift to get to the passenger seat, but once again, her positive attitude prevailed.

Everybody in the family thought I was crazy when they saw how I "fixed" the car, but I saw it differently. I wasn't crazy; I was desperate. We drove that battered and bizarre-looking VW Beetle until just before it was due for inspection. A clever friend of mine, when he saw my creation, remarked, "Hey, Pete! I see you settled your insurance claim." I thought his was a very funny comment and told many others about it. We were back on the road and back enjoying life as Janice and I moved us closer to our goal.

~~~~

Things also had improved for Ma. A constant theme in our nightly conversations was her planning to achieve financial stability without having to work full time. Her health was fairly good, but she just didn't have the endurance for working five full days. Her target date was January 2, 1969, when she would turn sixty years old and thus become eligible to receive Dad's full pension. On the evening of January 7, she was ecstatic because her first check arrived, and it was significantly higher than she had anticipated. She was still fragile and struggling with endurance. Of course, she continued to push herself to do all the things it takes to run a house, but that was Ma. She also went out with her old "boyfriend" Steve Steelguy a few times, but not with much enthusiasm. Dad was still her one and only who died on April 24, 1963.

She was off Disability in December of 1969 and was excited about going to California. She flew for the first time in her life in January of 1970 to visit Tommy, Karoline, and Thea. I think it may have been the greatest adventure of her life. She got to see and walk into the Pacific Ocean, walk on the Golden Gate Bridge, stand among the giant sequoias, go to Fisherman's Wharf, see Alcatraz, and do all the things visitors to San Francisco like to do.

Upon Ma's return home, she tried as best she could to resume her normal routines. It was, however, somewhat disconcerting when in that spring of 1969, Ma had two trips to the emergency room because of difficulty getting her breath. They didn't admit her because they thought she may have been getting the flu. As she said, "Nothing too serious," and she did return to work after each episode. The second episode did worsen into the actual flu, and she had to be off work for two weeks. I think I chose to think that she was fine and didn't worry about her. It was easier that way and allowed me to concentrate on my family, my education, and my life in general. We all may have done this to some extent because all our families were growing and required more of our attention.

Janice, Peter Jr., and I continued to spend Sundays with Ma, Pat, and whoever else showed up. Danny and Susie were still fighting and struggling, and so Danny was back and forth between their flat and Ma's house, depending upon his tolerance. Regardless, Ma really was enthralled with her grandkids and loved it when we brought them to see her. "The more the merrier," she always said.

Ma was very proud of how much I had accomplished and loved telling people (anyone and everyone) that I was a college senior studying to become an occupational therapist. After all the pain I caused her in my adolescent years, it was so good to see and hear the pride she now had in me. In our daily eleven o'clock phone calls, I loved not only telling her what I was doing in school but also updating her on my son's behavior and development and how much Janice and I were enjoying him. I know she was pleased to hear about the solid marriage Janice and I were building. It was my hope that Ma could not only have pride in regard to me but also not have to worry about me anymore. Crazy Pete and Tough Guy Pete were no more, and it was important for me to put Ma's mind at ease and erase these earlier versions of myself as much as possible.

My Last Two Internships

I successfully completed my last semester of on-campus classes and, on the first Monday in June of 1969, started at the Veteran's Hospital where I would work for the next six months as an OT intern. This was the first of two three-month internships otherwise known as level II fieldwork experiences that I would be doing. Just as the one I did last summer at the psychiatric unit, this was essentially a full-time job. Also, just like last summer, I was paid a stipend that was very helpful. I was still delivering pizzas to supplement my income and still driving my wrecked but "kind of repaired" VW Beetle with only one functioning door.

I was fortunate once again to be given excellent supervisors. There were three occupational therapists, and I was assigned to each of them at different times throughout my time there. The patients all liked and respected the OTs, as did the other staff. I felt very comfortable there.

The patient population in 1969 was a combination of young guys who were injured in Vietnam and a mixture of guys injured in World Wars I and II. Having tried to get into the Navy on two separate occasions without success because of my clubfoot, I had a high regard for these injured veterans. The focus and title of this internship was physical dysfunctions, and the conditions were complex, depressing, challenging, and rewarding in so many ways. I had the opportunity to work with patients with traumatic brain injuries, spinal cord injuries, strokes, burns, amputations, fractures, and peripheral nerve injuries.

Then there were the patients whose disabilities were not war-related, but these veterans had developed chronic and progressive conditions like multiple sclerosis, Parkinson's disease, and amyotrophic lateral sclerosis (Lou Gehrig's disease). Ma found it hard to hear about "these poor boys," so I didn't talk much about them during our nightly phone calls.

Because the VA was a component of the clinical teaching relationship with all the health sciences professions at UB, the staff and patients were very accustomed to having students work with them and seemed to enjoy facilitating our learning. It made for a good combination of clinical challenges along with great support. The three months went by very fast. I did well, and in September, I started my last internship, also with a paid stipend.

~~~~

My class of 1969 was the last OT class that had to complete three internships (level II fieldworks) of three months each. Call it bad timing on my part, but if I had gone into OT one year later, I would have been done in four years rather than the five we had to do. When the president of the university mandated that all bachelor's degree programs be restructured to enable students to graduate in four years, OT was one of the programs that had to be transformed, and it was the class coming behind me that was the beneficiary of this change. Many of my classmates were irate that they had to spend the extra year, but this is where disparity served me well. I didn't expect to ever even go to college, let alone graduate from a demanding program, so I was not upset about this. I also gained so much from the additional courses and the additional internship that I believe it made me a better occupational therapist.

The third and last internship was general medicine and surgery. My supervisor made sure that I had a good learning experience. Here, the patient population included men with diabetes, tuberculosis, cardiac and pulmonary conditions, and people recovering from different surgeries. Because I was so familiar with the VA procedures and had demonstrated my clinical competence in the first internship, the staff gave me a lot of autonomy. It was during these three months that I really got to appreciate the relationship between lifestyle and health. Many of the men I worked with had preventable conditions. These were not due to battles but to ignoring healthy ways of living. Of course, in 1969, this cause-and-effect relationship between the way you lived and how long and how well you lived had not reached the level of the health-conscious culture of today.

Smoking, alcohol consumption, sedentary lifestyle, obesity, and eating whatever one wanted were the causes of many of the conditions I was now treating. I was as ignorant as my patients about these healthy living concepts, which probably enabled me to be far more tolerant of these behaviors that I would be today.

One incredulous example that really exemplifies the thinking, culture, and laws related to health-care then as opposed to today is a patient who was paralyzed from his neck on down due to an obscure condition called syringomyelia. His favorite activity was smoking cigarettes, so after he exercised, the OT staff would set him up using a smoking robot, which held his cigarette, and then a small flexible tube went to his mouth. This was not viewed as aberrant in any way, and one of the OTs would often take her "smoke break" with this patient. Of course, his OT program was not smoking, it was building up his vital capacity with breathing exercises and neck flexibility stretching. I cannot imagine this smoking business happening today.

~~~~

I moved on through the last internship and received great praise for my knowledge, clinical skills, and the rapport I built with the patients as well as the hospital staff. So on the last Friday in November of 1969, I had officially completed my OT education. I wouldn't get my BS degree until the January commencement, and I still had to take the certification exam, but neither of these would preclude my getting a job as an OT. There was a shortage of OTs throughout the United States, and so I was getting job offers starting way back in

September. The VA wanted me to stay on and start my OT career with them, but I had other offers to consider. It was ironic that the first out-of-state offer of employment was from a hospital in Florida. I didn't take it, but the irony will become evident when Florida, becomes a significant part of my life at the end of my career. I also had offers from four or five facilities in the local area that appealed to me far more. I found the opportunity to work in the psychiatric unit to be the most interesting, and so I accepted the offer from Maria, the director, and with whom I had built a good relationship. She gave me the start date of December 1, 1969, that I requested. I finished my last internship on the previous Friday and started at the psych unit the following Monday. I did not want to waste a day on getting started on my career.

Although I had completed all the educational requirements for my degree in occupational therapy, I knew I would not become rich in this career. To confirm this, all I had to do was make a simple comparison. When I left the steel plant as a hooker/laborer in January of 1968, I was earning $8,400 per year, and my starting salary at the psych unit was $7,200 per year. One does not go into OT to become wealthy; it is the ethos of helping people that drives us, and I was proud to be a part of such a profession.

To supplement my salary, I kept my pizza delivery job at Pandora's Pizzeria. The hourly pay was not great, but it was the tips that made it worthwhile. So every Friday and Saturday from 5:00 p.m. to 12:00 or 1:00 a.m., I was driving all around downtown and the surrounding neighborhoods bringing people and businesses their dinners and pizzas. My wreck of a car (VW Beetle) with only one operating door was still going. It was due for inspection, but my risk-taking side took over, and so I decided to continue driving it until the license plates and registration came due. This was illegal and subject to a fine, but my logic was that the more miles I drove it, the less the accident was costing me. If I drove the car long enough before getting caught, then the cost of the fine would be negligible in relation to what I would have to spend to replace it. Another way this was risky had to do with my family's safety. With only one door to get us all out in the event of a fiery crash, for example, we may all perish. I did not allow myself to think of this and just kept on driving. This was not my brightest idea, but the income from Pandora's enabled us to save enough to buy another car before I got a ticket or we had a fiery crash.

A Big Change for Ma: Back to the Old Neighborhood!

Whatever was the draw the old neighborhood had for us Taltys? I don't know what it was, but it sure had a magnetic effect on most of us. In Ma's case, she had two compelling forces operating in favor of moving back. First, Pat found it very difficult to get to and from his work from out in suburbia, and second, Sue wanted Ma geographically closer to her. Pat was dependent on bus transportation, but the bus schedule from suburbia to where he worked was not in sync with his work schedule. He would get rides with friends of his from work, but these were not always reliable.

Sue and Ma continued to have a most powerful bond. Sometimes they were like silly sisters giggling and laughing, and other times Sue was Ma's counselor and advisor. They were always each other's confidants. Now they were faced with an obstacle. The distance from Sue's home to Ma's in suburbia had become too much of an obstacle for them to visit on a frequent enough basis for either of them. Two of their favorite activities, shopping and going for coffee, were not feasible unless Ma was geographically closer to Sue. They loved browsing through the various stores, doing errands and often paying bills in person, and then going to a drugstore where Ma would get her favorite treat, a Mexican Sundae, and Sue her hot fudge sundae. They would gossip, vent, joke, greet people they knew, and announce their plans for the upcoming week. It was a fabulous day for them both.

A Big Change for Ma: Back to the Old Neighborhood!

So with the strong desire to be back in the old neighborhood, for Pat to have more convenient proximity to his job, and Ma and Sue able to spend more time together, Ma broke the news to Tommy and Karoline. To give up her own, new, ranch home in a nice neighborhood in suburbia and instead return to a landlord's flat in the old neighborhood was incomprehensible to Tommy and Karoline. The old neighborhood was not what it once was; it was in decline with more unemployment and crime. Regardless of what may have negative consequences, Ma was adamant about moving. She never expressed any disappointment in the place where she ended up, but it sure was not the place we would have liked for her.

~~~~

Tommy sadly arranged for the sale of his suburban home that had served Ma and several members of the family in the time he owned it. Subsequently, Pat and Ma moved into an upstairs flat just half a block from Ma's beloved street for shopping and about a mile from Sue's flat. Pat could walk to work if necessary, but was now close enough that friends often drove him. Also, buses were far more frequent and compatible with Pat's work schedule. Sadly, the flat was not in the best of conditions. There were no screens on the windows, and Ma loved fresh air. The landlord was not eager to have screens and storm windows installed, so Ma solved the problem by thumbtacking cloth mesh over all the windows. It was not a perfect solution, but it gave Ma her fresh air without mosquitoes.

Another problem she had was inadequate water pressure. It took over an hour to fill their bathtub. There was no shower, so she and Pat had to plan their time so that the tub could be adequately filled. Of course, often, by the time the tub was filled, the water was cold. I felt bad for them, but this is where they wanted to be: back in the old neighborhood. I guess in Pat's and Ma's thinking being back there was worth whatever daily inconveniences and annoyances that came with it.

A Big Change for Ma: Back to the Old Neighborhood!

Now another negative for Ma besides the stairs to her second-floor flat was that she had a bigger trek to her job at the Big Store. Her legs were beginning to be painful once again when she had to walk or be on her feet even for just twenty minutes. This required her to take frequent breaks just walking the quarter mile to catch her bus to work. She was now outside of the routes her co-workers took to work, which precluded her getting rides. It was apparent that she and Pat had reversed their situations in relation to getting to work. Pat was now having it easy getting to and from work while Ma was struggling. Thankfully, things changed, and she didn't have to do this for long.

In our nightly phone calls, Ma would give me a detailed rundown of her day. It was usually a list of accomplishments (did up the dishes, did two loads of wash, got supper for her and the boys—Danny was back with Ma—and so forth) interspersed with comments of frustration about either how long each thing took for her to do or how tired she was at the end.

She never complained about the shortcomings of the flat, which were many, and focused instead about how she loved being back in the old neighborhood. She got to see Sue, plus her granddaughter Kathleen, who was now married and expecting a baby, Danny's kids, and the rest of us on a very frequent basis. She never spoke of being lonely, but I know she still missed my Dad, who had been dead for seven years on April 23, 1970. Within walking distance, albeit done slowly, she could visit her daughter Sue, her daughter-in-law Susie, and four of her six grandchildren. Sue usually took her shopping, and they often went to bingo a night or two each week. They also had dinner at each other's homes at least twice a week. With Danny back home, Ma didn't have room for Bernie, Annie, and Jill to stay with her when Bernie had a drum-playing job, and so she missed out on these visits. After Ma moved into the flat, they usually stayed with Janice and me, which was a lot of fun, watching Peter Jr. and Jill play together.

Pandora's Pizzeria

If I had known how such a menial job of delivering pizzas would change me, my life, and hurt everyone who knew me so much, especially Janice, I never would have taken that job. It was insidious the way it evolved. In the beginning, I was on the periphery of Pandora's social network, which is where I usually found myself in all social situations even those involving work. It was a family-owned and operated business by two brothers, Giuseppe* and Harry Pandora,* with a cousin Bobby* as their main bartender and one of the funniest guys I ever met. Then there was a close friend called "London"* (I don't know if I ever knew his real name) who made all the pizzas. There was a cook who, like me, was also on the periphery, but he had some strange ways and would always be an outsider. There was also a bevy of waitresses that came and went, but one (Cookie*) was Giuseppe's girlfriend, and she worked on a consistent basis, maybe even full time.

These people all knew each other for years, and it seemed quite insular from my perspective. I was just a part-time employee and thus happily existed on the fringe. I have actually always enjoyed being alone. In between deliveries, I got to know London, who had an explosive personality and always seemed ready to physically attack, but he and I got along fine. To avoid being overwhelmed when it got real busy, I would assemble pizza boxes way in advance. Sometimes I had one hundred boxes ready to go. London was a blacktop construction worker during the day and made pizzas on

Friday and Saturday nights. He appreciated my having boxes all ready, and that expanded into my putting tomato sauce and cheese on the pizzas London had previously rolled out into the pans. We would get twenty or more pizzas ready to apply the special toppings well in advance of when the phone started ringing.

I built a good working relationship with London. The Pandoras and the rest of the staff loved London, but he was not one that usually befriended people of no consequence like lowly delivery guys. So the fact that we connected was somewhat of a surprise, I think, to the others.

There was a *Goodfellas* kind of culture that prevailed at Pandora's that, because of my Irish heritage, would normally exclude me. They used a lot of Italian slang, had inside jokes about black and Hispanic people, played jokes on new and unsuspecting waitresses, and ridiculed unaware customers out of earshot, usually in Italian. I did not feel the need to understand their jokes but did find their banter comical at times. The interplay between London and the waitresses would have made a good sitcom in a less politically correct time and place. I noticed that they would alert me in advance when a joke or haranguing interplay was about to occur and then watch me as I reacted to it all. It was like they put on little skits for my benefit. It was a weird but hilarious use of time and energy.

They knew that I was married, lived on the predominantly Italian West Side, had recently graduated from college, and that I had a son. Beyond these basics, the rest of my life was of no interest to them. It wasn't that I was secretive about where I worked or that I was an occupational therapist, I just think they were not interested. Their communication was terse and staccato in nature. No prolonged monologues were forthcoming or solicited. It was a fast-paced, loud, busy restaurant kind of communication and atmosphere.

At the end of the night, there would be a gathering at the bar. They repeatedly asked (pleaded even) for me to stay and have a drink, but I always declined. Most social gatherings were usually stressful for me unless I got high or drunk. Except for the old days when I hung around with the crowd from the Big Store at my favorite taverns, I was never really a joiner of groups. I usually had one or two friends that I might play basketball, shoot pool, or have a beer with, but Janice and my family members were really my primary source of socialization.

Then one night I agreed to stay, and what a night it was. This was really somewhat of an exclusive club I was encouraged to join for just one drink. It was a real mystery to me as to why they wanted me to stay, and then why the great joy they exhibited when I finally sat down at the bar to join them was a second mystery.

It was either London or Giuseppe that a while ago had nicknamed me "Pietro" (the Italian form of Peter) and it stuck. The "inner group" consisted of Giuseppe and his girlfriend Cookie, Harry, London, Bobby, and then a mixture of other relatives and friends who stopped by after the restaurant closed. Because the "Big Four" (Harry, London, Bobby, and Johnny) were so patent in their high regard for me with lots of toasts to Pietro, the larger group as a whole also accepted me. I don't know if any of these other guys were "connected" or just "wannabe" mafioso, but regardless, it was great entertainment for me to watch and listen to their views of the world. London would cook up something special like a giant delicious sandwich that he cut into slices that we all shared. Giuseppe and Harry were so appreciative of the extra business I brought them by delivering to the dangerous neighborhoods that they would not let me buy a drink. Add to this interesting collection of unusual and humorous characters was a jukebox that they unlocked allowing music to be played continuously by anyone passing by. Because I (Pietro) was "in" and perceived by the group as "cool," the gathering became addictive, and I began to stay more frequently after making my deliveries, with disastrous consequences.

My First OT Job

Right from day one I knew I had chosen the right profession for me and the right job. Because of my success in the psychiatric unit as a fieldwork student last summer I was welcomed back by Maria, my supervisor and the director of OT, and all who remembered me. The OT staff was particularly pleased that I decided to join them. Besides the psychiatric unit where I worked, the OT department had two other divisions, which were also the director's responsibility. Maria's was a complex position that included an appointment at the university as a clinical assistant professor, but she also had to supervise the OTs working in the hospital providing rehabilitation services, and also the OTs working with children who had developmental disabilities who attended a special school that was on the hospital campus. She had a large responsibility and I had great respect for her. She was also a skilled psychiatric OT and clinical instructor. Her staff had learned a lot from her, but she had become so involved in her clinical work that the staff was thirsting for clinical leadership. My previous supervisor had left to return to graduate school in Boston, as did another therapist who did the same but at the local university. This left a void in clinical leadership that Maria was hoping I could help fill.

Ma loved hearing about my job and the kinds of things I did each day. Her interest in medical things was still strong, and so anything I shared with her about the patients and their diagnoses (no names or other identifying information, of course) made her day. She once said with pride, "I think it's wonderful that you can help these people, and just think of all our family who went through the psychiatric unit, and now you are there as a real professional." Great words, and they sure generated proud feelings in me.

~~~~

It was in February of 1970 that Janice found out that she was pregnant again and due in November. That sure was an exciting eleven o'clock phone call when I gave Ma that news. Janice's sister Annie and my brother Bernie's wife (they were one and the same) had a baby boy in March, so Ma was busy counting all her grandkids. Kathleen, Sue's daughter, found out she was also pregnant. This was going to be Ma's first great-grandchild, which just amazed and thrilled her.

~~~~

On the job front, Maria assigned me to an exciting team that was jointly led by two skilled young psychiatrists. Each of the six psychiatric teams was led by a psychiatrist and included psychiatric nurses, a social worker, an OT, a psychologist, and an array of paraprofessional staff known as mental health aides or technicians. Besides Maria, the OT director, and me, there was only one other OTR on staff. In occupational therapy, the professional person with the BS (now it is the MS) is considered the professional-level person with the COTAs (certified occupational therapy assistants) with the associate's degree as the technical-level person. I liked the clarity of roles these levels of education would seem to dictate, but I was about to be confused and frustrated by the abandonment of this supposedly long-established structure of professional demarcation.

Two of the teams did not have any OTRs, only autonomous functioning COTAs. It got more distorted whereby one team had our former secretary who "liked doing OT stuff," and so she was put in that position by Maria for some reason. This was crazy, at least it was crazy from my perspective. However, it was not crazy from the cultural perspective operating in the 1960s that was fostered in the community mental health model where everyone was viewed as equal. But they are not! Educational criteria and qualifications exist for a reason—to differentiate levels of clinical competency. Unfortunately, no one else in or out of the OT department shared my perspective. Mine was the lone and unpopular voice of dissension, and unwisely, mine was not a quiet voice on this topic.

To add to the craziness, for some unstated reason, Maria and the other OTR were both assigned to the same team, which made no sense when we had COTAs and a secretary representing the OT profession on their respective teams without any OTR supervision. I questioned this at meetings (big mistake) and in conversations with anyone who would listen (another big mistake). I was viewed by Maria and the other OT staff as antagonistic to the culture of the OT department and the whole psychiatric unit and teams system, and this was a very accurate perspective.

~~~~

After only being there a short time, I came to a depressing realization: I loved working with my team but hated working with the OT department. The team staff I worked with wanted to teach, learn, and collectively problem solve the complex needs of the patient population we were serving. It was interesting work because of the complexities of the diagnoses of the patients and the short time we had to impact the lives of these deeply troubled people. After ten or twelve days, most of the patients were discharged to home or else transferred to a state hospital for longer term treatment. It was exciting work, and I was getting pretty good at it. Also, my team's enthusiastic response to my ideas was very rewarding and even intoxicating.

In contrast, the OT staff was not interested in learning or in change. They were content with the status quo and enjoyed the ambiguity of the OTR and COTA roles. What made me crazy was that they verbalized a genuine interest in improving the OT program but refused to do the extra work it would take to effect these changes. My intolerance for their attitude was evident in all my interactions. The joy that they all expressed when I first came to work at the psychiatric unit was quickly evaporating and being replaced with silent resentment.

Because it was the hospital for the entire county, everyone who attempted suicide or became psychotic in the community was brought to one of the psychiatric teams for evaluation and treatment as needed. Each team mainly took patients from their catchment "area", which was a geographic segment of the county designated as each team's responsibility. The rapid turnover of patients made each day interesting because we never knew what problems would be thrown at us.

~~~~

After I had been on the job for just over two weeks, I received a phone call and was asked to come to the personnel office to meet with the director, Mr. B. A. Scumbag (you will soon see why I gave him this unflattering pseudonym). I assumed this was just part of the welcoming and orientation process for new employees. I was directed into his office, but he wasn't smiling or welcoming in any way. He walked around me, closed his office door, stared at me, and coldly said, "You lied on your application for employment. You said you had never been arrested or convicted of a felony. However, when we ran your fingerprints (every county applicant for employment had to be fingerprinted) through the system, it revealed that you are a convicted felon." Oh my god! What is going on? My case was adjudicated as a Youthful Offender, and mine was supposed to be a sealed record. I tried saying there must be a mistake. Maybe it's that other Peter Talty (fat chance, he actually was a policeman and maybe even a detective)? Mr. Scumbag was buying none of it, so I went to Plan B (whining and begging). "Please, sir, give me a break. I just started my career here as an occupational therapist. I've worked very hard to get to this point in my life. Isn't there something that could be done?" I was almost crying, and this time I wasn't faking. I was terrified.

Mr. Scumbag sat back in his chair and silently stared at me with what looked like a hint of kindness. Maybe Plan B was working. "Here is what you are going to do to keep your job. Take this pad of paper and write out everything that happened. I want dates, what you were charged with, convictions, penalties, the works. This will then be a part of your permanent employee file. Do this now, date and sign it, and I will notarize it. If you don't do it, you will be fired immediately." He left me alone, and I took the pad and wrote everything down about my 1959 arrest and conviction for second-degree grand larceny for the car I stole. I also put down the dates of my probation, and that this was a Youthful Offender case. He came back in, read my report, nodded, signed and notarized it, and put the report in my file. It was not in a friendly way he told me to go back to work. This was late on a Friday, so I only had to work for an hour or so and then I went home.

I was relieved that I saved my job, but my relief was short-lived. Once again, it took Janice's clear thinking to see the mistake I had just made. "Did he have the right to make you write all that stuff down? Wasn't all that confidential? If that is the only place where it is public, then maybe other people might find out about it too." She was absolutely correct. It was stupid for me to have panicked and put my criminal history all down on paper. I was desperate to get that report back before Maria or anyone else learned of my terrible past.

~~~~

It was so infuriating that my supposed confidential Youthful Offender status was for some reason apparently now voided. It took some analyzing, but then it came to me about how this all happened. Yes, my original arrest and conviction file was a sealed record, but that day I spent in the county jail was not. That was the day that they wanted us to experience jail prior to sentencing us to probation. Unfortunately, the admissions process they took us through resulted in an additional record existing outside of my Youthful Offender status and sealed record. Being two county institutions, they have access to each other's information. So that's what I believed happened to me. Now what can I do about it? It was a long weekend with lots of anxiety intermixed with rage.

~~~~

Right after punching in on Monday morning I resurrected some of my old reckless and aggressive behaviors of Tough Guy Pete and Crazy Pete days and went to the personnel director's office (Mr. Scumbag). I told the OT staff where I was going. People were always going to personnel for various reasons, so I knew no one would be concerned about my absence. Mr. Scumbag was not happy to see me and even less so when he heard what I was there for. "I want that report I wrote out for you on Friday. I checked with my attorney (a lie), and he said that you had no right to ask me to write it or for you to keep that confidential information in my file. I want the report back." He was cavalier and flippant as he said, "No, it is now a part of your permanent employee file. You should be glad I'm even letting you keep working here." It was with great restraint that I didn't punch his smug-ass face in, but I kept calm while still being intense and uncompromising. "I'm not leaving here until I have that report that I wrote because you illegally pressured me to write it." He gave me a look of "whatever" and pretended to be working with some files and papers on his desk and ignored me.

After an hour of waiting while he and his secretary worked around me, she asked me (nicely) to move so that she could access some files behind where I was sitting. He was not so nice in telling me in a raised voice to "get to work." I got up from the chair, and instead of leaving as he ordered, I sat on a corner of his desk after I moved his in/out basket out of the way. This annoyed and maybe somewhat enraged him, but I was resolute. I was amazed that he didn't call security and have me thrown out. After another hour or so of being uncomfortable on his desk while he unsuccessfully tried to ignore me, as we both tried to outlast the other, I could feel him changing. I don't think he realized that I was far more desperate than he. He caved! He pulled out my file, removed my confession, and said, "All right, here it is." Of course, I had to take one more shot. Giving him a cold stare, I said, "Just in case you made a copy of this and retained it, my attorney is preparing the documents right this minute to subpoena my file to be certain there is nothing pertaining to this is in it (a really big lie). So you are forewarned."

I left and went to my team meeting feeling that now my despicable past would not eradicate what I had worked so hard to achieve. If I had really contacted my attorney (which I no longer really had), I probably could have gotten this shameful part of my life really put into my confidential Youthful Offender file. However, I didn't do this and thus had another close call of almost being exposed once again forty-three years later in Florida.

~~~~

Sadly for me, my job did not bring the rewards and satisfaction I had anticipated. I continued to find the looseness of the psychiatric staffing model unfair, frustrating, and demeaning to me as well as the OT profession. I constantly queried Maria as to why should a person with just an associate's degree (or less when you think of the secretary) have the same status on a team as me with my hard-earned BS degree? She did not waiver on her belief that "this was the best use of our available manpower." Ever resentful, I was ever overtly critical. My perpetual carping about this inequity eventually got to her, and she brought it up to me at my three-month performance evaluation. My boss was an insightful clinician but a convoluted communicator. In any event, she moved me from temporary to permanent status in the civil service system, and I felt foolishly secure.

Obviously, Maria and I did not see the priorities of the OT department and the needs of the staff in the same light. I recognized that she had a difficult job trying to supervise three distinctly separate areas of OT practice spread out over a campus of three-quarters of an acre. However, by her own choosing, she spent the majority of her time working on her team where this most autonomously run team already had its own COTA and another OTR. To my naïve view, I believed she was enthralled with the revolutionary psychiatrist who was the team leader and the other members of this team that saw themselves as the vanguard of the community mental health movement. I thought they were all crazy and told anyone who would listen about their antics. My best, and only, friend in the OT department was the COTA on that same team, and I eagerly pumped him about what really went on when their doors were closed. He and I engaged in much juvenile fun based on the craziness we both saw going on around us, and we were not referring to the patients.

Although disgusted with my supervisor's lack of attention to the needs of the OT staff as she blithely went on what I viewed as a grand adventure with her team, I continued to offer much-needed but seldom-appreciated clinical leadership to the COTAs and the secretary. I really think they valued my guidance because they were often foundering as they tried to do the work of an OTR without the necessary education and background. I was good at clinical teaching and modeling the best way to carry out psychiatric OT intervention at both the group and individual levels. However, I was often dismayed because they lacked the rudiments of clinical effectiveness, and my instruction was wasted on them (in my opinion).

~~~~

It was while I was informally leading the OT department staff that I got the idea of getting myself promoted. Once the concept was formed in my brain, I couldn't wait to propose it to Maria. My proposal must have been persuasive because she bought it. The only problem was that what she bought was not the same thing I was selling. I wanted to take over the OT department. Why not? I had been on the job as a rookie therapist for all of six months. Conversely, Maria really saw me as a sort of "gofer" ("go for this, go for that"), whereas I saw myself as the "Czar of OT." Grandiose and somewhat delusional? Of course! Regardless, I announced to Janice, Ma, my team, my clique at Pandora's Pizzeria, and anyone within hearing distance that I was taking on a senior leadership position in OT. Everyone was very impressed, but not as much as I was with myself.

My staying late after my shift at Pandora's increased to once and sometimes twice a week. To demonstrate my new "coolness" at the after-hours gathering, I began drinking Dewar's scotch. It was still free for me, so I took advantage of it. I still do not know why they loved it when I stayed. I was not the center of attention. In fact, many nights, I hardly said anything. Perhaps they just needed an appreciative audience for their banter and antics, and I perhaps I met that need.

~~~~

Now, of course, my ever-present sense of disparity was not dispelled (another of those "dis" words that I love). I had my degree. I was a professional. I had the respect, and I even think admiration, of the non-OT staff and even more so from my team. I wasn't "Pete the janitor" or a laborer or scrap handler or a hooker anymore. There should be no reason to feel less than others. Right? Wrong! Because my job was replete with frustrations and what I perceived as gross inequities I felt disparity surging, raging, and spewing forth without restraint.

Why were people with less education than me able to have the same status on the other teams as I? Maybe I felt tormented by the fact that my starting pay as an OT was $1,200 a year less than I earned in the steel plant? Whatever it was, I was driven to improve our situation. That was probably why I pushed Maria to let me run things in OT during her absence and assist her in administrative matters and thus culminate in my being promoted. She did say that this was sort of an experiment to see how it went, and if it all went well, she would see if she could get me appointed to a senior therapist position in a year. I ignored the tentativeness in her eyes and in her words regarding my new role and proceeded to act as if I was already in that position and a lot more.

To increase my income and hopefully decrease my gnawing disparity, I began to seek another part-time position. The pizza delivery job was helping somewhat, but I wanted more. I found out that occupational therapists (registered occupational therapists) could work as consultants to COTAs working in nursing homes. The regulations stipulated that a COTA could work full time in nursing homes independently carrying out OT treatment programs based on an OTR's evaluation and formulated treatment plan. There was a group of OTRs who worked as consultants in the local area who met regularly for continuing education purposes, and I was told that it was through this group that I could learn where there might be open positions.

I attended the next meeting and quickly realized that I was an outsider. Most of the meeting revolved around a workshop this group was organizing. When asked to assist in assembling packets of handouts, sharpening pencils, and so forth, I willingly helped out. Working alongside these OTRs who I had not met before helped me gain entrée into this somewhat closed group. When we were all done, the chair of the consultants group asked one of the OTRs to give a report about any open positions for consultants. I was all ears with pen ready. I got the names of two places that needed a consultant. One was about three hours from home and the other ten minutes. I asked the group if there were any requirements I would have to meet considering that I was only out of OT school six months, but they said "No, just show up. If you can get a contract at the going rate of $10 per hour, that's all you need." They also recommended that I join the local OT association and that I attend their workshop coming up in a week. I joined the next day through my supervisor who was the past president and had membership applications in her desk. I not only attended the workshop at the member's discounted rate but I also helped out registering the attendees.

The very next day after hearing about the consulting opportunities, I contacted the nursing home. It was a small facility, only fifteen beds, and was located in a converted mansion. They did not have a COTA on staff but wanted me to advise the administrator and owner on how she could improve the facility. When I met with her, I was impressed with her caring attitude and sincere desire to provide a more stimulating environment and activities program for the residents. I was able to secure a contract for the glorious sum of $10 per hour for four hours a week on Saturday mornings. This was extravagant pay for an OT in 1970.

~~~~

Ma was very excited to hear about my consultant position and my additional income. She was struggling more now with her leg pain and lack of endurance. She hated to be dependent on other people and her being unable to keep up with her housework and regular activities. Talking with her each night began to become more difficult just because my life had gotten so busy, but she seemed to enjoy it so much that I just kept it going. On nights when I was delivering pizzas, Janice would call Ma, so we were always in touch with her. One of us had been taking her shopping, but because our car only had one door that opened, my sister Sue's car was better for this. Ma just couldn't climb over the gear shift to get in from the driver's side. I eventually did sell the much-fractured VW bug and bought a more staid car.

Once I became involved with the OT consultants group, I also became the treasurer of the local OT association. I had to pay the bills; send out dues notices, which Janice helped me with each fall; and maintain a roster of active members. As the treasurer, I attended the monthly board meetings and expanded my contacts within the profession. It was interesting to be a part of the decision-making process for our local OT association. This initial involvement led to an ongoing role of service to my profession in multiple ways throughout my career.

The Ramifications of My Unbridled Disparity

Now was I finally satisfied? Was my crazy obsession with how I was doing versus others' accomplishments finally been eradicated, and was I now allowing myself to experience peace and joy? Did the possessions of others pale in the face of my nice home and growing family? No, not really. My job was not what I had dreamed it would be. Not having the money to buy and do the things that I would like was a part of my discontent. Becoming rich was never anything one could achieve by becoming an occupational therapist, and I knew this going in, but I expected to be able to have a good life without having to scramble around consulting and delivering pizzas.

There were lots of frustrations for me at work, and after six months, I was also bored. Initially, it was fascinating to be working with such diverse and severe kinds of mental illness within the context of innovative thinking on my team. However, this was not the case with the OT staff. Some of my discontent may have been driven by the reading I was doing in the OT journal and books I had. I discovered some good program ideas that would have been ideal for our patients, but the OT staff was not interested in putting the time in to try new things.

In contrast to my OT colleagues, I sought challenges by independently organizing new programs like my "Job Clinic". This was a problem solving experiential kind of group where patients could practice filling out applications, role playing job interviews, searching for jobs, and how to answer awkward questions like your whereabouts during your hospitalization. I was able to get a few patients from my own team to attend but seldom anyone from the other teams. There are fewer sadder moments than when you prepare for a Job Clinic session (or any group session), and no one comes. I tried mentoring the COTAs, but they wanted to be autonomous and saw my mentoring as a hindrance. The mental health technicians and aides on my team were far more receptive to my suggestions, but they were really too busy to carry out what I saw as a better way.

~~~~

I met with Maria on a frequent basis and vented my frustrations without resolution. She was stretched pretty thin with her multiple roles and responsibilities, and a disgruntled new graduate (me) was not her main concern. Apparently, my issues were my own. It seemed she was always preaching patience and tolerance to me, which is not what I was interested in hearing. As a way to appease me, and I think to shut me up, she assigned an intern or level II fieldwork student to me. She would be arriving in about six weeks from an out-of-state prominent university and would be working with me for three months. Maria asked me to mentor her and be her clinical supervisor for the summer. In an effort to gain some control over me before I was off and running as I typically was, she cautioned me, "You know, Peter, the regulations state that a therapist must have at least one year of clinical experience before they can supervise a student. So, I will mentor you while you are mentoring the student. The three of us will meet frequently, and I will do all her evaluations with, of course, input from you." I didn't like it framed that way but also knew that she was so busy that I would probably end up doing it all myself the way I wanted eventually.

So, now I could add clinical supervisor to my roles of clinician, consultant, and pizza delivery guy. Even cumulatively, none of it was enough to lessen my disparity. I doubt that those close to me knew the level of disenchantment that I was experiencing, and that included Janice. It never seemed right to dump my worries on other people who have their own burdens. Janice had Peter to take care of, and now she was pregnant with our second child. Besides, she had a household to manage. This perspective was unfair to Janice and would prove unwise of me. Ma also never knew about my unhappiness. I kept our nightly phone calls light and funny. Hearing about the things my son did were a highlight of her days with decreasing highlights for her because of her declining health. It was probably a tacit understanding that we had to not talk about depressing things. We never expressed this, but our phone conversations sure reflected this silent pact.

Conversely, the staff at the psychiatric unit staff knew I was very unhappy because I was telling anyone, interested or not, how screwed up it was there. I think, on some level, I knew I was a corrosive substance. However, I was also ambivalent about my job because my work on the team was valued, but not so within the OT department. The OTs viewed me as annoying and intolerant of the way things worked in civil service. They were absolutely right on both points.

~~~~

One surprising place that offered respite from my pervasive negative thinking and poor attitude was my pizza delivery job at Pandora's. It was here where I had the full control, autonomy, admiration, and respect that I so coveted. This was a fun job with no real stress. I got along well with everyone, and no one questioned the way I went about my work. Because I knew the geographic area well, drove fast, and did not dally with the deliveries, I made a lot in tips. Of course, the after-work drinking and partying when the restaurant closed were great albeit decadent times. I often got very drunk and was not of much help to Janice on the day after one of these nights. She had never had any experience with a drunken person, so she just let me sleep it off.

~~~~

The Ramifications of My Unbridled Disparity

"Alcohol is a social lubricant." I don't know who said this, and I may not have the wording correct. Regardless, it was an accurate depiction of me. I was friendly when I met people, but not comfortable talking to them beyond the initial greeting. I never wanted to dominate a conversation, so I was relieved when someone took off talking away about anything. However, my relief quickly turned to boredom and aggravation as the person would go on and on about themselves or something I had no interest in listening to. But go on they did with me nodding and interjecting a few "wows" and "amazing" as they rolled on and on. My aggravation grew into such a level of resentment that I couldn't wait to get out of there. Alcohol helped to assuage my annoyance and increase my tolerance in these situations. Thus, it truly was my social lubricant.

Everything changed for me with booze. I could engage in more of a give and take in lieu of being a bored, frustrated, and counterfeit listener. After a few drinks, I might even take over the floor and become the boring one going on and on. None of this was truer than at the Pandora's parties after the restaurant closed for the night and all the crazy people came forth from the kitchen and the streets.

Because this group liked and maybe even revered me a bit because I was a college graduate working in a profession, they liked listening to me pontificate about all kinds of things (I think). One of the waitresses, Cookie, was also a graduate of the same university with a major in philosophy, and she was particularly interested in a perspective that differed from the predictable ones held by this aberrant group.

~~~~

The night before I was to pick up my student at the airport was a real disaster! I forgot I had to pick her up and proceeded to talk and drink a quart of Dewar's scotch whiskey until I was called to the phone at nine o'clock in the morning. It was Janice calling to save my ass. She was used to me staying late after I finished delivering pizzas, but never did I stay out all night. Knowing I had to be at the airport at ten thirty on this Sunday morning, she was concerned that I had forgotten. I thanked her, finished my drink (never leave a drink; that's bad luck), and drove to the airport in my still drunken state.

The student was amazingly poised for getting picked up by her supervisor who was drunk and someone she had never met before. I told her I had been out drinking all night, and she responded good naturedly and with a smile, "I know. I can smell it." How is that for an introduction to a professional therapist who will be your mentor for the next three months? I took her to my house first so she could meet Janice while I took a shower and got cleaned up (and brushed my teeth). In reality, I was still drunk and would have failed any sobriety test now or even then. No matter. Once I was more presentable, I drove Amber to the hospital where I had a room reserved for her in a dormitory they maintained on the grounds of the hospital for nursing and other students.

She was appreciative of the accommodations, and the next day I met her in the hospital's lobby and took her around and introduced her to everyone. Right from the first day, she became an asset to the OT department and to my team. She and I made a good team and were able to make several improvements in the OT program. The time went quickly, and her positive spirit, intelligence, and high energy resulted in me having a much better attitude about my job, at least for the moment.

And Suddenly, Ma Was Gone

August 4, 1970, was the worst night of my life. Janice called Ma that night because I was working on my treasurer's stuff for the OT Association. It was on a Tuesday morning sometime soon after midnight that my brother-in-law Jimmy called to say those terrible words, "They just took your mother in the ambulance to the hospital. You have to get there right away. Come right to the emergency room." His voice was matter of fact, but firm and business-like. Janice couldn't go with me because we had no one to watch Peter Jr. She also was six months pregnant, and more stress wouldn't be good for her or the baby. Hence, I was quickly out the door with Janice's words of "I love you. Please call me." trailing in my ears as I headed for the car.

It was another of those fast and crazy drives from the West Side to the hospital with me crying and praying all the way. "Please, God, please don't let her die! I will do anything, just don't let her die!" I rushed into the emergency room, saw Jimmy standing outside one of the cubicles with the curtains drawn. Too late. Ma was gone. Pat and Sue were just devastated as they stood over Ma on each side, each holding one of her little hands while Jimmy stayed out in the hall. Bernie arrived a few minutes after me. We all stood in shock and terrible grief around Ma. Sue had a wad of soaked tissues in her other hand. Pat looked like he was going to have a seizure. I pulled a chair up for him. Poor Ma. She looked so worn out and so old. I couldn't look at her for long. My usual crybaby response in these situations was under better control than usual. Calling Janice was hard, but I knew she would want to know right away. Saying the words "She's gone" was all I could get out. She, of course, had questions—"Are you all right? Did you get there in time? What happened?"—that resulted only in silence. She knew I couldn't say any more, and so she said, "I love you. I wish I was there." I grunted out, "I know" and hung up.

Sue, ever the organizer, was starting to think of what had to be done. We had to call Danny, who had gone back to Maryland where he had been living of late, and Tommy in California.

She asked me to call each of them because she said, "I can't take much more." I was worried about Pat going home alone to the flat, but she said he was going to go home with her and Jim. She knew it would be too hard for him. We all decided to go home and get some sleep. The nurse asked us if we had a mortician (what an awful name), and we gave her the name of the same place where Dad was laid out (another awful expression).

Even during this horrible time we were following Ma's thinking that "things always look better in the morning." Well, it surely didn't this time. Not having to go to work was good, but the rest was not. I called Danny and Tommy with a better presence of voice than I had last night when calling Janice. There was nothing to do but wait for them to arrive. In the afternoon, I went out to Sue's. The best news I heard that day was that Sue and Jim had invited Pat to come live with them. They had an extra bedroom in the flat they rented from Bernie in the two-family home he owned in the old neighborhood. So many times Sue and Jim came forth to rescue us, and here they were doing it again with Pat. I doubt Pat, or indeed any of us, could have stayed in Ma's flat without her. Even cleaning it out was going to be a terrible feat that will probably fall to Bernie, Sue, Pat, and I after Danny and Tommy leave. This is what I did during this time: with pencil and paper, I listed what had to be done, anticipated obstacles and problems, and then got on with getting things done. Having nothing to do would have been worse for me.

~~~~

Ma's funeral was a carbon copy of Dad's: same mortician (still hate the word), same church for the funeral mass, and she was buried next to Dad at the cemetery where most of Ma's family was buried. Ma was raised Episcopalian but converted to Catholic when she married Dad. She actually became more of a practicing Catholic than Dad. She always registered us at whatever Catholic Church was near where we lived and encouraged us to attend mass every Sunday. Ever since college I had gotten away from going to church. Janice and I went regularly when we were first married, but we fell into more of a sporadic attendance pattern especially after Peter was born. Regardless of my view of Catholicism at the time that certainly was contaminated by my liberal hippie perspective, Ma was going to have a Catholic funeral mass.

~~~~

Ma's wake, or "showing" (another dumb word), was well attended. Many of her friends and co-workers from the Big Store came. None of her friends or neighbors came from her suburban neighborhood probably because she had moved away and they hadn't seen or heard from her. Her present landlord and landlady were there, but she lived on her new street such a short time that no one else in the neighborhood knew her. The room was filled with our relatives, and the many friends of Bernie's and Sue's. The only people who came on my behalf were Maria, my boss, and her assistant. Isn't that bizarre? Even at my mother's wake I am counting people and experiencing disparity. How crazy is that? It made me even more sad and remorseful. I remember telling Bernie about this and that I was going to change. "I'm going to start making friends and stop being such a social recluse." He laughed, I think because he thought it was a stupid thing to say and also because he doubted that I could make such a large change. I was sincere at the time. Seeing how Bernie derived support from his friends while I stood about looking awkward and out of place just added to the pain of the loss of Ma.

~~~~

I returned to my pizza delivery job that weekend because there was no one to take my place. Staying around to party didn't seem right, so I went right home when I was finished with my deliveries. We had the funeral on Saturday, so I couldn't go to my consulting jobs (I now had two places where I consulted). I did stop in to each place late in the day to sign a few things but only for an hour or so at each place. Sue thought we should take advantage of everyone being in town and clean out Ma's flat. I loved this idea of getting this dreaded job done with more people around to absorb the emotional strife that was sure to surface as we wrapped up Ma's life. We did it in one day, and on Monday, I was back at work. Ma didn't have much, and so it didn't take long to get the flat cleaned out, and Pat all moved into Sue and Jim's. I didn't like to think about it, but this was now the third time I was involved in cleaning out one of Ma's flats without her. The first time she had left for Texas, the second time she was in the hospital, and now she was dead. All pretty sad times.

"The Eve of Destruction"[*]

As many people did in the 1960s, I added drugs to my alcohol consumption. Marijuana was easy to get and not very expensive. Some of us even did some convoluted math that said you could get high quicker and cheaper with grass than with beer and whiskey. We thought this deduction made us geniuses. Many of the professional people I worked with used grass to "relax and take the edge off from our stressful days." I bought this concept quickly even though I did not smoke cigarettes. I never did. I enjoyed smoking a pipe, and so buying a hash pipe and small hookahs seemed like sound purchases back in 1970. Did I say "sound?" That shows what my thinking was like in those days. Janice did not smoke because of being pregnant, and I only did the dope when I was in a social situation where this was appropriate.

 I became a hippie, sort of. I didn't follow the full Timothy Leary philosophy to "turn on, tune in, and drop out," but I did identify with "the movement" while continuing to be responsible by working (lots) and taking care of my family. After Ma died, Janice and I and Peter flew out to California to visit Tommy and Karoline and their daughter, Thea. Tommy commuted into San Francisco each day for his work, and I would sometimes join him and his commuting buddies for a trip to the Bay. While they worked, I went exploring the hippie

---

[*] A protest song written by P.F. Sloan in 1965 and also the title of a song recorded by Barry McGuire. The title captures my life at that time.

areas like Haight-Ashbury and San Francisco State University where a student and faculty strike had shut down the entire university. My hair was now down to my shoulders, and with my leather headband and peace symbol on a thong around my neck, I fit right in.

On one of my sojourns into San Francisco I was able to reconnect with the first OT I ever met: Corey Matthews. He was the guy I worked with a few years ago at the Big Store in the stock room. He was now a captain in the U.S. Army and was working as an OT at a large army hospital located in San Francisco. I visited Corey at the hospital and got to observe him in his clinical role working with a diverse patient population from kids to adults. He was even more impressive than he was when I first met him. While visiting with Corey, I got to meet a somewhat legendary OT who had become instrumental in my early professional life and would become even more so in later years. He was a senior officer and an OT and had written a very persuasive article in the *American Journal of Occupational Therapy*. The article entitled "The Derailment of Occupational Therapy" had galvanized the OT community, including myself. I had written to him commending his article and expressing how his thoughts were so compatible with my own at that time. He responded and mentioned that another guy from my university and home town was working at the same hospital and it was Corey Matthews. That's what prompted me to contact Corey while I was out there.

California, and particularly the San Francisco Bay area, really captured me. Just prior to going there, I had been exploring the idea of leaving OT and going to law school. One of the schools I was thinking of applying to was the University of California at Davis, which was about an hour and a half northeast of San Francisco. I had bought the LSAT (law school admission test) review manual and was conscientiously working my way through it. This was not a definite decision. I was just trying to lessen my disparity by perhaps changing careers.

~~~~

"The Eve of Destruction"

By the fall of 1970, I had grown angrier at work and more reckless and overt in my criticisms. I privately made fun of my boss and the other OT staff and did things to circumvent and subvert their efforts. I neither liked nor respected the OT staff but still admired my colleagues (love that word) on my team. When my student finished her internship and returned to her home, I didn't have an OT colleague to mentor or collaborate with. I was back as the lone wolf, black sheep, or whatever else they thought I was. Any good feelings I did have for this place had fully evaporated. No one outside of work knew how disgruntled I had become, even Janice. She knew I was depressed, angry, and withdrawn, but I was unwilling to disclose my reasons for my poor mental state. I didn't want to worry her that I might lose my job because of my poor attitude. However, with my position now made permanent, I stupidly thought it would be almost impossible to fire someone from a permanent appointment to a civil service position. She probably would worry even more if she knew the extent of my discontent and how foolishly blatant I was about it. So I continued to rave on at work, and then be silent as a Carthusian monk at home. This became my routine. It didn't register with me that I was actually causing Janice more stress in behaving this way. Being consumed with rage in a silent way surely must have taxed her extensive patience to the breaking point, but if it did, I surely didn't notice because of my increasing egocentrism.

My job angst was gratefully moved to the background on November 5, 1970, when Janice gave birth to our daughter, Beth Ann Talty. There was a girl who I kind of knew in the old neighborhood whose name Beth Ann I had always liked (the name not the girl). Beth without the usual Elizabeth connection was different, and I liked it. Janice liked it too, and that's how she got her name. She was delicate and a "girly girl" right from the beginning in contrast to Peter who each day was becoming more of a rough-and-tumble boy. It was both fun and fascinating to have two such different little people living in our home. I wished Ma could have lived to see Beth; she would have loved her.

~~~~

The happy times of Beth's arrival was diminished somewhat on November 19 with the sudden death of Janice's Aunt Florence who lived upstairs from us. She had helped raise Janice and had always lived upstairs when Janice was growing up. She loved helping care for Peter and was looking forward to helping out with Beth. Unfortunately, Aunt Florence had a very bad cold when we brought Beth home from the hospital, and thus she did not get to even hold her.

Aunt Florence's routine was to always come downstairs to visit with Janice and to feed Peter his breakfast. On this particular morning, Aunt Florence didn't respond when Janice opened our kitchen door and called up to her. Poor Janice, having just delivered Beth two weeks ago, now had to be the one to discover that her Aunt Florence had died in her sleep. She called a doctor who was a relative who lived across the street, and he came right over and said she was dead. I knew none of this until she called me at work with the sad news.

It was another sad time reminiscent of Ma's death with the wake, the funeral, and the cleaning out of her apartment. The closing up of a life is just so damn painful. Much of the closing up of Aunt Florence's apartment and life fell to Janice, along with caring for a new baby, an active toddler, and a crazy and angry husband.

~~~~

My craziness on the job was now reflected in my subversive efforts to organize the OT department. I assumed responsibility for things beyond the scope of my tentative position. For example, if my boss did not arrive on time for a meeting scheduled with the OT staff, I would run the meeting and often have all the business concluded when she arrived thirty minutes late. I sent memos to the staff and to other departments announcing changes in our programs and procedures. It was confusing to me when Maria responded angrily when I put completed evaluations of the OT staff in front of her for her signature. All this was done as part of what I considered my new role as the unofficial senior therapist and without the approval or knowledge of my boss. Accomplishing these administrative things gave me a sense of satisfaction, and coupled with my ongoing good work on my team, I was feeling much better about my job. Maybe I didn't have to go to law school to find job satisfaction after all.

My crazy house of cards collapsed on December 1, 1970, when Maria called and asked me to come to her office. I had no idea why she wanted to see me; I assumed it was some administrative task she wanted me to handle. I also thought maybe she was going to officially promote me to senior therapist, or at the least tell me how much of a raise I was going to get now that I had reached my one-year anniversary with the hospital. Wow! Was I off!

She was not smiling as she went through a list of things she considered to be forms of insubordination. Each of my decisions and accomplishments regarding administrative matters was discounted because in her view they were beyond my authority and competence. She was right. There were a number of things I did without adequate knowledge of the correct procedure just to get them done. She showed me how wrong I was while I justified my actions by saying, "I'm essentially doing your job for you, and you should be more appreciative."

This was my defense as she worked her way down her list of infractions with clear evidence that I really didn't know what I was doing. She then set all her papers or evidence aside and asked, "Peter, what do you think of me as your boss?" I was so glad she asked. I told her that she was disorganized, not aware of the needs and limited abilities of her staff, lacked follow-through on important matters, and was not good at time management. That felt good to say all that, but to balance my solicited critique I told her that she was very bright and an excellent clinician. All this from someone with just one year of experience!

Besides all that Maria asked, "What do you think of me as a person?" I gave her some more stuff about her being a good problem solver, and that she had the respect of the people on her team. She nodded, opened her desk drawer, and took out a wadded up piece of paper. After unraveling it, she slowly flattened it on her desk.

"The Eve of Destruction"

Handing it to me she asked, "Do you recognize this? Isn't this your writing?" On the crinkled up paper I was shocked to read what I had written a while ago, "Maria is an asshole." I wasn't shocked that I wrote it; I was shocked that she had found it. How's that for a professional? What could I say? I actually did remember writing it during a particularly frustrating OT staff meeting. I passed it to the only friend I had in the OT department, and he told me later that he threw it in the wastebasket. I suspect one of the other OTs that I had annoyed as their quasi supervisor dug it out and gleefully gave it to Maria. So what could I say, she had me. Out of desperation, I went on the offensive after a brief and insincere apology. "Yeah, I wrote it. I wrote it during one of our frustrating staff meetings a few weeks ago when you kept us waiting for twenty minutes and then spent another twenty minutes telling us where you had been."

"Well, Peter, you won't have to worry about those things anymore. I am terminating you from your position." What? Oh my god! She went on to say that she will let it go through as a resignation if I leave quietly. She also said that she would give me a fair recommendation saying that I "was a good therapist, but that it just didn't work out." Fair? What the hell was fair about that? Who would hire me with that paradoxical recommendation? Then I found my assertive, albeit reckless, voice. "Maria, you can't fire me. I have permanent civil service status, and my team loves me and values my work." She laughed in an infuriating, condescending, ridiculing way (supervisors have been shot for that kind of laugh) and said "Peter, Peter, Peter. You just don't understand civil service matters at all. I am your superior, and I have the authority to terminate you. Your team has nothing to say about it." I felt like a fool but still stood up in a confident manner (I think), opened her office door, and said something like, "Oh yeah? We'll just see about that."

~~~~

My bravado was emanating from remembering that I had three other job offers before I took this job. Every one of them told me that if at any time in the future I wanted to ever come work for them, all I had to do was call. I was also buoyed by all the praise I had received over the past year from my team. So I went upstairs and met with the two psychiatrists who were in charge of my team. They were appalled and agreed with me that my boss could not fire me because they saw me as such an asset to the team. It was their opinion that I had nothing to worry about. They convinced me that I was all set. So off I went to work with the patients.

By the end of the day I learned that I was far from "all set." One of the psychiatrists leading my team came and found me cleaning up the clinic after one of my group sessions. He was genuinely sad when he announced, "We lost. The personnel office and the hospital administrator agreed with Maria, and you indeed are fired. My partner (the other psychiatrist leading my team) and I both think it will be a terrible loss to the team when you go, but there is nothing we can do." I asked lamely, "But what about all the good things the team said to me and about me over the past year?" I learned the hard way what he meant when he said "it was false security." False in that the opinions of the team have no weight in personnel matters according to civil service, and that I was officially terminated. However, he did have some good news. He said that my boss said once again that if I left quietly, she would submit it as a resignation and not as a termination and that I could take a month to find another position. She also said that this was confidential and that I did not need to tell anyone why I was leaving. I felt only a little better after I heard all this. However, I was still fired from my first OT job, and nothing was going to change that.

~~~~

I went home and gave Janice the bad news, but also reminded her of the other positions I had previously turned down and of their promises to hire me whenever I was ready. Her calming and reassuring nature was unfortunately not as evident. Perhaps she was still reeling from finding her beloved Aunt Florence dead in bed two weeks ago, or just part of the adjustment to having a new baby. Whatever it was, she became very frightened about what we were going to do if I couldn't find another job. Janice's father was killed in an auto accident when she was only five years old, and it left her feeling scared in these uncertain extreme situations. Of course, I was not much help as I was consumed with the vagaries of my career and my old friend disparity that was now engulfing me.

So the next day I took a personal day that I had coming and called the three hospitals that had vigorously recruited me a year ago. I imagined they were going to be thrilled to hear that I was interested in joining them. The dilemma going through my mind was which position do I accept, and how do I tell the "losers" that I was turning them down a second time? However, this time there was a different tone with each of the people I spoke with. "No, we have nothing available at this time." They did not even give me that old phrase to "submit your resume, we will keep it on file, and notify you if something opens up." I also found out that one place hired a friend of mine two days after saying they had nothing available. My paranoia was fully aroused and got worse with each phone call. This was also true of all the other thirteen local facilities I called.

I don't think Maria blackballed me. She didn't have to. My behavior and attitude was so outrageous that the OTs I worked with must have enjoyed telling their OT friends of my antics. I imagined that "the word on the OT street was that I was bad news." No one wanted to take a chance on me when they had more stable and responsible people that they could hire. I began thinking that we may have to move far away in order to escape the despicable reputation I had built in twelve short months. Of course, like usual, I made this bad situation much, much worse by what I did next.

Egregiously, I Now Wreck Many Lives

Losing my job was not the only trauma I was bringing home to Janice. I managed for us to lose more than a job. It started at Pandora's. The late night drinking parties had changed for me. It seemed I was finding the banter and jokes too repetitive and racist in nature. My "hippiness" had fused well with the liberal views I had adopted earlier on in college and differed greatly from the culture at Pandora's. For example, I was greatly saddened by the assassinations of Malcolm X, Medgar Evers, Martin Luther King Jr., and Bobby Kennedy. I spent a lot of time watching the funerals on TV. I believed in these men and in their aspirations. I was against the war in Vietnam, capital punishment, and all things conservative. I had a framed picture of Martin Luther King Jr. on my living room wall. I felt sadness for the poor and very much supported the civil rights movement.

Because my value system and politics were so different from those gathered at the parties at Pandora's, it became a bad situation for me. It wasn't the fun it used to be. Little things became invisible wedges between us. For example, they used a word that they said was Italian, but I wasn't so sure. Whenever a black person came into the restaurant, they would call out to each other "Funge!" When I asked what it meant, they said it really meant "nigger," but they used the Italian word for fungi instead so the unsuspecting customer would not know they were interacting with racists. That wouldn't be good for business. They were so transparent in the way they said it and acted that the people must have surmised what the Pandora gang was saying and feeling.

The only other person who felt the same way I did was Cookie the waitress and Giuseppe's long-term girlfriend. As Cookie and I passed each other during the night, we had developed a private way of communicating our displeasure with the Pandora culture of bigotry and racism. Their thinking about everything was narrow, parochial, and simple. Cookie and I, on the other hand, had embraced the thinking and values of the 1960s and were both finding it increasingly frustrating to be silent and passive in the midst of these situations. She, more than I, verbalized her resentments.

In fact, Cookie was very outspoken and said whatever was on her mind. She was fiery, fearless, and confrontational. However, her vilifying attacks didn't happen during business hours. These came out at the parties afterward. When customers were around, she didn't want to do anything that would negatively impact her tips. She would vent in the kitchen with a stream of profanity. We would all laugh like crazy because it was funny to see this little redhead completely out of control and then switch back to the pleasant waitress when she reentered the dining room. The serious confrontations came out over the bar during the party after all the real customers had left. The Pandora gang just laughed at her. I didn't. I liked her, and I found her to be articulate and far more informed on social issues and history than I. She didn't have the medical and behavioral science background that I had, and so she deferred to me if the conversation went in those directions. There were nights I felt like a damn genius. No disparity on those nights. The group didn't take Cookie seriously, but me they did.

~~~~

It wasn't long before Cookie and I were having conversations that were more than intellectual. We were falling in love as terrible as that sounds for a guy married with two kids. Cookie took the first step, and I jumped right on board this runaway freight train to hell. She quietly asked me if I could get away during the day for coffee. Knowing I had a little flexibility in my schedule, I said yes, and we agreed to meet at a coffee shop not far from the hospital. The reason I could get out is that each team member was expected to build relationships with "resource people" who worked or resided in our catchment areas. These might be guidance counselors in schools, clergy, policemen, community workers, and so forth. This was a loosely structured expectation, and few of us really did much bridge building in this way. For my part, I saw this community outreach expectation as an opportunity to hook up with Cookie, and I took advantage of it. Another reason I was not concerned about leaving the hospital during the day was that I had already been fired. What else could they do to me?

So the following Tuesday, I slipped out at eleven thirty in the morning and met Cookie for lunch at a small and cheap restaurant across from the university and about a ten-minute drive from the hospital. I never saw her in street clothes before (she was always in her waitress's uniform at Pandora's), and she looked beautiful, cute, and sexy. It was the fastest ninety minutes of lunch and conversation of my life. It was also memorable because Cookie talked me into having my first bagel with cream cheese and jelly. Amazing what stupid things I keep stored in my brain. Being a direct person, she told me how much she liked (not loved) me, my look (hippies were in), as well as my "brain." Wow! We talked a lot about how much we thought of each other and laughed in a far freer way about the cast of characters at Pandora's. I was floating on a cloud driving back to the hospital and couldn't wait for Friday night when I would see her again at Pandora's. No one at the hospital asked me where I had been, so I didn't have to make up a lie about visiting my catchment area. It was at the point that I don't think anyone cared what I did.

The rest of the week was long. It was also long for Cookie. She told me so as soon as she saw me in the basement at Pandora's while I was folding my pizza boxes. We both knew how dangerous it was for us to be going down this road. Dangerous for me because I'm married, dangerous for her because she had been Giuseppe's girlfriend for the past two years, and then dangerous for both of us because we were getting this crazy relationship going surrounded by a bunch of volatile people. Did all this impending danger stop us? No, we went forward but in very clandestine and surreptitious ways. If stealth and foolishness could be inextricably linked, then that would describe us.

~~~~

I hung around after the restaurant closed to watch the action, not because I missed the gang but because it gave me the chance to talk with Cookie, albeit under the guise of our prior relationship. We were both careful not to have close conversations and kept our comments consistent with the way we were before. Before? Before what? Before we admitted to each other that there was a mutual attraction and met secretly for lunch.

Now I was not only negative and resentful on the job, but now I was also preoccupied with Cookie. I was scheming of ways I could see her without Janice or Giuseppe finding out. The only legitimate reason I had to be out of the house besides my full-time job was one of three reasons: working at Pandora's or my consulting jobs, attending meetings of the OT association where I was the treasurer, or to go out drinking with my friends or brothers ("stopping for a beer" or "meeting so and so for a drink"). I was energetically scheming how I could use any and all of these in some way.

I think, in a strange kind of way, it helped that Cookie was very accustomed to being the "other woman" because Giuseppe was also married. He didn't have any kids, and running the restaurant gave him opportunities to spend full days, some nights, and occasional weekends doing "other kinds of business" (implied *Goodfellas* stuff). Cookie was okay with being alone when Giuseppe was with his wife. So it was comforting for me when she said, "I know you're not going to leave your family, and so any time you can find for me will be fine." At least I wasn't going to have to deal with that kind of additional pressure.

Cookie had complete freedom to do as she pleased when she wasn't working at Pandora's or spending time with Giuseppe. She did not have to account for her time or activities. She shared an upscale apartment with a roommate who taught school during the day, which meant the apartment was available for liaisons. Giuseppe and Cookie took advantage of this, and she said we could do the same. Really? How could I get time away during the day? I couldn't, and I didn't.

My best time to meet up with Cookie was after I had been out for legitimate reasons. If I met my brothers or other friends for a night of drinking, I would leave them much earlier than usual and go meet Cookie at some other tavern. We tried to find places where there was little chance of running into anyone who would mention seeing us to Janice or Giuseppe. I did the same thing after the monthly meetings of the OT association. These meet ups took planning and some juggling. It also took a lot of lying and deceitful living, which should have made me so guilt-ridden that I would be unable to enjoy myself. Not so, I always had a great time with Cookie and was always scheming and looking for ways to get more time with her. No guilt, just lots of lying and conniving.

~~~~

However, all my juggling was not without angst. Keeping track of my lies reminded me of what Ma often told me about lying when I was growing up. "Remember, Peter, in order to be a good liar, you have to have a good memory." I know she was trying to dissuade me from lying, but instead, I worked on strengthening my memory. Trying to remember where I went and with whom was exhausting. If I told Janice that "I met someone for a beer," she would often ask lots of who and where kinds of questions. These were never asked out of suspicion; it was more out of curiosity or just making conversation. Janice was always very bright and perceptive, but she was also innocent and trusting. Regardless, I was busy trying to keep everything straight and without the benefit of a computer.

The relationship with Cookie was getting more and more intense. I began taking sick days from the hospital as a way to spend extended time with her. It was like being on vacation as we went to different parks, the zoo, museums, and sometimes just rides out in the country. My anxiety would get to me as I began to worry that Janice may be trying to reach me for some reason, so I would always call her just as I did when I was at work. Because of a glitch in phone technology, one of these phone calls resulted in the collapse of the house of lies I was trying to maintain.

Cookie and I had planned one of those "special days" with me using a sick-day scam. I was at Cookie's apartment and made my usual eleven-thirty phone call to Janice. The gods were against me because the phone line suddenly went insane. Another couple's conversation became intertwined with ours. It was bizarre because Janice and I could hear their whole conversation. I decided to have some fun and began answering the questions they had for each other, saying nonsensical things and laughing as they got more and more confused. After a few minutes, I got bored and hung up. I figured I would just call her back later, but Cookie had the terrifying thought that Janice might be trying to call me back at the hospital right now and urged me to try calling her back first. She was absolutely right! I called Janice, and as soon as I said "Hello," she said, "Where are you? I just called the hospital and whoever answered the phone said you called in sick this morning." Oh hell! Caught unprepared without a ready lie, I was stammering. I just muttered weakly that we would talk about it when I got home. Now I really was sick. So was Cookie. I told her I had to go and then drove home to have what was to be the worst conversation of my life.

As it turned out, we did not have the conversation I dreaded so much. It didn't happen because I didn't know how to tell Janice what I had been doing. Seeing her anxious and confused face overwhelmed me. It would devastate her to hear that I was involved with another woman. All I could get out was that something terrible had happened and I needed time to sort it out before I could talk about it. Janice's face was a picture of contorted fear melded into confusion, but I could say nothing to alleviate what she was going through because, strangely, I was as scared as she. Where was my compassion? Why could I only hold her and not be able to speak? Was I such a bastard? Who was this guy? How could I ignore Janice's tortured look? It wasn't that I was ignoring her; it's that I couldn't bear to think of her world disintegrating when I do tell her what I had to tell her. So I asked her to give me some time to "work this out" without telling her what "it" was. She had no choice because I offered none.

~~~~

Respites from facing the inevitable were provided through my part-time jobs, which had become ever more essential because I was about to lose my full-time job. I worked at my two consulting jobs on Saturday morning, which was a superficial distraction from "it." Working at Pandora's on Friday and Saturday nights was not a distraction in any way. Cookie was there, and of course, she had many questions about what happened when I got home from her place that afternoon. Being a direct and assertive person, Cookie could not comprehend why I had not told Janice the whole story about us.

Just as I had no answer for Janice, I had no explanation for Cookie. So once again, I was silent, and once again, I hurt and confused someone I cared about by my cowardly inaction. I did my deliveries both nights and was glad I was busy. Being busy was only a temporary haven, but forces beyond me were compelling me to take action. I went right home both nights, going to bed feigning more fatigue than I really felt or even deserved.

I decided to say nothing until Sunday morning ("things always looked better in the morning"). Tragically and coincidentally, that Sunday December 7, 1970 was also Pearl Harbor Day. I was unaware of this, being consumed with my own conflagration that I was about to ignite. After the kids were in for their naps, Janice and I sat down to talk. In my usual abrupt and insensitive way, I blurted out the worst thing I have ever told anyone: "I am in love with another woman."

Shock, grief, and fear filled the room as we sat in silence with Janice crying quietly. She gathered herself and asked, "Now what?" I had not thought much beyond this sad announcement that made me even sadder once I said it. "I don't know. I have to figure it out."

Janice wanted to know who it was, how did it start, when did it start, and other questions she had every right to ask. Providing each answer was like repeatedly sticking a knife into Janice's chest, pulling it out, and then plunging it in again with each answer. I still loved Janice and cared very much for her, and to answer each of her questions seemed beyond cruel. She wanted to understand, but the pain I caused with each word was too much for us both. So I became silent. Janice did not know what to do. To end this tortuous conversation, I said, "I have to see if I can find a job. One of the OTs from the OT consultants group told me that they are looking for a full-time OT at the Boondocks Home.* He gave me the administrator's name and I want to get my resume' ready so that I can send it out to him tomorrow." With that I got up and went to my desk to work on it.

The rest of Sunday was horrible. Janice had to pretend everything was fine when she talked with her mother and her sister Annie when they each called. I tried to not listen and kept busy with my resume' and cover letter as well taking care of the kids when they woke up; anything not to think of what I had just done. Blocking things out was not something I usually did, but I was doing a lot of it in those days. I remember wanting to just leave and go see Cookie. Was I that heartless and selfish? Yes.

~~~~

I got through Sunday and had to do more blocking when I went to work at the hospital on Monday. I was a pariah in the eyes of the OT staff because I was even more openly critical of them. They really were good people, but now I hated them because they had jobs, and I was about to not have one. I had told a few people that I was looking for another job, but I think I blocked out that I knew that they knew I had actually been fired.

Limbo was the state I was in both at work and at home. I always hated that ambiguous state of being "in between" and usually did impulsive and imprudent things just to get out of it. True to my character at the time, I did things where I made two bad situations much worse (home and work). Since I had been fired, there was nothing for me to be responsible for at work. I went to the daily community meetings with my team where all staff and patients on the unit gathered. It was where new patients were oriented, new staff introduced, the activities of the day were announced, and then it flowed into group therapy. These were always interesting and challenging sessions.

To offer insights and suggestions to the patients was something I had done in the past and continued to do so now, although now I was unrestrained and gave advice without the best judgment. Who was I to be offering advice to anyone about anything? I should have been removed or given hospital garb and been admitted. Luckily, there were always several staff members present to modify my comments, so no patients acted on my irrational suggestions. Thanks to my colleagues, I wasn't making the patients' lives worse by my comments and suggestions. That's how I functioned at work; no in-between for me. I did my work (minimally), interacted as little as possible with the OTs, and kept looking for a new job.

I still couldn't type in those days, so I asked my sister Sue to type my resume' and cover letter. I was too ashamed and embarrassed to tell the family that I had been fired, and so I lied some more and said I just decided to change jobs. It was awkward to talk with her and Jimmy when I took my handwritten resume' to their house. How could I tell them that I was "seeing someone else," that Janice and I were in turmoil, and in a few weeks I would be out of a job? This mess was exacerbated when I made the obligatory and usually fun visit to Annie and Bernie's, who now lived in the same house in the upstairs flat. Lying by omission is what I was now doing, and it felt even more deceitful to do it with Janice's sister and my brother. Getting out of there was all I could think about as I feigned being very busy and that I had to get home to help Janice. Terrible times and I was a terrible person, but I refused to look at myself and just pushed on. Alcohol and smoking marijuana did not cause the mess I was making, but it contributed to my being able to ignore the terrible hurt I was generating in Janice.

~~~~

Life at Pandora's had become too stressful for me because I was carrying on with the owner's girlfriend. So I gave him two weeks' notice and quit. Prior to this, Cookie had told Giuseppe that she was no longer interested in being his girlfriend. This did not go well. He loved Cookie and didn't want to see it end. To solidify her decision to end their relationship, she also quit Pandora's. She got a full-time job as an executive assistant to a VP of leasing at a large auto dealership. I do not know how an experienced waitress with a bachelor's degree in philosophy makes the transition to executive assistant, but she did. With us both now working days, there was no way for any daytime hookups, and that was a good thing because I was out of sick days and the tolerance of Maria, my supervisor.

I never stayed at Cookie's place overnight, and so evenings were the only time I could see her. It naturally aroused great ire and grief in Janice each time I went to meet Cookie, but my judgment and sense of what was right were absent back then. In an effort to appease Janice, I would help her with the kids and housework. In my distorted mind, I thought she would be less mad if she had less work to do. It was surprising to me that no matter what I did to help out (even doing the diapers in the days before Pampers), Janice remained angry when I said I was going out. "Going out" was my euphemism for going to meet Cookie.

My nights were as crazy as my days at the hospital. Roles both at home and at work were nebulous, contradictory, and confusing. This could also describe my behavior at the time.

From Disparity to Annihilation

During this crazy time even my sense of disparity was different. Throughout my life, whenever my sense of disparity was aroused, the difference between what I had and what I wanted was very lucid. I always knew exactly what I lacked and what I wanted. Not during these days. Disparity was not a factor because I didn't really know what I wanted in a career, a job, or a life partner. Being in-between in all things was definitely the deplorable state of my life.

To write now about what I did to Janice over forty-four years ago still causes a lump in my throat and still brings forth tears. What I did to her was so undeserved and unconscionable. She was, of course, very confused at first and was worried about all kinds of things, one of which was what caused my aberrant behavior. Was it her? Of course not. She was devastated when I told her that I had met someone else, but we still settled into an erratic and bizarre way of life together. My chaos was destroying Janice, and to compound it, she couldn't tell anyone what she was going through. Trying to sort out my job situation was actually easier because the control was taken away from me when I was fired and no one locally would hire me. However, the sorting out of the relationships I was involved in was evidently beyond me.

~~~~

Janice knew in the state I was in that I was incapable of figuring out what I was going to do. So when I told her that I thought it was best that I move out, she agreed. However, she was quick to request that if I went, I could not go live with Cookie because then I would still be confused about what I wanted. She felt that if I did not see her or the kids or Cookie for one whole week that I could more clearly know what I wanted. Janice had two other strongly stated requests, and these were not in any way suggestions. They were mandates. The first was that I wait until after Christmas to leave, and second, that I had to be the one to call everyone in the family to let them know that I was leaving. I agreed to both conditions. I had no choice really. If I decided to leave Janice and the kids in order to straighten my life out, she was setting forth conditions that I had to adhere to. Paramount of the conditions Janice stated was that I could not see Cookie. I wasn't convinced this last would be possible.

We got through the holidays, and then on Sunday morning, January 3, 1971, I packed up to leave. I found a place to stay, which was also on the West Side and only about ten minutes from Janice and the kids. This was a large house that had been subdivided into single rooms with a bathroom down the hall. As mandated by Janice, I called my sister Sue, and my brothers Bernie and Tommy. I didn't have to call Pat because he coincidentally called me. He wanted to come over for a visit and stay for dinner. I callously and flippantly told him, "Sure, you can come over, but I won't be here. I'm moving out today." He, like everyone else, was in shock. Calling Janice's mother may have been the most difficult of the calls I had to make. I didn't bother calling Danny because he had moved back to Maryland and probably wouldn't have cared that much anyway; he had his own problems. Each call made my leaving more real, but it didn't deter me. I was going no matter what. Why I was going was the question everyone asked, and when I said "I had to sort some things out," they must have been perplexed. I was not forthcoming with any more information. I just let the awkward silences sit and then just said good-bye. I had done what Janice had mandated: I informed everyone that I was leaving, and now I was.

Okay, I stayed through the Christmas holidays and made the phone calls Janice expected (dictated was more like it). I also did the food shopping, cleaned the house, did the wash, and cleaned up the kitchen. All I had to do was pack. We had a small nineteen-inch black-and-white TV that we agreed I could take. I just needed to pick out the clothes I would need, and whatever else a married guy and father of two takes when he goes off to live in a room.

As I packed I could not stop crying. I didn't know why. I soaked my handkerchief and switched over to Kleenex. I tried not to think about this terrible thing I was doing, but each decision of what to take aroused more and more emotion. Looking at Peter and Janice as they watched crazy me doing this crazy thing made me cry even more. Janice was crying too, and we were both trying to prevent Peter from seeing us cry. What was I doing? I couldn't say, but I knew I had to go.

In the midst of my crying and packing, my sister-in-law Karoline called me from California. Tommy obviously had told her what I was about to do, and she wanted me to know what she thought of it all. The disgust and rage in her voice was intense as she said, "Peter, you're a big shot, and now that you worked so hard to get through college you think you deserve a little treat?" I was unable to talk because of the crying, plus I had no idea of what to say in response. My brother Tommy came on the line and gave a softer message, "We love you and don't understand what you're doing. If there is anything we can do, I don't know what, just let us know." I choked out "good-bye" and hung up. I loaded up the car, kissed Beth, kissed and hugged Peter and Janice all the while choking and crying, and hurried out the door.

Was I Now a Bachelor or a Bastard? I Was Both!

I went to my room. No one else was around when I moved my stuff in. Where were the other boarders? I unpacked my clothes and put them away in the closet and the old dresser. I put all my toiletries out on the dresser in preparation for going to work on Monday. I had a sport coat, tie, and so forth in hopes of being asked to go out to the Boondocks Home for an interview in the upcoming week. I connected up the TV and was able to get adequate reception and a visible picture. There was a pay phone in the hall that I used to call Janice to give her the number. In spite of the pathos permeating our present situation, she was glad to hear from me, and I felt the same way about talking to her. Crazy, I know.

I then called Cookie and knew by the sound of her voice that I had made the right decision to leave Janice and the kids. Cookie was curious about the room. She grew up not far from where I was going to stay and knew the neighborhood quite well. In her usual direct way, she announced, "I'm coming to see your room. I'll be there in twenty minutes. I know right where it is." Without waiting for me to respond, she hung up.

There was a window in my room overlooking the street where I sat watching for her. My room did not impress her. It wouldn't impress most people. We sat there talking about how my departure went (terrible) among other things, and the assertive Cookie cogently said, "Look, if you want to stay here we can, but we can also go to my place. No matter where you stay, I'm staying with you." There it was! A declaration and invitation all in one! Her upscale apartment in the Affluent Towers* with a kitchen, two bathrooms, balcony, and living room made my room look like a dump (it was). I also had not figured out how I was going to do meals if I stayed in the room. So with her help I was repacked, and we were on the way to her apartment in less than ten minutes, she in her car, and I in mine.

~~~~

The relationship with Cookie went to another level with my moving in. Her roommate, Bernadette was fine with me moving in, but I don't know why. I only talked with her two or three times before, so she really didn't know me. No matter, she was happy I was moving in with them.

Cookie and Bernadette had been best friends for several years. So, now I was going to be the beneficiary of this friendship. They were respectful of each other's space and food and had no problem with either of them bringing home a guy for an overnight stay. I did feel a bit of foreboding that my more permanent presence was probably going to change these harmonious dynamics. However, in the beginning weeks, we were a happy triad living in a very nice suburban apartment. We shared meals, laughed a lot, watched TV, listened to music, and got high on wine and marijuana. I did learn from Cookie that Bernadette wanted desperately to be married and to have kids. She believed strongly in the sanctity of marriage, and my present actions were blatantly just the opposite of these values. The present bliss couldn't last. Could it? With me flaunting a lifestyle she absolutely abhorred in her shared home? How long would I be welcome here?

~~~~

Bernadette's soft knocking on our bedroom door woke me the following Sunday morning. This was very peculiar. Her cold response to my questioning "Yes?" was electrifying. "Peter, your wife is on the phone. She wants to talk to you." Oh my god! Someone is sick or hurt. I picked up the bedroom extension and was simultaneously relieved and alarmed. Apparently, everyone was okay. I knew this because all Janice said in a calm and matter-of-fact way was "I called your rooming house, and whoever answered the phone said you were only there for a little while the first night but you never stayed there. So I want you to bring the small TV home. You don't need it there." She was right; we didn't need it.

I hung up, and hastily began to disconnect the TV, but then Cookie asked incredulously, "What the hell are you doing? She doesn't want the damn TV. She wants you. Now get over there!" Now this was not said out of any concern for Janice; Cookie was dispatching me off on a damage-control mission. What a confusing and apprehensive Sunday morning.

On each of my visits home I tried to appease my sense of guilt by doing household chores. I was already planning to spend a few hours on that Sunday doing just that prior to Bernadette's alarming knock. Now I wasn't sure what I was doing. Janice's question of "Where's the TV?" when I walked in threw me. "I didn't really think you wanted it." I was wrong (or actually Cookie was). "I want that TV." I promised to bring it next time and then went into the basement to start the wash. There was not enough wash for me to stay down there for the day, so eventually I had to come up to face Janice. I knew my physical moving in with Cookie was even worse than my original disclosure about my being in such a relationship. In spite of all this, Janice was not devastated. She showed great strength as she went about the care of the kids and of the house. Shockingly to me, Janice's spirit was not broken. The house, the kids, and Janice herself all looked to be in fine shape.

~~~~

Meanwhile on the job front, things started to look up when I got a call from Mr. George Goodforme.* He was the administrator at the Boondocks Home. This is the call I was so desperately hoping to get. Could this be my lifeboat? I needed a job fast because my boss only gave me a month to find something, and my time was fast evaporating. Because I no longer had a role or purpose in the OT department, even my presence was intolerable for everyone. It was very clear that all the OTs neither liked nor respected me any longer. This wasn't quite true because the one other guy in the OT department did continue to be my friend throughout this dreadful time. My team was my salvation, but this too was not like it was before. They knew I was on my way out, so they were no longer investing their time or energy in me.

Could Mr. Goodforme be my deliverer from the occupational hell I had created? God, I hope so! Oh, what joy he wrought! He wanted me to come out for a visit to see the facility and to meet the staff. His tone and demeanor was so respectful (he kept referring to me as "Mr. Talty"), and he was so positive that just his voice was very rejuvenating. My job prospects had dribbled to nothing, so just about any interest in me was so uplifting. It was my good fortune that Mr. Goodforme was formerly a nurse and had been the director of nursing for the psychiatric unit for several years before becoming a nursing home administrator. His former position at the psychiatric unit meant he knew most of the people I worked with (not the OTs) and held them and the facility in high regard. So we scheduled my visit within a few days.

~~~~

My initial impressions of the Boondocks Home were not the best. It was a long and dreary drive out to the Boondocks Home and the array of gray buildings on the grounds were even drearier. However, this negative first impression quickly dissipated when I met Mr. Goodforme, and he enthusiastically took me all around the facility. He explained that the position for an occupational therapist had been approved and funded but unfilled for five years. They could not find anyone who would take the position. Okay, then who was more desperate, him or me? Great! If I did get this job, was it a job that no one else wanted? Why was that? I discovered why no one wanted to work there. There was no OT department! No one knew what OT was or what it could do for the patients. Equipment and supplies were nil, and the five women calling themselves occupational therapists were former nurse's aides, had no training in OT, and were happy doing crafts with the higher functioning residents and then selling their products in the gift shop. No matter, it was an OT job, and I would seize it if offered. I was desperate, and in a sense, I could tell Mr. Goodforme was too.

I was offered the position, and I eagerly accepted it with a starting date of February 1, 1971. Since it was a civil service organization just like the psychiatric unit, my thirteen months of seniority and civil service status transferred with me. Plus, it was a raise in pay. Because no one at the Boondocks Home knew exactly what OT was, I had the opportunity to establish my own department and also become a real supervisor, not like the one I pretended to be at the psychiatric unit. I was excited.

From Disparity to Devastation to Discovery

Although most of my sense of disparity was focused on my job as I tried to establish a new OT department in a facility where change was resisted vehemently, I had the competing attraction of Janice and the kids. The disparity here was that I was not there with them, and thus was living two lives: one with Cookie in a Shangri-la sort of way, and the other as a still married father of two and working to reclaim my professional identity and self-respect. My new job was challenging, but I had a good sense of where to go with it. However, when it came to my two home lives, I was at sea but didn't know it.

As I moved back and forth between these two disparate and desperate lives, my mental state was not the best. My life with Cookie was fun but strained because Bernadette was tired of my living there and silently and sometimes not-so-silently resented me for leaving my family. Cookie and I went out a lot when Bernadette was home in an effort to lessen her increasing anger. Surprisingly, Janice was coping fairly well with my absence and the way I had mangled her life and our family with my reckless and selfish behavior. Of course, none of this was as evident to me then as it is now, and so I carried on in my fragmented and destructive way.

~~~~

From Disparity to Devastation to Discovery

As the newest professional to join the Boondocks Home staff my fellow employees were curious about me, and many asked where I lived. This was especially true of people commuting from the city who were always in search of a person with whom to share the drive and commuting costs. I was often confounded by this simple question because I had three different addresses running around in my mind. Two was really more accurate because after renting the room, I never really stayed there. I tried to be vague and then quickly changed the subject. This seemed to work best. This way I wouldn't have to lie to any more people.

Janice and I settled into an uneasy routine living apart, but I tried to be as helpful as possible when I was home. In my twisted mind, Janice and the kids were "home" even though I no longer slept there. I needed to resolve this ambiguity and gather the courage to talk with Janice about where all this was going. Subsequently, on a Sunday afternoon, Janice and I sat down to talk while the kids were napping. It was remarkable to me how strong Janice was as I proceeded to talk about the future—a future that, in my view, was no longer an "us." I was being clear that I was not coming back, and that she needed to build a new life without me. How heartless I was. Janice became a little tearful but remained calm and focused. However, she shared with me how difficult all this was for her. The discovering of my many untruths, coupled with where I was really living was the final blow. It all came bursting forth in a clear and focused way, but with a request.

She had asked me in the past to go with her to a marriage counselor, but this made no sense to me because I was not interested in staying married. However, this time she presented it differently: "I'm having a real hard time dealing with all this. I need you to go with me to a counselor to help me get through it. Will you please go with me?" This got to me, and I also saw it as a way to extricate myself from the marriage without being as guilt-ridden as I had been feeling of late. "Okay, set it up for sometime at night, and I'll take you."

~~~~

Within a few days, Janice called me to say that she had made an appointment with a counselor at a social services agency for the next night at seven o'clock. I had told Cookie where I was going and that the sole purpose was to help Janice cope with the separation, but Cookie was suspicious of Janice's true motives. It was Cookie's view that Janice was going to get me into the counselor's office, and I would eventually be manipulated into returning to Janice and the kids. She didn't know Janice and that some of her many qualities were honesty and truthfulness. She was not a manipulative person, but of course, Cookie could not know this.

So on February 16, 1971, Janice and I went to see Karen Deliverer* at a local social service agency. She was nice and made small talk mentioning that she knew my uncle Pete who had worked at their agency in the past. My non-response was typical of me in these kinds of situations.

I never did have much tolerance for small talk before an important meeting; I viewed it as a waste of time when there was far more serious work to be done. Knowing that the purpose of the visit was to get Janice fortified in order for her to go on with her life without me, I wanted the counselor to get us moving in that direction. Thus, I purposely remained quiet, answered in one or two words, and kept reminding Karen that I was only there for Janice, not to repair our marriage.

The first visit was not productive at all from my perspective, but I reluctantly agreed to come back by myself while Janice also scheduled a separate visit alone. Karen explained that sometimes it works better if she can talk to each person separately. I reiterated in an annoyed way that I hoped these separate meetings were going to lead to the intended goal of making Janice stronger. Karen said that "she wanted to help us achieve what we wanted to achieve." Sounded good, but I wasn't convinced she really understood my objective.

~~~~

Arriving at the next meeting with Karen Deliverer a couple of days later reminded me of the times when I was the recalcitrant adolescent sitting in a chair outside the principal's office waiting to receive the consequences for my latest transgression. However, Karen was welcoming, and after we were settled, she began by asking questions exploring Janice and my relationship. I responded in a thinly disguised hostile manner again pointing out, "I am here to help Janice get used to living without me and so talking about our relationship was not why I was there." She took this frontal assault quite well, sat back, put her pen down, looked at me, and said, "Okay, I do not know what an occupational therapist is or what they do. Tell me about what you do." My work at the Boondocks Home had caused me to fall back in love with OT. So, off I went enthusiastically describing all the neat things OTs do with some examples from my work in mental health and, of late, at the Boondocks Home with patients with complicated physical disabilities. She asked some good questions and seemed genuinely impressed with my dissertation on OT. Then what captured my attention was when Karen Deliverer said, "With all your experience in mental health, I bet you think this counseling business is a lot of crap." Wow! Yes, that's exactly what I was feeling but was reluctant to say. I was beginning to like Karen Deliverer. She then endured herself to me even more when she said seriously, "Yeah, I kind of feel like it's all a crock sometimes too."

~~~~

With this established common understanding that counseling sucks, she asked me about my life before I met Janice. I told her about growing up in a home with an alcoholic father where we never seemed to have enough of anything, and how I was always trying in deviant ways to get the things we couldn't afford. She asked me about my teenage years and if I dated frequently. I explained that I hadn't dated much and that I really only had a couple of girlfriends before I started going out with Janice. In some convoluted way, I got around to talking about Ma and how much I missed her, and that I should have done more to help her out when she was alive. With that came a gusher of tears. I couldn't stop crying, actually sobbing.

In a calmer moment, I expressed my bewilderment. "I didn't even cry that much when my mother actually died." When I made this last disclosure, Karen sat forward, grabbed my wrist, stared at me, and said in a low voice, "I'm thinking something that may explain what has been going on with you. Hear me out. While your mother was alive, you had a heightened sense of responsibility toward her, your immediate family, your siblings, your career, and your job. When you buried your mother, you buried your responsibilities. What happened to you is common in people who do not let themselves grieve, especially when the loss is so devastating." That was the most words I ever heard from her, but they were powerful. As I sat there gathering and further calming myself, I got her point right away. Now my crazy behavior made sense. This explained so much. Karen asked me to think about all this and to come back the following week.

~~~~

Karen Deliverer was a wise woman to see in me what I could not see in myself. Intellectually, I understood the dynamics of unresolved grief. I even witnessed it when a man in a group therapy session I was co-leading with a psychiatrist at the psychiatric unit suddenly became so distraught that he convulsed into a fit of tears and anguish. His two-year-old son fell out of the backseat of the car the man was driving and was killed. We all knew this man well from previous admissions, but this was the first time we heard about this, and it was not in his chart history. This happened over twenty years ago. He said, "I didn't break down much when it happened. I had to be strong for my wife and everyone else." His life had been in turmoil of late with what he thought was just another midlife crisis. This pathological grieving was what Karen saw going on in me, and I was cautiously thinking she might be right.

The next day at work, the first thing I did was to read chapters in my clinical psychiatry textbooks dealing with pathological or unresolved grief and some journal articles that the librarian at work was able to find for me. The process of how unresolved or pathological grief can insidiously produce all kinds of dysfunction later on in a person's life was riveting. I could see myself in so many of the case histories that followed some of the articles. The psychodynamics of my behavior before, during, and especially after Ma's funeral was a textbook example of a disorganized and chaotic life—mine.

After reading and much thinking, I knew I was going back to Janice and the kids. Once I came to this realization, I also knew that living with Cookie was now going to be very difficult. I knew I loved Janice, and I was tired of my deceitful two lives. The difference between real love and infatuation was now quite evident in my clearer thinking mind. But I wanted to be sure that this wasn't just more of my crazy impulsive thinking operating. So I said nothing to Cookie or to Janice about this discovery and insight related to my abandoned sense of responsibility and my unresolved grief over Ma. I used the long drives to and from work to let my mind ruminate about Ma and how my life so radically changed when she died. I remember pulling off onto side roads on more than a few occasions to compose myself before walking into work or into Cookie's apartment.

I purposely did not smoke marijuana or drink alcohol during this time of intense introspection. I wanted to fully experience Ma's death without any masking or distortions. These were painful days but also very insightful. I became more and more confident that Karen Deliverer had discovered proof that counseling was not the crock that she and I had thought it to be. I also knew being distant or aloof was not going to work with Cookie, so I had to act as if our relationship was still intact even though I now knew different.

~~~~

My subsequent visits to Karen's office reinforced the idea that I was taking my life in a different and absolute right direction. I said nothing to Janice, Cookie, or anyone else that change was coming. Janice and I were scheduled for a joint visit on March 20, which was cataclysmic but in a positive way. I told Janice in front of Karen that I loved her and that I wanted to come back home. Instead of unbridled joy and enthusiasm, Janice shocked me with her reserved response, "Are you sure? I don't want you to come back if you are not sure." As I stammered to reassure her, Karen said something like, "I think I'll leave you two alone for a bit." Janice and I were both crying and hugging. It felt so good to be holding her and saying how sorry I was and that there was no doubt that I was doing what was good for us all. We thanked Karen when she returned and left her office a stronger couple but both with concerns. I was concerned about how I could get Janice's trust back, and how I was going to break this news to Cookie who loved me a lot. Janice was concerned that I might not be ready to leave Cookie. With uncertainties abounding, she returned to our home and the kids, and I to the Affluent Towers with Cookie and the now always angry, cupboard-slamming Bernadette.

~~~~

For some unknown reason, neither I nor Karen took time to explain to Janice about how my mother's death had instigated the downfall from my responsible life, and all because I never grieved her fully. This facilitated my launching a chaotic and senseless life path almost destroying my marriage and my career. It was a few days later that I was able to explain to Janice how this all happened. She took me back on faith alone, and I sure am glad she did. Who knows how my life path would have been if she had not got me to go see Karen Deliverer. In recalling those days, Janice says it was all divine intervention that gave her the words that got me to go to the counselor with her.

Without knowing just how to tell Cookie that I was going home and also afraid of her wrath, I again took the coward's route. I left work early one day to take advantage of the apartment being vacant while Cookie and Bernadette were both working. I packed up all my stuff in the few boxes I brought with me while being cautious to leave nothing behind. I couldn't face Cookie, so whatever I took with me now would be it. I was not returning here. I felt like the burglar that I used to be by quietly and surreptitiously gathering all my stuff. I carefully sorted through the stack of record albums and pulled out only those that I knew were mine. I even took my hash pipes but left the stash of marijuana as a goodwill gesture. Wasn't I nice? After an hour or so, I knew I had assembled everything that was mine, and then I sat at the kitchen table and wrote the note that would now devastate Cookie, whom I still cared about but was not in love with. I was again the bastard, but I was not to be deterred from following my path back home to Janice and the kids.

~~~~

Returning home was not the peaceful and joyful life I had anticipated. Janice and I were adjusting to life with me back home, which was not always smooth. It didn't help that Cookie reacted poorly (who wouldn't) to my unexpected, sudden, and thorough departure with rage and severe depression. My work in psychiatry taught me to recognize suicidal thoughts, and I was worried about her. She was so desperate that she called me at work and even at home several times begging me to come see her. I went each time she called even though it strained things between Janice and me. I felt I had to go because I was afraid Cookie would kill herself if I didn't. These visits did not go well. I was too close to her to be of any help to her psychologically. She needed an objective or neutral counselor, but she fiercely rejected any suggestions along those lines. She only wanted me to come back. Nothing else mattered. These were terrible times for Janice whenever I went to see her. Then, the calls stopped. I was worried about Cookie but decided I couldn't help her. So I did not attempt to contact her.

~~~~

About six months or so after this silent period of apprehension, I got a call from Cookie while I was at work. She was calling from a pay phone along a highway which made it hard for me to hear her.

What she told me was that a few months ago she had quit her job, moved out of Bernadette's apartment, put a lot of her stuff into her mother's house, packed up her car, and started driving south with no specific place in mind. I knew she had done this kind of thing in the past because she often told me how she always did it. To motivate herself to leave, she would play the Mamas & the Papas' song "Go Where You Wanna Go" several times and then just leave. She said she did exactly the same thing this time and ended up staying in a small city in South Carolina for no particular reason. She was working as a teacher's assistant in a grammar school and was seeing a counselor. She also got involved in a women's counseling group there that she said really helped her. This particular phone call to me was something her counselor recommended that she do in order to bring closure to our relationship. I was happy that she was in therapy, doing fine, and that she had made the call. Now we could both rebuild our lives, but Cookie would surprisingly reappear in my life a few more times. However, these encounters were not the harmful and destructive aspects like before. When we did meet again, we were each so different in so many ways that our meetings were of no consequence except for the remarkable uncanniness of the encounters.

~~~~

Our recently purchased VW camper, two really cute and funny kids, and a new job all helped Janice and I build a stronger and better life together. However, the love we had for each other was the real foundation for the "new us." We always enjoyed being with each other no matter what we were doing. I realized what I had almost lost and was resolute in that I was not going to endanger what we were building together ever again.

Rebuilding a Life

Physically moving back home was the easy part; regaining the trust of everyone again was much more difficult than I had thought. Some family members were just so glad I came back that they put my crazy times behind them. Sarah, my remarkable mother-in-law, was certainly this sort of person. She never treated me with anything resembling resentment. Based on a remark she made to Bernie during my absence, I was very concerned about seeing her for the first time after I came home. It seems that soon after I had moved out, Sarah said to Bernie in reference to me, "It was like he took a beautiful flower and just crushed it." She, of course, was speaking of what I did to Janice. In spite of these strong feelings, she was very pleased I was back. She was like many people in Janice's family and in mine that never made me feel like the pariah I was. Their interactions were as before. The discomfort I at times felt in their midst was all on my end. I just had to let their acceptance grow in me with each interaction. These people made the transition easy. There were also close friends who reacted the same way, so I just focused on all their welcoming ways and worked at showing them that their trust in me was justified and valued.

However, I had a few other family members and friends that felt so betrayed and were hurt so badly by my lies and breaches of trust that they seemed to find it hard to even be around me, let alone forgive me. Some were blatant about how they felt. They were not readily going to trust me again, and they even told others that they shouldn't trust me either. I understood why they felt this way because I knew how I hurt them deeply. I tried to not react to their coldness and worked to be the person I was before. These people were important to me, and I enjoyed being with them. In order to have it be as it was before, I would need to never deviate again and to accept the hard truth that only my consistent steadfast behavior over time would hopefully repair the hostile chasm I had created. Their trust was important to me, so whatever it took and no matter how long it took I was going regain it.

~~~~

Professionally, it was a little different. What I realized helped me to actually get my present position was the physical distance of the Boondocks Home from the city where all my professional and personal transgressions took place. It was over twenty miles outside of the city, and thus also outside of the OT gossip trail or grapevine. No one knew me at the Boondocks Home or of my crazy past. Mr. Goodforme and the rest of the management staff were so glad to have an OT on staff that where I had worked in the past or how I had acted was of no importance to them. This was truly a clean slate upon which I was free to write the next chapter of my OT life. I was so grateful and humbled for this second chance that I was not going to mess it up.

Within the OT network, I knew that my craziness was well-known. I surmised that the OT staff at the psychiatric unit could not refrain from sharing my deviant behavior with their OT friends in other facilities. I decided to ignore the tension I felt at the OT meetings I attended as the treasurer and act like nothing happened. Knowing that the OT profession was young and transitory, I felt that I could outlast the people and the rumors or stories that may or may not be circulating about me. I just had to now remain above reproach and be professional in all my interactions.

~~~~

Most important to me over all the other people was Janice. She was the one whose trust was now paramount for me to reestablish. Thankfully, she has a trusting nature and grew up in a stable and loving family. Her mother's philosophy regarding people was to always "give them the benefit of the doubt." Her mother never spoke ill of other people, and Janice had absorbed her mother's teachings and attitudes in many ways. This tendency to trust, coupled with my steady and consistent behavior, helped Janice to tentatively move to trust me once again. There were times I knew it was hard for her. I worked in a profession that was 95 percent female, so she had to realize that regardless of the odds and opportunities I would stray no more. What I had almost thrown away was too valuable to me to risk ever jeopardizing again. We had some difficult days, but both Janice and I diligently worked at getting our relationship back, but in even better and stronger ways.

~~~~

Just before we got back together I had bought the 1962 Volkswagen bus that nicely complemented the hippie persona I was still enjoying. We loved that bus. The previous owner had removed the backseats and replaced them with a platform bed. We traveled all around with this jerry-rigged camper. Janice, Peter, and I slept on the bed section, and Beth slept in what in those days was known as a "port-a-crib," which was like a small playpen that fitted nicely between the bed and the front seat. I attached harnesses to the floor of the deck so the kids could move around and play as we rolled through New England and the South on various vacations. The harnesses would never be approved today, but in 1971 front seat belts were all anyone cared about. Staying in campgrounds gave us a chance to inexpensively see a lot of places. We were not true hippies because I worked, and we took pride in acquiring things to make a nice home, but our appearance (yes, even Janice with her long straight hair was taking on the "hippie look") gained us acceptance by lots of interesting people we met along the way.

Challenges and Successes in the Boondocks Home

1971–1974

I had a job! I was a department head responsible for creating the first OT program in a large 650-bed facility. Although it was quite a distance from my home and somewhat isolated out in the "boondocks," it was a second chance for me and my career. I soon realized why no OTs found this facility enticing. If I was not so desperate for a job, I too may have driven on by this decrepit-looking place in pursuit of more modern and progressive-looking facilities. Alas, this was not me. I was extremely thankful for Mr. Goodforme giving me this opportunity, and I was excited to make the most of it.

What I was not prepared for were the four OT students sitting in the lobby on my first day waiting to attend an orientation and tour for new employees (like me) and students (like them). I think I was as befuddled as they. Unbeknownst to me, the head of physical therapy, who was also the head of rehabilitation and my boss, had agreed to have four students do their internship with me for eight weeks. Really? I didn't know what I was doing myself, and now I had four students to train? It gets better. When these students complete their internships, a second group of four would follow. These students were all enrolled in the two-year occupational therapy assistant (OTA) program at the local community college.

It was weird going around on a tour of the facility with students that I was supposed to train. However, I always liked clinical teaching, and this gave me another positive aspect of my new job that I had not anticipated. It had already been arranged that the students would be split up and would each spend a week in the different crafts room dispersed throughout the facility. This gave me some relief because the students had places to work, and I did not need to worry about them just yet.

The orientation tour was memorable for two additional reasons; one good and one not so good. This was when I first met Al Oldman,* the new director of social services who would become one of my best lifelong friends, which was good. The not so good was seeing signs over a half dozen rooms that said Occupational Therapy and being introduced to what were essentially nurse's aides calling themselves occupational therapists. They even had name tags with this title on it. It was Maria's, my former boss at the psychiatric unit, sage advice that I heard in the back of my mind that saved me from saying or doing anything stupid: "Don't try to change things right away. Take time to learn what the place is all about." It gave me the restraint I needed at the time. It felt good to fantasize tearing down invalid OT signs and destroying name tags, but Maria's way proved to be the better course of action.

Another not-so-good thing was the association of crafts with the practice of supposed OT. In the 1970s, the OT profession was distancing itself from crafts in favor of more scientific and therapeutic options. The OTs in this new era were embracing a more medically oriented way of helping patients in the rehabilitation process. We were paralleling and complementing (but not duplicating) physical therapy, and our fragile egos were ashamed of the OT profession's historical association with arts and crafts. For these latter not-so-good reasons it was a very long tour.

~~~~

While I was busy at home rebuilding my relationship with Janice, I was also busy rebuilding my career. It was a period of redemption in so many ways. It felt so good not to be so frenetically unstable. Being more in charge of me and being far less reckless and impulsive was invigorating and satisfying. Staid was now what I wanted my life to be, and it was my obsession to achieve it. Having the respect and trust of family and colleagues was far more important now than I had ever thought possible. I felt each day that I was redeeming myself a little bit more. Fortunately, I learned how fragile and tenuous respect and trust were, and I was cautious not to ever lose them again.

Reintegrating myself back into the family was going well. We attended numerous family gatherings, and no one made me feel unwanted, or brought up my leaving Janice and the kids. The initial awkwardness on my part was overcome with alcohol, usually beer. My brother Pat moved out of Sue and Jim's home and into an apartment just three houses from us on the same street on the West Side. He enjoyed the kids and visited with us often as well as staying for dinner as many times as he was asked. His motivation to move out was not his. Sue recognized the strain of having a moody and difficult person like Pat living with her and Jim, and so she asked Bernie to inform Pat that he had to move. Typically, this sad event became fodder for the Talty humor mill with Pat leading the way. He would often recall how Bernie said to him good naturedly, "Hey, buddy, want to go out for a beer?" As Pat often said, "Yeah, go out for a beer and then told to get out! Bastard!" This was all said with peals of laughter all around in typical Talty humor fashion.

The proximity of Pat's apartment and with Danny living back with Susie gave the three of us lots of opportunities for drinking and drugging, usually on Friday nights. This was one aspect of my life that still had some craziness to it and would have for several more years. I also included some of my new friends from work in our "outings" that gave us even more fun and laughs.

~~~~

Then there was something else that needed my attention: my status in the local OT professional organization that was a branch of the larger state OT association. Having been elected as the treasurer I had a financial record-keeping function as well as a role on the board that I could not shirk. Previously, I did want to resign so that I wouldn't have to face my colleagues who I'm sure were aware of my despicable behavior over the past six months. However, I wouldn't just walk away and bring more shame to my name. So I just sucked it up, did my treasurer's work, and attended the meetings with a fake confident manner. Offering neither explanations nor apologies, I acted like a normal person as much as I could. It worked! My colleagues were glad to see me, and the more normal I acted and spoke, the more their behavior became welcoming and warm.

So rebuilding my life on every front was not easy, but it was well worth it. The place where the rebuilding work was actually the easiest was my job. The staff at the Boondocks Home had no knowledge of my crazy era, and thus there was no need to convince them that I was okay. They just thought I was a bit strange because of my long hair and indomitable spirit. In contrast, many of the people working there were not happy in their jobs. They were hanging on waiting for retirement or hoping that something better would come their way. I think my upbeat personality and enthusiasm for OT at times confounded and probably annoyed them. Regardless, I was going forward and rebuilding my life as well as building an OT department from scratch.

Ironically, my nemesis and former boss Maria at the psychiatric unit (who fired me) gave me even more good advice in terms of how to proceed in my new role in a very different place. As crazy as her management style was, I had always known she was very smart. It was her smart words that were just what I needed at this time. "You know, Peter, you will want to rush in and change things because that's what you do. There are people there who are expecting this and at the same time are fearful of what these changes might be. Don't change anything for a few weeks. Tell your supervisor and your staff that you want to learn as much as you can about what they do and get to know the people there. After you have learned as much as you can, you would like to provide your boss with a long-term plan to implement an OT program where there has never been one before. You don't want to just make changes. You want them to be the right changes." I did exactly as she suggested mainly because I didn't know what else to do. Mr. Goodforme was very impressed with my planned and deliberate approach to my job.

Initially, I think the entire staff was taken aback by my appearance. My hair was long to the extent that I could put it in a ponytail on hot days, and I often did this because the facility was not air-conditioned. With my mustache and long hair, I looked very much like "Meathead" (Rob Reiner) on the popular TV show at the time *All in the Family*. In fact, once when we were traveling through Tennessee in our VW bus, a woman at a restaurant asked me if I was him.

Mine was not the prevailing appearance at the Boondocks Home, but because I conducted myself in a friendly and professional manner at all times, the staff and patients actually came to like and respect me. Politically, I had liberal views, which were also out of sync with the rest of the employees but I was never obnoxious or loud about my values. I let them know I walked a different path in subtle ways like the bumper sticker on my VW bus sympathetic to the 1970 Kent State student deaths: "They shoot students, don't they?" This was a takeoff on a popular movie of the time *They Shoot Horses, Don't They?* Maybe that wasn't so subtle. No one ever commented to me about my beliefs, and I didn't verbalize them to anyone.

~~~~

Fortunately, because no one knew exactly what my role was and what I was supposed to be doing, I could now embark on my mission of data gathering without interference. However, I had no office, no phone, no desk, no equipment, no supplies, no secretarial support, and when I tried to get these things, I was stonewalled. So out of frustration, I went to see Mr. Goodforme and told him of my plight in what I hoped was a mature and non-whining way. He listened and took notes about the things I needed in order to do my job. Then things got a bit tense, not for me but for the people he had his secretary call and summon to his office. His message was direct and to the point with each person that came in: "This is Mr. Talty. He is a professional occupational therapist that we are happy to have here. He is a builder, and he is going to build us a fine occupational therapy department. You are to give him any assistance he needs for him to do his job. Is that understood?" His tone was friendly but serious, and I think they were all chagrined.

The above meetings took place late in the day on a Friday. It was certainly a different place for me come Monday. The business manager paged me early that morning while I was on one of the floors. He wanted me to know that he had established an accounting center for OT, and he gave me the code to use. He also said that if I would put together a list of things I needed, he would procure them for me. At this time there was no money allocated specifically for major OT equipment, but he was confident he could transfer some funds to get me started. He also said that he had ordered a new phone line to be put in as soon as they built my office. What? Office? Built? Where? Who? How?

Later on that day, while I was in the midst of treating patients, the husband of the woman who ran the gift shop and worked for me appeared with two guys. I had begun using part of a large dayroom as my OT area where I worked with patients. He was the superintendent of buildings and grounds, and his attitude was not the one of dismissal that prevailed when his wife first introduced us a couple of weeks ago. In a somewhat deferential way he asked (that's right asked) if he could interrupt me for a moment. He said they were there to measure out where I would like my office. They were going to build me an office about eight feet by twelve feet, and he wanted me to decide which would be the best place for it. I picked a corner near the one entrance where I would have a window. Away they went, moving furniture, measuring, and outlining with tape on the floor where my office was to be constructed.

The whole week went like that. People saw me differently because Mr. Goodforme had clearly communicated to them that I was an important person whose requests were to be taken seriously. I purposely remained humble and appreciative of everyone's efforts to make me comfortable and productive. I was viewed as "Goodforme's golden boy," at least that's what people told me later on when they recalled their first impressions of this long-haired hippie in the white coat. I learned all this, of course, after I had become good friends with the other department heads.

~~~~

The staff was mostly older people who had been with the Boondocks Home for several years and were really not interested in change. Mr. Goodforme told me that he himself had encountered great resistance to change when he first came there a few years before me. When working at the psychiatric unit, I always found the rigid civil service system and accompanying mind-set tiresome and frustrating. My relief came from connecting with some newer and younger department heads. My new friend, Al Oldman, was one of these "new breed" with whom I connected. Al and I found that we had a lot in common. We were both in our mid-twenties, married, and each had two kids. It was when we stopped for a beer after work one day that we discovered that we both had firsthand experience and an affinity for the seedier parts of the downtown area. His came from being a cab driver, and mine as an out-of-control adolescent. We knew many people and places in downtown that most people we worked with did not frequent, and we had fun reminiscing and exchanging "war stories." Al loved people and parties. He was always having parties in his basement bar, and Janice and I attended many of them. He also liked to go to local taverns, and he loved golf. He tried to get me into golf, and I gave it a try for a year or so but gave it up because I was so bad at it.

I and the rest of the younger department heads had vision and energy. We all knew what we wanted to achieve with our professional expertise, and Mr. Goodforme tried to get us the resources we needed to achieve our dreams and along the way make the Boondocks Home a stellar facility. I probably had the biggest challenge because my role was not clearly defined, and I was somewhat encumbered by the entrenched women doing their crafts and calling themselves occupational therapists. This is where I had to ignore my previous boss's advice and institute change probably sooner than she would have recommended. I explained to Mr. Goodforme that the five women working for me could no longer legally call themselves occupational therapists and that they had to have new name tags and job descriptions designating them as OT aides. This was exactly what they were. He agreed and would order the new name tags immediately and that I should go ahead and change the job descriptions. Exerting a little caution into these drastic measures, I asked him not to do that just yet until I had time to explain it to my staff.

So in one of my first staff meetings, I explained the education of an occupational therapist and how their present titles were giving people the wrong impressions. They were depressed to have to get new name tags, and they found their new title of "OT Aide" degrading. They had previously all been institutional aides (nurse's aides) and had taken pride in not having that designation any longer. Regardless, I had a professional, legal, and ethical responsibility to correct this situation, and I set about to do it immediately. I did try to be aware of their emotions and continued to show that I respected them and their work in spite of their new job title.

~~~~

After the storm of the job title changes subsided we settled into a routine of establishing a new OT program in conjunction with carrying on the crafts program and the gift shop activities (ugh!). I was not comfortable with the crafts and gift shop baggage that went with my job, but I could live with it for now. These were hardworking women who took great pride in the craft projects they and the patients made. The gift shop was also an economic success, but surprisingly, the woman who had managed it for years under the title of "Director of Occupational Therapy" took the news of the title change the best. She understood why we had to make the change. It was her support that enabled me to move forward.

Not taking any other immediate action to change everything quickly turned out to be very good advice. The fact that this sage advice came from the person who terminated me from my first OT job was beyond ironic. However, deviating a bit further from her advice to do nothing and to just gather data or information for the first two weeks or so, I took some more bold action steps. Ignoring her advice, I went ahead and started individual treatment OT programs with patients brought to my attention by either the physical therapists or the nursing staff. Ethically and professionally, I couldn't ignore these needs once they were brought to my attention. By doing my best to help these patients, I also forged bridges with the other staff. Because I did most of my treatments in the midst of a large dayroom or the other areas used for the craft-production activities throughout the facility people got to see firsthand what was actually the value of OT. This was a challenging patient population because their diagnoses were often complex, long-standing, unfamiliar, and most had never had the benefit of OT services. I was also working with very little in terms of equipment and supplies.

My four students loved helping me "do real OT," which enabled me to spread myself around and thus help more patients. By working in public arenas, people could see firsthand the kinds of things OTs did to increase strength and range of motion of joints, improve coordination, prevent deformities, and increase independence in self-care. Because many of these patients had diagnoses that I was unfamiliar with, I was doing a lot of reading in order to do the right thing and not to do any harm. It was motivating to me because both the patients and the staff were so appreciative of my efforts. My staff, in addition to the students, in particular wanted to learn and to be a part of this "new therapy". However, the OT aides were a bit conflicted because they were still expected to produce crafts for the gift shop, and I needed their help as my caseload grew beyond what

I could handle by myself. In spite of being a bit conflicted, they were cooperative and followed my directives.

~~~~

Some fortuitous things appeared on the horizon that became impetuses in my efforts to extricate OT from the prevailing crafts-production mentality of the staff. The construction of a brand new building scheduled to open within the year was changing the culture of the Boondocks Home. It was adjacent to the present building and would house the three hundred or more patients in the skilled nursing facility along with modern OT, PT, and speech pathology services. We would also be getting the latest rehabilitation equipment that we had done without for far too long. I had so much fun going through all the rehabilitation equipment catalogs. It was like going Christmas shopping with someone else's credit card. The only proviso Mr. Goodforme gave me was to "order whatever you think you will need, but be sure to make use of it all." I respected him so much that I adhered to this principle in every way.

So, now me and the other progressive-thinking department heads were going to have a fine facility (it was even air-conditioned) and the resources we needed to provide the rehabilitation services our patients deserved. The only thing missing from an OT perspective were additional qualified staff, but this too was about to change. Mr. Goodforme realized that I could not do all that was expected of me with my present unqualified staff and students, and so he approved the hiring of two certified OT assistants (COTAs). Anticipating that I may have difficulty recruiting for this and subsequent positions because of the facility's location, not to mention my reputation, I built a relationship with one of the OT faculty members at the local community college. I did some guest lecturing there, and she, in turn, brought her whole class out to the Boondocks Home where I did demonstrations of OT with a wide range of patients.

~~~~

Proof that my terribly sullied reputation in OT had been erased or forgotten was the response I got when I ran the ad for two COTAs in the local newspaper with my name as the contact person. I intentionally inserted my name into the ad so if applicants had concerns about me professionally, they would opt out of applying. The response was amazing; about eight-five qualified resumes were received. Perhaps, foolishly, I decided to interview every one of them. It was time-consuming, of course, but gave me practice doing something I had never done before. I hired two excellent candidates that really helped me expand the OT services. Coinciding with these additions and moving us closer to becoming a real OT program was the enrollment of two of my OT aides into the evening OT assistant program at the local community college. They both successfully completed the program, and now I had four qualified OT assistants. All these additions made us a legitimate OT program.

~~~~

Things were also working out very well with Janice and me. The further we moved from my "crazy days," the stronger our relationship became, and the more I valued her and the family we were building. I had also successfully regained a respected and comfortable place in our extended families. We frequently hosted family gatherings at our house and had great times when the whole gang got together at either their homes or ours.

~~~~

We had three little mishaps that showed how Janice and I could weather storms of a different nature. One was entirely my doing, one was entirely an accident, and the other remains a mystery to this day. The first sounds bizarre, as I now describe it, because it was, well, bizarre. I loved playing and watching basketball, and I loved playing "pretend" basketball where I would run through our long kitchen, dining room, and living room, pretending I was playing basketball complete with imaginary dunks and alley-oops. On one of my "fast breaks" that included the use of a sponge for my "basketball," I went up to dunk next to our new and beautiful china cabinet. I misjudged something, struck the china cabinet with my shoulder, and caused the top of the china cabinet to slide off the base. I tried to grab it, but it was too massive. The best I could do was to prevent it from falling completely off the base as it tipped forward. The glass doors across the front all swung open, and our china and crystal came crashing to the floor. The loud noise of dishes and glasses crashing sequentially to the floor was a continuous roar that brought Janice running from the back bedroom to see her crazy husband trying to maneuver the top of the china cabinet back onto the base surrounded by piles of broken glass and china. All I said was "Don't say anything." She had to ask "Are you okay?" I nodded yes, and she left me to clean up the awful mess I had made. Typical of Janice, she found good even in this outlandish event.

She returned in a short while as I was shoveling the remains of our good china and crystal into a garbage can and said, "At least no one was hurt. Imagine if Peter had been playing in here when this happened. You know, it also was good that this happened today because a lot of our dishes and crystal were not in the cabinet. I hadn't had a chance to put all the dishes back in after yesterday's dinner." How many other people would have responded in this way? Janice is unique, and she, of course, was right. We had the family over for dinner the day before, and after washing all the dishes and glasses, they were sitting on our dining room table, waiting for Janice to put them back in their proper spots. There was lots of room for them now. This story has been told and retold by us throughout the years, and we still laugh about it. Janice does not hold grudges or resentments, and that was such a big help in moving past disasters like these.

~~~~

Subsequent to the "china cabinet fiasco," a large section of our plastered ceiling fell down, making a loud terrifying sound. We were fortunate once again in that Peter had just been playing in that area just prior to the crash. It was no one's fault. The only good part of this almost tragedy was having Peter take everyone who came to our house into the living room and pointing up to the gaping hole. He couldn't talk yet, but he pointed in such a cute way we loved to ask him over and over, "What happened?" With that, he would run into the living room and point up.

~~~~

The last mishap from those days remains a mystery, but it did make the local TV news under the heading of "Hot Wheels." One summer night while we were sleeping, we were awoken by our phone ringing and, simultaneously, a pounding on our front door. On the phone was our tenant from the front upstairs apartment. She could see what she thought was a fire that was in the rear of our house that she couldn't see clearly from her front apartment, and she was terrified that the house was on fire. At the front door was the morning newspaper carrier alerting us to a fire in the back of our house. The house wasn't on fire, but the five-car garage forty feet from the house was fully ablaze. I told Janice to call the fire department while I ran outside. She went first into Peter's bedroom and found him awake, standing in his crib with the curtain pulled back and watching the spectacle in our backyard. The whole garage was engulfed. The heat and flames were so intense that they were melting the paint off the back of our house and cracking the window panes. Someone besides Janice must have called the fire department because they arrived so quickly. However, there wasn't much they could do to save the garage. What their focus seemed to be was preventing the cars from exploding and the flames from reaching other structures. The gathering neighbors joined us as we watched spellbound as the flames raced through the crumbling structure. Janice had gotten the kids up in case we had to evacuate the house, and they all watched the spectacle from the bedroom window.

The next day we went out to survey the damage as the arson investigators went about their work. There were three cars lost in the inferno. Our cool, brand new, red Mercury Montego that we bought when we traded in our VW bus was destroyed. Also, the man next door who rented a garage from us lost his beloved Lincoln Continental, and the guy who rented one of our apartments was grief-stricken over the loss of his Corvette. My brother Pat who lived just down the street from us missed the fire itself, but he was entranced by the remains, especially the fiberglass Corvette that melted like the witch from *The Wizard of Oz*.

They could never figure out what or who caused this fire. We were afraid someone would come back and maybe set our house on fire. This kind of fear stuck with us all for many years. I, perhaps selfishly, felt an even deeper loss because now my basketball court was gone. Janice's calm response during these three mishaps simply reinforced the idea that this was a unique woman, and I was so glad I did not foolishly end our marriage.

~~~~

Coincidentally, I had moved out of my hippie phase and now felt we needed a more mature and practical vehicle. The Mercury Montego was a sporty-looking car that we were thrilled to own, but it was no more. The insurance money gave us the opportunity to take our transportation needs and recreational interests and combine them. Janice and I really enjoyed traveling and camping out in our VW bus, and so we bought a used pop-up camper to be pulled by the car that replaced the Montego—a Ford station wagon that Janice found and purchased. I had confidence in her to find and select our next car as long as it could pull a pop-up camper. She took a friend of ours who was a mechanic to look it over, and he pronounced it to be a fine car. The first time I saw the station wagon is when Janice brought it home. How's that for trust and confidence in a wife?

The station wagon and pop-up camper both worked out very well for us. We got to travel with the kids all over on vacations and took numerous short-distance weekend trips. The pop-up was a delight in comparison to the cramped VW bus. We now had two full-size comfortable beds and hookups for water and lights, and we were in heaven. Janice was able to make curtains to go with the large screened windows all around. Of course, Janice and I spent a lot of time basking in our luxurious outdoor accommodations.

The only negative thing about the pop-up camper was my inability to back it up. In spite of repeated trials, the popup was always jackknifing on me. I just could not make it go straight back. So the solution was for us to pull into a campground, find our site, disconnect the pop-up, and then Janice and I would push it into place. We did the same thing when we got home. I still cannot back up a trailer.

~~~~

Just before the garage fire, around Janice's birthday on May 4th, I decided to throw her a surprise party. She was going to have her hair cut by her cousin who lived across the street from us, so I set that as the night for the party. I put together a food and drink menu, but I couldn't have anything in our house because she would find it and the surprise would be ruined. So when I called to invite each person to the party, I also asked if they could bring some specific item on my list. Everyone was very agreeable. Pat kept the beer and soft drinks in his refrigerator until the big night. I then had to coordinate arrival times so she wouldn't accidentally run into any of the guests while going or coming from her cousin's house.

I had about thirty people all crammed into our master bedroom with the door shut when I called her to say that the baby (Beth) had thrown up. I knew this would bring her running, and it did. I was in the kitchen as she came flying in the back door, and frantically asked, "Where is she?" I said, "In our bedroom." She really got frantic then and exclaimed incredulously as she raced to the bedroom, "You left her on the bed (she was just six months old) and with the door shut?" It was with confusion, rage, and anxiety that she thrust open the door to thirty people yelling, "*Surprise!*" Boy, was she surprised! After she calmed down and saw that Beth was safe and asleep in her crib she was pleased that I would put this all together for her. Everyone had a great time, and Janice has a special birthday memory.

~~~~

I continued to improve my clinical skills as an OT by reading my textbooks and journals and by attending workshops and conferences on a myriad of topics. Once I rode a Greyhound bus for six hours across the state to attend a two-day splinting workshop that proved quite valuable throughout my career. It was also fortuitous that a physical therapist from the university offered a course in an advanced treatment for strokes known as neurophysiological facilitation one evening a week for fifteen weeks right at the Boondocks Home that I was able to take. Besides being very convenient, it paid off in many ways with my present caseload and a future offer for a faculty position (more on that later). Because the Boondocks Home was a ways from the city where much of the continuing education programs took place, a communications arrangement was provided. These were referred to as Tele-lectures, and were conducted through a speaker phone system, I could take advantage of many presentations. At the time I went to OT school, we did not have a course in management, so I tried to attend as many of the related Tele-lecture programs on management and supervision as possible.

~~~~

Another opportunity also came my way, which I seized immediately. Mr. Goodforme informed us at a department head meeting that able-bodied people who were receiving public assistance (pejoratively referred to as "Welfare") were now required to work in the various facilities, which included the Boondocks Home, in order to continue receiving their checks. The rest of the department heads were resistant and had concerns that these were unsavory people that could not be trusted. One of the department heads captured the mood of the group when he pronounced, "We don't need the kinds of trouble those people would bring us no matter how much help they might be." I felt differently and said, "I need help transporting patients to and from OT. So I will take all people I can get." The OT department was over a quarter a mile, plus an elevator ride, from where the patients' rooms were located. The transporting of patients consumed a great deal of OT staff time and thus limited the time we had available to work with the patients. I think just about everyone in the room thought I had lost my mind, but I didn't care. Ever since my internship and subsequent job at the psychiatric unit I knew the therapeutic value of work. My vision was that people receiving Welfare could help us while we gave them experience within a worker role that may have been lost or perhaps never even been established.

I was ready for these new workers, but they didn't come. I repeatedly asked Mr. Goodforme when they were coming, but he didn't know. I continued to press him until he gave me the name of the person in charge of the program and permission for me to contact him directly. I set up an appointment and went downtown to his office. At first he was not very responsive, but once I explained my vision, he went from skeptical to curious, and, ultimately, to very enthusiastic. He wanted to come out to the Boondocks Home to see the whole place and how I planned to implement my therapeutic work program with his Welfare clients. A few days later he came out with his assistant, and I showed them around the facility explaining the way I saw this program benefiting our residents as well as the workers. By the time they left, I could see that they were impressed with the training and supervision I intended to provide. I was now confident that my dream of a work program was going to happen.

I then convinced my staff that we could make this work and get a lot of free help if they would just follow my lead. I had a number of principles I wanted my staff to adhere to when interacting with our eagerly awaited (at least by me) volunteer workers. Why a person was on Welfare was a private matter and one we would not question them about. We also were going to treat each one of them with respect. I was going to have a name tag made for each one of them, but they could decide how they would like their name on it. If they wanted it to say Mr. or Ms. or Mrs. or their first and last name, it was up to them. I wanted them to interact with the patients and the rest of the staff in a professional and caring way and I would train them in how I wanted them to safely and respectfully transport our patients. What they would get in return was the freedom to select which days they wanted to work each month (the required number of workdays were set by the department of social services varying from five to nineteen days per month), but they could pick the actual days to work. If they were reliable and responsible, I would also give them a letter of recommendation to assist them in becoming gainfully employed and thus off Welfare. I also encouraged everyone to use the terms "Public Assistance" rather than Welfare which had such a negative connotation.

The first couple of workers arrived within a few days after the head of the program came to visit. Because they did not have cars, they had to gather downtown in front of the County office building where a school bus would transport them out to us. My staff was terrific in following the principles and procedures I modeled. They sounded like me in every way. The program worked! It grew to where we had ten to fifteen people coming out every day. Besides having very good patient transporters, I found a highly efficient secretary and an unemployed certified schoolteacher. Perhaps the crowning moment came when other department heads asked me to assign some of the workers to them. A few were even hired by the Boondocks Home and proved to be good and dependable workers.

It was ironic that the schoolteacher found his way to us at the time he did. We had just moved into our beautiful new facility, which had more space than was needed at the time. Coincidentally, one of the OT aides that I inherited when I first started working at the Boondocks Home was a former teacher. She and I had often talked about starting a school for the patients. Mr. Goodforme loved the idea and gave us a room in the new facility. We were able to get books and supplies donated through local schools, and we opened our school. It quickly became so successful that one teacher couldn't handle it all.

We had patients learning to read and write for the first time, others working on their GED, and some just exploring areas of interest like history and literature. When I assigned our newfound teacher to the school, we really were able to provide our patients with quality educational experiences.

~~~~

Once we had moved into the new facility, the county wanted to renovate what was known in those days as the "Health-Related Facility. Today it would be very similar to an assisted living facility. It housed a little over 300 people who were designated as "residents" to differentiate them from the 300 patients in the skilled nursing facility. They were all ambulatory, and many of them had little jobs like delivering mail for which they received a bit of spending money. The dilemma facing the county was where to house these 300 people while their facility was being renovated, and what about their jobs? They could not live in the building that we just vacated; it was eventually going to be demolished because of its poor condition.

Someone in the upper levels of county government came up with an ingenious proposal to solve the Boondocks Home's housing problem. There was an empty dormitory at that time on a local state college campus (a separate institution from the university) that once held three hundred students. Why not, he proposed, temporarily move the health-related residents into this dormitory for the year that the renovations were taking place and then move them back? Although I and several others thought this was a very creative solution, there were many of the department heads who shouted it down when Mr. Goodforme first presented it. A bitter argument ensued. There were those who envisioned our vulnerable residents being abused and neglected in this high-rise tower in the midst of an urban campus. They feared that the residents would wander off into unsafe areas, be robbed and beaten and left for dead. I championed an opposite view that this group was more resilient than they believed, and that I knew firsthand that the campus was in a much safer area than they thought. However, neither side really knew how well this population would or would not adapt to this drastic, albeit temporary, shift in living conditions. Because I have little tolerance for circuitous arguments without actual data, and being a risk-taker, I boldly volunteered to assess each resident to determine their ability to weather this drastic change. Because I had, by this time, established a high level of credibility with all the department heads, they readily supported me in this new venture, as did Mr. Goodforme.

~~~~

I took a few days to put together a cursory assessment of function that looked at self-care, cognition, and overall health including endurance, range of motion, and functional ambulation. I started by quickly reviewing each resident's chart and then took each resident through my assessment process. I was able to do about ten to fifteen of these assessments a day, so within a month I had written a comprehensive report with supporting data to endorse the idea that these were high-functioning people who could manage this change quite well. I actually believed that this change would be invigorating for many of them. When I put all my findings together into a report, I presented them to the department heads. It swayed the most vocal naysayers, and it was decided to go forward with this innovative solution. However, someone identified a concern that none of the rest of us thought was important at the time. What would the one hundred or so working residents do with their time once they moved, and what sorts of recreational programs would keep the total population from regressing? Mr. Goodforme gave me and the director of recreation the task of devising a plan that would keep the residents engaged in some purposeful activity while living on the campus. None of us wanted this group to deteriorate because of boredom or idleness.

~~~~

At the time, I was wrestling with an unrelated staffing dilemma of my own as we were planning for this big move. With the addition of the qualified cadre of COTAs to carry out the OT programs I devised after I evaluated each of the skilled nursing patients, there was no longer a legitimate role for the OT aides I had inherited. I had been attending a number of lectures on supervision and management and was concerned how to use what I had learned in the lectures to solve this dilemma. Of the five OT aides I inherited, two had graduated from the OT assistant program at the local community college, so they were fine. One was the teacher that helped me get our school up and running. Although I was ordered by Mr. Goodforme to transfer the remaining two OT aides back to nurse's aides positions, I was trying to find an alternative role for them. They were older and would probably now find the strenuous work as a nurse's aide far too taxing.

It then occurred to me that, once again, I could use my fondness for therapeutic work to solve two problems. The recreation director and I began meeting with a number of people on the college campus, searching for activities for our residents. This being the early 1970s, the students had a caring and helping attitude about them that was very encouraging. The various student clubs, like photography, were excited to have our residents join them. These kinds of activities, coupled with connecting students with individual residents, would help resolve the problem of idle time or vacant hours. This left the group that really was only interested in working, and there were almost eighty of them. So I approached the two OT aides about working with me to create and oversee a therapeutic work program on the college campus.

One did not want to make the twenty-mile trek into the city each day and so elected to transfer back to her nurse's aide job for the remaining year prior to her retirement. The other OT aide was thrilled to have this new responsibility in lieu of "returning to the floor."

So we started by identifying as many jobs as we could at the college campus that were similar to the jobs our residents held at the health-related facility. Mr. Goodforme agreed to continue paying the residents, which was very important to them. We were able to find similar and new jobs for all those who wanted to work. Some were working with student groups and departments of the college. Once we had the work program in place, the move took place with sixty residents a day transferred into the dormitory via school buses until all three hundred were moved in. The move went very well, as did the entire year the residents spent on the campus. My OT aide turned "work supervisor" did a fine job, and I was proud of her. She also retired when the move back was completed. When the year was up, the residents were moved back into their renovated rooms and were very happy. In the year they lived among college students, there was not one incident of mistreatment in any way. It was an all-around success, and I was pleased to be a part of it.

~~~~

With all the success I was having establishing a very successful and diverse OT program, plus forging a significant enhancement in my family relationships, you would think my sense of disparity would no longer be an issue. Wrong! I wanted the normalcy in a family and was working hard to provide a stable, fun, and supportive environment for them. However, we were struggling a bit to pay all our bills and still have enough money left over to do the extra things we enjoyed. So I had a form of self-induced economic disparity. Janice was always satisfied with whatever we had and was never hungering for more. Thus, the pressure I felt was all self-generated.

~~~~

Another source of disparity came from my feeling that I was not working in an elite facility with the highest caliber of staff. I looked at the big facilities in the area and wished I was the director of OT in one of them. It was this sense of disparity coupled with my usual willingness to take chances that caused me to always search for new ways to use my OT education. The nursing staff had developed two programs they called *remotivation therapy and reality orientation* for patients with varying levels of dementia. Today, a similar unit would be called a "memory care unit". I saw this as the next opportunity for me to expand OT's footprint in the facility. The nurses were very pleased to hear that OT was interested in partnering with them to advance the program further since a significant number of patients had dementia.

Mr. Goodforme was also excited about where I intended to take OT next, but he felt that I should go to the guru of dementia treatment at the University of Alabama for further training. I loved to learn, and I had read much of the guru's writings. In the late 1960s and early 1970s, he was a pioneer working with people most professionals were avoiding because of their poor prognosis. I was able to get approval to take a young man, who was one of the new OT assistants that I had hired, with me to Alabama.

We spent a week in Tuscaloosa, Alabama, learning everything we could about their signature program: "Reality Orientation". The training was conducted by a number of different staff members with the guru being the main instructor. Because the training went on continuously for many visitors throughout the year, the staff had the week highly structured and organized. Spending a week on the beautiful University of Alabama campus was a bonus.

When I returned to the Boondocks Home, the OT staff was nervous that I would make them abandon all the good work we were doing in OT and concentrate instead on people with dementia. I assured them that we were not going to drastically change what we were doing. However, I was excited to find a way to combine the new interventions for dementia with that of OT. Even though I was a risk-taker, I was not foolish enough to commit all our time to a population whose prognosis was not very promising. However, I was impressed with the reality orientation approach. In their view, if you could help improve function in one-third of the people with dementia, keep one-third from getting worse, and then provide supportive care for those who did not respond, you were having an impact. This is what I kept in mind as I ventured forth into this new area of my OT practice.

I should explain that in the early 1970s Medicare was not the controlling force in rehabilitation it is today. Now much of what therapists do with their time and who they work with and for how long are dictated not by the therapist but by Medicare regulations and reimbursement strategies. At the time I was at the Boondocks Home, Medicare was just beginning to become the force it is today. This meant that I had a great deal of autonomy and could deploy my OT staff in any way I chose. So it was off to work with people with dementia while maintaining the services we had already established. Rather than duplicate what the nursing staff was doing with their reality orientation and remotivation programs, I felt we could use our knowledge of the brain and the nervous system to effect change of some sort in a different way.

Through a series of sensory experiences, we found that people with dementia became more responsive. I also found support for this idea in the current literature. With the help of my OT assistants, we developed a structure and sequence of sensory experiences within a group context that was encouraging. It was fatiguing, demanding, and unrewarding work at first. However, I had a staff that believed in what I was trying to achieve. Eventually, we hit upon the kinds of sensory-stimulating experiences that increased attention and retention in some of the patients. The results were not spectacular, but they were encouraging. As our successes grew, the nursing staff began to extol the value of what I had named "Sensory Training". I wrote a training manual to help have consistency regardless of which one of us was running a sensory training group. I also made additional copies to give to the staff outside of OT so that they would understand what we were doing. The concept of sensory training got further impetus when Mr. Goodforme asked me to present it to a group of nursing home administrators to which he belonged. He was hosting the monthly meeting at our facility, and wanted to show them the good work we were doing in the area of dementia. I did the presentation, distributed copies of the sensory training manual to the forty or so attendees, and then we brought in a group of patients with dementia and demonstrated how we conducted the program.

Everyone was very impressed, and a number of them asked me to help them develop a sensory training program in their facilities as a paid consultant. Of course, I seized every one of these opportunities.

Subsequent to the above demonstration, Mr. Goodforme asked to meet with me and my friend Al Oldman, the director of social services. He told us that he got a call from a man who ran the office of the aging for a four-county coalition that was looking to provide training in community resources and treatment services for people with dementia in many of the nursing homes in a rural area of an adjacent state. He wanted to know if we were interested in helping them out. I immediately said yes, of course, because I was always looking for ways to earn extra money in order to reduce my sense of economic disparity, and I was not fearful of risky ventures into the unknown. Al was more of a conservative laid-back guy who was content with just managing the rigors of his everyday life. He had a lot of questions about how far away it was, what did they want exactly, how would he do that work and his regular job, and so forth. I'm thinking and shouting in my brain, *Shut up. You're going to blow this*. So to get us further connected, I volunteered to call this person to get more information. Mr. Goodforme was glad to get this off his desk and still be responsive to a colleague's request, and Al was glad that he didn't have to commit to something without knowing more about it.

I made the call with Al in my office. It turned out that the agency had already secured the grant, and it would be a rewarding contract for Al and me. We would need to travel the two or so hours each way to various locations out of state to provide the training. Since it would be providing educational services and enhancing the image of our facility, I convinced Mr. Goodforme to approve our paid absences for four trips over the next two months. This was a nice little bonus for us. Al was getting excited the more we learned about their training needs and how our combined expertise would result in a quality educational experience for all who attended. We agreed to the terms of the consulting contract and set the dates for the four visits. The training went very well and we got a lot of praise. I had been doing a lot of teaching of this nature at the facilities where I consulted on my sensory training program and was really falling in love with teaching.

It seemed that the more teaching I did as a guest lecturer at the university and the community college in their OT programs, the more requests I got for teaching opportunities both paid and unpaid. One paid teaching opportunity I was able to seize was the teaching of a course I designed on "Interpersonal Skills for Activity Coordinators" that met once a week for eight weeks. It was fun doing OT, but I discovered that it was also a lot of fun to teach. I had no intention of leaving OT to go into education but did enjoy the duality of these roles.

~~~~

The American OT Association (AOTA) gave me another opportunity to grow, which I also seized immediately. I read where AOTA had a large grant to develop leaders within the OT profession. As I read through the application process, I felt my progressive and diverse experiences as a department head building a new OT service delivery system would qualify me. I immediately put together the application and submitted it as soon as the notice came out. I felt I had a good chance to be selected, and I was! It involved two all-paid expenses to Boston, Massachusetts, with six months off in between. The training on leadership skills was very interesting because it had a community focus. The future of OT was for there to be far more practice in the community in addition to institutional settings, and AOTA wanted leaders across the country that could provide the necessary direction. I took Janice with me on the second session, and we had a great time touring about Boston when I wasn't in the training sessions.

A Scary Time for Our Baby

In August of 1972, when Beth was just nineteen months old, she became very ill. It started with a cold that quickly progressed to where she wasn't her usually lively and joyful self. Janice knew there was something more serious going on, and even though it was a Sunday afternoon, she called our pediatrician, Dr. Helpakid.* She left a message, and we waited anxiously for his call back. In the meantime, Beth was in a deep sleep, and we really could not arouse her. We were very worried.

Although it seemed like several hours, it was probably in less than an hour Dr. Helpakid called us back. After hearing Janice describe how Beth was not responding, he told us to bring her right out to his house. This certainly is not the norm these days. He told us later on that he knew Janice was not an over-reactive mother, and that is why he wanted to see Beth as soon as possible. So we quickly packed up Beth and Peter and drove to Dr. Helpakid's home. He examined her and told us to take her right to the emergency room. He was going to call the hospital and tell them to expect us. At the hospital, they took her right in and did a spinal tap. This confirmed what Dr. Helpakid's suspected that she had meningitis. Apparently, there were over twenty different types, but they could not tell just yet what type she had.

Coincidently, the resident on duty was someone who I had worked with at the psychiatric unit when he was working there as part of a clinical rotation while he was in medical school. He remembered me, and he was on our team before I lost my way or mind. So he was very helpful in explaining everything to us as were the nurses.

Beth was admitted and put in a crib on one of the floors. She looked so little in the crib. It was very hard to see our bubbly baby in a coma. They started her on antibiotics with an IV, which made us both sad and hopeful. One of us had to stay with Peter downstairs, while either Janice or I stayed with Beth. We were very worried because we did not know how serious this was and what the outcome was going to be. This is where my limited education generated terror in me that I kept to myself. Leaving her that night was very hard for us.

I didn't go to work for a couple of days, waiting until Beth's crisis was resolved. It was great joy when they told us that she was getting better and that she had the milder form of meningitis with an excellent prognosis. She came out of her comatose state and wanted to get up and play, but she had to remain on bed rest for a few more days. I used my OT skills and brought in several of her toys and decorations for her room. She had a pull toy that needed two hands to operate, but because of the IV and her hand strapped to a board, she only had one hand available. With lots of tape, I secured the toy to her crib rail so that she could spin the dial to the picture of a farm animal, pull the cord, and hear the sound of the corresponding farm animal. She loved it, and I loved hearing her familiar giggles filling the room. I also took several of her plastic Disney characters and hung them from the window frames, the walls, the ceiling, or anywhere else she wanted.

After a couple of more days, she was off bed rest but had to keep the IV in her arm. They gave her a wheeled pole with the IV attached and showed her how to maneuver it around the floor. She quickly became the nurses' favorite as she wandered in and out of rooms calling "nuuse" in the cutest way. After a total of ten days, she was discharged to the great relief of Janice and I and everyone else in our family.

The Grand Geriatric Facility

1973–1977

So after three dynamic and rewarding years at the Boondocks Home, I decided to see if I could parlay all I had achieved into a better position. By better, I mean better pay and larger scope of responsibilities as well as the opportunity to grow in whatever ways possible. Janice and I talked it over, and she was supportive of my need to grow and to lessen my sense of economic and professional disparity by seeking positions out of town. Most of both of our families were rooted in our hometown, and this would be a difficult adjustment for all if we were to move away. Regardless, I was going to explore the market to see what my value was and to see what kinds of opportunities may be out there. We did not make any announcements to the family about our potential for moving out of town because we knew it may not happen and so did not want to rile people unnecessarily.

I sent résumés to six or so facilities and two universities. There were two faculty positions that I found attractive, and at that time, you could be appointed to an OT faculty post without a doctorate. If you had the bachelor's degree in OT and significant related clinical experience, a college or university would appoint you to a faculty post with the understanding that you would obtain advanced degrees within a specified number of years. One of these was a large Midwestern university. It's ironic that the main thing that caught their attention on my résumé was the continuing education course that I completed in Neurological Facilitation. This was the course I took at the Boondocks Home taught by the physical therapist from the university. What I learned in that course and applied in practice was cutting edge information in 1974, and they needed someone with this background to teach a course in this area. They were so impressed with my background that they paid for my flight and a three-day stay at their campus. They also offered me a faculty position after I had been back home for a couple of weeks.

The other faculty position I applied for was in Canada. This also was an impressive campus and OT program, but they could not appoint a non-Canadian unless there were no qualified Canadian candidates. The officers at the bridge going into Canada gave me such a hard time about "taking a job away from Canadians" detaining me at the border for several hours that I was no longer serious about pursuing this position even if it were offered (which it wasn't).

In addition to the faculty post, I was also offered a position as director of OT at a large developmental center in Michigan, which was attractive for a number of reasons. It was a large OT department, well-established, and the executive director of the whole institution was an OT and a well-respected member of the OT profession.

The last place I interviewed at was the Grand Geriatric Facility,[*] which was only about three hours from our hometown. It was most impressive in terms of a dynamic future for the organization and hopefully me. They were getting ready to open a new thirteen-story tower to house 1,000 skilled nursing residents, including the most up-to-date rehabilitation departments of OT, PT, speech, and audiology. They had quite a campus with several levels of care, including a twenty-story tower for 240 well elderly living in their own apartments. Overall, the Grand was the most progressive facility and staff I had ever experienced. After spending two days interviewing and touring the existing and reviewing the plans for the future facilities, I was sold on them, and it appeared like they wanted me. Salary, resources, planning, and organization were all way above the other job offers I had received. Plus, we would not be far from our roots and our families.

However, what really sold me on the Grand was the interview with Dr. Way Insightful,* the medical director. His professionalism, management style, candor, and sense of humor were everything I wanted in a supervisor. But what really convinced me that this is a guy I could respect and work for was his response when I explained the kind of OT program I wanted to build.

After I explained how the type of OT program I wanted to build was different from what I saw, the COTA doing, who was already employed there, he listened carefully. I'll never forget his words, "Look, if we have you come here to build our OT program, you bring the concept of OT. By us committing to you, we are committing ourselves to the brand of OT you bring. We will support you in every way we can. You are the professional OT, and it is our job to get you the resources necessary for you to get the job done." That's all I needed to hear. I told him I would very much like to join the Grand staff, and he was very pleased. He explained that the final decision would be made by Mr. Walter Czar,* the executive director, who I would be interviewing with next.

Perhaps it was reckless to do on an interview, but one of the things I was doing during my rounds of recent interviews was to be somewhat confrontational in a professional sort of way. I felt that I could be brazen on the interview because I had a secure position at the Boondocks Home. It was my hope that they would see me as an assertive person who could effectively lead an OT department. I also felt that this was the time to establish some boundaries, and if this approach prevented me from getting a job offer, then it probably wouldn't have worked out anyway. So, it was with this mindset that I entered Mr. Czar's expansive office. He was impressive with his poise, dress, presence, and mannerisms. He was friendly but direct in his communication, so I felt my confrontational approach would win him over. It didn't work as well as I had hoped. Not knowing that he had designed the organizational chart, I openly criticized the structure that placed OT, PT, and speech pathology at a level below department head but then had the activities director at the same level as the medical director. I questioned his rationale for this inappropriate arrangement, but he did not flinch. "OT, PT, and speech are not needed by every single person who is admitted here, and this organizational chart is based on the principle that the disciplines involved in the lives of every person coming through our doors would be the department heads." His wording and speech was crisp and unwavering.

I explained to him that from my perspective, "OT was the discipline that could really enhance the lives of every resident far more than activities and that this perspective on OT he had adopted was too narrow and outdated. My expanded brand of OT is what this population needed." There it was; the line in the sand was now drawn. Who would acquiesce? Certainly not Mr. Czar.

I saved the day and perhaps the job I wanted by saying, "We obviously both feel strongly about our positions, but this does not mean we cannot work toward a common end: what is best for the residents." This gave us common ground. I knew that Dr. Insightful had already told him that I was the person he wanted to be the Chief of OT, so I felt Mr. Czar also wanted to endorse me. However, I did have to say one more thing on the way out the door to let him know I was not happy with OT's position on his personally carved totem pole. "I respect your position, but be aware that my objective is to convince you that when you see the kind of OT I bring that you will be making a place for me at the department head table." He laughed and said he "appreciated my drive and commitment to my profession and looked forward to being educated in this new way of viewing OT."

What ensued next was a round of interviews with the other professional staff, and they all went well. I ended up back in Dr. Insightful's office, where he quickly closed his door, shook my hand, and asked, "What did you say to Mr. Czar? Right after you left his office, he was on the phone to me all excited, but not in a good way. Regardless, whatever went on in there, he liked you, and that's all I care about, but he said something about you not liking his organizational chart." He was asking for a play-by-play of our exchange, which I provided in some detail and watched him become increasingly delighted as I told him the story of my interview with Mr. Czar. Apparently, according to Dr. Insightful, few people besides him spoke up when they didn't agree with Mr. Czar, and he enjoyed hearing about someone else who was not intimidated by him.

Dr. Insightful gave me a tip about negotiating my salary. "If you don't feel the salary they're offering you is fair, you could try what I did. I told them if you give me what I'm making in my three jobs combined, I'll come here. It worked!" So off I went back to Mr. Czar to hear the job offer. He was friendly, but I think I detected an edge to his voice as he laid out the salary and benefits package they were offering. I didn't get to use Dr. Insightful's strategy exactly because Mr. Czar went on the offensive. "I see on your résumé that you do a lot of moonlighting as a consultant. If you come here, we wouldn't permit this moonlighting. We don't think it reflects well on our organization if any of our professional staff is scrambling around the community just trying to make a buck." I was shocked, appalled, and enraged. How dare him! Not in the calmest of voice, I challenged, "How does the Grand have the right to dictate what employees do with their free time?" I may have gone too far. Did I just blow this great opportunity? If I did, I wasn't going to cower. If I didn't get this job, my confidence from the offers I had already received gave me the impression that I was a person that people wanted to hire. Without pause, he said, "Let's talk salary. Here is the salary range for the Chief OT position. What do you think?" Remembering Dr. Insightful's strategy, I said coolly, "I would love to focus all my energy on one job, and this is the position that holds the most attraction for me for a lot of reasons. I have four offers on my desk right now that are also attractive, but none have the unique vision as to what this organization is going to become. Your salary offer is more than all the others and your benefits package far superior. So I can forgo moonlighting." With that, he stood, put out his hand, shook mine firmly, and, with a smile (not a big one), said, "Welcome to the Grand Geriatric Facility."

~~~~

In a few days after my visit, I received a formal offer of employment from the Grand, specifying everything just as we agreed. This position brought a significant increase in my salary and thus reduced my sense of economic disparity commensurately. Naturally, I accepted, but I did realize that the path of establishing a unique, dynamic, and all-encompassing OT program was not going to be as easy as it was at the Boondocks Home. There I had Mr. Goodforme's support right from the beginning. Although I was viewed by some as Goodforme's "Golden Boy", I was also something of a wunderkind because I was able to accomplish a great deal even without the best of resources. Could I achieve all this and more now that I was joining a progressive organization rich in people and tangible resources? My concern at the Grand was Mr. Czar's entrenched view that OT was a limited service paralleling that of PT. I was intent on changing his mind and gaining his support ala Mr. Goodforme.

~~~~

Before I leave the Boondocks Home, I need to explain how a simple little book impacted Janice, me, and our life together. *I'm OK—You're OK* written by Thomas Harris, MD was a best seller in 1970. It was a practical and easy to understand approach to human behavior and interpersonal communication built around what Harris called Transactional Analysis (TA). After reading the book, I became enamored—no, actually, obsessed—with TA and attended several workshops on it. I bought copies of the book for all my OT staff and taught them ways of more effectively managing their own behavior and the behavior of our patients and one another. I eventually became sort of a TA guru and even did a presentation on it at the monthly meeting of the local OT association.

The best part of TA is what it did for me personally. It gave me a very good way of further understanding my own bizarre behavior following my mother's death. The multiple levels and aspects of TA provided the framework that I needed for dealing with my past, present, and future difficult interpersonal situations and people I was about to encounter.

I taught TA to Janice, and she was inspired to take a college course in it that helped her with the kids as well as the residual feeling from my sudden departure and overall craziness after Ma died. We used it to better communicate with each other and to move on from my past transgressions. She still says today that *I'm OK—You're OK* changed her life. I would agree, but it really changed all our lives. TA, of course, is not really relevant forty-five years later, but it was just what we needed back in 1971.

Accepting the position as the chief of occupational therapy at the Grand Geriatric Facility was both exciting and scary. This was the dream job I was hoping to find. Everything was new, including most of the staff. The Grand had amassed an amazing team of professionals from across the country heading every department and all led by the young and dynamic executive director, Mr. Czar. His vision for what the Grand was to become was so clear, organized, and unique that I was thrilled to be a part of it.

The scary part was leaving our hometown and our families. We had never lived any place but here where we could visit any family member within fifteen or twenty minutes. Now we would no longer have delightful pop-ins, and any family gatherings would not be easily or spontaneously arranged. We had season tickets to the local football team, which caused us to question how long we could make the somewhat extensive round-trip in for the Sunday home games. It was also an exciting time for the professional basketball and hockey teams, but I would have to follow them from afar through the newspaper with limited coverage. Leaving the town where Janice and I grew up and where our friends and family were based was indeed painful, but perhaps this would be the job that would eradicate my sense of disparity forever. So if this proved to be the case, then Janice and I decided it was well worth the ensuing emotional trauma.

~~~~

Another dynamic had to do with Janice's sister Annie and my brother Bernie, who had married a year and a half before us. Bernie and I were always very close: best of friends throughout our turbulent early lives and even more so since we married sisters. The four of us became a close family within our larger families that just became more so with the addition of two kids, each who were also becoming very close. In spite of the geographic distance now separating us, we knew that we would nurture these relationships in every way possible. This commitment was reflected in our spending all the holidays at each other's homes and visiting even if it was just for a few days and calling frequently by phone throughout the years (no e-mail, Facebook, cell phones, etc. in those days). So adjustments were necessitated within our psyches, family life, as well as my new job.

~~~~

Overall, the Grand treated their professional staff with a level of respect and support that was unusual for an OT position at that time. They paid for me to come down for the interview and then reimbursed us for the cost of Janice and me spending three days looking for a home. We had decided to buy a house because our income had risen to a level where this now became feasible. They also paid for the packing, moving, and unpacking of all our furniture and household goods. Because the Grand wanted me there as soon as possible, they paid for a hotel room and my food for the two weeks it took before we could move into our house. This is all normal for organizations outside of healthcare but rare indeed in OT.

~~~~

I made one error in leaving the Boondocks Home that I still regret. Foolishly, I did not take Medicare seriously back then. It sounds strange now, but for almost all my time working in nursing homes, they were governed with very few regulations. There were a few mandates about patient care, but those related to OT were not as important, or so I thought. It was not a big deal back then if a therapist did not follow through on a doctor's referral. I was busy getting ready to depart the Boondocks Home, and my mind was mistakenly on the Grand. This was in 1974, when the quality of care in long-term-care facilities was improving. Federal and state laws were establishing and implementing standards that specified the number of days a therapist had before doing an evaluation of a referred patient.

Several of these referrals came in during my last few weeks, and I just put them in my desk drawer, forgetting that the State was now seriously looking for negligent things like these. So after I left, the OT staff discovered the stack of referrals that flabbergasted everyone, including the nurses, PTs, social workers, and even the administration. This was stupid on my part because it was an easy fix. I could do six to ten of these in a day, depending on how involved the patients were. In my naïveté, I thought it would not reflect badly on me, and my successor would take care of these referrals without a lot of angst. Wow, was I wrong!

After I had been at the Grand for a month or so, I received a severely caustic letter from one of my best former staff members. She was bright, hardworking, and energetic. She believed in what I was building right from the beginning and supported me all the way. It was even she and her husband who hosted my going-away party at their house. She was a highly responsible person, and not surprisingly, it was she who discovered my unfinished work. Her letter was filled with disappointment, bordering on disgust, as she lambasted me for shirking my responsibilities and "leaving them in such a mess." It remains a sad memory for me whenever I think of the successes and good times I had at the Boondocks Home. She was absolutely right in her attack, and I should have known better. It was not the way to leave a job, and I would never do such a thing again.

~~~~

This sad corollary to my departure from the Boondocks Home was far from my mind as we went about finding a house and preparing for our move to a new city. I was sorry to miss the usually fun albeit arduous experience of loading our moving van truck with Jimmy and my brothers, but this time the Grand took care of our move. In the past, each of the times our moving team gathered for one of our numerous moves was a special day. The joking, kidding, reminiscing, and bitching that went on throughout these moving days were some of our best family times. Now for this move, all we had to do was pack our clothes and valuables, load the car, hitch up our pop-up camper, and drive to what I anticipated to be a disparity-free life.

A relative of Janice's was an attorney, and he graciously volunteered to meet us at the bank in our new town where we found our house to take care of the closing. I think our realtor was still in shock at the closing when she recalled how Janice and I walked in the front door of the house, quickly looked through each room, exited out the back door, and, after only twenty minutes in the house, announced to our realtor "We'll take it!" This may seem impulsive and foolish, but the house was so nice that Janice and I were both in agreement that this was the house for us. I think this was my risk-taking behavior contaminating Janice's usual sound but protracted decision making, but it all worked out.

~~~~

Success! Success in my job search! Success in housing! Success in family life! My sense of disparity really did seem to be rapidly dissipating. I finally had the job, the house, and the quality of life that I had so coveted. To us, we had found the ideal house. We were thrilled to have a split-level home in a nice suburban neighborhood. For some perplexing reason, I always thought that kids who rode a school bus were more affluent than those who did not. Outlandish logic, I know, but having lived in the city growing up and never riding on a school bus, I thought suburban kids came from rich families. I didn't take into account that many kids from lower socioeconomic backgrounds rode buses in impoverished rural communities or that those bused in the inner city may have come from struggling families. So although this perception was misguided and bizarre I was pleased that my kids would be riding on a school bus. It served as a real impetus in dispelling my sense of disparity in an admittedly peculiar way.

The house itself further dissipated my disparity in colossal amounts. Besides the suburban setting, the house had one and a half bathrooms, a family room, a laundry room, and an attached garage. These amenities were seldom found in the homes we were familiar with in our hometown. Janice and I have always been what I called "baskers"—"those who revel in and make the most of something pleasing." That was us, and we were fully engaged in basking in our new home and neighborhood. We meandered from room to room, sitting in different places to gain different perspectives of delight.

When cleaning out the basement of my mother-in-law's home, my brother Pat and I hauled up an oak piece of furniture that had at one time been the mantle that framed one of the fireplaces in this old home. It cleaned up quite well, and I made bookshelves in the opening that once framed the fireplace itself. With its beveled mirror on top and beautiful wooden carvings, it now occupied an honored place in the center of our living room, giving us one more thing to bask over. Basking may seem like we are obsessed with our possessions, but it's just that we appreciate the things we have and the aspects of them that we find pleasant to look at. But then again, perhaps I am rationalizing what others may view as bizarre behavior. Who cares, Janice and I love to do it, and it does wonders for one's (my) sense of disparity.

~~~~

For some people, feelings about a job can go through a downward spiral of emotion from excitement to disappointment, to despair, and then to depression as the honeymoon period subsides and reality sets in. I know all this now, but I didn't back then. Coming from the three highly successful years at the Boondocks Home I was anticipating more of the same but only on a larger scale at the Grand.

The Grand Geriatric Facility

I recall that it was with great energy and optimism that I entered the Grand in early July of 1974, and this feeling just got stronger as I went through the weeklong new employee orientation process. The history of the Grand going from a two hundred bed skilled nursing facility to evolving into a complex of multilevels of care in modern buildings was indeed exciting. When completed, the Grand would consist of a campus and care system of over one thousand beds, all oriented toward people over the age of sixty-two. Listening to how the buildings and care systems were designed with older people in mind specializing in the best care possible was inspiring.

As I listened to each speaker, I kept looking for ways that OT could be a major player in this unique care delivery system. I saw all kinds of ways OT could not only be an integral part of the Multidisciplinary teams but could be the voice that propels teams to higher levels of service. It was my emerging vision that OT would not just be one of the spokes on the team wheel but could share the hub with nursing. I had learned during my interview that my vision for OT was diametrically opposed to the executive director Mr. Czar's view. In my view, once he saw what OT could do, he would champion the role of OT in all of the Grand's venues. That was my dream, or was it my delusional thinking?

I guess Mr. Goodforme is to blame in part for my grandiose thinking. After only a few months of working for him, he proclaimed me an excellent builder. Of course, one cannot be a builder if they have no tools, supplies, equipment, staff, facilities, etc. Mr. Goodforme spoiled me in the sense that he gave me the resources and autonomy I needed to build a solid and dynamic OT program. Could I do it here where the resources were far more plentiful? What are the obstacles? How can I circumvent them? That was my thinking as I immersed myself into the Grand.

Mr. Czar was very explicit in that he wanted the people in charge of the various units (OT was a unit; not a department in his mind) to be big thinkers and not to be consumed with the details of providing services themselves. Translation: I should not have a caseload of patients whose care would prevent me from carrying out

The Grand Geriatric Facility

the administrative work that had to be done before the move into the new facility. I inherited an excellent COTA, who was loved by all and was extremely committed to the residents. Initially, her treatment methods were not in sync with my philosophy of OT, but she was very intelligent and quickly shifted her thinking in line with mine.

~~~~

Soon after I was working at the Grand, I read in the organization's newsletter that the man who was the director of environmental services was offering a dog for free. I called him and he explained that he had to get rid of the dog because pets were not allowed in his apartment complex. He had found her about six months ago wandering around the Grand's construction site and took her home. She didn't have a collar. However, she was so quiet and docile that he kept her in the apartment for the past six months without anyone knowing, but then someone reported him to the manager, so the dog had to go. I called Janice, and she was okay with my bringing the dog home even though she was not a natural dog lover.

After work, I went to check out the dog. She was a cute and friendly beagle-mix who may have been two or three years old. She and I connected, and I knew right away that I was coming home with a dog. He had given her a name, but I thought we could come up with a better one. The kids were thrilled with the new addition to our family, and even Janice found her to be a nice dog being that she was housebroken. We cannot recall who actually came up with her new name of "Taffy", but we all liked it, and that is what we called her. I loved Taffy right from the beginning, and she readily took to me. She loved to run and play, and I loved hiding on her as she frantically ran through the house in search of me. Her intelligence, coupled with her diligence, made it increasingly difficult for me to find a good spot to hide. Seeing her exuberance each time she found me was a real treat.

Taffy was a fine dog. I took advantage of her love of running and later on took her with me once I became a serious runner and nice weather arrived. Her endurance was greater than mine even if her

The Grand Geriatric Facility

legs were much shorter. Running became another way for me to enjoy Taffy. In fact, everyone enjoyed her. She was great with the kids and traveled well on our frequent trips back and forth to our hometown. Her favorite place to ride in the car was in the front seat curled up next to me or on the floor near Janice. She would nap for most of the trip but then become very alert and excited whenever our car approached Bernie and Annie's house because she knew they would be so glad to see her.

~~~~

Unrelated to Taffy, I became good friends with the speech pathologist, Dr. Ben Persnickety,* who had just completed his doctorate. Ben and his wife and Janice and I often went out to dinner together and visited at one another's homes. He had a quick sense of humor, and he too saw the shortcomings of Mr. Czar's view of the rehabilitation services. Ben had aspirations like mine that may have been bigger than the organizational structure of the Grand or what Mr. Czar would permit for either of us. Ben was a great sounding board, and although younger than me, he had far more emotional maturity than I possessed at the time. His keen insights into people were always right on the mark.

One of the many things I learned from Ben was that a professional rivalry existed between audiologists and speech pathologists even though they both belonged to the same professional organization (ASHA, the American Speech-Language-Hearing Association). They were at the same time colleagues and competitors. This rivalry came into play when Ben began to hire his staff. The staffing pattern for the communication disorders unit provided for Ben to hire and supervise an audiologist and an additional speech pathologist. Since audiological services were expected to be a prime service for the Grand's residents, Ben was directed to hire an audiologist as soon as possible. After interviewing several candidates, he hired Billy Rascal.* Right from the beginning, Billy saw himself as an independent service and did not want to report to Ben. As further action in establishing himself as a separate service from Ben within the communications disorders "unit" and, therefore, not subordinate to Ben, he set up his temporary office in the large sunporch I had taken for my office in the old building. There was plenty of room, and I liked Billy's company.

~~~~

Billy also lived in the same town as me and asked to join a car pool that the woman in charge of medical records and I had just started. Mine and Billy's senses of humor meshed beautifully and made all of our interactions a delight.

He was young and a bit wild in contrast to Ben, who was always professional and mature in his mannerisms. It was not easy being friends with two guys who were rivals and so different from each other, but I enjoyed both of them for different reasons. Ben was well-read, insightful, sensitive, and very deliberate in his demeanor. Billy was a bit crazy and appealed to my still-reckless proclivities. Being in the middle with one venting about the other and trying to remain neutral because I really liked and respected both of them gave me some stressful days unrelated to my role as Chief of OT. I don't know of a term that captures the complex dynamics that inextricably linked Ben and Billy to me, but a ménage à trois may come close without the sex, of course.

Everyone loved Billy. Women as well as men were attracted to him. His ability to relate to others was exceptional. Janice and my kids loved Billy. Being a graduate of the local university, he and I enjoyed going to their basketball games and then out drinking afterward. Many times we just went out drinking without the preliminary basketball game. He also liked playing basketball, which we did often on playgrounds or in the local high school gym. With a strong interest in football, he was often a dinner guest at our house on Sunday afternoons. His moving in and sharing my office was good for both of us but strained my relationship with Ben.

~~~~

The Grand Geriatric Facility

Knowing that I was going to have to recruit four registered occupational therapists (OTRs) when the new building opened in a few months and also knowing that there was a shortage of OTRs in the area, I set about making connections in the OT community to facilitate my upcoming recruitment process. By visiting OTs in their work settings, I would accomplish two things. First, I would get to meet local therapists who may be interested in making a job change or may know of someone who is looking to do so. Second, I would get to view OT in action, which would help me to understand how OT differs from what I had been doing back home. It may seem strange that the practice of OT could vary from region to region, but I knew it was possible and often the case.

The OTs were very receptive to my visits. OTs tend to be a friendly and welcoming sort, and we enjoy showing other OTs what we do in our practices. Unfortunately, none of them were interested in joining me at the Grand nor did they know of anyone else who was contemplating making a change. Although I didn't find any OTs to hire on at the Grand, I did make my presence known and extolled the virtues of the growing Grand Geriatric Facility organization. This latter activity was one of the things that Mr. Czar expected of all of us. I wrote this all in a memo to Dr. Insightful with a copy to Mr. Czar, but neither offered any praise or even acknowledged receiving the memo. So I asked each one separately what they thought of my visits, and both were glad I had ventured out but disappointed that I didn't reap greater rewards like signing on some OTs.

An unexpected gain from my visits was the meeting of OTs who were officers in the local district of the state OT association. They gave me a copy of their meeting schedule and invited me to a workshop they were conducting in a few weeks. It felt good to be included in a group of my colleagues. This was also something Mr. Czar was big on is, having high visibility among one's peers, carrying with it the Grand association. So anything Mr. Czar was big on became my focus. What a sycophant I was becoming.

~~~~

Something I soon discovered was that I was not educated enough about business and management principles or concepts. Mr. Czar and many of the other department heads had a big advantage over me because they had MBAs, MPAs, or MHAs: all degrees steeped in management knowledge and techniques. Changing majors a few times gave me a broad education beyond my OT education, but I never took any business or management courses along the way. In order to get better informed about management principles and strategies, I decided to take advantage of the Grand's education benefits and enroll in a graduate management course at the local university. The first course I took on Organizational Communication Structure and Communication was not only excellent in helping me become a better manager, but it also provided me with an understanding of some of Mr. Czar's thinking and methods. Until then, I felt like I was traveling in a foreign land where I didn't know the customs or the language.

Further along the lines of my obsession with understanding Mr. Czar's perspective better, I discovered that he had donated all of his college business and management textbooks to the staff library that the Grand was putting together. I checked out a number of these books and started using the concepts and principles in my proposals for the OT program that I was sending to him and Dr. Insightful. Surprise! No response! I naively believed that if my written communication was embedded in the language of management and followed the concepts and principles of management that my proposals would be well-received, supported, and eventually implemented. Dr. Insightful, being trained as a physician and not as a manager, was perplexed by some of my writings but remained supportive. He was pleased that I knew my job and was fine with me doing it the way I thought it should be done. I never got a response from Mr. Czar. I might have been Mr. Goodforme's Golden Boy back at the Boondocks Home, but I don't think Mr. Czar had that same perception of my value.

~~~~

I wrote policy and procedure manuals that were centered on the particular brand of OT that I practiced at the Boondocks Home interlaced with the most current knowledge in the field. This was incongruous with that of the COTA I inherited and with the OTR consultant that had ordered the equipment for the department prior to my arrival. By this time, the COTA had come to embrace my philosophy of OT and was one of my advocates. I then set about carefully reviewing the equipment list and replacing equipment that we now didn't need with equipment more compatible with my OT philosophy. As long as the total equipment cost remained the same, I had complete control over what was to be ordered.

Space also was not an issue. I had the largest OT footprint of any facility I had ever seen. It was almost twice as big as PT's. In addition to the big clinic, we had a great store room, a kitchen for teaching cooking, an ADL training bathroom, an office for me, and an apartment where residents preparing for discharge could try out living alone prior to going home. I do not know how OT ended up with such a large footprint, but I was going to make the most of it. It is not common for OT to have so much space, and I felt the pressure to use it in creative and innovative ways. I felt it was time for a coming-out party before we moved into the new building. I organized a formal presentation after conferring with the secretaries of the key administrative and clinical staff to determine the optimal day and time that would assure their attendance. After much haggling and conniving, I got my presentation on everyone's calendar.

The big day arrived, and I was ready. Everyone came, even (and most importantly) Mr. Czar! The presentation went very well. I was at my best: humorous, engaging, and informative. Everyone was impressed. The most common feedback I received afterward was "I had no idea that OT had that amount of education and that you could do all that." It was a happy day. I felt I now had the base of support I needed to move forward with implementation of my comprehensive plan for OT. Not so fast!

A few days after my remarkable presentation, I received a memo from Mr. Czar informing me that my planned use for the

OT Apartment must be changed because he was "re-designating the apartment space for offices for some of the twenty-five activities leaders that they were going to be hiring." Twenty-five? Why did they need twenty-five activities leaders when I was limited to five OT positions, not counting my own? Disparity was now fully engulfing me. Losing the apartment to the activities department in such a draconian way without any consultation with me was infuriating and embarrassing. It was symbolic of how Mr. Czar's view of OT had not wavered one bit from the stance he expressed during my initial interview. All my efforts were in vain. Some relieve came from my venting to Billy and Ben and the others at the Grand who supported me, but none of this changed the reality of my situation.

~~~~

I did not share all my angst with Janice because I didn't want her to be worried that our future was uncertain. I did my best to keep it from her. To alleviate the frustration I was feeling at work, I became active in the local OT association and eventually became the chair of the district where my leadership was welcomed and appreciated. I also coordinated the state annual OT conference and even got my picture in the newspaper. Along these same lines, I contacted the local college and got an opportunity to teach in their OT program. I knew that teaching was something that Mr. Czar did not view negatively and as "moonlighting". However, I was not teaching just to impress him. I did it to save my sanity and to salve my severely damaged ego.

A Sad Distraction

My attention to my job was diverted when my sister Sue called to tell me that she got a call from the Veterans Hospital to say that our Uncle Wasson or Waddy had died. Sue said she could not handle taking care of whatever needed to be done and asked me to come back home to handle it. This was a rare moment when Sue was not letting herself be sucked into a Talty family tragedy. In fact, she and Jimmy were always the first and often the only ones to step into the breach. No more. Rightfully, she had done enough and at the cost to her own family's sense of peace and her own health. I said, of course, I would take care of it and left the next morning to wrap up Waddy's life.

~~~~

Waddy wanted to be cremated, and I found out that we could have his "cremains" (a new word for me that meant the remains of a human body that was cremated) interred (buried) at his family's cemetery with Ma (his only sibling). I also learned that, because he was a veteran, the Veterans Affairs would provide a marker without charge. After conferring with the rest of the family, we decided to wait until summer and then hold a memorial service and internment because it was still winter.

After I got the administrative details taken care of at the VA, the cemetery, and the funeral home, I had to go to his little room and clean it out. This was one of the saddest moments of my life when I viewed how little he had in his room. He lived in a home where his longtime landlady rented rooms on the second floor to three men. For the last several years, Waddy was her only remaining boarder. It was dark and bleak upstairs as was his room. What hit me first was the mirror on his old dresser. Around its inner frame, Waddy had wedged pictures of his nieces and nephews, mainly Bernie's and my kids. His beloved nineteen-inch black-and-white portable TV sat next to the one chair. He borrowed the money from Tommy to buy the TV several years ago and was diligent in paying Tommy back. I started crying when I saw the mirror and didn't stop for a long time.

I felt so bad about leaving him behind when I moved out of town. Janice and I were his primary source of support and companionship. Sue and Bernie filled in for us as much as they could, but with just the two of them to provide a weekly place for Waddy to visit, it may not have been enough. I knew that Janice's caring and loving ways made a special connection with Waddy. Perhaps he saw his daughter Alice, who died of cancer at a young age (ten?) in Janice or perhaps in our daughter Beth. Whatever it was, he beamed when he interacted with each of them. I took all this away when I selfishly moved us away in order to advance my career. I didn't see him much after we moved. Several times I offered to pick him up and bring him to our house for a weekend visit, but he was fearful of his arthritic knees being unable to tolerate the long drive. This lack of contact over the past two years made the cleaning out of his room even more painful for me.

I had brought four or five cardboard boxes with me but only needed two. His clothes were probably not even worthy of Goodwill, but I picked out what may have been of use to someone, and it only half filled a garbage bag. There were no mementos of his life. We knew he needed money, so for his birthday and Christmas, that's what we always gave him. He had no friends or other family members to give him things. There was nothing on his wall except a few notices from the VA about upcoming appointments he would not keep. I took his TV and his pictures off his mirror and closed the door on his little room where he had lived for over thirty years. I had trouble thanking his landlady because of my choked crying voice, but she seemed to understand. I stopped at a Goodwill drop-off box and carefully put the remnants of Waddy's sad life inside. I then drove tearfully back to my full life and loving family, but with a heavy heart.

The Grand Ain't So Grand!

Even though I was in despair due both to the dealing with Waddy's room and the strife of the Grand, there was an excitement about moving into the new building, hiring all the staff, and setting up the equipment, and supplies. I evaluated almost all the 520 residents and assigned the ones who could benefit from OT to the different therapists I had hired. With the large number of residents being admitted, it did not take long to fill everyone's caseloads. I knew that it was not appropriate or ethical to put residents needing OT on a wait list, so I had to drive the staff to do more and to stretch each one of them as much as I could. My thinking was to demonstrate how effective OT could be in as many ways possible with the staff I had and, with this base of effectiveness built, then ask for additional therapists. I was not popular with my staff, but I knew no other way to proceed.

~~~~

What helped during these days of disparity and despair was eating and drinking. I ate more, gained forty pounds (I had not begun running for exercise just yet), and drank far too many Manhattans and gin and tonics on weekends. Prior to this time, I only drank beer and seldom hard liquor. These times required stronger medicine. Although unhappy at work, Janice and I were happy in our new house and neighborhood, and Peter and Beth had a great time playing with their many new friends. Janice became close to the woman across the street, and they became lifelong friends. Her husband and I became drinking buddies, and we went to a lot of university basketball games as well as played basketball at the local playground along with Billy Rascal. Of course, both of these activities were followed with lots of drinking and crazy behavior.

After we were settled into the new building, Mr. Czar announced that he was bringing two administrative interns to the Grand for six months of training under him. They were from his alma mater, and just like he, they were finishing their masters in healthcare administration with a specialty in long-term care. They were a young man (Guy Lost*) and a young woman (Wonder Woman*) who were as different as their genders and pseudonyms.

A weird set of dynamics then followed as the interns were given various administrative projects interfacing with me and the other clinical supervisors. They were often unsure of how to proceed, especially Guy, and Mr. Czar did not have the time or inclination to mentor them. So he either sent them to me or encouraged them to find mentors among the senior staff. I wasn't considered senior staff because I was not a department head, but they still ended up seeking my counsel. This was an informal mentoring relationship that evolved but was especially necessary for Guy because he was far more overwhelmed by Mr. Czar's assignments than his female counterpart. As a result of our frequent conversations, Guy and I became good friends. He often came to my house for dinner and we discovered that we had a common interest in trains (model and real). His demeanor was timid and shy, and he was eager to find a girlfriend. My friend Billy, the audiologist, was mentoring him in this area. Being from out-of-state, he did not have any friends in the area and was very appreciative of being invited to our home. He also liked Manhattans, which gave him and me another connection. So Guy, Billy, and I became fast friends both at work and after work.

~~~~

As an OT, I knew well the value of being engaged in things that had meaning. I had time each evening and on weekends to help Janice with the kids but also time to play with them. If they were with their friends, I let them play together, knowing kids needed that peer interaction.

However, if they were doing something by themselves, like swinging on our swing set or climbing a tree, playing with dolls or cars and trucks, I got on a swing, climbed the tree, sat in little kid's chairs to play house, or got down on the floor with the cars and trucks. This was how I connected with them and had a good time doing it.

~~~~

We continued to take family camping vacations using our pop-up camper, but once Beth and Peter were in school full-time, things changed. Because of their school schedule, we no longer could go camping during the less busy times of the year like the fall and spring. Part of my love of camping was the solitude, peace, quiet, and the beauty of the outdoors. No more. We were now forced in with the hordes of families that converged on the campgrounds in the summer months. After one summer of this madness, we decided to abandon camping and sadly sold our pop-up camper. We felt a little better when we were able to sell the camper for significantly more than we had paid for it three years ago.

~~~~

As I became more interested in model railroading, I built an HO layout in our basement. This is where the kids had a lot of their toys and where they usually played when indoors. Thus, we could engage in parallel play: me with my train layout and Peter and Beth with whatever they happened to be into at the time. Peter liked watching me build the mountains, roads, houses, etc., and I would show him the model layout in my model railroad magazines that I was trying to replicate. He often had good ideas, and I liked it when he became engaged in what I was doing.

The wooden car I built for the kids with Peter's help was a lot more fun to build than it was to drive. I never could get the steering to work properly, which was frustrating when the kid driving it would try turning it, and the wheels would jam up on one side or the other. None of this dismayed the kids, and they still look back on their car with good feelings, especially Peter.

Janice and I went to every event that the kids participated in at their elementary school as well as those outside of school. If either of the kids joined a sports team, I would often volunteer to help coach, and we would attend every game. They liked having me there, and this gave us another opportunity to engage in a common activity. We didn't push the kids into anything, but if they showed a glimmer of interest in something, we would support and encourage them all the way without being really concerned about winning or losing. Just for them to be involved and to have fun was all we expected.

~~~~

Being home with Janice and the kids was really a great respite from the frustrations of my job. Of course, the Manhattans also helped. I sought activities at work that would give me meaning and lessen my frustrations. I enjoyed mentoring the administrative trainees and assumed they would mention the fine guidance I provided on their assignments to Mr. Czar and that he in turn would come to value me to some degree. I was wrong once again!

Outside of the personal satisfaction that came from my coaching and guidance, there were no other rewards for my efforts. If anything, I earned criticism from my staff for spending time with the interns and not taking some of the load from them. Oh well, another round of Manhattans will make us all feel better.

~~~~

One of the most unpalatable aspects of moving into the new building at the Grand was that I was confronted daily with the physical reality that I was not a department head. Mr. Czar's office and that of each of his department heads were all located in an exclusive U-shaped configuration of offices right off the lobby on the first floor. Since I, along with the other entire medical and rehabilitation services, were on the ground floor, my sense of disparity raged almost out of control. I longed to have my office on the U because I felt this would tangibly legitimize my position as well the rightful place for OT in the Grand's organization. Deep inside, I knew the chances of my ever achieving this were negligible at best, but then they were just about annihilated when we received the results of our first comprehensive inspection from the State health department.

When I established the OT department, I did so with the intention of meeting the residents' needs in a comprehensive way. This meant that we had residents receiving OT who had disabilities resulting from strokes, arthritis, Parkinson's disease, cardiac, and pulmonary conditions. This type of OT was traditional and not contested. It was the people with psychiatric conditions and various levels of dementia that was deemed to be beyond the province of OT and that these residents could best be served through the activities department. The State then declared that the OT department was overstaffed and that two of the positions should be converted to activities leader positions to help them meet these additional needs of our residents.

Dr. Insightful went over the report with me, which I found absolutely confounding and potentially ruinous for OT at the Grand as well as for me professionally. It was a major blow to OT and to the direction I was leading the department. To his credit, Mr. Czar told Dr. Insightful that he was going to contest the survey team's findings and recommendations, and wanted my help in formulating the response. I went to work immediately and crafted a strong response justifying OT's historic and ethical responsibility in serving our resident population in the way I had designed. Quoting OT national publications and research extolling the benefits of OT for people with psychiatric conditions and those with cognitive deficits stemming from dementia was the crux of my response. Dr. Insightful felt the wording and tone were just right: objective and not too caustic. Mr. Czar agreed and attached it to his own attack on the survey team. Then we waited.

In a few weeks, we received the State's response. They tempered their earlier message about changing the staffing recommendations regarding OTs and activity leaders but held firm that OT had overstepped its bounds in addressing the mental health needs of our residents.

This was now a mandate that could not be ignored, and so we had to adjust our caseloads, documentation methods, and policy and procedure manuals to reflect this narrowest of views of OT practice. I was enraged as well as very depressed. Where do I go from here? I was not interested in continuing in a position where my autonomy was so reduced and my sense of disparity so inflamed. I had to leave.

Moving On

So after three years of mostly silent and sometimes not-so-silent frustration at the Grand, I decided to look for another position where my profession was more respected and my talents more appreciated. Janice was very supportive and understood why I had to move on. I hated to disrupt everyone in the family because we were really settled in and happy in our town and neighborhood. Janice had followed her best friend's lead and got her permit and began the training to become a school bus driver. The kids loved their school and the neighborhood where they had so many friends. Regardless of the disruption it would cause, I had to find a new job.

I applied for every department head position I saw advertised in the *American Journal of Occupational Therapy* without concern about their locations. I had some phone interviews and had some interesting in-person interviews. Wanting to avoid the level of unhappiness and frustration that permeated my every effort at the Grand, I put together a three-ring binder with photographs depicting the type of OT that I both practiced and preached. I showed the binder to every person I interviewed with and had some curious exchanges. I had really enjoyed teaching and felt that the ideal next position for me would be one with a combination of practice, management, and teaching.

~~~~

There were three in-person interviews that had intriguing results. The first at a major medical center in the northeast appeared to have everything I wanted. However, when the physician who was the head of physical medicine and rehabilitation explained how at this facility they did not believe there were any differences between OT and PT, my antennae went up. I questioned the validity of such a belief, and he countered this by giving me a copy of the job description for OTs and PTs with just the term "Therapist" across the top. With that, I brought out my binder and had him reluctantly look at every one of the fifteen or so pages of photographs depicting my brand of OT. He was neither happy nor impressed but remained cordial and professional. This experience was repeated several times as I went through the subsequent interviews with key staff throughout my first day. I knew I confounded and even antagonized these administrators and clinicians, but I didn't care.

The schedule was for me to have another set of interviews with other key staff the following day, but back at my hotel room, I made my decision. Arriving on time at the administrator's office the next day, I was quite direct: "It is apparent to me that your philosophy of OT here at this medical center is far different from mine. I don't think I want to work here, and I suspect you don't want me to work here." He concurred. I then stood up, shook his hand, and caught a cab back to my hotel to checkout after rescheduling my flight. Although the visit to the medical center was disappointing, my aborted trip had more of an impact on my career than I ever could have imagined.

~~~~

In the 1970s, the American OT Association (AOTA) had completed the move of their operations from New York City to Gaithersburg, Maryland, just outside of Washington DC. The association was becoming involved in lobbying the Congress and other political advocacy activities when they called me. Me? I was, of course, very surprised and pleased. They explained that they were forming a new national committee to be known as the Government and Legal

Affairs Committee (GLAD for short), and they would like me to join them. Why me? I didn't know why, but I said, "Yes, of course." Serving on a national committee was a big deal.

I had visited the AOTA headquarters that previous summer, but it hadn't gone too well. Janice and I and the kids were traveling about in our pop-up camper and ended up camping in a state park not far from the AOTA offices. I decided to take a drive to Gaithersburg to see the AOTA headquarters while Janice and the kids hung out at the campground. It was an impressive outer office, and I felt a real sense of pride viewing the large, raised, silver letters spelling out "*The American Occupational Therapy Association*" on the richly paneled lobby wall. This was my professional association!

There was a busy receptionist on the phone behind a sliding glass window who asked too rapidly with her hand over the phone, "Can I help you?"

I stammered, "I'm Peter Talty, and I'm an OTR from out of state, and I'd like to tour the offices." Like most people, when I stammer, I also slur my words.

This apparently annoyed the receptionist because she raised her voice level and said, "What? What do you want?" More stammering on my part. She raised a finger—not the middle one—for me to wait, slid the window almost all the way over (I could still hear her), pressed a number on her phone, and said lowly, "There's some OT out here from out of town that wants to look around the offices. Yes, I'll tell him." She slid the window open a bit, leaned over, and said, "Take a seat. Someone's coming out." Take a seat? I wanted to take off. Why did I bother coming here?

In a few minutes, out came a woman with a welcoming smile. She introduced herself as Jan Sheridan (I forget her title at the time, but I knew she was a senior member of the executive staff). Her handshake was firm, and she said a very funny thing, "I must apologize. We encourage our members to visit the national office, but few therapists do. So when they do appear, like you, we don't know how to act." With that, we both laughed, and then she took me on a tour of the whole operation. It was a great visit following an awkward beginning.

I think I bored the heck out of Janice around the campfire that night, telling her all about my visit to AOTA.

So having previously visited the AOTA, I was excited about returning there and joining a national committee but had no idea why I was selected. It became more nebulous and intimidating when I heard the backgrounds of the other committee members seated around the large conference table at our first meeting. These were the leaders of my profession who all had extensive experience at the national level. The chair of the committee introduced each person and provided impressive summaries of each person's career as an explanation and justification as to why they were chosen. I was the last, and surely the chair had the least to say in terms of my accomplishments. However, I doubt I will ever forget her words, "And last but surely not least, we have Peter Talty. Peter was first brought to our attention when he went up to a large medical center and caused such a stir that they called our office to complain about his boldness and unusual view of OT practice. In fact, his presentation of OT was so unusual that they would not even consider his folder of photographs. He then came to visit our offices, and no matter how rudely we treated him, he would not go away. We then looked further into what he has done in leading his local OT association and his building of two OT programs. We knew that we had to have him on our committee, and we are so pleased he said yes." I should get all that put on my tombstone. Regardless of her kind words, I was still in search of a new job.

~~~~

The next interview was a return to Canada, but this time I was wiser than the time I applied for a faculty position at a Canadian university three years ago. When asked at the border about my reason for entering Canada, I said, "To visit occupational therapists at the medical center." They waved me by, and off I went to have a repeat of the other medical center experience with one exception: the OTs here were captivated by my notebook depicting the kind of OT I was doing and my explanations or rationales for this approach. Albeit the OTs liked what I was espousing, the heads of administration were not so moved. At the end of the one-day round of interviews, the administrator who oversaw all the therapies was genuinely conflicted when he said, "As impressive as you (me) are and as intrigued as our OT staff are with your work, I just don't think we are ready for you. We are trying to rebuild our therapy departments and feel that you are just too different from what we are used to from OT." What a nice way to put it. I said I understood (I really didn't) and returned home with another potential high-level position jettisoned from my short list of prospects.

~~~~

Last, I got to travel to the South to apply for the most enticing of all the positions I coveted. If I was hired, I would be the director of OT at a large medical center overseeing thirty OTs providing OT services in diverse areas throughout the complex and also be appointed as assistant clinical professor of OT at the local university. The two days I spent interviewing there could not have gone any better. It was mutual attraction with everyone I met. My skills and experience were exactly what they needed, and this I heard repeatedly.

I loved the diversity of the position. Teaching, managing, and practice all rolled into one. The salary and benefits were far superior to what I was receiving at the Grand. There was no doubt in theirs or my mind that, for this combined position, I was the best person for the job. Apparently, they had looked at a number of people prior to me, but no one had my background. The vice president made a verbal offer, which I accepted without hesitation. They wanted me there as soon as possible, but I explained that I needed to give the Grand four weeks' notice prior to leaving, and he said he understood. He said he would get the letter of employment offer to me within a few days but that I should go ahead and give my notice to expedite my departure from the Grand. I flew back home in more ways than one.

The first thing I did the next morning was to meet with Dr. Insightful to inform him that I would be leaving. He was disappointed in some ways, but he said in his usual honest, dry, and humorous way that I so enjoyed, "It is probably best that you are leaving because Mr. Czar was never going to become a lover of OT." Humorous but sad at the same time. Oh well, I just landed my dream job, so I didn't really care.

It was now excruciating trying to pay attention to my daily responsibilities at the Grand when my interests were now on my new job in the South. I had given Dr. Insightful a nice letter announcing my resignation and thanking him for his support over the years. In my magnanimous mood, I even thanked Mr. Czar in the letter and sent him a copy. I felt I could now be kind, and plus I wanted to leave on good terms. However, there arose an obstruction of sorts. It was an agonizing time calling Janice each day to see if my letter had arrived and to hear that it had not. This was not limbo I was in; it was definitely hell.

At the end of two weeks, I started calling Dr. Wimp,* the vice president who offered me the position, but he was either not in or not available whenever I called. I left message after message expressing my increasing concern about not having received his letter but to no avail.

At the end of the third week, I resurrected my old reckless ways and made a different kind of call to Dr. Wimp's office. Borrowing my friend Billy's office where no one could hear me, I held the phone away from me, distorted my voice, and said I was Dr. Omnipotence* (Dr. Wimp's boss). I said in the best authoritarian voice I could muster, "I'm outside at a conference, and I need to speak to Dr. Wimp immediately." His secretary assured me that she would find him right away. Within a minute or so, Dr. Wimp came on the line. After he offered greetings in what I'm sure was a pretty obsequious manner, I said, "This isn't Dr. Omnipotence. This is Peter Talty." I think he gasped, maybe not, but he was certainly rattled as well as apologetic as he spoke too quickly. His explanation for not sending me the letter or taking my phone calls was disastrous.

Apparently, after I had left, Dr. Wimp had submitted the paperwork to appoint me to the position. However, he was informed that because this was a civil service appointment, he could not appoint an out-of-state candidate unless there were no in-state qualified candidates interested in the position. Regrettably, an in-house and in-state candidate had come forth, and they had no recourse but to appoint her to the position (my position!). He contritely admitted that he had been avoiding me because he did not know how to tell me this devastating news, and he was hoping the candidate would decline and that he could then appoint me. He was delusional and I was devastated. Short of saying "Screw you," I hung up and tried not to panic. It didn't work too well.

I shifted into my old false bravado, walked quickly up to Dr. Insightful's office, and announced, "Great news! I'm not leaving. The position didn't work out, so now I can stay. So I won't be leaving."

He looked at me for just a second and blew me away with his response. "Oh yes, you are. The way Czar (not Mr.) looks at you is that you are no longer loyal to the Grand, and he won't let you stay."

Trying not to panic more than I already was panicking, I just about blubbered, "Look, I need this job. There must be something I can do."

He thought for a moment and, in a conspiratorial whisper, said, "Go down to your office, close the door, and think big thoughts. Think of a new OT program that will capture Czar's attention and get him to be glad you want to stay."

I exclaimed, "I don't have to go to my office. I can tell you right now of an idea I've had for a long time: cardiac rehabilitation."

He grabbed a pencil and his notebook and said, "Tell me about it. What do we need in terms of staffing, equipment, training, space, and so forth in order for us to have a cardiac rehab program?" I took off and told him everything I knew without embellishment. He wrote as quick as I talked. When I was done, he looked over his notes and said, "This is good, very good. Wait here. I'll be right back." He went up the hall to Mr. Czar's office as I waited anxiously. After about ten minutes, he returned, put out his hand, smiled broadly and, while shaking my hand vigorously, said, "Welcome back!" I was breathing again.

Moving On! Really? Really!

I tried to get reenergized about the OT program and made a superficial effort at researching cardiac rehabilitation, but I doubt anyone was fooled by my lackadaisical attitude. Then another guardian angel appeared in the form of a voice on the phone. It was Cal Emancipator,* who was the coordinator of rehabilitation at the medical center from whose psychiatric unit I had been fired six years ago. I had not actually met Cal but knew of him as a Rehabilitation Counselor from my days at the psychiatric unit. I was, of course, very curious as to why he was calling me. He was calling to offer me a "lifeboat" (my word; not his). He said that they were looking for an OT Director at the medical center and that several people had suggested that he contact me. This position was a dual position with a clinical appointment to the faculty of OT at the university. The chair of OT at the time was Art Advocate,* and he and I had become good friends before I left the area. He too had been telling Cal that he would like it if I were to take this position. So the following week, it was off to our hometown to meet with the key personnel at the medical center and the university.

The interviews at both the medical center and the university were actually more like friendly meetings among old friends. Everyone I met was so pleased that I might accept this dual position that they talked as if I was already on board. At the end of the day, the position was offered, and I accepted it. What a lifeboat! I got exactly the kind of position I was seeking, plus we would get to return to our beloved hometown. A few days after my visit, I received the letter signed by both Cal and Art, specifying everything we had talked about. It was another raise in pay, and the most amazing thing about this whole thing was that I was going to now have the position of the same person who fired me almost six years ago: Maria. What a powerful way to instantly eradicate my disparity. What irony! The strange twists and turns life takes, especially mine.

Just about one month after Dr. Insightful had saved me by pushing forth my cardiac rehabilitation ruse with Mr. Czar, I was telling him about my new job. Dr. Insightful asked in his rueful but humorous way, "Are you sure you're going this time?" When I confirmed that the new position was completely legitimate with everything stipulated in writing and that I was leaving in a month, he was genuinely glad for me.

My friend Billy, the audiologist, organized a nice going-away luncheon for me, and they gave me a wooden penholder for my desk. Mr. Czar came and said he enjoyed working with me (I bet) and wished me the best in my new position. It was a good way to end my experience with the Grand Geriatric Facility.

~~~~

The Sunday after I accepted the position, Janice, I, Taffy, and the kids drove to our hometown to make the big announcement to the our family in person. Janice's mother and her husband, Frank, along with Janice's sister Annie and my brother Bernie, were all there along with our kids. After everyone was gathered, I said, "Janice and I have something to tell you. I have accepted a position at the medical center and the university, and we are moving back home." I will never forget the rampant joy that erupted following that announcement. Bernie was shaking my hand, and everyone was hugging and crying. What a memory of a wonderful time! The joy just permeated the room that day and still makes me emotional recalling that scene today!

We Become Bernie and Annie's Neighbors

What a tumultuous beginning I had in my new joint position as the head of OT at the medical center and assistant clinical professor of OT at the university. Because we had not yet sold our present home or found a new home in our hometown, Janice and the kids stayed there, and I slept on a cot at my brother Pat's apartment. Starting a new job and being disgusted with the almost forty pounds I had gained, I decided to start running on a daily basis. I ran every day up until Friday when a cataclysmic event occurred, which I'll describe in some detail below.

I started my new job on January 24, 1977, and spent my first few days dealing with an unforeseen problem. The disconcerting piece of information that emerged was that one of my long-time friends with whom I went to OT school was passed over when I was appointed to my position. She had been at the medical center ever since graduation, and naturally, she and everyone who knew her assumed she would get the position. The hurt, disappointment, and antipathy she felt toward me made it hard for us in so many ways. I just worked at doing my job while trying to respect her space and highlighting her skills and abilities in any way I could.

~~~~

The cataclysmic event that impacted all of us on January 28, 1977 was the "Blizzard of '77", and I was thrust into the worst of it.

We Become Bernie and Annie's Neighbors

While working that first week on Friday at about 11:30 a.m. there came an announcement over the public address system that stunned us all: "There is a severe blizzard fast approaching the area, and all noncritical healthcare personnel have permission to leave the hospital immediately." Because all of us in the rehabilitation services were considered "noncritical healthcare personnel," we all quickly packed up our stuff and left the hospital. I had intended to drive home for the weekend anyway and was thankful for the early start.

However, it was shocking to step out into that subzero temperature with howling winds greater than I had ever experienced. The abrupt cold was so brutal that it was hard for me to catch my breath as I was half blown across the icy parking lot to my car. There were no weather apps or other forms of data sources for current road conditions, let alone cell phones. The car radio was all I had. When I got in my car and started heading toward the Interstate, I had no idea what awaited me or the how really disastrous this storm was to become. Also, I did not take time to notify anyone of my intended route because there was no way to contact anyone, and I had no idea exactly where I was going except to find my way home.

There was no new snow falling but what was on the ground and sitting out on the lake was picked up by one-hundred-mile-per-hour winds and whipped into quickly towering snowdrifts. It took me seven hours to drive a little over seven miles. I had heard on the radio that the Interstate was closed, and so I was attempting to take a side route, which paralleled the Interstate. None of this was possible as I sat for almost two hours in one spot in a four-lane highway that became essentially a bumper to bumper parking lot in both directions.

Recognizing that staying in my car could cause me to run out of gas and potentially freeze to death, I decided to abandon my car and try walking. Where to? I didn't know where I was or what was around me. As I opened the car door, I was hit with the full brunt of the blizzard. Standing upright was a chore, let alone trying to walk. Out of desperation, I started opening the car doors of those that were still running to get some respite from the coldest cold I had ever experienced. Everyone was as confused about what to do as I was, but all let me share their warmth for a few minutes before I pressed on. That is all but one man who pushed me back out as I tried to enter his car. He will not be the poster guy for the City of Good Neighbors!

Eventually, I could see some people through the blistering snow moving slowly toward a building with lights on and a door opened. It was now about 7:00 p.m., and people were giving up on trying to get home and, just like me, were abandoning their cars. We were all trying to find some kind of shelter, knowing that our cars would not be suitable once we ran out of gas. I made it up the steps and just about collapsed into a deliciously warm elementary school. Someone had broken a window in the door and got the school opened. Over 150 people gratefully found their way into the sanctuary of that school that night. Another resourceful person got the emergency phone number off the door that was that of the janitor and, using the pay phone in the hall, called the janitor at home. Luckily, he lived nearby and came to the school on a snowmobile and unlocked the gym so we could sleep on the exercise mats, the cafeteria refrigerators so we could have food, and the office. What a wonderful person he was to come out of his nice warm house just so we could have access to food, sleeping mats, and a most appreciated phone. Since this was long before the now-ubiquitous cell phone, we all had worried loved ones wondering where we were.

~~~~

After thawing out, I stood in a long line to use the phone in the principal's office to call Annie and Bernie to let them know I was okay, safe, and warm. They, of course, were all quite worried about me because Janice had called the hospital when she heard about the blizzard. Whoever she talked to said I had left the hospital at eleven thirty that morning, which, of course, had everyone alarmed because no one knew where I was, and it was now close to 8:00 p.m. Because I couldn't make a long-distance call from the principal's phone, I asked Bernie to call Janice so she wouldn't have to worry any longer.

We Become Bernie and Annie's Neighbors

I was safe and warm and could smell a wonderful soup someone was cooking.

Thus began a saga of waiting for the blizzard to stop and watching for the opportunity to dig our cars out. The long hours were made even more difficult for me by a man that was an incessant loud talker whose volume of voice made rest impossible, no matter what room he was in. He was a nice guy, but with nerves stretched a little thin I think his constant loud chattering was irritating to most people but downright intolerable for me. Then surprise! I heard him say something about wishing his wife would find a job as an occupational therapist in Arizona or someplace warm. Stupidly, I told him my name and that I was an OT and then inquired as to who his wife was. He yelled loudly, "Peter Talty! Peter Talty! We heard you were coming back here. Where are you working?" A bombastic stream of other questions and loud exclamations followed without me given a moment to respond to any of them. I did figure out that he was the husband of an OT I knew quite well through the local OT association. I spent the next two days trying to hide out in rooms as far away from his booming nonstop voice as possible.

On the morning of the second day (Sunday), the blizzard had subsided enough that people were able to get their cars started. However, because of the amount of snow on the cars and in the engine compartment itself, many of the cars wouldn't start. The local police arrived on snowmobiles and helped people get their cars started using emergency trucks that also appeared. We were all gathered at the windows, watching for our cars to be uncovered. It took quite a while to move down the eight lanes of abandoned cars to get a lane open in each direction. Once someone saw that it was their car about to be ready, they would dash out and jump in their cars. I heard my OT friend's loudmouth husband yelling my name, saying that I was going home with him (the hell I say!) when his car was cleared, so I hid behind a large man until the loudmouth was gone.

They finally got to my car, and out I went. Bad luck! My car wouldn't turn over at all. I checked the lights but nothing. When I opened the hood, I was aghast. There was nothing related to the engine visible. I was staring at snow encasing my entire engine compartment. A man next to me remarked that I may have to junk my car (it was only a year old) unless they could tow it into a warm garage and keep it warm so it could dry out. He sure did sound knowledgeable and convinced me that all was lost. Now what to do?

While I was deliberating my dismal options, I cleaned as much snow as possible from the engine and battery. I then flagged down a guy in a tow truck and asked him if he had jumper cables and the extra power I have seen that some tow trucks possess. He said he did, and he would see if he could start my car. He connected the cables, revved his engine for a few minutes, and then signaled for me to try starting it. Surprise! After a few tired groans, it sprung to life. I was so happy. The guy wouldn't take any money, but I finally convinced him to take $5.

~~~~

I then resumed the trip that I had started three days ago. It was Sunday morning as I meandered my way over to a parallel route because the Interstate was still closed for sixty or more miles in the direction I was driving. My hope was that this alternate route would be snow free, and I could eventually enter the Interstate at some point and make it home. This plan was working surprisingly well. There were no cars on the roads because there was a driving ban in effect that I was choosing to ignore. My recklessness and risk-taking tendencies were going to be called on repeatedly over the next few days.

Alas, all came to a standstill after I had been driving for about an hour. I came upon a wall of snow that filled the entire area from the road to the bottom of the viaduct that traversed the road I was on. There were two cars already stopped and pulled over onto what was thought to be the shoulder. As I sat there wondering what to do because, unlike Friday, I was in farm country with nothing around me. No schools around to escape into this time.

Then I heard a loud engine behind me and saw a thrilling sight: the biggest snow blower I ever saw. It was a National Guard vehicle that went to work clearing the road for us with a gigantic auger. Me and the three cars followed him on through, and with jubilant beeps of our horns, we resumed our journey. The rest of my drive was thankfully uneventful.

When I had gone about sixty miles on this secondary road, I was able to enter the open section of the Interstate and arrive home, while Janice and the kids were still at church. Taffy was very glad to see me. I went in and took a much-needed shower, made coffee, and waited for my family to return. They were also happy to see me and were shocked that I had made it home. Could any homecoming ever be better than this? I doubt it.

~~~~

I was concerned that if I wasn't able to get into work, I would not get paid for those days when I was absent. I had to pay for the whole move back to my hometown myself, which caused me to be quite concerned about our finances. Thus, getting back to the medical center and on the job so I would be getting paid became an obsession with me. That Sunday night, as I watched the news and weather, I decided that we should all head to our hometown the next day. My plan was to drop Janice and the kids off at Annie and Bernie's, and I would go to work.

This is where my recklessness and risk-taking behavior put my whole family in jeopardy. The next morning I loaded up the car with all of us, including Taffy and all the clothes we would need for a week. We were able to drive the Interstate for about fifty miles but then had to exit because the Interstate was still closed. I planned to take the same parallel roads all the way that I had taken on Sunday. Besides the roads being treacherous, the counties we would be traveling through were all closed except for emergency vehicles. This trip was foolhardy and illegal, but in my mind, these were desperate times.

All went well for the first twenty miles or so, but when I had gotten two-thirds up a steep icy hill, we skidded up onto a frozen snowdrift that was more ice than snow. I must have had some intelligence and foresight operating because I had put a snow shovel in the trunk, but the icy snowdrift couldn't be broken through with my puny shovel. My wheels just spun as I tried going alternately between Drive and Reverse to no avail. I then had Janice drive while I pushed, which was also pointless. We were stuck!

As I peered back down the hill we had just driven up, I could see through the blinding snowstorm that had arisen that a state trooper was parked at the bottom of the hill with his emergency lights flashing. I told Janice to wait in the car while I ran and slid down the hill to the state trooper's car. He was not smiling as this exchange took place: Me: "Hi. Hell of a day, huh? Look, can you use your two-way radio to get me a tow truck to pull us off that snowdrift?"

Trooper: "If there are people in that car, get them out. There's a county snowplow coming up the other side of this hill, and they will never see your car in this whiteout. I'm also giving you a ticket because this county is closed to all but emergency vehicles."

Me: (Time to resurrect Tough Guy Pete): "Listen, I'm not out for a Sunday drive. I'm a physician on my way to the medical center. There are not enough doctors available, and I'm on my way to help out. Now can you please get me a tow truck so I can get there?" My tone was authoritative but yet respectful.

Trooper: "I'm sorry, Doctor, but all the roads ahead are impassable. I'm sorry, but you'll have to go back. Let's get your family out of the car, and I'll drive you down to the Fire Hall, where you can wait for the tow truck."

Me: "Well, that is disappointing, but I understand."

The trooper and I trudged up the hill with the wind and snow whipping us in the face. We got everyone out and down the hill and into the trooper's car, including Taffy. My Doctor sham was almost all lost when Peter heard the trooper refer to me as "Doctor." I had always told my kids that I wasn't a doctor even though on some of my jobs I wore a white coat. I was always proud of being an OT and often took them to work with me to see firsthand the different ways I helped people. Peter started explaining, "He's not a doctor. He's an occupational therapist." Thankfully, the voice coming through the two-way radio, coupled with my loud comments about the storm, prevented the trooper from hearing Peter. We made it to the Fire Hall and waited for the tow truck.

Eventually, the tow truck arrived, and I went back up the hill with the driver. After surveying the situation, he determined that it would be best for him to winch me off the snowdrift from below while I was driving and steering my car. He did so, and in short time, I was turned around and heading downhill. We reloaded everyone and drove back home. A tiring and disappointing day for us all, but it could have turned out so much worse. We were so thankful to return to our cozy home and wait for the roads to be cleared. I did talk with my boss, Cal Emancipator, and he assured me that I would be paid for any missed days. Wasn't that nice? Start a new job, work four days, and get five off with pay.

~~~~

Living with my brother Pat worked out well for Janice and me. This saved me the cost of a motel during the week, and I could travel back home on weekends to help get our house ready to sell. Because money was a little tight, we decided to try selling the house ourselves in order to save the realtor's fee. We also had to find a house in our hometown, but we got some unexpected help at a dance we attended with Annie and Bernie. One of the guys we met at the dance happened to be a realtor, and he had just listed a house he thought we might like. The next day was a Sunday, and we were the first people to see it. The house was very nice, and it had a number of things updated that we were looking for in our next home. A bonus was that it was on the same street as Annie and Bernie! So once again, Janice and I moved quickly and decided to buy this house.

Things also moved quickly with our present house. We placed an ad for our house in the local newspaper and put several signs around the neighborhood. Janice and I felt we knew how to prepare and show a house even though we had never done this before. At the end of two weeks, we sold our house, validating our belief that we knew how to do this. While continuing to live at Pat's, I organized a two-truck move with Danny driving one truck and me the other.

In a very short time, we were moved into our new house, had the kids enrolled in school, and I set about trying to master my two new jobs.

The Medical Center and the University

I was fortunate to have two bosses, Cal and Art, whom I both liked and respected a great deal. It was refreshing in that neither saw themselves as my boss. They apparently respected me enough to grant me complete autonomy while trying to get me the resources I needed to do the best jobs I could. Art had me co-teaching a course in physical dysfunctions OT with a new faculty member who was very easy to work with and glad to be paired with me. She and I were a good team. Our course was actually fun to teach and well-received by the students.

At the medical center, I was in an awkward position that took all of my interpersonal skills in order to avoid generating more resentment amongst the therapists. Knowing that my friend was devastated when they recruited and appointed me to the position she and the other therapists felt she deserved, I had to be extremely wary. By being vigilant, I was able to prevent my inadvertently or intentionally being cast as her nemesis and archenemy. I genuinely believed that she was a better OT than me in this setting but not a better manager. In spite of the ample frustrating experiences while at the Grand Geriatric Facility, I learned an awful lot about being an effective manager and supervisor. By deferring to her clinical expertise in all things related to patient care and OT, I avoided what could have been a highly contentious relationship.

Coincidentally, the house we ended up moving into was less than an eighth of a mile from where my friend lived as a single parent with her little boy. She and I would sometimes ride to and from work together, and she and Janice got to know each other better as neighbors. As I think back to long ago of when I attended my first class in gross anatomy, I recall how I first met this friend, sort of. I knew nobody in the class on the first day and was overwhelmed before the class even started because just about every student had lab coats on, dissection kits in front of them, and a stack of anatomy textbooks that they had previously purchased. How did they know what to buy? Desperately trying to catch up fast, I leaned over and asked the girl seated next to me where she got everything. That girl was this same woman, and without even looking in my direction, shushed me. We eventually became friends and worked together on a number of projects, and now here we were, eight years later, trying to adjust to each other in a difficult job situation.

However, regardless of the tension between us, I was basking in the joy of now having the job of the person who fired me six years ago. It was such an exhilarating feeling that my sense of disparity was just about obliterated. I had always coveted this position because it had so much prestige associated with it, and for me to now be "the guy" meant that I had gained the respect of the OT community. Disparity, be gone!

~~~~

Now what direction did I want to take my new department, and how far could we go? The answers to both questions were less within my control than I thought. I knew I had the support of my supervisor (Cal), but I was very cognizant of the fact that the OT staff members I inherited were far more aligned with my friend than they were with me. The other even greater impediment to my changing the direction of OT at the medical center was the permanent civil service status that all the therapists enjoyed. Thinking I could terminate any of them would have been naïve on my part, but I already knew this from my past experience in a civil service organization at the Boondocks Home.

So my approach was to be patient, be a hard worker, be an advocate for my staff at every opportunity, and be a resourceful and willing problem solver. I knew that I was dealing with entrenched ideas about OT and the organization as a whole. My approach was not to force people into areas of incompetence but to lead by example and never be in a reactive mode if I could help it.

There were a number of external forces at work that could facilitate my maneuvering my mired ship into open water. First, they were completing the construction of a state-of-the-art medical center adjacent to the present outdated buildings we now occupied. Second, a new director of physical medicine and rehabilitation had just been appointed to head up the rehabilitation department at the medical center and to also serve as the chair of rehabilitation medicine in the medical school at the university. He was a scholar and a visionary and would bring a new impetus to the whole rehabilitation department. Third, Cal Emancipator, as the coordinator of rehabilitation and the chair's assistant, was creative and resourceful at circumventing the impediments of a somewhat stagnant organization and staff. Any or all these forces would be my allies in generating change.

~~~~

An unexpected additional impetus to my quiet change efforts arose when Art, the chair of OT at the university, sent me an announcement about federal grant money available from the Comprehensive Employment and Training Act (CETA). He was wondering if I had any program ideas that might qualify for a CETA award. I had several ideas and arranged to meet with him in a few days to look at each of them in relation to the grant funding criteria. By the time we met, I had read the details of the grant and whittled all my ideas down to one.

There was an abundance of unemployed certified OT assistants (COTAs) in the area in 1978, and this grant could employ some of them for a year, enhance their skills, and thus increase their potential for employment. I also knew that the medical center had about two hundred patients occupying hospital-level beds but with only nursing home-level needs. It was my idea to hire and train eight COTAs that would then work with these patients to make them more independent in self-care. Art loved the idea, and so we went to work putting the application together and submitted it. We were notified in a few weeks that ours was one of the applications approved for funding.

This CETA grant gave me the opportunity to hire eight COTAs who would not have civil service status. I also had enough funding to hire a grant manager and a secretary. For the grant manager, I decided to see if a former patient of mine from the Boondocks Home might be interested. As a young man, he was injured in a swimming pool accident and was mostly paralyzed from the neck down but still had some movement of his arms. While a patient at the Boondocks Home, he was able to earn his GED and then obtain a bachelor's degree in business. I worked with him to adapt his tape recorder, work surfaces for his wheelchair and room, and some self-care routines. He was thrilled to hear of this professional job opportunity, and I was able to hire him as my grant manager. He selected and hired his secretary and facilitated the hiring of the staff I selected.

Although I couldn't fill all the positions with COTAs, the conditions of the grant permitted the hiring of people with some experience in healthcare. Adding these ten new people into my department helped to establish some momentum of change. I also was able to exchange a COTA that I inherited who was not highly productive or motivated with a PT open position. I used this acquired position to hire the first hand therapist at the medical center, and she added to the feeling of what I called "a new day; new way" of thinking and working.

~~~~

In the midst of the above changes, my friend was dealt two terrible blows. Her little boy was struck by a car and was critically injured. Not knowing what the outcome was going to be was an awful time for her. We all supported her as best we could. Except for her former husband, she had no relatives in the area, so her friends and fellow employees were her support system. Her son recovered fully, but a few short months later, she was diagnosed with Hodgkin's lymphoma. She handled this news better than most people I know. Because she was diagnosed early, her oncologist was optimistic as she underwent the standard treatment regimen. She fought it for a few years but then did succumb at a very young age. She passed away after I had left the medical center. What a sad end for a fine woman and fine OT.

~~~~

Totally unrelated to my job, Annie was planning a surprise birthday party for Bernie but wanted it to be at our house so as not to arouse his suspicions. Janice and I decided to change things up a bit and make it a surprise party for both Bernie and Annie since their birthdays were less than two weeks apart. Janice called all the people that Annie had invited to tell them about the change. We also called other people that Annie hadn't invited to make it even a bigger party. The plan was for the four of us to go out to dinner that night, with them picking us up.

Knowing that Bernie knows everyone's cars, I recruited our sons, Peter and Bernie, to direct the guests to park around the corner on the next street out of his sight. That all went well. As guests arrived, we directed them to our basement where we had snacks and drinks available. Finally, we saw them pull into our driveway, thinking they were coming to pick us up. Getting all the fifty or so people to quiet down was done quickly, and all was ready. When they came in, I said to Bernie, "Can you check out my junction box in the basement before we go? I think I smell smoke."

He remarked, "Yeah, I can smell it" (of course, he could because a lot of people smoked in those days). I led the way down the stairs with Bernie, Annie, and Janice coming close behind, and then the room exploded with "Surprise!" It was great. They were both shocked because of the people who came. Some of the guests were people they hadn't seen in quite a while. It was a memorable party.

~~~~

I continued my distance running that I had started just prior to the Blizzard of '77 and was consistently running three to five miles a day during the week and longer runs on weekends. We lived close to a nice park, which provided pleasant routes for running with Taffy. She loved to run. I kept her on a leash until we got to the park and then unleashed her. This was our routine, and we both enjoyed it very much until she took on a skunk and lost. The skunk's spray caught her full in the face. I left her hooked up outside when we got home because she reeked too bad to be brought in the house. Janice was now driving a school bus and wouldn't be home until nine thirty or so in the morning.

She read my note about what had happened and where to find the smelliest dog in that part of the state. Janice went to work problem solving our latest crisis and called the vet. His advice was to give Taffy a bath in tomato juice, which was known to be the best solution. She left that part for me to do. What she did was to call a dog grooming shop right near our house to see if they could help Taffy. They had Janice bring Taffy in, and they worked on her for the afternoon. However, Janice said that when she picked her up, the shop smelled terrible, and Taffy was improved about fifty percent. When I got home, I gave her two or three tomato soup baths, which resulted in her being house worthy once again. There were, however, consequences from Taffy's skunk fight. The one was that whenever she got wet, the pungent skunk smell returned. We don't know if this next event was coincidental or a direct result of Taffy's visit, but the dog grooming shop went out of business soon after.

About a year later, our wonderful dog became ill. Janice thinks it started with her eating a large chocolate rabbit she was able to get out one of the kid's Easter basket, but we really didn't know what was going on with her when I took her into the vet's. He ran some tests that were inconclusive but thought it best to keep her overnight to better monitor her condition. The next morning, when I was getting the kids off to school, the vet called to say that Taffy had just died. Oh no! My running buddy gone! I was so sad and then had to tell the kids that our good friend was gone. I called Janice from work to give her the awful news after I knew she would be home. It was a very quiet house that night.

ARMI

Throughout all the staffing machinations with the CETA grant and the managing of the OT department itself, Cal Emancipator was my guide and expediter. Although on paper he was my direct supervisor, he truly was more of a colleague. After the emotional trauma of trying to win Mr. Czar over and being unsuccessful at it, I welcomed Cal's unfailing support and encouragement. He was a wizard with administrative matters. He knew all the medical center and university procedures and how to get things done whenever the red tape seemed like the strongest duct tape ever. He was a wordsmith too but was always ethical, honest, and straightforward in all of his interactions. Our working relationship evolved into a friendship and from that into a business partnership.

    Cal and I both wanted to achieve great things in our professional lives, and we also both recognized that we had to follow a path beyond our professional endeavors if we wanted to gain the wealth and autonomy we both desired. Another person with similar aspirations was one of my and Bernie's best friend Bob Wrestler. Bob went to high school with Bernie and, when we were in our early twenties, hung around the local taverns with both of us. Our connection with Bob grew to where he became more like a brother than just a good friend. He was working as a sales engineer but was interested in going into business for himself at some point. Cal was already involved in a partnership of sorts with a psychologist, and they maintained an office offering counseling and testing services in an office building not far from the medical center.

Cal, Bob, and I began meeting on Saturday mornings to explore opportunities for a business combining our different talents. Both Cal and Bob possessed a tolerance for conversation and discussion that far exceeded mine. Being a person with a high task orientation, I was impatient and wanted to be engaging in the work that would achieve the financial independence and autonomy that we all sought. At first, these were fun meetings; but as week after week went by without any tangible results, our relationships regrettably became strained. I think I was the only one that was both intolerant of the rambling conversations and the one with the most inherent need for recklessness and risk taking.

Finally, we came to the agreement that we would become management consultants combining Cal's and my social science and communication skills backgrounds with Bob's knowledge of business and sales. I had a friend who had a small business specializing in public relations and the design of marketing materials that joined us for one of our marathon Saturday sessions. We hired her to help us come up with a name for our company and a brochure and business cards to help promote our services. After hearing all that we wanted to accomplish, she came up with a concept and a name that we all liked: "ARMI" (Applied Resource Management Incorporated) along with our motto, "Sometimes it takes an army to solve your organizational problems." Our six-paneled brochure described all the services we offered: vocational testing, conflict resolution, creative problem solving, motivation strategies, communication skills training, stress management, time management, etc. We also put together a training manual that we gave out at the workshops we conducted.

We were able to secure a few contracts that convinced us that we had hit on the right types of services to offer. What kept getting in the way of us expanding our services was the time that we had to spend at our day jobs. It was also a problem that often the companies wanted our services during regular working hours, and that was when we were not available.

A conversation between Art Advocate, the chair of OT at the university, and me provided a possible way out of our dilemma. Art encouraged me to think about joining the OT faculty on a full-time basis. I saw a university appointment as an opportunity to gain a lot more control over my time and the flexibility to get ARMI really going. So after a year and a half, I agreed to resign from the medical center and join the OT faculty as an assistant professor. The prestige of being a university professor helped to squelch my usual feelings of disparity. My thinking was to stay at the university just for a few years and then enjoy the rewards of being a high-paid management consultant.

I planned to commit all my free time to ARMI, but neither Cal nor Bob was interested in abandoning their day jobs like I did. We also found it harder to have a united focus. So after several discussions, Bob and Cal acquiesced to my request that they turn ARMI over to me. Being the good friends that they were, they were very understanding of my desire to go this ARMI journey alone. We parted friends.

I was able to get a few more contracts, but I became frustrated with the amount of time I invested in soliciting contracts without coming away with a sale. I took a few salesmanship courses, but I was finding out that I lacked the personality for sales. So I was spending less and less time in this endeavor. You could say it "Petered out," although I never liked that expression for obvious reasons.

The University

1978–1982

It sure was exhilarating to be a professor. From high school dropout to university professor was no easy transition, but I did it. This position was rewarding in so many ways beyond its prestige. The students were very motivated and eager to learn. Because of my strong clinical background, the students enjoyed my firsthand accounts of what it was like in the real world of OT practice utilizing the best science available at the time. The OT faculty was a mixture of seasoned instructors, recent graduates who were new to both teaching and practice and those like me with a moderate amount of teaching and practice experience. Art was a wonderful colleague who was passionate about OT. He gave us all the freedom to grow in the directions we chose. There were some internal conflicts among the faculty with resultant warring camps and cliques. I prided myself in having good relationships with the entire faculty and was not viewed as a member of any one clique. I listened empathetically when a faculty member would vent about someone else, but I never agreed with them. I kept taking the high road and thus maintained the respect of the entire faculty and hence stayed above the fray.

~~~~

It was while I was at the university that I discovered that I really had a gift for teaching. However, the gift was all I had because I had never taken a course in education or had any guidance or mentoring around the teaching process. My position as an assistant professor was provisional in that after six years, I would have to stand for tenure; and if I did not meet the criteria for promotion and tenure, I would be forced to leave my university post after one more year. Looking ahead, it was easy to say that I had plenty of time. Also, initially, I didn't expect to remain at the university very long, but now I wasn't so sure. ARMI was no longer the exciting and rewarding option we originally envisioned. Academia seemed a better way to go.

One of the first conditions I would have to meet in order to be granted tenure was to earn an advanced degree. My bachelor's degree had to be augmented with at least a master's degree but preferably a doctorate. With my newfound love for teaching and wanting to become far more competent at it, one advanced degree available at the university seemed ideal for me.

Within the School of Health Related Professions, of which OT was a part, they offered an MS in Health Sciences Education and Evaluation. Most of the courses were offered late in the day to accommodate practitioners in nursing, PT, OT, dental assisting, and any other healthcare discipline. The whole program seemed to be tailor-made for me, plus because I was now a member of the full-time faculty, my tuition was waived.

All was looking good, and then I encountered a major obstacle. For some reason, the creators of this program had decreed that all the PT and OT graduate students must take BIO 517 Neurophysiology. I knew the reputation of this course and how demanding it was. I also felt my science background was not adequate to meet the demands of this course and professor. I met with the chair of the health sciences department and tried to convince her that I did not need this course to complete this degree. I was not convincing, and she was resolute that if I came into this program, I must take neurophysiology.

Although this decision seemed to be final, I, as usual, was not convinced that this was the final word. I went to see another professor in the program I was interested in whom I knew from some committee work we both did, and I knew her to be a reasonable and thoughtful person. I explained to her how I wanted to use the intended master's degree to teach management and clinical skills to OT students as my primary focus and how neurophysiology was not foundational to this career path I was interested in pursuing. She agreed with my rationale and thought an alternative educational plan would meet my educational goals and at the same time satisfy the requirements for the major. However, she explained that neither she nor I could ignore the edict of the chair of the department. Her caring attitude prevailed, and she suggested that we go see the Dean of the whole School of Health Related Professions together. So down the hall we went to find him. Once we were seated in his office, my friend was fantastic as she explained the whole situation far better than I could have done. He listened carefully and then completely agreed that I should pursue the course of study that I had outlined. He signed the forms I had brought with me, and I was on my way into graduate school. I can now add two more guardian angels to my increasingly long list.

~~~~

It felt like I was going back in time with working and going to school. My job as a professor was demanding from the preparation, lecturing, testing, and grading point of view; but because I loved teaching, I did not find the work dissatisfying in any way. In fact, I discovered that being a university professor may be the best job one could ever have.

My sense of disparity did propel me to extend my work beyond my professor's role. I began to obtain contracts to serve as a consultant to as many healthcare organizations that I could squeeze into my free hours. I did all this because I wanted a bigger house in a better school district. I believed that living among professionals would be more satisfying for me, and it would give our kids a stronger education and preparation for life. With all my consulting, we were accumulating additional funds, which were further augmented through Janice's working. Janice completed the training for driving a school bus and was now working for the local school district. I felt the time was good for us to move up and get the house we always dreamed about.

~~~~

When I wasn't going to school or working, I was usually working at home. I did not want to isolate myself away from the family, so I created a work area in our living room with a card table and chair set up behind our couch. This work area kept me in the mainstream of family life while I wrote lectures or research papers for my graduate courses but could readily jump into a game of Candyland whenever the opportunity arose.

At Art's request, I became the Coordinator of Undergraduate Admissions and Advisement for the OT department. I also designed and taught a new OT course ("Therapeutic Interaction") that had almost three hundred students enrolled each time I taught it. Besides teaching and advising, I helped Art with some administrative functions, which often included interviewing prospective faculty members. In this area, I had two interviews that I will never forget. Imagine my shock when Art asked me to interview the same person who had fired me from the psychiatric unit several years ago. Maria had gone on to earn a doctorate and was now seeking to join our faculty. What a strange position for both of us. We both just laughed and laughed. She said in between giggles, "Peter, Peter, Peter. It is quite ironic with you sitting there with me trying to get a faculty post." Then more laughter and giggles from both of us. It was the strangest interview I ever did. She left after just twenty minutes. I don't know what happened between Art and her, but she didn't get the position. Art didn't ask for my input, so I knew I did not impact his decision not to hire her.

~~~~

Art, being a creative and energetic person, had secured a grant to outfit an old RV bus as a mobile OT, PT, and speech pathology clinic to provide services to children with developmental disabilities living in hard-to-serve rural areas. I was not involved in this program because it was outside of my areas of clinical expertise, but whenever Art needed a second or third faculty member to interview prospective clinicians for the bus project, he would ask me if I were in my office. It was on one of these occasions that I was shocked to receive the résumé of Cookie Cutter (a fictitious name). I wondered, *Could this be the same Cookie that I moved in with back in 1970 when I was insane?* It was she, and she was feeling as awkward as I to be in this situation. Unbeknownst to me, she had gone back to college and became a speech pathologist. She was looking for a job and saw Art's ad in the local newspaper. We visited a bit and caught up on each other's lives and talked a little bit about the bus project. After she had left, Art came in to get my impressions of Cookie. I told him that because of my previous relationship with her (I offered no details), I didn't feel comfortable giving him my opinion. He was fine with that because he had enough input from the other faculty members who interviewed her to make his decision. I know he hired someone else for whatever reason, and that was that except I had to tell Janice about this whole crazy thing. We both laughed about the irony of it all.

Oh No, They're Moving Again!

Although working and studying a lot, I still found time for crazy fun in two areas that could not be more different. The younger OT faculty at UB had a custom of going out for a drink on Friday nights. On some Fridays, I would call Janice and stop at a local tavern or go to the faculty club. It was fun to talk about our courses and university politics as we drank Manhattans or Martinis. Competing with partying with the OT faculty was my need to go out with my brothers Danny and Pat and visit the taverns in the area of our roots: the old neighborhood. Regardless of which temptation I succumbed to, the result was always the same. I stayed out late, got very drunk, and was hung over the next day. Fortunately, this was not an every-Friday-night event. Also I was fortunate to avoid getting stopped by the police or having any accidents. I honestly believed it was Janice's prayers that kept me from any driving-related tragedies on those crazy nights.

It was after one of my drunken Friday nights with the OT faculty that I was woken up by Janice early in the morning out in front of our house. I was so drunk that I did not remember driving home at all and just slept in my car all night. Considering what catastrophic events could have occurred in my state scares the hell out of me even today.

While I was recovering the next day, Janice suggested that we not waste the day. We had been looking at houses in the more upscale towns near us, and she thought we could do some "drive-bys" to check out some houses. Janice's cousin was a realtor and knew the kind of house we were looking to buy and was going to sell our present house for us when we were ready. To expedite our search in the days before people had home computers, she let us borrow her multiple listing book that had the details on all the homes for sale. In one of my more sober moments, I had gone through the book and noted which houses I thought had potential for us. Janice had done the same thing, and now she was strongly encouraging me to go with her to see the houses we had each selected at least on the outside. So we did just that.

I was too nauseous to drive; the best I could do was lay across the backseat and raise my head up when she announced that we had arrived at one of the prospective houses. As time moved forward, my stomach stabilized, and my pounding headache receded. I had even made it into the front seat at this point. Many of the houses we drove by had looked better in the book than they did in person. Then things changed when we viewed a home on Belvoir Road in an upscale village we always admired. We decided to have lunch in a restaurant close by and to call Betty, our realtor, to see if she could get us in to see the inside. The information about the house included everything we wanted and more. Betty arranged to meet us at the house right after lunch. Because the house was vacant and had a lockbox on the front door, she was easily able to gain us access to what we saw as our dream house.

Once inside, we were sold. All we had to do was convince the buyers to sell it to us for our offered price. In spite of our excitement, we were a little reluctant to put in an offer because neither we nor our realtor could figure out why this great house was on the market for three months. It was an English Tudor design with four bedrooms, two and a half baths, a beautiful family room with a wet bar, a brick fireplace framed by bookcases, and a large living room and a separate dining room, a two and a half car garage, and an in-ground swimming pool. We had never considered a house with an in-ground pool, but when we saw this beauty, we were enchanted. It was heated, had a diving board, a slide, and a self-cleaning system. So my risk-taking wont took over, and we decided to seize what appeared to be a great opportunity to get the house we always wanted. The sellers accepted our offer after a bit of haggling, and Janice and I rejoiced.

A few days later, our excitement was greatly amplified when on our way home from a play we had gone to see, we decided to take a drive past our new home. We had not closed on it yet, but we were eager to grasp any piece of experience we could related to this great house and the neighborhood. Whatever it was, we just had to drive down our new street. This was the Christmas season, and our curving street looked so beautiful with the lights in the trees, and many of the houses were decorated and lit so tastefully amid a pretty snowfall. We stopped in front of our new house and basked (there we go basking again). Being emotional people, Janice and I were both on the brink of crying as we sat looking at a home that was about to be ours.

~~~~

However, we had one misstep in our exuberant transition to our new house; our present house did not sell immediately. In fact, we were paying for two homes for a few months. We were fortunate that we had the added income from all the extra consulting work I was doing to cover our double expenses. Looking on the positive side, as Janice always did, this move could be more gradual with plenty of time to prepare our new home to get it just the way we wanted it. I painted all the rooms that we didn't have wallpapered. I remembered being so enthralled with the house that I would frequently interrupt my painting to wander around and just bask.

The kids had to change schools, but it was not as difficult as we had feared. It helped that our neighborhood was replete with kids both Beth's and Peter's ages with whom they made quick friends. Because many of these kids went to the same middle school with Peter or to the elementary school with Beth, their transition was almost seamless. The in-ground swimming pool that was heated most certainly helped our kids build relationships.

Oh No, They're Moving Again!

~~~~

About four months after we moved into our Belvoir Road house, our old house had finally sold, and I completed my master's degree in Health Sciences Education and Evaluation. Obtaining an advanced degree and moving into our beautiful new house combined to destroy any sense of disparity that I was previously feeling. Life was very good indeed. It got especially good when I convinced a large contingent of Taltys and Rileys to come to a downtown theater where the commencement exercises took place, and I formally received my master's degree. Janice and I decided to really celebrate this double big event in our lives. We invited a lot of people, including extended family, colleagues, friends, and an unusual assortment of people from my past. One of the people who I was so pleased to see there was Herman and his wife. Herman was the guy who I worked with as a janitor for seven years at the grammar school. My Uncle Bern hired me when he promoted Herman to be the fireman. He trained me but also encouraged me to continue my education. He knew me as a former punk who was trying to become a competent janitor under his tutelage. Herman and all the family and friends who came to celebrate with us made for a wonderful time. Hosting this big party in our beautiful home was the culmination of years of work, risk taking, and sacrifice. Having so many people who knew me when now see this house was something I will always treasure. I knew there was not a shred of disparity present in our house or in my heart that night.

~~~~

My combined roles as OT professor and OT consultant were demanding, but with the role of student now completed, I could enjoy a simpler life. However, I felt our beautiful home was missing what I thought was an essential element. I so enjoyed the ambience of a tavern that I decided to create one in my basement. By this time, Bernie had become a skilled carpenter and all-around handy guy; so with his direction and assistance, we built a paneled recreation room complete with a bar and pool table. It was very conducive to getting drunk and high as my brothers Pat, Danny, and I often did on Sunday afternoons.

~~~~

Danny had assumed care of his two daughters, Shannon and Heather, and he was working sporadically. Pat had moved out of the apartment near our former home on the West Side and into a brand-new subsidized apartment complex near the city hall and adjacent to downtown. He initially loved living there and getting to know the diverse people who inhabited the many other apartments. Coincidentally, one of his neighbors who also became his good friend, was my former grant manager from the CETA grant at the medical center. That job led to his being discharged from the Boondocks. Because neither Danny nor Pat had cars, I had to pick them up and take them home after a long afternoon of drinking and smoking dope at my house. Once again, Janice's prayers enabled me to get Pat, Danny, and his daughters home safely and without my getting a DWI or having an accident. Absolutely undeserved miracles!

~~~~

It was during the usual abundant basking that Janice and I were engaged in that one of the worst things to ever befall the Talty family occurred. The facts are still muddled even today, but the damage done will remain for years to come and probably forever. We were all confused as to why my sister Sue had become withdrawn and why she and Jim refused to come to any family gatherings. Bernie and I thought if we went to see her together, we could learn what the problem was and perhaps help. We spent an evening with Sue with no more information coming forth. All we knew is that something had happened between Pat and Jimmy and that whatever it was, things were very bad. She told us that we should no longer invite them to any family gatherings where Pat would be present. We readily acquiesced to her request. Sad and befuddled and unsuccessful at learning what had actually happened to cause this attitude of rejection of Pat, Bernie, and I went home.

My siblings and I grew up in a fractured and chaotic home but remained close because of the immense efforts of Ma and my sister Sue. Now here, Sue was obviously in turmoil, and we were helpless to help her because she would not tell us the nature of the problem. When we finally did find out what happened, we knew beyond a doubt that the cohesiveness of our family was destroyed forever.

Eventually, pieces of Sue's terrible plight came out. Jimmy had lost his treasured job as the number two driver in seniority with the trucking company, and apparently, my brother Pat was to blame. I couldn't and wouldn't believe Pat would do such a thing to Sue and Jim after all they had done over the years to keep our family together. They may have even done more for Pat, including taking him in three times; the last was after Ma died. I also believed Pat when he vehemently denied having anything to do with it. In any event, Jimmy lost his high-paying and prestigious truck-driving job that he took such great pride in and gave them the best financial security they had ever had. Because he was such a hardworking man and so responsible toward his family, he was not unemployed very long. However, the only job he was able to get was driving a school bus transporting kids with disabilities to their various programs. He did this low-paying job with class and dignity and never spoke again of his better days (at least in my presence).

There then evolved a strange and strained set of relationships within our once strongly bonded family. No longer could we have a big gathering like my graduation party, where we all came together to joke and laugh in celebration. Sue would not come to any event that Pat was going to attend, and out of respect for Sue and Jim's feelings, the rest of us would not even bring up Pat's name. This got so weird that for some occasions, Janice and I or Bernie and Annie put on separate parties: one for Sue and her family without Pat and another one with Pat. Complicated and crazy!

It was a year or more before Bernie elicited the truth from Pat. They went out for a few beers one night, and Bernie got Pat to tell

Oh No, They're Moving Again!

him what he had done that cost Jimmy his job. When Bernie told me how Pat had duped me and the rest of the family all that time, I was disgusted and furious. I tried to understand why he did what he did, but it was apparently only driven by spite. It was very hard for me to be around Pat for a while.

~~~~

Unrelated to the chasm between Sue and Pat and in spite of our great house and neighborhood, my sense of disparity was aroused when I ran several miles through the even more upscale neighborhoods adjacent to Belvoir. These homes I now coveted were larger, more opulent than ours, and the settings were just beautiful with mature trees and well-maintained grounds. Through my interactions with the professors at the university and the administrators at the facilities where I consulted, I knew it was these neighborhoods where they lived or wanted to live. I wanted to live there too. However, Janice and the kids were very happy on Belvoir. They loved having their own swimming pool as did all their friends. Janice continued to drive a school bus and had continued the running program she had started in our previous neighborhood. We ran many of the 5K and 10K races in the area together. She also had become good friends with the women on our street, and they often did crafts together. So with all this bliss, why was I contemplating another move? I know now that I was trying to quench the unquenchable thirst of my disparity. I was incorrectly assuming that if I had enough money, a large enough house, and the right job, I would be happy. I was wrong, but of course, I proceeded in ignorance to try to appease the unappeasable monster of disparity within me.

My distance running got me searching for a bigger and better house. As I ran in and out of Chapel Woods, Woodstream Farms, Wellington Woods, Farmington Woods, and on and on searching for a house for sale that we could afford. I knew that this was not going to be an easy sale with Janice, but I also knew that she liked the kinds of houses I had identified and enjoyed just looking at them with me.

We were mostly content with our Belvoir house and neighborhood (Janice completely and me not so much), so we did nothing for a while. But then I saw an ad for a home in the local newspaper that started with "For Sale by Owner." I knew that these homes can be less expensive because the seller does not have to pay the realtor fee of 7 percent. The description was enticing to both Janice and me (once again more to me than to her), and I called the owner to get more information and the address. We set up a time for that evening to go see it. In the meantime, I took a running route that gave me a chance to see it from the outside, and I was impressed. It was a two story Mediterranean style brick home in one of my favorite neighborhoods: Wellington Woods. I was half sold before we even saw the inside of the house. Now I hoped that seeing the inside would also sell Janice.

Driving into Wellington Woods that evening, I was eager to either see a house we didn't want or a house we wanted and could get at a price we could afford. Janice was not interested in moving but was going along out of curiosity and to shut me up about it. Pulling up in front of the house caused the same reaction in Janice as it did in me. Janice knows quality, and this house had quality construction throughout. The two-story foyer, large rooms throughout with first-floor laundry room, and amenities that continued to impress us throughout. The price was already lower than any house I had seen in this area, but we offered even less. The couple who owned it had raised their kids there, and they were looking to downsize. After some haggling, they accepted our price, which was quite a leap from what we could expect to get for selling Belvoir. I wasn't as concerned as Janice that we could swing this deal, but she was never the crazy risk taker that I was. Good thing too! Someone had to be stable and practical in this relationship.

We had decided that in order to pull this off, we would have to sell Belvoir ourselves in order to avoid paying 7 percent of the selling price to a realtor and at a price that was above the norm for our street. The next week was spent readying our house for an open house we planned to conduct. I made a large hand-painted sign for the front lawn, wrote an ad for the local newspaper (no Craigslist or Internet back then), and put flyers with a picture of the house and a brief description of its highlights, like the in-ground pool and finished recreation room in the basement in all the supermarkets and any place else they would let me. The notice also included our outrageous price and details about our upcoming open house. The open house was a great success, and we sold it at our asking price and with a closing date that would dovetail nicely with the closing on our new house. I had a lot of fun painting SOLD diagonally across my For Sale by Owner sign in front of our house.

~~~~

So after three happy years, we had to now clean out Belvoir, and we felt the best way to do this was to hold a garage sale. A mega garage sale! From a practical perspective, we needed extra money for hiring movers because we no longer had the Talty moving crew as a result of the rift in the family (the collapse of Pat and Sue's relationship). I had a number of metal storage shelves in my basement that I planned to take with me to Wellingwood. I arranged these shelves in rows in our large garage and organized all our stuff into sections and marked each row with what could be found there: Tools, Toys, Kids Clothing, etc. We also had large items, like desks, a refrigerator, chairs, etc. Many people said that ours was the most organized garage sale they had ever seen. I also put signs all around our neighborhood and on the main streets to advertise our garage sale. Janice and I really pushed the stuff we had for sale and sold things we were not certain people would buy. The profits from our garage sale paid for our move and more.

Wellington Woods

Now was I happy and content without any vestiges of disparity? Yes! What a house! Janice and I were basking more than I would have ever thought possible. I then thought about expanding our sphere of happiness in a direction that surprised everyone, even Janice. Before we moved into Wellingwood, I had been thinking about how hard it was for Janice's mother, Sarah, to live by herself now that her third husband had died. Bernie and Annie had moved out of town, and Janice's brother Frank now lived outside of Philadelphia. This left just Janice and me to provide assistance as Sarah tried to remain independent in a ranch home about twenty-five minutes from us. She was lonely because she had not connected with her neighbors, and her friends and relatives did not live near her. The house we were moving into was so large that I felt we could all live together without a problem. I also felt that Sarah had always been such a giving person that we could now do something for her. Janice was very pleased that I would propose moving my mother-in-law in with us but thought Sarah may prefer her own home.

After more discussion, we decided that we should go talk with Sarah in person and that I should be the one to propose the idea of having her move in with us. So off we went to present my latest brainstorm to Sarah. At first, she was reluctant to accept our invitation because she thought we wanted her to contribute to the cost of our new house (which we didn't) or that we were going to charge her rent that she couldn't afford (wrong again). Once she saw that we wanted her to move in with us without any cost to her, she was very pleased and accepted. She then became very anxious about what she would do with her house and all her stuff. She had known how well we did in selling our houses, and when Janice suggested that we sell her house for her and give her the money, she liked that idea too.

Janice and I then set about organizing another house to sell. Annie and Bernie came in to help us clean up and clean out Sarah's house to maximize its attractiveness to potential buyers. Once again, I painted signs advertising House for Sale by Owner and nailed them up all around Sarah's neighborhood. We also ran an ad in the local newspaper, extolling the amenities of this desirable ranch-style home. The results of our efforts were shockingly successful.

We sold Sarah's house and most of the furniture to the first people we took through the house. Sarah didn't expect to sell the furniture, but this couple liked the way everything matched and seemed to fit so nicely in each room. So it was a package deal that thrilled Sarah as well as Janice and I. Maybe we should quit our day jobs and go into real estate. Just kidding.

~~~~

With both homes sold, it was time for us all to move in, which we did in July of 1983. This house was of exceptional quality that impressed us more the longer we lived there. Unfortunately, both Beth and Peter had to change schools. Peter having completed his freshmen year at one high school had to change to another in the same district, which was not an easy transition for him. Beth adjusted easier perhaps because she got more involved in school activities. Regardless, we all loved the house. It was great for basking! However, there would be other adjustments all around as we all got used to living with Sarah and she with us.

~~~~

My vigorous basking got a jolt when I was looking through the Wellington Woods Home Owners' Association's phone directory. I read each name to see if I knew anyone. There was one name that I found shocking. I was reading both the husbands' and the wives' names when up popped Cookie _____. This could not be happening. She had told me when I interviewed her who she was married to, and there it was, his name next to hers. There could be no mistake. I noted the address, and on my run the next morning, I tried to find her house. I found it! Cookie was living right behind us on the next street! The corners of our backyards intersected each other. This was the irony of ironies. How was Janice going to feel about our latest dream house when she finds out that Cookie, the woman I moved in with, was now our neighbor? Until I could figure out how to tell her, I thought it best to forewarn Cookie to avoid any public awkwardness. This was a highly social community with a gourmet dinner club, crafts club, gardening club, and so forth. I didn't want us to run into Cookie in one of the prevalent social gatherings. So with all this in mind, I called Cookie from my office soon after I discovered where she lived. She took the news good-naturedly; she even laughed heartily when she thought about the odds of our families living so close to each other. It turned out that she and her husband did not participate in any of the social functions in the community. This lessened the potential of an accidental encounter but did not lessen my angst.

I briefly debated whether to tell Janice about our neighbor or not because I did not want this to ruin her happiness over our new home or, worse, that she would misinterpret my feelings. I loved Janice and knew that Cookie's unexpected reappearance would never change that. I had worked hard over the past thirteen years to earn back her trust, and so I did the right thing and told her. She was as shocked as I, but now she trusted me enough to know that this was not planned in any way; and in spite of what some people may think, this was not the result of any diabolical long-range planning on my part. Janice and I weathered this minor storm and moved further on with the great life we were building together. We still laugh about the crazy paths our lives took to put Cookie and me in such proximity to each other at this stage of our lives.

While living with Cookie right behind me, I always checked to see if she was out in her backyard whenever I had work to do in my yard just to avoid any awkward interactions. This bizarre coincidence was a secret only Janice and I shared, and we told no one until now. It was a private joke we shared every time we saw her or heard the name "Cookie." It seemed there were more dogs or cats or characters on TV or in movies that were named Cookie. Regardless of where we were when the name "Cookie" was mentioned, Janice and I gave each other a knowing smile. We both understood that our relationship was so strong that my long-ago aberrance was irrelevant to the life we enjoyed today and ever more.

~~~~

After I had been an assistant professor of OT for about three years, I began thinking seriously about how I would fare when I stood for tenure at the end of six years. I knew I had to earn a doctorate, do research, and get published in peer-reviewed journals. In terms of teaching excellence and service to the university and the community, I felt very confident in these areas. The doctorate seemed to be the next thing for me to attack. My fellow faculty member and good friend Jerry O'Man* encouraged me to pursue a PhD in Higher Education, which is what he did. I looked over that curriculum and found it doable and interesting. I submitted an application and had my transcripts forwarded to the department of higher education. The interview was with four or five faculty members, some of whom did not seem very enchanted with my response to some of their questions. After forty-five minutes of listening to what seemed to me to be a mini-filibuster from one of the faculty members, I was ready to forget the whole thing and just walk out. The chair of the admissions committee cut off "Professor Filibuster" in mid-sentence and announced that I had been accepted into the program. How about that? I was now a doctoral student.

When the next semester started, I enrolled in my first doctoral course. I don't remember the name of it, but I doubt that I will ever forget the first lecture. It was a small class: about ten students. The professor went on and on defining the difference between authority and responsibility for two hours with a ten minute break. There was no discussion. It was clear that he didn't want any. The next day I dropped the course and formally withdrew from the doctoral program.

By withdrawing from the doctoral program, I was essentially deciding to leave the university. The choice was between being an OT professor or being an OT practitioner. As a practitioner, I could earn far more than as an academic, albeit putting in far more hours and work days. The actual nature of OT practice was more challenging and interesting to me at the time. The best part about academia for me was teaching and interacting with the students. However, being an academic is much more than teaching. It is serving on committees, doing research, obtaining grants, and publishing. These last four components of an academic position did not appeal to me. So at the end of five really good years, I resigned from the university.

~~~~

Leaving the university was somewhat sad for me mainly because of the students. They were bright, enthusiastic about OT, eager to learn, and unintentionally funny as hell. I always tried to engage students when I taught, not just that class but also every student for every minute in every class. This may seem unrealistic, but with this grand objective in mind and the knowledge I gained in my master's program, I achieved this in my courses. It was hard work to reach this level of competency, but it was recognized when I received the Outstanding Teacher Award for the university's School of Health Related Professions in 1980. I was notified in advance that I was going to receive this prestigious award and thus brought Janice, Beth, and Peter along to witness me receiving this public recognition of my good work.

~~~~

It was two years later in 1982 that I left the university in a most moving way. The OT students organized a surprise going-away party that was memorable for a number of reasons. When some of the faculty said they were going for a drink right after work at a tavern we frequented I was eager to join them. It was located right across the street from the campus and was a place we often went to on Friday nights. So I did not suspect a thing and called Janice to let her know that I was going out with the faculty. I said I wouldn't be late. I had no idea that the students had already called and invited her to the surprise party.

When I walked into the tavern, I was surprised at how crowded it was. You could hardly get to the bar. I was also surprised at the number of students that were there. It must have been the full student body, plus the entire OT faculty, faculty members from other departments, some clinicians, and the best surprise of all: Janice. What a good time we had. There must have been two hundred people drinking, dancing, and laughing. Then the organizers quieted folks down and told me that I meant a lot to them and that they appreciated how interesting I made my courses. The surprises weren't over. The students brought out a large box the size a console TV might come in (not a flat screen). It was decorated on the outside with gift wrapping, and their silence told me that most of the people in the room knew what was inside. Of course, the inside was filled with lots of crumpled up paper, and I was told to dig down to the bottom. I did and found a small box also wrapped. Opening it up, I got one of the most thoughtful gifts I ever received. The students chipped in and bought Janice and I season tickets to my favorite professional football team! What a gift and what a night! Disparity was nowhere to be seen on this night.

BEDLAM HOSPITALS*

1982–1987

While I was at the university, I maintained consulting contracts practicing OT in home health, community agencies, three nursing homes, and a psychiatric and chemical dependency facility. This last, Bedlam Hospitals, was the place I targeted for my next career move. Bedlam was a unique organization in that it was a hospital, privately owned, and adeptly managed by a father-and-son team (Marvin* and Scott* Entrepreneur, respectively). Because it was privately owned, I knew that my work as a manager would not be encumbered by the constraints I had experienced in the two civil service organizations in which I had worked in the past. It was very difficult to terminate an unmotivated or underproductive employee from a civil service position who had permanent status (I may have been the exception). Bedlam was private, and they also did not have a union. They paid well, usually well above the local average for comparable positions in the area. However, they would terminate anyone who was unwilling or incapable of meeting their expectations, and I liked that. I viewed Bedlam as a high-risk, high-reward opportunity, which dovetailed nicely with my risk-taking personality.

    The son, Scott Entrepreneur, was the executive vice president and the one who ran the day-to-day operations of the hospital and the guy I dealt with throughout my two years of weekly consulting services. He was bright, willing to invest in people and programs

Bedlam Hospitals*

and, with his MBA, had an excellent grasp on managerial concepts and methods. His father, Marvin, was the guy who built Bedlam up from a small psychiatric hospital that was always suspect in the local healthcare arena because of its extensive use of ECT (electroconvulsive therapy or pejoratively known as "shock therapy"). Although ECT has fallen out of favor with present-day psychiatrists who rely more on medication to treat depression, ECT is still accepted treatment for people with severe depression that does not respond to medication. Coincidentally, my Dad was a patient at what was the forerunner of Bedlam Hospital where he did receive ECT.

Recognizing the decreasing market for inpatient treatment for mental illness, the entrepreneurs astutely diversified Bedlam's services to include inpatient and outpatient chemical dependency treatment, including detoxification. In fact, at the time I was consulting with them, approximately two-thirds of their beds were devoted to patients with alcohol or drug addictions. It was clear that these resourceful owners saw that the future of Bedlam was tied to addictions, but they were not going to abandon their mental health services. This area still provided significant revenue for them and an important service for the area.

The OT department consisted of five OT assistants (COTAs) with the most senior one being the supervisor. I got to know each of them in my role as a consultant, and I found them all to be bright, eager to learn, hardworking, and very motivated. I felt confident that these COTAs would welcome my leadership and clinical expertise if I were to join them on a full-time basis.

I scheduled an appointment with Scott the next time I was there. When I made my pitch about leaving the university and coming to Bedlam on a full-time basis, he was both pleased and surprised. He said he had often thought about asking me to come there full time but thought I would never leave the university. As a matter of protocol, he wanted me to meet with both he and the medical director, Dr. Howard Benevolence,* to make sure he was not opposed to my becoming their director of OT. I knew Dr. Benevolence a little bit from the psychiatric unit where he was the clinical director of psychiatry. I didn't know this until later on, but Howard (that's what everyone called him) was suspicious of me. He thought I would bring some of the outlandish and poorly managed methods that some of the OT staff (mainly Maria) employed from the psychiatric unit that he found intolerable. Howard and I spoke in the hall while waiting for Scott to finish up another meeting. He feared that I would be too much like my old boss. Whatever I said in response to his questions in the hall must have been just right because he quickly became very enthused about my joining them.

Scott definitely deferred to Howard whenever the discussion came to the care of patients or to personnel decisions related to the healthcare professionals. I was not anxious at all during the interview because I had other options if Bedlam was not interested in hiring me. Not to worry, they were very interested, both Scott and Howard. It was agreed that I would take over OT, and that Scott and I would work out the details. After Howard left, Scott asked me what I was looking for in terms of a salary. I gave him a high figure as a starting point, but he countered with something that was very good but not what I wanted. When I felt I had gotten as much out of Scott as I was going to get, I proposed a compromised position. I agreed to accept his offered salary (which was substantially more than all the directors of OT were getting in the area) but suggested that it be for four days a week rather than five. My thinking was that I could continue consulting at two nursing homes both within the same block as Bedlam Hospitals and thus have the higher income I proposed. He liked my unique approach to resolving our stalemate, and we had a deal. As a further inducement, they also provided a very attractive benefits package.

The COTAs were ecstatic that I was going to be their boss. I was well-received by all the staff and felt very comfortable right from the beginning. Howard and I became good friends and started car pooling to work a few days a week when we found out how close we lived to each other. We found out that we had enough in common to have both a good professional and personal relationship. I also was given the opportunity to continue teaching one of my favorite graduate courses at the university each fall semester: Management for Occupational Therapists.

~~~~

Within a few days, I had drastically changed my career path going from the security of an academic position (that is if I had attained tenure) to the high risks, high rewards of the world of a healthcare business. Yes, Bedlam was a business and a healthcare organization operating in a highly competitive environment. I realized this right from the beginning. In fact, the risk-taking side of me was attracted to this job where my success or failure was dependent on my knowledge and skills. In order to continue to be successful, which the owners of Bedlam were, they had to be alert to opportunities in the marketplace and to seize them before the competition. It was an exciting place to work.

I felt this conglomerate of roles I had orchestrated for myself (manager, consultant, practitioner, and professor) was good for my short attention span when it came to jobs. Could this combination of roles in this job at Bedlam hold my attention and finally dispel my ubiquitous sense of disparity? At the time, I thought it would; and for a time, it did.

~~~~

Besides enjoying the risk-taking aspects of my roles, I always liked the intrigue, subterfuge, manipulation, and clandestine aspects of being a manager; and at Bedlam, I chose this path far too often. It was risky to operate in this realm, but I also discovered that I had a big chunk of Machiavellianism in me. The owners of Bedlam, Marvin and Scott, strived to always take the high road but sometimes had to operate in this way out of necessity. At these times, we had a common bond.

I made no big moves for the first six months or so. However, I was constantly searching for opportunities while enjoying a good salary. My first opportunity came in the form of my being instrumental in helping Bedlam out of a difficult situation. The difficulty came in the form of Bedlam Hospitals having problems during a major inspection by JCAHO (The Joint Commission on Accreditation of Healthcare Organizations). Bedlam took its accreditation seriously and was usually recognized for its high quality of care.

This time the Joint Commission focused on the way we documented information in the patients' charts. It was not patient care that was being criticized; it was our documentation methods. This was serious not because our quality of care was deficient; it was not. It was serious because JCAHO said it was a problem. "Up in arms" and a bit of justifiable catastrophic thinking would somewhat describe the mood of everyone right on down to most of the department heads. In an effort to respond effectively to JCAHO deficiencies with a plan of corrections, Scott formed a task force consisting of the healthcare department heads related to patient care, including Howard and I.

Scott appointed Terry Sagacious* as the chair of the task force. Terry was very knowledgeable about hospital regulations and probably was one of the most influential people in Bedlam and had excellent relationships with the owners. She had worked with Marvin for over twenty years initially as a secretary and then as his informal assistant administrator until Scott finished his MBA and came on board as the executive vice president.

Coincidently, Terry lived near Howard and me and had joined our car pool. This provided a lot of time for problem solving without having to take the time out of our busy schedules at work. We each had a different perspective, and this enabled us to learn from one another as we looked at the various problems facing the hospital each day. All three of us were committed to making Bedlam Hospitals the best that it could be. I learned a lot in our drives back and forth from Howard and Terry. They had far more knowledge than me about Bedlam, but I had the advantage when it came to management.

The people on the task force had been with Bedlam long enough to be a bit intimidated by Terry, but I was not. I liked and respected her very much. She had thought she knew exactly what the problem was that caused us to have difficulty with our latest JCAHO inspection and was organizing a solution that I could see was faulty in some key ways. So I made my "ballsy" move at the first meeting of the task force. After Terry had distributed copies of what she said "was absolutely the best and only way to fix our documentation problem" and began assigning tasks, I interrupted her. This was risky. No one interrupted Terry except Marvin and Scott (who were not present). Looking at Terry in a firm but kind way, I said, "Terry, you have articulated the solution so well that I am almost hesitant to disagree with you." There was a brief awkward silence that Howard broke by saying "Notice he said 'almost,'" and with that, everyone laughed, even Terry. She then gave me the floor, and I took over outlining how I believed we had to change the way we documented our services.

Bedlam had quality services being delivered, but JCAHO viewed it as fragmented, not well-coordinated, and not provided with a multidisciplinary focus. The problem I said was the way our medical chart was structured. Rather than having tabs in the chart for each discipline, I proposed that we change to what we used at the Grand (I didn't tell them where I got this), where the chart was organized around the patient's problems that all related disciplines documented around.

What I did was propose something so big and disruptive that people seemed to almost be afraid of it, and thus they fiercely resisted it. Undaunted, I pushed on with an implementation plan that required everyone to change their ways of documenting what they did, noting the cost of restructuring the charts in such a radical way. Knowing that nurses, social workers, pharmacists, OTs, physicians, and psychologists needed to be trained in this new approach, I volunteered to do the training for all staff and on all shifts. I also volunteered to help Terry train the secretaries on how to physically restructure our charts. It worked! Terry acquiesced, and we went forward with my solution. Terry thanked me in front of the group and then again on the ride home. She said, "You really bailed me out!"

I did all the training and got the charts restructured in plenty of time so that when JCAHO did their reinspection, we passed! In fact, the surveyors (inspectors) were so impressed with the documentation system that we now had in place that they wanted our permission to pass it on to other facilities that were struggling with this same thing. This was announced in a public meeting of all the department heads and executive staff. Terry stood up and gave me all the credit, and everyone applauded. I was a hero!

The timing of all this could not have been better. At holiday time, Bedlam gave out bonuses if they had a good year in terms of revenue. The individual amounts were highly secretive because bonuses were based on performance as ultimately perceived by Marvin and Scott. I knew when I opened my check that I had made the right decision to come to Bedlam. In appreciation for my work in leading the hospital in becoming fully reaccredited with JCAHO, the owners gave me a bonus that was equal to one-third of my annual salary. This made for a very nice Christmas and significantly dispelled disparity, at least for a little while.

Unique Relationships and Special Times

Unrelated to Bedlam Hospitals and my new position, Bernie and Annie and their two kids (Jill and Bernie II) became established residents of a village 75 miles east of us, and we settled into our beautiful home on Wellingwood Drive. With their move out of town, our joint Christmas, Thanksgiving, and Easter holidays evolved into real extravaganzas and into something really special. We alternated between one another's homes for these holidays, usually staying overnight. These were rich and deep relationships that were made deeper and richer as time moved forward and the kids got older. Bernie and I had gotten to be best friends once I grew up and became a responsible adult. Janice and Annie, who had eight years difference in their ages, now shared the same stage of life as wives and mothers and also became best friends. As couples, there were no other couples within our social and family relationships that had the cohesiveness and joy that we four experienced when we were together. Bernie II and Peter Junior became best friends, and it was great to watch them rush to greet each other and then rush off to do boy things and share boy secrets. Beth absolutely worshiped Jill, and Jill, being the oldest, became the leader of this little pack that could not wait to see one another at every opportunity. The depth and richness of these unique relationships were indeed special and will always be treasured by each of us no matter where we are, who we are with, or what we are doing. There is no word in my *Pocket Thesaurus* to fully capture it.

To make these holidays even more memorable, Janice and Annie prepared great meals and snacks. I added to the festivities when I started buying goofy Christmas gifts with even goofier quips for each person. They brought me great pleasure as I raptly watched their expressions and listened joyfully to the kiddingly scornful remarks as each one opened their gifts. Wonderful memories!

During these days, disparity was not present in my life. I could say this with confidence because we owned a home in a neighborhood that I never would have thought possible. I had a job where my talents were needed, appreciated, and rewarded. I had two bosses, Howard and Scott, who I genuinely both liked and respected, and I knew that they felt the same way about me. I was able to keep myself involved clinically by evaluating each patient referred to OT and did a lot of clinical teaching to make the COTAs more effective. Teaching at the university on a part-time basis and continuing my nursing home consulting gave me real diversity in my OT practice. In short, I had interesting and rewarding work in three OT arenas. My family life was also great, and we were really living the good life. So how could disparity possibly have a place in my great life? Oh, it will! But, not for a while.

More success at Bedlam Hospitals

I knew joining Bedlam Hospitals would give me the high-risk-high-reward environment I was seeking. Here I was solely dependent on my own skill and acumen. As I worked building the OT department, I lobbied Scott and Howard to consider a name change from Occupational Therapy to Therapeutic Activities because we were becoming a more diverse program. I was able to arrange to have art therapy students from a nearby college work under me as part of their required internships. One of them was outstanding, and I was able to hire her. I also did the same thing with recreational therapy. So changing the department's name to Therapeutic Activities made a lot of sense, and they agreed to the name change.

With OT now having its own identity under the Therapeutic Activities umbrella, I expanded and strengthened our role through the addition of OT students from local colleges and universities. By training students, I was able to increase the presence of OT on the different units. One of the services we provided was an evaluation of function using a standardized OT assessment that gave a clear picture of a patient's cognitive functioning. This proved to be increasingly useful to physicians, nurses, social workers, and substance abuse counselors. It was time consuming to administer these assessments and do the necessary documentation. I then figured out that the hospital could bill for these assessments and generate additional income. OT thus became a revenue-generating service in addition to being a valued clinical service. Bedlam was a for-profit organization, and anyone who enhanced this objective was recognized and rewarded. So once again, I was rewarded with another raise and more accolades from my bosses.

~~~~

It was my next challenge that resulted in not only one of the biggest successes of my career but also especially in my life. I recognized that in spite of my successes, my department as well as I were in a precarious situation because of the hospital's bed allocation and usage. Bedlam Hospitals' mission had changed from being solely an acute care psychiatric hospital to an increasing commitment to becoming an inpatient substance abuse treatment center with a detoxification unit. Of the 185 total licensed beds, only fifty-five were allocated for psychiatric patients, and these were seldom all filled. Conversely, the substance abuse beds were always filled with people waiting to be admitted for inpatient treatment. The future of Bedlam Hospitals was clearly in substance abuse services, but at that time, OT had a negligible role with this population. We provided an afternoon crafts group as a respite for patients going through treatment and some recreation using a gym and swimming pool located in a high school across the street from the hospital. That was it. OT was certainly not a mainstay of the substance abuse treatment program.

I decided to expand OT's role in substance abuse but was rebuffed by the vice president of chemical dependency who oversaw these services. How dare him! He explained that their patients did not need OT to become clean and sober, and in fact, "OTs and other professionals often focus on the wrong things and interfere with the actual addiction treatment process." I was not used to being rebuffed. In fact, I viewed myself as the wunderkind of Bedlam Hospitals (like I was at the Boondocks Home), and I was not to be denied, only delayed. How was that for arrogance?

As a way of saving face and pushing myself and OT into a place where we were obviously not welcomed, I proposed a different path. In trying to be open to the possibility that I could be wrong (can you imagine?) about OT being an asset to the substance abuse treatment program, I said, "Look, you may be right that OT is a detriment and that I need to understand alcoholism and substance abuse treatment better. What do you think of my sitting in on all your service components? I would respect confidentiality and not attend any session where either the staff or patients were uncomfortable. This would apply to detoxification, lectures, individual and group therapy sessions, family groups, AA, NA, after care, outpatient, and community functions. Then when I have been through everything, lets you and I get together to see if my perspective has changed. What do you think?"

He surprised me by saying, "That is an excellent way to go. Let's do it. I'll explain to the staff what you are doing at our next staff meeting. Actually, could you come to our next meeting this coming Thursday at eleven thirty? We could explain it together so the staff knows we are on the same page." What a great response. I then let Scott and Howard know what I was doing, which they applauded. They liked initiative, and I, of course, had a lot of it in my lifelong quest to dispel disparity.

Something I did not anticipate was the lack of enthusiasm on the part of the COTAs when I told them of my plan. They had a negative view of the patients with substance abuse problems because they did not see them as being sincere about getting clean and sober. They also were disgusted with the inappropriate way some of the patients interacted with them during the recreational crafts programs we ran on a seven-day-per-week basis. I asked them to be patient as I went through my data-gathering process. I also assured them that I would not make any decisions about future OT services without including them. They liked this approach but also remained skeptical.

~~~~

As a result of my taking on this new venture, I was pretty busy trying to do my regular job, but I also was attending as many of the substance abuse programs as possible. The first startling insight that I came to was that I was not as informed about alcoholism as I thought. However, this was not the biggest insight that I discovered. Sitting in all these different sessions, I saw myself in so many of the stories the patients and families shared. It was disconcerting to discover that I was not much different from the patients. Perhaps the biggest difference between us was that I had not suffered the devastating consequences of drinking and drugging that they had. I never received a DWI for driving drunk, but I deserved a thousand for all the nights I drove drunk or high or both. I never was terminated from a job for drunkenness or lost my OT license. Also, my drinking and drugging did not lead to a divorce mainly because of the patience and love of Janice. I also was never jailed for drunkenness. Outside of me dodging these painful consequences so far, the patients and I were absolutely the same.

I did not share any of these insights with anyone. Keeping the idea that I was an alcoholic to myself was a way of further denying it, plus I didn't want to see myself that way. Who would? Running through my mind were the usual denials, minimalizations, and rationalizations: "I only drink and drug on weekends. I can quit anytime I want. I have a lot of stress in my life, and a drink or two or a joint now and then helps keep me calm, and on and on . . ." I had learned that these are the typically overused defense mechanisms that people with a drinking and drugging problem employ, but I was not 100 percent convinced just yet that I was one of them. However, that would all change on July 25th of 1982.

~~~~

It was always a big event when Tommy and Karoline came to visit us. This particular visit coincided with Bernie and Annie's eighteenth wedding anniversary, and they were also in town for a weekend of celebration and, of course, lots of drinking. Making good use of our bar and pool table in our basement tavern on Belvoir, we commenced to drinking early on in the afternoon with more than the usual disastrous results. Tommy and I loved to drink Manhattans, followed by wine at dinner enjoyed by all, and finishing off with after-dinner cordials like Drambuie or Bailey's Irish Cream. I drank a lot of everything that day and night because I was overjoyed to have all these people that I loved so much all together. Janice and I loved entertaining, and we especially loved entertaining this beloved group. Adding lots of alcohol to the Talty humor always made for a great time.

However, I had too much of a great time on that day. Drinking myself into a state of drunken unconsciousness dampened or maybe even ruined the celebration. I forced the cancellation of a special dinner we had planned for the next night at a recently renovated downtown restaurant. Janice and I had eaten there a few weeks ago, and we couldn't wait to take everyone to see how this old restaurant had been renovated. Alas, it was not to be, and it was because of me. I was too nauseous and hung over to even get out of bed until about three o'clock of the next afternoon. When I came down to the basement where Bernie and Tommy were enjoying cold bottles of Molson's Blue ale while seated at our great bar, Bernie hopped up to get me a beer. It was then that I said the words that may seem melodramatic now, but I know changed my life forever: "No, don't get me a beer. I'm not going to drink ever again. I am disgusted with myself." My words must have seemed incredulous to Bernie and Tommy. I know they may have thought I was just overreacting to a severe hangover. Regardless of what they thought or said, I was resolute in my declaration to not ever drink (or drug) ever again.

It was the shame I felt about getting so drunk, coupled with the insights gained through all the substance abuse sessions I sat in on and the reading I had been doing, that gave me the will to stop drinking and drugging. When I told the rest of the family of my decision, I did not go so far as to declare that I was an alcoholic, but I now knew it was true. In support of me, Janice also decided to quit drinking. This was not really ever a problem for her, but she always supported me in whatever I did. As of this writing, we have over thirty-three years of sobriety. This commitment to a life of sobriety was the key I was missing in my previous attempts to dispel my sense of disparity. Recalling the bonuses I received from Bedlam Hospitals, none can compare to the bonus of a life of sobriety I inadvertently received and without it costing me a dime. Now that was one giant bonus that still pays dividends every day! Thank you Bedlam Hospitals!

The Parlay!

The discovery that I had a drinking problem did enable me to transform this insight into a parlay or into something of greater value. In fact, it was several things. It started with the way I transformed OT's role in the substance abuse treatment process. I keyed on this simple concept: "Changing people, places, and things is the way to sobriety." This is a slogan often said at AA and NA meetings. I had discovered myself that I needed new interests and new friends in order to fill my now-ample vacant time in a meaningful way. For me it was the outdoors, specifically backpacking and canoeing, but I also felt OT could help people strengthen their recovery through what I called the Life Skills Groups.

I organized all my thoughts into a set of group experiences that would enhance but neither compete with or duplicate what the counselors were doing. I took the approach that counselors got people clean and dry, and OTs could help them get sober or into a life that was satisfying and full without drugs or alcohol. All this became a proposal that, when presented immediately, won the support of the counseling staff as well as my bosses, Howard and Scott. My personal epiphany about my alcoholism was certainly a key component driving this, and I looked forward to implementing this dynamic program.

With the help of the COTAs, I developed five Life Skills Groups that all patients going through the twenty-eight-day rehabilitation program would need to complete prior to discharge. The five groups were: communication skills, creative problem solving, healthy living, leisure time planning, and stress and time management. Collectively, these groups would be the underpinnings of recovery and sobriety. Using my teaching skills where I strove to engage every student every minute of every class, I now did the same with people with addictions. As a result, the patients gained much from these Life Skills Groups. This was evinced in the follow-up surveys the hospital conducted where former patients repeatedly said that the Life Skills Group were one of the most important things in helping them to maintain their sobriety. If I had not had the epiphany about my own addiction and recovery processes and the courage to disclose this when conducting the Life Skills Groups, I doubt the groups would have been nearly as effective.

~~~~

I also parlayed my new found knowledge and skills in the integration of OT into substance abuse inpatient treatment into a national presentation. Each year, the American OT Association conducts a national conference with presentations that spans the full gamut of OT practice areas. That particular year, the conference was being held in Atlanta, Georgia. Substance abuse was not a common topic on the previous programs, but I felt it should be. So I submitted a proposal to conduct what was known as an "Institute", which is a two-day intensive workshop that preceded the conference itself. It was approved, and I was excited to have this national platform to inform and inspire other OTs so that they might see another place where our skills were needed. I took the same approach that it took the expertise of an alcoholism counselor to get a person clean and dry, but as OTs, we could enhance the recovery process by giving the person the skills to maintain sobriety through the alternative use of free time or what we called "vacant hours". The program was well-received, and I enjoyed presenting it, although two full days of presenting was stressful and exhausting.

~~~~

The Parlay!

As my usual stress reliever, I went on daily runs through the downtown streets of Atlanta. I usually ran in the morning, but on one of the days, I ran in the late afternoon. On this particular day, I had an experience that resonated with me for several years and culminated in Janice and I having another of our many great adventures. After my run, I was walking to cool down when my attention was caught by a store ablaze with promotional media about Atlanta hosting the 1996 Summer Olympics. It was quite spectacular. There were about twenty televisions spread across one wall with each showing a past Olympic event, and every four minutes of so, all the televisions would coalesce into one giant picture showing an athlete winning an event with great crowd reactions. They did the same thing showing the reaction of the Atlanta Committee when it was announced that the 1996 Summer Olympics had been awarded to Atlanta. The whole place was electric, and I was more than smitten. I wanted to attend these Olympics but knew it was probably something we could never do because of the costs involved. So I just added it to my growing bucket list.

Up, Up, and Away: Part 1

Returning to my job at Bedlam Hospitals after the excitement of Atlanta, I was aware of some disenchantment stirring within me. Not the outright disparity that usually engulfed me, just some nagging feelings. Once the Life Skills Groups were up and running, I became bored. I started thinking on a larger scale. I firmly believed that there was a lot that could be done to make Bedlam an even better hospital. Scott liked my ideas, but he was sensitive not to do anything that Howard did not support. Howard, being the medical director, had the ultimate responsibility for patient care, and Scott and Marvin both respected Howard's perspective too much to do anything that would alienate him. I expressed to Howard that I would like to be doing more. I also told him that I would probably look for another position where I could advance myself with more challenging work. This was not a threat; it was just some confidential rambling between friends as we continued to ride back and forth to work.

It was in this state of disquietude about my future at Bedlam that we (Howard, Scott, and I) came to an agreement that I should be promoted to the vice president of Patient Care Services and assist Howard in the administrative and staffing aspects of his position. I was ecstatic. I didn't have to change jobs or disrupt my family with a move out of the area. We saw the position as one that would evolve as we identified functions that I could handle as directed by Howard. It would require my full commitment, and therefore, I would need to resign my consulting positions at the two nursing homes and hire the replacement for my position as Director of Therapeutic Activities. I would be well-compensated financially and also receive the significantly better benefits package reserved for executives, so resigning from the nursing homes would not be a problem. They felt that my teaching the course in management at the university was the type of outside work that I should continue doing because I liked doing it, and it enhanced the image of the hospital in the healthcare community. We were all excited about this new role and position the three of us created.

~~~~

The first and best person I could think of to replace me as the Director of Therapeutic Activities was one of my former graduate students and friend who was in charge of OT at a community mental health center adjacent to a local medical center. She had the expertise and personality that the department needed to take it to the next level. When I called, she was quick to say that she was not actively looking to make a job change but was intrigued enough to come for the interview. Everyone she met was impressed with her, and she was attracted to the position. So we worked out the salary and a starting date. Coinciding with her arrival, I was officially promoted to my new position.

~~~~

I loved the diversity of my new position. Because Howard oversaw the departments of nursing, social work, pharmacy, therapeutic activities, and the substance abuse program, I was involved in a myriad of functions that required new learning on my part. Learning new things was something I always enjoyed, but I also felt my prior education and experience provided a different perspective on the problems that were being addressed at the senior management level of the hospital. I was privy to information that was both intriguing and daunting. Howard and Scott both had major responsibilities regarding the functioning of the hospital as well as its future, and I was soon immersed in some of these significant issues.

My Machiavellian ways were given a workout as I tried to understand the complexities of long-standing covert conflicts among the key players in the organization. I always had the ability to gain entrée into different factions within most of the organizations in which I worked while not being perceived as a member of any one faction. I achieved this by always being straightforward, hardworking, observant, a good listener, and a resourceful problem solver. I also asked questions in careful ways so as not to arouse defensiveness while learning as much as I could. However, not many of these well-honed attributes were of any value in my new job. In spite of this, I continued to strive to influence major decisions at the corporate level. I thought I was being persistent, but the other executives saw me as just annoying. I learned this in various ways, but I just assumed the other executives that tried to guide me were misinformed. I had all the answers. This was dangerous thinking.

One of the things I felt bad about in my new role was the erosion of the good relationship I had built with Howard. He was a good and intelligent man who had found a way to be a very effective medical director within an administrative environment that I would describe as pretty challenging. My narrow perspective precluded me from seeing the onerous responsibility that Howard, Scott, and Marvin carried, and thus my suggestions were often naïve and sophomoric. I can see this now, but I couldn't back then.

~~~~

The owners and operators of the hospital had complete authority over everything as indeed they should. It was the two of them that had the ultimate responsibility for determining the success or failure of the hospital. As I put forth contrary opinions and suggestions, I ignored the guidance from Howard and the other executives who were trying to caution me.

In an effort to get some data regarding what our employees were thinking and feeling, I suggested an altitude survey that I would send to each of the executives for their feedback and suggestions. The owners liked the idea as did the rest of the executives.

In addition to working on the attitude survey, I also had the idea to send a memo to the owners suggesting that we make a name change. The name Quality Assurance Committee was the name given to the most powerful group in the organization. It was comprised of the owners and the executive staff of vice presidents (now including me) and senior vice presidents. I explained in my memo that a name that better described how we functioned as a group was "Executive Council". This idea everyone liked. So this change in name was enthusiastically endorsed by all. Of course, the challenge was to get this group to function with more objectivity and become a true executive council, not just in name, and I arrogantly believed I was the one to bring this about.

~~~~

As promised, I had the draft of the attitude survey ready and in everyone's mailboxes (no e-mails back then) within a week. It didn't take long to put it together because I had some models that I used as a management consultant with Cal and Bob back in the ARMI days. I added a bunch of new questions directly relevant to Bedlam at that time. At our next meeting of the executive council, the group gave me some good suggestions, which I used to modify the attitude survey. The final version was approved, and I set about to get as high a return as possible by meeting with each department and shift in the hospital. At these meetings, I emphasized anonymity and encouraged the employees to include handwritten comments. I also explained that since I was having our secretary type up all the comments, no one had to worry about being identified by their handwriting. No one but she would see the originals, and they would then all be shredded after she typed all the comments.

~~~~

The attitude survey was brutally successful. I had an almost 95 percent return rate, there were extensive handwritten comments, and the employees' responses clearly demonstrated that many of them mistrusted and had little confidence in the administration. Using a 1 to 5 Likert scale, I was able to tabulate what percent of employees felt changes were needed in specific areas. To say that the employees used the attitude survey to vent and "rip" on the administration would be an understatement. However, I was impressed with the mature and professional way the owners handled this unbridled and often unjustified criticism. They also were very complimentary to me for coming up with the idea and for the work I did to make it all happen. The bad news was that the attitude survey set expectations on the part of the employees that things would change, and change fast. I knew it was not realistic for all the things the employees identified to be changed, nor could they be changed immediately. I did, however, feel that the owners needed to be forthright and forthcoming through an all-employee memo that I volunteered to draft.

The results of the attitude survey strengthened my position regarding the need for change, but I was disappointed to see how easily the data was ignored and the owners and executives reverted back to their old ways of relying on assumptions, rumors, and innuendos to make major decisions. I, of course, found this very frustrating. Also, typical of me, I did not keep my frustrations to myself. I was operating under the illusion—or was it delusion?—that the owners wanted to hear my observations and perceptions, and thus, I continued to share these in private with the owners and the rest of the executives in the executive council meetings. Howard and a few of the other executives tried to advise me that I was pushing too hard. Howard was also concerned that my comments were going to bring more work onto our desks than we could handle. Howard always had clearer vision than me when it came to taking on projects. He was an intelligent and reasonable man, and who could blame him for wanting a manageable and relatively stress-free life? This difference in our visions produced some tension between us that made our car pooling strained at times.

Up, Up, and Away: Part 1

~~~~

While I was busy acclimating myself to my new role as the vice president of Patient Care Services and unintentionally aggravating my peers and bosses, I received a phone call from a "headhunter" with a very intriguing opportunity. One of the biggest and most renowned rehabilitation facilities in the world was looking for a director of OT, and they had contracted with this executive search firm to find the best person possible. He explained that he began his search by contacting the American OT Association and two other organizations and asked them for a list of people who they believed could lead this department of over one hundred OTs. It turned out mine was the only name that appeared on all three lists, so he felt he had to contact me first. Nice introduction! It got my attention. So it was off to the big city for two days of interviews and wooing.

The facility was very impressive in every way. I felt the interviews were going well, but my best presentation came at the end of the first day when I met all one hundred of the OTs for an hour in an amphitheater classroom within the facility. Not sure what questions they may have of me, I decided to give them an abbreviated résumé by starting off saying, "Let me start by telling you what kind of OT I am by explaining where I worked and the kinds of things I accomplished." Along the way, I described my style of management and some of the clinical problems I encountered and resolved. I had the gift that day. They were mesmerized and gave me a resounding round of applause when I finished. It was evident that the group of OTs viewed me as the right person for one of the most coveted jobs in the OT profession.

I had dinner that night with the headhunter who was very positive. He had canvassed the people who I had met with that day, and they all strongly felt that I would be ideal for the position. I could tell that he was very pleased. It was almost like his work was done. The only thing I had to do was to not screw up the next day of interviews.

I did not screw them up. In fact, the second day went even better than the first, and in a month or so he called and, I was offered the position. Now what to do? Did I really want to disrupt my whole family and move to the big city? Could I go from being a lifelong fan of local sports to a zealot supporting "them?" Because I really didn't want to move and because the big city was a far more expensive city to live in than my hometown, I responded with a ridiculous figure when the headhunter asked what kind of salary I was seeking. He was a bit shocked with my exorbitant salary demand, but I felt I was in control because they wanted me more than I wanted them. As a way of explaining how out of line my salary demand was, he explained how far above my proposed salary was in relation to a comparable position at the facility such as the director of PT who had been there for sixteen years and was earning about two-thirds of my proposed figure. With more than a hint of arrogance, I suggested that this position should also be elevated. In any event, we parted friends with the assumption that I would not be joining them because they could not meet my salary expectations.

~~~~

  I returned to my Bedlam vice president's job but without much zest. Going through the motions in a lackluster and resentful way would aptly describe my state of mind and attitude in those days. I did find it interesting to mentor two new managers in our division and conduct a management course for supervisors throughout the hospital. As is typical of these kinds of in-house courses, those who needed it most chose not to attend. It was my adamant belief that the main reason the managers at all levels at Bedlam did not manage effectively was that they lacked training. Following my faulty logic further, I assumed that once they were trained, then their managerial behavior would change for the better. I tried not to be a nagging voice of criticism, but I'm afraid I was unsuccessful at this. I was a nag without restraint. My daily five-mile runs at lunch time were not enough to arrest my percolating frustration, discontent, and rage.

  Now did my sense of disparity come charging forth during these unhappy days? No, not really. This was partly due to the status I enjoyed as a vice president and the affluent neighborhood and home in which we now lived. So my discontent was not present at all in my home life, but it sure was rampant in my work life. The money was too good to just walk away, and so I just ran more miles to get rid of the rage I felt toward Bedlam and the position I had put myself in and tried to carry on.

Two Possible "Lifesavers"

Traversing the landmines of Bedlam in my desolate and negativistic mood was not good for obvious reasons. However, in this state, I was miraculously thrown not one but two lifesavers that I desperately needed. The first came from the big-city recruiter. Surprise! I thought that position was dead, but I was wrong. According to the recruiter, the facility wanted me so badly that they got creative in putting together a financial package that would meet my demands. They elevated both the OT and PT director positions, and then they arranged for a part-time faculty appointment for me at a nearby university that accounted for a portion of my stipulated salary, and last, they were able to secure the final amount from a foundation within the organization. The benefits and relocation packages were also very attractive. Did I seize this great opportunity? No, of course not, because I still did not want to leave the area. Did I use it to alter my position at Bedlam? Of course, I did. Once I received this fine offer, I knew I had a new card to play. This was lifesaver number one, and I was able to use it to seize lifesaver number two as described below.

Rather than accepting the attractive offer outright, I chose to think about it for a few days. I then went and talked with Scott about my interest in a comparable position within Bedlam Hospitals: the Vice President in Human Resources. This position was currently open, and I thought I would be able to handle it. Then I put forth my crazy idea: "I think I could be very good as the vice president of human resources. What do you think?" He then asked a lot of astute questions that revealed several gaps in my background in human resources. Undeterred, I pressed on and reminded him of what I had achieved at Bedlam in the past four years through learning on the job. Scott was not overly enthusiastic about me taking on this big responsibility, and was also concerned about my leaving Howard without an assistant. He said he would think about it and, of course, talk it over with Marvin. He said he would get back to me in a few days.

Up, Up, and Away: Part 2

I didn't have to wait long. The next morning Scott had his secretary contact me to arrange a meeting that afternoon. What he said caused great jubilation on my part. "I talked it over with my Dad, and we are willing to give you a chance. The human resources job has become far more complex than any of us could have anticipated, and because of that, we want to invest in your education. We have attorneys available to guide you and outside consultants that you can call on as needed. You also have two experienced assistants to help you." We worked out the details on salary, reporting process, and a transition plan so Howard wouldn't be left in a mess.

After wrapping up some things with Howard, I moved into my new job and office. It was interesting right from the beginning because the employees had begun to organize a union, and as the VP of human resources, it was my job to thwart this movement while strictly adhering to the laws of the NLRB (National Labor Relations Board).

Within a few days in my new job, I came to the realization that human resources had very little authority but had major responsibilities. This would be the epitome of madness that would be my yoke throughout my tenure in the position. Oh well, I asked for this job, and I was going to master it. I found the new language and concepts of Human Resources interesting and easy to grasp, so my new job immediately eradicated the boredom I was experiencing.

I felt bad that Howard was hurt by my leaving him and tried to assuage his negative feelings without success. We still rode to and from work together, but not as frequently nor with much of the old joviality. Eventually, he did seem to have moved on, and we got back some of our old relationship. He had found an excellent replacement for me in the former director of social services. He was, in many ways, a far better fit for the position than I, and I think he really helped Howard get over what he saw as my betrayal.

~~~~

Around this same time, I was able to help my brother Danny get a job at Bedlam that led to profound changes in his life. My work as an OT in the substance abuse program had resulted in a useful by-product in the form of good relationships with the counselors and administrators within the program. One of the things I had learned is that there is a somewhat impregnable culture within the alcoholism staff and community that excludes people who do not have a history of addiction. I was able to gain entrée into this insular group once I disclosed my problems with drugs and alcohol when I ran all those Life Skills Groups. I also wrote about my history in the hospital's newsletter. So when I asked for help in getting Danny a job as a chemical dependency aide, the people in charge were very accommodating. Danny, like I, had "seen the light" and was actively attending AA meetings. This was a critical component in his getting hired, as well as the many college courses he took in alcoholism studies and workshops he attended. He was able to work his way up and into a sort of junior counselor's position and eventually become a credentialed alcohol and substance abuse counselor. He was then promoted into a regular counselor's position and went on to have an outstanding career in that field.

~~~~

Unfortunately, my career in human resources was not going as well. I was new to the executive role. I foolishly believed that I could counsel the other executives toward a more proactive and balanced mode of responding to staff issues, but this was vehemently rejected at every turn. My constantly pointing out what I believed to be a better way was eroding the previously good relationships I had forged with the other members of the executive council. Another misjudgment on my part was to overexaggerate in my mind my value to the hospital.

The owners, Scott and Marvin, showed great faith in allowing me to operate a major component of the hospital's operations with so little experience and training in human resources, and for that confidence, I will always be grateful. I was trying very hard to master my new job. I took advantage of every learning opportunity. I joined the human resources professionals group and attended their monthly educational meetings as well as different workshops they offered. The owners had provided me with subscriptions to two publications that were filled with very useful information. I also was developing good relationships with more experienced human resources directors that I could call on as needed. The attorneys and specialized consultants were also great advisors and guides for me. The one attorney who I spent the most time with was a labor relations expert who guided all of us through the process of legally trying to prevent the union from getting a foothold in Bedlam Hospitals without breaking the law. He was a great strategist, and I followed everything he said to avoid violating any labor laws that would result in a mandate for us to become unionized. In spite of our best efforts, the union movement moved forward to where a vote was to be conducted overseen by the NLRB.

There are specific rules regarding who were the employees that were eligible to vote in the election, and it was my job to enforce these rules. There were some jobs that it was unclear as to their eligibility, and these were resolved at a series of NLRB hearings attended by me and our attorney. Once all employees were properly classified, the vote was conducted.

~~~~

This is where I erred. A major mistake I made was to delegate a critical task that I should have definitely done myself. Instead of personally scrutinizing this critical list that identified employees eligible to vote, I gave the task to one of my assistants. She was not diligent enough, and two employees voted who were not actually eligible. My error was in not checking her work prior to the vote. The result was that we lost the election by two votes, and Bedlam Hospitals had its first union. This was not the first error that this assistant made, and so I fired her, which proved to be another stupid move on my part.

~~~~

As they say, February 27, 1987, was a day like any other day. I was working in my office at 11:25 a.m. when Scott and Marvin's secretary called and said they needed to meet with me right away in Marvin's office. This was a common thing that happened once or twice a week. I thought I might be in for some more browbeating over the union snafu, but I wasn't concerned. I was told cheerfully by Marvin's secretary to go on in. Marvin was seated behind his large desk at the opposite end of his long office with Scott seated in a chair to the side facing me. I turned to shut the door, but before I could do so, Marvin stood up, buttoned his suit coat for some reason, and said in his most authoritative voice, "Mr. Talty, as the president of Bedlam Hospitals it is my duty to inform you that you are terminated immediately from your position as vice president of human resources."

I immediately turned my back to them, reopened the almost closed door and said "fine," and began to exit.

He then raised his voice in anger and shouted, "We do not like your management style, and security is escorting you out. You are to take nothing with you, and—"

I didn't listen to the rest and said "fine" again trying to be as cavalier as possible. I walked on past the rotund cherubic security guard who must have been secreted in Scott's office when I first came up the stairs awaiting this assignment to make sure I didn't become violent. I went down to my office, showed the security guard who was plainly embarrassed to be a part of this whole thing that I was taking nothing but my day planner and my own keys (I removed the Bedlam keys). Without any explanation to my staff or speaking to anyone, I left Bedlam and my high-paying executive position forever.

Soon after I left, the owners put out a printed announcement to all departments that I had been terminated and that no one at Bedlam was to have any communication with me. Now that I had been deemed a pariah (my word), my friends were put in a difficult position. A few chose to ignore the owners' dictate and called me, and a few others even came to see me. There was understandable silence from the majority, especially my colleagues on the executive council. Not even Howard called me or stopped by, which I understood completely.

It was sad that I destroyed the faith that Howard, Scott, and Marvin had placed in me. They supported and rewarded my efforts on their behalf for over five years, but I disappointed them.

The Process of My Rehabilitation

There was a day when getting fired in such a terrible way would have resulted in me getting justifiably drunk, but I knew I was not going to let this happen just because I got fired again. I had gone fifteen years between firings, and plus I had almost eighteen months of sobriety. So now I was out of a job. How do I tell Janice? What are we going to do? Where do I get another high-paying job to pay for our upscale home and lifestyle? I decided only God could help us, so instead of going to the nearest tavern, I caught the twelve o'clock Mass at our church. Before Mass started, I made a promise to God: "If you can get me out of this mess, I will attend daily Mass forever." I felt confident that I had struck a deal that would save us in more ways than one.

After Mass, I went home and told Janice. Her calm demeanor did not surprise me, but what she said took me aback: "Good! I'm glad you're out of there! That place was killing you!" She was right, of course, but it still shocked me to hear it from her with such raw emotion. I then had to tell Janice's mom, who responded in a simple and wonderful way: "It will be all right. You are a good man. You will find something." I was moved to tears with her response. I also called all my family members, giving them all the same reason for my termination: "They just didn't like my management style." Of course, it was much more than this, but how could I explain something so painful and complicated? I felt it was much better to put the emphasis on the future and my going forward to find another job right away.

Danny, of course, didn't need to be told. He heard about my ousting while at work. All my family members were both sad for me and very supportive. Bernie, who was living out of town, promised to send me their Sunday newspaper that had the most job ads. Tommy offered to do the same for the Washington DC area. I had learned a lot in the past year about how to handle being fired through counseling others. I also knew the value of keeping a positive attitude as I vigorously started my job search. This was, of course, a very stressful time, but I didn't feel I was in this by myself.

~~~~

The next day the Maintenance staff delivered all my stuff from my office, including my university chair. This was the chair I received when I won the teacher of the year award in 1980. Janice's mom and I were the only ones home that morning, and because I was too embarrassed to interact with the guys I knew from Maintenance, we did not answer the door. After a short wait, they left after depositing all my stuff on my grand front porch. It was depressing moving all my stuff inside.

~~~~

As I turned more and more to the church and to prayer to get me through this stressful time, I also prayed a great deal to St. Therese of Lisieux, known as the "Little Flower". Ironically, it was the woman who was the assistant that I fired that was the same person that introduced me to St. Therese. Of course, this was when we were on good terms and long before I fired her. She also attended our church, and one day at work, she told me about St. Therese and gave me her (St. Therese's) prayer card. It is interesting how much solace this prayer card gave me during the dark days following my firing and the ironic way I came to know St. Therese. Many prayers to St. Therese and attendance at daily Mass gave me a great deal of hope as I valiantly scoured ads for open positions from all sources and dutifully applied for every one of the ones for which I had the qualifications.

~~~~

Because I previously had two vice president positions plus a series of department-head-level positions, I was confident that I could qualify for another executive-level position. Following everything I had learned and taught to others about what to do if you get fired, I called everyone I knew that might be able to help me secure an executive position. I was honest with everyone telling them that I had been fired and asked for their help in my job search.

The other thing I did was that I kept myself busy in many different ways. My sister Sue had been diagnosed with breast cancer, and so I took her to some of her chemotherapy treatments. She was feeling well enough to type my revised résumé and cover letters as I began applying for various positions. It was coincidental and fortuitous that I and her husband Jim had both just been fired, and we were both actively searching for new jobs. We were both able to encourage each other in our respective depressing job searches. I think what made this search so depressing for us is that we were both jettisoned from very lofty positions.

As a backup plan, in case my search for an executive position did not work out, I wrote to the OT licensing department in the state capital to have my license moved from inactive to active status. Years earlier, to save money, I had placed my OT license in the inactive category when I moved into administration. I was now going to apply for OT positions as well, and I would need a current OT license to qualify for them.

~~~~

I also did mundane things like getting my lawn mower serviced to be ready for the spring and did some home repairs that had been waiting for my attention. Another mundane but humbling task I did was to apply for Unemployment, something I had never done. Not surprisingly, they had no vice presidency positions listed in their catalog of open positions. They also did not have any OT positions listed. Janice accompanied me to daily Mass at 7:00 a.m. each day, which was a good way to start each of these difficult days. It was my objective to do everything and anything I could to not have to disrupt my family. I wanted to keep all of us, including Janice's mom, living in our beloved Wellington Woods home. Beth was particularly upset when I told her that I had been fired. She said, "It makes me feel so insecure." Her response was very disconcerting and propelled me to work even harder to maintain a stable and secure home for all of us. I called everyone that I thought could help. The results were disappointing. No one had any leads on local open executive positions.

I then went on some out-of-town interviews but nothing came of them. Since nothing was coming from my search for an executive position, I had to pursue some OT positions. This was not a bad thing because I enjoyed OT and had gotten pretty good at it. The first ad I saw for an OT was at a local community agency providing a range of services for adults with developmental disabilities. Having had limited experience with this population, I was not confident that I would get the opportunity to even interview for this position, but I sent my résumé in anyway because you never know. Surprisingly, I got a call from the OT that was vacating the position, and she was very excited about my background. So we scheduled a time for an interview and tour of the day treatment facility where this position was based. Thus, began the most amazing transition from fired to hired and from a difficult organization (for me) to one of the most stable and healthy organizations with which I have ever been associated. I had taken the tact right from the beginning to be completely open and honest about my firing. So when I met with the Director of Day Treatment and the OT that was leaving the agency, I told them the whole story of my meteoric rise and fall at Bedlam Hospitals in a non-blaming way. My thinking was why hide anything. One phone call to Bedlam would finish me anyway because I was not expecting good words to come from them about me. Surprise! I got the job! They were impressed with me and my honesty. It was a three-day-a-week job with a salary higher than I expected. In fact, the pay I received excluded me from qualifying for Unemployment.

It was a great feeling to be working again, and the staff at this agency was very helpful in getting me acclimated to the agency and to this client population that was so new to me. Going from the stress of a vice presidency where I was in over my head to the practice of OT where everyone was open and honest was truly heaven and just what I needed. It was as if I had St. Therese to assuage my diminished spirituality and this agency to salve my damaged ego.

On the two days when I wasn't working at the day treatment program, I worked in home care, seeing patients of different ages and diagnoses, all thanks to Cal Emancipator, my former supervisor at the medical center. This was also new to me, and I enjoyed helping patients and their family members become as independent as possible. Home care paid very well, and by doing the documentation at home at night, I was able to see several patients on each of the days when I wasn't working at the agency. The combination of the salary I received from the agency coupled with my pay I received for each home care patient visit was keeping us economically stable. However, I saw an opportunity for me to increase my income much more by hiring therapists and creating an OT private practice business.

It was also at this time that I saw an ad in the local newspaper where a major university outside of my hometown was looking for instructors for their local management courses. I applied immediately and was called for an interview within a few days. They needed someone to teach two courses, management and interpersonal skills, both in their evening program. I was hired and began teaching two courses two nights a week. The assistant director was very concerned about maintaining a high quality of instruction in all the courses and frequently sat in on my classes because I was the newest instructor. I didn't mind because I knew how to teach and how to engage students. She was very impressed and always gave me high praise at the end of the night whenever she sat in on my classes. The students also gave me strong reviews. Thus, I had another source of income and was doing something I loved: teaching. I stayed with this university for two years but had to resign when my other ventures required more of my time.

~~~~

I had also picked up a contract with a skilled nursing facility where I met a significant person from my past. As I looked through the medical charts of the new patients I was going to evaluate that day, I noted one name that intrigued me. It was the same name as my bookkeeping teacher who saved me over twenty-five years ago. I went to see him and found him to be completely lucid even though he had had a mild stroke. It was the same guy! He didn't remember me specifically but remarked that what he did for me is what he believed teachers should do for students. What a remarkable encounter this was but I think far more significant for me than for him. He did well and was discharged to home after a few weeks.

I Become an Entrepreneur and Live the Life

1987–1997

In 1987, there was a shortage of OTRs in the area of my hometown, and I set about to exploit it by building a business of providing OT services. Through my teaching (which I was doing again with a course each semester at the university plus the out-of-town university), serving as an officer in different capacities at the local, state, and national levels and having worked in several facilities, I was well-known in the OT community. It also seemed that my crazy past and even my most recent spectacular firing were not even issues in securing contracts or in recruiting therapists. There was no Craigslist or Internet back then. So the best way for me to find OTRs is by word of mouth, and the best place to find facilities and agencies to contract with was the newspaper classified section and also word of mouth.

None of this was planned out. I just started saying yes if someone called looking for OT services. When they asked, "What kind of OT do you do?" I would respond, "What kind do you need?" My thinking was that if I could not provide the expertise they were looking for, I would either take it on myself and master it on the job or canvas my growing cadre of OTs that I knew and recruit them to provide it. This may seem bold and reckless, but my risk-taking nature, coupled with lots of prayers to St. Therese and attendance at daily Mass, all provided the impetus and courage necessary to venture forth in spite of the uncertainties involved.

~~~~

I called my growing company "Peter Talty and Associates." The name was not very creative, but it met the requirements of a "DBA" (Doing Business As) and enabled me to operate as a legitimate business in the state and to open a company bank account. By using my own name, I got the added benefit of getting my name known even more so in the OT and healthcare communities. My prior relationships helped me to land my first contracts, and right from the beginning, I established a routine where I did many of the contracts in the beginning myself. This enabled me to get the systems all in place and to build the relationships with the key staff members to ensure a smooth delivery of OT services. An added benefit to my doing the OT myself is that I could identify the potential "landmines" that could result in the loss of a given contract. Some could not be resolved for various reasons, but by taking certain measures, we could avoid the contract blowing up on us. All this information was imparted to the therapist taking over each contract and gave me the necessary information about each contract to guide and mentor each of the therapists.

~~~~

I was busy, but I was nowhere near as stressed as I was at Bedlam Hospitals. I loved the autonomy and control I had over my growing business. It was a perfect time to be doing this because OT was a mandated service in schools, nursing homes, hospitals, and home care. OT also was a way for facilities to generate income through reimbursement from private insurance companies, Medicare, Medicaid, and Workers' Compensation. The problem was that there were not enough OTs in the area to meet these growing needs, and my company was where facilities and agencies regularly looked to when they needed OT services.

A somewhat downside to my business is that I had to be gone two nights a week as I expanded my business into the rural areas about two hours from home. I also had to drive over forty thousand miles a year in those days.

It was on one of my overnight trips that Janice's brother Frank gave me a surprising response to my saga at Bedlam Hospitals. He had a degree in accounting and had spent several years in upper management for the Big Store before going into business for himself and then into a series of sales positions. This was early on after my being fired, and I felt I should explain what happened to me to both him and his wife, Gerry. They happened to be vacationing at their summer home on a lake that was right on the route I drove in between facilities, so I stopped by for a quick visit. After I finished my sad story of ascension and demise at Bedlam Hospitals, he dismayed me when he said, "I would have fired you too. They made the right decision. Neither incompetency nor disloyalty can be tolerated especially at the vice president level." Well, how do you like that? I thought he would be more supportive and understanding, not join in with Brutus and Cassius. It took some time and a lot of miles of running for me to stop being mad at Frank and hurt by his cruel comments before I saw how absolutely right he was about my being fired for my lack of competence and absolute loyalty. It's a lesson I will never forget.

~~~~

My company grew so fast that in the second year, I had doubled my previous salary from Bedlam Hospitals; and at the end of the third year, I had tripled it. The child in me wanted to send a copy of my balance sheet to the owners of Bedlam Hospitals, but my adult prevailed. However, I honestly think Scott felt bad about having to terminate me, and I kind of think he would be glad that I was doing so well. Regardless, I never sent it or had any contact with anyone from Bedlam Hospitals. I felt sadness when I learned that a few of the executive staff had died at different times in subsequent years, but I sent no notes of condolences. Not because I was bitter; I was not. I just didn't think it would be appropriate. The owners and the medical director supported me and certainly were essential to my successes at Bedlam, and I am still saddened about my inability to meet their expectations. They were right to fire me; they probably should have just done it sooner.

~~~~

I took a number of one-day workshops on various aspects of running a business that were put on by the Small Business Administration that proved very helpful. I also found two attorneys who were also trained as CPAs that were very reasonably priced and would often meet with me at seven o'clock in the morning prior to my heading off to my various contracts. I had early starts to my day as my business grew into the surrounding counties, and some of the agencies and facilities with which I had contracts were sometimes two or more hours away. Since most of my therapists wanted to stay closer to my hometown, I took these contracts on as my personal responsibility until I could recruit someone in those areas. Because of the distance involved, I would usually stay in a local motel for two nights each week. I didn't like leaving Janice and her mom alone (Peter was traveling with the band, and Beth lived on campus during the semesters), but I did not have an alternative at that time. Within a short time, I was managing over thirty contracts spread out among eight counties. I had a combination of full- and part-time therapists (OTRs and COTAs) that also totaled almost thirty.

Our added income enabled us to travel a bit. No, these were not cruises to exotic places. Janice and I often traveled on weekends around the state and to adjoining states to see and hear the band that had hired Peter. He was now doing the sound and also the lights because the guy previously doing the lights had quit. We got to know the band members who turned out to be Peter's good friends and excellent mentors. Peter always enjoyed it when we showed up. It also gave us the opportunity to visit with him during the day after he woke up after his late nights. We missed Peter badly, and these weekend sojourns helped us cope with his being on the road. It was also during this same time that Beth left for college. So our house was a bit lonely for us even though we had Janice's mom living with us, our dog, Nikkie, and two cats, Duke and Mandy. Our big house now seemed bigger and emptier.

Our dog, Nikkie, and our one cat Mandy all had a Bedlam connection. I got both from one of the COTAs that was in the department I managed. She had a great sense of humor, and when her mother expressed concern that she may get pregnant before she and her boyfriend married, she said, "That's okay. If I get pregnant, I'll just have the baby and give him to Peter and Janice."

~~~~

In an effort to assuage our sad feelings about not seeing Peter enough, we bought him a car for Christmas. It was not a new car. We bought it from my brother Bernie, and it was in very good condition. Janice was able to find a large ribbon and bow that we put on the top after we parked it in Bernie's garage after we had it detailed. Peter had a few days off from the band that Christmas and was able to join us at Annie and Bernie's for one of our many special holiday gatherings. This gathering was made even more special when we had Peter go into the garage for his gift. The combined shock and joy he showed made the cost and all the clandestine doings all worthwhile. Janice and I felt that if Peter had a car, we would get to see him more when he had a few days off. It turned out to be delightfully so.

With our enhanced financial position, we were also able to help a number of our family members. This made us feel so good. We also helped out our church. A young priest joined our parish who was an avid runner. He organized the first road running race under the auspices of our church, and I supported him with a significant donation that got the name of my company—now known as "OT Works—on all the shirts the runners received. I also continued my commitment to go to Mass each day. It required diligent searching to find Masses in the rural areas where I traveled, but I did it. When I was home, Janice and I continued to go together.

~~~~

John Updike, one of my favorite authors, wrote over twenty novels, but four of them involved a character named Harry "Rabbit" Angstrom with whom I felt an affinity. The reason these novels about Rabbit are mentioned here is that these particular Updike novels at times seem to uncannily parallel my life. It was striking to me that whenever I read the latest Rabbit novel, his life was almost a duplicate of mine at the given stage. *Rabbit, Run* and *Rabbit Redux* were like looking into a mirror, and his musings and concerns were strangely also mine. Then the economic and professional success I was experiencing with my group OT practice was very similar to *Rabbit Is Rich*. We lived well, and on one of our winter vacations to Marco Island, Florida, I almost fell out of my lounge chair when I read how Rabbit's life of prosperity was so in sync with mine. Before his death in 2009, John Updike wrote the last book in the series. It was entitled *Rabbit at Rest*, which I have just finished reading. It was difficult for me to read at times because his life took unfortunate turns that I have avoided and some I did not. The ending was particularly depressing for me for many reasons. In spite of the sadness *Rabbit at Rest* generated in me, the power of Updike's writing style is something I would love to someday emulate.

~~~~

In 1993, the World University Games, which is an Olympics-type of international athletic competition, came to my hometown. Having experienced the Olympics media extravaganza in Atlanta, I knew that the World University Games was something I had to do and in a grand manner. I was one of the first people to go to the university's ticket office where you could purchase tickets for all the events. I got tickets for opening night for Janice and me, Peter and Chelli (his girlfriend at the time), and Beth. Knowing how Bernie loved swimming competitions, I got tickets for several swimming competitions for him, Annie, Janice, and me. I did the same thing for Beth with gymnastics. Janice and I went to several other competitions, including track and field and the closing ceremonies. The whole thing was exciting and moving, and this confirmed for me that we would be going to Atlanta in 1996 for the Summer Olympics.

Janice and I not only went to Atlanta for the Summer Olympics, but we went twice! We flew down, rented a car, stayed at a bed-and-breakfast outside of Atlanta, and attended the amazing opening ceremony and events like basketball, volleyball, and swimming. Then we flew home, only to return in two weeks to attend baseball, track and field and some other events. The Centennial Park bombing occurred on June 27th, just after we returned. The security that previously was rigorous became even more intense after it was decided to continue the games in spite of the bombing. The feeling of nationalism was certainly magnified throughout all the events we attended. We feel attending the Olympics the way we did is something that for Janice and me was a special memory that we will never forget. It was extremely expensive, especially the way we did it, but we didn't care. This was something Janice and I always had in common: if something is unique and an opportunity that may not come our way again, regardless of the cost, we do it. Some may think this is imprudent, but we had gained a level of economic comfort that enabled us to do these things without anxiety or guilt.

The Talty Family's Interest in the Macabre

For reasons that I cannot explain, many members of the Talty family, including me, have a fascination with true crime; the more grisly and gruesome, the better. Ma and Dad as well as my sister Sue "enjoyed" (a bizarre word, I know, but highly accurate) reading about true crimes. *True Detective* magazine was a favorite of theirs. I can recall each of them at different times reading these magazines in bed each night. Two of my brothers (Bernie and Pat) and I shared this interest, however, not relying on magazines like *True Detective*. Investigative crime novels were more to our liking. We exchanged books on actual killings, with Ann Rule being one of our favorite authors.

People are surprised and I think a bit disconcerted when they hear of the genre of books I like to read and genre of TV shows I like to watch. Many erroneously think that my true crime interests are like that of many millions of viewers who watch *CSI*, *Bones*, *NCIS*, *X-Files*, *Criminal Minds*, and on and on. Wrong! I watch none of these. Give me the real murders with interviews with the actual perpetrators who committed these heinous deeds or the investigators who pursued and apprehended them. My favorite shows include *Snapped*, *On the Case with Paula Zahn*, *Dateline on ID*, *Unusual Suspects*, *Lockup*, and *Locked Up Abroad*, and so on.

I am enthralled with these kinds of shows and books for a number of reasons. First, it has to do with the motivation of the criminals.

Why do they do what they do? How do they deal with the guilt and remorse they must feel? If they feel none, then what parts of their brains have gone awry? What elements in their environments played a role in fostering such deviant behavior? The occupational therapist in me wonders how do they deal with life in prison without the possibility of parole? How do they find meaning and hope when neither is the intent of incarceration? These shows cannot answer these questions with certainty, but I enjoy analyzing the behavior of these dangerous people in the safety of my own home.

Janice has come to like the same kinds of shows as I with what could best be described as morbid curiosity. We always have a backlog of our shows ready to be called up for watching while we have dinner. I also have a backlog of real crime books ready to be devoured in my free time. Bizarre? Perhaps, but it's what we do. I do not openly share my interest in real crimes because people may wonder about my own inclinations. This is my first public disclosure about my reading and watching pleasure. To be of interest to me, it must be true crime.

Merging Entrepreneurism with Academia

Although having my own business was lucrative, it had many other benefits as well. I loved the freedom of not worrying about a boss. This business was also the epitome of one of my favorite configurations in which to immerse myself: high risk, high reward. I could now control the direction and pace of my business. There were, of course, stressful times. I was always in the position of trying to be sure that I had enough contracts to keep all therapists working at a productive level. It was also a cash flow problem at times when I first started out because as an employer, I had to pay therapists every two weeks without delay, whereas the companies where we provided services didn't pay me for thirty, sixty, and sometimes ninety days after the OT services had been provided. In the beginning, I was sometimes paying therapists on credit card money, my credit card. Luckily, this stressful time passed once we started to receive payments for the services we rendered. The cash flow crisis was brief; and then prosperity was ours!

There was one unique set of circumstances that captured the confluence of our financial commitments and the receipt of funds back in the early days of my business. I had taken on a large contract providing OT services to preschool kids with developmental disabilities in multiple sites that required the hiring of five additional therapists. Using my credit card, I had paid these therapists for the weeks they worked. Meanwhile I was sweating the bill that was coming from Beth's university for tuition, fees, and room and food for her second semester. This confluence of debt versus income occurred in our mailbox when we received the tuition bill and the first large check from the new contract on the same day. The amounts were within a few dollars of each other. From that time forward, we were always in the position of having more income than expenses, which, of course, is the definition of a successful business.

I always said to myself that if I had the opportunity to run my own organization, I would do it differently. For example, I never liked meetings no matter where I worked. I found them boring and not very effective. So I ran my private practice OT company for ten years, and during that time, I only had one meeting. There was no e-mail or cell phone communication systems like today. So I did it all through face-to-face interactions or phone calls. Another thing I never liked were forced social functions, like company picnics, luncheons, home barbecues, house parties, and so forth. So they also were not part of our operations. I went to two weddings of my therapists, but that was the extent of social networking for me.

Another thing I committed to was non-manipulation and honesty in dealing with both my employees and the places where I had contracts to provide OT services. I had forsaken my Machiavellian methods having learned the hard way through my Bedlam Hospitals vice presidencies how truly harmful and counterproductive these methods were. The straightforward and honest way made my life so much simpler. Without deceit at any time, I was often told that people saw me as a person of integrity, and I needed that trust from my therapists as well as the agencies and facilities where we provided services. For the most part, this approach served me well, but there were therapists as well as administrative personnel at some of the agencies that at times took advantage of my trusting ways. However, these few aberrations didn't change me or my management style. I took the high road in every instance. Of course, there was some residual rage that I released through running, cycling, and prayer, but I remained honest throughout.

My hiring of people was something else that was outside the norm. I hired several people over the phone, sent them off to an agency or facility to provide OT services, got their time sheets every week, and sent them their paychecks. Some of them worked for me for as long as three years, and I never met them. We had no performance evaluations, no job descriptions, and no policy and procedure manuals. It was each therapist's job to meet the needs of the agency that contracted with us and in the manner in which I had established by my working there initially, as dictated by the clients (agency, facility, or organization). I did not want a cumbersome bureaucratic structure, and so I didn't create one.

Like always, once things were running in a predictable fashion, I looked to do something else, like returning to teaching. In reality, I had never really stopped teaching. Soon after I was fired from Bedlam Hospitals, a friend who I went to graduate school with and was now the acting chair of OT at the university gave me the opportunity to teach kinesiology when she heard I was looking for a job. This was a complex course that I struggled with throughout the semester, but it led to another amazing path in my less-than-ordinary career and life.

~~~~

The place I will refer to as the College was a small private college in a rural area upstate, and in 1986, they had established a new OT program. Their first class had progressed into their junior year and now needed to take kinesiology. However, none of the OT faculty members or the natural sciences faculty at the College had the expertise to teach it. The founding chair of OT was a very resourceful person. She called all the OT and PT schools within two hours of the College to get the names of their kinesiology professors in hopes of finding someone who could teach kinesiology as an adjunct instructor while maintaining their present full-time appointment. When she talked with the chair at the university, she gave her my name. I, like everyone else, said to myself, "Where the hell was this College?" Regardless of where it was, I would check it out because of being an opportunist, I checked out everything. The chair of OT and I arranged to meet late in the day after I had worked in a school district providing OT services that was only about forty-five minutes from the College.

~~~~

What that first meeting led to was nothing that I would have ever expected. The College was small and one could tell right away that it was not a place of affluence. It had been established in 1890 as a woman's, liberal arts, Baptist college, but had recently become coed, nonsectarian, and had diversified by adding professional programs like business, social work, nursing, criminal justice, and, most recently, OT. I was impressed with the chair who had come to the College from a major university three years ago to develop the OT program. She was a genius at making do with less, but she was also a realist and knew that for someone like me to make the trek to the College to teach kinesiology offering me the minimum wage was not going to do it. We worked out a deal that was mutually beneficial, and so I was then teaching kinesiology at both the university and the College. I taught at the university on two mornings a week and at the College on Thursdays from 4:00 p.m. to 9:00 p.m. So, besides running my business and practicing OT in several places where I did not have therapists, I was now teaching a lot. However, everything I was doing I loved, so it was nothing like the drudgery that some work can become.

~~~~

The other good news about the hectic schedule I had engineered for myself was that we had more discretionary money than we ever had. We were able to take great vacations to Florida, have season tickets for Beth's university's basketball team where we could watch her cheer, help out family members, and take sojourns on weekends to see Peter and the band. We also did some remodeling in our house to make our great house even more spectacular in our eyes.

So with this prodigious life that I was now enjoying, whence was my sense of disparity? I absolutely had no sense of disparity in those days. There was no one else's life or goods that I coveted. There was peace and joy in abundance in my life spiritually, economically, socially, professionally, and within my immediate family. I missed Peter and Beth terribly but found ways to keep connected to them while adjusting to their moving away as they built their own lives. Being able to support them as they pursued their dreams felt good and helped me to accept the way life works. So disparity was gone!

~~~~

Since I was traveling for two and sometimes three days a week, Janice decided to get more involved with a company that I'll refer to as "Skin Care Cosmetics." She had started with Skin Care Cosmetics a couple of years before I was fired from Bedlam but decided now to use her new free time to get really serious about it. She started as a consultant but quickly progressed to team leader and eventually to sales director where she won seven new cars. I was proud of her accomplishments and happy that she found a job and a company that was extremely compatible with her values and interests. She developed a wide circle of friends, customers, and colleagues that provided the social outlet she needed very much. I have always been somewhat of a recluse by choice, and we thus differed in how much we needed socialization. Therefore, Skin Care Cosmetics was just what we both needed.

~~~~

Unfortunately, during these very good days, we continued to have to endure the great family rift between Sue, Jim, and their daughter Kathleen on one side and Pat on the other. In between, trying to maintain relationships with all parties were Bernie and me. Bernie and I continually tried to remain neutral and made no overtures about trying to include Pat in any family functions that Sue and Jim were attending. Pat's name was not even mentioned at these gatherings even to the extent that we told no family stories that included him. Running two separate holiday functions became a bit tiresome, but Bernie and I were not going to exclude Pat from our families. He loved our kids, and they loved him, so we were going to keep Pat connected to us all as much as we could.

I spent a great deal of time reliving the thing that had so severely split our family in two. In my heart, I had resolutely believed Pat when he swore that he had nothing to do with Jimmy losing his job. I felt strongly that the shunning he was experiencing was not justified. I had no proof of his innocence, only his sincere declaration that he had nothing to do with the whole mess. I was wrong! Pat admitted to Bernie when they were out drinking one night that he was the one that brought disaster upon Sue and Jim. The why was never clear nor was the how. The essence of it was that Pat had been lying to me and everyone else about his role. One part of me was enraged, but the other part felt great pity for Pat, who would do what he did to Sue and Jim after all that they had done for each of us individually and for our family as a whole. They sacrificed their youth and their happiness so that we could stay together and grow up in a safe and secure home as much as possible. I have no words to express the pathos for this shameful and painful chapter in my family's story. Time was never going to heal this wound.

~~~~

On top of the monumental grief Pat brought to Sue and Jim, Sue's cancer worsened with metastases to other body systems. Unfortunately, we didn't know how bad it was. She was tough, and she tried her best to carry on in spite of her declining health. One of the things I loved about having my own business was that I could do things like stop in to visit Sue and other family members when my travels took me near their homes. On one occasion, the visit was not at Sue's home but at the hospital where she was admitted for a few days. She was tired and irritable, but I saw this as no reason to cut my visit short. Sue had other ideas, plus something on her mind.

In a firm and uncompromising voice, she told me, "I do not want Pat coming up here to see me. You tell him that for me. I couldn't take it if he came up here, and if he ran into Jimmy up here, Jimmy would probably kill him. So make sure you tell him." I assured her that he would not even think of coming up here, but to appease her, I said I would tell him. Then in her businesslike. no-nonsense way, she dismissed me, "Well, Pete, you better take off. I'm too tired for visiting."

With that, I kissed her goodbye for the last time, but I had no idea that this was the end. I did stop at Pat's apartment and gave him Sue's mandate about staying away, but he adamantly said, "I would never go up there."

Oh, Pat! He lied again or at best he changed his mind. After I left him, he went to see Sue at the hospital that very night. I found this out when Sue called me after he had left. She didn't give me the hell I deserved for not being more forceful in keeping Pat away. She explained that he called first and asked if he could come up to see her, and for some reason, she said okay but specified when he could come so as not to run into Jimmy. Although I never would have expected it, she told me she forgave Pat for the awful thing he did to cause Jimmy to lose his job that subsequently wrecked their lives in so many ways. That she could do this was another example of her inner strength even when she was so sick. She even had the presence of mind to caution me not take it out on him. Her justification for this was "because he (Pat) is a sick (she meant mentally) man." Although my first response was not to go after Pat for his disobeying Sue's request, but I did call him to tell him that Sue had called me. I was matter-of-fact about it and was not reprimanding him just as Sue entreated. Strangely, he was actually jubilant when saying that Sue forgave him and they had a good visit. What can I say? This was God at work here, no doubt.

~~~~

A few days later, I was at an OT faculty meeting at the College, helping them revise their curriculum, when the secretary excused herself to tell me that I had a phone call that was an emergency. With the dynamic nature of my business, there were always crises from the facilities or the therapists themselves that I dealt with on a daily basis. It was not unusual for one of these folks to deem their present crisis an emergency, so I was calm when I picked up the phone. It was Jimmy, and his message was terse, and his voice was one of resignation: "You better come quick, Pete. She's going fast." What? Who? How? I knew the terrible answers. I just hung up, walked back into the meeting room, and announced with a choked voice: "I have to go. My sister is dying." With soft voices of condolences and offers to do anything from a concerned group in the background, I gathered up my stuff and began the long drive to the hospital. I don't know how I drove through the tears and choking sobs, but by the time I got there, I was composed and ready to face whatever was to come. Or so I thought.

As soon as I walked onto the floor where Sue was and I saw Janice, who was already there, I followed in my mother's footsteps and went all to pieces. Janice hugged me firmly and whispered in a firm but loving way, "You have to be strong." I was not. Surprisingly, Sue was alert, up and moving around her room but in a confused and agitated state. She was in and out of bed, moving about like she was looking for something. Karoline, who had come into town to help Sue before she was hospitalized, was there, and she and Janice were very good at calming and redirecting Sue back to bed. We couldn't understand what she was mumbling or what she was looking for. We were a confounded inept group surrounding our sister as she was going through some sort of pre-death gyrations. She eventually exhausted herself and accepted Karoline and Janice's guidance and assistance back to bed.

Sue was so much to me. She was always our family's rock and anchor in the most turbulent of times. Beyond this, she was my best friend, my confidant, my mentor, my advisor, and my second mother. I learned so much from her. I wish I could have had her assertiveness.

She feared no one. I know I made her life hell as I foundered in my teenage years, but I knew she was proud of what I had become and the way I had done it. I'm so glad she got to see a better me in spite of some big missteps along the way. Her sardonic and humorous take on things and people was something I will never forget. Going forward without Sue in the wings was going to be very hard.

~~~~

Our good friend Bob Wrestler, at Bernie's request, picked up Tommy from the airport and brought him up to the hospital. We then sat once again in a sad vigil at the all-too-familiar hospital awaiting the end of another one of our family member's lives. I felt so bad for Sue. Not as sad about her dying as I felt for the sad and difficult life she lived. All the burdens of our troubled family all found their way to Sue and Jim's door, and they did their best to help. She struggled as a teenager as our drunken Dad left Ma alone to deal with a house full of demanding kids and without any money to meet our needs. So it was always Sue to whom Ma turned and turned and turned. Without respite, Sue was struck with blow after blow of the crises that befell our family and us as individuals. This was so unfair.

A large hole was cut out of us all in the morning of June 2, 1988, when Sue died. In an effort to help Jimmy, we (Bernie, Tommy, and I) began talking with him about the arrangements. We didn't find out until weeks later that what we thought were helpful suggestions were perceived by Jimmy as us taking over. For example, I remember mentioning that I knew Sue resented a certain church because of some long-ago slight by a priest there that I don't remember now what, and I suggested instead that we look into another church where I knew she had more positive feelings. At the time, I thought I was being helpful, and Jimmy seemed to appreciate my suggestion. I was wrong! We all were!

The day of her funeral, I remember driving with Janice, Peter, and Beth in the car and just crying in choking sobs all the way. I learned how harmful unexpressed grief can be and was not going to let it do to me what it did when Ma died. It was a sad day made even sadder by Pat's unwelcomed presence. He sat in his dilapidated car across the street from the church. I was concerned that Jimmy would see him, or worse yet, Pat would try to attend the Mass. Not to worry. Pat just stayed in his old car and followed the funeral procession at a distance out to the cemetery where Sue was buried. A breakfast was prearranged at a nearby restaurant where we got to see old friends and family members that we usually only see at events like funerals and weddings. Wisely, Pat did not attend. He instead visited Sue's grave after we had all left for the restaurant.

In saying goodbye to Jimmy, Kathleen, and Shawn, I was emphatic in saying that we must keep connected. I also offered to help Jimmy in any way he needed. He thanked me, and we all returned to our lives, lives that now had a large void.

~~~~

A few days after Sue's funeral, I asked Janice to go for a ride with me. I wanted to go down to the waterfront. I needed to be in a place where I could really feel alive. The waterfront was a nice place to walk and talk. This is when I shared with Janice an idea that has been percolating in my brain for a few months now: *Ah, Wilderness!* This title of Eugene O'Neill's 1933 comedic play was the focus of my next venture but not the play itself. The idea of spending time hiking, backpacking, and canoeing in the wilderness is something I always enjoyed ever since as kids Danny, Pat, and I hiked out to "Old May Woods" from the trailer park. In later years, Janice and my recreational camping with our VW bus and later on with our pop-up camper gave me a real sense of joy that I wanted to experience again but at a more adventuress level. It seems I was always being drawn to the outdoors, and now I was going to do something about it in a small way. Even though Janice was more of a "girly girl" than an outdoors person, she was almost as enthusiastic as me. I explained that to get us on our way on this new path, we needed to do something tangible along those lines. So off we went to an outdoors store where we purchased two life jackets and two paddles. This may sound crazy to buy these things when we didn't have a canoe, but I knew that these purchases would solidify our pact to become wilderness people. *Ah, Wilderness!*

~~~~

Early on in the next week, I stopped out at Jimmy's to see how he was doing and to see if I could do anything for him. He was distant and not very talkative. I mistakenly thought it was his way of dealing with Sue's death. Unbeknownst to me, this was the beginnings of Jimmy and Kathleen's absolute severance of their connection to all of us Talty's. This was never stated but was evident in their refusal to attend any family gatherings, never calling any of us, and the cold way in which they responded to our efforts to engage them. Part of this may be due to Jimmy remarrying and becoming close to his new wife's family. I cannot be sure, but I suspect this rejection of us by Jimmy and Kathleen was related to Pat's awful deed that caused so much pain for their family and that we supported Pat because we stupidly believed him. This whole mess was beyond me to fix, so I just ignored it and focused on Janice, our family, and the fine life we had built.

Ah, Wilderness!

Did I really have the time back then for getting involved in the wilderness? I would truly be a novice, and therefore, how would I find the time to learn all I needed in order to be safe and able to enjoy these new ventures? What it also came down to was how much juggling would I be able to handle while still keeping my business viable and my teaching at the level necessary? One of the benefits of not drinking or drugging is that my mind became so much sharper, and my memory astonished me on an almost-daily basis. Add to this my natural tendency to take risks, and the answer to all these questions was a resounding yes! Yes, I will find a place in my busy schedule to make the outdoors or wilderness an integral part of my life for some very good reasons.

First, was my lifelong attraction to being out in the woods hiking and exploring. Second, I could clearly see how the wilderness could support and enhance my sobriety. The AA mantra of how "changing people, places, and things" strengthens one's ability to resist the temptations of drugs and alcohol always made complete sense to me as an OT. Knowing how hard it is to change an ingrained habit and to adhere to a new way of living has been something very familiar to me personally ever since July 25th of 1982. That is when I quit drugs and alcohol, and I consciously went about changing people, places, and things in my life. I intended to take this a step further and to use the wilderness as a way to forge an even stronger commitment to sobriety.

Third, I like taking risks and adventure. I like it when things are not predictable and safe but not to the point of chaos and being overwhelmed. The idea of going off in a canoe and paddling an unknown waterway was enchanting and at the same time scary. To me, the wilderness offered so many opportunities to take on new challenges, to learn new things, and to meet new people who also had a passion for the outdoors.

Another of those crazy coincidences occurred that affirmed that this wilderness idea had merit. I accidently came upon the vehicle that would be a great facilitator in my becoming more of an outdoors guy. In a seeming totally removed activity related to the outdoors, I was doing some painting at my house when I ran out of paint. So I left all my painting stuff lying out and rushed off to the Big Store, which was located in a shopping mall. Because my focus was on finding the paint and getting back before my brush and roller dried out, I was not really cognizant of an outdoors show going on throughout the mall. In spite of my preoccupation with paint, there was one display that caught my eye: a display for the Adirondack Mountain Club. I grabbed a brochure and application off the table as I hurried past, never imaging what would come from this fortuitous trip for paint.

By joining the club, I began receiving a newsletter that told of upcoming and past canoeing and backpacking trips. The backpacking trips sounded like something I could handle because of how my running had built up my endurance. Canoeing also became a reality when I bought a used tandem Kevlar canoe with caned seats. My brother Danny was also interested in canoeing, so I registered us both for some canoeing lessons taught by volunteers within the club. We also took several canoeing trips with some great people who taught Danny and me a lot about canoeing. In those days, many of my weekends were taken up with overnight canoe trips. I also took Peter with me on some trips when he was available, and he too loved the whole idea of canoeing and exploring with some degree of risk. Our skill level was such that no matter who I went with, we ended up capsizing the canoe and swimming down the rapids of many rivers.

Regardless, it was great fun and well worth the stress it generated in my work life because of my absence.

~~~~

Managing my company without any partners was expeditious because the decision-making process was simply me. I had control over my time, but I was not about to skip off to the woods (as much as I would have liked) and allow my company to collapse. To say that I was my own boss was not entirely accurate. In reality, I had sixty bosses. I maintained a war chest of approximately thirty agencies or facilities where I provided the staffing for their OT services, and I had about the same number of therapists full- and part time. Keeping all these entities happy was an ongoing challenge, and so they were my bosses in that sense.

A weakness I had as an entrepreneur was an aversion to "schmoozing" (talking in a cozy or intimate manner to someone, typically in order to manipulate, flatter, or impress them). I didn't like it and was not very good at it. I tended to provide the professional OT services as stated in the contracts without any extracurricular networking. I had competitors whose calling was that of a schmoozer, so perpetual vigilance on keeping customers happy was my job. I did this by providing quality OT services with professionally performing therapists, not through "BS". Most of my customers valued this in me and my company, but I did lose customers to competitors whose middle name could easily have been "schmooze". So, I couldn't be in the wilderness and unavailable when schmoozers were lurking about.

The other constraint on my time was the constant recruitment and replacement of therapists. Everyone wants to earn more, work less, and have better benefits. I tried to pay equal to or just above the rate of private organizations. I could not compete with the school districts for paid days off and short work days. I also couldn't pay at the same level as the state and federal agencies. I accepted the fact that my best recruit was often a new graduate, and I also recognized that once they had enough experience or got a better offer, they would move on. New graduates meant I was putting rookies into positions that often exceeded their skill levels. This necessitated time on my part for training and ongoing mentoring. Overwhelming a rookie was not something I could afford. It was bad for the patients, the customers, and the rookie's self-esteem. This is where my teaching skills dovetailed nicely with staff recruitment and training.

~~~~

So, I taught my OT classes with an eye to recruiting. Being an effective instructor required preparation, but it paid off in gaining the respect of the students who could potentially become one of my employees. It was fairly easy for me to recruit therapists because many of them knew and liked me as their instructor, and others with whom I had been colleagues for over twenty years spoke highly of me. It also helped that my present employees spoke highly of me. Then there were those I hired without meeting them in person. I got a good feel for people through phone interviews coupled with talking with their former employers or instructors. It was always quite comical to meet one of these over-the-phone hires at a wedding or somewhere else and to discover that they had been one of my employees for two years or more. There was one group of three therapists that I recruited and hired about the same time who dubbed themselves "Charlie's Angels" in reference to the old TV show of the same name.

Most people would think my hiring practices were strange and reckless. On the surface, I would agree with these observations. However, what I always knew was that occupational therapists are a most trustworthy and conscientious group. I have met very few of them who were otherwise. So hiring an OT over the phone, assigning them to a facility or agency a distance from my home office, and leaving it to them to carry on without direct or even intermittent supervision was not really risky at all.

The ability to trust OTs plus having a level of comfort with things fluid and dynamic enabled me to operate a diverse and fluctuating private practice. I was also never a person who liked just socializing. I actually like being alone. That is not to say that I lack the interpersonal skills to be an effective supervisor, teacher, occupational therapist, friend, neighbor, or family member. I just didn't need to be a member of an ongoing work or social group for social purposes. Being alone in the woods was fine with me, and if Danny, Janice, or Peter couldn't go with me, I was okay with going alone.

Down But Not Out

Keeping my business going was certainly a priority for me but so was exercising. My education as an OT taught me long ago about how exercise can relieve stress and prevent a number of diseases. With my family's history of heart disease and early death, I was determined to beat heredity by adhering to a lifestyle where daily exercise was a central part. When my deteriorating ankle and knees precluded me from engaging in distance running, which I loved, I switched over to walking and bicycling and then later on incorporated an elliptical machine routine. Perhaps I could not eradicate my genetic predisposition for some diseases, but for those where exercise was a deterrent, I was determined to stave them off as long as possible.

This dual commitment to maintaining a business and exercise came together in 1992 on a routine thirty-mile bike ride with my friend Barry Counter*. We were neighbors but had been running partners for a couple of years before we both switched to cycling. Like me, he liked long bike rides at a moderate pace and liked to ride even if it rained. On one country road, we were pedaling along through a rainstorm that suddenly worsened. He was about twenty feet in front of me, but at one point, I couldn't see him because of the driving rain. I could see headlights in my mirror, but the rain distorted the image in my mirror so much that I could not determine how close they were to me. Unbeknownst to me, Barry had stopped under a tree and was standing alongside his bike as I blindly approached him. At the last second, I saw him; but for some reason, he took a step back, still supporting his bike right into my path. I struck Barry, catapulted over him with my feet still clipped into my pedals, and landed harder than I ever remember hitting in my life. I can still feel the hit when I recall my fall. I sustained what is known in orthopedics as a "FOOSH" injury (Fall On Outstretched Hand). The fall was absorbed by my left hand and arm, but the force was transmitted up to my shoulder and ribs. Of course, I didn't know it at the time, but I had a type III AC (acromioclavicular) shoulder separation and three fractured ribs. All I knew was that the pain was some of the worst I ever experienced.

I was fully conscious, and the pain quickly became almost intolerable. I told Barry as he quickly got to me, "Don't move me. I'm hurt bad. Call an ambulance." There were no cell phones in everyone's pocket like today, but the guy in the car that was following us saw me go over and had stopped. He brought a blanket to put over me (it was still raining furiously) and volunteered to go up to a nearby house to call an ambulance. What a good guy.

The ambulance was on its way, and in a short time, we could hear the siren. I then thought about my mangled bike. How would we get it home? So I asked Barry to go to the same house and to call Janice and tell her to bring my SUV to accommodate my bike but not to alarm her. A police car arrived and provided traffic control even though this was not a well-traveled road. The EMTs in the ambulance were very gentle and efficient as they loaded me into the ambulance. A worried but calm Janice arrived just as they were about to shut the ambulance doors. I told her I'm okay (a lie) and asked Larry to put my bike in the back of our SUV.

Then began one of the worst parts of this very bad day. For some unknown reason, the ambulance driver chose the longest route to the hospital and drove about 20 miles per hour on roads where the normal speed was 45. Janice followed in my SUV with my bike in the back. The pain was killing me, but they told me that there was nothing they could give me. Are you crazy? This is an ambulance! My whining finally convinced them to call the hospital, and they got clearance to inject me with something that only reduced the pain slightly.

At the hospital, I had X-rays and was seen by the emergency room doctor who called an orthopedic surgeon. The orthopedic doctor looked at the X-rays and told me about the three rib fractures and the shoulder separation. I wish all this took as short of time as it took to retell it. I was there for five hours. There was even time for Beth to come by for a visit after Janice called her with an update. As always, it was good to see her, but not under these circumstances. I still have no idea what took so long as I watched other patients come and go. Another thing, I was never good at was waiting. I hate waiting, especially when nothing was happening, and I had no control.

Finally, they came in and fitted me with a complicated sling to support and immobilize my shoulder. The doctor and nurses were a bit puzzled by it as they tried to follow the printed directions in getting it on me. The plan was for me to follow up with the orthopedic surgeon regarding possible surgery next week. Then they said, "As soon as you pee, you can go home."

The fact that I didn't have to pee was not important; I had to stay until I peed. Oh yeah? I don't think so. I told them, "I'm leaving, so do what you have to do to finish everything up as I get dressed because I'm not waiting any longer and I don't have to pee." This got things moving, and in spite of Janice's and the nurses' protestations, we were out the door and on our way home.

Danny and I had an extended canoe and backpacking trip planned into northern Canada into the backcountry of Algonquin Park, but I had to withdraw. There was no way I could carry nor paddle a canoe nor carry my big backpack. Undeterred, Danny took his wife, Cheryl, on her first and last trip to Algonquin. They did a very challenging trek for which she gets kudos.

As for me, it was impossible for me to sit, walk, or lie down because of the pain. I was very tired from the pain medication, but through much trial and error, I discovered that the only way I could rest or sleep was in a firm chair with an additional seat cushion that doubled the height of the chair. This elevated position seemed to lessen the movement of my fractured ribs and thus eased the pain. Walking with a cane on the fractured rib side also was less painful, but it was cumbersome with the shoulder sling. I slept poorly in bed, but by sitting semi-upright with couch cushions supporting me, I was able to get some sleep.

~~~~

The next day I had paperwork to do for my business and for the College. Although it was summer, I was expected to attend meetings at the College that were important for the OT program. My job was to protect and advance the department of OT, and being at the various meetings was the best way to do this. This was before the electronic age where working from home was so highly effective. So I had to drive the 112 miles regardless of my pain. There were also clinical responsibilities I had that no one else could do. This meant more driving and staying in a motel on my way to the College.

At home, I had to work at my desk that was in our family room. That's where all my payroll and time sheets were awaiting my processing so I could bill the facilities and agencies so that I got paid in a timely manner. Realizing that my desk chair would not give me the support I needed, I set about to get the one chair I could sit in across the living room carpeted floor, through the foyer, and across the carpeted family room up to my desk. There was no one home, so it was up to me. By using my cane as a hook, I had maneuvered the chair across the living room and was midway through the foyer when a very surprised Pete walked in from work. He took over and got the chair to where I needed it. The chair worked well, and I had a productive day. Pete never forgot the image of me dragging this big chair with my cane with my shoulder immobilized in a very grotesque-looking sling.

~~~~

The next day started my four-day trek to some facilities where I had OT evaluations and treatments that had to be done and then on to the College and back home Thursday night. Bernie, as a traveling salesman, was sometimes working in the same areas where I traveled, and he talked to Janice to find out which motel I was staying at and came to visit. He had called ahead of time, so I knew he was coming. However, when he knocked on my motel door, it took me a bit to get up and across the room. He was taken aback when he saw the condition I was in with my sling, cane, and how my pain was so damn debilitating. There was nothing he or anyone else could do for me. My hope was that when I saw the orthopedic surgeon at the end of the week, he would be able to help me. So for now, it was just suck it up and deal with it. We went out for dinner, but it was not fun.

I shocked the patients that I saw at the two facilities I visited the next day. One guy said good-naturedly, "Hey, boy! You look worse than me. How you going to help me?" I did my best with each patient, but it was more writing than treating on those visits. The faculty and our secretary at the College were very surprised to see me but were all glad that I showed up for the meetings. Working at my desk, getting to and from my dorm room, and sitting through meetings were all hell, but I did it.

My colleagues, family members, friends, and employees all thought I was crazy for trying to carry out my responsibilities in such a debilitated condition. They did not realize the negative impact my absence would have had on my business and my academic career. I was also fueled by my continuing efforts to stave off my feelings of disparity, which no one but me understood, and there are times when even I don't get me.

~~~~

The orthopedic surgeon's evaluation and prognosis was pretty grim. Apparently, my type of shoulder separation does not respond well to surgery, so that was not an option. He said in an unenthusiastic way, "You can try some therapy, but I don't think it will do much good. Just keep wearing the sling, and when the pain is more manageable, try doing some exercises. You're a therapist. You know what to do. The ribs are going to take time to heal, and nothing can be done until they do. Here's another prescription for pain medication. If you need more, call the office. Good luck." Good luck? That's it?

I went home and started researching exercises for shoulder separations. I knew the sequence to follow in general but got some good ideas about what to do at this early stage of recovery. To let my shoulder sit in an immobilized position over a long period would not be good. Wherever I went to do clinical work, I would confer with other therapists (OTs and PTs) to see what suggestions they might have. Each one gave me little tips, which I followed on a very consistent basis. I kept at my shoulder exercise routines regardless of where I was staying and eventually got my shoulder to where I could move it in all directions without pain.

Being able to move my shoulder without pain was not enough. I needed it to be stronger. I had to lift and carry a sixty-pound canoe and a seventy-pound backpack. So now I added some strengthening exercises that were pretty minimal at first, but I got the strength back to where I needed it to be. I was looking forward to a follow-up appointment with the orthopedic surgeon I had scheduled back when I first saw him. I wanted him to see what could be done as opposed to his negative prognosis. He was very impressed and even remarked, "I am amazed that you got the full motion and strength back. It just shows what a person can do if they are motivated. Most of my patients don't follow through like you did. Good job!"

I, of course, had to say, "You know, if I had listened to you when you said that you didn't expect much from therapy, I would not have been motivated. But I set out to prove you wrong. Tell your other patients about me." He said he would, but I doubt he did. I didn't care. I got my shoulder back.

Chair of Occupational Therapy

Prior to my cycling accident, the College had become an increasing important part of my professional life. The College was vastly different from the university in terms of size (twenty-six thousand versus one thousand students) and many other ways, but the key difference was the importance the College assigned to teaching and the support of students. I loved how closely student evaluations of instruction and faculty observations of teaching were scrutinized for decisions relevant to reappointments, promotion and tenure. My evaluations were excellent, and the comments by students of how much I taught and inspired them made the long drive to the College well worth it. Also, because I was practicing OT at the same time I was teaching it, I had numerous and current clinical examples that helped me engage students at all levels.

I had taught at the College for two years but then had to resign in order to manage my growing business. During this year away, I missed teaching; and so when I saw that the College was recruiting a new Chair of OT, I decided to apply. I had been teaching three days a week prior to my resigning, and the College was very accommodating, allowing me to stay in one of their empty dormitories two nights a week. This three-day-a-week schedule for two semesters enabled me to maintain the full-time salary of an assistant professor and thus remain in the same retirement system I had started at the university. It was my thinking that if I could hold down an assistant professor's position, then why not the chair's position? I had never been a chair, but I felt I knew enough about the role that I could do it and also keep my business going.

My plan was put in motion when I submitted my curriculum vitae (that's what a résumé is called in academia because it includes all presentations beyond the classroom, research endeavors, publications, etc.). The OT faculty members were very excited about me applying, and they arranged the on-campus interview to coincide with their senior class celebration where the students who I had taught gave me a plaque in appreciation. I took Janice with me, and we stayed in a local bed-and-breakfast (no dorm room for her). The series of interviews with the Dean, the professional standards committee, the OT faculty, and the president all went extremely well. I had kind of thought that they might want me to live closer to the College, so while I was interviewing that day, Janice went around with a realtor who was also the husband of one of the OT faculty members, looking for a possible house for us to purchase. She did not see anything that was comparable to our Wellington Woods house, plus I was not going to disrupt Janice's mother and move to the College area unless it was absolutely necessary.

By the end of the second day, I had a verbal offer that was a bit underwhelming. Apparently, the College was still recovering from the 1970s, where it almost closed, and the faculty worked without pay just to keep it going. The president was a young guy with excellent financial management abilities, and he had stabilized the College as an institution. He had instituted changes to attract more students, such as becoming coed, increasing athletic programs, and starting the OT program. He had come from another private college where OT was one of the most attractive majors and thus supported OT's efforts at the College in every way he could. This was reflected in a substantial equipment budget for outfitting the OT laboratories, which I had done last year in my role as an assistant professor. He had also secured the funding to renovate the College's main academic building in which OT was also given ample laboratory, office, and classroom space.

~~~~

Now came some risk taking on my part by asking for changes before I even started in the position. I verbally accepted the position as chair and at the rank of associate professor (I previously had been an assistant professor) even though the salary was less than I would have liked. My start date was set for June 7th of 1991 (about a month from what the dean had wanted). I explained the reason for moving my start date was so that I could complete a cycling trek across the state that was scheduled for the first week of June. I had been training pretty hard for the past three months and was not certain I could complete the 411 mile trek over five days from Niagara Falls to Lake Placid, New York. He was fine with the change in dates, but now began the real risk-taking part: juggling two major, normally full-time jobs (managing a diverse and extensive private OT practice with multiple elements and managing an academic OT program while teaching half of what full-time faculty taught). It had the potential to be disastrous for either my OT practice or the College's OT program or possibly even both. As usual, I was not dissuaded and thus set forth to do both.

Riding a Bike from Niagara Falls to Lake Placid, New York

This bike trek (a long, arduous journey) I had committed to do was another of those things I decided to do without a lot of thought or preparation. I was inspired by an ad I saw in my Mountain Club magazine. It described a cycling trek across New York State, through the Adirondack Mountains, and finishing in Lake Placid, the home of the 1980 Winter Olympics and the "Miracle on Ice." I had fallen in love with the Adirondack Mountains, and the idea of riding a bicycle through them was too much to resist. It was sponsored by the American Lung Association, and I had to solicit donations from friends and relatives, which I set out to do after making up a promotional slinger. I hate asking people for anything, so this for me was a big thing to have to ask for donations. Surprisingly, I easily raised the entry amount, plus enough to move me into a level for some additional prizes. The staff at a lot of the places where I was providing OT services were very generous. My new colleagues, the OT faculty at the College, even contributed. So along with contributions from family and friends, I had the financial hurdle behind me.

    I didn't own a bike, so I used my son's old Takara that he left behind when he started traveling with the band. There was also a nice incentive for me to complete the trek because Peter's band was playing in Lake Placid for a few weeks, and one of them included the day we were scheduled to finish. So I took Peter's bike in to the bike shop for a tune-up and new tires and began training. Because of the ice and snow in the area, I actually couldn't get out on the road to train until March, just a little over three months before the trek started. Endurance-wise, I was in good shape because I continued to run three to five miles every day, but I probably never rode a bike longer than three miles at any one time in my life. Obviously, I had some work to do.

I had a Chevy Blazer SUV at the time, so I could take my bike with me everywhere I went on my overnight trips. I had been doing a lot of reading about how to train for an extended bike trek, but finding the time and weather conditions to train were a challenge. The other challenge was getting enough hill work in to prepare me for the mountains. My hometown is rather flat, but I did have some substantial hills around the College that I took advantage of on my overnights there. It was just over forty-six miles around the lake that the College sat on with some moderate hills, and that served as my weekly training route. In addition to my round-the-lake route, on alternate days, I climbed the really big hills that seemed to go on forever. All this built my confidence and cycling endurance.

~~~~

Unfortunately, the day of the start of the bike trek arrived before I was fully ready. I knew that one of the days, we were going to have to cycle over ninety miles, but the most I had done was eighty. I also had not cycled fifty to seventy miles on each day for five consecutive days. I hoped and prayed that I would be ready. A truck, referred to in the lexicon of cyclists as the SAG Wagon (SAG being an acronym for "Support And Gear") would transport our camping gear (we would stay in State Parks on two of the nights), our change of clothes, extra bike parts, tire pumps, and so forth. A bike mechanic to assist with flat tires and minor repairs would ride in the SAG Wagon along with the driver. The dreaded other purpose of the SAG Wagon was to transport the riders and their bikes who were unable to complete the trek for various reasons. I certainly did not want to end up in the SAG Wagon! I knew that just seeing their flashing lights in my rearview mirror would propel me to find extra energy and strength to keep going.

Janice dropped me off in Niagara Falls (not in the falls itself, but in an area near the falls) on the morning of the start. The plan was for her to drive to Lake Placid in time to arrive the day before we did, and we would then get to visit with Peter for a couple of days before returning home. My hope was that Beth and her friends from her university would come to the start of the trek, which was not far from her campus, and then Peter would see me finish. We had become close to Beth's college friends through attending many of the university dances, almost all the home basketball games where Beth was a cheerleader, and by having them to our house for football games. Her roommates had also seen me cycle the fifty miles between our home and their university on a regular basis as part of my training, so I thought they knew I was getting ready for the Adirondacks trek. Apparently, I didn't make it clear when I was going and how much their being there at the start would mean to me because none of them showed up. They also may have had a busy weekend. Whatever, it was just Janice who was seeing me off. I didn't know any of the other fifty or so riders and most of them didn't seem to know one another.

Janice took some pictures, somebody from the American Lung Association wished us well, and off we went. It was a quiet beginning without the spectacular fanfare I had envisioned. Now the real work began. I had learned from running numerous distance races that going slower in the beginning and not getting caught up in the excitement of the moment works out better, and so that was the approach I took. The first day we rode fifty some miles, and I was very tired and sore. I didn't drink enough water at the rest stops they had set up for us along the way, and I paid for it in the form of muscle cramps in my legs. In setting up my tent, I had to crawl around the ground, hammering in the stakes to keep it upright. While I was getting my tent set up, a guy came around and handed out some sheets of paper stapled together that had a description of each rider's background. We then all convened where they had set up a cookout for us where we all ate plenty.

Exhausted, after a shower and eating, I went into my tent when it was still light out in order to rest up for the next day. It was light enough that I could read the handout they gave us, and I found it intimidating to hear how experienced many of the other riders were. At the same time I was reading my handout, I heard two or three riders in tents adjacent to mine saying, "Some joker had only started training for this trek three months ago and had never ridden a trek before." They were all in disbelief as they laughed, and this shook my confidence a bit more because the "joker" they were talking about was me. Maybe this whole trek thing was not such a good idea.

The next day was the worst. It didn't help my confidence that a cycling team from our group in full regalia appeared, mounted their beautiful high-end bikes; and when their leader yelled, "Lock and load!" off they sped, looking like something from the Tour de France. They were impressive but at the same time a bit demoralizing for a novice like me. The temperature had risen into the low nineties by midday to correspond wickedly to the distance we had to ride of ninety-one miles! This was really the test of my endurance, saddle sore pain tolerance, and perseverance. It was the delicious fresh fruit all cut up for us at the rest stations along the way that was a big help. I avoided the mistake of the day before and drank an abundance of water. However, it was not enough to stave off the leg cramps in muscles that had never been taxed like they were on that day. It was more crawling around on hands and knees to set up my tent; shower, eat, and go to bed (in the tent).

The next day we were delivered a bunch of miracles. After a relatively short ride of seventy-two miles, we got to sleep in a real bed in a motel, plus we got to soak our sore asses in bathtubs. Eating in the motel's restaurant gave us another level of joy and pleasure. It was not a gourmet meal, but it sure did taste good. The mood of the whole group was uplifted with these simple pleasures. I had gotten to know some of the other riders from riding alongside of them, and one was my roommate.

~~~~

I don't know what happened to me, but the next day I awoke inordinately energized. I felt like I could ride forever as we moved through the foothills of the Adirondacks. Riding faster and faster with ease, I found myself riding just behind the lead riders who were, of course, the cycling team. As I rode up behind the last cycling team rider, he asked, "Could you take a turn up front and help the team out?" This I learned is what cycling teams do to take advantage of the drafting effect. So off I went pedaling like a crazy person to catch and pass the lead rider. He said thanks as I took my place in front. I rode there for a half mile or so with chants of "Peter Power" emanating from "my team." That day we rode sixty miles; but to me, in the surreal state I was experiencing, it felt more like twenty. I rode with the cycling team and enjoyed riding a fast pace as the miles flew by. Before I knew it, we were being waved into a right turn onto a college campus, and the exciting ride was over. We stayed in a dormitory at SUNY Potsdam and had another great meal. There was lots of kidding about "Peter Power" and many references to me being the second rider in that day. I was feeling like a real cyclist! The guy leading the trek and the organizer of it even commented within earshot of several riders that "Peter rode with the big boys today!" That's right. I did! Not a shred of disparity could be seen, heard, or felt at that moment. I went to bed (in another real bed) basking in my new identity as a rider with the big boys and the camaraderie between the riders of which I was a part was oozing among us. Each day and at different times, I became friends with more of the riders, and it felt great to be a member of such an interesting group of people all with the same objective: to make it to Lake Placid but not in the SAG Wagon!

~~~~

The next day we hit the mountains, and the glory of the day before was gone along with my motivation. It seemed it took forever to get to the top of some increasingly difficult climbs, but then we darted down the other side. We all hated to apply our breaks even though we were going dangerously fast because we wanted to save our hard-earned momentum for the next climb. The numerous climbs were exhausting me, but I pushed on not wanting to even see that SAG Wagon, let alone have to ride in it because I had to quit the trek. There were already two riders in the back of the truck, and two others had pulled out all together, and someone had picked them up. Although sad for each of my fellow riders who had to drop out, I was naturally fueled to persevere to avoid the shame I associated with dropping out.

We were stretched out over several miles with each rider experiencing their own pain and battle to keep going. However, for me, this was seeing the beautiful Adirondack Mountains from a whole different perspective. Each strenuous climb was rewarded with great vistas and then came the exhilarating downhills. The plan was for us to spend the night in another college dormitory, which was a college that had always intrigued me. Paul Smith's College sat on Lower St. Regis Lake surrounded by the natural beauty of the Adirondack Mountains. I first heard of Paul Smith's from some friends of Beth's who had transferred to her university in order to complete their bachelor's degree in hotel and restaurant management.

At that time, Paul Smith's was just a two-year college but had since become a four-year institution. I looked forward to seeing the college, and it was even better than I had imagined. Certainly, its location was unique as were its collection of modest buildings. I have always enjoyed touring college campuses and marvel at the uniqueness of each one. Paul Smith's was a wonderful place for an Adirondacks' lover like me to meander about which I did after a hot shower before we ate.

We had a very good dinner and enjoyed more camaraderie. I was feeling a bit melancholy about this being the last night we would be together. I always get this way when things I am highly invested in come to an end. I had become very connected to this group of strangers who came together with a single purpose and who supported and encouraged one another in order to achieve it. I knew I was winding down one of the most exciting things I had ever done.

Tomorrow we would ride together for the last time. I doubt that we would ever meet again, but even if we did, it would not be like this unique experience we shared on the trek.

The next morning we had another fine breakfast, filled our tires and water bottles, stuffed snack bars and fruit into our shirt pockets, and gathered at our starting point. Our leader suggested that we ride into Lake Placid as a group by meeting up just outside of town. He gave us a rendezvous spot where we would all gather. I had an image of us all riding in together, and Janice and Peter cheering us on to the finish. With that picture in my mind, we started off.

I rode with various people that day as a way of saying goodbye as we climbed and descended through what are known as the High Peaks. We eventually meandered through the villages of Tupper Lake, Saranac Lake, and finally, we started seeing signs for Lake Placid. Throughout the trek, our leader had ridden out ahead of us each morning and spray painted inspirational and humorous messages on the road. We looked forward to seeing them, but now the messages were messages about the end coming: "You're almost there! We are so proud of you! You made it!" Just after the "You made it" message, I came upon the spot where our leader said we would meet before our triumphant collective ride into Lake Placid, but no one was there. What the hell was going on? This was the spot without a doubt. I had rode at a moderate pace this day and was pretty sure over half the riders were ahead of me and should have been here. A few more riders pulled in, looking as puzzled as me. Confused and somewhat angry, I decided to ride on to see if I could catch up with the others. I caught up with and rode with some of the guys who I had gotten to know pretty well who offered various explanations as to why they didn't wait for the rest of us. Some didn't hear the announcement, some stopped briefly and then continued on when they didn't see anyone, and still others just elected to get it over with.

Oh well, I knew I was going to finish something that was quite remarkable for me. I was never able to run a marathon because of the problems with my surgically corrected club foot. I was, however, able to complete several half marathons of 13 miles and numerous

5k and 10k races; but every time I would try to train for a marathon, my ankle would swell up, and I was almost unable to walk. So this bike trek was my marathon!

I came over a small hill, made a turn, and there I entered the village of Lake Placid. There were no crowds of people like at the Tour de France or like I had imagined in my mind. There were tourists and shoppers ambling in and out of shops, paying no attention to a few bike riders pedaling by. Then I saw Janice and Peter, and I got choked up. They looked so happy to see me. I rode up to the finish line, stopped my bike, shook hands, and hugged some of the other riders hanging around; and by then, Janice and Peter had walked up to meet me. It was a wonderful feeling to hug them and bask in the glory of finishing the trek on my bike (actually Peter's bike) and not in the feared SAG Wagon.

That night I took Janice and Peter with me to the farewell banquet. Once again, we ate well. There were a few short talks and offers of congratulations to all of us who left Niagara Falls six days ago and were now completers of a significant journey. I think we all knew that what we had was a special time, and it would not be replicated. No one asked me for my phone number or address (no e-mails back then) nor did I ask for anyone else's. We all knew this was it. A special experience to be treasured but never to be again.

~~~~

We had a good two days visiting with Peter. We were staying at the same inn where the band was also staying and playing each night. When we checked in, I got another special treat in the form of a telegram from Annie and Bernie that said for me "to stop pedaling my ass all around the Adirondacks" along with congratulations.

We meandered in and out of the shops, looking for some post cards to send out announcing my completion of the trek. I found a unique one. It was a wooden post card bigger than the standard size with Lake Placid pictures on it. I bought several, addressed them to all our relatives and friends, and wrote that I was successful. Because of their size and weight, we had to take them to the post office for mailing. It was well worth the time and cost of sending them out.

During the second day, we enhanced my special trek experience by taking the tour of the Olympics. We visited all the places that made the 1980 Winter Olympics so memorable. Janice and I had watched a lot of it on TV and read about the athletes and their accomplishments, and now we were standing in the places where great things happened eleven years ago. I was proud of what I had just accomplished but felt even prouder to stand in the places where so many American athletes showed the world what they could do. We stood at the top of the 120-meter ski jump to see what these super ski jumpers see before plummeting down and across the land of snow. It was a terrifying perspective. Standing next to the long speed skating track where Eric Heiden won five gold medals and broke four Olympics records and one world record was amazing. Of course, the ultimate experience was to stand in the arena where a bunch of U.S. college kids shocked the world by defeating the powerful Russians in a hockey game known as the "Miracle on Ice" and went on to win the gold medal. It was very emotional. USA! USA! USA!

At night, we listened to the band and visited with Andy, Paul, Tom, and Dave with whom we had become close after all the times Janice and I traveled about seeing them play at different venues. After a great trek, great Olympics tour, and a great visit with Peter, it was time to say goodbye. It was another ending; another time for melancholy, which, of course, was not atypical for me. However, Janice and I had a nice ride back through my beloved Adirondacks and back to my world of responsibility. I had the new job to look forward to plus whatever crises in my business that had arisen since my departure.

The crises I always feared would occur and then exacerbate because of my absence fortunately did not happen. Things were actually quite calm and stable. I was thus able to start my new position as the chair of OT at the College the following week with a clear head. In reality, my mind was still in the Adirondacks. So much so that when I saw that Paul Smith's College was hosting members of the Mountain Club for long weekends, Janice and I seized this opportunity to enjoy canoeing in the Adirondacks while having meals at the college, hot showers, flush toilets, and real beds in the dorms. It was a great way for us to explore this part of the Adirondacks and to practice our burgeoning canoeing skills. This all took place just about six weeks after I had stayed at Paul Smith's on my Bike Trek. We had a great time and couldn't wait to come back. How could anyone tire of this beautiful area?

~~~~

In addition to the various canoeing and backpacking adventures and misadventures I had with Danny, Pete, and Janice as well as on my own, I decided to take advantage of the Paul Smith's summer experience the following year. However, rather than Janice and I going, I thought it would be good to get the Talty boys together along with my nephew Shawn Riley (Sue and Jim's son)and my future son-in-law Dan Russ (I didn't know at the time he was going to be my son-in-law). The group of eight also included Bernie's son Bernie II and my brother Pat. After getting commitments from everyone, I made the reservations.

~~~~

After getting everyone organized into roommates and car pools, off we went. We had the best time. I brought my two canoes, two bikes, lots of snacks, and plenty of insect repellent. On the second day, we all climbed St. Regis Mountain, which involved a 3.4-mile hike each way with a climb of 2,874 feet. It was a very hot and humid day, but most of the boys were undeterred as they made their ascent. Those who made it to the top were rewarded with a spectacular view of the surrounding lakes and mountains.

The evenings were filled with Uncle Bernie regaling the group with tales of yesteryear and lots of kidding and reminiscing. There was a lovely swimming area in a cove, and I can still picture all of us just lounging about in the cool clear water of lower St. Regis Lake after an active day of canoeing, hiking, and cycling. The accommodations enabled us all to be together, having an outdoor experience without the roughing aspects that Danny and I were accustomed to, but some of the others were not. Paul Smith's College gave us the opportunity to enjoy one another's company in a beautiful setting.

Let the Juggling Begin!

I like to work. It is a fact that I cannot hide. I especially enjoy working where I have many challenges, a lot of control, and the potential for commensurate rewards. My private OT practice had all these elements, so why did I seek even more of the same by taking on the OT chair position at the College? Not to be too grandiose about it, but I think it might be something like what George Mallory, the famous mountain climber, answered when asked in 1924 about why he wanted to climb Mount Everest: "Because it's there." The position of OT chair in a struggling small private college was an opportunity to achieve something entirely different but also similar to what I had done before. I knew that I knew how to practice OT as well as teach it, and I knew how to manage people and a business. I think I also was a bit bored. The crises in the business were multiple and many times poorly timed, but they were repetitious in nature. Yes, "it was there," a job with interesting elements that I wanted to do.

As a part-time faculty member, I was aware of the obstacles facing the College. I was also aware that the OT program was expected to be the primary major to drive the College forward onto a stronger financial footing; just how I was to do this was unknown. I decided to use the remaining weeks of the summer to learn as much as I could about the College's and OT department's strengths and weaknesses. Along the way, I intended to build relationships with administration as well as the chairs of the other divisions. A strength I recognized was that OT was a mystery to almost everyone on campus, so no one had any expectations about what we were or could become. They only knew that OT meant lots of new students, and that's what this struggling college badly needed.

~~~~

An initial problem that I identified in my budget was the exorbitant cost of teaching one particular course: neuroanatomy and physiology. It was presently taught by a faculty member from a relatively close medical school who drove the sixty miles each way once a week to teach a lecture and a lab to the OT students. He was an excellent instructor with a CV (Curriculum Vita) that I imagined one would look like for a candidate for the Nobel Prize in physiology or medicine. The students loved him and his teaching style. The only downside was the cost to the college. Not having an alternative, since no one in natural sciences or OT had the necessary background, my predecessor was able to convince the college to pay him an inordinate amount to have this critical course taught. It was more than six times what was normally paid for a course like this.

While ruminating about this financial dilemma, an unsolicited letter was given to me by the chair of natural sciences. It was from a young man who had just completed his PhD in neurosciences at Penn State, and he was inquiring about a potential faculty post in a private college that valued teaching and was located upstate. Sounds like good fortune and opportunity was knocking. I called him immediately, and we had a good conversation. He was familiar with the area where the College was located, having grown up not far from it, and he had earned his undergraduate degree at a major university nearby. His interests were not in research and publishing as an academic career but in teaching and working with students. He had taught PT students at Barry University in Miami, so he kind of knew what OT was about. I told him to fax me his full CV, and I would get right back to him in a day or so. I then went to see the Dean.

On the way, I conjured up how we could create a position where there presently was not one. Conjure, or "to summon by magic," was an apt description of what I needed to do in this financially struggling institution. The Dean was the leader and administrative head for the academic side of the College, and I needed for him to be a fellow conjurer. My proposal that I formulated on my walk across campus was to take the money we were paying the "Nobel-guy", add enough to it from courses being taught by the present faculty as overloads, and create a joint appointment for this new guy between OT and Natural Sciences. The Dean could be intimidating, but I liked him and found him approachable if you were logical, and I was that. He hated paying the big amount to "Dr. Nobel" and saw how my plan could work. He told me to schedule the new guy for a visit and a round of interviews.

"Dr. Neuro"* came to campus, was well-received by the OT and natural sciences faculty, did an impressive lecture for our students, and was found more than qualified by the professional standards committee as well as the Dean. He was offered the position, accepted It, and he joined us that fall. Dr. Neuro, or "Dr. N." as the students came to call him, became a stalwart member of the faculty and served us well for many years until his sudden and premature death at age fifty. He and I became good friends and had offices next to each other for the eight years preceding his sad and untimely death. On the morning that his wife found him after he suffered a massive heart attack and died, he and I had tickets for that night's NCAA basketball tournament. What a shock!

Dr. Nobel did not take the news well that I was replacing him with a recent doctoral graduate, but I was resolute that this was the best decision for the College. The hiring of Dr. D. and his success as an academic who fit so well into the College's culture established me as a mover and a shaker in an institution that needed lots of moving and shaking.

~~~~

Let the Juggling Begin!

I was always concerned that my education did not include a doctorate whereas almost everyone else on the faculty except the librarians possessed earned doctorates. Would this auspicious group look down upon me and not hold me in high regard? I didn't need to worry. There were no concerns about this. My predecessor had done a fabulous job at establishing OT as a respected profession within the academic structure without a doctorate. So I just piggybacked on her good work and took the OT department to the next level.

~~~~

It was surprisingly uplifting to move back and forth between the two different worlds of running a business where profit was the focus and academia where learning was the focus. What some may find overwhelming and stressful, I saw as interesting, complementary, and rewarding work. Keeping on top of everything was not easy, but I had to become even more skilled at time management in order to make the juggling work. I could not use anything as an excuse for something not being done or being done incorrectly either with my business or with the College. There was no tolerance for errors or omissions from the patients, my employees, my colleagues, the students, or the organizations with whom I had contracts to provide their OT services. It was a constant juggling act to keep everything running and moving forward. In between all this, I found time to immerse myself further into the wilderness with Janice or my brother Danny and sometimes just going off by myself. The woods, lakes, and rivers and the overall natural beauty of the outdoors always relaxed and energized me.

~~~~

I was also constantly learning. There was no Internet, so my learning took the form of reading, attending workshops and conferences, and interacting with other professionals out in the field and within the College. Reading was critical for both the clinic and the classroom. I could not be misinformed or use outdated information in either arena. At times, it almost seemed people were expecting me to be omnipotent. Both the therapists that worked for me and the students I taught seemed shocked whenever I said, "I don't know." I never felt omnipotent. More often, I was humbled by all that I did not know. What was amazing to me was not how much knowledge I had accumulated over the years from reading and attending workshops and conferences, but how much I had learned from listening to and watching others. Over and over, I would draw on this pool of knowledge in giving lectures, running a lab, treating a patient, consulting to an agency, guiding a new therapist, and doing the ongoing problem solving in running the business. I worked hard to keep informed, but the reality was that I was stretching myself pretty thin. Luckily, the College's academic calendar was what saved me.

~~~~

The College as a whole had a unique component of experiential learning in their overall curriculum known as the Field Period. There were no classes held on campus during the month of January. This is when all students in every major worked in their field in order to gain practical hands-on experience. Each faculty member had fifteen to twenty-five students whom they advised in preparing them for their Field Periods and evaluated the student's performance in order for them to receive three credit hours for each of the four required Field Periods they completed over their four years. Since our work as professors was done prior to the Field Period (four weeks each January) and during the first few weeks of the spring semester, this meant that the College's faculty had the month of January off. Our fall semester ended the first week of December, so with some astute scheduling of course material and exams, a professor could be off for almost seven weeks each winter. That's just what I did, but I had to be sure everything in the OT department and my courses were all in order. However, I also was available by phone throughout the time I was not on campus.

The other big block of time off was for the summer. I had a 1twelve-month appointment, which meant my responsibility as chair was ongoing. However, I did not have to be on campus except for meetings or administrative duties, most of which I could do from home. So, although I had a full-time, twelve-month faculty appointment as the department chair, I had organized everything in such a way that I could effectively manage the department from afar from about June 1 until August 25. This provided ample opportunities for the wilderness, my business, and family.

This allotted time off was also one of my best recruiting tools when it came to replacing or hiring faculty. The salaries were low and the hospitalization coverage poor in that the college provided no support for family coverage, only individual. Also, being a rural campus, as beautiful as it was, potential faculty did not like the ruralness of the College's location. Potential faculty members wanted the accoutrements of a more suburban or urban environment. So my best selling point was time off, and I used it to attract and retain faculty.

Marco Island and MFR

I used the January or winter break at the College to escape to Marco Island, Florida. Our good friends, Bob and Babs Wrestler,* introduced us to Marco Island in 1988, and we loved it. Every year, I would search for a workshop or conference held on or near Marco Island. By attending a learning experience that was required for retaining my OT license, I could deduct my related expenses from the profit from my business. My attornets/CPAs had guided me in only claiming legitimate expenses so if I was ever audited, I would have the necessary records and rationales. This allowed me to rent a large and comfortable car and thus transport Janice, Beth, often one of her friends, and once even Peter with all the gas and tolls plus the cost of this luxury car all being deductible. I was also able to deduct some of the costs for the upscale condo we rented depending on the number of days that the workshop or conference ran.

There was one conference I attended on Marco Island in 1990 that still resonates with me today. It was on a new practice technique at that time called Myofascial Release or "MFR" for short. A father-and-son team were PTs and had developed several three-day workshops that were attended mostly by PTs, a few chiropractors, OTs, massage therapists, social workers, and I even met a few alcoholism counselors. The first MFR workshop I attended aroused both my skepticism as well as my curiosity. Skepticism because I could not find any scientific evidence that MFR could do all that its practitioners claimed it could do in terms of decreasing pain and increasing function and my curiosity because I had directly seen the benefits of MFR in my practice. What the instructors said whenever asked about the lack of research was, "We are so busy helping people become pain free and back to full function that we don't have time to do research. We will leave that to others."

An often usable by-product or takeaway from the many workshops I attended was that I was able to experience a myriad of teaching styles and strategies, and these instructors really were excellent teachers. There was very little lecturing in their workshops; it was almost all hands-on all day every day. They would demonstrate a technique, and then we would apply it to each other with frequent changing of partners in a large room in a hotel with forty or fifty tables set up as the one hundred or so attendees moved about the room applying the latest technique that was first demonstrated. The instructors then moved about the room coaching us on the various techniques.

MFR I was the introductory course that I completed just to satisfy the IRS requirements for continuing education. I was not impressed because the instructors openly admitted that there was no creditable research to prove the merits of MFR, and most health insurance companies did not reimburse a therapist who used this technique in their treatments. Since I had already paid for MFR II, which was termed "Unwinding," I attended the second course but without much enthusiasm. Why would I spend my time and money to learn something that was not creditable or reimbursable? To satisfy the IRS and give my family a great Florida vacation away from the cold and snowy north in January! That's why!

~~~~

During the first course, I had become friends with a PT from Minnesota who had moved to Marco Island a few years ago and established his PT private practice right on the island. He had begun picking me up at my condo each day in his sports car and continued to do the same for the second course. We shared a negative perception of MFR but were both committed to finishing the second course. It is important to mention here that every time my friend moved his manual gearshift toward the front of his car, he winced in pain and grabbed his right shoulder. We talked about various causes of his pain like therapists like to do but came up with nothing that could explain it.

He and I thought we had lost our minds during MFR II or "Unwinding" when we watched and participated in what we saw as generalized madness throughout the large room. The same format as in MFR I was followed of watching and then practicing the various techniques demonstrated on each other, but this time the instructors took the patients to another level of semiconsciousness. Without really much demonstration of specific hands-on techniques from the instructors, the "patients" suddenly began crying. These were real tears accompanied by some wailing. In a short time, there was a cacophony of sounds that mystified me as I stood back and watched this response being replicated throughout this crazy room. I looked for my PT friend and found him volunteering to be a patient for one of the instructors. This surprised me because I thought he and I were equally skeptical, disgusted, and resistive to getting any further involvement in these therapy shenanigans (my description).

My friend whom I will call Corey* for reasons of confidentiality was lying on his back on one of the cushioned tables as several of us stood around to watch how this craziness was generated. With some maneuvering of Corey's neck and what seemed to me like nothing more than cradling his head, the instructor asked for volunteers to each take a limb and his trunk and lift Corey off the table and to turn him over. Corey's eyes were closed, and he seemed to almost be dozing. Then he started yelling and crying like a baby. There were no intelligible words. This went on for three or five minutes. When he was calmed down and quiet, the instructor assisted him to a seated position. He then got up and walked over to me. Of course, I was stunned at his participation, let alone his complete breakdown. I asked, "What the hell just happened to you?"

He didn't answer my question and just said, "I'll be right back. I have to make a phone call." Off he went while I meandered around the room, seeing what can only be described as an emotional catharsis being produced in different ways. I listened as the instructors gently asked the patients what they were feeling. The patients described a long-ago injury they sustained in a fall, an auto accident, a sports-related trauma, and so forth. All spoke of chronic pain that no medication or treatment had helped, but now they were pain free.

After fifteen or so minutes, Corey returned and motioned for me to go with him outside into the lobby. He told me his remarkable experience. He said, "I felt like I was being born and that someone was relentlessly pulling on my arm. They wouldn't stop no matter how much I cried." The phone call he made was to his mother in Minnesota. His question was simple: "Was my shoulder ever injured when I was a baby?"

The answer was not so simple as she went on to explain, "When you were being born, you got stuck in the birth canal, and the only way the doctor could get you out was to pull on your arm. The doctor as well as us were worried that you were going to have some kind of nerve damage, but you never did. You played sports just like all the other kids." When told it was his right arm, Corey was shocked because that's the arm that he felt being pulled while he was being "reborn."

Throughout the rest of the day, I witnessed more experiences and stories like Corey's. How this was all happening was a mystery to me. I began to suspect some kind of mass conspiracy to entice me to become enthralled with MFR and thus become an advocate. This was ridiculous, and I knew it. That night going home, Corey enjoyed showing me how he could move his gearshift in all directions without any pain. We were both puzzled by the whole day and especially Corey's experiences.

When we returned for our second day of MFR II or "Unwinding," I had a lot of questions. Apparently and unfortunately, my questions were not going to be answered. Our instructors announced that we would "have more of what we had the day before." More what? More crazy stuff? Riding to the hotel with a pain-free and amazed Corey was too much wonderment and rejoicing for me. It was also frustrating that he was not interested in analyzing how the whole crazy MFR thing that he went through yesterday resulted in full pain-free mobility of his right shoulder. I wanted to know how and why, but tooling down the beach road with Corey singing the praises of MFR was a bit much. And now the instructors are saying, "We don't have time to figure out how this all works. We just know it does. So we will leave it to researchers to figure it all out as we go on helping people get beyond what have been their pain-wracked lives." Great! Not what I wanted to hear.

Corey urged me to volunteer to be a patient, but I wanted just to coast along watching until it was over. Finally, after seeing and hearing all these people getting over their pain, I decided to venture forth and join what I felt were a bunch of crazy people having psychotic experiences. I got my chance at a table just behind me when the instructor asked, "Who else wants to be freed from their pain?" I stepped forward, and he had me lie down on my back. I explained that I have pain in my lower back, and I would ask that he be aware of this vulnerability as he engaged in his voodoo crap (I didn't really say it that way, but I sure felt like saying it).

As I lay there with my eyes closed, the instructor massaged my neck, and then he said, "He has to go up. Pick him up." I felt a whole bunch of hands all over me, and then I was being held aloft. With that, he gave another directive to turn me over, and before I could tell them to be careful of my sore back, I was gone. Gone back forty years! Back to the trailer park where I was having that fight with Carl Boyer. It was like I was experiencing the fight all over again. I felt every one of the three flips he gave me when I landed on my lower back. I can feel the shame of getting beaten so easily in front of so many of my friends. It was also weird that I was watching the fight out our trailer window in the same way my Dad must have seen it. I was crying just like I cried when I got flipped and pretended to be too hurt to get up to fight on. I was sort of half asleep during the whole MFR "Unwinding" experience, hearing and feeling everything in the present as I re-visited the past and Carl Boyer's three flips. Now here comes the real crazy part: I had no pain in my back no matter which way I moved. I had joined Corey and the rest of the crazies. However, having just gone through a remarkable but unexplainable experience that caused the eradication of my back pain, I was humbled. The rest of the day, I helped many other patients go through "unwinding" mainly because I didn't feel like talking. I wanted to quietly reflect as I watched, helped, and listened.

I told Corey about my experience, and we both marveled at how the MFR "unwinding" had changed us both. I was quiet with Janice and Beth that night as I continued to quietly analyze and process what I had experienced. The next and last day of the MFR workshop was looking at ways we could take what we learned and go forward and help others. We identified a number of obstacles like the lack of credibility of MFR and it not being a reimbursable service by health insurance companies. Our instructors remained resolute in their commitment to the merits of MFR and offered as evidence all the personal experiences of those in the room (including me) that were now shared by those who felt comfortable in doing so. Neither I nor Corey shared our stories because ours paled in comparison to what we heard from the other patients that day. And then it was over. There was a third MFR class starting the next day, but I had not preregistered for it, and it was already filled. Corey drove me back to the condo for the last time.

~~~~

Now what? Did I become a MFR zealot and go about championing the value of MFR? No, there was still enough of a skeptic in me to still question it. However, I did discover that there is a place in the world and in my thinking for things that are not logical, scientific, or clearly understandable. MFR sits in the place where things work best when they are not micro-analyzed and dissected. So I try to just accept it as is and go forward appreciating the results without trying to dissect and categorize them. This was a whole new way of thinking for me the one that loves facts, logic, structure, predictability, scientific evidence, and control. This experience expanded my way of thinking for the better. From that time forward, I allowed for crazy things that science can't explain while still holding science in the highest regard.

That night I explained in detail to Beth and Janice about my MFR experience, but I could tell from their responses that they could not really appreciate what I had learned. So I just left it at that and savored my MFR metamorphism. My efforts to apply MFR (the stretching, not the unwinding part) to my real patients was not successful, nor was I successful at teaching it to my OT students. MFR remains a mystery that changed me in more ways than just eliminating my back pain. Years later, my low back pain returned, and I have resorted to chiropractic, which seems to work as well as my MFR catharsis without all the wailing.

Crises in the Wilderness

My brother Danny and I fell in love with Algonquin Provincial Park. It is not a park in a citified way but a true water wilderness with a vast network of lakes and rivers located in northern Ontario, Canada. Seeing bears and moose wandering freely was always a thrill, and the abundant birds, raccoons, and howling wolves all made each trip memorable. Using a map provided by the park rangers, we made numerous trips there; and even after ten years of extended trips, we probably only saw 30 percent of this special place. On some of our trips into the backcountry or what's known as the Interior, we could go for days without seeing another person. We would go on two-week excursions paddling my sixty-pound canoe that we had to carry overland on one of our backs and shoulders using a yoke, plus all our gear for sleeping and eating. This wilderness was so pristine that in the backcountry you could drink the water right from the lakes, but we seldom did this after we got a water filter for safety's sake.

As our canoeing skills and map-reading ability improved, we ventured further and challenged ourselves more each year. One trip we will never forget was the one on the Petawawa River. Prior to driving to Cedar Lake, which was our starting point, we were feeling good after a fine breakfast and just so happy to be back in a place Danny and I both loved. We spent from about eight in the morning until three in the afternoon on a ninety-degree day in July doing more carrying and portaging than we did paddling because of the low water levels on the river. We had an extensive fifteen-day trip planned with a route laid out that would take us into areas we had not seen before. At around noon, we were both so exhausted that we took naps along the trail; but stupidly, we did not drink much water. Why not? I just said it. Because we were stupid! Consequently, we were in the throes of hyperthermia but didn't know it.

Finally, we came off the Petawawa River and into beautiful Radiant Lake. This lake was already ominous because this is where some early loggers lost their lives. A makeshift cross was erected by someone many years ago in tribute to them. We felt ready to join these loggers that didn't make it.

There are only a few designated places where we could set up our camp, so we set off to find a site early on and rest up for another tough day that was to follow. The mosquitoes and deer flies were having a feast on Danny and me. To escape them and to cool off, we went for a swim after setting up our tent. My thigh muscles kept cramping up on me and thus prevented me from really enjoying what should have been a luxurious swim after our exhausting day. In addition to the severe cramps, I became so nauseous that I couldn't eat the meal we had prepared. Not eating and not drinking anywhere near the water we required was "the perfect storm" brewing on Radiant Lake.

I was really in a quandary: If I attempted to lie down in the tent, the cramps would savagely arise, driving me up and out of the tent into the hungry mouths of voracious mosquitoes and deer flies that our DEET did little to deter. They were feasting while torturing us. In a vain effort to get some sleep, I put all my clothes on to give me some layers of protection and tried propping myself against a tree where I could quickly come to my feet if leg cramps seized me in a painful frenzy. All this could be resolved if we had the common sense to drink ample amounts of Gatorade (which we had with us in powdered form) or even water and stretched our muscles far more frequently. Alas, we took neither of these simple remedies and suffered through a long night. We learned after this ordeal that people suffering from hyperthermia lose their normal powers of judgment, resulting in calamitous decisions, which certainly did fit our predicament.

The next morning I told Danny of a possible solution to our situation and a way for us to get out of here. "We can paddle to the opposite end of the lake and try to find the railroad tracks. I'll hike back to my truck and see if I can drive back in here to pick up you, the canoe, and all our gear." He looked at me like I had just said I was going to fly. My plan to hike along the abandoned Canadian Pacific Railroad line that was in the process of being removed seemed ludicrous to Danny. According to the map, it would be about a ten-mile hike that I was confident my five-mile runs every day had conditioned me to do. Assuming I could make it, getting back to pick up Danny and everything else was something I hadn't fully figured out yet since so few navigable roads existed in the park. A canoe was the principle means of transportation.

As we were discussing my obviously doomed plan, a man went by in a small boat with an outboard motor. It was loaded down with lumber. Apparently, Danny wasn't as hyperthermic as me because he suggested that we wave to the man in the boat if he came back again and see if he could get us out of there. In my hyperthermic-damaged thought process I rejected this idea for reasons I don't recall, but I'm certain they were not very sound.

Eventually, we again heard the motor of the little boat. We both rushed out onto a prominent outcropping of rock near the water's edge waving and yelling like Robinson Crusoe must have done every time he thought he saw a ship. He saw us and turned his boat toward our campsite. When he got closer to shore and cut his engine, I told him of our leg cramps and our decision to give up on continuing our journey. I also told him of my idea of hiking out. The look on his face said everything we needed to know in terms of the value of this idea. "Well, I don't think you'd make it all the way back to Brent (where my truck was left). Those deer flies up on that railroad bed would eat you alive." Well, that settles that. Desperately reaching for a way out, I asked, "Is there any way you could get us out of here?" He stood in his boat thinking and not talking for more seconds than I could stand and then offered a plan of rescue replete with a scary bunch of "ifs." "If I can get your canoe tied onto my Subaru Outback and if we can fit the two of you and all your gear in my small car and if the tracks have been removed as far back as Brent and if the railroad workers are not working today and if there are no obstructions along the way, I will give it a try." Oh joy! Maybe . . .

Danny and I broke our camp down and packed up our gear in record time so that when our esteemed rescuer pulled his little car down to the lake's shore, we had our canoe unloaded. My canoe looked gigantic when we got it centered on the roof of his Outback, but we got it secured with a combination of his ropes and mine. We introduced ourselves and found out his name was Ivan. The Outback was pretty low to the ground when all our gear and the three of us were all on board, which brought out another concern about shocks and springs breaking.

Ivan explained that he was repairing an old cabin, and that was why he was moving the lumber across the lake when we first saw him. We drove slowly along a dirt path that really didn't seem to be an actual road. Our trust was in Ivan as he explained that we may be coming back if the railroad bed wasn't clear of ties and rails. Driving over railroad tracks and ties just would not be possible.

God was with us for when the railroad bed came into view. It was clear! The railroad ties and rails were lying to each side of the cinder railroad bed, leaving what appeared to be a drivable road of sorts. Up the embankment, Ivan took us bouncing along what was surely not intended to be a road. With cinders and rock hitting the underside, Ivan cautiously drove along the track route for at least fifteen or so miles. Each turn brought anxiety because Ivan did not know at what point we might encounter obstacles necessitating our return to Radiant Lake. And then what? To me it seemed the only route was to make it back to Brent on Cedar Lake, where my truck was parked, and then head for home. If necessary, I felt Danny and I could hike on out with the canoe and our gear if Ivan could just get us as close as possible before he was forced to turn back.

Then like the Emerald City in the Wizard of Oz, the broken-down and abandoned buildings that comprised the old railroad station of Brent appeared. I could have cried with relief. Ivan was happy for us and refused to take the money I offered him. I was insistent telling him that he may have to get a new tire or something. He finally accepted the money. From this day forward, he would always be known by Danny and me as "Ivan, the Wonderful!"

We loaded the canoe on the top of my truck and, with all our gear inside, started the long ride home. I had to stop several times to stretch because of the cramps that kept on coming regardless of where we were along the highway and increasing traffic as we approached Toronto and then across the bridge to the USA. I was far more relieved than I was disappointed that our long anticipated big trip into Algonquin was over in less than twenty-four hours in the park itself.

After I dropped Danny and his gear off, I headed to Wellingwood, where Janice as always greeted me with the excitement of a teenager. She knew I loved the outdoors but worried a great deal because of the dangers inherent in such isolated backcountry trips that I particularly sought. Arriving home safely was the answer to her prayers and, in this case, mine too.

Even being home didn't stop the leg cramps. I was exhausted from the long drive, arduous portaging, and little sleep the night before on Radiant Lake as well as the stress of the whole disastrous trip. However, the leg cramps would not let me sleep. Seeing the pain I was in, Janice called the pharmacist who suggested copious amounts of Gatorade to replace the electrolytes I had most likely depleted, which she promptly went out and bought. It was the answer along with the pharmacist-suggested heating pad! In a short time, my cramps decreased to where I could finally sleep.

Someone from our canoeing group remarked when I told him about our abbreviated trip into Algonquin that "it's the misadventures of a trip that makes it an adventure and often results in a good story." This was so true. It seemed Danny and I had a misadventure of some sort on at least 50 percent of our trips, but it never deterred us from going again. There was always enough good that came out of most trips to keep us coming back for more.

These wilderness experiences were ample opportunities for me to experience my familiar sense of disparity but in a different way. My equipment, knowledge, and skills were far less than that of my canoeing friends and, in fact, inferior to the demands of the environments where I placed myself. However, the Adirondack Mountain Club people were a supportive and encouraging group without being judgmental or intrusive. They were not braggarts, nor did they ever make me feel inadequate. In this sense, disparity was my objective assessment of where I was lacking in equipment, knowledge, and skills, and I set out to lessen this disparity by reading, watching, asking, and building the necessities of wilderness living to where I could actually relax and enjoy the outdoors in a safe way.

As much as possible I included Danny, Peter, and Janice in my learning process. Their skills grew as did mine and thus enabled me as well as them to take on increasingly risky outdoor adventures with both good and not-so-good results.

~~~~

On one solo canoe trip I had planned, I encountered my own mishaps and misadventures. I had read about a little traveled canoe sojourn in the Adirondack Mountains whereby one could eventually canoe and backpack through a network of lakes, ponds, and streams from Little Tupper Lake to Lake Lila. Both of these lakes were in the backcountry and were two of my favorite lakes on which to canoe and camp. To traverse between the two lakes was too palatable to ignore, and the risk taker in me decided to do it alone. By this time, Danny and I had bought matching solo canoes, his in green and mine in red. Now I could do what is known as solo-tripping (not the kind from the '60s). Many times I couldn't find someone else who was free to go, but I could now go off by myself, which provided me with many pleasant memories.

However, this particular trip from Little Tupper Lake to Lake Lila had enough angst to cause me to consider abandoning the wilderness forever except from a car window. The first day and night were quite pleasant as I paddled the six-mile length of Little Tupper Lake and spent the night on an island in the middle of Rock Pond with no one in sight. It was a beautiful campsite on a ridge with a nice place for my tent. I made a small fire and sat up enjoying the quiet and solitude: *Ah, Wilderness!*

The next day was hot and humid as I started to carry my canoe on the two-mile trek to Hardigan Pond, where I planned to stop for lunch. I was not strong enough to carry my seventy-pound pack along with my sixty-pound canoe at the same time, so I had to use what we called the "leap frog" approach to portaging. I would carry the canoe for a few hundred yards, put it down, and come back for the pack. The next step was to then carry the pack about fifty yards past where I had left the canoe. All morning I did this without seeing another person. It was kind of eerie. Knowing that black bears inhabited this area, I sang songs and talked out loud in prayer in order not to surprise or awaken a bruin, especially one with cubs.

By the time I reached Hardigan Pond, I was out of water, and I had learned in Algonquin Park what happens to dumb people like me who do not drink plenty of water on hot and strenuous days like that day. So my first priority was to paddle out to the middle of Hardigan Pond, fill my collapsible water bucket, pump it through my filter, and fill all my water bottles. I scooped the water and was in the midst of filtering the water when the pump broke. I've had problems with it in the past, but none of my usual remedies worked. I then decided to throw some purification tablets in the bucket, but I couldn't find them. I would have to get to shore in order to do a more thorough search of my pack.

Since I was already in the middle of the pond, I decided to paddle the rest of the way to the far end where I planned to go anyway. The place that looked like the best place to get out was full of mud. I heaved my pack onto the muddy shore, got out, and hoisted the canoe onto my shoulders to begin the next portage to Little Salmon Pond. The ground was spongy, and after four or five steps, I sunk into the muck up to my waist. I was stuck!

There was no one around to help get me out, and I knew very few people ever took this route in either direction. So, it was up to me to get myself out of this true quagmire. The first thing I did was to thrust the canoe onto what looked like a more solid section of land. I was praying that I was not in quicksand where the more you move, the lower you sink until you are no more. I saw this in an old movie and was terrified of it happening to me. After fifteen minutes or more of maneuvering and shifting my weight back and forth, I got my right foot on more solid ground and, with a big sucking noise, extricated myself from the smelly muck.

I now had to decide whether or not I had enough time and energy to make it to Lake Lila before nightfall. Pitching a tent and setting up camp in the dark in an unknown area was not part of my plan. I also had the water issue. Finding those purification tablets was critical no matter which direction I decided to go. The way behind me was known to me from just having spent the better part of the day leap-frogging it. So, as disappointing as it was, the sensible decision was to head back to Rock Pond, spend the night there, and head down Little Tupper Lake and to safety the following day.

It was a quick reloading of the canoe and paddle back across Hardigan Pond. On the shore, I took off my muddy boots, shirt, and pants, washed them in the pond, and redressed with dry socks from my pack. It was so warm that my shirt and pants dried quickly as I frantically searched for my vital purification tablets. When I finally located them, I was alarmed to see that I only had four, which was only enough for two quarts of water, and I needed three or four times that amount to get out of there. I filled my canteen and two plastic bottles, and put in the purification tablets in hopes they would do their job and that I would have enough to get to Rock Pond. It was my thinking that once I got to Rock Pond, I could set up camp, get a fire going, and boil enough water in my cook stove to prevent cramps that were sure to come that night.

It was now about one thirty in the afternoon and approaching the hottest time of the day. Without any delay, I was packed up and began the long trek back along the same trail I had worked so hard to get over just a few hours ago. Except for being long and hard, the trek back was uneventful. The only difference was that I was so weakened by the day's rigors that I could no longer lift the canoe up onto my shoulders. So when the trail had sufficient grass and not rock-laden, I just put my gear in the canoe and pulled it as if it were a sled.

Just before sunset, I arrived at Rock Pond in an exhausted state. I was too tired to paddle out to my beautiful island campsite from the night before and elected instead to just stay along the shore near the stream leading out. I got my tent set up, a fire lit, and began a continuous process of boiling water, filling my canteen and plastic bottles and then boiling more. In a short time, I had a number of various containers filled but because of the boiling aspect, I had to wait for it to cool down before I could drink it. I had some powdered Gatorade, which I mixed in for flavor as well as to replace my electrolytes and was waiting for my water supply to cool when it began raining. It quickly turned into a downpour that put out my fire. I jumped into the tent but took my cooling water containers along with me.

It was a long night. I had to drink a lot of water/Gatorade to stave off leg cramps, which led to frequent trips outside to urinate. The rain became torrential with plenty of thunder and lightning. I had my wetsuit on, which kept me dry, but the continuous in and out got the floor of my tent and sleeping bag pretty wet. I was oblivious to the mess I was making because I just wanted to sleep. Of course, the competition between urinary urgency and the rain was no contest. Urinary urgency won out. Thankfully, the lesson learned in Algonquin about inadequate fluids saved me from a night of leg cramps but did not result in a restful night's sleep.

The next day brought more of the rain, but what was of concern now were the winds. I knew that once I paddled out of the meandering stream connecting Rock Pond to Little Tupper Lake, I would be at the mercy of the infamous winds that made crossing this open water so treacherous. I also was concerned that I would be too fatigued to adequately maneuver my canoe in the strong winds intent on capsizing me. Getting turned sideways against a strong wind can easily flip a canoe unless the correct strokes are employed as preventative measures.

I was going to try waiting out the storm, but it seemed to be worsening. So I decided to break camp and start paddling out. It was about nine in the morning, but because of the storm, it was still quite dark. I knew the way out would not be a problem because the meandering stream I was paddling was protected with trees on both sides. I just had to haul my canoe and gear over three beaver dams, paddle past a large beaver lodge, and I would then be paddling for my life across the biggest part of the lake. I planned to use the lee (the side away from windward) of a small island and then use a canoeing technique known as ferrying to cross the lake on an angle. This was not something I was very skilled at, but to do otherwise would put me in even greater peril.

It was getting lighter but not enough to see the distant shore as I ventured out from the protection of the island. Keeping the proper angle of the canoe in relation to the wind is the safest and the easiest way to cross a windblown lake, but holding that angle is not so easy. With lots of prayers and concentration, I made it safely to the other shore. I tried to pull into the shore to rest, but the waves kept driving me into the rocks protruding out into the lake. I decided to just turn the bow toward the end of the lake where I came in and just paddle hard against the wind and rain. Staying near the shore made me feel safer, but it also thrust me into more turbulence and waves. In addition, there came two places where I had to cross large bays where the proximity of a safe shore was nonexistent. So paddle on I did, praying with every stroke.

A ways down at the end of the lake, I began to see a light through the driving rain. I hoped it was the light from the ranger's station because it became my destination. Finally, it became clear that I was going to make it out of there. The closer I got to the end, the more the winds subsided. With all my clothes, sleeping bag, and tent being soaked and the accumulated rain water sloshing about in the bottom of my canoe, I was paddling a pretty heavy load. Seeing the sandy shore next to the ranger's station in calm water made me start to cry.

I was so relieved. I said lots of prayers of thanks for getting me back to safety.

It was when I stood up and got out of the canoe that I realized how completely spent I was. Pulling the loaded canoe up onto the sand was much more difficult than I would have thought. I got my pack, paddles, and extra items up and into the back of my truck, but I did not know about my canoe. I had to get it off the beach, across fifty yards or so across a parking lot, and then up onto my truck. This seemed beyond me. I noticed a crew of park workers getting organized for the day, and when one young guy came across the parking lot, I asked pathetically, "Hey, look I've been fighting the winds out on the lake all morning and I'm pretty beat. Do you think you could carry my canoe up from the beach and help me get it on my truck?" Expecting to hear that they weren't allowed to help people, I was shocked when he said, "Sure, just give me a minute." He went in the shed briefly, came out, went down to the beach, carried my canoe on his shoulders like it was a pillow, and placed it right on the top of my truck right in its rack. I could have hugged him, but I don't think he would go for that. I offered him $5, but he refused it and, with a big smile, continued on to his work. What a guy!

It had stopped raining, but I was freezing even though the temperature was in the fifties. I quickly started my truck and got the heater going while I hurriedly tied my canoe in place. Changing into the dry clothes I left in my truck never felt so good. Getting in that truck, feeling that heat, and knowing that I was safe was very emotional. I drove into the village of Long Lake, where they have a gas station with the best coffee and homemade and slightly burned chocolate chip cookies. I love burned cookies for some reason. Driving back through the mountains, listening to Travis Twit, sipping coffee, and eating burned chocolate chip cookies was pure rapture.

On the way home, I called Janice, who was at a Skin Care Cosmetics conference in Dallas, Texas, but got her voice mail instead. Whenever I went off into the wilderness, Janice always wanted me to call to let her know that I was out safely and on my way home. So I left a singing message for her that was right out of the Wizard of Oz:

"I'm out of the woods. I'm out of the woods." She got the message in between sessions and had a good laugh with her friends about the way I let her know all was well.

~~~~

One of my last canoe trips was with three seasoned canoeists into Killarney Provincial Park in western Ontario, Canada. This was another wilderness area and one I had always wanted to see. I may have met these guys (two of which were brothers) at a Mountain Club meeting or even on previous canoe trips, but I didn't remember them nor did they me. After a few phone calls back and forth, it was settled that the four of us would make the trek to Killarney. For reasons that will be made apparent, I will call the brothers Frick* and Frack,* and my traveling partner Superman.*

I picked up Superman at 5:00 a.m., loaded his canoe and gear on my truck, and went to one of the brother's home designated as our rendezvous point. Superman was a bit tentative as he inquired as to my experience with Frick and Frack, and when I had no recollection of either one, he began to caution me about pending disasters, which I chose to ignore. I never liked forming opinions about people, places, or things from other people's impressions. So I just blocked Superman's comments and entered a room of chaos in Frick's home. His family room floor was covered with all kinds of camping equipment as the brothers went about deciding which items to take and which to leave behind as Superman gave me the I-told-you-so look.

In a surprisingly quick manner, the decisions were made, packs packed, their canoe tied on their car, and off we went. Not so fast. Frick's car needed gas, which required driving around a bit to find a gas station open that early on a Sunday morning. All this time Superman was muttering and growling under his breath that they should have got the gas last night, been all packed and ready to go, followed by a good dose of: #%&^#@$%@. Frick announced at the open gas station that we finally found that he knew the way and would lead us to Killarney. That was fine with me but not so fine with Superman. He had been to Killarney with Frick and Frack last summer, and they got lost twice on the way. There were no GPSs in those days, just AAA maps and memory.

Once on our way, I found Superman to be a delightfully funny and entertaining traveling companion. He regaled me with stories of previous canoe trips, many of which I had done with Danny, but not at the same time as Superman. We also found that we had a lot in common in terms of distance running, family turmoil, and careers (he and his wife were both recently retired special education teachers). It was a long drive to Sudbury, Ontario, and beyond to the entrance to Killarney Park by a route chosen previously by the trip planners: Frick and Frack. Their trip planning was actually quite good in that we missed no turns until one just before the park entrance, which was no big deal (except to Superman) as we turned around and entered Killarney about two thirty on a very hot August afternoon after an eight-hour drive.

Superman and I each paddled our solo canoes while Frick and Frack led the way in their tandem. After a couple of hours of steady and hot paddling across a large lake, Superman summoned us over to his canoe to announce in a controlled rage that "we are going the wrong @#$%&%$ way." I was the least capable of determining direction, so I just hung out alongside as Superman did his best to convince Frick and Frack for us to go in a more westerly direction than we were headed but to no avail. The brothers pedantically went over and over the route using the Killarney map we had all purchased at the ranger's station. Reluctantly, Superman acquiesced, and we followed the brothers across the lake and down a narrow channel. Oh no! Superman was right! We paddled a needless distance of at least a mile that we had to paddle back to the point where Superman had first alerted us to our errant path.

Back on track, over two moderately lengthy portages, and we were on the lake where we had planned to spend our first night. It was another of those pristine Canadian glacial lakes, cold and clear. Superman and I quickly set up our tents, took a swim to cool off and wash off the substantial sweat of the day, and cooked our dinners. We did all this as Frick and Frack continued to micromanage each other's decisions and actions from the placement of the tent to what to make for dinner. Because we Taltys take great glee in kidding, teasing, and absolutely antagonizing volatile people like Superman, I pretended that I too was befuddled by the various camping decisions I encountered. Catching Superman with my peculiar sense of humor gave us both fits of laughter.

With everything cleaned up for the night, we all settled down around a nice campfire that Superman (who else?) had built. We shared stories of previous trips, and these three did have extensive histories of adventures in exotic places. My trips were not unique, and they had all been to the places I had hiked and canoed. However, I did wow them with the story of my feet, finding my shoe-buying partner, and getting written up in the *National Enquirer*. None could top that, and it was pleasant to find such an attentive and appreciative audience when the topic was as mundane as my feet and shoes. After some star watching, we decided to all hit our tents and sleeping bags early because we had another hard day ahead of us.

~~~~

The next day we were woken up by thunder, flashes of lightning, and strong winds but no rain yet. It was imperative that we eat quickly, break camp, load up our canoes, and paddle as fast as possible across the lake where we could follow the trail before rain made seeing our destination too difficult. Superman and I realized that to delay would be foolhardy. As we packed up efficiently but without delay, Frick and Frack deliberated which items to put in what pack in order to have the most stable and balanced load. Superman and I were moving with such exorbitant alacrity that I did not even take time to send forth any Talty humor. I was too worried about crossing that expanse of open water if the wind became dangerously strong.

After donning our rain gear, I led the way with Superman close behind while the brothers deliberated, sorted, re-deliberated, and re-sorted. Just as we reached the halfway point of the lake, a monsoon arose. I had never experienced rains of this magnitude. Blindly, I reached the far shore and pulled my canoe up on the beach, making room for Superman. Directly facing us was a ten-foot climb up a muddy embankment with water cascading down it. Climbing it was our only option in order to access the trail. I put on my seventy-pound pack and climbed to the top, slipping down a few times. I ran as best I could down what I hoped was the trail. It was unclear because we were in an area that was not well-traveled, plus the rain and wind obscured the trail.

When I could run no further, I walked a few more feet and threw my pack off, returning for my canoe. I passed Superman as he hustled on by portaging his lightweight pack and canoe all in one trip. I slid down the mudslide and looked out across the lake to see if the brothers were on their way. They may have been, but the storm precluded my seeing more than thirty feet out into the lake. With the canoe balanced on my shoulders using the yoke and my paddles stowed up inside, I climbed the now even muddier embankment. It took a few tries, but I made it and moved down the trail as fast as I could, leap-frogging my pack for another fifty yards. This is how I spent the next couple of hours.

Then the rain stopped, and the sun came out. I could now really appreciate the natural beauty of this remote wilderness. My wonderment was interrupted by Frick on one of my return trips for my canoe when he asked, "Have you seen my brother? I haven't seen him since he took the canoe and headed up the embankment during the storm." He looked very scared when I told him I had only seen Superman. Neither Frick nor Frack were young guys. They were both in their late sixties, so we were concerned that he might have been hurt or gotten lost. We each had whistles and began blowing the three short blasts to summon Superman and also help Frack find his way to us. In a short time, Superman appeared and joined us as we moved off the trail in different directions, blowing our whistles in hopes of locating Frack, but nothing.

Superman volunteered to climb to the highest point possible in hopes of getting a signal on his cell phone to call for help. Frick and I decided to continue to blow our whistles and search deeper into the thick woods. It was at least an hour before Superman descended from the ridge he had scaled and gave us the good and bad news. The good news was that he was able to make his 911 call and reached the volunteer firemen who work with local Boy Scouts to carry out search-and-rescue missions. However, the bad news was that it was too late in the day to send out a search party this far into the backcountry for fear they would get lost or injured. So they would send them out at first light the next morning, but unfortunately, Frack would have to spend the night out in the woods.

Feeling saddened by Frack's plight but buoyed by the possibility that he could be found safe the next day, we headed off to set up camp. I set up camp on a small stretch of land at the edge of one of the deepest and clearest lakes I had ever seen, and Superman was across from me on a rock outcropping. Frick wanted to stay closer to the trail in the event his brother wandered into camp in the middle of the night. It was just about sunset when Superman and I heard Frick blowing his whistle like crazy. Assuming the worst, Superman and I dropped what we were doing and ran as fast as we could to Frick's campsite a bit down the trail.

I was so relieved to see Frack standing there with Frick that I did not think about the other problem that Superman brought forth: what about the volunteer firemen and Boy Scouts that were going to paddle in looking for Frack? Superman saved the day once again. Without a moment's hesitation, he announced, "I'll go back down the trail and climb up on that same ridge and try to reach them." Off he ran! That's right—ran!

Then I found out that we had another problem. Frack told us that he lost the trail in the storm and mistakenly followed a deer path for quite a distance to the point that the woods became so dense that he could no longer get the canoe through the trees and had to put it down. He continued on lost and confused for hours until he finally stumbled onto the real trail and eventually to us. The additional problem now facing us was how do we get four guys and their gear out in two solo canoes if we can't locate their canoe? We three were busy fretting over this, while Superman hiked and climbed, trying to halt the now unnecessary rescue mission.

After about an hour of beginning darkness, Superman appeared dirty and sweaty after another climb up to the magic ridge. Success! He reached the dispatcher, and the search was called off. Great news! Then Frack gave Superman his not-so-great news: "I lost our canoe." The look of disgusted rage on Superman's face seemed apparent only to me as Frick and Frack engaged in a calm discussion of where the canoe could be. Superman, in a voice filled with frustration and fatigue, said, "Let's just finish setting up our tents, eat, get some sleep, and search for the canoe in the morning." We all liked that idea. Frick and Frack stayed where Frick had originally set up their camp just off the trail, while Superman and I hiked out on our little peninsula overlooking a resplendent lake. I did not tease Superman that night. He did not need any more aggravation. After a quick swim in some very cold water, he and I then used the remaining daylight to paddle out in our separate canoes onto the calm lake and peer far down into the crystal clear water to great depths seeing large fish swimming among long-ago sunken logs. It was very relaxing and captivating to have this unique vantage point.

~~~~

I awoke refreshed as did the rest of our group and in surprising good cheer; even Superman had lost the doleful look he had worn for most of the trip. As we drank our coffee and ate our oatmeal and whatever (the brothers always had elaborate meals—no freeze-dried packaged foods for them) we formed a plan to find the missing canoe. What made it so difficult to plan the search is that Frack could not recall with certainty which side of the trail he came out on, so this meant we had to search both sides for extended distances. It was decided that we would split up, search both sides of the trail, spreading further and further out, and blow three long blasts on our trusty whistles when the canoe was found. I was feeling pretty hopeless after an hour and a half of searching in woods and grass that was the same color as their canoe when I heard the joyful whistle blasts. I followed that pleasant sound back onto the trail to find a smiling Frack with his found canoe!

Superman announced that he voted (I didn't know there was an election) in favor of abandoning the trip and heading for home. Frick and Frack elected to leave also. I hated to leave without seeing more of Killarney, but I was not motivated enough to try convincing the rest of them to continue on. So it was decided to pack up and head out, but we all knew we had a great story of misadventure to tell around a future campfire. Portaging my canoe and pack down the trail, Superman earned his moniker once again when he came back after unloading his stuff at the lake and carried my canoe all the way back for me. It was a fun ride home with Superman as we relived that crazy trip.

Big Surprises for Janice

I wanted to do something really special for our thirtieth wedding anniversary, which is on October 30th. Knowing that it is very cold with early snowfalls in Algonquin at that time of year, I began suggesting a trip there for a long canoeing and backpacking weekend. Janice thought I was a bit crazy, but she knew I love it there and will go late in the year but never this late. She always loved doing anything with me, and so she was in from the beginning. To keep the ruse going, I assembled our mounting piles of gear in our family room as she looked on with more than a little trepidation.

I had no intentions of going canoeing. This was going to be a weekend at one of the best hotels in Toronto with tickets for the play Sunset Boulevard, which she had wanted to see. I also made reservations for Bernie and Annie to stay in the room next to ours. So it was going to be a weekend of many surprises for Janice.

I ran into a bit of a snag when I found out that the hotel we were staying at only had underground parking, and it could not accommodate the canoe on top of my SUV. Janice knew that you cannot go to Algonquin without a canoe, so I had to come up with a story. What I said was that the yoke on my canoe needed to be replaced, so I had arranged to rent a canoe from an Outfitter that had a base near where we were going.

Now I had to enlist the help of Beth to pack Janice's good clothes for going out to dinner and to the theater. She surreptitiously packed all Janice's good clothes, including jewelry, and her spare good glasses in an extra suitcase that she wouldn't miss. I added my good clothes to hers, and we were all set. On the day of departure, I made sure the suitcase with our good clothes was under the mound of camping gear packed in the back of my SUV.

I hit snag number two when I could not find the entrance to the hotel in busy downtown Toronto. She was curious as to why I wasn't taking the usual route to Algonquin that bypassed Toronto, but I just said it's more interesting the way I was going. Now came my dilemma. If I stopped to ask for directions to the hotel, she would know right away that we were not going to Algonquin. Also, because I retain very little when people give me directions, she usually accompanies me for these kinds of conversations. Knowing she would never leave a running car, I quickly pulled into a parking lot, jumped out and ran across the lot to the attendant. It worked! She stayed, and I got the directions, which were really quite simple, even for me.

Then it was three quick turns, and we were going down the ramp into the parking area under our hotel. She asked expectantly, "Are we stopping here for dinner?"

I said something like "You'll see" as I pulled into a parking spot. We got out, and when I opened the tailgate, I pulled out the suitcase and announced that "We are not going to Algonquin. We're staying here for the weekend. Happy anniversary!" She was surprised, but I think relieved more than anything that she didn't have to paddle out onto a bitter cold windswept lake in search of a place to camp.

~~~~

We got settled into our room while I wondered if Bernie and Annie had found their way to their room next door yet. The plan was for them to already be in the hotel's restaurant and seated using the reservations I had previously made when me and Janice arrived. Something got screwed up because they were not there when I checked at the restaurant's reservations desk. In fact, the maître

Big Surprises for Janice

delivered snag number three when he said, "Talty, reservations for four?"

I quickly said, "No, just two."

With that, he took us to our table that happened to have four large Queen Anne chairs just right for hiding.

After we had ordered some nonalcoholic drinks (we had both quit drinking alcohol over thirteen years ago), we went to the salad bar. Obviously, my mind was not on the vast selections at the salad bar. My thoughts were on Bernie and Annie. Where were they? Then, I looked across the room, and there they were! I was actively waving them to our table when Janice caught my antics. She asked with lots of consternation, "What are you doing?"

I quickly turned my waving into a dance and exclaimed, "I'm just so happy to be here with you that I felt like dancing."

Thankfully, Janice's trusting nature prevailed, and she just smiled and said, "That's really nice!"

Then we headed to our table. Janice told us later on that she saw the top of Annie's gray hair, and was thinking that they had mistakenly sat someone at our table while we were at the salad bar. As we got closer to our table, Bernie poked his smiling face around his chair, and jubilation abounded! It was so good to see Janice so happy to see them. She was even happier when she told them how I had tricked her and the great job Beth did packing her stuff.

We had a delicious dinner and lots of laughs as always. It was another nice surprise for Janice when she saw that Bernie and Annie had the room right next to ours. The next day after breakfast, we decided to go exploring. Actually, this was another ruse to get to York, where the play Sunset Boulevard was being performed. We had arranged it ahead of time that Bernie would say that he wanted to go out to this area to see and hear some jazz musicians he had heard about. So we all boarded the subway and headed to York. Then came the last surprise of the weekend full of surprises. We were meandering through the streets in an effort to show Janice some bell Bernie and I had seen earlier while the girls were shopping. It was quite fortuitous that we ended up right next to the theater with the marquee blazing, "SUNSET BOULEVARD." When Janice saw the large marquee, she turned to the rest of us saying, "I would really love to see that . . ." I stood holding four tickets for the next performance. Her response, like all her responses that weekend, made it all worthwhile. We all had a great weekend and came away with another fun story.

Peter Jr. Comes Home!

We missed Peter so much, but he was doing what he loved and having his own adventure traveling with the band. To help lessen our grief of Peter's growing up and moving on, Janice and I traveled to many places around the northeast to visit him. The car we gave him did serve its intended purpose because we did get to see him more often. He also was so appreciative, and he thanked us numerous times. He even drove it to Disney World when the band was playing down there.

After Pete had been traveling with the band for about five years, he had progressed with his skills to the extent that he was now effortlessly doing both the sound and lights. He happened to be home for a long weekend as the band transitioned to a new venue, and he and I were just talking in the family room as he finished his wash and was packing up. A conversation took place that proved epic in both of our lives. It remains fused in my brain even today to the extent that I can recall it almost verbatim. I believe my words and timing were divinely inspired and that I was just the conduit for delivering the message:

Me: "Is traveling with the band and being a roadie wearing on you?"

Pete: "Yeah, it is, but what else can I do?"

Me: "What do you think about moving back home and going to college? You can live here for free, and we will pay your tuition and for any books you need just like we did for Beth. You would just need to get a part-time job to pay for your gas and other expenses. What do you think?"

Pete: "I'd like to do that, but I don't know what I want to be. I wouldn't want to come home and waste time and money if I didn't know what I wanted to study."

Me: "Remember my friend David Shrink* the psychologist? Well, he does prevocational testing and counseling to help people figure this all out. Do you want me to give him a call and set up a time for the next time you're in town for the testing?"

Pete: "Yeah, that sounds good. I'll get the new schedule tonight, and I'll call you tomorrow with some dates."

I couldn't believe how well this spontaneous conversation went. I always tried not to interfere with my kids' lives once they became adults. Knowing each person needs to live their own life in their own way, I felt I could best show respect for their decisions and the paths they chose by supporting them without judging or coercing them to do it my way. Actually, who in their right mind would choose to it my way? I tried not to be advising them unless they sought my advice which was not very often. This was the way I mentored therapists, advised students, and supervised employees. Perhaps I should have been more assertive in guiding all these people, but it just wasn't my way. There were some times where I found it hard to be silent as the course of action they were pursuing did not seem the best, and when I did speak out, I came on too strong, creating tension and distance between us. So I held back on the advice-giving in order to build better relationships with people, including my kids, students, and employees.

So things with Pete moved quickly. He was able to take the tests that David recommended that showed Pete's strengths were in mathematics and creativity. The careers where he had high compatibility in terms of interests were photography and architecture to name a few. He was always very bright, and I felt he would be successful with whatever career he chose. Having been on the faculty at the university plus having received both my BS and MS degrees from there, Pete was open to my insights about admission to the university. I knew that their evening division operated under an open admissions policy where Pete could take courses, demonstrate academic competence, and then transfer into a day program that he chose. This was exactly the path I took into the OT major, and he was eager to try college this way.

He completed the application process for the evening program of the university, gave notice to the band, moved back home, and started classes the following fall semester. I was impressed that he took Calculus 142, which was known as a killer course by anyone I knew who took it. He passed it along with a full semester load and earned a GPA of 3.7 on a four-point scale. I was thrilled to have him home and pursuing his college degree. He had decided to apply to architecture once he had earned enough credits and satisfied all their prerequisites.

~~~~

I was able to hire him for some computer projects for my business, but he needed more than that to support himself. Then another of those fortunate things came our way that solved this problem. Janice's Skin Care Cosmetics business had grown to where she became a sales director, necessitating the hiring of a part-time secretary who also typed up my invoices each month. I would often drop off the therapist's time sheets at her house if we hadn't received them all when she left after working for Janice each week. On one of my extended bike rides, I brought the time sheets to her house. She wasn't home, but I got to meet her husband. He and I were chatting in his driveway when he mentioned that he worked for UPS. With that, I asked if he could get Pete a job there. He said yes and gave me the contact person! Pete followed through and got the job. It paid well and had the hours he needed to attend classes and enough money to pay his expenses.

~~~~

One of the things I did when Pete was back home was reacquainting him with canoeing and backpacking. He loved the camping trips when he was in the Boy Scouts, and we had some great trips after he moved back home complete with plenty of misadventures. I introduced him to Algonquin Park, where we had one particular misadventure that I doubt either of us will ever forget.

It was during the fall when the leaves were turning, and we encountered few people on the water or on the trails. We set up our camp one afternoon at the confluence of two flowing streams that was quite picturesque and so peaceful. Some previous campers had their creative juices flowing because they made a nice shelf between two closely growing trees using pine branches and scraps of rope. My stove fit nicely on the shelf, and I was contentedly getting ready to start cooking our dinners when another wilderness tragedy swiftly unfolded.

Pete was getting our tent and sleeping bags set up as I was boiling water for our dinner. A crazy sequence started when my lovely tree-limb-shelf collapsed and the pan of boiling water poured onto me. I tried to jump back, which saved my body and legs from getting burned but not my foot. Like a running outdoor spicket, the boiling water poured right into my right hiking boot, searing flesh as it flowed. I was in so much pain that I could think of nothing else to do but to jump into the adjacent stream. This only helped to a little extent because my sock was filled with very hot water burning the hell out of my foot. I then threw myself down into the shallow water and tore savagely at my laces and finally got my sock and boot off.

My movements were not done too quietly because Pete appeared with a puzzled look on his face. What was I doing sitting in the water with my clothes on and one boot off with a pained and contorted look on my face? He found out quick when he heard me yell, "The @#$%%##@ shelf broke! I burned my foot. Get me a towel and the first aid kit."

I dried my foot carefully (after getting out of the stream) and saw the repulsive two-by-three-inch red bubble on the front of my ankle extending onto the top of my foot. It hurt a lot, and the first aid cream did nothing for it. I then tried a combination of Vaseline and cooking oil that gave me some relief. It was actually surprising how much better it felt after only a half hour of applying my homemade burn ointment. I was able to wrap it in a gauze bandage over the ointment and felt good enough to get a sneaker on and enjoy the rest of the night. The next day my foot was feeling good enough that I was able to get my hiking boot on, and we were able to complete the rest of our trip without much difficulty.

Once we got out of the woods and were headed back to the States, I stopped at a drugstore to get some real burn ointment that helped to ease my pain. After dropping Pete off at the apartment he now shared with a couple of other architecture students, I headed back home and resumed my usual busy schedule. In fact, I was so busy that I tried to ignore my burned foot and ankle. However, after a week of futilely trying to ignore my worsening pain, I went to the nearby walk-in clinic. Once fully unwrapped, I think the site of my infected burn oozing a greenish-yellow pungent slime alarmed me, the nurse, and the doctor. When the doctor asked how long ago this happened and I said a week ago, he shook his head and said, "You are either the toughest man or the dumbest man I ever met. Why did you wait so long?" My answer of being busy did not impress him. He lanced it, released lots of ugly and smelly pus, applied some antibiotic cream, gave me a prescription for oral antibiotics, and sent me on my way. It healed well, and I have no residual scars, only the emotional scars related to the doctor's comments. Regardless, Pete and I have a shared memory of a misadventure culminating in the doctor's direct but somewhat rude remark that still makes us laugh.

Janice's Mom

Janice's mom, Sarah, was a remarkable woman of great strength, practical intelligence, kindness, and resiliency. Her first husband, Lou, was killed when he was just forty-four years old, and she was left to raise three kids. Her resolve was further tested when she was stricken with stomach cancer and given little chance of surviving. She rallied, overcame the cancer, and went on to work full-time and see her three kids married and enjoy eight grandkids and three great-grandkids. Her spirit of positive thinking and always giving people the benefit of the doubt served her well, and this attitude was passed on to her kids especially Janice. I still see these qualities in Janice today.

Prior to coming to live with us, Sarah had outlived two other husbands besides Lou Pepe (Tom DePaul and Frank Eppolito). Although left alone, she maintained her independence and continued to value relationships with family and friends to a high degree. Her biggest burden was her loss of hearing. She struggled with a variety of hearing aids and was constantly trying to find the right ones and the right adjustment so that she could be a full participant in her family and social life. Unfortunately, nothing gave her the level of hearing that she and we desired. This left her out of the conversations that she so treasured. Undaunted, she persevered in her efforts to relate to others, although I'm sure the outcome was less than satisfying for her. We in the family, with the exception of Janice and Annie, were not as tolerant as we should have been, and I regrettably may have been the least tolerant of us all. However, because I was always a taciturn person, working a lot at home, or away a few days each week, I doubt that she was aware of my low tolerance. What also helped was her credo in life to" always give people the benefit of the doubt."

~~~~

It seemed her coming to live with us gave her a sense of peace in that she didn't have to worry about caring for a home and was not alone. With her own car and large bedroom and sitting area, TV, and her own phone line, she was able to keep and talk with her friends and relatives, which she valued greatly. However, as time went on, Sarah got confused more easily and then became very agitated when she could not remember things. She needed constant and repetitive reassurance and information, which was exhausting for poor Janice. It was Janice who had to deal with her mother's confusion and agitation on a daily basis. Ours was a hectic household in the early stages of her confusion, and she strove so hard to understand it all and become a part of our crazy lives. Janice had become deeply and successfully involved in Skin Care Cosmetics as a way of coping with my absence, first when I was traveling three days a week building my private practice and then later four days a week when I became the chair of OT at the College. With Beth away at college and Peter traveling with the band, these were lonely days for Janice, and the friendships she formed with other Skin Care Cosmetics consultants helped her to not only survive but also to actually flourish. She grew in confidence and business acuity through the supportive way Skin Care Cosmetics as a company supports the entrepreneurs in all the consultants and leaders.

So as a result of our busy work lives, Janice's mom was alone a lot and was in dire need of a family connection that we now found difficult to provide. She never complained and never gave up trying to be included in a family that was not always present or able to visit with her as much as she would have liked. Janice valiantly tried to fill this void by having meals and conversations with her as much as possible but was busy working in her office or on the phone a great deal of the time. She also took her with her to her many Skin Care Cosmetics functions, which she enjoyed very much. It was not that the rest of us were intentionally avoiding her; we just were all caught up in our own lives and activities. I think we all feel bad about this today whenever we think back on those days.

~~~~

Then our crazy home life got even crazier when a few things coincided. When Peter left the band to come home to attend architecture school and Beth graduated from her university, there were now two more people moving in and out and around in our house. Beth had a busy schedule working at the day care program at the Jewish Center, working for me doing the payroll, and getting involved with Janice in Skin Care Cosmetics. Peter, like the rest of us, had an erratic schedule of working at UPS nights and going to school days. To compound the comings and goings of us all, Peter met Costelli,* who initially lived in another city. After a bit, Costelli moved in with us, and now Janice's mom had someone else with an erratic schedule living within this crazy house. However, in many ways, Costelli may have been more tolerant than any of us toward Sarah and, along with the steadfast and ever-caring Janice, gave her the socialization she desperately craved.

Eventually, Costelli moved out into her own apartment, Peter moved in with some fellow architect students, and Beth got an apartment with a friend with whom she graduated from college. With me gone a lot or when home working on my business or my courses and Janice immersed in Skin Care Cosmetics, this left Sarah often alone and lonely. We had two cats and a nice dog to help keep her company, but of course, they were no substitute for people.

It was fortunate at this time that she met and began dating Dom Pleasant.* He was a nice man with whom she had a lot in common, both being Italian, alone, having both grown up on the West Side, and had known each other in earlier days. He was a widower independently living in his own home. They talked every night on the phone where she could hear fairly well using an amplification device. They also went out once a week for lunch, had dinner out every Sunday, and once in a while attended a dance on a Saturday night. Dom helped Sarah deal with the loneliness, but for a number of reasons, their relationship never progressed to marriage.

Sarah subsequently developed health problems, specifically intractable lower back pain, beyond her severe hearing deficit and her seeming overnight great confusion meant that she could no longer be alone. A sequence of cascading events starting with her having even more severe back pain necessitated her being hospitalized. I expected the foreign environment of the hospital to make her more confused and thus cause her to become extremely agitated. I shouldn't have worried. I could see that God was at work when Sarah thought she was on a cruise ship and was quite content. She was happy as she misinterpreted the nurse' station to be a bar where one could be served drinks. To her, all the patients in the day room were others on the cruise ship and the staff were the waiters and waitresses. She showed more enthusiasm and liveliness than I had seen in her in a long time. With medication, they were able to get her back pain under control without sedating her. She still knew all of us and enjoyed our visits.

Our sense of calm that we were feeling because Sarah's back pain had been resolved was soon dispelled as we became embroiled in the Medicare nursing home morass. Although Sarah was enjoying her "cruise", she was at the same time going downhill in terms of her overall functioning to the extent that she now required nursing home care. We had initially thought that we could keep her at home through the use of home health services, but this was no longer feasible.

Nursing home placement became our only option, which put Janice in a terrible position. Her mother had always wanted her to promise that she would never put her away in a nursing home. Janice, being ever-truthful, would respond that she would take care of her at home for as long as she could. She did not want to make a promise she couldn't keep, but now we had no choice. Sarah had seen too many of her friends and relatives living and dying in nursing homes, and she was adamant that this was not the way she wanted to live her final days. Janice went through a great deal of anguish over this decision. With Annie living out of town, and her brother Frank and his family living outside of Philadelphia, all this fell on Janice. However, once again, Janice showed her great strength as we began the painful and arduous placement process.

Besides the emotional trauma of the placement decision, we now had to find a nursing home that would accept her. The hospital's discharge planner gave us a list of about thirty local nursing homes and asked us to select five. Having worked in many of these facilities myself, I had my top five in terms of care that the residents received and thus indicated these on the list. We were surprised to hear that none of these facilities would accept her because she did not have enough money to support the level of care she required. I then picked my second best five but got the same result. This process of selecting and rejecting continued until the list of thirty facilities was exhausted. The hospital was adamant that we had to find a place for her because she no longer qualified for hospital-level care.

I then went to see a nursing home administrator who I had gotten to know by my working with him in a facility that was not on the local list. However, he was now the administrator of another facility, and I went to see him. His was a good facility that was clean, well-run, and provided good care. It was not one of the new and high-end facilities, but one I knew would still be good for Sarah. So I went to see him and explained our plight. Because I knew he respected me, I felt I could ask him to help us out, and he did.

In 1995, Sarah was transferred to a nearby skilled nursing facility. She was initially confused, but the staff was friendly and caring, and she quickly settled in. Her confusion continued to get worse, but she knew us, and we were able to take her out for family gatherings either at our house or a nearby restaurant. Her hearing deficits were compounded with her growing confusion, making long visits difficult, but this placement proved very satisfactory, and I am forever grateful for the administrator who accepted Sarah for placement in 1995.

These were sad days for Janice because with me gone three and sometimes four nights a week to the College, Beth and Peter living in their own apartments, and Sarah in the nursing home, Janice was alone in the big house in Wellington Woods. Thankfully, her Skin Care Cosmetics friends and her growing success in building her business helped her through these difficult days. We lived this way for two years when disparity began to swell in me, providing the impetus for another move.

Changes to My OT Private Practice

I was in the midst of a real struggle with trying to keep my business going against several forces beyond my control when I picked up a vague message from my answering service one day in 1996. It was from a physical therapist that I didn't know, but I will refer to by the pseudonym of Richie Weelrdealr.* Richie was very friendly and complementary when I returned his call, but he was somewhat vague about why he wanted to meet with me for "breakfast, lunch, or dinner, you name it. Pick the day, time, and place." Because I have attended enough of these obscure meetings that turned out well, I agreed to meet with Richie Weelrdealr.

We met for breakfast at a place convenient for us both and on a day where I had adequate time without another appointment until later on in the day. Richie was a nice person and, in spite of his overboard sales efforts, seemed genuine, and I liked him. As part of his string of complements, he said, "I asked a lot of people about Peter Talty, and not one person had anything negative to say about you, and that's why I wanted to talk with you." He was associated with a new company that was from out of state, and they wanted to build or acquire PT, OT, and speech pathology practices in this area and integrate them all under the concept of a "one-stop-shop." The company and the company's president and CEO will also have humorous and appropriate pseudonyms: Jay Confounder* was the

CEO of Services for Health and Ancillary Medicine or SHAM.* The reasons for these pseudonyms will become evident as this bizarre story unfolds.

What Richie was presenting in a vague way was that the company he worked for, SHAM, was interested in purchasing my company, which I had previously incorporated under the name of OT Works, PC. In my mind, I was questioning the business competence of these guys right from the beginning because why would a company want to acquire a practice like mine that was at great risk from the many new OT graduates in the area competing for OT contracts and positions? Either they knew something I didn't know or they were really ignorant of the fiscal realities of the local OT market. Regardless of which it was, I was going to hear what the big cheese from SHAM had to say.

Jay Confounder flew in to meet with me. Over dinner, Jay and I engaged in a sort of chess match (not that I can play chess) because neither one of us knew what Richie Weelrdealr had told each of us about the other. I never had a high tolerance for chatter, gobbledygook, banter, and other kinds of time-wasting talk. This has always been one of my shortcomings because, unfortunately, this is what a lot of people do before they get to the main purpose of a meeting. I listened, asked direct questions, and showed more patience for this kind of communication because he was paying for dinner, and this could be a good opportunity for me.

~~~~

The bottom line was that SHAM would buy my company provided my accounts were as I stated and that I would remain with SHAM for one year as a consultant to facilitate an orderly transition. I was honest with Richie and Jay right from the beginning about how volatile the rehabilitation market (and my company) was in this area because of the surplus of OTs that were now available. Jay was confident that their business practice model would do fine in this area and wanted very much to purchase OT Works, PC. We just needed to agree upon a price. I, of course, wanted far more than they were willing to pay and thus began a process of negotiation that continued for a few weeks. Finally, in September of 1996, we had a deal that was satisfactory to SHAM and to me.

I had to convince as many of my contracted facilities and agencies as well as the therapists, to remain with SHAM, which turned out to be much easier than I thought it would be. Apparently, since I was still involved, and they all trusted me, the transition was in a lot of ways seamless. SHAM took over the payroll, did all the billing, paid the therapists and the operating expenses, and paid me a substantial salary as per the purchase agreement. They even paid Beth for her services until she decided to become more involved in Skin Care Cosmetics and left the company.

Richie ran the business on a day-to-day basis while conferring with me on issues relevant to OT. I also helped him prepare proposals intended to expand the business. Jay liked the idea of my mentoring Richie, but we did not share the same approach to the management of people. I was not a micromanager. My philosophy was to hire good people, train them in the beginning but, as soon as possible, let them function independently. I also was distancing myself from the chaos and confusion that was quickly becoming the way SHAM operated.

The deal that Jay and I signed was a far better arrangement for me than it was for SHAM. Jay's approach was to drive Richie to find more contracts as fast as possible because the OT Works aspects were a drain on SHAM's limited resources. They needed more revenue to offset the major expenses they had taken on, and they were learning that OT Works was not the cash cow they originally thought it was. It served me very well for years, but the market had changed. I did not deceive them. Everything they were learning was made clear right from the beginning, and I have the correspondence to prove it.

After we had been operating under the erratic auspices of SHAM for about eleven months, I got a phone call from the State Office of the Professions. They were investigating me because someone had lodged a complaint against me, stating that I was assisting an out-of-state corporation in becoming a rehabilitation service provider in this state, and this was considered unacceptable practice. The agent went on to say that this could jeopardize my OT license. I assured them that this was not my intent and that I would terminate the agreement with SHAM immediately.

That phone call was disconcerting for a number of reasons, not the least of which was that my excellent professional reputation was being besmirched without my knowing it, and my OT license was now at risk. Before I signed the contract with SHAM, I had the whole agreement scrutinized and much of it authored by a local attorney I found who specialized in these types of contracts. He was very expensive, but SHAM paid his bill as per our contract. When I contacted him about this current issue, he too was surprised by this threatened investigation and promised to research it and get right back to me. After a few anxious days, he called to explain that the state's case was weak, and he found out that it was a competitor of mine who had lodged the complaint. He was confident that we could win the case in court, but it would take a while. I was not interested in fighting the case, so I thanked him for his time and decided to take another course of action.

~~~~

Prior to getting the phone call from the State's Office of the Professions, I had really grown disenchanted with the whole SHAM organization. Jay must have known from his accountants that expenses for OT Works were far exceeding revenues especially since they had to pay me my money every month, pay the therapists I had on the payroll, and plus pay even higher salaries to some new therapists that Richie decided to hire. Jay was pushing Richie, who tried unsuccessfully to push me, to find more and better revenue-producing agencies and facilities with whom to establish contracts. They simply were not there in this area, which I had explained to them from the beginning, but I think greed, impulsiveness, and ego clouded their vision.

So in September of 1997, I decided to end the madness and protect my OT license and professional reputation. What I did was compose letters to all the contracting agencies and facilities announcing my termination of my association with SHAM. I just said I was going to concentrate on my teaching responsibilities instead. In the same letter, I told them they should feel free to enter into an employment relationship with the therapists presently providing their OT services. I also composed a similar letter to the therapists and explained that they could investigate becoming an employee of the facility or agency where they were presently working. I sent copies of the two letters to Jay and Richie giving thirty days' notice of these changes. All the letters went out at the same time.

In my personal letter of termination that I sent to Jay, I explained about the notification I received from the OT licensing board and this was the primary reason for terminating our agreement. I sent a copy of this letter to the Office of the Professions so they would see that I was taking the appropriate action to preserve my OT license.

The fallout from all my letters was not what I expected. Most of the therapists quietly signed on with their respective agency or facility. All parties seemed to be pleased with their new relationships. I heard nothing from Jay, but Richie called me in anguished shock and confusion about what I had done. I provided Richie with no more details than what I put in my letters. It was not at his level that I formed the contract with SHAM, and thus, he did not need to know the details regarding my decision to terminate it.

~~~~

SHAM continued to operate for another few months or so, and then they closed up their area office. Richie went back to being a physical therapist working in one of the facilities. I had one phone conversation with him several months after we parted ways. I called him just as a friend to see how and what he was doing. He was extremely contrite and apologetic for getting me involved with Jay and SHAM. I assured him that I did very well through the SHAM contract and had no regrets. Unfortunately, Richie was still just as sad for me at the end of the conversation as he was in the beginning. He needn't have been so remorseful because in spite of the abundant angst that I experienced during the sojourn with SHAM, it did inadvertently enable me to profitably extricate myself from the business, which was struggling desperately at the end anyway.

Pat Becomes a Trailer Owner

My brother Pat's life had gone progressively downhill for a number of reasons. Of course, becoming estranged from Sue and Jim because of the sinister thing he did that devastated their lives and divided our family was only part of his sad life. He had undergone numerous surgical procedures, two on his back, one on his shoulder, and one on his wrist. All these gave him some relief from the various and constant pain he was experiencing. However, his most drastic surgery were those he had on his brain in an effort to eradicate his seizures. Although these were initially promising, his seizures continued to be the most disabling of his entire myriad of ailments.

Eventually, because of his uncontrollable seizures, it was pronounced that he was unable to work around machines or drive a car. It was determined that he was permanently disabled, and thus he began receiving monthly payments through Disability Social Security. This stable income provided initial relieve from his numerous creditors, but as time went on, he was experiencing economic strife once again. He was always an impulsive shopper, and very soon, his expenses far exceeded his monthly check. His living situation had deteriorated to where he and his dog, Dino, lived over a tavern in one of the worst parts of the city, which was adjacent to a high-crime area.

Reluctantly, I did forgive Pat for what he did to Sue and Jim because I still loved him and forgiving him was the Christian thing to do. He was still the same self-centered Pat who did little to help

Pat Becomes a Trailer Owner

himself. Living over a tavern was not the best for a Talty who liked the taste and effect of alcohol. The good thing about his living arrangement was that if he had too much to drink, he did not have far to go to sleep it off.

He had a nice woman as his girlfriend who moved in with him. Whatever peace or pleasure Pat was expecting to derive from having her move in was quickly eviscerated when her daughter and son also moved into Pat's filthy, poorly furnished, and depressing apartment. That they would elect to inhabit such a place tells a lot about their economic status. The result was predictable chaos. It escalated to the point that Pat came home drunk one night and threw them all out.

~~~~

Pity, frustration, guilt, and sadness were the prevailing emotions I experienced whenever I thought about Pat and his sad life. Having been catered to by Ma and Dad for whatever reason, having uncontrollable epilepsy, and then being institutionalized in a State Hospital at the age of fourteen gave him an ill-fated start in life. Having an erratic and unsuccessful educational experience coupled with a checkered work history all resulted in his being a pretty unhappy guy. I felt guilty because when we were kids and even as an adult, I always teased and ridiculed him. He also had become very obese, exceeding three hundred pounds ("that's as high as my scale will go").

Now I truly had become my brother's keeper, doing whatever I could to help him. However, his biggest need was for a better and safer place to live, but neither his nor my economic position was able to change this. At least I didn't think I could. Then wonderful and caring Janice shocked me with a solution to Pat's living situation. Knowing that I always wanted to visit Alaska, she had been secretly saving to make this possible. She had saved $5,000! It was her plan to surprise me for my birthday, but now she offered me a choice: visit Alaska or help Pat get a home and get out of his terrible tavern flat. She knew what I would choose and was fine when I chose to help Pat. What a woman!

Pat Becomes a Trailer Owner

We learned that the best option for Pat with the money we had to work with was a trailer. Living in a trailer was something Pat always aspired to do but never would have thought possible. Living in that thirty-five-foot Ironwood in the Trailer Park may have been some of the happiest days of Pat's forlorn life. He was so excited when I told him what Janice had offered to do that I was fearful of his having a seizure. He didn't and immediately began looking in the local newspaper and making phone calls about trailers for sale.

After a quick search of trailers on the market, Pat found one in a suburb north of us and just fifteen minutes from our house on Wellingwood. He was one excited guy when we got everything finalized, and he was a home owner. The trailer park he was in was not opulent with amenities, but it was clean, safe, and the people were friendly. With the help of Danny and his grandson Devon, we got Pat all moved in to his own trailer. He loved his trailer and the trailer park life. His dog, Dino, became an indoor dog when Pat became a trailer owner and seemed as content as Pat in his suburban environment.

~~~~

Pat was always pretty handy and was overjoyed that his trailer included a shed that he quickly outfitted into a nice little workshop. He was always creative and enjoyed modifying the inside of his trailer, adding shelves and cabinets. Each time I stopped to see him on one of my bike rides, he had something new to show me. His love of music, especially loud music, could now be realized because his place was his own. He made friends with several people in the park who took him shopping and to his doctor's appointments. That was the one downside with his location. He had to rely on his neighbors for rides, and he hated asking them. In addition, he didn't tend to show a lot of appreciation, nor did he seek out ways to reciprocate.

~~~~

Pat Becomes a Trailer Owner

Could life get any better for Pat? Yes! Besides the pride that comes with home ownership, he found a girlfriend. She wasn't really a girl and may have even been a few years older than Pat's fifty-two years of age. He had an interesting pickup line that she and he both liked telling people about. One day, when Pat was sitting on his porch, Carolina,* whom he had not really met, was walking by with two of her granddaughters when Pat yelled out, "Hey, do ya like fish?" She said yes, and Pat invited her for a fish dinner that night that he prepared. They got along very well and spent more and more time together.

We included Carolina in our family gatherings, and she seemed to really enjoy herself. She was a nice person, quiet, and seemed pretty easygoing. Because she worked as a nurse's aide I felt she would be into the caretaker role, which Pat needed and wanted very much. Their relationship progressed to the point that after a while, she moved into Pat's trailer while her adult daughter and granddaughters stayed in her trailer. Carolina also was able to purchase a small pickup truck, so now they had transportation.

~~~~

I could not believe how well Pat's move to that trailer park worked out. It was so good to see him so happy. He and Carolina seemed like they were very compatible. She made a delicious chicken dinner for Janice and I one night, and it was so nice seeing Pat in such a normal living situation. The conversation got around to marriage with me, probably steering the conversation in that direction. I felt there was a risk that she might tire of Pat's moody ways and self-centeredness. Empathy was certainly not one of his strong points. My concern was that Carolina would decide that Pat was too heavy a load. Surprise! She liked the idea of getting married, but she was concerned that they didn't have money for any kind of reception. No problem. I offered to pay for a small reception and asked her and Pat to check out some places and to make a list of whom they would like to invite. It seemed to take forever for Pat and Carolina to take these next steps, and being a person that hates loose ends, I continued to push them.

Finally, they had a place with a buffet right in the area that was not expensive, and their list of guests was not extravagant at all. However, they still didn't have a date set at the church Pat attended. Then Carolina revealed what the real holdup was: she didn't have a dress! That was it? I gave her enough money for a dress, and we were on our way.

~~~~

I was pushing for this marriage not just because I thought Pat and Carolina were very compatible but because Tommy and Karoline were going to be coming in from New Mexico for Bernie and Annie's daughter Jill's graduation in OT from the College. My thinking was to have the wedding, while Tommy and Karoline were in town. Finally, I got the date set, and it did happen just a few days before Jill's graduation. It was a brief and simple ceremony in Pat's little church. With all the Talty brothers together, we had a lot of laughs, but more importantly, the wedding did finally happen. Pat's friends from the trailer park and a few from the tavern he lived over were also there. With Carolina's family and ours, we had about thirty-five people. It was so good to see Pat so happy; nervous but happy. Carolina's daughter and her granddaughter really seemed to like Pat, and it was good to see him becoming a part of her family. For their honeymoon, they were going to drive around the state and see where they ended up. This sounded crazy to me, but it was their life. I orchestrated enough.

Out of Town Again

The termination of my business in my hometown coincided with a housing crisis that was emerging for me at the College. My living in empty dormitories at the College was coming to an end. The success I had in doubling the enrollment for OT corresponded with growth in many of the other programs and led to more students living on campus. They were running out of empty dormitories, and thus I was losing a free place to stay. I was also tired of living away from Janice. These factors all contributed to my thinking that we should sell our Wellingwood house and buy a townhouse in the same development as Annie and Bernie. This way, I could be home every night because this was only thirty-five miles from the College. I was attracted to the idea of a townhouse because Bernie and Annie had just sold their own large home because their two kids had moved out, and downsizing made a lot of sense. They loved living in their village and a developer had just started building a new section of townhouses near their former home, one of which they decided to buy and move into once their home sold. Everything worked out, and they were very happy with their new townhouse and lifestyle.

So once again, I followed my usual way of thinking about something a lot on my long drives back and forth to the College but saying very little about my concerns or potential solution to anyone. Even to Janice. As a result, my proposal to move did not receive the reception from Janice I had anticipated. "Are you crazy? I love this house. I don't want to move. I have my Skin Care Cosmetics business and my mother in a nursing home here. Our kids are here. What are you thinking?" That didn't go well. I really only had four selling points: I would be home every night, we would be right near Annie and Bernie, I could keep my tenured position, and we could be free of the responsibilities of owning a large home that we no longer needed. As attractive as these things were to Janice, the move just did not make sense to her. However, maintaining the status quo had risks associated with it that we needed to consider.

~~~~

The first concern was my housing situation at the College. I was told by Conference Services that they would not be able to accommodate me next year because the students were going to be occupying all the dorm rooms in the fall. I couldn't afford to rent or buy a house nor rent a motel room. I had earned tenure and been promoted to full professor, so to walk away from this position didn't seem like the smart thing to do. Also, I loved my job. I had autonomy, flexibility, and a great deal of time off. I was also well-liked and respected by the students, faculty, and the administration. In addition to three Excellence in Teaching Awards, in 1995, I received the Professor of the Year Award for the entire college. I had to find a way to stay, and moving closer to the College seemed like the best option for us.

Another driving force was the OT practice environment. Prior to the SHAM arrangement and at the time I started my private practice, there was a great shortage of OTs in the area, and it was even greater in the rural areas. Also, the facilities were willing to pay my fees because they couldn't find an OT. Everything changed when a new OT program at a local college graduated their first class of sixty OTs. The majority of this class was from the area and wanted to get their first OT job there. Within months, I started losing contracts to new graduates. The facilities and agencies could hire a new graduate full-time, which was more attractive to them rather than pay my high fees.

My therapists also wanted more pay and better benefits, putting a further strain on my company's profit margin. I never intended this to be a nonprofit enterprise. Providing quality OT services at an above-average fee was my objective. If I pay the therapists more and increase their benefits and if I could not obtain a rate increase from my contracted facilities and agencies, then I would be losing money. Talk about disparity!

Some of the therapists were offered positions by my contractees, which presented quasi legal and ethical issues. My original employment contracts with the therapists contained a noncompete clause to prevent them from taking such a position or attempting to obtain such a position. However, I learned from my attorneys that non-compete clauses are not enforceable in this state, and so I removed them. Of course, the subsequent SHAM venture and the closing up of my private practice negated all these issues.

~~~~

So after many discussions with Janice, she agreed that moving would be the best option for us for all the reasons I mentioned above. Right after we decided to make this move, the first people we called were Bernie and Annie. They were very pleased, and as evidence of how pleased they were, that evening they drove in to give us the developer's book and other papers describing the various townhouses available. Their excitement got Janice excited, and the plan was put into effect. With Pat happily married to someone with transportation, I also felt comfortable leaving Pat. He wouldn't have the support of Janice and me, but I was comfortable in Carolina picking up our yoke.

~~~~

But now began one of the most challenging times of Janice's and my lives. It started with the irreversible illness that forced us to have our wonderful dog Nikkie put to sleep. Janice could not go with me to the vet's because she had just developed a herniated disc producing terrible pain for her. We had Nikkie for fourteen years, and he proved to be a wonderful companion that I still miss today.

Janice's pain prevented her from sleeping and doing much to prepare the house for selling or helping us get ready to move. We went through a number of fruitless medical and surgical evaluations and different medications, all to no avail. Finally, we went to see a neurologist who gave her a steroid injection in her back to treat the inflammation. This helped, and then she went through a series of physical therapy treatments, including water therapy that really helped her get back to normal. She was now able to help me with all we had to do in order to make the "Big Move."

~~~~

First, we arranged for a friend of ours who was a realtor but more importantly also lived in Wellington Woods to list our house. This meant that she could extol the features of our beautiful neighborhood in the process of selling our house. It was not our first choice to go with a realtor because Janice and I had sold three previous houses ourselves. However, with me away at the College and us wanting a quick sale at a good price, we thought listing with a realtor was our best option.

What we hoped was going to be a fast sale of our house ended up taking almost nine months to sell. In many ways, we found ourselves in a perfect storm or what I think of as a real estate maelstrom. First, it was somewhat of a downturn in the local real estate market, but this was not the only reason our house didn't sell. We were surrounded by a great upturn in new home construction. These new homes were contemporary in design with open floor plans and light neutral colors. Our home was unique and well-crafted, but it did not capture the interest of people shopping for a home in our price range. In all, we had ninety-five showings, including special showings to groups of realtors themselves. We had lots of positive comments, "it shows beautifully, very well maintained, impressive curb appeal" and on and on, but no offers.

Keeping the house in a perpetual state of readiness and then staging it for the ninety-five actual showings were both fatiguing and frustrating. As part of preparing the house, we had to get rid of a lot of stuff. On several garbage days, I had thirty to forty large trash bags filled with stuff Janice allowed me to remove. In addition, Janice had a great deal of stuff that we didn't need or want but had great sentimental value to her. She also thought she might use this stuff someday or that someone in the family or one of her Skin Care Cosmetics friends might find a use for these things in the future. So these things could not be put out for the garbage. The problem was that this mass of stuff made our basement look small and cluttered (it was). So we elected to rent two storage sheds in our new town to store all this excess stuff until Janice could go through it and decide who might want it. So every week, when I headed off to the College, it was with a full cargo in my SUV destined for one of the storage sheds.

We dropped the price drastically just to get it sold, and finally it did sell but not until September of 1997. We delayed the actual purchase of the townhouse until Wellingwood sold so we wouldn't have to be paying for two homes at once. The timing did work out. The townhouse design we selected and had constructed to our specifications was completed, and we made the move. We were going to live one section over and right behind Annie and Bernie, and they, like us, were thrilled. The process of finally getting to the townhouse was an arduous one, but I felt it was going to be well worth all the stress and strain we experienced.

A Simpler Life That Was a Godsend

Driving to and from work on a daily basis was a new experience for me. Having dinner with Janice and sleeping in my own bed every night was so easy and so pleasant. I now had lots of "nots" in my life. I did not have to drive 112 miles through backcountry roads that many times were treacherous with snow, ice, and wind. I did not have to worry about my OT business and the chaos that my association with the SHAM Corporation generated. I did not have to leave the comforts of home and live in an empty dormitory. I did not have to worry about getting a room. I did not have to worry about a large home, including its roof, gutters, outdoor painting, and so forth. I did not have to worry about any other jobs except being the chair of OT at the College. Sadly, I did not have the pleasure but also the responsibility for animals. Nikkie died before we moved, and we gave our two cats (Duke and Mindy) away; Duke to Jill and Mandy to Danny. Lots of "nots" were gone, and now a far simpler and calmer life prevailed.

The townhouse we selected was cleverly designed with two bedrooms, two and a half bathrooms, fireplace (electrified), and a two-story open loft that served well as my office. We had an extra-large deck built off the family room, and with high privacy fences on each side and open grounds and woods behind us, we had our own little haven for tranquil meals, especially breakfast. We had the basement finished into a large open office for Janice and extensive storage closets and shelves to accommodate her ever-increasing collection of Skin Care Cosmetics products, promotional materials, and paperwork. There was so much stuff that we had to keep one storage shed to hold the stuff that Janice couldn't part with but that we had no room for in our neat and tidy town house.

~~~~

Unfortunately, things were not simpler for Janice. She was now the one who had to make the drive back and forth to our hometown to run her weekly Skin Care Cosmetics unit meetings and for every other area Skin Care Cosmetics function. Her main customer base was in our hometown area, as were the women she recruited and trained to be members of her unit. It was hard to maintain the personal contact she once enjoyed so much. Beth had also built a unit of Skin Care Cosmetics consultants under her to the extent that she also became a sales director, and thus that made Janice a senior sales director. Both did quite well with their businesses, each winning numerous sales awards and cars.

Janice also tried to visit her mom in the nursing home as much as she could, but because of Sarah's increasing confusion, visits were very difficult. Combining a visit with her mom with a Skin Care Cosmetics function did not always work out. So it was more trips to our hometown. It was Janice's plan to become close to the local area Skin Care Cosmetics directors, but this did not work out. Janice missed her Skin Care Cosmetics friends and the camaraderie she enjoyed for so many years. However, in spite of these negative aspects of having departed our hometown, Janice did find a lot of joy in having me home every night, our townhouse, and the proximity to Annie and Bernie.

~~~~

Another pleasant event that happened in the same year that we moved to the townhouse was that Beth got married to Dan Russ.

A Simpler Life That Was a Godsend

Besides the usual good feelings surrounding any wedding, Beth and Dan got married in a most unique and special way. They had been together for a few years and wanted to get married. However, they did not want the typical big church wedding. So they instead decided to have a sort of "secret wedding." They found a quaint old mansion known as the Samuel Morgan Inn not far from where we lived. It was an old mansion restored as a great bed-and-breakfast that was just the right size for our intimate gathering.

The only people who knew about the wedding were Beth and Dan and, of course, Janice and me. Janice and Beth were reluctant to tell me for fear I would accidently slip and tell people what really was going to happen. However, they had to eventually tell me so that I could assist with some of the preparations. Everyone else thought they were coming to a Skin Care Cosmetics recognition dinner in Beth's honor. It was a small group consisting of Beth and Dan, Dan's mom and Dad, Bernie and Annie, Jill and her boyfriend Jim Bassett, Peter and his girlfriend Kathy, and Bernie II.

So on a snowy and cold December 28th of 1997, we all gathered at the inn. Beth was upstairs in their room, getting into her wedding dress as the rest of us mingled about waiting for Dan's mom and Dad to arrive. They had gotten lost on the way but in a short time arrived safely. Beth's Pastor and her husband also drove down from our hometown in order to conduct the ceremony, but they were also secreted away.

By way of announcements, Dan took his mom and Dad aside and told them that he and Beth were going to get married in a few minutes. Dan was concerned that his parents would be too shocked at this sudden news with no forewarning. Then as Dan and Bernie chatted away, he asked Bernie, "Are you up for a wedding?"

Bernie, a bit confused, responded with questions of his own, "You mean coming up? Right now? Here?" When Dan said yes to all the questions, there was great jubilation among our little group as everyone heard the news. With that, we moved into a larger room that was tastefully decorated for Christmas. A poignant moment occurred when Janice invited Annie up to the bedroom where

Beth was getting ready. I was in charge of starting the music as Beth, looking absolutely beautiful with her usual resplendent smile, descended the stairs.

The pretty room was robust with the joy we all felt for Beth and Dan and even greater for me as I drank in the collective sense of family and love that prevailed. Beth's Pastor added to the warmth and love in the room with the way she interacted with us all and performed the simple and meaningful ceremony. Beth and Dan danced as did I with Beth in a dance I dreaded ever since she was a little girl. I was always secretly emotional whenever we attended a wedding and watched the traditional father-and-daughter dance. Sad because it was the finalization that Beth was a little girl no more and another guy was now her number one.

Beth and Dan certainly gave our family a unique and rich memory that will always be special. They stayed the night at the bed-and-breakfast, and the next day they stopped to see Janice and me on their way home. They also brought us gifts: sweatshirts and mugs with the Samuel Morgan Inn emblazoned on both. Every time I put that shirt on or drink out of that mug, I reflect back on that exceptional night when our daughter got married in a most unusual way. They certainly added a significant page to the Talty saga, one that we all love describing to other people.

~~~~

After the wedding, we settled into life in our townhouse. We had not lived away from our hometown ever since our return in 1977 after three years away. This time it was different. We were different, but also there were other factors. The other time when we lived out of town, we were in a new city without our family or friends. Now right down the hill, Janice had her sister, and I had my brother. Bernie and I walked together almost every day. Janice hired Annie to help her with the secretarial parts of her Skin Care Cosmetics business. Bernie and Annie had become mainstays of the local community and knew everybody and everything about this pleasant small town. I also got to see Jill and Jim all the time at the College as well as in my courses as they progressed through the OT program. Jill was an outstanding student, and it gave me great pride for the other students and faculty to know that she was my niece.

~~~~

    Living in the townhouse also put me ninety minutes closer to one of my favorite places in the world; the Adirondack Mountains. I was able to suspend both of my canoes in our two-car garage so I could quickly load one on top of my SUV and head east and north. Janice and I, and sometimes just me, took numerous canoeing trips where we paddled onto some spectacular lakes with outstanding scenery. We pitched our tent, cooked meals on my backpacking stove, built campfires at night, and immersed ourselves in the outdoors. During the day, we took hikes, climbed mountains, and explored the area by canoe. Janice had not been an outdoors person, but she grew to love it as we progressed from our VW Camper to a pop-up camper that we pulled on the back of our station wagon when the kids were young to where we could really rough it on the ground, in a tent, in all kinds of weather. She even progressed to the ultimate test of backcountry camping where no toilets were available, and digging a hole was the only option. I was so proud of her!

    Janice and I were never as gregarious or as socially oriented as Bernie and Annie. They were far more engaged than we would ever be. I think people were surprised that we were not jumping into the multiple social activities that abounded in that other Talty household, but they were all still friendly toward us; and on the rare occasion we elected to participate, we were warmly welcomed.

~~~~

    A mixture of joy and sadness permeated our happy days in 1998, when two very happy events were sullied by one sad event that none of us anticipated. It was, of course, one of the most joyful days when Jill and Jim earned their B.S. degrees in OT from the College. It was like Jill had two sets of beaming parents, her mom and Dad and Janice and I, watching her walk up onto the Chapel steps to accept her degree from the president of the College. As is almost always the case, the weather on that Memorial Day weekend in 1998 was glorious. Sitting on the lawn in our chairs in front of the historic chapel overlooking the pretty lake could not have been a better scene. Also, as always, I processed (walked in) with the faculty to the cheers of the OT students, some of whom I had known for four years. It was a special treat to have Tommy and Karoline at the graduation and at Pat's wedding, which was the other very happy event. It turned out that Pat's wedding was the last time the five of us brothers would be together.

Janice's brother Frank and his wife, Jerry, had also come to town for Jill's graduation, and they were staying with Bernie and Annie. Jerry had previously been diagnosed with oral cancer but had been declared to be in remission. Unfortunately, the day before the graduation, Jerry became very ill and was unable to attend the graduation. In fact, her illness was so severe they left the next morning to return to Philadelphia. We found out later on that her cancer had returned. She resumed treatment, but it was in vain. She died that same summer.

~~~~

1998 was an eventful year for the Talty's with a mixture of blessings amid the tragedy of Jerry's reoccurring cancer and subsequent premature death. But we were not done with cancer and death. It was in 1999 that we got the call that Sarah was dying. Janice and Annie went in by themselves for some reason. I don't know if Bernie and I couldn't get away because of our work or if it was uncertain whether Sarah was gravely ill or not. Regardless, the girls undertook this sad vigil by themselves. Sarah survived the night and passed the following morning on May 6 of 1999. Getting her things from the nursing home was sad when one's whole life is reduced to one cardboard box plus a painting that wasn't Sarah's. This painting was not really ours, but whoever had gathered up Sarah's things included it with her other things. Annie said to take it when I asked about it, so I did. Interestingly, at some point, Beth asked for the painting, had it reframed, and it is now over Beth's family room fireplace.

Sarah's funeral was sad not only because of her passing but also that she had outlived all her siblings and that of her first husband's siblings except for Father Bob, who happened to be in town and was able to officiate at her funeral Mass. It was also sad to hear him speak about all those who had gone before Sarah. I also found it sad that with Sarah's death, our kids and Bernie and Annie's kids lost their only grandparent. I was heartened to recall that although Sarah abhorred the idea of ever going to a nursing home, by the time she was admitted to the skilled nursing facility, she was not really cognizant enough of her surroundings to realize it. She thought she was on a cruise and later on thought that she was living in a grand estate that Janice and I owned. These were certainly comforting thoughts. Sarah could rest well knowing that she had lived a remarkable life, always thinking of others first and "always giving others the benefit of the doubt."

~~~~

The simple life I had anticipated living in a small town, working just one job with many days off, and living in a townhouse with far less homeowner's responsibilities worked out pretty well until midway through 1999. We had the death of Sarah in May, and then soon after, Annie began to not feel well, and she feared that her tumor in her jaw had returned. Her oncologist examined her and said that there was no evidence that it had come back. It was a great relief for us all, and we returned to our simple and tranquil life.

However, it was that fall when Annie was seeing her dentist for a routine appointment that he discovered that the tumor was back. This was terrible news especially when she and everyone else believed her to be in complete remission based on the oncologist's evaluation just a few months previous. We were confused and enraged, but we all just hoped and prayed that it was caught in time and could be treated. Our simple life was further complicated when Annie ordered us not to tell anyone about the latest diagnosis that was confirmed with further testing and examination. Their daughter Jill was marrying Jim Bassett on November 6th of 1999, and with a honeymoon planned in Hawaii, Annie did not want to spoil it all with her bad news.

Jill's wedding took place in the chapel at the College and her reception at the classy Club 86 in a nearby town. Annie looked beautiful, and she and Bernie worked hard at pushing the bad news into the background so that Jill's special day would not be spoiled in any way. It was so hard to pretend that everything was fine. The four of us—Annie, Bernie, Janice and I—were the only ones laden with this awful news. I think we all just focused on the present and ignored what may be happening to us all down the road.

~~~~

God's hand was at work not only in helping us get through Jill's wedding but also in the decision to move to the townhouse and for me to just have one job. This simpler life with much free time would enable Janice and me to be a big help to Annie and Bernie in their difficult days ahead.

"Morning Has Broken"

"Morning Has Broken," the spiritual song popularized by Yusuf Islam (Cat Stevens), plays in my mind whenever I think of Annie. I picture a summer day, with both doors open at the back of St. Patrick's church, as we, what I think of as the "Big Four" (Annie, Bernie, Janice, and I) are exiting after the 8:00 a.m. Mass with "Morning Has Broken" playing. Annie is wearing a summery dress, smiling, greeting her many friends, and trying to persuade us to join them for coffee at their house or to go out for breakfast. She is pretty, confident, and eager for the day ahead to unfold regardless what it is to be. Regrettably, I usually declined these invitations because of my reclusiveness. Why did I not say yes every time? It would have made her and Bernie so happy.

~~~~

"Leiomyosarcoma." That is the terrible word that changed everything. Up until Annie was given this scary diagnosis, we never ever thought of her as having cancer. Leiomyosarcoma. She no longer had a recurring benign tumor of her parotid gland. Leiomyosarcoma of her head and neck is now what Annie had to face, and thank God Janice and I were living right near Bernie and Annie and had the time to support and accompany them on their dreadful journey.

Annie adopted a firm belief that she could get well. She would do anything that would help her overcome her cancer. Life was precious to Annie. So began an almost two-year odyssey of surgeries, radiation therapy, chemotherapy, hospitalizations, and doctor's appointments with specialists of many types. Annie tried to schedule her appointments around my schedule as much as possible so that the Big Four could share the ride and the emotional load. Janice and Annie began giving each other Christmas ornaments and little caricatures depicting the four of us as a team. The doctor's messages were sometimes vague and sometimes shockingly optimistic in comparisons to what other doctors had told us. We were often confused and depressed after many of the visits. It seemed it was best at times not to press the doctors too much because we all wanted to believe she would get better.

~~~~

It was Annie's wish that we keep things as normal as possible and to keep the more negative pieces of information to ourselves. In this vein, I asked her to come to one of my classes to act as a model for my clinical demonstrations. She was thrilled that I asked her. Annie's radiation therapy had resulted in some muscle weakness in her neck and shoulders, and since my course taught students how to do manual muscle testing, she would make a great model. The students loved her. She was funny ("You better take me to lunch after this."), and she really enjoyed helping students learn. The students sent her a nice card with lots of encouraging words. She treasured the experience as did I.

As her cancer progressed, the treatments became more extensive and aggressive. The residual pain and distortion of her appearance were challenging for Annie, but she persevered in her quest to live life as best she could. In addition to all she was going through personally, her health insurance was rejecting most of her claims, which generated stress she didn't need. I did my best to write appeals for every rejection and eventually persuaded them to pay the claims. It helped her in that she could just hand the denials to me, and I would take care of them. This, at least, removed one of her many worries.

As close as the Big Four was, we became even closer as we together navigated through the morass of Annie's cancer treatment and health insurance denials, appeals, and reversals. This was far more than any one person could handle, but we did our best to help her until we all became overwhelmed, anxious, and depressed. I had known Annie for over forty years, and what strength of character she demonstrated under these most adverse of situations. We were all praying like crazy that the next specialist or the next treatment would be the answer. I also prayed that I would have the strength to handle whatever was to come.

On October 16th, 2001, after a valiant fight of almost two years, Annie could fight no longer. Janice and Bernie were with her when she decided to sign a DNR (do not resuscitate) order after they talked it over. With that decision came her being taken off the medications that were sustaining her, put on a morphine drip, and hospice notified. Janice called me, and I picked up Jill and Bernie II and brought them with me to the hospital. We notified the rest of the family and close friends. Annie slipped into a coma and could no longer respond to us. For two days, the support of our family and prayers sustained us through this anguishing time. I was feeling the loss of my brother's wife, my wife's sister, my friend of over forty years, and a key element of the Big Four.

When the evening of the second day of our sad vigil arrived, everyone had left except for Bernie, Janice, and me. By midnight, we were all exhausted. The nursing staff was wonderful and brought in two recliners, which Bernie and Janice fell asleep in, while I stretched out and slept on four metal chairs I had arranged in a row. All we could hear as we drifted off to sleep was Annie's slow and rhythmic breathing. Then a most extraordinary thing happened. The three of us all awoke simultaneously around 3:00 a.m., when Annie stopped breathing. There were no sounds of distress; just silence. We called the nurse and, after checking her vital signs, said, "Yes, she's gone." How could we be shocked? I don't know, but we were.

~~~~

What a funeral Annie had! The funeral home was packed with Annie's many friends and family members from Victor and our hometown. The night before the funeral, I got inspired and composed a sort of homily combined with a eulogy. Janice and I delivered it with humorous allusions to Annie that was well-received. At the end, the packed church applauded enthusiastically. I'm sure Annie was very pleased with our message:

A Tribute to Anne Marie

Peter

"Let not your heart be troubled: you, who believed in God, believe also in me. In your father's house there are many mansions: if it were not so, I would have told you. I go to prepare a place for you. And if I go and prepare a place for you, I will come again, and receive you onto myself, that where I am, there you may be also."

14:13 John

Janice

Those mansions have just become a little brighter with special touches in each room. There are little throws, matching items in all rooms, and every item has little labels on the bottom in case they get misplaced. Anne Marie is very busy. There is a lot to be done to get our mansions ready for us, plus enhancing the mansions for all those who have gone before her. This is, of course, in between lots of visiting and catching up. There is also much shopping to be done. Heaven's QVC shopping network is experiencing a great surge. The clothing and jewelry departments are particularly stressed.

A Tribute to Anne Marie

Peter

"Now it came to pass, as they went, that he entered into a certain village; and a certain woman named Martha received him into her house. And she had a sister called Mary, who sat also at Jesus' feet, and heard his word. But Martha was cumbered about much serving, and came to him and said, Lord, dost thou not care that my sister hath left me to serve alone? Bid her therefore that she helps me. And Jesus answered and said unto her; Martha, Martha, thou art careful and troubled about many things: But one thing is needful: and Mary hath chosen that good part, which shall not be taken away from her."

Luke 10:30

Janice

Martha now has help. Anne Marie is moving about filling dishes and asking, "What else can I get you?" The newly enhanced mansions now have ample and delicious food served effortlessly by Martha, Anne Marie, and a legion of trained staff that move about all the mansions, asking, "What else can I get you?" Guests are particularly enthralled with the new dinner and desert items that draw on Anne Marie's extensive familiarity with the Food Channel. However, some of the gatherings lack a certain levity, but she assures everyone that when her husband, Bernie, gets here, look out!

Peter

We all remember that you could not be in Anne Marie's home for more than a few minutes before she would ask, "What can I get you?" It was one of her ways of welcoming guests, but it was also, and more importantly, the way she led her life. Thinking of the needs of others without ever thinking of herself. She found joy and pleasure in making those around her feel comfortable and valued.

Peter

"Paul wrote to Timothy, 'The time of my departure has come. I have fought the good fight, I have finished the race, I have kept the faith.'"

Timothy 2: 6–8

Anne Marie also has fought the good fight, finished the race, and kept the faith. The way Anne Marie fought the good fight impacted all of us here and countless others she met along the way. My daughter Beth wrote a letter to Auntie Anne while Anne Marie waged her last battle this past Sunday at Strong Hospital. Let us read parts of Beth's letter that says what we all feel in our hearts.

Janice

We love you very much! You mean the world to us! There are not enough words to express how we feel about you. We feel such love and admiration towards you. You have been such a wonderful example of how to live. You have taught us about courage, love, caring, parenting, friendship, the importance of family, acceptance, tolerance, determination, perseverance, will, about being a fighter, and, most of all, about truly loving life!

Peter

We know that we, your family, are not the only ones whose life you have touched in this way. You have passed these traits onto all those who were blessed enough to cross your path. Your friends, your neighbors, your coworkers, your customers, your doctors, your nurses, all were inspired by the way you lived with adversity. You are a special person. Your spirit is huge, and you brought joy to everyone with whom you interacted.

Janice

Our family is so incredibly special, and you are such a big part of that. The memories and stories are endless. Things that so bizarre that only our family could understand. Any occasion to get together became an event. We love each other so much and have so much fun together. You can always count on our family dinners ending up in an explosion of laughter. Even the quiet moments, which were rare, were so comforting and peaceful. I had such a tremendous childhood because of it. Your presence in our family gatherings will be greatly missed but will never be forgotten. Your spirit will be with us forever!

Peter

Even now, as we are gathered together, we experience your presence. This is not a holiday, but it is a celebration. A celebration of greatness! Greatness in the impact you had on so many in such an unassuming way. A celebration of life lived to the fullest and with a focus on the needs of others. A celebration of how you bettered the lives of others expecting nothing in return.

Janice

Notre Dame had its Rudy, and now so does our village. He didn't give up, nor did you. You were able to dance at your daughter's and son's weddings. You brightened many holidays, were part of the birth of two beautiful grandsons, saw your children become parents themselves, witnessed the baptism of Jeb, and experienced the ongoing love of your family as they took care of you in your final days.

Staying with this movie theme that I seem to be into, I am reminded of a character in the movie Steel Magnolias. When the character played by Julie Roberts passes, her friend said:

"That's all she ever wanted was to take care of all those that she loved so much. Unfortunately, her body was too weak to allow her to do that. Now that she is in heaven, she can watch over everyone that she loves, without the limits of her sickness."

This is how we can think of Anne Marie now. We have a special friend in the highest of places ready to help us. We can take comfort in knowing that you will always be watching out for us. We are counting on it. We will draw on your spirit in difficult times and rejoice in recalling the laughter of better days and times.

Peter

And Jesus said to Anne Marie: "Now about those mansions... Anne Marie, Anne Marie, Anne Marie. When you finish helping Martha... Your work on earth is done, but we are way behind up here. The gifts you left below will strengthen your friends and loved ones until they join you. The mansion you are preparing for you and Bernie will require a large stage and seating for thousands, a dance floor, and a bandstand with an elevated area for a set of drums."

Janice

And Anne Marie said to Jesus, "Yes, I have thought of all that and I have some ideas about colors, but before I begin, what else can I get you?

~~~~

Now came the pain of life without Annie. Trying to reengage in the activities of work and home seemed meaningless. We each, in our own way, tried going forward but would get that kick-in-the-stomach feeling whenever thoughts of Annie seeped into our consciousness. This was a terrible time for us all, but especially for Bernie. His life made no sense without his "A". I don't know how he did it, but he found the inner strength and resolve to go on. Janice and I tried to support him in any way we could, but we too were struggling.

~~~~

After almost four years of going through the motions of living, Bernie met Ann King. She lived in the same group of townhouses as Bernie and she was a widow. They found they had a lot in common and began going out together. They have been together for over ten years as of this writing. They bring happiness to each other, and Ann has been a fine addition to our family. At times, I think she saved Bernie's life; but in reality they made each other's lives so much richer. So as Bernie says, he got lucky twice, but I think we all did.

Grandparents? Us?

My son-in-law, Dan Russ, had bought an older home in a nearby suburb just north of our hometown, and he commenced to remodeling it with his usual skilled diligence. Dan's talents and expertise resulted in some amazing transformations as he gutted and rebuilt each room. Beth had moved in, and they subsequently married in the unique way I previously described. Beth and Janice had some great times planning and organizing sales meetings and attending local and national Skin Care Cosmetics functions.

Beth and Dan's lives changed in 2004, when she became pregnant. On October 25th of 2004 Luke Daniel Russ was born, and he was our first grandchild. I never thought much about being a grandparent and was surprised at how emotional it was for me at the hospital when Dan came out and told us that Luke was here. It was also emotional going in to see Beth and her newborn son. I think "surreal" is an overused word, but it really captured my feelings at that moment. When our kid had a kid, it was surreal.

Luke had some health issues that took a bit to resolve, so he was unable to go home with Beth. Of course, she spent a lot of time at the hospital; and eventually, everything stabilized enough that Luke was able to go home wearing a monitor. Once Luke was home, he required a lot of special care, and so Janice went in to help Beth while I stayed home and taught my courses. She stayed at Beth and Dan's during the week, helping in any way she could, and then returned home on weekends when Dan wasn't working. This routine continued for almost a month until Beth felt she could handle everything, and so Janice came home.

~~~~

However, Janice had to rush back because Dan had had an accident at work. He was at his brother's shop using a table saw when a sharp piece of wood flew back and punctured his abdomen. They rushed him to the hospital where they had to schedule him for surgery to close the wound. So, Janice went back in to help Beth. I was very worried about Dan and went right up to the hospital. I found Dan's mom and Dad in the surgical waiting room and visited with them while the doctors were examining Dan.

Then a nurse came in and said they were taking Dan to surgery right then, but we could see him for a moment. Like many things in my life, the next scene remains a permanent fixture in my brain: just as Dan's mom, Dad, and me exited the waiting room, they were wheeling Dan's bed out into the hall on his way to surgery. He beamed when he saw us all and quickly gave one of the best lines ever uttered by someone on their way to surgery: "Hey, I don't entertain under the best of circumstances. "This generated just the tension release we all needed, and after a few handshakes and hugs, off he went. I waited a bit but then drove home, knowing that Beth or Janice would call me when Dan was out of surgery. The surgery went well as Janice reported when she called me later on that night.

These were difficult days for Beth, but the way she handled it all was admirable. I was so proud of how she took care of Luke, delegated tasks to Janice, managed the house, visited with Dan until he was discharged, and then took care of him when he returned home. Janice stayed with Beth and Dan for another two weeks, which they both appreciated very much.

~~~~

Bernie and, before her death, Annie were familiar with the grandparent experience because Bernie, Junior's wife, gave birth to Michael, and Jill gave birth to Jeb both in 2001. Janice and I were novices. So after Luke was all better, Beth drove down to our townhouse with him to spend the day with us. We were pretty excited. Luke was so little and so cute. Janice and I slipped easily into the doting grandparent roles. Beth let me hold him as I turned pages in a colorful kid's book that he liked. I can still see him looking at the pages and then intermittently looking up at me. It was fun watching him being fed and watching him watching us and smiling. I still have those images cemented in my brain and a picture of me reading to Luke as he sits on my lap in our rocker is on my desk.

Being a grandparent was not what I expected. Naively, I never thought I would become like all the other people who became grandparents, always talking about every little thing their grandkids did. Now I was just as obsessed as everyone else who experiences this stage. Our visits to our hometown and the holidays had significantly more zest to them now that Luke was here.

My Sabbatical

One of the benefits of earning tenure at a college or university is that you can apply for a sabbatical leave to do research, engage in new learning, travel, and a variety of things that promote your professional growth, provided it is approved at a number of levels. At the College, a faculty member can elect at the time of application to be absent from their post for a full year at half pay or a half year at full pay. I knew you had to be in your faculty position for at least seven years and at the rank of full professor to even submit an application for a sabbatical. After I had surpassed my seventh year, I started figuring a way I could be approved for a sabbatical. However, an essential element of the application at the College is that you must submit a plan demonstrating how your teaching and administrative responsibilities will be covered during your absence. "Therein lies the rub." None of the other OT faculty were ever willing to serve as the acting chair. Thus, as the division chair, I was essentially precluded from ever going on sabbatical because I had no one to cover for me. I found this so frustrating, but there was nothing I could do about it. Or so I thought.

In 2001, a change came about in my role at the College that I never could have envisioned. It occurred in a most extraordinary way. I was in the midst of an interview with a prospective faulty member, Vicki Virtuoso,* and I was struck by the idea that the person sitting across from me could be our next OT chair. I was looking to step down anyway because I had been the chair for ten years, and most faculty members only do it for three or four years. So I audaciously said, "You know, looking at your curriculum vitae, I can see that you could be the chair of OT here at the College. What do you think?"

She was stunned and asked, "I hadn't thought about that. What would you do?" I explained that I would step back into my professor faculty line and teach the full complement of courses rather than the typical half-time release from teaching that chairs were granted. Then shockingly, she said, "I never thought about being a chair. Let me think about it for a minute . . . Yes, I would like to apply for the chair's position." Hot dog! "Barkis is willing!"

This then required me to make a series of phone calls to the Dean, to the members of the Professional Standards Committee (PSC), the OT faculty, as well as students who were all preparing to interview a potential faculty member, not a chair. They were all surprised that I wanted to step down, but all were agreeable as long as this is what I wanted. Wanted? I was dying to just be a faculty member without all the administrative aggravations that the chair's position entailed.

Vicki impressed everyone. The Dean and the PSC were particularly impressed that she was just finishing up her doctoral dissertation and would be in possession of her doctorate when she joined us in the fall of 2001. So the Dean made her an offer, which she readily accepted, and I was on my way to a new and better life.

~~~~

Vicki did not disappoint us. Her drive and organizational skills made it an easy transition for us both. She took over at a good time. I had weathered the storm of the depleted enrollment that struck the OT profession in the late '90s and planned and oversaw the transition of the OT program from a bachelor's to a master's degree. The program was now stable and back on track to regain its position as the flagship program of the College. Vicki was doing a masterful job at leading the program and required my guidance less and less. I was pleased that, at one point, she was so impressed with what she had inherited she remarked in private to me, "You (me) had the department running so well all I (she) had to do was not muck it up."

So now that the OT department was in Dr. Vicki Virtuoso's most capable hands, it was time to apply for my long-delayed sabbatical leave. I had taken some workshops and did extensive reading about a teaching methodology known as Problem Based Learning (PBL) and had taught several courses using this format. It has been used in medical schools, nursing programs, PT, OT, and numerous other healthcare professions' educational programs. For the past five years, I had used it in one of my upper-level courses that taught students clinical reasoning with good results. I could tell from the reading I did that there were different interpretations of PBL, and I wanted to see firsthand how various OT programs around the United States implemented PBL. I discussed all this with Vicki, and she was very supportive. She had the background to take over some of my courses, so that would not be an obstacle.

~~~~

As part of my sabbatical, I planned to canoe, camp, and hike in as many of the national parks as possible. I celebrated my sixtieth birthday by taking a sixty-two-mile round-trip bike ride from my home to the Women's Rights National Historical Park in Seneca Falls, New York, to get my Golden Eagle Pass. This would allow Janice and me to have free entrance to all the national parks. It was a beautiful day for a bike ride and well worth it.

I then did an online search of all the OT programs in the US that used some form of PBL and were in proximity to a national park. I planned to use the fall semester for my sabbatical leave, so because of the Academic Calendar at the College, I would have from June through January to complete my objectives. There was one problem in that none of the OT schools taught courses using PBL during the summer. The other problem was that camping out in a tent in Maine in November wasn't in our plans. So for those winter trips to visit cold-weather universities, I drew on a niece and a nephew of

Janice's that were very receptive to our staying with them. It also was serendipitous that one of the mecca's for PBL was at the University of New Mexico (UNM). With Tommy and Karoline living just outside of Albuquerque, New Mexico, this gave us a place to stay while visiting the UNM.

I eventually found eleven OT programs that used PBL, were near a national park or a family member, and the chair and faculty were receptive to my coming to visit. With these commitments solidified, I put together the sabbatical application packet with all the background and supporting information required. I also put together a budget to help offset the cost of gasoline, books I needed to buy related to PBL, and other expenses as we traveled about the country. Both the proposal and the budget were quickly approved and so for eight months learning about PBL was going to be my primary occupation with an ample immersion into *Ah, Wilderness!* What a country, or should I say, what a college!

Packing for my sabbatical was interesting for Janice and me. Because on a daily basis we would be camping in national parks, our clothing would be the usual stuff we wore when we canoed and backpacked in places like the Adirondacks. However, this would not be appropriate attire for visiting college campuses and meeting OT faculty. In addition, Janice planned on attending some Skin Care Cosmetics functions and thus needed her dress suits. So to accommodate our good clothes, I rigged a cargo net that was suspended from the inside roof of my SUV. This kept our good clothes clean and reasonably unwrinkled so that we could do a quick change as circumstances required. They also would not be dirtied from the moving of our camping gear in and out throughout our travels.

~~~~

I spent the summer taking care of the details related to the different excursions I planned for the fall and reading my PBL books. Rather than be away from the family and our home for five or six continuous months, I organized the sabbatical visits into five separate trips with plenty of downtime in between. These are the five trips and the universities I visited:

- St. Augustine University, University of North Carolina, and Scranton University
- Ithaca College: this was just a two hour drive from my home.
- University of Eastern Kentucky, University of New Mexico, University of Kansas Medical Center, and University of Missouri
- University of New England, Tufts University, and University of Sacred Heart

For this New England leg, we stayed with Janice's nieces Linda and Laurene near Boston.

- Mercy College: we stayed with Janice's nephew Greg Pepe in Manhattan.

I have always been enchanted with college campuses, and getting to visit these varied places in different climates was a joy in itself. At each one, the faculty were gracious and welcoming. The similarity among the OT students was interesting. Apparently, we all recruit or attract the same kinds of people. Even though there was significant variability in the way PBL was implemented, I learned so much from each visit. It was good to directly observe and help facilitate PBL sessions. I was thus able to teach as well as learn.

Driving enabled us to see beauty in different forms as we traveled south, north, east, and west. The only part of the country where our meanderings didn't take us was into the northwest. We really came to appreciate the national parks. We camped in eleven of them and visited a few more. The experiences that we had will be with us forever. How could we ever forget riding a mule down into the Grand Canyon, canoeing through the rapids of the two thousand feet deep Mariscal Canyon between Texas and Mexico on the Rio Grande river, camping on the isolated island of Dry Tortugas sixty miles out in the Gulf of Mexico, hiking the trails of Zion in Utah, or sleeping on the wooden platform called a "Chickee" in the backcountry of the Everglades? Never!

Our schedule of doing five separate trips with time back home in between worked out so well. It gave me time to reflect and read as well as time for Janice and me to reconnect with family members. Besides learning about PBL and connecting with family, we also had those wonderful outdoor experiences. The Internet was valuable in finding places of interest, but in most cases, we had to do what Janice and I often do, and that is to get information but then just go on faith. The number of times we have done this successfully throughout our married lives would astound most people.

I returned to campus in the spring of 2006 fully rested and even more enthused about teaching. There was some negative fallout from my being absent that I had not anticipated. Most of this came from the students that were the first to be going through our new master's degree program. They had become somewhat dependent on me and hadn't gotten to know Vicki very well. Vicki was an accomplished instructor and was very familiar with the material that was the focus of my course that she was teaching to this group of anxious students. I had given her all my notes and books, so she was well-prepared. Then a disaster struck. Just prior to the fall semester beginning, Vicki found out that a new edition of the textbook I used had just been released and that the edition my course was centered around was no longer available. Also, the new edition was totally changed, and so my notes and handouts were no longer useful.

It was a challenging semester for Vicki, but being the experienced professional that she was, she was able to adapt. She delivered the course the best she could under adverse circumstances but not to the satisfaction of a disgruntled group of students. She jokingly told me that she was so sick of hearing the students say things like: "Peter said" or "Peter told us to do it a different way" or "Peter said that's not the way to do it." What a time of undeserved madness for poor Vicki. However, I am still so grateful that she took over as the OT chair and supported me with my sabbatical leave.

Pat's Mercurial Life as an Adult

What I thought were now the beginnings of the good years for Pat were far from it. The good relationship between Pat and Carolina was short-lived. Why it didn't work is left to supposition. Whatever it was that caused her to pack her things and walk back up the street to her old trailer is not something we ever knew. He insisted that he did not know why she left. However, I do know that the person who signs on as Pat's life partner must be long-suffering with extraordinary forbearance. I don't think Carolina was that kind of person. Her work as a nurse's aide in a nursing home may have sapped all the care-giving she possessed. Also, she probably did not want someone as moody, needy, and self-centered as Pat. This is all conjecture on my part based on having tried to help him for many years and under a number of circumstances. I also lived with Pat for about a month when I was in the process of moving back to our hometown. His self-centeredness, moodiness, and lack of empathy made living with him difficult, and I was only there a month. So I can certainly see why Carolina opted for her old trailer and a life without the baggage Pat brought to their marriage.

Pat was very depressed over Carolina's leaving. Also, with us living out of town, we were not able to provide the kind of ready support we had provided when we lived on Wellingwood. With Carolina gone, he was back depending on Danny and his neighbors for transportation to the store, his doctor's appointments, and visits to the vet for his new dog "Sue". That dog's name in itself was strange.

Why would he name his new dog that replaced Dino with "Sue"? This was our revered sister's name, and as to why he chose to name a dog after her would take Freud, Jung, Carl Rogers, and the most brilliant members of the American Psychiatric Association years to figure out.

With Carolina gone, Pat spent vast amounts of time on the Internet doing research on things from our early lives like our neighborhood, the New York Central Terminal, downtown, other points of interest as they were when we were kids, and so forth. He also discovered various chat rooms and communicated with various people about who knows what.

He loved to do all this with his head phones on and his favorite tunes blasting through his brain with Sue asleep on the couch. His once-beloved trailer had lost its appeal, and he was now disgruntled about all the things that were breaking down and the overall decline of the trailer park. Sadly, like many people, the Internet became his refuge.

~~~~

He began talking a lot about a woman named Sleazy Cat* who lived in California. She was divorced and was supposedly quite wealthy as the result of a sports memorabilia company that she and her ex-husband operated. It was quite a shock to us when Pat announced that Sleazy was coming for a visit and staying with Pat in his crumbling trailer. What magnetism did Pat exude online that enticed Sleazy to make this trip from sunny California to the snowy northeast after only knowing Pat a few months? What a mystery this presented. Puzzling indeed!

When Sleazy arrived at the airport, she rented a car and found her way to Pat's trailer. Everyone in the family was asking the same questions: Who was Sleazy? What was she like? Why was she here? All we did knew was that Pat was quite happy, almost giddy after she arrived. We got to meet Sleazy in person at Peter's and Kathy's house

---

* The reason I chose to use unusual pseudonyms like these will become very apparent before this strange and tragic tale comes to its pernicious end.

when they hosted Christmas Eve. This was Luke's first Christmas, and so that added to the festive atmosphere that Peter and Kathy so aptly fostered.

However, on that night, Pat was very lethargic and kept falling asleep. Sleazy was very indulgent toward Pat, employing a sickening sweet voice: "Are you feeling tense? Do you want to take a little nap?" Who was this woman? I tried to learn more about her using the little bit of information Pat had told me. Pat told me she was once a high-ranking executive for Area 51 at Edwards Air Force Base near Roswell, New Mexico. I had asked her about this and other positions she supposedly held in the past and about the sports memorabilia company that she and her ex-husband owned, but she was not forthright or forthcoming. It was a difficult night for me.

She was reticent and actually quite evasive. Her answer to the big question about why did she leave sunny California and come to the cold and snowy northeast was bizarre: "It gets too hot in California. I love the brisk air here in the northeast. It's much better for my sinuses." Whacky! My continued efforts to learn more about her were unsuccessful as she continued to simply ignore me and dote on Pat. Whatever!

I think we in the family really wanted whatever would make Pat happy and for him to have the economic, emotional, and transportation support he needed. Sleazy seemed to provide all this regardless of what we thought about her bizarre decision making, unusual behaviors, obtuse style of communicating, and weird thought process. With her rented car, she was able to take Pat shopping, to his doctor's appointments, and for social and recreational rides around the area. They seemed content in Pat's trailer and in the trailer park. So our view was if he was happy, then we were too.

As the weeks and then months passed and Sleazy didn't return to California, I was confused. Pat didn't help to clarify things as he just laughed and said, "She loves it here, and she loves Sue (his dog) and my trailer." He was enjoying her apparent substantial largess as they went out to eat frequently and seemed to be having a great time. After a few fun-filled months, she did eventually return to California with a promise to return. They maintained their intense online communication, but Pat missed all the "services" Sleazy provided. Pat only had one bed and a small couch that would not accommodate either one of these heavyweights. Therefore, I suspect that their relationship would not be considered strictly platonic.

~~~~

On September 25th, 2004, Peter and Kathy got married. It was a beautiful wedding, and they arranged to have a big band with an excellent soloist to provide the music at the reception. Everything was so well done. Sleazy regrettably was unable to attend the wedding, but she asked Pat to "take plenty of pictures" using the disposable camera she provided. Pat was irritable and withdrawn throughout most of the day, and it took Bernie and me to cajole him into a more receptive mood. I found it sad that he wore his only suit coat: a bright green one that he bought when he and Carolina got married. Oh well, he had moved on, and now it was all about Sleazy.

Sleazy did return to the trailer. In fact, she moved in permanently. Confusing things even more, Pat disclosed that Sleazy was not divorced and that she was, in fact, still living with her husband, Wimpy.* According to Sleazy, as explained by Pat, Wimpy was fine with her moving in with Pat. Was this the crazy California lifestyle at work here or just two crazy Californians that Pat found on the Internet? We didn't have to wait long for the answer.

~~~~

Once Sleazy moved in, it became apparent that she was a germaphobe. She instituted all kinds of crazy rules like anything purchased had to remain on the enclosed porch for three days before they could be brought into the trailer. She made an exception for perishable items, but not for the mail, newspapers, and so forth. Because Pat's medications to control his seizures came in the mail and because he often waited just until he needed it before placing his order because of the costs involved, he was often at risk for seizures. This enraged me. Leaving his medication on the porch for three days was ridiculous and dangerous. His seizure medication was essential to any sense at all that he had for peace and well-being, but this was denied to him because of Sleazy's distorted and aberrant thoughts and behavior.

Another rule that was really more of a mandate was the prescribed ritual she instituted for every time Pat went outside. Terrified that he would bring in germs on his clothes or body, she made him strip in his enclosed porch, leave the clothes on the porch, and then take a shower. He did find it frustrating to have to adhere to this strictest of rituals every time he took Sue out or went out to get the mail or for any reason he went out. However, for whatever reason, he complied with Sleazy's unreasonable and bizarre directives.

Why did Pat, who would seldom do anything he didn't want to do, now do crazy Sleazy's bidding? My best analysis and conclusion was to put it simply: they were made for each other. She was fairly bright but certainly no genius. Any productive use of what intelligence she had was consumed by her deceitful and manipulative ways. Sleazy knew how to manipulate Pat for what I believed were unknown malicious reasons. He was, for whatever reason, a willing participant in her crazy games.

I say willing because throughout his life, he never allowed himself to be uncomfortable for long if he could help it. Long-suffering he was not. He remained a spoiled kid throughout his life, and he was getting his current needs met through Sleazy. What was frustrating for me is that he would whine and complain about Sleazy's ways, but I could not persuade him to throw her out no matter how strange and difficult his life with her became.

Another crazy Sleazy rule was that no one could come into the trailer except Pat. This prevented Bernie, Danny, and me from stopping in to see him, which each of us did on a routine basis. Sleazy also took to her bed (actually Pat's bed) and refused to get up except to go to the bathroom or to eat, which she did a lot. I learned all this through e-mails that Pat secretly sent me. These e-mails alarmed and enraged me. I was enraged at Pat for getting involved with such a crazy person and enraged at my own inability to do anything about it because he apparently didn't want anything done about it.

Sporadically, she would be less controlling and return to glimpses of her doting personality, which Pat loved. She had stopped renting a car for the duration and instead would rent a car just for a few days at a time to do shopping or other errands.

Then this incredulous story gets even weirder. Sleazy announced that her husband Wimpy was coming for a visit. We now knew that she was still married. That she originally said Wimpy was her ex-husband was just another of the zillion lies that she told. According to Pat, Wimpy was a nice guy. Like that mattered? He and Pat even became best friends. The three of them got along so well that they decided that Pat should come out to California and move in with them. Pat thought it was a great idea and didn't want to talk about anything else. I tried to talk him out of it, but to no avail. The three of them rented an SUV, and with Sue (Pat's dog), they drove across the country. They supposedly bought Pat a T-shirt and an ice cream sundae in every state. A highlight of the trip was a detour to Talty, Texas, an actual town just outside of Dallas so that Pat could take a picture of the town's name. They were going to stop to visit Tommy and Karoline in New Mexico, but Tommy nixed it because Karoline was not feeling well.

~~~~

Karoline and Tommy, mainstays of our family for so many years, were going through a very difficult time when Pat called wanting to stop by for a visit. Karoline's health problems had become much worse to the point that soon after Pat's phone call, she went on Hospice care. Janice and I got to see her before she died on May 30th of 2007. As a teenager, I lost Karoline's respect because of my deviant ways but gained it back by finishing college and building a solid family. Then I lost it again when I left Janice and moved in with Cookie. Fortunately, I did regain her respect by the way I led my life and supported my family thereafter.

~~~~

We found out later that the great cross-country trip that Sleazy and Wimpy took Pat on was paid for with Pat's credit card. They had no money. There was no lucrative sports memorabilia business. Wimpy was a supervisor for a large winery and probably was earning a good salary since he supposedly had been there for several years. However, besides being a germaphobe, Sleazy was also a shopaholic. I saw the direct evidence of this when I helped Pat clean out his trailer after Sleazy had returned to California. She loved to order things online. Lots of things. Things they didn't need. Sometimes two and three of the same thing. If she bought a rug shampooer, it would still be in the box; never opened, never used, and there would be two of them. Pat's trailer was jammed with brand-new stuff. She had enough toilet paper and cleansing pads to last years. The sad thing was that all this impulsive, uncontrollable buying put Sleazy and Wimpy in tremendous debt. That is why Pat had to finance the cross-country trip, which put him in even greater debt than before.

~~~~

Once they reached California, Pat sent me pictures that he secretly took of Sleazy and Wimpy's house. It was a small, weather-beaten, somewhat decrepit-looking ranch in an older neighborhood. However, it was the photographs of the inside that were very disturbing. The clutter and the chaos of each room made it difficult to even figure out what each room was. Every room was filled with clutter just like the homes seen on that TV show *Hoarders: Buried Alive*. Every room was filled. There was no table, countertop, or chair that wasn't stacked precariously with a conglomeration of papers and boxes. It was also very dirty. How does a supposed germaphobe live in such a place? There was floor to ceiling and end to end trash or whatever in the garage with only a path to the washer and dryer. I still have the pictures that show the hell in which Pat chose to live.

He chose this willingly because he believed Sleazy, who said that she and Wimpy were going to "get this all cleaned up before you get here." One day, after Pat had been there for a few months, Sleazy announced that she had bought a large fan that sprayed a mist. This fan was intended to cool the three of them as they cleaned out the garage. This magic fan was still in the box, and the clutter was worse a year after the fan was delivered. "Queen Sleazy" had decreed that the de-cluttering could not go forth, so nothing was done about the squalid conditions in which Pat now had to live.

On one impulsive buying binge, Sleazy bought three La-Z-Boy recliner chairs: one for each of them. I remarked to Pat that they were "Just like the three bears." The picture of the living room shows the three new lounge chairs surrounded with piles and piles of stuff. Pat said that he stayed in his bedroom as much as possible or else he went out on his scooter to get away from the chaos and the squalor (my words).

~~~~

Apparently, Sleazy was extremely tyrannical in controlling her clutter. She would not let Wimpy or Pat throw anything out or rearrange her things. Tantrums coupled with loud bellowing (Pat's word) were her common responses if anyone tried to straighten up or clean the filthy accumulations she vehemently controlled.

Because he was immersed in the chaos of life with Sleazy and Wimpy, Pat was able to witness firsthand just how impulsively they spent money. According to Pat, as their little nondescript house increased in value, Sleazy and Wimpy would take out a home equity loan and then just go on a spending spree. Again, according to Pat, they did this twice. They did it once before he knew them and then again when he was living with them in California. The La-Z-Boys were a part of one spending spree along with some gambling excursions (oh yes, she had a gambling problem too) to a nearby casino where Pat was their guest.

There were bright spots in Pat's otherwise miserable life. He loved the California weather, and he spent a lot of time riding around the little town in a motorized scooter that he or they bought. I was never sure who was paying for all this. In his travels around the community, he made friends in a little coffee shop, met some friendly neighbors, and became a regular attendee at a small church. Beyond that, his only peace came within his bedroom with his beloved dog, Sue. There, he could watch his TV and replay some of his favorite old shows like *The Honeymooners* and *Green Acres*. He had bought the complete set of some of his favorite shows and enjoyed watching them over and over again. His music and headphones provided another escape from the hell in which he chose to live.

~~~~

After several months out West, Pat fully realized what a big mistake he had made. This was confirmed one day on the phone. As he so succinctly put it, "I fucked up big-time this time, boy!" Yes he did, but extricating him from this mess was beyond anything me or anyone else in the family could do. Even if we had been able to bring him back home, the question was, then where would he live? His trailer was gone, and none of us had enough money to buy him another one. Then there was the extreme high cost of his non-generic seizure medication, which is covered by California's Medicaid program, but not in our state. No, the grim reality was that he had to stay in California, and worse, his monthly income from his Disability Social Security was not sufficient for him to move out of Sleazy's and Wimpy's stressful and disgusting house. Tragically, he was stuck. I felt bad for him, but I also knew that there was no alternative. Unfortunately, it only got worse for him.

Because of all Sleazy's bizarre behavior and rituals, life was hell for Pat. I think she was able to manipulate Pat as well as Wimpy to the extent she did because they were both inadequate and needy men. Bewilderingly, Pat and Wimpy both loved Sleazy and were taken in by her clever talk. She fostered a dependency in them. On Pat's part, he was sucked all the way in and followed all her demands, and then it was too late.

I realize now that we lost Pat once he found Sleazy. He was no longer interested in spending time with anyone in our family or even hearing what was going on with us, our kids, or our lives. It was like Sleazy was this great enchantress with whom he had become completely mesmerized. Her insidious ways became fully entrenched when she moved into his trailer. He would, on occasion, go out with one of us (she absolutely forbade any of us from entering Pat's trailer), but his life was consumed with following Sleazy's erratic and eccentric directives.

~~~~

The whole living arrangement when she stayed with Pat in his trailer was very contradictory. One moment, Pat would be complaining about Sleazy and her queer ways but then the next moment talking about something Sleazy had promised him or about their great sex life. He took great delight in sharing the latest episode with peals of laughter. We never understood why she stayed or why he let her stay. When I would offer a suggestion about sending her back to California, he was quick to say things like, "But she is good to me. I get lonely, and it's nice to have her here." So obviously, he was finding enough positives that suggestions about changing the situation were summarily rejected. He even got angry with me for suggesting such a thing. These cyclical discussions happened frequently enough that I lost interest in participating in them and just laughed along with him as he described her latest antics.

Why? That was the big question. Why would Pat remain in such a relationship? One in which his daily life was now so replete with strife? All my education and clinical experience in mental health leads me to formulate one hypothesis: they were both nuts! Speaking more professionally, I think we have two very inadequate personalities with overlays of numerous dysfunctions. His lifelong struggle with seizures, multiple medical conditions, and his extreme self-centeredness found acceptance and feigned understanding in Sleazy's imagined self-importance, germaphobia, obsessive compulsiveness, manipulativeness, emotional lability, profound sense of self-pity, narcissism, and denial of reality. Add to this morass was the fact that they were both very obese where eating provided them with great pleasure. What resulted was an extremely dysfunctional symbiotic relationship where each of their abnormal needs and behaviors dovetailed perfectly.

Once he abandoned his trailer and sold or gave away most of his possessions, he had no way of returning. He was stuck forever in the madness of life with Sleazy and Wimpy. I could really no longer be my brother's keeper because of the enormity of the mess in which he had become entangled.

~~~~

Pat's sad life got even sadder during the two years he was living in California. His despondency was worse each time we talked, and then he got very sick in November of 2007. He had terrible back pain and flu-like symptoms, but Sleazy would not take him to the doctor's. She had convinced Pat that he didn't have to go, and he accepted it until the pain was just too great. It had me so enraged and frustrated because she was so nice to me on the phone saying that "Pat was getting better, and I'm taking very good care of him" and would not take him to the hospital or to his doctor. Sleazy always portrayed a sense of omnipotence and that she always knew best. Pat was, in fact, quite enamored with Sleazy's stories of career successes and medical expertise, but his pain was so great that nothing she prescribed was working. According to Pat's e-mails, which she always read, he was not getting better, only worse. He was always guarded about what he said about life with Sleazy because she would go berserk if he said anything negative about her. However, now Pat's pain was just too great to ignore or deny.

Eventually, they took him to the doctor's, and after an examination, they told Sleazy to take him right to the hospital where he was admitted in January of 2008. He was diagnosed with advanced and untreatable pancreatic cancer. His doctor was very open and told all this to Pat. I had many phone conversations with Pat, Sleazy, and Pat's oncologist who turned out to be a very kind and sincere man.

He was direct and clear but also genuinely sad as he explained that nothing could be done. I was devastated. We all were. Because of my anger toward Sleazy's protracted response to Pat's pain, I could not, at the time, hear the oncologist when he said that even if Pat had come to him in November, when the pain first started, the outcome would not have been any different. The type of cancer Pat had was usually untreatable at the point the patient first experiences the characteristic back pain. Regardless, perhaps getting him in earlier could have reduced his pain. I don't know.

As angry as I was at Sleazy's reticence to get Pat to a doctor, I could tell she had feelings for Pat and may have been as sad as the rest of us. At least she sounded genuinely bereft over the phone when she talked about losing Pat. It seemed I came to trust and believe her more during this time than I did in the past. It was she who kept me informed about Pat's daily status. She spent hours at the hospital with Pat, and Wimpy was there a lot too.

~~~~

Since Pat was not going to survive, I became obsessed with getting him away from the craziness of Sleazy and back home with the family that cared so much about him. As my brother's keeper coupled with my love for him, I could not let him die in a place where he had lived miserably for too many years. This was a lot to ask of Janice, but I had to ask. Janice once again showed her great heart when I asked her what she thought about my bringing Pat back here to die in our house. Without hesitation, she said, "I would like for us to do this. We have the spare bedroom, and he could have his own bathroom. How would you get him back here?" This was just the way she is: not thinking about what it will do to our lives but only what Pat needed. She was and continues to be an amazing person. She even began looking into home care and hospice services that we expected to utilize once I got Pat back here.

I asked Pat's doctor about his ability to fly back East, and he said, "I think he will be fine for traveling, but it must be soon. He doesn't have much time." I then had to convince Pat to come back East to die, and once I said we would bring his dog, Sue, back also, he agreed.

My plan was to rent a large SUV that would accommodate a large crate for Sue to get us to the airport. At this time, I was communicating a lot with both Sleazy and Wimpy about travel plans and Pat's condition. I asked Wimpy to purchase a large dog crate to accommodate Sue and that I would reimburse him for it once I got out there. I wasn't sure if Pat was up to a large and boisterous black Lab jumping on him during the two-hour drive to the San Jose airport, and thought a crate would be best. Bernie offered to come with me, which I was glad of because who knew what I was going to find out there.

~~~~

Janice and Ann went to work getting airline reservations for the next day and return flights for Bernie and me and Pat's dog. We had to fly into San Jose, pick up the SUV, and drive the few hours up to where Pat lived with Sleazy and Wimpy. Sleazy said the hospital was not far from their house. We changed planes in Chicago, and I decided to call Pat before we boarded our flight to San Jose to let him know what time we expected to be seeing him. He was agitated and lethargic, and when I said something lighthearted, he chastised me with, "Peter, this is bad. This is no joke." I told him not to worry. We would be there as soon as we could, but our conversation had to end because the plane was getting ready to take off. Unbeknownst to me, this was the last time I would talk with him.

We had a very difficult time getting the SUV at the San Jose airport. Apparently, they did not have the Ford Expedition that I had reserved, but they didn't tell us that. We spent an enraging hour there pacing an empty car rental agency, and then they gave us the news that they were giving us a Cadillac Escalade instead of the Ford Expedition. It seemed to take forever before the transaction was complete and we could depart. Bernie and I were looking forward to Pat seeing this high-end vehicle we were going to use to get him to the airport. We reminisced a lot about Pat as we made the two-hour drive to the hospital near where he lived.

Walking into the hospital at about 7:00 p.m. was unsettling, but not just because of Pat. The very large waiting room was filled with sick little kids being held and comforted by their worried parents. There had been a flu epidemic in the area, and the hospital's emergency room was overwhelmed. We were directed around to the unit where Pat's room was, but we couldn't find him at first. We mistakenly went into a room where a large bald-headed man with big glasses was seated slumped over a bedside table. Bernie and I looked at each other, asking if it was Pat? We checked the name on the door plate and found out that it wasn't him. At the nurse's station, they directed us to another room where we found Pat in a semiconscious state. Our efforts to arouse him were unsuccessful. The most we elicited was a low moan.

Bernie and I got to meet Pat's doctor whom I had spoken with several times by phone over the past few days. He explained that Pat was deteriorating much faster than they had anticipated. He did not feel Pat would live very long. I knew he was very sick, but to hear that his end was imminent was sad beyond words. It was very emotional to see Pat like this. In many ways, it reminded me of seeing him so many other times after he had been through his surgeries. Of course, in those instances, we were confident that he was going to survive each of those other surgeries and then be better for having gone through them. Knowing that he was not going to be going home from this was depressing indeed. I could not stop thinking of all the sad times Pat had in his life. I'm so glad Bernie was there to help me through all this.

Sleazy had been at the hospital all day and had gone home because she was exhausted. She came back that night with Wimpy. The four of us kept that loneliest of vigils, waiting for Pat to pass. It was an awful time for us all. Even though I now knew that Sleazy was dysfunctional on many levels, during this waiting time, she seemed genuinely sad for Bernie and me. Wimpy seemed normal, and he too was sad. Because Bernie and I had not eaten, we decided to go get something to eat and then come back. Sleazy had our cell phone number and promised to call us if anything changed.

We drove to an Italian restaurant that Wimpy suggested. It was a subdued dinner. We were anxious to get back to the hospital. We ate quickly and returned to join Sleazy and Wimpy. We spent the time in Pat's room, meandering out into the hall or sitting and talking in the little waiting area across from his room. The staff paid little attention to us, which I found deplorable. This was not a warm and supportive environment for loved ones anxiously awaiting death. Unrealistic as my thinking was, I had hoped Pat would at least know we were there or better yet wake up. He did not wake up, and he died after a few hours of labored breathing. It did help to have Sleazy and Wimpy there to talk about Pat, but I would later learn that it was all a sham. I was duped by Sleazy. Her pleasant and caring demeanor led me to believe that she truly was a caring person and that all the things Pat had said about her were exaggerations or outright fabrications on Pat's part. It would not be the first time Pat's depiction of a person was not accurate or that he didn't tell the truth. Throughout the whole ordeal, Sleazy presented herself as a woman who was about to lose a loved one, and I felt a real affinity with both her and Wimpy.

Then at one thirty in the morning on February 9th of 2008, Pat was gone. I tried to view his passing as a blessing, but I selfishly missed him terribly. I then called Janice to give her the sad news in my choking and stilted way. We both just cried on the phone, unable to talk, and with "I love you," I hung up. Janice was going to call the rest of the family in the morning. She and Ann then went to work to get our airline reservations changed so that Bernie and I could return home after we made the arrangements. Sadly, we were coming back without Pat or Sue.

Making the arrangements was sort of comforting. I had to become very task oriented to help me move through my initial devastation. Sleazy was helpful as she came across as a model of efficiency with a wealth of information about the area. She rapidly told us about a motel, nearby restaurants, a funeral home, and so forth along with detailed directions. Wimpy would return the dog crate. "Glad I saved that receipt." We arranged to have Pat cremated as he had requested. Also, following his wishes, we would have his ashes (the cremains in funeral director's parlance) buried (interred) with our Dad at the family cemetery. Knowing that Sleazy and Wimpy were strapped financially and that they had incurred some significant veterinary expenses for Sue, I suggested that they sell Pat's scooter and his TV as compensation. She appeared cavalier as if money was no problem for them, but I could see that Wimpy was very appreciative and relieved.

Bernie and I then went to a Sleazy-recommended motel for some needed sleep. We were exhausted, but I was still surprised we slept as well as we did. The next morning we went to an early Mass at a nearby Catholic church they told us about at the motel, had breakfast, and drove to the funeral parlor where we had previously arranged to have Pat cremated. I don't remember why, but we couldn't take Pat's cremains back on the plane with us. They had to be shipped to us in a week or two. After we paid for the cremation, we made the two-hour trek back to the San Jose Airport, dropped off the car, and boarded our plane for home.

~~~~

It was good to be home and to see Janice. Bernie had to still drive home, so he left right away. I had Monday to get ready for my class that I had to teach the next day, pack my stuff, and talk with everyone. Once again, keeping busy was helpful, but I knew from past experience that not taking time to grieve can be harmful in the long run. So I did plenty of crying to the extent that reading and preparing lectures along with talking on the phone took much longer with my intermittent crying. The tears were not only about missing Pat, but I cried much more whenever I thought about how much of life he had missed. I also cried when I thought about the disparity between my full and rewarding life and the one he had to live. Very sad! Rest well, my brother.

Sleazy's Final Blow

Throughout the time we were with Sleazy in California, she impressed me with how distraught she was over Pat's death. Because she was so distraught, I was reluctant to press her on our wanting to see Pat's room and just where he had spent the last few years of his life. When she said, "I just can't go into his room right now," I stupidly believed her. So regrettably, we left California without gaining access to Pat's room. We knew he had photographs of the family and other things that we valued, but alas, we left with nothing, not even a glimpse of his room.

Now I was the one that was distraught. Of course, I was distraught over losing Pat, but now this was compounded with us having nothing of his to help keep his memory alive. Sleazy told us to call her, and she will "get up the courage to go through his room and send us things of value that she found." Fair enough. However, after a few weeks without any calls or e-mails from her, I began calling her. No one ever answered, but I left messages on at least ten of the several calls pleading with her to call me back. Finally, she called. The conversation was more of a circuitous monologue on her part. I had to eventually wrest the control from her and ask if it would be okay for me to come back out to California just to go through Pat's room. She reluctantly agreed to my coming back out, and we settled on a date that would work for both of us.

~~~~

Janice and I were taking a trip to New Mexico to visit Tommy and Karoline, so we thought we would fly up to San Jose from Albuquerque, rent a car, and drive to Sleazy's house. Sleazy said it was fine that we come. She even said that "maybe our being there would give her the courage to go into his room." Feeling that I was imposing on Sleazy and Wimpy, I offered to take them out to dinner on the night we arrived at a place of their choosing to show my appreciation. Sleazy suggested that we meet at an Applebee's near their house, and that is what we did. This ended up being the most boring and enraging dinner I ever experienced. Sleazy talked nonstop for three hours! It was all absolute balderdash! She talked so much that she hardly ate, and by the size of her, it was obvious that this was rare. Pat often talked about her excessive eating: "One night she got up and made herself five sandwiches, ate them all, left all the stuff out on the counter, and went back to bed." I was completely powerless to get her to answer my questions directly. She would go off on tangents of circumstantialities that none of us, including Wimpy, could follow.

As we finally concluded our dinner monologue, the conversation went as follows:

Me: "We must leave on our flight in three days, so can we come over tomorrow?"

Sleazy: "No, that wouldn't work. I have to go to my mother's."

Wimpy: "I get home at five o'clock tomorrow. You could come over any time after that."

Sleazy: "No, no. You have to come with me to my mother's to help me. Call me tomorrow, and we will work something out."

Me: "Okay, great. I'll call you first thing in the morning. I really appreciate this."

~~~~

Janice and I returned to our motel room ranting and raving to each other about what an idiot Sleazy was. The question that we kept asking was why did she say it was okay for us to come there if she was not going to let us in? We went to significant expense with airfare, car rental, motel, and food, but she seemed unconcerned about this. Her only concern was herself.

Whatever impressed Pat about Sleazy's supposed great intelligence escaped both Janice and me. Wimpy seemed a decent fellow but was absolutely under the control of crazy Sleazy. I knew we had to pretend that we were impressed with her and really believed all her concocted stories of accomplishments and the detailed descriptions of the numerous good deeds she performed for Pat. I knew from Pat's many stories that Sleazy was a liar and exaggerator, and now Janice and I could see it so clearly for ourselves. How and why did he ever tolerate such a deceitful, self-centered, and bombastic person for all those years?

So then began the frustrating game of calling and waiting. As agreed, I called Sleazy the first thing the next morning, got her voice mail, and left a message to please return my call. I left this same message at least twenty times, but she never called me back. We had Pat's address, and so we went to Sleazy and Wimpy's house at least six times, and we varied the time of day in hopes of catching one of them at home. We rang the bell and knocked but to no avail. There were no windows in the garage for me to see if their car was there, but then I remember the photos of the garage that Pat had sent me, and I knew there was no way a car could get in that cluttered garage. Also, there were no windows that were without shades or curtains for us to see in, so that was of no help. Strangely, there were also no neighbors around to ask of Sleazy's and Wimpy's whereabouts.

Out of sheer desperation, I went to the local police department to see if they could help me in some way, but of course, they could not break in or help us since no crime had been committed. Although no real crime was committed, the life Sleazy forced Pat to live should have been punishable, but of course, it wasn't.

~~~~

So sadly, our time was up, and we had to leave California. Janice and I were so angry at Sleazy. What was Sleazy's motivation for agreeing to have us come and then thwarting my efforts to get in to Pat's room? I am not sure, but I think it was shame. How could she let us see the squalor in which she and Wimpy lived? Her ego would not permit us to see the reality of what we saw in Pat's photos of her cluttered house of disarray. In order to protect her fragile and overinflated sense of self, she had to lie and talk nonstop at dinner, hoping that we would just go away. When this proved unsuccessful, she had to avoid us by not answering her phone or returning my calls.

We were out of time and had to leave. It seemed my rage temporarily supplanted my grief. She knew how short our window was, and so I believe she waited until it was safe to return my call. We were at the airport when she finally called. She was all apologies, giving excuses about having to take care of her mother who had fallen or some other story. I could hardly listen and cannot recall now what she gave as the reasons she gave us. Janice, being more tolerant than me, patiently explained that if we had had known, we could have changed our flight. She got more of Sleazy's ramblings, and I told her to just hang up. What was the point in listening to her babble on and on? We were screwed.

When I got home, I contacted the life insurance company where I knew Pat had a small policy ($5,000) that he had bought years ago, naming me as the beneficiary. Surprise! The insurance company informed me they had already been contacted by Sleazy! She was trying to get his insurance, but she couldn't find the policy. Of course, not being named as the beneficiary and not being a relative, she had little success in doing so. I didn't have the policy either, but by being able to provide all the information the insurance company required, they were going to make payment to me. Tommy, Bernie, and Danny all agreed that this money would be used to cover all the expenses we had incurred for our two trips to California.

~~~~

Sleazy's Final Blow

The enraged child in me caused me to make one more call to Sleazy. Of course, no one answered, but I left this message: "Hi Sleazy and Wimpy. This is Peter Talty. Hope you both are doing well. I just wanted to save you any more trouble. I talked with the Prudential Insurance Company, and they told me that you were inquiring about Pat's life insurance. Well, you can stop your painstaking search of Pat's room. Because I am the beneficiary named on the policy, they are making payment to me even though I do not have the policy itself in my possession. Take care, Peter." A very satisfying phone call indeed! She certainly did deliver the final blow, but I got some satisfaction in leaving my message.

About three or four weeks after I made that pleasurable phone call, I received a large envelope with Pat's insurance policy in it. There was a note enclosed that just said something like, "Here's Pat's insurance policy. We thought you might want it." The note was signed "Wimpy." What a bizarre ending to the bizarre Sleazy and Pat saga. I do end it here because Pat is gone along with all the things he loved. I sure hope and pray his new life is far better than the one he had. Rest well, my brother.

More Grandkids?

We were so enjoying Luke, and then we got news that more grandkids were coming! Both Beth and Pete's wife, Kathy, became pregnant, and both were due in June of 2006. This was great news, and the way we came upon this news was an interesting sequence of events. It started with Peter calling us and asking us to check out an e-mail he had just sent us. So when I opened his message he had sent us a copy of a sonogram that was his way of informing Janice and I that Kathy was pregnant. I didn't know what it was, but Janice knew immediately and started crying. However, he asked us not to tell anyone else because he and Kathy wanted to tell everyone at Thanksgiving. Unbeknownst to us, Beth was also pregnant, but she kept her news quiet so as not to spoil Kathy's and Peter's surprise (he had called her with their news). Before Kathy made her big announcement, Janice was telling Beth that she (Janice) had had a dream that she (Beth) was pregnant. Beth and Dan laughed about Janice's dream, which she told us later was only off by about a week.

So now here comes my old friend disparity. We were living out of town, and seventy-five miles away are living our two kids, their spouses, and our soon-to-be three grandchildren. It is now customary that when disparity is awakened in me, change is soon to follow. The change I was pondering was another move: could we sell our townhouse and find a home near Peter and Beth? When I told Janice my thoughts, she was in total agreement that this is what we needed to do.

More Grandkids?

A couple of years ago, we never would have considered leaving Bernie and moving back to our hometown, but God was at work in our lives once again. Bernie had had such a difficult time adjusting to life without Annie that we knew he needed us close by, and we knew we would never leave him as long as he needed us. However, things changed when he wandered up the street one day to a garage sale and met Ann King.

I now had the question about my job. As part of my sabbatical agreement, I was expected to remain at the College for one more year. The old housing issue I had experienced before was still present and was even worse because there were even more students wanting to live on campus. It seemed either resigning or retiring effective next year were my only options. It was too far to commute from our hometown, and I could not afford to rent an apartment for use during the week. I then went to talk to Vicki, the chair of OT. She was alarmed that I was looking to leave. I really had become a mainstay of the OT department as well as the College, and she did not want me to leave. So when I told her that the only reason I was leaving was because of housing, she told me about an option I had never considered. The College had a two-bedroom, fully furnished, two-story Cape Cod-style house that they rented out to various guests visiting the campus on weekends. During the week, an English professor from Vermont lived there. I knew him well. I just never knew where he stayed.

So I contacted him and also Conference Services who were both fine with me sharing the house. I set it up that I would start staying there beginning in the following fall semester. Vicki was so pleased that I was staying that she made sure my courses were all scheduled on a Tuesday through Thursday basis, so I only had to be there three days a week. Considering that the semesters were only fifteen weeks long, it was only thirty weeks a year and three days a week that I actually had to be on campus. Of course, I still had all the preparation for lectures and the administrative tasks that went with my position. However, this left ample time for canoeing, backpacking, cycling, family, and grandkids!

The Sale and the Search

Everyone in the family was pleased that we were going to move back to our hometown to be near our growing families. Even Bernie thought it was the right thing for us to do. Peter and Beth had bought homes within eight blocks of each other, and so we decided to concentrate our search for a home in the towns near our kids. We also wanted to find a ranch-style home because the stairs involved in living on three floors in our townhouse had raised havoc with Janice's arthritic knees. So all we had to do now was to sell our townhouse and find and buy a ranch-style house near our kids.

On our end, Janice and I decided to sell our townhouse on our own, but we needed information about what comparable homes in our area sold for and what would be considered a reasonable price for our home. This is information realtors provide as part of the listing process, but I didn't want to pay the realtor's fee. What I did instead was call the most successful realtor in the area and ask her if she would be willing to give me the information I needed with the condition that if we were not successful in selling it ourselves, we would give her the listing. She agreed to this, came right over, went through the house, and gave us the information we needed about comparable houses sold and a price she thought our house would be able to command. We thanked her and went to work.

Something Janice and I had learned was how to prepare and present our houses. We had to learn all this through experience because in 2006, the *Home and Garden* TV show didn't exist. Realtors

The Sale and the Search

often told us that open houses didn't really sell a house, but they do help realtors find prospective home buyers and sellers. This had not been our experience. We sold all our houses by running open houses, and we planned to do the same thing again.

We cleaned out as much as we could. Cleaned and shined the chrome and brass throughout the house, washed windows and mirrors, and got every piece of glass shining beautifully. To give the house a fresh smell, we put an apple pie in the oven. Then came the staging, and this we knew can turn a looker into a buyer. Everything had to look lived in yes, but lived in by the two biggest neat freaks ever. The flyer we put together bulleted the numerous amenities and improvements we added to the house, especially the finished basement. We set the price significantly higher than any of those that previously sold because we were confident our house was a cut above. I advertised in the local newspaper and put signs up all around the neighborhood, at our church, and the local supermarket announcing the open house.

The open house was a big success based on the number of people it brought in. We had lots of people saying the price was fair and that they were going to be putting in an offer. Of course, saying and doing ain't the same. In spite of the numbers of people we got to come through our townhouse and their very positive comments, we received no offers. After a few more days of no offers, we decided to list it with the realtor that I had first contacted.

~~~~

Janice called the realtor the next day, and she once again came right over. One of the things that concerned Janice (I was at work) was that the realtor was insisting that we provide a list of the people that came through our open house. In this way, if she ended up selling our house to one of them, we would not have to pay her the realtor's fee. Unfortunately, we did not have such a list. This posed a problem for both the realtor as well as us. The way it was left, the realtor took pictures of the different rooms and put her sign in the

The Sale and the Search

window with the understanding that Janice would talk it over with me and decide what we wanted to do about the list.

Janice was quite distraught after the realtor left and sat down almost in tears over the situation we were now in and prayed for some sign about what we should do. Then God went to work. The doorbell rang, and it was a woman who had gone through our open house, and she was very anxious because she saw the realtor's sign. She was both nervous and eager to put in an offer. Because Janice hadn't signed anything, we were still free to sell it ourselves. It was a brief conversation with her willing to pay almost our full asking price, and we had a deal. Janice notified the realtor of this sudden and wonderful development. It was now on to find a home in the areas we selected and to pack.

~~~~

I began collecting cardboard boxes from the College and several stores. As the boxes grew in our garage, I was filling them almost as fast. A lot of my life was now spent packing, taping, and marking boxes and stacking them in the garage. As the pile of boxes grew, I had to park my car outside, and soon Janice had to join me. I am faster at packing than Janice, and so I have become the packer. She has become the sorter. This division of labor works well unless the packer has nothing else to pack because the sorter has not been able to sort or decide about certain items. So the resolution we adopted was to pack it all and sort it out once we got to our new house. This, of course, led to an inordinate number of boxes that were unsorted and had to be moved as is which greatly increased the mass of stuff that had to be moved. In a short time, our two-car garage was filled from floor to ceiling with packed boxes.

"Peter, I Think I Found Our House"

We had decided to use a realtor to facilitate our search for a ranch-style home near Peter and Beth. Bernie knew of a friend of Annie's that was a realtor that he suggested we call. He lived in one of the areas we had selected and knew the other areas pretty well where we were interested in living. Between our searching the multiple listing of homes online and our realtor's efforts, we saw a number of homes that could work for us. We then toured a few that had possibilities, but there was always something they lacked. There was one home that had potential if some remodeling could be done at a reasonable price. We reached out to our son-in-law Dan and his brother to give us their opinion. However, we canceled out when we explored the neighborhood further and found it wanting for a number of reasons. It had become frustrating and depressing to travel in each time a house looked promising in pictures but proved to be so disappointing in person.

~~~~

Then one day Janice came up from her basement office where she had been searching online for houses and, in an almost awestruck voice, said quietly, "Peter, I think I found our house." She had found a home on a by-owner website that really did look exactly what we were looking for. The photographs were quite enchanting. We studied each one, trying to be objective in assessing the home overall.

"Peter, I Think I Found Our House"

To drive in and not have the house be something that matched the pictures was not something either one of us wanted to do again. However, there was just no way of telling for sure unless we saw it in person. So we called the owner who said the home was vacant and unfurnished but that her son and his family who were visiting from Florida were camping out there for the Christmas holidays and that he could show it to us. We set a day and time to go see it but, of course, with some trepidation.

Pulling up in front of this contemporary ranch home impressed us immediately. Its stone front with a soaring peak of two-story windows was captivating. The inside was the open floor plan we had wanted with a two-story fireplace in the large family room. It had three bedrooms, two full bathrooms, a dining room, and first-floor laundry. These were all the things we had on our wish list. We arranged for both Peter and Dan to go through it to get their input. The house had some issues but had all the things we wanted in our next house. I hired a structural engineer to assess the house, and he pronounced it sound in every respect.

~~~

So once again, we went ahead on faith, which was our wont, and negotiated a great deal on the house with a mutually agreeable closing date. Then on April 22, 2006, we formally purchased 10 Bluebird and arranged for Dan to renovate the kitchen, the two bathrooms, and the laundry area. While he was doing the renovating, he also oversaw the installation of new carpeting, painting inside and out, new gutters and downspouts, and the installation of a sprinkler system. All because of Dan's excellent work and wonderful suggestions, in May, we moved into one beautiful home.

~~~

Now came the move itself. Unfortunately, our stuff filled a very large moving van from end to end and from floor to ceiling. It took me eleven trips with my SUV completely filled just to get the stuff

"Peter, I Think I Found Our House"

from our storage shed into my garage prior to the moving van's arrival. Even after the van was loaded, there were still a number of items left over that we then tried to squeeze into our two cars. Then after these were as full as the moving van, there was still stuff that Bernie and Ann said they would bring in to us in a few days.

Because we were not having our furniture and stuff delivered until the following day, we stayed in a motel that was not far from Bluebird. Then we had a disaster strike us when Janice's knee became so painful that she couldn't walk without using a chair for support. She was in agony trying to move around the room at the motel. So in the morning, I took her to the emergency room, got her settled, but then had to leave because I had to return to Bluebird. The moving van was due to arrive early that morning, and I had to open up the house for them.

Once the van arrived and they were busy unloading our stuff, I left and went back to the hospital to get Janice. They had taken X-rays and said nothing was broken. They gave her crutches, pain pills, told her to rest the knee as much as possible, and to follow up with an orthopedic surgeon. When we got to Bluebird and the movers saw the state she was in, they quickly located and set up our rocker and footstool so she had a place to sit. Now she could sit in the front window and direct the movers in the placement of our furniture and the numerous boxes we had accumulated. This, plus the labeling we did on the boxes as to the room they were intended to be placed in, greatly helped to at least get things somewhat distributed so it wasn't as overwhelming as some moves can be.

Janice's directing the movers from her seated position enabled us to get settled fairly quickly. In fact, we were settled enough that we hosted a family party for about fifteen people on Memorial Day, which was only three days after we moved in. Of course, our basement was jammed with boxes, but we were so glad to be moved into Bluebird that we didn't even care. I did have to return to the College for their commencement on the Sunday before Memorial Day, so that made a shortened day for me in terms of unpacking. Everyone loved our new house but, of course, not as much as Janice and I did.

~~~~

"Peter, I Think I Found Our House"

Janice hobbled around for about a month, and then we returned to our previous town so that she could have arthroscopic surgery on her knee. She and I both liked the orthopedic surgeon who did the surgery on her other knee, and so we went back there to see him. She did well with this most recent surgery but was told that she is going to need a knee replacement in a few years. However, she bounced back from this surgery and was back to full function in a short time. Just in time to enjoy our new house and our grandkids.

Walton Woods and Audubon

Once we settled into Bluebird, I began exploring the area around where we lived. I had become an avid walker for exercise to complement my bike riding in nicer weather, and now walk I did. We were living in a real paradise but didn't know it. Walton Woods, which was what our little enclave was called, was a group of diverse homes built around a network of paths meandering through bucolic woods and past three picturesque lakes. Each day I took a different path and arrived home all excited about what I had seen that day. In the evenings, I took Janice for a short walk to Lake Audubon, where we would sit on one of the benches dispersed around the lake and just enjoy the serenity of it all. We were so thankful to have found such a beautiful place to live.

The larger Audubon Community of which Walton Woods was a small part was designed as a multiuse community that included a library, small technology firms and medical practices, the police department, the senior citizens center, and a network of houses, townhouses, and apartments. It was as if we had found this little oasis with immediate access to the expressways and businesses without the hassle of traffic found in other communities. The way this whole area was designed was very clever. Within a one-minute walk from our house, we could enter onto one of the many meandering walking paths that were nicely wooded. There were small playgrounds discretely placed on many of the paths providing additional surprises for the kids. I walked all the paths at various times and thus got to experience our woods in all the seasons. The green of spring that replaced the blazing fall colors reflected in the lakes were both just a delight. It was if we found a special place to give me a taste of the outdoors without the work and dangers. Winter was also a spectacular time to walk around the frozen lakes with snow flurries being strewn about their clear icy surfaces. The cycle repeating itself with trees and flowers coming forth each spring was always uplifting. What a place!

Each day we rejoiced and basked (yes, more basking) in our home and in the surrounding Audubon Community. It was a real joy for me each time I returned to Bluebird after my days at the College or from my many canoeing and backpacking trips.

Little did we know how much the Audubon Community network of paths and lakes would mean to our grandkids and enhance Janice's and my feelings about this spectacular place she found.

Hey, Papa?

Oh, the emotion those two words arouse! Once Luke could talk, Beth asked if it was okay for Luke to call me Papa because Dan's Father was already called Grandpa by Dan's brother's kids. Papa was perfect because that's what Peter and Beth always called me until they didn't think it was cool and switched over to Dad or Pop. I loved Papa then and was glad to be Papa again.

Janice and Beth searched for an alternate term for Grandma because that name was also already taken. Janice discovered that the Italian term for grandma was, in fact, *nona*, and so that is who she became. We now had our own names and identities as grandparents.

I knew with my own kids that they liked it best when I played with them on the floor and entered into whatever fantasy activity was capturing their interest at the time. I played house in a tree where each branch was a different room. I sat at Beth's little table and had pretend lunch. Peter and I played with trucks and trains, built with Legos, and made wooden cars for his Cub Scouts' Pinewood Derby. I played table games with them like Candyland, but we played them on the floor and only moved to the table when they got older. Reading to them was something else they loved. Because kids love adventure, I always looked to do adventurous things with them, but not those that were really dangerous. I have always been very good at introducing an activity to make it sound far more dangerous than it actually was. It was the turning of ordinary things into adventures that was the most fun for them as well as me.

~~~~

I missed those days when I was one of my kids' favorite playmates, and now I was going to get the chance to do it all over again with my grandkids, starting with Luke. This is not something I planned to do; it just happened naturally with both my kids and my grandkids. From the first time Beth brought Luke to visit us in our townhouse, I felt that he and I connected as I played with him, rocked him, showed him pages in his little book, and fed him. I just felt that he and I were going to be buddies.

Once we moved to Bluebird, we got to see Luke far more frequently. Both Janice and I were becoming people whom Luke enjoyed seeing. Janice often helped Beth with Luke and the housework, including some cooking. A part-time job opportunity came my way (actually, I sought and obtained it) that afforded me additional contact time with Luke. I started teaching at a nearby college as an adjunct instructor in OT one day a week during the year and then two days a week during the summer.

Driving to or from the college, it was very easy to drive a route that took me right near Beth and Dan's house. This gave me additional opportunities to stop in to see Luke, play a bit, and then head off to the college or home depending. As he started to walk holding on to things, I would get on the floor (where else?) and let him use me for balance or climb on me. If he was in for his nap, I would let him know I had been there by putting his toys in obscure places like the tops of curtains or squeezing a stuffed animal inside one of his trucks. When Beth knew I was going to be stopping by while Luke was having his breakfast, she would leave the front door unlocked for me. I would slip in sort of quietly (I purposely made noise to alert him) and let Luke discover me and rejoice as he exclaimed, "Hi Papa!" Great words and a great welcoming!

Luke was not our only grandkid for long. On June 6 of 2006, Samantha Jade Talty was born to Peter and Kathy; and then on June 30, Andrew Peter Russ was born to Beth and Dan, giving Luke a little brother. Janice and I were able to be at the hospital for both births, which was our original intent when we decided to sell the townhouse and move back to our hometown and onto Bluebird Lane. What a great decision that proved to be!

It surprised me that I was so moved when watching my two kids (Beth and Peter were really no longer kids) taking care of their own kids. I guess this is something every grandparent knows about, but it caught me by surprise. It's something I loved seeing every time it happened and still do. They love being parents, and we are so happy to be here to witness these interactions.

A New Home for Beth and Dan

Once Andrew was born, Beth and Dan decided to look for a bigger house. Dan preferred to buy a house that he could rehab it to his immaculate standards and beauty. I saw what he did with our house and knew his talent was immense. So in 2007, they eventually settled on a large four-bedroom, two-and-a-half-bath home in a beautiful section known as Farmington Woods. I was very familiar with this area from my running days because this is one of the places I enjoyed running through when we lived in Wellington Woods.

It was a busy time for Beth and Dan. Janice and I tried to help whenever we could. Having a newborn and a two-year-old made it hard for Beth to find time to pack and help Dan get the house ready to sell. They were selling it themselves, so Dan had two big jobs: get the present house in excellent shape so it sells quickly at a high price and renovate their new house. While I was at the College, Janice helped Beth with the kids and the housework; and then when I returned, I helped with packing and anything else they asked me do. Dan sold the house at their first open house and at a very good price. I then shifted my efforts along with Dan to their new house. Lacking the ability to do the skilled work, I was fine with taking direction from Dan and doing cleanup work. Dan demonstrated his masterful ability to renovate a house and thus created a home of real beauty. Beth and Dan moved into their Walnut Creek Court home in 2007, and Dan has continued to improve their house both inside and out to provide his family with one of the finest homes I have ever seen.

A New Home for Beth and Dan

Beth and Dan's Walnut Creek Court home was just about eight miles from Bluebird. This made a nice bike ride for me of sixteen miles round-trip that I could extend by taking a ride on a bike path right next to their house for another twenty or so miles if I wanted. I, of course, also got to see Luke and Andrew on my rides, which made my ride that much more enjoyable.

A New Home for Peter and Kathy

Not long after Beth and Dan moved into their Walnut Creek Court home, Kathy and Peter announced that she was pregnant. So on December 17, 2008, Simon James Talty was born. We now had a total of four grandkids. The one downside was that now there was a bit of crunch for Peter and Kathy since their home on Courier Road only had two bedrooms. The idea of subdividing Samantha's bedroom proved impractical for a number of reasons, and there were really no other options within their budget.

So now I have disparity in another form: my son and his growing family need a larger home. And when disparity exists within me or those close to me, I am driven to resolve it. So within this state of disparity bordering on despair, I got an inspiring thought. When I told Janice about my idea, she too thought it was a good one but was not sure Peter or Kathy would find it as attractive as we did. The only way to know for sure was to go talk with them. It was late in the evening when I called to be sure they were going to be home and just said, "We have an idea that we want to run by you." They were fine with us coming over, and so off we went.

~~~~

The idea was a simple one that I put forth: "Would you like to sell this house and move into a larger house if we helped you do it?" Both Kathy's and Peter's face lit up as they almost in unison said "Yes!"

This was in 2009. So the first priority was readying their Courier Road house for sale, but a close second priority was finding a home that would meet their needs. Then commenced a flurry of activity that was at times overwhelming for all of us. We had to empty out a number of the rooms so the house would be attractive to potential buyers, and I decided that the best option was our two-car garage on Bluebird Lane. Searching on Craigslist under "Free," I found a few troves of moving boxes that I began accumulating in their basement. After packing, taping, and marking many boxes, we then had to get them out so we had room to paint the rooms. So at the end of each day of painting the inside rooms, I would fill my SUV with boxes and other items that I then stored in our two-car garage. Before the move took place, I had filled the garage wall to wall and floor to ceiling. It was well-organized so that it did not resemble the cluttered mess that I saw in Pat's photos of Sleazy's and Wimpy's garage. Instead, my garage was more reminiscent of our neatly packed garage in our townhouse prior to our open house and subsequent move.

~~~~

Painting their house had a benefit that I never could have anticipated. I was concerned that our only granddaughter, Samantha, seemed afraid of me. She would quickly and in an almost panicky way climb into her mother's lap as soon as I entered the room. This was sad for me because I liked kids and usually got along with them quite well. Not so with three-year-old Samantha. Thus, I used an approach that I usually employ whenever I feel a student, patient, colleague, or just anyone doesn't like or trust me: I ignore their behavior, limit my interactions to a minimum, keep the conversation brief and restricted to the business at hand, do nothing to increase their dislike or mistrust of me, and then just give it time. I did all this with Samantha without anything changing. Unfortunately, I still scared the hell out of her.

The change came about when I was painting the walls outside and near her bedroom where she was confined with a children's safety gate. Avoiding eye contact and gently talking to myself, I would pose little puzzles about the painting like "Oh, oh! If I paint this dark color on this wall, I might get some on the white wood." Knowing Samantha was very bright and observant, I also knew that she would be curious about these little puzzles I kept fabricating. I also said all this in a low, nonthreatening way so as not to alarm her. Then I would express quiet excitement by exclaiming the solution: "I know! I will put some of this painter's tape that Samantha's mom bought for me on the white wood." It was fun watching her watching and listening to my quiet ramblings of puzzles and solutions.

After a few days of this approach, Samantha no longer moved away from her gate to play in her room when I was there painting. Our fragile but growing relationship took a big leap forward when I announced, "Today is going to be the most fun day ever!" Before I got my paint and paint brushes out, I began removing the painter's tape and rolling it all into a ball.

I then threw the ball of tape into her room. Then it was with the delightful sound of her giggle that she picked it up and threw it back out at me. This began an ongoing activity and a bridge-building event for us that she still laughs about today. I can definitely say that painting Peter's and Kathy's house was the best thing for helping me connect to Samantha, and it gave us the foundation for a wonderful relationship.

~~~~

After all of us working hard, we got the Courier house at a level of presentation that made it spectacular for the area and could command the above-average asking price they had set. Kathy's mom and Dad, her sister and brother, plus Janice and I could all be proud of the way we transformed the house. It sold at the first and actually only open house they held and at just about their asking price.

While preparing their house to sell, Peter and Kathy had also been scouring the Internet in search of a home that would meet their needs. Janice and I usually went with them and looked at these homes, but they were all found to be less than their pictures and descriptions indicated. Finally, they found a home on Sprucewood Terrace in a fine neighborhood that was just what they were looking for, and it was within their price range. They made an offer, and with a bit of good work by their realtor, an agreement was reached.

Once the Courier Road house was sale-ready, I shifted my attention to their new house on Sprucewood Terrace. The house was in good shape, but Peter and Kathy wanted to change the color scheme on the inside. So they picked the colors, and I commenced to painting. With no furniture or people in the house, the painting went quite fast. The two-story living room and stairway was a bit tricky, but the walls needed minimal patching; and in a short time, the house was ready for new carpet. They had a real showplace when everything was done, and at the end of the summer of 2009, we got them all moved in and the boxes out of our garage. It was a very happy time for us all.

A Grandkid We Didn't Know We Had

One day in the fall of 2009, Peter called to see if we were going to be home. He arrived quickly and told us that we had better sit down. What? Why? What devastating news was he preparing us to hear? Janice and I were very nervous!

Then Peter shocked us when he said, "It seems I have another son besides Simon." Now not only was I was shocked, but now I also was confused. What was he talking about? What happened was that Peter was contacted through Facebook by a young man living in Florida. He had apparently Googled Peter's name, and with some e-mails exchanged, they deduced that Peter was most likely his father. After talking this over with Kathy, Peter arranged to fly to Florida to meet his son. While there he had a paternity test done that confirmed that we did, in fact, have another grandson: Phillip. Well, that was quite a surprise.

Phillip was twenty-four years old and had been raised by his grandparents in Florida, but he was in frequent contact and often visited with his mom and stepsiblings who lived about an hour and a half from Peter. It turned out that he was going to be coming to the area for the holidays. We arranged to meet him for breakfast once he was in town. He was a nice guy who was very happy to meet his other grandparents. He quickly fell into calling us Papa and Nona, and it all felt quite natural. Janice and I could see a lot of Peter in

Phillip. We also arranged a family gathering at our house on Bluebird and invited other members of our family so they could meet him. This was a good way to get him connected to the rest of the Talty's. Whenever his schedule and ours permits, we try to get together. He has also included many of the family members in his Facebook messages, including the exchanging of birthday greetings.

Life sure is full of surprises. Discovering that we had a fifth grandson was a nice surprise.

The Unexpected and Abundant Joys of Grandkids

As Luke, Andrew, Samantha, and Simon each started talking and walking, they each brought a new level of joy for Janice and me. It was a thrill for me to take a bike ride that took me past their houses and then to see the excitement they expressed upon seeing me. I would take time out to play with them, push them on their swings, climb up into their tree houses with them, or even go into their kiddie pool with my biking clothes on. They loved it all as much as I did. Their parents also loved the connections I was building with each of them.

I always appreciated the differences in Peter and Beth. The differences made them each fun to be with throughout their lives but for different reasons. Now we had four more individuals that were each fun and funny in their own ways. Being with each of them one at a time brought its own joy, but then it became magnified as each of them grew and their personalities emerged, and we brought them all together. It was such a thrill for Janice and me to watch the grandkids jump out of their parent's cars with such excitement and watch them bound across the grass up to our door and ring the doorbell with such enthusiasm. Upon entering, it was constant treasured chatter with "Papa" said about twenty times. I designated two closet door knobs as the "Russ Boys Hooks" and two other ones as the "Talty Kid's Hooks", where they diligently hung up their coats with a sense of pride in ownership.

Sometimes we would only have Luke and Andrew, and other times just Samantha and Simon. However, it was at our house where the four kids were together the most. Regardless of which ones were there, I was always promoting good relationships by extolling the virtues of whichever of the grandkids were not present. I wanted them to like and respect each other so that as time went on, they would look forward to playing with and spending time with each other.

For about a four-year span, the grandkids viewed me as a real fun person who was full of surprises and adventures. This was before they discovered video games and peers. In those days, our home provided a great place to play hide and seek, to build with Lego's and Lincoln Logs, race pull-back cars, construct forts, and so forth. All this was on the first floor, but then we had our basement. It wasn't a finished basement, but it was painted, well-lit, and carpeted. They loved working out on our exercise equipment and playing air hockey. There wasn't an extensive amount of exercise equipment, but they loved to show off all that they could do on the elliptical machine, weight bench, or the recumbent bike. It was so cute to see them moving their little legs and arms as fast as they could to break their personal bests. Throughout all this was a pleasant cacophony of our grandkids' voices. Janice could hear them upstairs and loved hearing the excitement and genuine joy in their voices as she prepared lunch.

Lunchtime was always a big deal not because of the food itself but because of its presentation. I had bought plastic cereal bowls for each of them that were shaped like race cars. They loved them almost as much as the mac and cheese Janice put in them. Janice also showed her cleverness by creating a face out of fruits and pretzels for each of them that they also loved. Each lunch was topped off with a choice of Oreo cookies from our ever-popular cookie tin.

Once the snow was gone and the temperature warmed up, we moved our activities to our yard. We had a screened gazebo in the backyard where we would then have our spectacular race car bowl lunches outdoors. We also used our big front yard for baseball and football. Then to ratchet up the excitement, I would take whatever grandkids were visiting onto the paths leading to the playgrounds and the lakes surrounding our home. The generating of suspense and curiosity was something I did well in everything I did with the grandkids, and the Audubon Woods and lakes gave me ample opportunities to provide safe adventures in many forms. In this vein, I had fostered a sense of mystique around one particular playground that I called the "Hidden Park." It was off the main path but hidden from view by the woods surrounding it.

The Hidden Park had the basic swings, but it also had a tire swing that was the source of great excitement. I had created a way of pushing two or three grandkids at the same time in a vigorous circular pattern that was to them as thrilling as the biggest roller coaster ride around. The excitement built with my commentary about increasing the speed and distance to the extent that the tire they were sitting on would bounce against the support posts on each side. They would scream and yell for me to get them going faster so that they could experience the resounding jolt of striking the side posts again and again. No one fell off, and no one got hurt. I let them each decide how vigorous they wanted the tire swing ride to be and adjusted accordingly.

~~~~

Janice and I also did some day-long excursions with all four of the grandkids to local attractions, which were special for all of us. I have pictures in my mind of all four of them standing on a fence rail and holding onto the fence watching the little steam engine come in to pick us up. We then sat on the tops of the cars of the trains as they took us in and out of woods and across a bridge. I had Simon sitting with me because he was still pretty young, but the other three all rode independently on the cars right in front of Janice. This was just one of many special days we had in our special house on Bluebird Lane and amid the special environs of Walton Woods and the Audubon Community.

During these memorable days, our family gatherings and holiday celebrations were certainly embellished with the presence of grandkids. Seeing them come in with their excited chatter was wonderful only to be exceeded by that thrilling (for me) question of "Where's Papa?" I loved playing with them or just watching them play. Seeing them grow and develop language, cognitive, fine motor, gross motor, and social skills was fun, but it was even more fun to use my OT background to offer them what we in OT call "the just right challenge" to facilitate the acquisition and enhancement of these skills through play.

The relationship with the grandkids was now the source of basking for me and Janice. It was a period of four or five years of wonderful times, and then like all things, they run their course, and the inevitable change occurs. As with all kids, as they got older, their classmates, peers, and technological devices became far more attractive to them than their grandparents. We know they love us, and they are always glad to see us, but the intensity of the Bluebird days has dissipated. It saddens me that those days are gone, but the rich images I glean from the repository of my mind several times each day will never dissipate. Janice and I love to reminisce about those days. We also know that we have a strong foundation of relationships with each of them that will withstand time, distance, and competing elements. Our relationships with our grandkids will, like all things, be shaped by various forces that we cannot control. Hopefully, we will remain connected regardless of where life takes each of us over the years.

A New OT Job!

With my working only three days a week and for only thirty weeks a year, I had time to explore other things. I e-mailed my friend Chris Einstein,* who owned and operated an OT private practice. He and his wife, Carol,* owned Therapeutics Extraordinaire* with two areas of OT specialization: hand therapy and pediatrics. It was the hand therapy that interested me the most. My timing was perfect because they needed help with their hand clinic two days a week, which was perfect for me.

    Chris and I had been colleagues and friends for several years. He was the first full-time OTR that I hired when my private practice began growing. He was a big help in helping me expand clinically as well as geographically. After a couple of years, he left to head up his own OT program and eventually became one of the most respected OTs but not only in the local area. His good work as a member of the National Board for the Certification of Occupational Therapists earned him the title of president of this august body.

    Our paths crossed again when he joined the OT faculty at the College as our field work coordinator and professor. He was a great clinician as well as a great teacher and once again helped me build an OT operation. He had obtained his clinical doctorate, and he and Carol opened Therapeutics Extraordinaire that was highly successful.

~~~~

I would be spending my Mondays and Fridays with Carol at their Hand Clinic which was about twenty minutes from Bluebird Lane. I met with Chris at the hand clinic on a Saturday morning, and he got me oriented. I looked forward to working with Carol, who was a very experienced hand therapist as well as pediatric therapist. She and Chris were a very good team. I was excited to get started, and we set it up that I would start the following Monday.

In spite of all my experience, I was still nervous when Monday morning arrived. My anxiety came from not having done this type of clinical work before. I had made splints, and splinting was one of my main things I taught at the College, so I was fine with that. It was everything else that went into hand therapy that was going to be the challenge.

~~~~

The Hand Clinic was adjacent to the office of a noted hand surgeon who referred all his patients to Therapeutics Extraordinaire. This would give me a chance to work with a wide variety of acute conditions, including trauma, infections, postsurgical conditions, fractures, dog and cat bites, and some conditions that I had only seen a few of in my career. I learned that some of the patients had been injured at work or in auto accidents and were coming to OT for several months because of the severity and complexity of their injuries. Then we had the people who were just injured or had had emergency surgery over the weekend and had come in to see the surgeon for follow-up on Monday morning. In the midst of his seeing these patients, he would send his nurse over to get us. It was interesting, but I'm sure some people might think it gruesome to see the awful injuries people had sustained. Not me. I found it fascinating to see these wounds or surgical repairs and enjoyed the dialogue with the surgeon in terms of what type of splint the patient needed or what type of exercise their hands could tolerate.

To bolster my knowledge and skills, I took some continuing education online courses and attended some in-person workshops.

I felt like a rookie at times and was anxious because I certainly did not want to do anything that would make the patients worse or to neglect to do something that could help them. Adding to the stress was the rapidity of the pace. Trying to move back and forth between two rooms, applying modalities to patients, answering the phone, seeing new patients who just appeared and had been referred by other doctors, making splints, seeing the impromptu patients the surgeon summoned us to see, and documenting all that I did in the prescribed manner to maximize reimbursement made for stressful but rewarding days.

As my competencies grew, Carol was able to leave to attend to other aspects of their private practice either in their separate clinic or in the community. I was pleased with the way my skills increased as well as my confidence. I enjoyed interacting with the patients and using my considerable interpersonal skills to manage the more difficult patients. This new area of practice also enhanced my teaching because I had current clinical examples to share with my students to help them understand the concepts I was presenting. It was great to be out in the field on Mondays and Fridays (and sometimes also Saturdays) and then bring those experiences into the classroom on Tuesdays through Thursdays.

~~~~

Because of the fast-paced and dynamic environment of the hand clinic coupled with my several years of clinical experience, I grew quickly into a competent hand therapist. Carol was a very good teacher, and we worked well together. I continued to study hand therapy literature and took workshops that gave me additional insights into this highly specialized area of practice. This evolution was not without stress and strain. The anxiety I felt whenever Carol left me alone came from my fear that I might not know enough to help the next patient coming in the door or one just brought into the surgeon's office. To be responsible for not doing the wrong thing was what drove me to be as prepared as possible for whatever condition needed to be addressed.

I became close to the long-term patients who had complicated conditions like complex regional pain syndrome whom I worked with every Monday and Friday for six months or more. This became the nucleus of my caseload that was then augmented by the constant influx of acute patients that were just injured or had just had surgery. Seeing and treating open wounds using the different modalities like Fluidotherapy, whirlpool, ultrasound, various massage techniques, plus splinting made for busy days.

After just about a year, a couple of events occurred that changed how I spent my Mondays and Fridays. First, I was tiring of the stress and strain of the unpredictable dynamics of the hand clinic. When I wasn't working, I was consumed with reading and learning. I was also finding it harder and harder to keep up with my teaching. I also missed not seeing my grandkids. So just around the same time that I was considering resigning, the surgeon took the decision out of my hands. A local hospital gave him the opportunity to move his practice out of the present building where the hand clinic was also located and into the hospital itself. This was a very attractive opportunity for him, and he took it. He would now use the therapists at the hospital and no longer refer patients to Therapeutics Extraordinaire. With the surgeon went the majority of the hand therapy business, and I was no longer needed. So by mutual agreement, in 2010, I said goodbye to hand therapy, but I took away a most rewarding year in a new area of OT practice.

Ah, Wilderness! No More

Another ending that occurred in 2010 besides my hand therapy experience was my decision to end my wilderness adventures. I cannot say exactly when I ended my obsession with the outdoors, but I knew it was time. It seemed to be a myriad of coalescing events that brought me to this decision that shocked my family and friends and even Janice. Getting older made me more vulnerable and less capable of effectively responding when things went awry. A few too many close calls and feelings of inadequacy in terms of strength, endurance, and diminishing skill certainly played a part.

    I was also at a crossroads with my equipment. My canoes were heavier than the modern ones, which posed significant problems for portaging as well as loading and unloading them onto the top of my SUV. My loaded backpack that could weigh as much as seventy pounds for long trips was now exceeding my strength. Everything I bought over the years was now being manufactured in much lighter forms. So as I was contemplating the expense of upgrading my equipment, reality set in. The cost was quite significant and the gains questionable. The question ruminating through my mind was: if I did go to the expense of buying new lightweight canoes and modern equipment, would I use it all enough to make the investment worthwhile? The answer was no. At this stage of my life, I was enjoying time with Janice and my family, especially my grandkids. So to be off backpacking in the woods and paddling remote rivers and lakes was not as pleasurable as in the past and was becoming more precarious each year.

Another factor was the anxiety my canoeing and backpacking trips caused Janice. This was especially true of my solo trips. Some of my regular canoeing partners had moved away, some became ill, and others, like my brother Danny, had lost their zest for the outdoors. Janice still loved going on these trips with me, but her knees had made the more strenuous trips beyond her ability, especially climbing mountains and long hikes. So my trips became more and more alone. However, I was never lonely on these solo trips. In fact, I enjoyed the solitude. Plenty of time to read, think, pray, meditate, and, of course, bask. However, the fact was that poor Janice and other members of my family were sitting at home worried about me. This wasn't fair to them and not too prudent of me.

~~~~

So without prior discussion, I announced that I was no longer going to venture into the wilderness for my recreation and that I was selling all my equipment. This process where I analyze and analyze, gather data, analyze and analyze, identify the problem at hand, generate solutions, analyze and analyze, select what looks to me to be the best option, announce it, and move immediately into implementation has generated great consternation over the years on the part of my family, especially Janice, and my friends and co-workers. My justification for doing problem solving in this silent way was to avoid burdening people with my problems, and I saw no point in telling people my thoughts because I knew more about my situation and potential options than they ever could. So predictably, all were shocked with my decision.

My peculiar problem-solving and decision-making processes have been difficult for Janice for the fifty-plus years that we have known each other. She has always been a wonderful listener, has a keen mind, never overreacts, and has the gift of pragmatism. So why then would I not include someone with all Janice's talents in my mental processing? I'm not sure, but it's a good chance that under all of it is my need for control. I am working on this, but like all entrenched habits, change is not easy.

~~~~

So after making the big announcement, it was on to Craigslist. I knew from selling our houses and our garage sales that advertising was the key, and I was not concerned about being too obnoxious in promoting my sale. I placed an ad for my one-day camping sale, listing the canoes, tents, backpacks, and the various other items I had accumulated over the years. One of the best things I did was also getting it into the Mountain Club newsletter. This would attract the canoeists and backpackers. I cleaned everything up, polished the canoes, and organized tables in my garage to display all the things I had priced. I then put big empty boxes weighted down with rocks along the main road that courses through the area. On each side of the boxes I had painted in large letters CAMPING SALE with an arrow directing them to our house. On the day of my sale, I put my canoes and set up tents out on the front lawn to attract attention.

It was a busy and rewarding day. I felt no regrets about selling all my stuff. There was no sadness in seeing my once-beloved canoes and tents go because I had already come to the decision that this was the right thing to do. There were some things like a great hatchet and Swiss Army knife that Peter gave me and a walking stick that Annie gave me that I kept for sentimental reasons. For more practical reasons, I also kept a small backpack, a walking stick for Janice, and our canteens. These would be useful on any day hikes we wanted to do.

There were some things that did not sell, but a man called me from an inner city church where he ran a program for youth. He was trying to gather enough backpacking equipment so that he could take some teenagers on a backpacking trip into the Adirondacks. He was thrilled that I donated everything I had left.

~~~~

Now in 2010, I was no longer connected to the wilderness, and I was fine with it. Janice was concerned that I had moved too quickly (what's new about that?) and that I would not have anything to do with my free time. This did not concern me because there were so many things that interested me, and now the grandkids were becoming even more fun to be with. So I was able to devote more time to them and other areas of my interests. I knew that I no longer needed the outdoors as an alternative to drinking and drugging; my life had become exciting and full without drugs or alcohol.

Alaska: First-Class Style!

A place I always wanted to see was Alaska, but we were always so busy that we never took the time to even look into traveling there. With my work, grandkids, canoeing and backpacking, and our usual stuff, we thought that the amount of time it would take was not something we could do. Then an opportunity presented itself through my brother Tommy. Janice and I had always found time to visit Tommy and Karoline wherever they lived and welcomed them into our various homes throughout the years. Since Karoline had passed away, Tommy had sold his home and moved in with his daughter Thea and son-in-law Jack. Then one day Tommy told me that Thea and Jack were taking a trip to Alaska that Jack had won through his job and that Tommy was going too. This got Janice, and I talking about maybe we would go also. It would be great to take a cruise to Alaska, and to do it with Tommy would make it that much more special.

Janice went to work on trying to book us on the same trip, but it was sold out. So we were disappointed but just had to accept that we were too late. Then a little later on that same day, Janice got a call from the person she originally talked to at the cruise line. They had a cancellation! Janice called me to give me the good news and bad news about the cancellation. The good news was that we could now make the trip to Alaska with Tommy; but the bad news was that the only room left was a high-priced balcony room on the back of the ship. This room was a deluxe room, and it came with its own butler who served breakfast in the room each morning and provided other services as requested and its own concierge. After about twenty seconds of consideration, I said, "Let's do it!" Janice was in complete agreement that this was a once-in-a-lifetime opportunity to experience an Alaska cruise with Tommy, in a spectacular room, and with some exceptional amenities. We were very excited and couldn't wait to call Tommy to tell him the news.

~~~~

One of the many things Janice and I have in common is the philosophy that life is short, and seizing opportunities that may not come our way again is what we need do. Janice losing her Dad when she was only five years old and my Dad dying at age fifty-four was harsh evidence of how true this was, and thus we had a sense of urgency about life. We had adopted the view that doing it now was the thing to do, and this epic Alaskan cruise was certainly in that vein.

Besides the trip itself, there were options like side trips that all sounded so engaging that we wanted to do them all. However, we had to be selective because the cost of the cruise was far more than anyone I knew ever paid for a cruise. First class comes with an exorbitant price, and we were fine with that, but we couldn't do every side trip offered. We chose three that we thought would give us three additional perspectives on Alaska and British Columbia, Canada.

~~~~

This truly was the trip of our lives. It was not just an Alaskan cruise. It was the way we did it that made it special for us. Having never done anything in our lives at the first-class level, Janice and I had no idea of what to expect. From the moment we walked on the ship, we were recognized by the crew that we were first-class passengers once they saw our tickets, and they treated us accordingly. No standing in line to check in for us. We were whisked past all the regular passengers and right up to the priority lounge along with the other first-class passengers where pastries, beverages, and comfy chairs were available. Our personal concierge introduced herself to us, gave us her contact information, assured us that she was available to assist us twenty-four hours a day for anything we needed, and then summoned a young man who escorted us to the upscale (what else?) Cagney restaurant where we were served a delicious lunch while our cabin was being readied.

After lunch, we found our way to our cabin and opened the door to a bevy of opulence. "Cabin" certainly seemed an inappropriate term for our plush and spacious suite with a large private deck in the middle of the rear of the ship. We were in awe with the room, amenities, furnishings, and the panoramic view from our deck. Our luggage arrived along with Andrew, our personal butler. Andrew offered to unpack our things, which we declined, and then gave us the menu for our breakfast that he would serve us in our room at any time we would like. So this is how rock stars and other VIPs travel! What a way to start our magical trip!

After getting settled, we went and found Tommy, Thea, and Jack and brought them back for a tour of our cabin. They were quite impressed as we all sat comfortably on our spacious deck overlooking the 180-degree view of the ocean and the shores of British Columbia. The deck became a great place to read, visit, and nap on the comfortable lounge chairs. It was mesmerizing to watch the changing scenery, spot whales, and really luxuriate.

We found out that we could include Tommy in our in-room breakfasts each day, which we instituted on the second day. Janice, Tommy, and I started each day with workouts on the different pieces of equipment available in the large fitness center in the upper bow of the ship. My love for the elliptical machine was greatly enhanced while looking out at the ocean. After we all worked out, we went to our cabin to await our breakfasts. Andrew arrived with our elaborate breakfasts as scheduled. The three of us were like little kids as Andrew served us our scrumptious breakfasts.

The first side trip Janice and I took was aboard the Alaskan Railroad that took us into the Alaskan wilderness and through bucolic scenery that never stopped. Sitting in the comfortable restored passenger cars while viewing the mountains, streams, and picturesque countryside was something Janice and I will never forget. The views were just like the ones I longed to see in person every time I saw a TV show about train rides through Alaska, and now we were having that same experience.

I have always wanted to get up close to a glacier and see an iceberg calve. We got the opportunity to see this when we took another side trip where we left our cruise ship and boarded a smaller ship that took us into a bay where we could view a glacier and watch the dramatic calving. Our route to the glacier took us past more magnificent scenery with radiant blue images of the ice and water cascading down the cliffs surrounding the bay. Although it was raining and cold, the raw beauty of this extraordinary place made the rain and cold insignificant. To add to the excitement of this side trip, we got the opportunity to step from our glacier ship back onto our cruise ship while both vessels were moving. The two captains had both ships going at the same speed abreast of each other, so the transfer was easy. However, it was daunting looking up at the huge cruise ship and down at the cold water moving below us. All part of our great adventure!

Seeing the mountains, valleys, and forests of remote British Columbia from a float plane was our third side trip that was almost spiritual in nature. There was just Janice and I and another couple along with the pilot who took us past scenes that could only be seen from the seat of a small plane roaring down hidden valleys and over mountains. It was part-travelogue and part-amusement park ride. The pilot skillfully landed on an isolated lake, and then drove his float plane right up to a beautiful waterfall so we could get a close up look. Taking off was another thrill. We hated to see the flight come to an end.

After eight days in Alaska, our cruise ship brought us back to Seattle. We said goodbye to Thea and Jack the night before, but Tommy joined us in our estate room for our last scrumptious breakfast served by our butler Andrew. It was then time to say goodbye to

Tommy and our sojourn into the life of the rich and famous. We were not sad because we had a bushel basket of memories, which served as great fodder for future basking for me and Janice.

    Our schedule gave us an extra day in Seattle. After saying another goodbye to Tommy, Thea, and Jack, Janice and I decided to explore downtown Seattle. We had another one of those unanticipated special days that are typical of what I call a mini-adventure within the greater adventure. Walking all around the "Emerald City" was fun and relaxing. We rode the monorail, went up in the Space Needle, walked through pleasant neighborhoods, and hung out in a park with a big wading pool complete with a sporadically showering biosphere-like fountain that delighted lots of kids. On a side street, we had a delicious dinner in a quaint moderately priced diner. The next day we flew home, reminiscing (and, of course, basking) about all that we had seen and done.

The Great Opportunity I Didn't Get to Seize

I have always spent a lot of time thinking of things that can make our lives better. In the car or in my canoe or at my desk, my mind wanders, and I imagine better days and better ways. It's probably that old disparity thing at work. It was one night in my office at the College that I got what I think was one of the best ideas I ever had. It dovetailed with the current mission of the College and my personal mission of earning more money in a very exciting way.

My idea was to hitchhike on the College's current thrust of providing educational opportunities not only online but also on-site. We offered criminal justice degree programs for police officers all over the state partnering with community colleges; nurses were taking graduate courses offered at area hospitals; and over six thousand business students were getting a degree from the College enrolled in six universities in China and another two hundred in Vietnam. All these external degree offerings got me thinking about OT.

~~~~

I knew from personal experience that many COTAs (certified OT assistants) living and working in the area of my hometown would love to earn a master's degree in OT and become OTRs. However, because of family commitments and economic constraints, they were unable to enroll in the local universities that usually only admit full-time students. There are some universities that offer a master's degree in OT that is conducted on weekends, thus enabling COTAs to continue working full-time. The problem was that the closest program of that nature was four hours away.

So I contacted one of my former students who was also one of my former employees in my private practice at a local community college where I was hopeful that we could hold classes in their classrooms and labs on weekends when they were not being utilized. In 2011 she was the chair of OT and was having difficulty recruiting students because most high school students chose to go directly into an OTR program. We both thought that it would help recruiting if she could tell prospective students that if they completed the OTA program at the community college, they could go directly into the College's OTR program to be offered on weekends. This could be a win-win-win arrangement for the community college, the College, and the local COTAs.

~~~~

I arranged a meeting at the community college with the chair of OT, the vice president spearheading these kinds of programs for the College, and his marketing manager. The meeting was very productive with everyone thinking this was the best idea since sliced bread and night baseball. We also met with the current group of students who were very excited to learn about this potential way for them to become OTRs and not have to quit their day jobs.

About one and a half hours south of my hometown was another OTA program whose chair of OT was a former student of mine from the College's first OT graduating class. She and I had been communicating back and forth for several months about how she could partner with us so their graduates could come to the College. Because of the almost three hours between our two campuses, we never were able to establish a viable pipeline for her students. She was very enterprising, and to assess the level of interest in a weekend OTR program to be hosted at her college, she held an information-gathering lunch where over fifty COTAs showed up. This confirmed that there was a market for the kind of weekend OTR program I was putting together. Unfortunately, for this community college, I saw the more populated area of my hometown as having an even far greater number of potential students, and so I had to decline her gracious offer to host my new potential program at her college and instead looked to house it at the community college I originally approached.

~~~~

Vicki, the chair of OT at the College, was also excited about my proposed program and was a big help in putting together a budget, which showed significant revenues for the College. Because we wanted the weekend OTR program to be covered under the College's accreditation from ACOTE (Accreditation Council for OT Education), the curricula for both programs had to be identical. Converting our BS and MS curricula into a weekend format for COTAs was a nightmare, but we did it. We submitted everything to ACOTE and received provisional approval to enroll students. Then we hit a landmine that I never anticipated.

~~~~

While waiting for the agreement between the College and the community college to be signed by the OT chair and her superiors to be returned, I received a distressful e-mail from her. She had decided that our use of her classrooms and labs on the weekends would be too disruptive for the OT faculty. It seems they set up their classrooms and labs on Fridays so that when Monday came, they would be all set. So she said they would not be able to host our weekend OTR program. I was shocked but not dismayed. I knew this program was a winner, so I just had to find a new home for it.

I knew I had put together a strong curriculum, and I also knew that there was a large market of potential students eager to enroll in a weekend OTR Program. Because I had worked as an OT in numerous facilities in the area, taught many OT students at the university for five years, and had served on the board for the local OT association, my name was well-known. This name recognition would be of great value in recruiting students as well as faculty for the College's proposed weekend OTR program. The only things we needed were classroom and lab facilities.

The withdrawal of the local community college from the proposed partnership with the College was disappointing but did not deter me from trying to implement this very worthwhile program. Then I happened to see in the local newspaper that one of my former students and colleague was still the president at another community college just outside of my hometown. He was a progressive thinker and had made significant improvements and acquisitions at his college. I knew that his college did not have an OTA program, but they did have a well-established PT assistant program. So I sent him an e-mail and explained what we were doing and asked if he might be interested in partnering with us. He suggested that we meet in person, which I arranged to do the following week.

He liked what we planned to do and wanted me to meet with the chair of the PT program whose lab spaces we would be using and the various deans with whom we needed to interface. All these meetings went very well with everyone being very cooperative, probably because my program had been endorsed by their president. We just had to work out the details on things like parking, keys, scheduling, and so forth. We now had a home!

~~~~

Vicki and I were working hard at getting the curriculum and sequence of courses in place when we came to some areas of disagreement. She did not want to give credit to the COTAs for work experience, and I felt differently. I believed that experienced COTAs would be more attracted to a program where they could earn credit through their jobs. It would not just be the simple granting of credit. There would be a rigorous scrutiny of papers submitted justifying the appropriate level of learning, and the number of credit hours allotted for this method of learning would be limited. We also disagreed on the extent the COTAs would have to retake courses they had already taken in their COTA education. I wanted to give them some credit and then have them take a modified and shortened version of the courses that fell in this realm. This was a cordial and professional disagreement about how best to provide higher education in a nontraditional way.

While Vicki and I were wrangling over our differences in educational philosophies, we had to put together our projected budget. The budget had to be approved by the vice president, who was responsible for all off-campus programs. He liked the whole idea of our weekend OTR program and how it fit nicely with similar offerings of this nature at the College. From my perspective, I knew that my presence would be key to the program's success. I needed to be involved in marketing, recruiting students and faculty, assessing transcripts, advising students, training and evaluating faculty, and teaching in the program myself. This was going to be far more than the three days a week for thirty weeks I presently enjoyed at the College, and so I put in a salary that was significantly higher than my present faculty salary. I put this in the first version of our budget that we put together a few months ago, and it was never questioned until now.

In reviewing our final proposed budget, the vice president commented that my salary would be comparable to my present faculty salary, and not the one I put in the budget. Are you serious? In response to my expressed disappointment, he explained that the figure I put in the original budget was "just a placeholder" and was never an approved amount.

That evening I sent an e-mail to all the principals involved, announcing that I was resigning from the weekend OTR program. I stated that the reason I was resigning was because the program was not going in the direction I had originally intended. No one expressed any concerns about my abrupt resignation nor did anyone question my decision. Apparently, no one else was interested in

The Great Opportunity I Didn't Get to Seize

running the weekend OTR program, and it was removed from the list of future projects and from the ACOTE list of programs granted provisional status. Oh well.

I had invested a lot in getting the weekend OTR program to a state ready to launch and was disappointed that I wouldn't get to implement it. It was the loss of this exciting opportunity that hastened my decision to retire. It was not the only thing. I simply needed a change.

Retirement!

In the summer of 2011, as I prepared my fall courses, I came to the conclusion that I didn't want to work anymore. I have always been cognizant that the longevity genes were in short supply in the Talty family. Heart disease was and still is a major problem in my family, with my mom dying of it and all my four brothers having had cardiac or vascular surgery because of the occlusions coming from the buildup of atherosclerotic plaque. Losing Sue, Annie. and Pat to cancer was another concern. Knowing this history had committed me to a daily exercise regimen to maintain weight, reduce stress, and try to keep my arteries clear that I started in 1977. But will that be enough to offset heredity? In 2011, I was sixty-nine years old. I had worked long enough, and now it was time to enjoy a life with more freedom to choose how I wanted to spend my time.

Janice and I had previously met with our two different brokers to see how it would all work out financially. There was good news all the way around. The hard work and sacrificing of all our yesterdays were now going to comfortably sustain us for the rest of our lives. In addition, working more years would have had a negligible impact on our future income. Once we were set financially, it was time to let everyone know of our decision.

Coinciding with my decision to retire, I also decided to bike across America. There was a fund-raising event that I wanted to participate in that required the soliciting of donations from friends, students, colleagues, and relatives. By raising the stated amount, I would be one of the thirty or so riders that would ride from Seattle to Washington DC over a forty-five-day period. A truck (SAG Wagon) would transport our gear and provide bike repairs and first aid along the way. This was something I always wanted to do, and if I was retired, I would have the time to train and actually make the ride.

The first person I told after Janice was my department chair Vicki, and we agreed that I should tell the rest of the OT faculty at our upcoming meeting. Everyone was a bit surprised, but I think they really all knew that I was less engaged and would soon retire. There is no mandatory retirement age for professors. So I could have stayed indefinitely, but for all the reasons I described, I felt it was time.

When I told the OT faculty they all expressed concern for the students because they knew how connected I was to each of them. So we agreed that I would personally make the announcement to each class all within a half hour. This would circumvent rumors and misinterpretations relevant to my decision. To also promote my bike ride, I wore my cycling jersey to make the announcements and rolled out a three-foot map of the USA with my intended route highlighted. I made the announcement brief and with a lot of positive energy. It all went well, and my final year was underway.

Once I decided to retire, a number of events occurred that were exciting but complicated. Whenever I left a job, there was always the question of how to best do it. Of course, when you get fired, which happened to me twice, there is no farewell party or closure ceremony. It's over in a flash. But in most of my other departures, the staff or faculty were saddened by my decision to leave. They were sad, and I was glad. I was going to something better, and they were staying behind. I was giddy with anticipation, while they were sometimes distant with me. It's all part of saying goodbye.

Some places gave dinner parties in my honor; others organized drunken bashes of celebration. Some gave me dignified luncheons and gifts; others did nothing but offer comments of congratulations. I had attended roasts for my colleagues who were leaving different organizations, which I found very distasteful. For people to stand up and say unpleasant things about someone who may have invested a great deal in the organization always seemed to me to be wrong. Why make the last gathering a preponderance of negativity? Roasts have never appealed to me, and I told people who were organizing any of my going-away parties that if it was going to be a roast, I would not be attending. Many thought I was being too sensitive and that it would all be in good fun. To hell I say! In every place where I was employed, I worked very hard and made it a better place. I always wanted to have positive memories of the places and the people with whom I worked, not the barbs of roasts. Also, and probably most important, I knew a roast would arouse my sense of disparity.

So after my announcement, different ideas began to emerge about what to do on my behalf. My departure this time was different from any of my other ones for two reasons: it was retirement, and it was leaving a place where I had worked the longest, twenty-five years. Of all the places I had worked, I think the College was where I had the greatest impact. This is not to say that I was sad about leaving the place where I had invested so much. Actually, I was elated to be leaving it all behind and starting a new chapter in my life with Janice.

~~~~

As ideas came forth, of course, one of them had to be a roast, which I immediately rejected, giving the reasons I previously mentioned. There was talk of a dinner or a picnic in the spring, but I had another idea. Borrowing from the dying professor at Carnegie Mellon University, I decided to do what he did and give what he called "The Last Lecture." I was very inspired by the way he did his last lecture, and although I wasn't dying, I was ending my academic career. He delivered his last lecture in front of his colleagues, his present and former students, his family, and the administration of his university. It was my intent to give my last lecture on a day and time that would allow the people who mattered most to me to attend. So it was set for Sunday, May 20, 2012, at 2:00 p.m. in the Norton Chapel at the College.

~~~~

I also met with the staff of the development office, who were very interested in establishing a scholarship in my name. That's pretty good. Here I was a high school dropout that went to college, graduated, earned an advanced degree, became a college professor, and now was about to have a college scholarship established in my name. I thought this was both remarkable and ironic. Of course, I gave my permission to use my name and to assist the development office in any way I could to raise the money to support it.

One of the graduating master's students, who also had a background in journalism, approached me about writing a book. Having been a student in a few of my courses, she saw firsthand how I used my extensive and diverse clinical experiences as a way of teaching OT. It was her idea that I write down all my stories but, of course, not providing any identifying information related to my patients. She would edit the stories, and my stories could be recorded for those interested in reading them. So in the early part of 2012, I began writing and sending my stories to "my editor." She provided great feedback and suggestions, and in the fall, *Occupation as the Key to Change* was published by AuthorHouse. After I retired, I returned to campus soon after its publication and conducted a book signing and sale in the lobby of Hegeman Hall. It was fun to see everyone again as I autographed the books.

~~~~

A group of OT students decided to have a T-shirt made up with my picture and name on it along with some of my infamous sayings. It was the student OT association that designed and sold the T-shirt with the proceeds going to their treasury. I bought several shirts for Janice and I as well as our grandkids. Several members of my family also bought shirts, but we all value the shirts so much that few of us actually wear them.

~~~~

Retirement!

One evening in the spring of 2012, while working in my office, I looked at all the books I had accumulated and wondered what to do with them. I did not want to take them home because we were already overwhelmed with books at our house on Bluebird Lane. Then I got the idea for a book lottery. The way it worked was that students purchased lottery tickets with a hidden number on it. The lowest number would get to pick a book from my library, and I would write a personal note in it for them. Within a few days, all my books were gone, and I had money to donate to the Peter Talty Scholarship fund. Everybody won!

~~~~

The Last Lecture was everything I had hoped it would be. I titled it *Changing Addictive Behavior through Occupation*. Almost three hundred people attended. As they entered the chapel and were waiting for the lecture to start, we had a slide show playing on the large screen showing Janice and me and the rest of my family doing all kinds of things. This was my way of showing those at the College about my life away from the College. Many of the people who attended were a surprise. My brother Tommy even came in from New Mexico. It was great to have all my family there, including our grandkids, along with present and former students. The lecture was well-received, and I enjoyed demonstrating my teaching talents to friends and family who had never seen me in action. The faculty gave me a beautiful plaque with my picture on it (now my face is on a plaque as well as a T-shirt). The inscription on the plaque says:

In Recognition of
Professor Peter Talty
For His 25 Years of Dedication to The
Keuka College Division of Occupational Therapy
And In Honor of his Retirement May, 2012

Retirement!

We honor and thank Professor Peter Talty for 25 years of dedicated teaching in the Division of Occupational Therapy and the profound influence he has had on our students, faculty, and staff.

Peter served as Chair of the Division of Occupational Therapy for ten years and guided the transition from the Undergraduate to the Graduate Program. A tribute to his exceptional teaching career is the endless comments from students regarding his depth of knowledge and versatile teaching skills. He has taught generations of occupational therapy students and mentored numerous colleagues over his academic career.

Professor Peter Talty has had a remarkable impact on the future of the Occupational Therapy profession through his dedication to his craft, his knowledge and wisdom, his ability to share his life lessons and infectious passion for life.

I was given a smaller version of the large plaque that was to be hung in Hegeman Hall outside the office I had occupied for several years. I was proud of my work at the College and took pride in my plaque.

After the last lecture, the faculty hosted a wonderful reception in my honor in the OT labs. I received lots of congratulatory greetings from people I had not seen in years. I was also asked to have my picture taken with numerous students and colleagues, which was fun.

All in all, it was a great way to retire. My family and friends got to see what I did and where I did it, and my students and colleagues got to see my family in pictures and in person.

Florida!

Thanks to our good friends Bob and Babs Wrestler, Janice and I fell in love with vacationing each winter on Marco Island, Florida. We would spend two or three weeks there in a high-rise condo on the beach overlooking the Gulf of Mexico. They were great vacations, but our financial situation changed as well as my interests. Because I had my private practice, I could deduct many of my expenses because I usually attended a workshop or conference in conjunction with our vacation. Once I no longer had the business, the cost was just beyond us. In addition, we were quite engaged in the outdoors with our canoeing and backpacking activities. Thus, I no longer thought about Florida vacations. This all changed in March of 2011, when Bernie and Ann invited us to join them for a week in a condo they rented from a friend in Sarasota, Florida. It wasn't Marco Island, but it reawakened my dormant feelings about Florida.

    Like most changes in my life, they are instigated by information and experience. This time the information came while we were staying in Sarasota with Bernie and Ann. I had forgotten how wonderful the weather was in Florida. I was curious about where Ann's mother and father had stayed when they spent some winter weeks in Florida and how long they stayed and so forth. Her information got me thinking. Her parents had an older trailer that got them out of the cold snowy northern winters. I began to plan to do the same thing. After searching through the Sunday morning homes for sale, I found some manufactured homes in Sarasota that could work for us. I explained to Janice, Ann, and Bernie about my latest brainstorm: "Just get a place. Who cares what it looks like? Just have a place where we can get out of the cold and snowy winters." They must have thought I was not thinking clearly, but they were enthusiastic about going to see the homes I found.

As soon as I saw the newly paved roads and neatly lined trailers in Mobile Estates, I felt we were moving in the right direction. The homes were much nicer than I anticipated. Watching Janice and Ann interacting with some women at the swimming pool, I discovered another reason to get a place in Florida: Janice would have friends in a place like Mobile Estates, which is something she didn't have on Bluebird Lane, where younger people and families prevailed. Here she would have people more compatible with her age and interests. After looking at about eight homes, we put in an offer on the one we liked the most.

After we returned home, we had second thoughts, not about Florida but about the home on which we had made a verbal offer to the owner. I called her that day, and it turned out that she was as ambivalent about selling her home as we were about buying it. We agreed to cancel our offer, and then Janice and I were on to the great search.

~~~~

Every night, me at the College and Janice at home on Bluebird Lane, we scoured the Internet searching for a winter home that we could afford all along the Gulf Coast stretching from Tampa to Marco Island. In the process of our searches, we learned a lot about the pros and cons of different communities and different types of houses. As each of us found a home with potential, we would send it to the other. On weekends, we would discuss our findings and search some more. It quickly became apparent that we had to see these homes in person in order to determine which ones were viable options for us.

In the process of inquiring about various homes online, we connected with two realtors who were both very knowledgeable but in different areas of Florida. One was knowledgeable about one area, and the other knew a lot about some other surrounding areas. I had not retired yet, but I had seven weeks off in the winter. So in early January of 2011, Janice and I flew to Tampa, rented a car, and drove south. In talking with our realtor for one area, Janice found out that we could rent a manufactured home in a community that I will call "Idyllic Lakes" for two weeks at a very reasonable price. So our plan was to drive there and to see homes we identified online as having potential, and then meet our other realtor to do the same thing in her area. Little did we know what lay ahead and the direction this trip would take us.

The flight and two-hour drive to Idyllic Lakes made for a very long day, but we were quickly wide awake once we checked in and drove into this lovely gated community. The holiday decorations and lights made for a very impressive entrance. The lakes on each side of the road were also pleasantly lit. I'm sure our jaws dropped as we turned onto Sugar Mill Court. Idyllic Lakes was laid out in a cul-de-sac configuration, which was something we had not seen when looking at other communities where the manufactured homes were arranged in rows like a typical trailer park.

I know our jaws for sure dropped when we walked into our temporary home. It was so expansive with a large family room, dining room, fully equipped kitchen, a den, two bedrooms, two full baths, a two-car garage, laundry room, and large lanai. It was nicely decorated with modern furniture. We went to bed that night in wonder about what we had stumbled into and were excited to see what everything would look like in the daylight.

The next morning I took my usual forty-five minute walk; but this time it was around the Idyllic Lakes community. Although I only saw a small portion of this 850-home community, I was enthralled with the natural beauty of this place. The extensive number of pine and palm trees interspersed on the cul-de-sacs, and roadways provided a real sense of tranquility. From the walking path behind our place, I could see that our lanai was situated right on a large lake with the golf course on the other side and a picturesque bridge to our right. I walked the path behind our place and found a beautiful swimming pool, tennis courts, bocce courts, shuffleboard courts, and a luxuriant clubhouse as the centerpiece. Walking through other courts or cul-de-sacs just impressed me even more. I was very excited when I got back home. Janice was making coffee as I rambled on about all that I had seen on my walk. We had our breakfast out on the lanai and watched birds flitting about as golfers played the eighteenth hole across from us. It was a warm pleasant morning made even more pleasant by our surroundings.

I couldn't wait to show all that I had seen on my walk to Janice. Our place included the use of a golf cart that we wanted to use for a driving tour of Idyllic Lakes, but we didn't know how to start it. Luckily, a young man delivering packages for UPS using a golf cart was driving past, and I hailed him for assistance. Although his cart was gasoline-driven and ours electric, he was able to show us how to start ours. With that, we were off on a driving tour of Idyllic Lakes with stops at the clubhouse and swimming pool. Janice was as impressed as me. We couldn't wait for our realtor to pick us up so that we could check out homes for sale in this peaceful and bucolic setting.

~~~~

Our realtor was not only knowledgeable about local real estate but also very honest. We came to respect her very much because she pointed out deficits we didn't see because we were so taken with certain things. She showed us several homes in Idyllic Lakes and some others in some other communities in the surrounding area but nothing compared to Idyllic Lakes. In addition, we also still went with another realtor to look at communities further north of this area. She too was an honest person and told us that she had never seen anything like Idyllic Lakes (Janice had sent her information for comparison purposes) and said that she did not have a community superior to it in her listings. So after spending a day with this kind and straightforward realtor, we returned to Idyllic Lakes even more interested in this unique community.

We spent a lot of time gathering information about Idyllic Lakes by interacting with home owners whenever we could. The swimming pool, Coffee Social on Saturday mornings, and my walks gave us the opportunity to get the insider's perspective. It was all positive. I had never met a more content group of people. Of course, the usual Talty pessimism was operating as I probed their level of satisfaction with living in the Idyllic Lakes. The question I asked everyone was "What are the best and worst things about living in Idyllic Lakes?" It was remarkable to me how no one could come up with a real negative aspect; everyone said it was their best decision to move here. What also struck Janice and me was how friendly everyone was.

~~~~

Before we left for home, we decided to put in an offer on a home that was designated a "Short Sale", but it turned out to be anything but a "Short Sale." Numerous phone calls went back and forth between all parties throughout the fall after we returned home. Then after an extended nightmare of poor follow-through on the part of the bank holding the title, we decided to withdraw our offer. We also decided to wait until December and then rent a Idyllic Lakes home for seven weeks and recommence our search for a home to purchase. Bernie and Ann came for a visit, and they too were impressed with Idyllic Lakes.

~~~~

Returning to Idyllic Lakes felt so good. I realized that my obsession with finding a place in Florida was mainly driven by two things: Janice and my increasingly intense dislike of the northern winters and my concern that Janice did not have enough of the socialization that she enjoyed so much. In spite of how much we loved living on Bluebird Lane within the pleasant surroundings of Walton Woods and the Audubon Community, we were living among younger families whose interests were quite different from ours. In addition, ever since Janice had stepped down as a Skin Care Cosmetics sales director she lost the social network she had so enjoyed for several years. Also, with Beth and Peter being so busy with their own families, it was not possible for them to spend as much time with us as we would have liked. Janice really enjoys people, but there were not the opportunities for her where we presently lived. When I saw how Janice blossomed in the Idyllic Lakes community, I knew this is where we should spend our winters.

My Dreadful Past Roars Again!

Since we eventually expected to be living in Florida, I decided to apply for a license to practice occupational therapy there. There were some part-time OT jobs that I thought I might pursue after I retired, and the first step was to have an OT license. I already had my license for New York, and getting one for Pennsylvania was a pretty easy process back in 1987. I had no idea of how significantly different Florida was going to be, plus this was now 2011. Time and geography made for a whole different experience.

My previous licensure application experiences in New York and Pennsylvania were both entirely paper processes. I just filled out the form, produced proof of my having successfully passed the National Board for the Certification of OT Exam, enclosed a check for a specified amount, and, several weeks later, received my license. Not so in Florida! I had to be fingerprinted and produce a urine sample at a specified date, time, and place to be sure I was drug-free. Driving around unfamiliar streets with a full bladder looking for the lab was a painful experience. With everything finally done, I just waited for my OT Florida license to arrive.

My Florida OT license did not arrive as expected. Instead, I received a certified letter from the Florida Agency for Health Care Administration specifying my criminal record. I was instructed to contact an investigator from the background screening unit, submit the required information within thirty days, or be automatically disqualified. I finally reached the investigator who was responsible for my case. He explained that the screening process for felony convictions was far more rigorous in Florida. He said, "It was similar to the scrutiny that an applicant to become an FBI Agent goes through." Are you kidding me? For an OT license? Regardless, my application was potentially being denied because of my arrest and felony conviction back in 1959 for stealing a car. I explained that this was a sealed record and that I was given Youthful Offender status, which, in a sense, meant I did not have a record. Not so in Florida. The investigator explained that their screening process has access to everything. It was now my responsibility to have the records of how my case was adjudicated faxed to his office before my application could be processed.

I was embarrassed, anxious, and enraged. Apparently, all that I had overcome and achieved since 1959 had no bearing on my application. Things were further complicated because I had already taken a part-time position as an OT with my actual start date dependent upon receipt of my license. I was also renting and living in Idyllic Lakes at the time, so getting records sent from New York and the County, where my case was adjudicated, was going to be an anticipated nightmare. Undaunted, I knew I had to see this through, but I knew from experience that navigating through the bureaucracy of the County was going to be very difficult long distance. Surprise! My first phone call led to an "angel" in the records department that was proved to be my savior. When I explained what I needed, she explained that the records from that far back (fifty-two years ago) were archived in the basement of another building and that it would take her a little while to locate them. She took my phone number and said she would call me back once she located my records. Later on that day, my angel called me back. She had my records! I read to her what Florida said they needed notarized and faxed, and she took care of it all. Within a few weeks, my license arrived!

I was able to start my part-time job, but it was not what I expected. My plan was to find a facility where I could be a temporary part-time therapist, where I could work whenever I was in Florida for a few hours two or three days a week. The nature of the kind of OT they practiced at this facility was not something I found very satisfying. So after one half day, I quit! My supervisor was surprised and I think even disappointed, but it just wasn't for me. I didn't need to work after I retired, and so I was not going to do something that wasn't rewarding to me.

Upon my return to my hometown, I went down to the courthouse, located my angel, and thanked her in person. This unassuming, courteous, and diligent woman restored my faith in the civil service system. She also gave me copies of everything in case I had another problem in the future. It seems that one day that they gave us a day in jail so we would appreciate probation was a record that the Florida scrutiny uncovered.

IMMERSIONS INTO THE IDYLLIC LAKES COMMUNITY

The next time we went to Idyllic Lakes, I brought my bike back with me, which allowed me to explore the larger surrounding communities. Cycling around the areas demonstrated to me that Idyllic Lakes was ideally situated. It was a distance away from the rest of the congested areas of the surrounding towns, confirming that we once again had found our "Shangri-la" (a remote beautiful imaginary place where life approaches perfection: utopia). Bluebird Lane was our first Shangri-la, and now Idyllic Lakes was our second.

It made me so happy to see how Janice flourished socially in Idyllic Lakes. This was not only exactly what I hoped we would find when I began focusing on getting a home in Florida, but it was much more than I had envisioned. The people were just so genuinely friendly that she quickly made friends. This was something she missed ever since she had retired from her Skin Care Cosmetics directorship. No matter where we went in Idyllic Lakes, we found friendly and welcoming people. I always thought of myself as a social recluse, but now I really enjoyed being with these unpretentious folks. We didn't encounter any braggarts or people who only talked about themselves and their success. Being a typically suspicious Talty, I was skeptical of the sincerity of these people, but they all passed my scrutiny. There was not a loquacious one among them. They really enjoyed living in and talking about the present, and any past accomplishments were seldom brought forth. I felt that if we lived here for any length of time, we would quickly find ourselves a part of this fine social network. All we had to do now was to find a place to buy.

Buying a home definitely seemed the way to go. Renting had advantages in terms of not having to be concerned about a home when we were back north, but we liked the idea of owning our own place where we could come here whenever we wanted and stay as long as we liked. I also felt that the longer we were here and involved in the many activities available, the more immersed we would become in the social fabric of Idyllic Lakes. Janice needed and deserved this, and I wanted to find a way to give it to her.

~~~~

Between the homes we toured on our own and the ones that our realtor showed us, we looked at thirty-two homes in the Idyllic Lakes community. Because we had our list of what we wanted in a home, there was something lacking in each of them. Then one day, when out on my bike ride, I spotted a For Sale by Owner sign in front of a very attractive home. Next to the sign was a tube with flyers in it. While I was removing a flyer, the owner came out and invited me in, but I declined. I was sweating quite a bit, plus I would not want to go through it without Janice. The flyer was well put together with pictures of all the rooms and views of the lakes and golf course from the spacious lanai. When I got home and showed the flyer to Janice, her response surprised me. She said, "Why did you show me this? It's exactly what I want, but there is no way we could afford it." With that, we made a decision: we decided not to decide. That is, we would relax, enjoy our remaining time at Idyllic Lakes, and cease our searching. Our thinking at that time was that we would come back to the Idyllic Lakes but as renters, not owners.

Going Forth on Faith

It was good to be back home on Bluebird Lane and to see our kids and grandkids again and the rest of our family. It was scary to see how fast our grandkids grew in the seven weeks we were away. What would they be like if we were gone longer?

I returned to the College for my last fall and spring semesters. I really felt no sadness about retiring; only an excitement about becoming free of the many career responsibilities I had borne for so long. My mind was now on a future where time was my own. Time to do things without concern for upcoming lectures to prepare, labs to organize, papers to grade, exams to construct and administer, patients to evaluate and treat, or progress notes to record. The idea of sleeping in my own bed every night and not have to leave Janice on the nights I was staying at the College was something else I was eagerly anticipating. Also, never having been very tolerant of meetings, I could not wait to be free of them. It was thus with a constrained sort of joy that I taught my classes while counting the days until retirement.

We were discouraged by the poor outcome of the Short Sale fiasco but were still very much in love with Idyllic Lakes. Everything we learned convinced us even more that this was the place for us. As I looked over our finances, I could see where we were going to be comfortable in retirement and got thinking about the home Janice and I thought was perfect. However, this was all based on photos on the flyer I picked up and just a brief look at the front and back of the home. Our only knowledge of the inside was based on photos and the description in the flyer. So I said to Janice, "I've looked over our finances, and we could 'make a run' at the Frenchman's Court home that you liked so much. I know we haven't seen the inside, but what do you think of asking our trustworthy realtor to go through it and let us know what she thinks about us putting in an offer? She has always been so honest with us, and she certainly knows our tastes."

Janice was uneasy about it but said, "Let's see what she says."

Our realtor's response to my e-mail asking her to check out the house for us is something Janice and I will never forget: "I just took someone through it, and it is a knockout house. It has everything you're looking for. There are at least two offers going in on it, so you'll have to move quickly if you want it." This is where our going forth on faith came in. We decided to put in an attractive offer and learned the next day that it was accepted. At long last, we were going to be homeowners in Idyllic Lakes and with an exceptional house at that even though we had not set one foot inside. How is that for faith?

~~~~

Now that we had purchased our Florida home, we were thirsting to be there. Janice created a stopgap experience for us with pictures. We once again called upon our realtor to go through our newly purchased winter home and take pictures for us. Janice then took these photos and the flyer, put them in plastic sleeves, and made a three-ring binder for our viewing pleasure. Every night in bed, we would go through the binder in anticipation of living in this great home. We were like two kids at Christmas who knew what presents they were getting.

Many times the homes in Idyllic Lakes were sold furnished, but unfortunately, this was not our situation. We had all our appliances but would need everything else. Very early on Easter morning, while searching through the Fort Myers Craigslist furniture listings, I saw where a guy was selling a houseful of furniture. He had posted some excellent pictures that depicted high-quality furniture in what's known as the Tommy Bahama style. When Janice got up, I said to her, "Take a look at this furniture and see what you think." She sat down at my desk and, after scrutinizing each photo, announced, "That's exactly what I want!" The collection included a wicker master bedroom set with two dressers, mirror, armoire, nightstand, and king-size bed; another complete bedroom set with a dresser, mirror, two nightstands with matching lamps, and a queen-size bed also all in wicker; a unique dining room set with four chairs and a round glass-top table; a kitchen table with six chairs; two easy chairs, two more armoires; a futon; a trundle bed; a unique coffee table, and finally, a decorative lamp with an unusual shape. All this furniture, along with what we planned to take with us from Bluebird Lane, would give us just about all the furniture we would need.

Even though it was Easter morning, I called the guy. He had just posted the furniture the day before, and I did not want to take the chance of losing this find. It turned out that the guy had all this furniture because he had closed up his mother's condo in Orlando and had now had it all in his house which was about fifty miles from Idyllic Lakes. Because all the furniture was occupying a lot of space in his own home, the guy wanted it all gone as soon as possible. This created a problem for us because we would not have our Idyllic Lakes home for almost another two months. I asked the guy to take my phone number and to give me the chance to counter any offers he received while we figured out what we wanted to do. Should we buy it relying on just pictures? How would we get it from his house to Idyllic Lakes? Where would we store it until we moved in? What to do? What to do?

I then called the present owner of our Frenchman's Court house. I knew that he had moved to his new home, and so I asked about the possibility of us having the furniture delivered and put in the garage until we arrived. He was fine with it and even gave me the neighbor's name and phone number who had the key. Returning to Craigslist, I found a guy who would pick up all the furniture, drive to Idyllic Lakes, and put it in the garage.

It was now back to the owner of the furniture to confirm that we were going to purchase all of it, have it picked up within a few days, and agreed to wire him the agreed-upon amount for the purchase. I still needed to find someone to help me move everything from the garage into the house and found this guy through U-Haul and scheduled him for a tentative date to be confirmed once we knew for sure when our closing was going to happen.

The whole crazy thing worked! The furniture was great, the movers were reliable and delivered everything intact, the neighbor opened and closed the garage as requested, and we got everything moved inside as hoped. Once again, Janice demonstrated her good judgment by having the mattresses placed inside the house. This was to not only protect them, but to also give us a bed to sleep on if we were delayed in getting everything moved in. All this was another example of our going forth on faith. I'm sure many people would think we were crazy, but it's worked for us so many times that we didn't care and still don't.

~~~~

But we were not done with Craigslist and our quest for furniture just yet. In spite of the houseful of furniture we just bought, we still needed a dining table and chairs for our lanai. I did find a unique set on Craigslist that Janice loved. The photos were enticing and the price reasonable. I called the owner who had the set in his consignment shop. The problem was that the store was sixty miles from Idyllic Lakes and our car was too small to transport it. He agreed to hold onto the set and to deliver it to us after we moved in. Once again, everything worked out. He delivered it as promised (after we moved in), and it was even more beautiful than the pictures.

Janice enlarged the pictures of our new furniture (including the lanai dining set), put each one in a plastic sleeve, and added them to her three-ring binder containing the photos of our new Frenchman's Court home. Now we had a really big book to look through in bed each night and commiserate about our dream home that was on the brink of becoming a reality.

After my last lecture and reception at the College on May 20 of 2011, Janice and I started driving to Florida to hopefully close on our new home. The problem was that we did not have a definite closing date. So to say that we had mixed emotions driving south would accurately capture our feelings. I was now retired. The way I looked at retirement was that I now I was going to be paid for doing nothing. What a concept! I no longer had to worry about getting everything done for work. It was also exhilarating for us to reflect back on how well all the elements of my retirement process had gone. Although we had the uncertainty of our house closing, the good feelings about where we were with our lives far overshadowed it.

For a backup plan just in case our closing did not happen immediately, Janice had tried to arrange for us to rent a home in Idyllic Lakes in the interim. Unfortunately, she couldn't reach the person that handles the rental properties, and so we did not have a place to stay. However, our good fortune continued because on the second day of our journey South, more good news emerged. We were on Route 75 and only a few hours from Idyllic Lakes when the Title Company called to say that the closing was set for that same day at 2:00 p.m. Hallelujah! So Janice and I basked and just enjoyed the moment as we motored South.

Our timing was such that we had the opportunity to do a walk-through with our realtor to be sure everything was okay. We previously had had a thorough home inspection done, so this was just a pleasant formality. The fun continued as we drove down Frenchman's Court and into our driveway. Opening the front door and walking through our new home was made even more resplendent by the simple fact that this was the first time either of us had set foot inside it. The glow continued as we also briefly examined our new furniture for the first time. We would not need our picture book anymore. Now it was all real, and it was soon going to be all ours.

We then followed our realtor to the title office where real estate transactions are processed in Florida. Because there was no mortgage involved, the whole purchase transaction was quite fast, but the paperwork still had to be finalized, so we used that time to go to the water authority to get our water account established and to have our water turned on. We then returned, signed all the documents, and received our treasured keys to our new Florida home. What a fun experience that was to drive into Idyllic Lakes and announce to the guard that we were now homeowners. We gave him all the necessary information, and we both smiled broadly as he applied the permanent parking pass to our windshield. We were in! We were really Idyllic Lakes owners! Bask? Over a parking sticker? You bet we did!

After unloading the car, we headed off to Walmart to do what we could to strengthen the local economy. I don't remember the total amount that we spent, but it was substantial. We needed everything to establish our new home with all the necessary staples plus regular food.

It was a long day, and once we had the groceries all put away, we crashed. We made up the bed, did a quick dusting, went to bed, and were quickly asleep.

~~~~

The next morning the guy I hired through U-Haul arrived, and he and I commenced to move all the furniture from the garage into the house. He was an experienced furniture-mover. His experience saved much time and our backs. It also helped that he had various furniture dollies that made the moving of the real heavy pieces so much easier. Janice, having studied the photos of the furniture as well as the ones of our new home, had a vision of where every piece should go. It was uncanny to me how well every piece of furniture worked out in every room and in every place she designated. Each piece just enhanced every room. Even the carpets we had bought up north worked out perfectly. The furniture was all set in place within two hours. Thanks to the skill, strength, and work ethic of the U-Haul guy, we were all settled by eleven o'clock in the morning. Soon after the U-Haul guy left, the guy holding our dining set for our lanai arrived with the set as promised. It too was as beautiful as the pictures and looked great on the lanai.

So again and again, our going forth on faith and the trusting of people we didn't know was successful. I had used this strategy numerous times in my private practice where I agreed to provide OT services over the phone and hired therapists without meeting them face-to-face. The whole purchase of our Frenchman's Court home and furniture were all in that same vein.

~~~~

Then our son-in-law Dan Russ arrived! He had previously arranged to drive down to the east coast of Florida to pick up a dog he had bought online. Yes, this may seem crazy, but Dan is one of the most rational people I know, and so be assured that this was not an impulsive irrational decision. Dan had offered to tow a trailer with any things we wanted moved to Florida and drop them off on his way to pick up their new dog, Fenway. So before leaving Bluebird Lane, I rented the trailer, Dan picked it up, and he and I loaded it with the things that would not fit in our car. So when Dan arrived with our stuff, we had all the furniture in place, and we were pretty well-settled. We were so glad Dan got to see Idyllic Park and our new home. He was on a tight schedule, and so soon after unloading, he was on his way to pick up Fenway.

Life in Shangri-La II

Of the seven homes we owned, none could compare to Bluebird Lane in terms of the joy that house brought us on a daily basis for over seven years. This had to do with the design itself with its impressive appearance from the street, and the excellent configuration of the rooms all on one level. Add to it the excellent renovation our son-in-law Dan Russ did for us, and we had a house everyone loved, especially us. The physical space was, of course, greatly enhanced with the presence of our grandkids. So Janice and I viewed Bluebird Lane and the surrounding Audubon woods and community as our Shangri-La. Now with our Frenchman's Court home in Idyllic Lakes, we had another Shangri-La that I designated as Shangri-La II. Now we had two great homes.

But now it was now time to enjoy our new home in Florida. It was wonderful to sit on our lanai overlooking the thirteenth fairway of the golf course and the two lakes on each side with the section of forever-wild trees stretching across the far side of our paradise. We could watch alligators stealthily swimming about, turtles migrating back and forth between the two lakes, eagles flying overhead or grasping fish in their big talons and flying off, or herons and egrets foraging along the shore. So peaceful and beautiful! What a place! Boy, did we bask! Actually, it was perpetual basking combined with a large dose of reveling!

However, we still needed to make the purchase of a critical piece of equipment: a golf cart. Even though we don't play golf, Janice and

I had a great time purchasing our own golf cart. We had learned from our renting experiences that everyone has a golf cart, and it is the preferred way to get around in the community. We picked out one in a burnt-orange that had all the extras we wanted. Because it was a new golf cart, we were able to have our names painted on the front. We thought it was another thing to gloat about to each other as we viewed *Pete & Jan Talty* on our own golf cart as if it was a Lamborghini. As a culmination, I attached my New York State TALTY OT vanity plate as well as some hometown-related decals and a flag. We were all set for classy transportation within the community. This was also further evidence of our immersion into this special place.

One of the things the previous owner of our home said to me about retirement still resonates with me today: "Peter, you'll find that the best thing about retirement is that you can now do whatever the hell you want each day." He really captured the feeling I craved, and now we had it for ourselves. We could decide to read on our lanai, take a cruise around the community in our golf cart, take a bike ride, swim in the great community pool, or take part in the ample array of activities available.

~~~~

I also used this freedom to help Janice establish friendships in this vibrant community. I knew that whatever I would do, Janice would like to do also simply because as she always says, "I just love being with you. It doesn't matter what we're doing." Because of her reluctance to participate in social things that did not include me, I knew I had to push myself to initiate these things. Therefore, I became "Mr. Social". I not only went to the Saturday morning Coffee Socials, but I also invited ourselves into tables of people whom we didn't know. Everyone was very friendly no matter where we went. We joined the bocce league, became members of the Idyllic Lakes Theatre group, and even became cast members in the spring play. Janice joined the women's group, and I the men's group. The daily afternoon swims in our community's beautiful swimming pool were great for her. She would float on her noodle and socialize with other women in a circle talking about anything and everything. Janice also participated in what was known as "Idyllic Lakes U", which were weekly classes on a wide range of topics. She also took art classes and unleashed some hidden talents in painting. In addition to the activities we joined, we also got to know our neighbors on our court. We attended dances, shows, and just about everything we saw advertised in the community's newsletter known as the *Whispering Pines*. I was not always eager to attend all these of these social functions but did it for Janice to help her become integrated into this very friendly community. Mission accomplished!

~~~~

What made my mission so easy to accomplish were the friendliness of the people and the diversity of activities available. However, besides their natural friendliness, there were two other factors that made living in Idyllic Lakes a joy. First, as friendly as they were, the people respected each other's privacy. I liked being greeted by people who also left you alone at the pool to read or just to be quiet at a coffee social if you didn't feel like talking. If you needed help of any kind (a ride to the airport, a tool, information, where to get the best products or services, and so forth), they were very responsive without being intrusive. I didn't have to worry about people being what my skeptical sister Sue would describe as being "just a little too friendly."

~~~~

The other thing about the inhabitants of Shangri-la II was what linguists and philosophers call their worldview. Wikipedia defines *worldview* as: "A comprehensive world view (or worldview) is the fundamental cognitive orientation of an individual or society encompassing the entirety of the individual or society's knowledge and point of view. A world view can include natural philosophy; fundamental, existential, and normative postulates; or themes, values, emotions, and ethics." The worldview I found at Idyllic Lakes was centered on living in the present. Few people dwelled on the past. I seldom heard people speak of their careers or accomplishments or regrets or disappointment in their lives. They also did not worry about what laid ahead. Their way was to enjoy the great weather, our beautiful community, and just being alive in safe and bucolic surroundings. This was quite an adjustment for me who spent many miles driving, running, or cycling, ruminating about past mistakes, or worrying about things like the health of my loved ones, natural disasters, potential economic crises, and so forth. However, it was an easy transition for me both because of the positive spirit that was infused in Idyllic Lakes that was so prevalent and because it made life so much more pleasant to enjoy the present. For Janice, this was not an adjustment in worldview in any way because the present was always her focus. Now she was surrounded by people who shared her worldview.

Was Shangri-la II la-la land a place where people denied the realities of the past and potential consequences of ignoring the future? Not at all. They anticipated problems by maintaining their homes, their cars, their minds, and their bodies. They also learned from the past and avoided repeating the mistakes of yesteryear. I often pondered what made these people the way they were and decided that to overanalyze things leads to missing the essence of them. So now I just enjoy what we have and am thankful every day that we found our way to the Idyllic Lakes.

A Real Sod (Not Sob) Story

In 2013, our beautiful front lawn of our Idyllic Lakes home was not looking so good. It was brown, dry, and no matter how much I ran our sprinkler system, the grass did not revert back to its usual rich green color. I asked a neighbor who was pretty experienced in lawn care and Florida vegetation in general what he thought my problem was, but he wasn't sure and suggested I call a pest control company. The pest control guy diagnosed my problem as an infestation of chinch bugs that are lethal for St. Augustine grass, which is what we have. Sadly, nothing could be done, and the only solution was to tear up the dead stuff and replace it with sod. His company didn't do this kind of work, but he said there were a few companies in the area that I could contact.

After checking out the process for installing sod online, I knew this was beyond me. I found two sod installation companies in the area, but an online check of their previous customers' reviews were confusing. Company A was rated as the most knowledgeable, and Company B the most workable and friendly. Apparently, the owner or manager of Company A was condescending and arrogant and often outright rude to the customers. He also charged twice as much as Company B. In spite of his poor interpersonal skills and high prices, all the customers said he was "the Man" when it came to sod.

A peculiar thing was that both of these sod companies were right across the street from each other. So after measuring off the area we needed to have sodded, Janice and I went off to visit both places to

A Real Sod (Not Sob) Story

see if we could decide which one to go with to get our lawn resodded. The guy from Company A was just like everyone said: expensive, abrasive, and belittling. How could this guy stay in business? He helped us make our decision when he said our job was too small for him. He said, "Write your name and phone number on this piece of paper, and if one of my guys wants to do your job on his own time, he'll give you a call." After saying all that, he walked away. I was pissed, but I was desperate to have a lawn again, so I sullenly wrote down the information.

We then went across the street to Company B, who was exactly like the reviews said. He was friendly, seemed disorganized, and was almost half the price of Company A ($450 versus $900 that we were quoted over the phone). I agreed to have company B do the job and gave him a check for half the amount up front. A date for the work to begin was arranged, but before the job could begin, we left for home when Sandy Kish (Kathy's mom) died in September. I contacted Company B and asked them to wait until I returned before putting in the sod.

When I returned, I tried calling Company B but their voice mail said the number was disconnected and no further information was available. Janice told me that they had cashed our check for $250. Then more bad news: their website was no longer operating.

After repeated phone calls, I decided to go to their shop early the next morning to see if they were there. The place was all locked up. I inquired at a mechanics shop on the same property and was told "They're gone. Everybody's looking for them." This whole thing shook my faith in people and my going forth on faith now looked pretty dumb.

With a mixture of depression and rage, I wandered around Company B's building and parking lot and was pleased to see their large landscaping trailer with several landscaping tools and a wheelbarrow on it. A dormant part of me came forth ("Crazy Pete"), and I decided to take what I considered to be the equivalent of my deposit in tools. The wheelbarrow was a heavy-duty version that I couldn't lift into my car, so I settled for an assortment of ten or so tools (rakes, hoes, shovels, and so forth).

While unloading the tools into my garage, Janice came to see how I made out. When I explained why I had all these tools, she became very nervous that I would be arrested. I wasn't concerned because I thought it was all justified.

A few days later, the secretary from Company B called, and this is the conversation:

Secretary: "Mr. Talty, this is Company B calling to let you know that the crew will be there tomorrow to remove your old sod and prepare the ground for your new sod."

Me: "I'm shocked because I thought you were out of business. No one answered your phone, your website was down, and your neighbor the mechanic said you had left town."

Secretary: "I don't know why he said that. We are still in business. It's just that we grew too fast and couldn't handle all the business we had coming in. So we had to shut down for a few days to get reorganized. Anyway, we are all set to come tomorrow to get your sod in for you."

Me: "Well, that sounds good, but there is a problem. Because I thought you had left town with my money, I took all the tools out of your trailer as compensation."

Secretary: "Really? Let me see what they want to do. (She tells someone about the deed) He says that won't be a problem, and they will pick up the tools when they come tomorrow."

Me: "Okay. Fine. I'll be here."

They came, did a fine job, picked up their tools, and we now have a nice lawn once again. I tell this story to show that we do not live in Shangri-la 100 percent of the time and that Crazy Pete has not been fully eradicated.

Teaching Again!

"Chose a job you love, and you will never have to work a day in your life." This wise quote was from Confucius and really captures my feelings about my job, or actually my two jobs. Throughout my professional life, I fortuitously found two interrelated careers that provided me the kind of satisfaction and rewards that Confucius was describing. In my professional life, I always seemed to be intertwining practice as an occupational therapist with that of a teacher. If I was working full-time as a therapist, I always sought a part-time teaching position. The motivation was usually the extra income, but the real rewards came in the teaching process itself. Engaging students was my quest, which I refined over the years into a sort of obsession to engage every student every minute of every class. As unrealistic and grandiose as this sounds, it led to me becoming an excellent teacher to over two thousand OT students and receiving the Outstanding Teacher Award at two institutions: the College and the university.

When I joined academia as a full-time professor, first at the University, and then later on at the College, I continued to practice OT on a part-time basis. Having a job in what the students regarded as the real world enhanced my credibility with them. This part-time practice also gave me the opportunity to explore doing home care, hand therapy, and ergonomics. The students loved my stories from the real world of OT practice, which, of course, led to me publishing my first book, *Occupation as the Key to Change*.

So whether it was in an OT clinic or in some facility or in a classroom at some college or university, I was always doing a job that I loved. To abandon this rich and rewarding work when I retired was not as easy as I thought it would be. Just prior to retirement, I found a tutoring opportunity through the infamous Craigslist that proved very successful and rewarding for both the person I tutored as well as myself. This recent graduate was having difficulty passing the NBCOT (National Board for Certification in Occupational Therapy). We found each other on Craigslist, and I tutored her twice a week for about eight weeks. She passed! I thought tutoring might be something I could do in retirement, but I was not going to rush into anything work-related, or so I thought.

~~~~

Located about a half hour south of Idyllic Lakes was Another University. It was the newest branch of the state system of higher education with about fourteen thousand students enrolled. They also had an OT program whose chairperson was from the northeast whom I knew a little bit from attending national conferences of OT educators. So I sent her an e-mail inquiring about possible part-time teaching opportunities and attached my curriculum vitae. It turned out that she remembered me well, and she did have a course available that was right in line with my expertise and availability. So we worked it out that I would teach one course each semester. Yeah! I was back in the classroom!

~~~~

Another University turned out to be a great place for me for a number of reasons. First, it was a brand-new campus with all the latest electronics for teaching and cutting edge clinical laboratory equipment. The OT faculty members were also very professional and welcoming right from the beginning. Then after lecturing for a few weeks, I learned the real reason why Another University was such a great place to teach: the students. I had never taught a group of students that were not only very bright and well-motivated but at the same time respectful and appreciative. Having taught at four other colleges or universities, I can definitely say that the Another University students were the best. This was confirmed by the full-time faculty members who had been there for several years. They felt it was a combination of their intense selection process, the culture within the OT department, and being located in the larger culture of the South. Whatever it is, teaching at Another University is another example of my doing work that I love. I teach one course each fall and spring on a one-day-a-week basis that works out just fine.

Sadness amid the Joy

Unfortunately, our abundant joy was interrupted with the death of two beloved family members in 2013. On January 26, John Russ, our son-in-law Dan's father, died after a long and sad struggle with a respiratory disease. His death was the first that our grandsons Luke and Andrew ever experienced. Since John and his wife, Sue, lived right across the street from Beth and Dan, they saw firsthand the slow and painful decline of this fine man. Someone either online or at his memorial service described John Russ as "a gentleman and a gentle man." What an apt description! The family had decided to wait until spring to have his memorial service, which worked out well for me because I was now teaching at Another University, and we had just gotten back to Florida. We were then able to attend the memorial service and offer our condolences in person.

My daughter-in-law Kathy's mom, Sandy Kish, had been stoically and valiantly battling a form of cancer that eventually took her life on August 31, 2013. However, prior to her death on April 5, 2013, Sandy's insights about family traditions and transitions were recorded by the local newspaper in a poignant article she penned. She titled it "Spreading the Wisdom Learned from Mother's Voices," with a wonderful message about "passing the torch." The timing and relevancy of her article still resonates with us all today. We were able to attend her wake and funeral in person.

~~~~

Sadness amid the Joy

Our family was certainly diminished in many ways with the passing of John Russ and Sandy Kish, and I personally miss them both. It was fortuitous that we were in town and able to attend Sandy's wake and funeral. It was further fortuitous that when we stopped at Beth's house to say goodbye before we headed back to Florida, Dan told us that one of the duplex apartments they owned was going to become available. This was good and unexpected news for Janice and me. We had been talking about our future housing needs, and one of the possibilities was to sell our beloved Bluebird Lane house and then rent one of Dan and Beth's duplexes.

It was stressful to be in Florida and worrying about our house back north during the snowy and bitter cold of the winters. As much as we enjoyed Bluebird, it was becoming a burden we didn't need at this stage in our lives. With each of our visits back home, we explored various housing options, but none appealed to us. There were some requirements we had that we just did not see as we explored various apartment complexes. We then thought living in a trailer park might work, but we found the closeness of the trailers unacceptable. The lot rents and distance from our kids and grandkids were additional negatives. The apartments we looked at in several complexes were also too small for us, and we needed a basement for our exercise equipment. Since I did our laundry, I also hated the idea of sharing a washer and dryer with other tenants and having to work my laundry time around their schedules. The apartments we saw that were duplexes or added on to existing homes were of low quality and not close enough to our kids and grandkids. Boy, were we were fussy! However, we were not willing to accept less than what we had worked so hard to achieve.

So Dan and Beth's duplex was in many ways ideal. Instead of paying rent to a stranger or a corporation, our money would go to Beth and Dan. Over the years, Dan had done so much for us, including the complete renovation of our Bluebird Lane home. It was great that we could do something for him. Because Dan had done the renovations himself, both of the apartments were impeccable in every way. We would be living in a home that Dan would take care of with his usual diligence. Thus, we could relax in Florida without any concerns about our northern home. Also, his hard work would pay dividends because we would only be living there for three months or so each year, and we always took good care of our homes. The other pluses were that it was a half a mile from Beth's and four miles from Peter's. This provided ample opportunities for pop-ins, which meant a lot to us. So as they say, this was a no-brainer.

While we were flying back to Florida on September 8, after Sandy Kish's funeral, Janice and I talked it over; and by the time we changed planes in Baltimore, we had decided that 6000 Newhouse Road (the duplex) was where we wanted to be. Janice, with her usual financial acumen, had run the numbers and selling Bluebird, and renting from Beth and Dan was definitely the way for us to go. As soon as we got settled back in Idyllic Lakes, I sent Beth and Dan an e-mail saying that we definitely wanted to be their tenant as soon as their present tenant departed. We didn't have a definite date of when we would move into the duplex, but we had to sell Bluebird as our first step.

The Craziest of Days for Janice and Me!

There were several times in my life where I had to put myself, as well as Janice, through hell in order to seize an opportunity that presented itself; and this was definitely one of those times. Traveling a lot in a short period of time was crazy, but we had to do it. On September 17, we flew back home to Bluebird just to get ready for a meeting with our realtor. Although we had had great success in the past selling our homes, we decided to use a realtor this time because we were now in Florida for at least nine months.

The realtor we contacted was not only one of the top agents in the area, but she was also instrumental in negotiating the purchase of Peter and Kathy's home on Sprucewood Terrace. She and her husband arrived a few minutes early, and he commenced to photographing the outside of our house from several angles. Once inside, he photographed each room, consulting with his wife to get the best perspectives. We then sat down with them and heard their approach to selling houses. Janice and I were very impressed with both their professionalism and aggressiveness. We had wanted them to see Bluebird Lane at its best, and so we had a lot to do to get it ready. Our thinking was that if she could get inspired about our house, she would inspire prospective buyers to pay our price. We didn't need to worry. We had compiled a list of our home's strengths, but then they brought out additional selling points we hadn't considered. Their approach using social media and technology was impressive, but we were really impressed when we saw our home online. It looked and sounded great, which, of course, it was.

We had to fly back to Florida on September 22 in order for me to teach my course at Another University, so we had to trust them to get our house sold. Our realtor took an unusual approach in that she held an open house on a Wednesday night. It was surprisingly successful in that over sixty people showed up. Then two days later, we had three offers on our house, and two of them were above our asking price. It was a fast and easy decision as to which offer to accept, and a deal was made. With a little searching, I found out that the purchaser was an architect, so I assumed that he valued the unique design of Bluebird as everyone seemed to do whenever they saw it. Our realtor did her job!

~~~~

It was fortuitous that the course I taught at Another University was held on Mondays, and that year, Veteran's Day fell on a Monday. So with the university closed, we had from November 4 through 10 to accomplish the seemingly impossible task of getting Bluebird ready to sell. We flew to our hometown in the afternoon of November 4 after I taught my morning class and had scheduled our return flight on Sunday, November 17 so I would be back in time to teach the next day. It was going to be crazy, but I had done things like this all my life where I had to go through a bit of hell in order to make our lives better. Janice was a great partner on these crazy but highly beneficial forays.

~~~~

Now we were faced with the Herculean feat of cleaning out Bluebird. We had decided to contract with the most well-known estate sale company in the area to help us achieve this in the most expeditious way possible. Unfortunately, some hard decisions had to be made in terms of what to keep and what to put in the estate sale. This arduous and gut-wrenching responsibility was on Janice because it was she who found it so difficult to let things that she was so emotionally attached to be sold or donated. It was a fact that we did not have any place for the majority of the stuff occupying our basement and closets. Neither our Florida home nor the duplex we intended to rent from Beth and Dan could absorb our glut of stuff. It had to go!

We had a very short window of opportunity to clean out and make some very difficult and emotional decisions. This is not work that could be delegated to people even if they were available. No, it was all on Janice and me. Since we did not know when the duplex was going to become available, we decided to use PODS (portable on-demand storage) units to store everything in until we could move into one of the Newhouse Road duplexes. I arranged to have two of the large (sixteen-by-eight) containers to be placed in our driveway. I then purchased over one hundred boxes of various sizes from U-HAUL along with sealing tape, blankets, several boxes of wrapping paper, three large rolls of bubble wrap, several thick magic markers, and two hundred feet of rope. I was now ready to become "the Packing Machine."

In between feverously packing, taping, and marking, I also became "The Shredding Machine." Because Janice is paranoid about identity theft; not just ours, but every customer to whom she sold a Skin Care Cosmetics item to, everything had to be shredded. She would not permit me to throw any receipts that had a customer's name on it into the general garbage or recycling bin for fear this would in some way result in identity theft for her former customers. All had to be shredded. This was twenty-two years of receipts from her highly successful Skin Care Cosmetics business and all our personal receipts and records for almost fifty years. Thus began my new role as the shredding machine. Fortunately, we had previously purchased a heavy-duty shredder that would accommodate seventeen pages at a time. I set up my shredding operation in the spare bedroom and shredded every chance I got in between packing and stacking. Then around midnight or so every night, I would take several bags of shredded receipts and other documents Janice designated as shredding necessities over to our church that had a bin for recycled paper. When I started this shredding operation, the sizable bin was empty, but I filled it with shredded paper. I knew it was most likely all my shredding because there was nothing else added in the week I dumped in my shredding. That's a lot of shredding!

Janice and I were both exhausted as she continued to sort and make painful decisions (for her) about what to keep, give away, sell in the upcoming estate sale, or put out for the garbage pickup while I continued to pack and shred. As I packed and shredded, I kept thinking of the old essay by Albert Camus, "The Myth of Sisyphus." Sisyphus was a figure of Greek mythology who was condemned to repeat forever the same meaningless task of pushing a boulder up a mountain only to see it roll back down again. These were terrible days for us both, and our usual harmonious relationship was severely strained. I knew that our present onerous plight was temporary, and when this hell ended, we would be as we were before. I also knew that Janice and my work ethic, diligence, and focused effort would get this done. Actually, we had to get it done because we had the estate sale scheduled in a few days, PODS to be packed, and all done in six days before we had to fly back to Florida in time for me to teach. Even the term "nightmare" does not come close to describing what Janice and I experienced in those six horrendous days.

The packing of the PODS with all our furniture and household goods destined for our duplex was all done by my son Peter, my nephew Justin, and a good friend of Peter's Mark Superpacker*. Those three guys worked nonstop masterfully, packing each of the PODS. Peter's experiences at UPS as well as having spent five years as a band roadie paid great dividends. He strategically placed each piece of furniture and boxes, floor to ceiling, so that nothing would shift during movement of the PODS to and from the storage warehouse. Both PODS were filled to capacity, locked, and ready for pickup on the night before we left for Florida.

~~~~

The Craziest of Days for Janice and Me!

The estate sale certainly got rid of a lot of stuff, but there were still many things left unsold. Everything had to go, so I arranged to donate everything we had left to a guy we found who helped set up homes for people coming out of prison or were trying to overcome the loss of their stuff in fires or floods. I called him, and he stopped by one night while we were packing, shredding, and sorting, which had become our usual activities. He agreed to pick up everything we had left behind, but once again, we needed Bernie and Ann to bail us out because we would be gone back to Florida when he came to pick up our significant donations.

To compound things and confound the vacaters of Bluebird Lane (us), the pump for our laundry tub in the basement sprang a leak. I wanted nothing to deter the sale, so I contacted a plumber who scheduled an installation of a new pump on the day Bernie arranged to be at Bluebird when the donations were getting picked up. Thank God for Bernie. All went well as did the final sale. Within a few days after we flew back to Florida on November 17, the sale was completed, and we had our money. All we had to do was await the vacancy of one of the duplexes, have our PODS delivered to 6000 Newhouse, and move in. In the meantime, we could bask (Janice and I can never get enough basking) as retirees in our new Florida home and lifestyle.

New Frontiers

"Space: the final frontier. These are the voyages of the starship Enterprise. Its five-year mission: to explore strange new worlds, to seek out new life and new civilizations, to boldly go where no man has gone before." These words of Captain Kirk were sort of my unspoken mantra in my first few years in Idyllic Lakes. As an occupational therapist, I knew too well what happens to an idle body and mind, and I was determined to oppose nature and the Talty genes by challenging both to a moderate degree. This is especially true once a person retires.

The great actress Helen Hayes captured this perspective so succinctly when she said, "If you rest, you rust." I certainly did not want Janice or I to rust just as we are embarking on what was shaping up to be the best chapter in our life together. This, of course, applies to the body as well as the mind. I knew my cycling and workouts on my elliptical machine would keep my body going, but what about my mind? Teaching courses at Another University was both stimulating and rewarding in countless ways. I also became involved in the Idyllic Lakes Homeowners' Association and became a board member serving as the secretary. It was the challenge of learning new things that was the antidote to the rust that comes from idleness, and an unchallenged lifestyle. However, there is also the uncomfortable feeling that comes with trying to acquire the skills necessary in order to become competent enough to really enjoy a new endeavor.

Regardless, I was going to push myself into new frontiers. A case in point was softball.

I decided that one way of stretching myself while living in Idyllic Lakes could happen by my joining the softball team. Idyllic Lakes played in a league against nine other communities. The league was very well organized with umpires, lighted fields, uniforms, and all the necessary equipment. It would be good for my physical as well as my mental health, or so I thought. It did not turn out too well. I tried my best after purchasing a new glove complete with rubbing oil to make it more flexible and attended all the practices. I was never a good baseball player in my youth, and now at seventy years of age, I was absolutely terrible. This was not too surprising because I completely lacked the essential skills and abilities of running, catching, throwing, and hitting. Plus, I didn't really know the basics of the position I played (usually catcher).

Because I was such a liability, I often spent each game in the dugout encouraging my teammates. Janice came to all my games along with my brothers Bernie and Danny when they were visiting. In spite of my dismal performance, I enjoyed the challenge of trying to gain at least the rudiments of the game and the camaraderie of being a part of the team. After one season, I resigned but made some new friends who never made me feel that I didn't belong. I realized that my fragile feet and ankles just could not hold up to the rigors of softball. I had to find something else.

Janice and I both learned how to play bocce, and my skills improved to the point that in the spring of 2015, my partner and I went undefeated and finished in third place out of thirty-nine teams. That was a far more successful venture than softball.

We also went to dances, and I actually danced. I think my dancing is comparable to my softball prowess, but I'll keep working at it because Janice enjoys it so much. We are looking into taking a ballroom dancing course at some point to help me become a bit more competent on the dance floor.

Then came the biggest risk of all: I decided to try acting. We have the Idyllic Lakes Theatre group in our community that puts on a play every spring, and I got a part in the upcoming play. In 2013, the play was *The Sunshine Boys*. This was the Neil Simon play and subsequent movie with George Burns, Walther Matthau, and Richard Benjamin. I auditioned for the part of Al playing opposite an experienced actor who once performed this play off Broadway with Alan Arkin. I got the part, but initially, it was intimidating to work opposite such an experienced actor. However, he proved very supportive and encouraging. His wife was a good director, so between the two of them, my competence and confidence as a novice actor was growing. It was over halfway through the rehearsals that a sad and tragic thing occurred. The other sunshine boy had a stroke and the play had to be cancelled. Thankfully, he recovered quite well and was back on the golf course that summer. Unfortunately, he was unable to continue acting.

The rehearsals for *The Sunshine Boys* really got me excited about acting. I explored taking an acting course at a private school, but after sitting in on a session, I did not find it very useful. My acting friend who had the stroke told me that "the best way to learn acting was to act." So with that in mind, I tried out for a big part in the play the following year: *Lend Me a Tenor*. It worked out real well, and many people complemented me on my acting. Of course, the standing ovations were what really got me hooked. The following year, I had the lead in *Whose Wives Are They Anyway?* This was an even more challenging role for me because I had to alternate between being a man and a woman. Throughout the play, I was switching back and forth between genders that required my wearing a dress and wig and talking in a falsetto voice. Now I'm looking to get involved in a community theater when we return to our hometown. I also may take an acting course at Another University, depending on my teaching schedule. Janice also had roles in the last two plays, and also did quite well. She also joined the Board of the theatre group.

~~~~

Writing this autobiography has been another venture into a new activity. The part of writing about my life has been both emotionally paralyzing and exhilarating. Whatever I'm writing about, I need to emotionally revisit the events. The ones that are painful, embarrassing, enraging, or depressing take forever to write and put me in a funk for many hours afterward. Forcing myself to recall details like people's faces that I have hurt or betrayed is very difficult because I cannot write about these things in the abstract. I must mentally and emotionally be back there to the fullest extent possible in order to achieve the level of authenticity that I feel is necessary. Learning to write in this way has been challenging but rewarding. Writing about the good times has been a joy.

Move Number 20

From my birth until now, I have moved twenty times. I had moved nine times before I met Janice, and she not at all. Hooking up with me resulted in her moving eleven times. Why did I move so much? Disparity and opportunity that's why. I was constantly looking for opportunities that would give us a better life and reduce my sense of disparity. Move number 20 was actually an extension of move number 19.

When we decided to sell our Bluebird Lane house and move into Beth and Dan's duplex apartment, there was a delay. They wanted to be fair to the present tenant and give her enough time to find another place. So that is why we put all our furniture and stuff into the two PODS that were kept in a warehouse for us for thirteen months. We, of course, had our wonderful Florida home on Frenchmans Court in Idyllic Lakes, so we were fine with waiting. We had everything we needed because of our going-forth-on-faith approach to buying and purchasing a home. When we came to our hometown, we got a suite at the nearby motel that worked out quite well; and one time, we were able to stay at Dan's cousin's house, which was vacant and much appreciated.

~~~~

In December 1 of 2014, we initiated one of those crazy ventures that have been pretty commonplace throughout our marriage by driving to our northern home. This was move number 20 where our stuff stored in the PODS was going to be moved into our new residence at 6000 Newhouse Road. We stayed at the motel for one week while our apartment was being freshly painted in preparation for our moving in. I had arranged to have both PODS delivered and contracted with a small moving company I found on Craigslist who moved our stuff in on December 8. Thanks again to some great help from Ann and Bernie, we were quickly settled and even put up Christmas decorations. We hosted Christmas Eve and had our friends the Wrestlers join us along with Bernie and Ann for dessert after going out for dinner. We still had a bit of work to do to get fully settled, but that could wait until our return next summer. On January 2 (Ma's birthday), we returned to Florida in time to teach my spring course at Another University.

~~~~

Florida was now our home for about nine months of the year (September through late May minus a month back on Newhouse Road for Christmas). I believe that shifting between Florida and our northern home is challenging but stimulating. Preparing for the journeys each way, closing up one home and opening the other, the drives themselves, adjusting to different climates, saying goodbyes, and adapting to everything is at times tiring and daunting. But it does challenge and refresh the mind. Why do we do it? Because we love Florida, our home there, and the life we are building there. So we will keep our two homes and move back and forth until we decide it's not worth it. This will then necessitate a hard choice as to where to live out our final days. We talk about it without deciding.

Surprises!

With Janice and I both in the play (*Whose Wives are They Anyway?*), our time for other activities in the spring of 2015 were quite curtailed. We were in our last week of rehearsals, and anxiety was running high. These sessions now included use of the recently constructed set and costumes. The expectations were that we would have our lines memorized at this point, but we were all struggling with them. I personally found it overwhelming trying to remember which voice to use where, when to have the dress and wig on or off; which of the seven doors I was supposed to be using, and my lines. In an effort to reduce my confusion, I typed up cue sheets briefly describing each of the nineteen shifts in character, costume, voice, and room. These were in large print and taped backstage next to each of the doors I was going to be entering. Even with these crutches, I was foundering.

~~~~

It was while I was in my foundering state and awaiting my next entrance from one of the bathrooms during one of the dress rehearsals that I caused a great ruckus. I was sitting on a chair that unbeknownst to me was precariously perched on an unstable board. With a slight shift of my weight, the chair slid out from under me, causing me and the chair to cascade through the side curtains and onto the floor. On the way down, I shattered one of the support trusses and a decorative tree. There was a cacophony of loud noises when I painfully hit the floor and brought the cast and many others rushing to the crash site. I felt a lot of pain in my lower back and right wrist, but I quickly checked for fractures by moving every joint with no problem. In the midst of people clamoring around me was an EMT who just happened to be part of a fire inspection crew going through the clubhouse. While taking my pulse, she kindly asked if I was hurt. Knowing Janice was nearby and very concerned about me, I attempted to reassure her that I was okay by responding in my falsetto voice with one of my lines from the play: "I just feel a little faint." This brought great laughter and relief to Janice as well as the rest of the cast.

I sat out the rest of that rehearsal, applied ice packs, and rested. At some point, one of the maintenance guys conveyed a message from the property manager that they needed me to fill out an incident report at the receptionist's desk whenever I felt up to it. Since I was feeling fine, I went out to the receptionist's desk still in my dress sans the wig. The receptionist was filling in information on the form as I responded to each of her questions when she suddenly started giggling. They wanted her to check either male or female on the form, and my dress made her and me laugh quite a bit. I left early so that I could get home where I could apply proper cold packs and start a regimen of pain and anti-inflammatory pills. My tumbling episode got around the community pretty fast, and I had numerous expressions of concern from so many people that I was really moved. This truly is a caring community. I healed quickly and was right back at it the next day.

~~~~

On Thursday, the day of our dress rehearsal, I was working out on my stationary bike in the garage and going over my lines while Janice went looking for hair bands. The wig she was going to wear in the play was problematic for her, and she had been checking out hair bands for the past week. I was therefore completely unsuspecting of anything at all when she drove into the garage. I looked up when the passenger-side door opened, and to my great surprise, my son Pete got out! He had decided to fly down to see Janice and me in the play. Janice knew about it (she had to pick him up at the airport), but it was a wonderful surprise for me.

Besides Pete, we also had my brother Danny and his wife, Cheryl, who drove down from North Carolina to stay with us (good thing we have three bedrooms) and also see the play. To add to the pressure to do well in the play, our good friends Bob and Babs Wrestler drove up from Marco Island to attend Sunday's performance. And then we have the students. About ten of my students from my current class at Another University made the thirty-mile trek to see their professor on the stage alternating between a man and a woman.

~~~~

There was one more really big surprise for Janice and me that was just amazing. Cheryl told us that she was driving up to visit her aunt who is over one hundred years old, which she has done before and thus did not arouse our suspicions. I arranged a bocce game with Pete, Danny, and my good friend and co-star in the play Bob Margrett at 11:00 a.m. before our all-day rehearsal starting at one o'clock. In the midst of our intense bocce match with Pete about to throw his ball, he paused and informed Bob what was about to take place. I heard a voice that caused me to turn away from Pete to see the smiling face of Beth! Cheryl did not go to see her aunt. At Pete's request, she had picked up Beth at the airport and brought her to our house to surprise the heck out of Janice, and then they all came to the bocce courts to surprise me. We were both so thrilled to have Pete and Beth there and for them to see our play.

It was pretty impressive to hear of all the machinations Pete and Beth went through to surprise us. What great kids we have! They make us more proud every day. Pete had been to Idyllic Lakes last spring when he and Kathy and the kids flew down, and we all went to Disney World for a great time. However, this was the first time for Beth to see our home, community, and see firsthand the life we are enjoying.

~~~

The play went well, and it was so good to have our friends and family see the fruits of all our hard work. It will remain a special memory for me of the eight of us (Danny and Cheryl, Bob and Babs, Beth, Pete, and Janice and me) all sitting around our dining room table and enjoying the flow of Talty humor. What a great time!

Oh, Danny Boy

The caller ID read "Danny." How could this be? Danny was having surgery that day to remove an 80 percent blockage in his carotid artery in North Carolina, while we were back on Newhouse Road. How could he be calling me? It was him! He was out of surgery, everything went well, and he called me by mistake because he thought I had called him. He was in a great mood but had to go because he had to call back the guy who had actually called him. I said my usual goodbye in reminiscent of our canoeing days, "See you at the end of the portage," and we hung up. We would never speak again.

That day was Saturday, July 25 of that year (2015), a big day because it was Annie's and Bernie's wedding anniversary and the date that I stopped drinking and drugging thirty-three years ago. The coincidences of life continue to amaze me.

Danny's heart attack of the previous week was a blessing because that is when they discovered the blockage in his carotid artery plus valve malfunctions as well as other blockages of the arteries in his heart. He had the additional surgery on Monday, July 27 to resolve these problems, and he was very enthused about getting it all done. I was enthused because I was optimistic that he would then go through cardiac rehabilitation, take charge of his health, adhere to an exercise regimen, lose a hundred pounds or so, change his eating habits, and therefore perpetuate for many more years the great life he and Cheryl had built in North Carolina.

Apparently, the surgery was successful, but he still had difficulty regaining consciousness even several days after the surgery. Also, his heart rate was erratic with episodes of atrial fibrillation that kept him in the ICU much longer than was expected. We were all very worried about him. Janice and I had previously scheduled a dinner date with Bernie and Ann and the Wrestlers at one of Janice's favorite restaurants for that Wednesday, but I did not want to go because of the anxiety I was feeling over Danny's condition. I decided to cancel out, but when I called Bernie that afternoon, he said he too was worried about Danny, but he was already on his way in and he felt we should still do it. He also said it would be better for us to be together. So although not very motivated about going and very worried about Danny, we reluctantly drove to the restaurant.

We were early, but surprisingly, they were already waiting for us in the lobby. After some quick greetings, Bernie hustled us into a side room that the restaurant had remodeled that he wanted us to see. I'd seen it before but went on in to appease Bernie. Then a great shock. In the room were all our family (except, of course, Danny, Cheryl, and Tommy), including all our grandkids (even Philip) and many of our good friends all there to celebrate our upcoming fiftieth wedding anniversary. Bernie, Ann, Beth, and Peter had put this all together now because they knew that we would be back in Florida when the actual date (October 30) occurred. What a great job they did in surprising us and arranging such a wonderful dinner and evening. They thought of everything, including a slide show that depicted the great life Janice and I have enjoyed. It was so good to see everyone. Danny was, of course, on all our minds, but we still had a great time.

Unrelated to Danny and our anniversary, I was also in the throes of trying to master a new computerized teaching system that Another University had implemented. There were several training sessions for faculty in July and early August, but we were back on Newhouse, and thus I missed all of them. There were some online courses that I was attempting to complete, but I was just not getting it. Since the entire faculty and student body was attuned to this new system, it was imperative that I be able to comprehend and use it when I began teaching on August 24. However, the importance of this all evaporated in one phone call.

On the Thursday morning after our anniversary party, Cheryl called and asked if we could please come to North Carolina because she and her daughter Michelle "needed an adult". I said we would leave as soon as we could. So the computerized teaching system was pushed right out of my mind, and we got ready to leave. Thankfully, Beth came over and helped Janice pack, while Dan helped me move our outdoor furniture into the basement. There was a lot that we had to cancel and rearrange besides packing everything in the car, but by 7:00 p.m., we were on our way.

We got to Morgantown, West Virginia, about midnight, went to bed, slept poorly for a few hours, and were back on the road by 6:00 a.m. We drove straight to the hospital in North Carolina. Cheryl met us in the lobby and led us through the maze to the cardiac ICU. Both she and Michelle were very appreciative of our coming, and I was so glad she asked us to come.

I had seen family members and patients in ICUs before, but it still was very hard seeing Danny in his unresponsive state. I feared I would not be capable of being the adult that Cheryl and Michelle needed, but I tried to be strong. He was quite swollen, and added to the weight he had gained over the years, he looked immense. Although unresponsive to our voices and touch, he did seem to be sleeping peacefully.

Each patient in the ICU had their own nurse stationed at a computer right outside their door, and they were constantly monitoring the data coming from the multiple screens in Danny's room and making adjustments as they saw changes. Cheryl had alerted us to the chilly temperature in the ICU so we were prepared with our fleece. Only two visitors at a time could be in the room with Danny, and so we rotated out whenever someone else buzzed the nurse's station to come in. Two of Danny's grandkids (Devon and Kelsey) had relocated to North Carolina, and they, along with Cheryl and Michelle, helped us keep a constant vigil. Both Cheryl and Michelle were employed by the same hospital system, and so they were trying to attend to their job responsibilities in between visiting the ICU to check on Danny and hoping to catch his doctors.

It was a feeling of confidence that prevailed with all the staff taking care of Danny. Each day, Janice and I wore our fleece, brought our books, which we never read, drank our coffee, and sat with Danny, praying that he would wake up and be okay. I quizzed every nurse, nurse practitioner, and physician's assistant as to how they thought Danny was doing, and their responses were very encouraging. They were having difficulty stabilizing his heart rate with periodic episodes of atrial fibrillation for which various medications were being administered through an IV. Cheryl and Michelle told us that the day before when they tried to lower the dosage to wake him up, he awoke briefly with a terrified and agitated look on his face, and his blood pressure shot way up, so they increased his medication again to restore him to a restful state. It was good to see him resting peacefully even though that was not true for the rest of us.

We stayed at Danny's and Cheryl's house each night, but it was very hard for me seeing Danny everywhere in his garage, backyard swimming pool, his beloved porch, and throughout his house. However, I was glad we could be there so that Cheryl did not have to return alone to an empty house each night. I tried working with the new computer system for my teaching, but I couldn't concentrate or retain anything. All I could think of was Danny. I noticed that the bookshelf next to where I was working had a lot of Danny's mementos, including a picture of him and me standing with an arm around each other on the shore of Rock Lake in Algonquin Park, Ontario, Canada. He had a Hoppalong Cassidy bowl that he found years ago in an antiques store, a patch from the Appalachian Trail, and photos from some of our canoeing and backpacking adventures. His bookshelf contained some surprises. I didn't know he was so taken with Janice Joplin as well as the Hell's Angels. There were also two exercise books, which were pretty new. Maybe his interest in exercise had been aroused. I was also pleased to see that he had my first book, *Occupation as the Key to Change*, among the few books he had.

For the next five days, things were increasingly worrisome. He slept, and we watched and prayed. It seemed like they kept adjusting different medications to stabilize his heart while hoping he would wake up. However, I was not told this by his doctor because all the information flowed from the nurses and his assistants. It did seem that Danny was having some organ failure in that his kidneys were not working well, which caused a number of problems, not the least of which was his generalized swelling or edema. As a result, they started him on dialysis, which was initially successful in reducing the swelling, but then he went into atrial fibrillation, and so they had to put him on an every-other-day schedule.

I was quietly overwhelmed and was praying very, very hard that Danny would get better. In the midst of my deep prayerful state, a sense of calm came over me, and I just felt—no, knew—that everything was going to be all right. I shared this with Janice, and I felt the most hopeful since we first arrived.

Danny's nurse said that his cardiovascular surgeon was concerned that there may be something else going on internally, like pancreatitis or some other problem that they couldn't see with an MRI, CT scan, or X-ray. He asked a general surgeon to see Danny and to perform abdominal exploratory surgery to make this determination. They told us it was risky, but that it was more risky not to do it. It would be done laparoscopically in an effort to reduce the risk. So on Thursday, August 6, they took Danny back into surgery, and we all (Cheryl, Michelle, Devon, Kelsey, Janice, and me) waited in a different waiting room to await the surgeon's findings.

It didn't seem to take too long, maybe an hour or so, and the surgeon came in to see us. He said that the surgery was done, and that all he found was a small amount of pancreatitis. Then we were struck with his terrible words: "We lost him twice but brought him back. He is back in the ICU, and you should go back to that waiting room. His doctor will come and talk to you there." So off went our confused and scared little group to that other waiting room. After about fifteen minutes, his doctor came in to see us. I don't remember his exact words, but his meaning was clear: "We lost him again, and you can all come see him now if you want." All? Not just two at a time? What is going on?

I asked him, "Are you saying he may not make it?"

He said, "Yes. He is very sick."

With that, we were quickly out the door and down the hall. They must have known we were coming because both ICU doors were wide open, which was very unusual.

What an awful scene: Danny was all covered up to his neck with a very heavy blanket. One of his regular nurses was on a stool leaning over him doing CPR, while a respiratory therapist was air bagging him. Seeing all this was a scene I will never forget. After a few minutes of stunned silence, Cheryl then asked his doctor "Is this all that's keeping him alive?" How brave she was to ask that terrible question. His doctor just nodded, and with that, Cheryl said firmly, "Stop!" And with that, Danny died at 6:50 p.m. on August 6. What consummate grief then seized us all! "Shock" is too gentle a word for what we experienced. We were kissing and gently rubbing Danny and telling him that we loved him. I said, "I love you, boy. See you at the portage." If he could hear us in his last moments, we wanted him to take our love and good words with him on his last journey. The doctor and the nurses left us alone with Danny and our awful grief. His nurse brought us cups of water and more tissue boxes. It was all so final and so unexpected. We truly believed he would recover, and the staff never led us to believe otherwise.

Cheryl went to call Shannon and Heather (his daughters living in our hometown), and I went into the hall to call Bernie and Tommy and our kids Peter and Beth. We had been keeping everyone updated throughout the week, but they, like us, were bowled over by my devastating message: "He didn't make it." Oh, the anguish this brought was horrible for me to hear and just catapulted me further into my own despair. Some adult I was turning out to be. My emotions are back there now as I wipe more snot and tears into tissues and my handkerchief.

Handkerchiefs. Handkerchiefs played a role throughout Danny's life and in his death. Ma always told us to carry a "hankie" (her term for a handkerchief), and Danny really internalized this message. He even taught his grandkids to carry one. Ma took the hankie idea a bit further when we were kids and bought us each a package of handkerchiefs with our initials monogrammed in one corner for Christmas. Perhaps this was a remnant from her days of prosperity in the Big House. As a result of our frequent moves, packing and unpacking, and other forms of family turbulence, our monogrammed hankies got mixed up, and we ended up with one of our brother's hankies never to be returned. In the throes of my tearful state in the ICU after Danny died, I noticed that the hankie I was using had a "D" on it. Another one of those crazy coincidences in my life!

Then came the decisions that all loved ones dread. How do we proceed? Where and when shall a service be held? What kind of service? Danny wanted to be cremated, and so that had to be arranged. We decided to have two services. One would take place in our hometown where his daughters, grandkids, and other family members as well as many of his friends all lived. This would be held at the Irish Center in the heart of our old neighborhood on Friday, August 14. The other service would take place in North Carolina the following week to accommodate Danny's friends and the friends of Cheryl, Michelle, and Todd.

In order to attend the hometown service, Janice and I drove back to our Newhouse home, foolishly opting to drive all night. Cheryl, Michelle, and Todd with their two kids did the same thing, but they did it in a more sensible way. Danny would have been pleased with how well the service went and that over one hundred people came. Seeing Danny smiling broadly in the four hundred plus slides in the slide show Devon put together reminded us all that Danny was a happy guy who really enjoyed life. It was good to see people we hadn't seen in years, but it could not ease the pain we all felt in losing Danny so suddenly. When Cheryl's brother sang "Oh, Danny Boy," it was so difficult to not, in Ma's infamous words, "go all to pieces," but we were getting stronger.

When it came time to us to offer some remembrances of Danny, I found the courage to stand up and read some simple thoughts I put together:

Eleven Things I Learned from Danny

1. Enjoy and treasure family.
2. Keep it simple. If it's complicated, ignore it or break it.
3. Make a friend of everyone you meet whether they want to be your friend or not.
4. Build and enjoy a comfortable nest wherever you are.
5. Enjoy life.
6. Regardless of the time or place, be sure to take a nap.
7. Be aware of the past, but do not be bound or saddened by it.
8. Live in the present.
9. Look forward to the future.
10. Laugh, tease, kid, joke, and laugh some more.
11. Remember that the Oakland Raiders are the only real professional football team.

Rest well, my brother and canoeing partner. See you at the end of the portage.

We had to leave on the following Monday so that I could be back in Florida in time to teach and try to master the computer teaching system that had been making me so crazy. Sadly, this prevented us from attending Danny's North Carolina memorial service, which I very much regret. I was honored that Todd, Danny's son-in-law, read my "Eleven Things I Learned from Danny." This service also was very well done with the "Friends of Bill," arranging everything and offering great tributes of what Danny meant to them.

We all now have the sadness of going on with our lives without Danny. We all try to remember the good times, and I have a wealth of intertwining memories spanning our seventy years as brothers and friends. We were playmates as kids; budding athletes in baseball, football, street hockey, and basketball; delinquent adolescents;

drinking and drugging buddies as adults; watchers of all sports; pool players; fellow home moving guys; and paddlers of canoes and capable campers. I miss all these parts of us terribly, but I am so thankful I had these times with Danny.

It was during our early days of our canoeing adventures and misadventures that Danny gave me a gift that I will treasure even more than when he first gave it to me. It is a print on a metal sheet that depicts two guys struggling on a portage with roaring water behind them as they climb a hill on the trail. It surely was a glimpse of us. The title *Cruisers on the Portage* as well as the image, depicts well something we did hundreds of times.

St. Therese of Lisieux to the Rescue Again

The suddenness of Danny's death has impacted me terribly. I see him all around Idyllic Lakes. He loved it here and came to visit as much as possible. The swimming pool took him back to his high school days as a competitive swimmer. I can see him swimming laps and thoroughly enjoying the pool regardless of the temperature. Even in one January, when the heater was broken, Danny was in the pool every day to the shock of us Floridians.

We played bocce a lot and revisited our drinking and pool hall days by playing pool in our clubhouse. He loved napping on our lanai and touring about the community in our golf course. Danny loved life and especially life in Idyllic Lakes. I see him everywhere and tear and choke up with each memory.

I realize that I need help in order to move on with my life and my responsibilities. I have to teach, which includes learning the new computer teaching system at the university, researching literature for lecture information, preparing exams, and so forth, and I find focusing very difficult. Completing this autobiography is another of those tasks that is taking me forever to complete because of the sadness that engulfs me.

Knowing how my mother's death and subsequent unresolved grief caused me to experience a crazy life, I knew I needed help in adjusting to the loss of Danny. I considered calling my primary

St. Therese of Lisieux to the Rescue Again

physician and getting a prescription for an antidepressant but decided that this might only mask my grief and not really move me forward. Then also this respite from my grief may roar up and wreck my great life in the future. It was then that St. Therese of Lisieux came to my rescue once again.

It was the prayer card and my praying to St. Therese that got me through the mess I generated with my getting rightfully fired from Bedlam Hospitals in 1987. Now my church here, St. Therese of Lisieux, is conducting a nine-week support group for parishioners struggling with the death of a loved one. It starts next month and has a most appropriate title, "Friends of Lazarus." Janice wants to go also, so I registered us both.

These coincidental things like a saint I never heard popping up in my times of need are really remarkable and appreciated. I am very encouraged that the Friends of Lazarus will be the answer to our prayers and help me move forward in my good life.

Our close family of six siblings has now with Danny's passing been reduced to three (Bernie, Tommy, and me). I know we three will cling even more tenaciously to one another as we forever mourn the loss of Sue, Pat, and now Danny.

What If . . . ?

What if I wasn't crazy? Then again, what if I was crazy with that whole disparity thing operating but was raised in an affluent and stable family instead of the one where dysfunction reigned? What if my sense of disparity did not even exist because all my wants and needs were taken care of? Then what would I be? How would my life have been different if I hadn't lived a life of wanting? What would become of my relentless drive to make a better life? Could I have been content with less? Or without being encumbered by disparity, would I have been freed to excel at an early age to achieve great things, success, wealth, and peace? These questions, of course, can only be answered through speculation aided by some introspection, which I do a lot of; but in the end, we cannot truly know.

What if I had been more like Danny and not have a brain so infused with disparity? He was always happy with what life gave him while I was not. We were also so different in our worldviews that it was a wonder that we got along so well. It seemed that we always found areas where we shared the same perspective and thus spent little time on areas where our ideas and feelings diverged. Those eleven things I learned from Danny were unfortunately not a natural part of my being as it was his, but I'm working on them.

Now perhaps a corollary question is what if I had married someone other than Janice? How many women could or would be supportive of a restless husband who was always looking for something better? In contrast to me, Janice was always content with wherever we lived and whatever we had. One would think that a person easily contented like Janice would abhor the frequent upheaval of moving to new houses, changing schools for the kids, having to get used to new neighborhoods, finding new friends, and having to adjust to leaving behind the comforts and roots of the other place. However, Janice only questioned my motives not to oppose me but to better understand why I believed a change was necessary. Once she understood why my present job or current house was lacking in my view, she became the steadfast partner I needed in moving forward. Ours thus evolved into a formidable partnership that continues to serve us well today coupled with a lot of good humor along the way.

~~~~

Janice had suggested that we renew our vows in church during the four o'clock mass at St. Therese one day after our fiftieth wedding anniversary on October 31. I thought it was a good idea. We went to the parish office and made the arrangements. When Janice mentioned our plans to one of our good friends, she wanted to attend, and she also organized a reception in our honor back at the Idyllic Lakes Clubhouse. We sent invitations to fifty-four people and fifty-one showed up. Several of them came to the mass to see us renew our vows, and some were not even Catholic. It was all very touching. We have made some great friends here, and it was so nice to have them attend our reception. So we ended up having two great celebrations of our fifty great years together.

Conclusion, Maybe

Writing this autobiography has caused me to reflect on the decisions I have made throughout my life and the results of the paths I chose. In retrospect, I now wonder why I had to make my life so difficult by constantly striving to improve it and why I could not take the easier path. There are many men who I have known who chose a simpler path. They had one or maybe three jobs throughout their entire adult lives whereas I had eight different full-time jobs, managed a diverse private practice, taught in six different colleges and universities, and personally practiced OT in over fifty different organizations on a part-time or consulting basis. These same men only moved two or three times into different homes, not eleven. In total, I moved twenty times. What if I had stayed at any one of my full-time jobs or could have been content in our first or second house for forty years? Certainly, things would be much different today, and much I would have missed.

My unquenchable thirst for betterment and the eradication of my sense of disparity was the fire that drove me to actions more rational men would have wisely eschewed. I cannot say all this came from a deprived childhood. None of my siblings were cursed with this relentless strive and drive that caused me to take Janice on our high-speed and erratic roller-coaster ride of life. What if I could have tamed this inner beast of disparity? I perhaps could have given Janice and my family a more tranquil life experience. However, I know the

Conclusion, Maybe

beast within would not permit me to rest when opportunities were to be found and seized.

The path I chose had its rewards in terms of excitement and prosperity, but it also brought with it much stress, toil, and strain. If I could have been satisfied with a more ordinary life, what may have been different? What would I have missed? The written words of Tony Arata and made popular by Garth Brooks in a song entitled "The Dance" may answer these questions:

> Yes my life is better left
> to chance.
> I could have missed the pain
> But I'd have had to
> miss the dance.

Wikipedia says this fine song has two meanings: it is "both a love song about the end of a passionate relationship, and a story of someone dying because of something he believes in, after a moment of glory." This may have been the artists' description of its meaning, but to me, "The Dance" describes my engagement in whatever it took to wrest success from the various forces of doom real or imagined. For some bizarre reason, I found great satisfaction in being engaged in struggles of all kinds. If not, would I not have chosen a less stressful path? No. I was not content with simple things. I loved engaging in the work, the learning, the risks, and the problem solving that went with each adverse situation in which I found myself regardless of the outcome.

~~~~

Some may wonder if my present contented life in Idyllic Lakes will wane and that I will then be off on another path. It may be my age that fosters the joy and peace that I now feel, so I think not. The life I built with Janice and resulted in where we are right now has real sustainability. I know deep in my heart that this life we have been living in this place for the past three years is the life of our dreams. We bask every day and multiple times. The only thing that could alter it would be changes in our health.

~~~~

So what can a reader of my autobiography take with them and perhaps use in their own life? I really don't think there are lessons for others in my life story unless, of course, they possess the "disparity gene." For saner folks who are satisfied with their life as it unfolds, my way would probably strike them as strange at best. Regardless, my life's story demonstrates that the path one takes in life is far less important than the way one behaves on their chosen path. My behavior was both my ally and my yoke as difficulties arose. What I did in response to adversity, whether internally or externally generated, has the capacity to inform and inspire others regardless of the results I engendered. Enjoy my dance as well as yours.

Edwards Brothers Malloy
Thorofare, NJ USA
April 27, 2016